W9-BRI-649

Salads

FAVORITE RECIPES FROM SOUTHERN KITCHENS

Table of Contents

ACKNOWLEDGMENTS

We wish to thank the many women who submitted their recipes for inclusion in this book. Without their help, this book would not have been possible.

We wish also to express our appreciation for the use of photographs supplied us by the following: Front Cover – United Fresh Fruit and Vegetable Association (recipes on pages 283, 334 and 358); and Frontispiece – Florida Citrus Commission (recipe on page 304).

Title page and additional photographs were supplied by the following: Western Growers Association; California Foods Research Institute; United Fresh Fruit and Vegetable Association; Diamond Walnut Growers, Inc.; McIlhenny Company (Tabasco); National Dairy Council; Spanish Green Olive Commission; California Avocado Advisory Board; Sunkist Growers; National Live Stock and Meat Board; Seven Seas Dressing; South African Rock Lobster Service Corporation; National Macaroni Institute; Processed Apples Institute; Pickle Packers International, Inc.: General Foods Kitchens; Pineapple Growers Association; Evaporated Milk Association; and Tuna Research Foundation.

The Progressive Farmer MCMLXVIII
Library of Congress Catalog Card No. 67-30671
Printed in the United States of America

Introduction

The Southern farm homemaker, ever conscious of her family's health, serves salad frequently. Her modern salads are mouth-watering combinations of luscious fruit, tasty vegetables, succulent bits of meat, fish or cheese—all arranged on crisp, fresh greens or molded attractively in gelatin.

Each of the recipes in this Salads Cookbook has been generously submitted by Southern farm homemakers. Each homemaker has served her contribution to her family frequently and proved it a winner. You can use it with the utmost confidence.

A citizen of ancient Rome tossed salt on some lettuce one day to make it more tasty, and presto—the dish we know as salad came into being. "Salad" is from the Latin "sal," for salt.

Salads were introduced into England by Catherine of Aragon, one of Henry VII's queens. Catherine kept her chefs traveling the continent gathering green vegetables until her English gardeners were able to produce the desired plants.

Although salads were little used in the United States until after World War I, they are now a familiar and important item on all American menus.

The variety of salads in this Favorite Recipes from Southern Kitchens Cookbook is limitless. Almost every type of food has been incorporated into a delicious, nutritious salad. You'll find hot and cold salads; crunchy, tangy, wilted and spicy ones—any kind you could possibly want.

The Southern farm homemaker knows green salads are rich in vitamin A and that fruit salads are packed with vitamin C. So, she serves light salads to the family dieters, rich ones to those trying to put on weight, and hearty salads to the entire family.

A "bonus" in this cookbook is the tasty selection of appetizers—cheese deviled eggs, avocado dip, ham and chutney canapes, tidbits to make a hit at any party.

Each of the recipes in this Salads Cookbook that you and your neighbors have sent The Progressive Farmer proves once again that Southern farm homemakers are the best cooks anywhere. And your willingness to share them confirms once more that your hospitality and generosity are unequaled.

Lena Sturges, Foods Editor
The Progressive Farmer

Abbreviations in This Book

Cup	c.	Large	lge.
Tablespoon	tbsp.	Package	pkg.
Teaspoon	tsp.	Small	sm.
Pound	lb.	Dozen	doz.
Ounce	oz.	Pint	pt.

MEASUREMENTS

3 tsp. = 1 tbsp.
2 tbsp. = ⅛ c.
4 tbsp. = ¼ c.
8 tbsp. = ½ c.
16 tbsp. = 1 c.
5 tbsp. + 1 tsp. = ⅓ c.
⅝ c. = ½ c. + 2 tbsp.
⅞ c. = ¾ c. + 2 tbsp.
4 oz. = ½ c.
8 oz. = 1 c.

2 c. granulated sugar = 1 lb.
3½ c. powdered sugar = 1 lb.
2¼ c. brown sugar = 1 lb.
4 c. sifted all-purpose flour = 1 lb.
1 lb. butter = 2 c. or 4 sticks
1 qt. = 4 c.
A Few Grains = Less than ⅛ tsp.
Pinch is as much as can be taken between tip of finger and thumb

CAN CONTENTS

Average Contents	Can Size
1 c.	8 oz.
1¾ c.	No. 300
2 c.	No. 303
2½ c.	No. 2
3½ c.	No. 2½

Choose Your Salad

In the not too distant past, salads were considered strictly summer fare. But homemakers have learned to vary the contents of salads so they now have an honored place at the table 365 days a year.

Salads also have changed from side dishes only to main dishes as well.

It wasn't so long ago, either, that salads consisted of greens garnished with tomatoes, sometimes cucumbers, scallions and perhaps a little pepper and celery.

Today, there are as many salads as there are ideas . . . attractive side dishes of fruit or vegetables; big, elegant main dishes . . . great for family, tops for company.

Which salad to choose? It depends on the rest of the meal. A small, crisp green or fruit salad is an excellent accompaniment to a meal. If the salad is to be the entire meal, choose a hearty one that contains generous amounts of meat, seafood, poultry, eggs or cheese.

A simple rule of thumb to remember when choosing a salad is that light salads go with hearty meals. Tart salads are particularly good with seafood. Fruit salads are delicious as appetizers, desserts or as side dishes.

Special occasions call for special salads. What would the Fourth of July be without cold potato salad? Labor Day without bean salad or Christmas without cranberry salad? Try rich-looking tomato aspic on Valentine's and maybe a molded cherry salad on Washington's birthday.

COLORFUL SALADS

Dash your salads generously with color, being sure the color combinations are pleasing. Ingredients also should complement each other in texture, form and flavor.

Mix fruit and vegetables for an unusual taste treat. Or try soft and firm-textured foods together.

To enhance flavor of salads, sprinkle lemon juice on fruits, seafood, meats, poultry or vegetables. The lemon juice also keeps salad foods from developing unattractive brown spots.

Main Dish Salads

A main dish salad is a meal in itself—nutritious and filling. These salads are usually built around meat, fish, eggs or cheese combined with salad greens and a tangy dressing.

A light main course salad, however, may be just a generous serving of fruit topped with sherbet or cottage cheese.

Menus featuring main dish salads are perfect any time: for suppers, bridge luncheons, baby or bridal showers, or just when you're having a few friends in. They're ideal for spur-of-the-minute meals, too, since preparation and service are so easy.

Usually a main dish salad menu includes hot soup, the salad, bread, dessert and beverage.

Because canned meats are used so often in main dish salads, remember these tips. For easy slicing of canned meats, chill well, remove both ends from the can, push the contents out in one piece, then slice as desired. Canned meats may be sliced several hours ahead of serving if the slices are tightly wrapped and refrigerated.

Cube, sliver or slice luncheon meats, corned beef or small sausages and add to tossed green salads, potato, macaroni or cabbage salads.

As a real time-saver, use a packaged mix in preparing bread to accompany the salad. Or, vary hard rolls or French bread with garlic butter, a sprinkling of poppy, sesame or celery seeds, or a topping of grated cheese.

FOR SPECIAL OCCASIONS

Special occasion salads may be colorful fruit arrangements, gelatin molds or unusual frozen salads. Gelatin and frozen salads are especially well suited for entertaining when much of the food must be prepared in advance.

Use a special serving tray or platter for these salads—your most elegant silver, china or crystal trays, for example. Garnish the salad neatly and attractively.

A large gelatin ring looks particularly nice with mayonnaise or dressing piled high in the center.

Breads to accompany dessert salads are usually fancy party sandwiches or tiny rolls.

To Accompany Meals

Probably the most popular and most often served of all salads are those that accompany a main course.

The accompaniment salad may be used to garnish a main dish serving platter; it is sometimes a first course appetizer.

These salads are served in small to medium-sized portions and complement the rest of the menu in color, texture and flavor. They may be varied easily by the dressing or topping. This way they adapt to luncheon, supper or dinner menus.

There are several ways to serve these accompaniment salads. Individual salads arranged on greens on a large platter may be passed. A small salad for each person makes an attractive place setting. Arrange on small plates or in wooden or pottery bowls and put to the left of the dinner plate.

Crisp, tossed green salads, fruit or vegetable arrangements garnished with greens are attractive in a large salad bowl.

Bread sticks, cheese sticks or appetizer crackers are good when salads are served at the beginning of the meal. Assorted breads or dinner rolls are appropriate when the salad is served with the main course.

Try these suggestions for dressing up these accompanying salads:

With a fruit salad, use canned pineapple chunks. Lift them from the can and while they are still wet with syrup, dip in chopped nuts.

For a fruit salad topping, roll balls of cream cheese in slivered or chopped nuts, plain or toasted coconut.

To prevent apple or banana slices from turning dark, dip in pineapple syrup or juice.

Use whole spiced peaches, crab apples or apricots to garnish meat platters. These are especially tasty with canned meats.

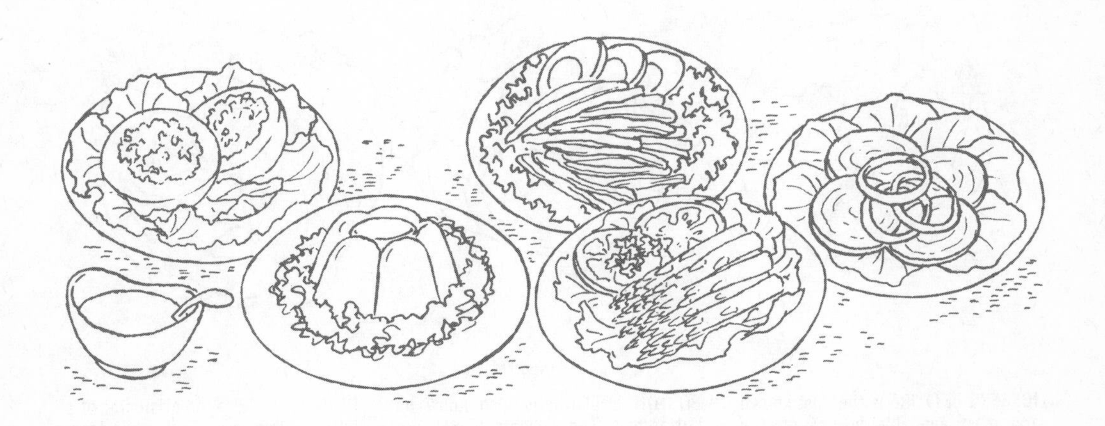

Garden-Fresh Greens

Shades of green from deep emerald to chartreuse signify spring has arrived. Spring, when salad ingredients are rushing to maturity.

Watercress is reaching its season. Tender, young spinach leaves, crisp iceberg lettuce and endive are being harvested. Soon, all greens will be in homes enlivening every type of salad: one-of-a-kind Caesars, chefs, aspics, seafood salads.

All salad greens should be young and crisp, clean, tender—and green. Remember, darker salad vegetables are richer in iron and vitamins A and C than are the paler ones.

Use one, two or three—even more—greens in your salad to give them contrast, texture and flavor. Liven up otherwise-ordinary salads with zesty endive, chicory, escarole or romaine. Adding vitamins, interest and color to salads are spinach, celery leaves, kale, dandelion greens and Swiss chard.

Choose crips lettuce that is firm and heavy for its size, unless you plan to use the leaves for cups. Then choose a loose head.

Chicory, endive and escarole have a few dark, tough outer leaves, but the inside ones are tender. Spinach should have dark, small, tender leaves.

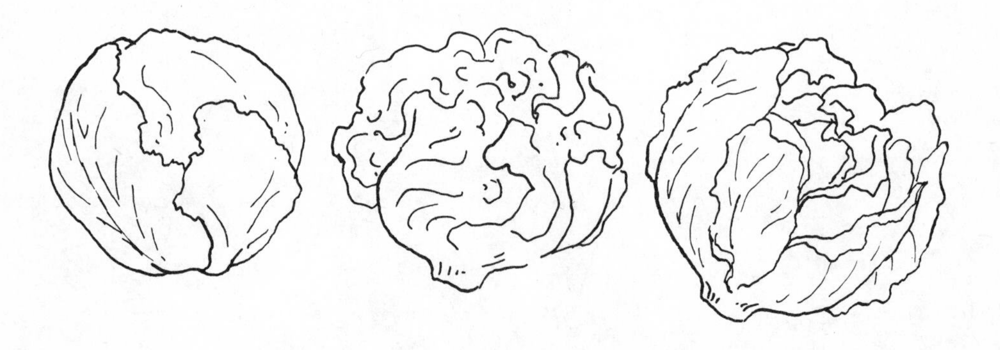

ICEBERG LETTUCE is the best known and most available lettuce on the market. Heads are large, firm and crisp textured. Outer leaves are medium green, inner ones are pale green and tightly folded. It adds "crunch" to salads because it doesn't wilt.

BOSTON LETTUCE is also know as butterhead. The delicate leaves are green outside and light yellow inside. They have a buttery, oily feeling. It is very perishable and should be used the day it is bought.

BIBB LETTUCE is the aristocrat of all lettuce. Dark, succulent green leaves are loosely held together. It has a tender mild taste.

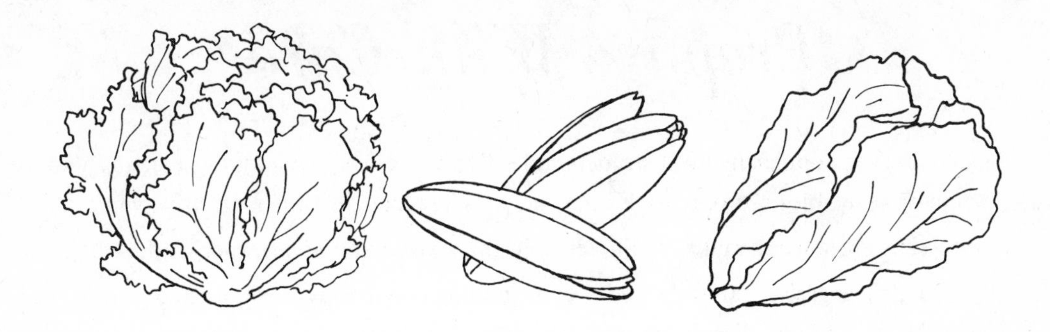

ESCAROLE has large, broad pale green leaves. The edges are slightly ruffled. It is crisp and has a slightly bitter taste.

FRENCH OR BELGIAN ENDIVE has elongated, crisp yellowish-white leaves and looks like a young unshucked ear of corn. Its bitter flavor mixes well with blander lettuces in a tossed salad.

ROMAINE OR COS lettuce has an elongated head and stiff leaves which are medium dark to dark green on the outside and become greenish white near the center. Its pungent flavor gives tang to tossed salad.

WATERCRESS has small, dark green glossy leaves on sprigged stems. The leaves and tender part of stems are spicy and peppery additions to salads. This aquatic plant is sold in bunches.

SPINACH leaves are tart and tangy. They add color variation to salads.

CHICORY has curly fringed leaves. It adds a bitter flavor and rather prickly texture to salads. It is also called curly endive.

LEAF LETTUCE is an unheaded type. Its loose leaves branch from a single stalk, are light or dark green and have ragged edges.

GREEN CABBAGE is an all-year winner for coleslaw. The spring variety is bright green, winter is silvery green. The compact head has large leaves.

CHINESE OR CELERY CABBAGE is about the size of a bunch of celery. Its closely packed, whitish-green leaves are crisp and firm.

Prepare With Care

Salads, an ever popular menu item, demand only the freshest, crispest ingredients. Watery, wilted fruits or vegetables not only look unattractive, they have lost their nutritive value.

How greens are washed makes a difference in the texture and appearance of the salad.

Generally, rinse greens carefully under cool running water to remove outside grit. Remove tough outer leaves and any discolored or wilted leaves. If the outer leaves are not bruised, save them. Shredded, these are good as salad beds or in sandwiches. Although they are not as tender as inner leaves, these outer leaves are especially rich in vitamins and minerals.

Drain all greens after washing them. Shake off as much water as possible, then gently blot the greens dry with a paper towel. Or spread them on a clean tea towel or paper towel. Roll up loosely and put in the refrigerator until it is time to prepare the salad.

Store washed greens in a vegetable crisper in the refrigerator. If you find it necessary to keep them any length of time, put them in plastic bags or cover them with plastic wrap.

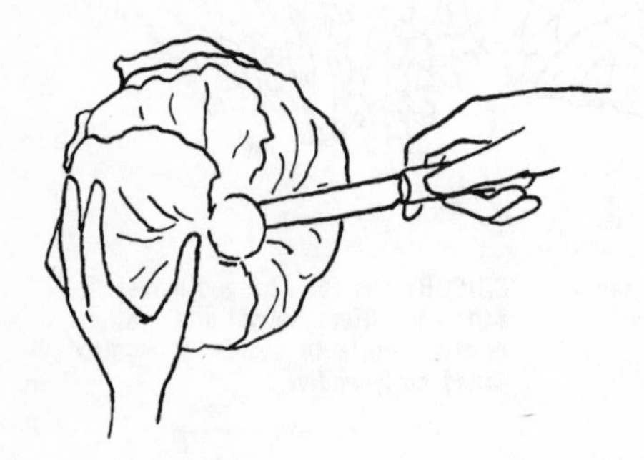

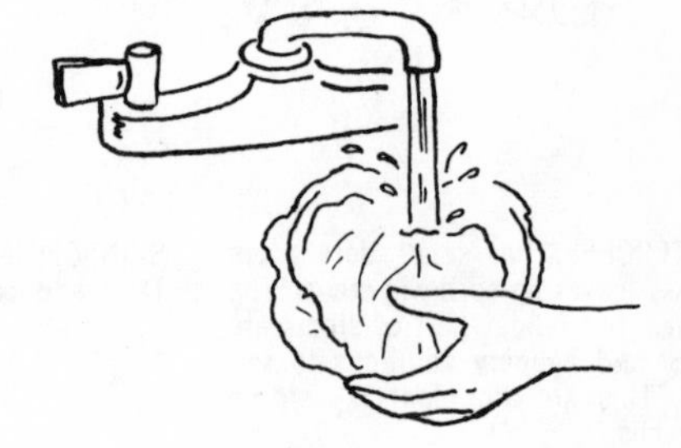

Tips for handling certain greens:

LETTUCE—remove any bruised outer leaves. Cut out the core with a sharp knife. Then hold the head, core cavity up, under cool running water. The water will separate the leaves.

CHICORY, ESCAROLE, ROMAINE—leave the root end on. Wash the heads thoroughly under cool running water.

SPINACH—cut off roots and remove any bruised leaves. Swish leaves in a sink full of cool water, changing the water several times. When the leaves are clean, blot them dry between paper towels.

PARSLEY, WATERCRESS—wash, dry, then store in tightly covered jars, plastic bags or plastic wrap in the refrigerator.

Care For Bowls

Treat a wooden salad bowl with tender, loving care, and it will be a favorite for years. These bowls develop a fine patina with age if they are properly cared for.

The harder the wood, the better the salad bowl. Hard wood does not absorb too much of the liquid dressings. The flavor of dressings, particularly garlic, will "season" the bowl if you do not thoroughly wash the bowl after using it.

It is this seasoning that produces the patina—and even seems to add a special something to the salad itself.

Drain a wooden salad bowl after use, then rub dry with absorbent paper. As an added preventive to keep the bowl from cracking, polish it with oil paper.

If you feel you should clean the bowl more completely, rinse it quickly in clear, lukewarm water. Rinse again quickly, this time in cold water, then dry it completely.

Before using an unfinished wooden salad bowl the first time, rub the inside thoroughly with olive oil, then dry it.

ONE BOWL FOR GREENS . . .

If at all possible, use one bowl for green salads alone. Have another, preferably a large pottery or glass bowl, for salads which are mixed with mayonnaise. The bowls should be chilled before the salad is added, and of course, washed each time after they are used.

Handle the pottery or china bowl carefully. They are apt to chip easily if you toss the salad too hard. Ceramic bowls, though less likely to chip, may do so if treated roughly.

Clear glass bowls demand the least care, and they are relatively inexpensive. They are perfect for displaying mixed greens or fresh fruit salad.

For the ultimate in elegance, present your salad showcase in a silver bowl. To protect the silver, toss the salad in a glass bowl, then put this glass bowl in the silver one before serving.

To Make Good Salads Better

Why is one salad a masterpiece and another just a bowl of greens?

Often it's the garnish that makes the difference. Besides decorating the salad, a garnish adds to the taste. Think how much better a green salad tastes when it is topped with strips of meat and cheese, olives or pickles, anchovies or hard-cooked egg. And, the salad is far prettier with these good-to-eat garnishes.

A garnish provides contrast and interest to salads, but it is not the center of attention. With garnishes, use a light touch, just enough to make the salad pretty, not enough so it becomes gaudy.

Often the way a salad is placed on the serving dish is all the garnish that is needed, so let your imagination take over in this department.

WHICH GARNISH TO USE

Type of Salad	Garnish
TOSSED GREEN	Apples, artichokes, avocado, bacon, cheese, meat, eggs, citrus fruit, grapes, olives, radishes.
TOSSED VEGETABLE	Anchovies, bacon, bleu cheese, capers, eggs, grated lemon rind, nuts, pickle relish, sardines, dill pickles, pimiento.
FRUIT	Cheese, cheese spreads, nuts.
MEAT, SEAFOOD	Fruit, cheese, cucumbers, olives, tomatoes, pickles, mushrooms.
POULTRY	Asparagus tips, avocado, cranberry jelly, fruit, olives, nuts, watercress, dill, mint, parsley.

GARNISH TRICKS

TOMATO FLOWERS

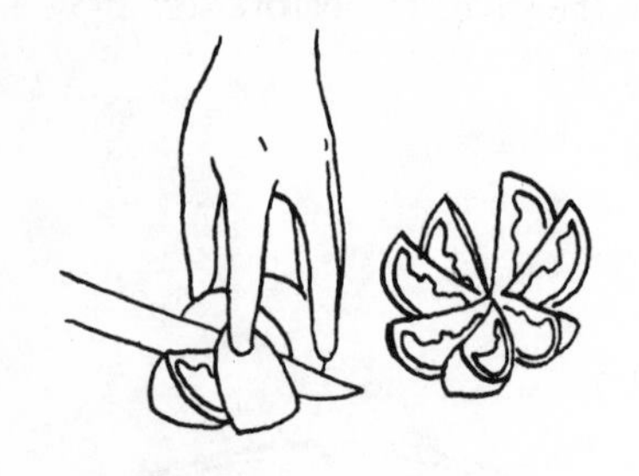

Using a sharp knife, cut tomato into wedges, making sure that it is not cut completely through. Lightly spread wedges apart.

CARROT CURLS

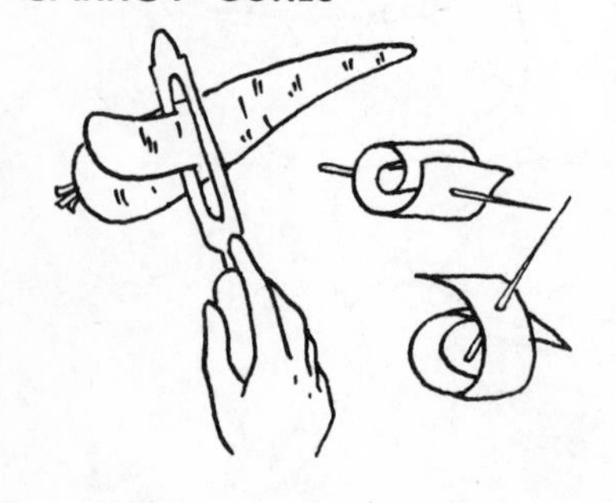

Scrape raw carrots to remove tough outer skin. Using potato peeler, slice carrot lengthwise into very thin strips. Roll up strips; secure with toothpicks. Place in ice water to crisp.

CELERY CURLS

Cut celery sticks about 4 inches long. Slice into narrow lengthwise strips (to within 1 inch of end). Place cut celery in ice water to curl.

RADISH ROSES

Cut off radish root. Leave some of the stem and leaves. Cut down side close to skin in several places to make petals. Place in ice water. Do not try to separate or spread the petals apart. The ice water will make them bloom.

FLUTED CUCUMBERS

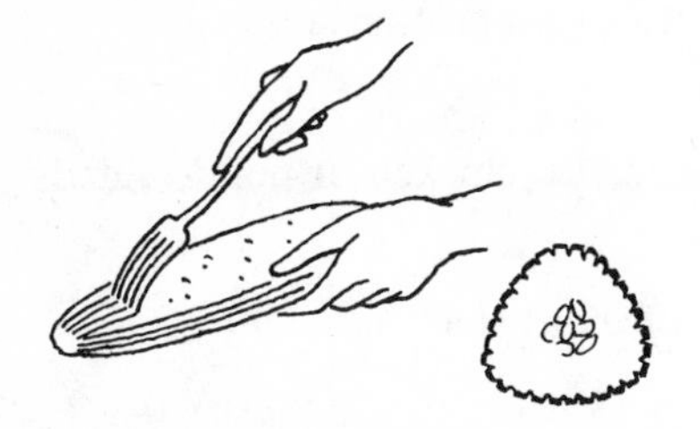

Cut off end of the cucumber. Peel if the cucumber is tough. Leave young cucumber unpeeled for added color. Draw tines of a fork firmly down the length of the cucumber. Cut into thin slices. Chill in refrigerator.

CHOPPED PARSLEY

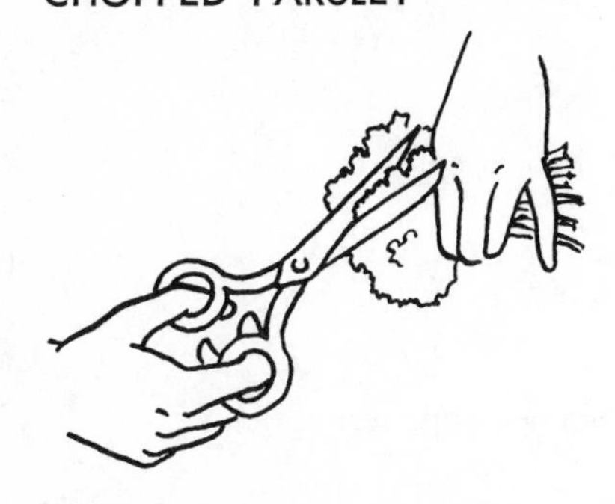

Pull parsley bunch through hand to form close bunch. Snip with kitchen scissors.

CELERY PINWHEELS

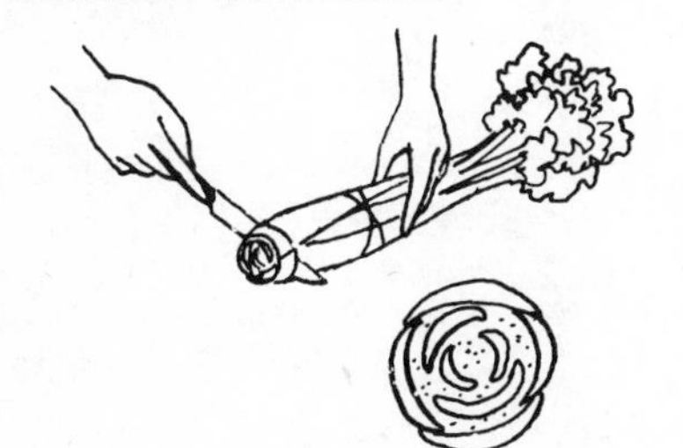

Separate celery stalks. Trim ends. Wash thoroughly. Fill stalks with cheese. Put together, tie, chill, slice.

In Favor of Flavor

To give your salads a tasty lift, add seasonings or cheese to them. The chart below will guide you in using seasonings which complement the salad.

Herbs and spices should be stored tightly covered away from heat or cold. As soon as they lose their delicate aroma, replace them.

Cheeses should be refrigerated for best keeping. However, they are served at room temperature for the most distinctive flavor. Exceptions are cream, cottage and Neufchatel cheese which should be chilled when served.

HERBS	USE WITH
BASIL	Tomato salads, fresh tomato slices
CARAWAY	Coleslaw, beet salads
DILL SEED	Coleslaw, potato salad
MARJORAM	French dressing, fresh tomato slices, meat salads
OREGANO	Potato or tuna salads
ROSEMARY	French dressing or mayonnaise for chicken or potato salads
SAVORY	Tossed salads
THYME	French dressing marinade for diced chicken

CHEESE	USE WITH
AMERICAN CHEDDAR	Tossed salads, dressings, appetizers
BLEU	Tossed salads, dressings, appetizer spreads
BRICK	Salads, appetizers
CAMEMBERT	Fruit salads, appetizer spreads
COTTAGE	Fruit, vegetable salads
CREAM	Fruit, vegetable salads, dressings, appetizer spreads
GORGONZOLA	Salads, dressings
GOUDA	Appetizers
MUENSTER	Raw vegetable appetizers
NEUFCHATEL	Salads, in dips
PROVOLONE	Appetizers
RICOTTA	Salads, appetizers
ROQUEFORT	Dressings, appetizers
SWISS	Fruit, vegetable salads

SPICES	USE WITH
ALLSPICE	Fruit salads, fruit salad dressings
CINNAMON	Tomatoes, cottage cheese garnishes
GINGER	Pear salads
MACE	Whipped cream dressings for fruit salads
MUSTARD	Mixed with water for commercial mayonnaise or French dressing
PAPRIKA	Add to oil and vinegar for additional color
CAYENNE PEPPER	Salad dressings, meat, fish and vegetable salads

BLENDS	USE WITH
APPLE PIE SPICE	Waldorf salad
CURRY POWDER	French dressing for chicken salad
HERB SEASONING	Sliced cucumbers, sliced tomatoes, French dressing
ITALIAN DRESSING	French dressing, tossed green salads
PICKLING SPICE	Beet salads
SALAD LIFT	Add to oil and vinegar for French dressing or stir into prepared salad dressing
SEASONING SALT	Substitute for salt in oil and vinegar dressings

Salads In A Hurry

FRUIT

START WITH	COMBINE WITH	SERVE WITH
Crushed pineapple	Chopped cranberries Chopped nuts	Mayonnaise
Pineapple chunks	Melon balls	Mint French Dressing
Pineapple slices	Banana slices Peanuts	French Dressing
Pineapple slices	Cream cheese Chopped nuts	French Dressing
Pineapple slices	Grapefruit sections Orange sections	Fruit Dressing
Pineapple slices	Prunes, stuffed with cream cheese	French Dressing
Apricot halves	Soft cream cheese Chopped dates	Fruit Dressing
Peach halves	Cottage cheese Chopped chives or onion	No Dressing
Red apples, sliced	Spread apple slices with cream cheese	French Dressing
Red apples, sliced	Grapefruit sections	Fruit Dressing
Diced apples	Halved raw cranberries Diced celery	Creamy French Dressing
Diced apples	Chopped celery Nuts Seeded grapes	French Dressing
Bananas, sliced	Grapefruit sections Orange sections	Honey French Dressing
Bananas, sliced	Pineapple slices Red berries	French Dressing
Bananas, sliced lengthwise	Spread with peanut butter, press together. Slice crosswise. Sprinkle with chopped salted peanuts.	Creamy French Dressing

VEGETABLES

START WITH	COMBINE WITH	SERVE WITH
Cooked Peas	Sliced celery Cheese cubes	French Dressing
Green Beans	Egg slices	French Dressing
Sliced beets	Thin onion rings	French Dressing
Asparagus spears	Tomato wedges	French Dressing
Cucumber slices	Green or sweet onion slices	French Dressing
Cucumber slices	Sliced radishes Green pepper strips	Onion French Dressing
Cucumber slices	Sliced onions Lettuce chunks Tomato wedges	French Dressing
Shredded cabbage	Chopped onion Thinly sliced carrots	French Dressing
Shredded cabbage	Chopped green pepper Chopped pimiento	Garlic French Dressing Dash Tabasco
Shredded cabbage	Drained pineapple chunks	Fluffy Cream Dressing
Shredded cabbage	Chopped celery Chopped parsley	Thousand Island or French Dressing
Shredded cabbage	Unpared red apples, diced Nut meats, broken	Cooked Mayonnaise
Shredded cabbage	Chopped sweet pickle Minced onion Vinegar	Mayonnaise
Tomato, cut into eighths	Head lettuce, broken into bite-size pieces	Onion French Dressing
Tomato, cut into eighths	Capers Chopped onion	Celery Seed French Dressing
Tomato, center removed	Diced cooked chicken	Creamy French Dressing
Tomato, cut in very thin slices	Minced parsley Minced green onions Freshly ground black pepper	French Dressing
Tomato slices	Sliced cucumber	Garlic French Dressing
Tomato slices	Avocado, pared and cut into strips	French Dressing
Tomato slices	Cottage cheese	Chive French Dressing

What Terms Mean

BLANCH—Parboil in water for a minute, or to pour boiling water over food and then drain it almost immediately

BLEND—Mix two or more ingredients

CHILL—Refrigerate until thoroughly cold

CHOP—Cut into pieces with a sharp knife

CUT—Divide food materials with a knife or scissors

DICE—Cut into small cubes

FLAKE—Break into small pieces; for example, with canned tuna fish

FOLD—Combine by using two motions, cutting vertically through the mixture and turning over and over by sliding a spatula across the bottom of the mixing bowl with each turn

GARNISH—Decorate; for instance, decorate a salad with hard-cooked eggs or parsley

GRATE—Cut food into minute bits by rubbing on a grater

GRIND—Cut food into tiny particles by putting through a grinder

MARINATE—Let food stand in an oil-acid mixture such as French dressing

MINCE—Cut or chop into very small pieces

MIX—Combine ingredients in any way that evenly distributes them

PARE—Trim off the outside covering

PEEL—Strip off the outside covering

SCALD—Heat milk to just below the boiling point

SHRED—Cut fine with a knife or sharp instrument

SLIVER—Slice into long, thin strips

STIR—Mix food with a circular motion to blend it so it has uniform consistency

TEAR—Break or tear into bite-size pieces

TOSS—Lightly blend food ingredients

WHIP—Beat rapidly to produce expansion due by incorporating air as with cream, egg and gelatin dishes

Calorie Counts

CHEESE	Amount	Calories
Blue or Roquefort type	1 oz.	105
Cheddar or American:		
Ungrated	1-in. cube	70
Grated	1 cup	445
Cottage cheese:		
Creamed	1 cup	240
Uncreamed	1 cup	195
Cream cheese	1 oz.	105
Parmesan, dry, grated	1 tbsp.	20
Swiss, natural	1 oz.	105
MEAT, POULTRY, FISH, SHELLFISH, RELATED PRODUCTS		
Bacon, broiled or fried crisp, drained	1 slice	50
Chicken, cooked:		
Meat and Skin, broiled	3 oz. without bone	190
Canned, boneless	3 oz.	170
Ham, baked, lean and fat	3 oz.	245
Boiled ham, sliced	1 oz.	65
Crab meat, canned	3 oz.	85
Salmon, pink, canned	3 oz.	120
Shrimp, canned, meat only	3 oz.	100
Tuna, canned in oil, drained	3 oz.	170
NUTS, RELATED PRODUCTS		
Almonds, shelled	¼ cup	210
Brazil nuts, broken pieces	¼ cup	190
Cashew nuts, roasted	¼ cup	190
Coconut, flaked, packaged	¼ cup	150
Peanut halves, roasted, salted	¼ cup	210
Peanut butter	1 tbsp.	95
Pecans:		
Halves	5 halves	70
Chopped	¼ cup	185
English Walnut:		
Halves	6 halves	65
Chopped	¼ cup	165
VEGETABLES AND VEGETABLE PRODUCTS		
Beans:		
Kidney, dried, canned	½ cup	115
Lima, cooked	½ cup	90
Snap, green, cooked	¾ cup	25
Beets, cooked, diced	1 cup	70

Cabbage:		
Raw:		
Finely shredded	½ cup	12
Cole slaw with mayonnaise	½ cup	85
Cooked	¾ cup	25
Carrots:		
Raw:		
Whole, 5½ x 1 in. (25 thin strips)	1 carrot	20
Grated	½ cup	20
Cooked, diced	½ cup	20
Cauliflower, raw, flower buds	⅓ cup	10
Celery, raw:		
Stalk, small inner	3 stalks	10
Pieces, diced	1 cup	17
Cucumbers, 7½ x 2 in.:		
Raw, pared	1 cucumber	30
Raw, pared, center slice, ⅛-in. thick	6 slices	1
Endive, curly (including escarole)	2 oz.	10
Lettuce, headed, raw:		
Head, loose leaf, 4-in. diameter	1 head	30
Head, compact, 4¾-in. diameter, 1 lb.	1 head	60
Leaves	2 large or 4 small	5
Mushrooms, canned, solids and liquid	½ cup	20
Onions:		
Mature:		
Raw, 2½-in. diameter	1 onion	40
Young, green, small, without tops	6 onions	20
Parsley, raw, chopped	1 tbsp.	1
Peas, green:		
Cooked	½ cup	55
Canned, drained	½ cup	70
Peppers, green; raw:	1 med.	15
Chopped	1 tbsp.	2
Canned, pimentoes, medium	1 med.	10
Potatoes, medium, about 3 per lb.; Boiled		
Peeled after boiling	1 potato	105
Peeled before boiling	1 potato	80
Potato chips, medium 2-in. diameter	10 chips	115
Radishes, raw, small, without tops	4 radishes	5
Sauerkraut, canned, including liquids	1 cup	45
Tomatoes:		
Raw, medium 2 x 2½-in. diameter, about 3 per lb.	1 tomato	35
Tomato juice, canned	½ cup	25
Tomato catsup	1 tbsp.	20

FRUIT AND FRUIT PRODUCTS

Apples, raw, medium 2½-in. diameter, about 3 per lb.	1 apple	70
Apple juice, fresh or canned	½ cup	60
Applesauce, canned:		
Sweetened	½ cup	115
Unsweetened	½ cup	50

Food	Portion	Calories
Apricots:		
Raw, about 12 per lb.	3 apricots	55
Canned, heavy syrup (pack)	4 halves	105
Dried; uncooked halves	10 small	100
Avocados, raw:		
California varieties	½ avocado	185
Florida varieties, peeled, pitted	½ avocado	185
Bananas, raw medium	1 banana	85
Blackberries, fresh	¾ cup	40
Blueberries, fresh	⅔ cup	60
Cantaloupes, medium	½ melon	60
Cherries:		
Fresh raw, sour, sweet, hybrid	1 cup	65
Canned, sour, red, pitted	½ cup	105
Cranberries, fresh	1 cup	50
Dates, fresh and dried, pitted, cut	2 cups	40
Figs:		
Fresh, 1½ in. diameter	3 figs	90
Dried, large, 2 x 1 inch	1 fig	60
Fruit cocktail, canned in syrup	½ cup	95
Grapefruit:		
Fresh medium white	½ grapefruit	55
Pink or red	½ grapefruit	60
Raw, sections, White	½ cup	4
Grapes:		
American slip skin	1 cup	65
European adherent skin	1 cup	95
Green seedless	1 bunch	80
Lemons, medium	1 lemon	20
Lemon juice:		
Fresh	¼ cup	15
Fresh	1 tbsp.	4
Canned, unsweetened	¼ cup	15
Limes, medium	1 lime	15
Lime juice, Fresh	¼ cup	15
Fresh	1 tbsp.	4
Oranges, fresh:		
Navel, California	1 orange	60
Other varieties	1 orange	75
Orange juice:		
Fresh:		
California Valencia, summer	1 cup	120
Florida varieties:		
Early and midseason	1 cup	100
Late season	1 cup	110
Canned, unsweetened	1 cup	120
Frozen concentrate:		
Undiluted, Unsweetened, 6 oz. can	1 can	85
Water added	1 cup	110
Orange and grapefruit juice:		
Frozen concentrate: water added	1 cup	110

Food	Amount	Calories
Peaches:		
Fresh:		
Whole, medium, 2-in. diameter	1 peach	35
Sliced	1 cup	65
Canned, syrup pack, heavy	1 cup	200
Frozen:		
Carton, 4 oz.	1 carton	99
Can 16 oz.	1 can	355
Pears:		
Fresh, 3 x 2½ in.-diameter	1 pear	100
Canned, heavy syrup pack, halves or slices	1 cup	195
Pineapple:		
Fresh, diced	¾ cup	55
Canned, syrup pack:		
Chunks	10 med. with 2 tbsp. juice	75
Crushed	½ cup	95
Sliced	2 small or 1 large slice and 2 tbsp. juice	90
Pineapple juice, canned	¾ cup	105
Plums:		
Fresh, 2-in. diameter	1 plum	25
Canned, syrup pack	3 with 2 tbsp. juice	100
Prunes, dried:		
Medium:		
Uncooked	4 prunes	70
Cooked, unsweetened	4 with 2 tbsp. juice	95
Prune juice, canned	½ cup	100
Raisins, dried	1 tbsp. scant	30
Raspberries, red:		
Fresh	¾ cup	50
Frozen, 5 oz. carton	1 carton	138
Strawberries:		
Red, capped	¾ cup	40
Frozen, halves	5 oz.	155
Frozen, whole	5 oz.	131
Tangerines, medium	1 tangerine	40
Watermelon, 4 x 8-in. wedge	1 wedge	115

FATS AND OILS

Food	Amount	Calories
Oils, salad or cooking	1 tbsp.	125
Salad dressings:		
Bleu cheese	1 tbsp.	80
French	1 tbsp.	60
Italian	1 tbsp.	85
Home-cooked, boiled	1 tbsp.	30
Mayonnaise	1 tbsp.	105
Thousand Island	1 tbsp.	75

Source: Yearbook of Agriculture, U.S. Department of Agriculture

APPETIZERS

Recipe for Cocktail Curry Sauce on Page 31

Appetite Pleasers

For today's busy homemaker planning a party or dinner without help, appetizers that can be made in advance allow more time to spend with guests.

Appetizers are just what their name implies—appetite-teasers. They are to whet the appetite for the meal that is to follow.

Appetizers or hors d'oeuvre are usually simple finger foods, so it is unnecessary to provide forks when serving them. Toothpicks are good for spearing small sausages, tiny meatballs, cheese cubes, etc. Have napkins within easy reach, of course.

When planning appetizers, keep your full meal in mind, if you plan to serve one. Fresh, crisp vegetables or tangy marinated vegetables are excellent if the meal is to be rich or heavy. If a light meal is planned, the appetizers can be creamy or rich.

TANTALIZINGLY ATTRACTIVE

Make your appetizers attractive. They will be more tantalizing. Arrange them on pretty serving platters, bread-boards or even in baskets.

Shells of fruit, such as melons or pineapples, make unusually attractive serving "dishes."

Have an alcohol lamp handy so guests can toast their own tiny meat appetizers. Or keep them hot in a pretty chafing dish and let guests help themselves.

Arrange seafood appetizers on beds of shredded ice. Embed a cup of zingy sauce in the center of the ice. Surround mounds of dip with crackers and chips.

THE HOSTESS' CHOICE

There are no rules governing where to serve appetizers. It's whatever best suits the convenience of the hostess.

Vegetables steeped in seasoned marinades and chilled before serving do double duty as an appetizer and salad course at the table, or they can be served ahead of time with cocktails.

Appetizers can replace the soup course at dinner. They may be passed around or served buffet-style. Weather permitting, set up a table on the patio or near a barbecue pit and serve appetizers out-of-doors.

As with all foods, make sure with appetizers that the cold ones are served well chilled and the hot ones piping hot.

Variety of Appetizers

ANCHOVY—Small, smoked, herring-like fish. Very salty and pungent. Used especially for relishes and sauces.

ANCHOVY PASTE—Paste made of anchovies.

ASPIC—Jelly of fish or meat stock used to make cold vegetable, meat or fish molds.

CANAPE—Appetizer of small pieces of cracker, toast or bread topped with caviar, anchovy or other savory food.

CAVIAR—Processed salted roe of sturgeon. Very expensive.

RED CAVIAR—Salmon roe. Less expensive.

COMPOTE—Mixture of fruits cooked in syrup.

CROUTON—Small cube of bread toasted or fried crisp.

DEVIL—Chop food fine, combine with sharp seasonings and cook with a crumb topping. Or crumbled food which is cooked and served with a sharp sauce.

FOIE GRAS—A fat liver, especially of goose, usually served in the form of a paté.

HORS D'OEUVRE—Appetizers served with cocktails or before dinner usually accompanied by small crackers or toast.

PATÉ—Seasoned paste usually made of poultry, seafood or meat. Used as spread for canapes or crackers or cut into thin slices and served with a garnish.

PATÉ DE FOIE GRAS—Paste of fat goose liver and truffles, sometimes with added fat pork. Sometimes made with chicken livers.

PUREE—Vegetables or fruits which have been put through a sieve to form a smooth paste.

SPANISH OLIVES—Green olives stuffed with pimiento.

TRUFFLES—A dark, rich, edible fungus which grows underground in some parts of Europe. Used in some patés. Very expensive.

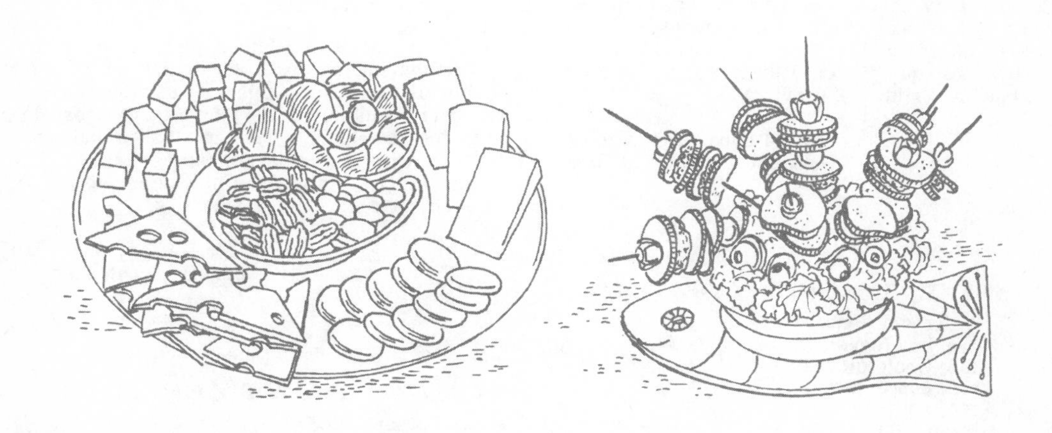

AVOCADO DIP

1 lge ripe avocado
¼ tsp. onion juice
Dash each of pepper, curry powder and cayenne
1 tbsp. white wine vinegar
¼ tsp. salt

Peel avocado and remove seed. Mash to smooth pulp and mix with remaining ingredients. Use as dip for potato chips, cauliflowerets, diagonally cut carrot slices or tiny cheese crackers. Use horseradish or Worcestershire in place of curry powder, if desired. Yield: 1 cup.

Mrs. Homer E. Melton
Woodlawn, Virginia

BACON-AVOCADO DIP

6 slices bacon
2 ripe med. avocados
1 c. sour cream
½ tsp. monosodium glutamate
1 ½ tsp. onion salt
2 tbsp. horseradish
2 tsp. lemon juice
1 tsp. Worcestershire sauce

Cook bacon until crisp and break into small pieces. Mash avocados to smooth pulp. Add remaining ingredients with bacon. Chill. Serve with corn chips, crackers or with celery and carrot sticks.

Mrs. M. E. Cobb
Rosenberg, Texas

TERIYAKI APPETIZERS

½ c. soy sauce
2 tbsp. brown sugar
1 clove of garlic
1 tsp. cracked gingerroot
1 ½ lb. round steak

Combine soy sauce, sugar, garlic and gingerroot. Cut steak into 1/2-inch cubes; add to above mixture and let stand overnight. Remove meat; cook quickly on Hibachi and serve on toothpicks. Yield: 6-8 servings.

Donna Franquemont
Asheboro, North Carolina

FESTIVE TOMATO COCKTAIL

4 c. tomato juice
3 sm. bay leaves
½ tsp. whole cloves
⅛ tsp. peppercorns
¾ tsp. salt
1 ½ tsp. diced onion
3 tbsp. sugar

Simmer all ingredients together for 30 minutes. Strain. Taste and add more ground cloves, sugar or other seasonings as desired. Serve either hot or cold. Yield: 8 servings.

Mrs. Peggy Shomaker
Lenoir, North Carolina

PINEAPPLE APPETIZER

1 tall can unsweetened pineapple juice
1 bottle ginger ale

Freeze pineapple juice in ice cube trays. Thaw until slushy when ready for use. Pour ginger ale over the frozen crushed pineapple juice.

Mrs. R. E. Hayes
Louisburg, North Carolina

SEVEN-UP HOLIDAY APPETIZER

1 pt. peppermint ice cream
1 qt. milk
4 7-oz. bottles chilled Seven-Up

Put semi-soft ice cream in bowl. Add milk and Seven-Up. Stir until ice cream floats in small pieces. Garnish with maraschino cherries and mint leaves, if desired. Yield: 12 servings.

Mrs. Ernest Waddell
Fort Worth, Texas

STRAWBERRY AND PINEAPPLE COCKTAIL

1 c. orange juice
½ c. lemon juice
Sugar
1 c. strawberries
1 c. diced pineapple

Combine orange and lemon juice sweetened to taste, keeping mixture rather tart. Chill. Wash and drain the strawberries. At serving time, cut the berries in half, reserving 6 large ones; mix with the pineapple. Place in glasses and cover with fruit juice. One large, perfect berry set on a tiny circle of pineapple may decorate the top of each cocktail. Yield 6 servings.

Mrs. Peggy Shomaker
Lenoir, North Carolina

TOMATO APPETIZER

Tomato juice
Sprig of mint or watercress

(Continued on next page)

Freeze tomato juice to a slush. Serve with a sprig of mint or watercress.

Mrs. Beulah Gibson
Athens, Alabama

TOMATO JUICE COCKTAIL

- 2 c. tomato juice
- Lemon juice to taste
- Lemon slices

Chill tomato juice with lemon juice to taste. Serve with lemon slice on each glass.

Mrs. Herbert Beaman
New Bern, North Carolina

AVOCADO DIP

- 3 avocados, mashed fine
- 3 or 4 sm. pkg. cream cheese
- 4 tbsp. mayonnaise
- Juice of 1 lime
- Juice of ½ lemon
- ½ sm. onion, grated
- 1 clove of garlic
- 1 tbsp. sherry
- Salt, pepper and paprika to taste

Blend all ingredients well and chill.

Lola A. Harris
Shelbyville, Kentucky

BASIC DIP FOR APPETIZERS

- 1 8-oz. pkg. cream cheese
- 1 carton sour cream
- Pinch of salt
- Pinch of onion and garlic salt

Combine cream cheese, sour cream and seasonings to blend smooth. To this basic dip may be added chili peppers, chopped shrimp, crushed nuts, crushed pineapple or mashed avocado as desired. Serve with corn chips, potato chips or crackers.

Mrs. Frank Groessel
Clint, Texas

BAKED CHEESE BALLS

- ½ c. butter
- 8 oz. sharp cheddar cheese, grated
- ½ tsp. paprika
- ½ tsp. salt
- 1 c. flour
- Green stuffed olives

Mix all ingredients together except olives until smooth. Wrap 1 tablespoon cheese mixture around each stuffed olive. Bake 10 minutes at 400 degrees.

Mrs. John E. Adams, Jr.
Follis, Oklahoma

CHEESE-OLIVE COCKTAIL SNACK

- 1 c. grated medium cheddar cheese
- ¼ c. butter
- ½ c. flour
- ¼ tsp. red pepper, ground
- Salt to taste
- 25 med. stuffed green olives

Combine all ingredients except olive; blend until smooth and creamy. Mold mixture around each olive. Bake at 400 degrees for 10 to 12 minutes. Yield: 25 servings.

Kate Cullum
Batesburg, South Carolina

CHEESE STRAWS

- 2 c. flour
- 1 tsp. salt
- 2 tsp. baking powder
- Pinch of red pepper
- ⅓ c. butter
- ¾ c. grated cheese
- 1 egg
- ½ c. milk

Stir together flour, salt, baking powder and pepper. Work butter and cheese into the flour. Beat egg and milk until light; add to the flour mixture. Mix smooth. Roll into 1/2-inch thick and 4-inch long strips. Bake in hot oven.

Mrs. French L. Dove
Garrison, Texas

EXOTIC HORS D' OEUVRES

- ¼ c. grated sharp cheddar cheese
- ¼ c. chopped ripe olives or pickle relish
- 1 med. onion, grated
- ½ tsp. curry powder
- Mayonnaise
- English muffins

Combine all ingredients except muffins with enough mayonnaise to moisten; spread on muffins. Broil until slightly browned and bubbly. Cut into serving pieces.

Helen V. Childs
Covington, Virginia

PARTY PICK-UP OR APPETIZER

1 3-oz. pkg. cream cheese
½ c. margarine
1 ½ c. flour

Combine cheese and margarine and mix until well blended. Gradually add flour and blend. Chill for several hours. After chilling, roll pastry and cut in 2-inch rounds. Cut pieces of foil in 2-inch rounds and lay circles of pastry on each. Pinch foil and dough together in 5 points, forming a cup. Bake at 450 degrees for 10 or 12 minutes. Cool and remove foil cup. Fill each cup with jelly or preserves. Yield: 2 dozen.

Mrs. W. M. Cavin
Stanley, North Carolina

FROZEN LOG

½ lb. yellow sharp cheese
8 slices bacon
½ tsp. Worcestershire sauce
2 sm. onions
1 tsp. dry mustard
2 tsp. mayonnaise

Put all ingredients through food chopper; blend well. Roll into a log the size of a 50-cent piece; freeze. Slice and place on bread rounds, crackers or split English muffins. Broil until browned; serve.

Mrs. Mary Evans
San Antonio, Texas

CHEESE BALL APPETIZER

1 8-oz. pkg. cream cheese
1 jar Roka-Blu spread
1 jar old English sharp cheese spread
2 tbsp. beer
1 tbsp. grated onion

Cream all ingredients thoroughly. Form into 2 balls. May be frozen. To serve, roll in chopped parsley or nuts. Center on plate and surround with crackers.

Mrs. Harold McLeod, Jr.
Greensboro, North Carolina

SWISS SANDWICH PUFFS

16 slices tiny icebox rye bread
½ c. salad dressing or mayonnaise
¼ c. finely chopped onion
2 tbsp. snipped parsley
8 slices process Swiss cheese

Toast bread on both sides. Combine salad dressing, onion and parsley; spread on toast. Cut out rounds of cheese to fit toast; place a cheese round atop each slice, covering salad dressing mixture. Broil 3 to 4 inches from heat until cheese is puffy and golden, about 2 to 3 minutes. Trim tops with sliced olives, if desired. Serve hot. Yield: 16 servings.

Mrs. Earl Ramond
Bay St. Louis, Mississippi

CHEESE BALL

1 lb. soft type cheddar cheese
1 8-oz. pkg. cream cheese
Dash of onion salt or juice
Dash of garlic salt
Dash of Tabasco sauce
Dash of Worcestershire sauce
Dash of salt
½ c. nuts, toasted
Paprika

Soften cheeses and blend. Add seasonings to taste. Form the seasoned cheese into a ball and roll in the crushed nuts. Roll the ball in paprika. Chill cheese slightly in order to roll more easily. Serve on decorated platter.

Mrs. Jack J. Durham
Amherst, Texas

CHEESE BALLS

1 12-oz. carton cottage cheese
Milk
2 tbsp. grated onion
Salt and pepper to taste
Chopped parsley

Blend cottage cheese and enough milk to make a smooth paste. Add grated onion, salt and pepper to taste. Form into small balls. Roll in chopped parsley. Chill. Serve with picks.

Mrs. Della Brown Little
Johnson City, Tennessee

CHEESE DELIGHTS

1 stick butter or margarine
1 jar Old English cheese
1 c. sifted flour
½ tsp. salt
½ tsp. cayenne pepper

Combine all ingredients; mix well. Shape into ball or log. Chill. Serve with crackers.

Mrs. Mary Chandler
Marquez, Texas

GARLIC-CHEESE ROLL

½ lb. cheddar cheese, grated
1 3-oz. pkg. cream cheese, softened
1 sm. clove of garlic, finely chopped
1 tsp. salt
¼ c. chopped pecans
Paprika
Round salted crackers

Combine cheeses, garlic and salt; blend in pecans. Form into roll the diameter of round crackers. Roll on waxed paper sprinkled with paprika; wrap. Chill overnight. Slice; serve on crackers. Yield: 10-12 servings.

Mrs. Cary King, Sr.
Tullos, Louisiana

GARLIC-CHEESE ROLL

½ lb. mild yellow cheese
2 lge. cloves of garlic
1 c. pecans
1 3-oz. pkg. cream cheese
Chili powder

Grind yellow cheese, garlic and pecans in food grinder. Add mashed cream cheese and mix thoroughly. Roll into long roll any size desired in waxed paper sprinkled generously with chili powder. Leave rolled up in the paper and refrigerate at least 24 hours before serving. Cut slices of desired thickness and serve on round crackers.

Mrs. R. E. Taylor
Victoria, Texas

CHEESE LOGS

1 lge. pkg. cream cheese
½ lb. pimento cheese, grated
½ lb. sharp cheese, grated
½ lb. cheddar cheese, grated
2 c. pecans, chopped
1 onion
2 cloves of garlic
2 pimentos, chopped
Red pepper to taste
Salt to taste
Paprika

Soften cream cheese; add remaining cheeses and pecans. Grind onion, garlic and pimentos together; blend with cheese mixture, pepper and salt. Form three logs; roll in paprika. Wrap with waxed paper; store in freezer. Thinly slice; serve on crackers.

Mrs. Abe Daigle
Lafayette, Louisiana

CREAM CHEESE BALL

1 16-oz. pkg. cream cheese
1 c. cottage cheese
2 ½-oz. Roquefort cheese
¼ lb. sharp cheddar cheese, grated
2 tbsp. Worcestershire sauce
1 sm. onion, grated
¼ tsp. grated garlic
1 tbsp. monosodium glutamate
1 or 2 dashes Tabasco sauce
½ tsp. seasoned salt
1 c. finely chopped parsley
1 c. finely chopped pecans

Mix all cheeses and seasonings with one-half the parsley and pecans. Mold in round greased mold. Mix remaining parsley and pecans; pat on outside of ball. Chill for 24 hours. Serve with crackers or corn chips.

Mrs. P. H. Loh
Morrilton, Arkansas

CHEESE BALL PICK-ME-UPS

1 8-oz. pkg. cream cheese
1 4-oz. pkg. bleu cheese
1 5-oz. jar Old English cheese
1 6-oz. roll smoked cheese
1 tsp. monosodium glutamate
Dash of salt
¼ tsp. garlic powder or 1 clove of garlic, crushed
1 tbsp. Worcestershire sauce
⅛ tsp. Tabasco sauce
1 c. finely snipped parsley
1 c. finely chopped pecans
Pretzel sticks

Soften cheeses to room temperature. Blend well with monosodium glutamate, salt, garlic and sauces. Add 1/3 cup parsley and 1/2 cup pecans; blend. Chill cheese mixture until easy to handle. Form into 1-inch balls and roll in reserved parsley-nut mixture. Refrigerate. May be stored for several days. Insert a pretzel stick in each cheese ball just before serving. Yield: 90 balls.

Mrs. Lura Lee Davis
Sweetwater, Texas

NIPPY NUT LOG

1 8-oz. pkg. cream cheese, softened
¼ lb. bleu cheese, crumbled
1 tbsp. grated onion
1 tbsp. Worcestershire sauce
½ c. finely chopped toasted pecans

Blend cheeses. Add onion and Worcestershire. Mix thoroughly. Shape mixture into a log. Roll in pecans. Chill. Yield 6-8 servings.

Thomas O. Davis
Waynesboro, Mississippi

OLIVE-CHEESE BALLS

1 lge. jar Spanish olives
1 sm. pkg. cream cheese
1 tsp. garlic powder
1 tbsp. lemon juice
Chopped salted peanuts

Drain and dry the olives with a paper towel. Mix cheese, garlic and lemon juice and spread on olives to cover. Roll covered olives in peanuts and chill.

Mrs. Wm. Droenner
Giddings, Texas

CELERY PINWHEELS

Cheese
Mayonnaise or salad dressing
Bunch of celery

Soften and mix favorite cheese with enough mayonnaise to spread easily. Separate celery; fill each stalk with cheese mixture. Reassemble the bunch; tie with cord if necessary. Wrap in wax papper and chill thoroughly. Cut crosswise to serve.

Mrs. Arver L. Britt
Soperton, Georgia

ROQUEFORT ROLLS

2 3-oz. pkg. cream cheese
⅛ lb. Roquefort cheese
2 tbsp. finely chopped celery
1 tbsp. finely chopped onion
Dash of cayenne pepper
Salad dressing
1 ½ c. finely chopped walnuts

Blend cheeses; add celery, onion, cayenne and salad dressing. Form into tiny rolls or balls. Roll in nuts; chill. Yield: 16-20 rolls.

Mrs. Jo Frances Weimar
Alto, Texas

COLLEGE INN SPECIAL

1 sm. bottle stuffed olives
¼ c. chopped sour pickles
¼ c. green pepper, chopped fine
1 tbsp. chopped onion
1 3-oz. cake cream cheese
¼ c. mayonnaise

Mix olives, pickles, green pepper and onion with soft cream cheese; add mayonnaise. Spread on crackers or for sandwiches.

Mrs. C. W. Rook
Beaumont, Texas

GOURMET CHEESE SPREAD

1 lb. Edam cheese
1 slice onion, ground
1 tbsp. Worcestershire sauce
½ tsp. mustard
½ tsp. horseradish
Salt and pepper to taste
Garlic salt to taste
Cream

Slice top of cheese round about 2 inches from top. Hollow out center, forming a bowl. Combine mashed cheese with all remaining ingredients. Add enough cream to obtain spreading consistency. Place mixture in shell. Serve with assorted crackers.

Mrs. LeJeune McCracken
Arlington Halls Sta., Virginia

PARMESAN DELIGHTS

1 c. mayonnaise
½ c. Parmesan cheese
2 tsp. Worcestershire sauce
1 tbsp. minced onion
Toast rounds

Blend all ingredients well except toast rounds. Spread on toast rounds and sprinkle with a little additional cheese. Brown under broiler and serve very hot.

Nan Hollingsworth
Hollandale, Mississippi

THREE-WAY CHEESE TREAT

BASIC CHEESE BASE:

1 ½ lb. cream cheese
1 ½ lb. cheddar cheese, grated
¼ c. milk

Blend cheeses with milk. Divide mixture into three portions to be used as base for caraway, anchovy and coffee loaves.

CARAWAY LOAF:

4 tbsp. caraway seed
1 tbsp. horseradish
1 tbsp. Worcestershire sauce

Thoroughly blend all ingredients with one portion of the basic cheese base. Shape into a long loaf; chill for 4 hours or until firm. Slice. May be served on crackers.

ANCHOVY LOAF:

2 oz. anchovy paste

Thoroughly blend anchovy paste with another portion of the basic cheese base. Shape into long loaf; chill for 4 hours. Slice. May be served on crackers.

COFFEE LOAF:

1 tbsp. instant coffee
2 tbsp. sugar

Thoroughly blend coffee and sugar with remaining portion of basic cheese base. Shape into long loaf; chill until firm. Slice. May be served on crackers.

Ann Williams
Angier, North Carolina

ONION SNIP-SNACKS

¼ lb. butter
2 ½ tbsp. dry onion soup mix
1 can refrigerated buttermilk biscuits

Melt butter in skillet; stir in onion soup mix. Cut each biscuit into fourths. Place biscuits in skillet. Cook over very low heat for about 20 minutes, turning to brown evenly on all sides. Yield: 40 servings.

Mrs. James N. Holeman
Sturgis, Kentucky

ROQUEFORT FRUIT DIP

1 c. Roquefort cheese, crumbled
1 3-oz. pkg. cream cheese, softened
1 c. sour cream
⅓ c. milk
1 pkg. low-calorie Italian salad dressing mix
Peaches, pineapple chunks, fresh strawberries, bananas or orange slices

Mix Roquefort cheese with cream cheese and sour cream. Gradually beat in milk and beat until well blended. Gradually beat in salad dressing mix. Chill until ready to serve. Serve in a bowl with a tray of fruit pieces. Yield: 2 cups.

Letetia Davis
Goode, Virginia

COCKTAIL CURRY SAUCE

¼ c. butter
1 green onion, minced
2 tbsp. flour
1 tsp. minced gingerroot or 3 tbsp. chopped crystallized ginger
½ c. apple
1 to 2 tsp. curry powder
1 tsp. each salt and sugar
4 whole cloves
Dash of cayenne
2 c. milk
½ c. shredded coconut
¼ c. lemon juice
Thin cream

Melt butter in chafing dish blazer. Cook onion until transparent, stirring occasionally. Blend in flour until mixture bubbles, then add ginger, apple, curry powder, salt, sugar, cloves and cayenne. Remove from heat and gradually add milk. Stir constantly until sauce thickens. Place over pan of simmering water and cook 30 minutes, covered. Remove whole cloves. Stir in coconut. Gradually add lemon juice. Cream may be added if consistency is too thick. Fresh vegetables, in bite-sized portions such as flowerets of cauliflower and broccoli, sticks of zucchini, celery, carrot, green pepper and radishes, may be used for dipping. Yield: 3 cups.

Photograph for this recipe on page 23.

CHEESE DEVILED EGGS

- 6 hard-cooked eggs, chilled
- 1 tsp. prepared mustard
- 1 tbsp. parsley, chopped
- ¼ tsp. salt
- ⅛ tsp. pepper
- ½ c. mayonnaise
- Paprika
- ½ c. cheese crackers, finely crushed

Slice eggs in half lengthwise. Remove yolk and press with a fine sieve. Add mustard, parsley, salt, pepper, mayonnaise and half of the crumbs; blend. Refill centers of whites with yolk mixture. Press halves together. Dip one end of egg in mayonnaise and remaining crumbs. Sprinkle with paprika.

Mrs. Jack J. Durham
Amherst, Texas

PICK-UP CHICKEN STICKS

- 3 lb. chicken wings
- ¾ c. melted butter
- 1 ½ c. flour
- ⅓ c. sesame seed
- 1 tbsp. salt
- ½ tsp. ginger
- Juice of ½ lemon

Cut wings in three sections disposing of the webbed meatless portion; dip sections in melted butter. Mix flour, seed, salt and ginger; roll chicken sections in mixture. Place in foil-lined pan. Bake, uncovered, at 350 degrees for 1 hour. Sprinkle with lemon juice before serving. Yield: 6-8 servings.

Mrs. Jack McKain
Sarasota, Florida

SLICK CHICK

- 1 whole fryer or stewing chicken
- 1 stalk celery, sliced
- 1 lge. onion, chopped
- 1 tsp. salt
- Freshly ground pepper to taste
- 1 14-oz. bottle barbecue sauce

Cover chicken with water; add celery, onion, salt and pepper. Simmer, covered, for 1 hour to 1 hour and 30 minutes or until tender. Cool slightly. Remove meat from bone; discard skin. Dice; place in a saucepan. Cover with sauce. Simmer, uncovered, for 30 minutes. Serve hot. Yield: 50 cocktail buns.

Mrs. G. R. Gislason
Johnson City, Tennessee

HAM AND CHUTNEY CANAPE

- 1 c. Virginia ham, ground fine
- 1 c. chutney
- ½ c. whipping cream
- Melba toast rounds
- Parmesan cheese

Mix ham and chutney; moisten with cream. Spread thickly on rounds of melba toast. Sprinkle with Parmesan cheese. Heat in 350-degree oven a few minutes just before serving. Yield: 20 canapes.

Mrs. John H. Tyler
Thomasville, Georgia

APPETIZER MEATBALLS

- ¾ lb. ground beef
- ¼ lb. ground pork
- ¾ c. rolled oats
- ¼ c. finely chopped water chestnuts
- ¼ tsp. Worcestershire sauce
- ½ c. milk
- ½ tsp. onion salt
- ½ tsp. garlic salt
- Few drops Tabasco sauce
- Margarine

Combine all ingredients except margarine; mix well. Shape into about 75 small balls. Brown well in margarine; drain on paper towels and cover with Sweet-Sour Sauce.

SWEET-SOUR SAUCE:

- 1 c. sugar
- ¾ c. vinegar
- ¾ c. water
- 1 tsp. paprika
- ½ tsp. salt
- 3 tsp. cornstarch
- 1 tbsp. water

Combine sugar, vinegar, water, paprika and salt; cook for 5 minutes. Add cornstarch mixed with water. Simmer for 30 minutes. Serve warm. Yield: 15 servings.

Mrs. George Green
Albuquerque, New Mexico

CHINESE MEATBALLS

1 egg
½ c. water
½ c. bread crumbs
2 tbsp. horseradish
1 c. sliced water chestnuts
1 lb. ground chuck

Beat egg and water; stir in bread crumbs, horseradish and chestnuts. Add beef and mix gently with hands. Shape into 1-inch balls. Bake on cookie sheet at 350 degrees for 12 minutes.

SAUCE:

⅓ c. orange marmalade
1 clove of garlic, minced
2 tbsp. lemon juice
¼ c. soy sauce
⅓ c. water

Combine all ingredients; bring to a boil. Serve hot as a dip or place in chafing dish with meatballs. Yield: 44 meatballs.

Mrs. Kenneth R. Hanson
Tucson, Arizona

SOMBREO SPREAD

1 lb. ground beef
1 c. chopped onion
½ c. hot catsup
3 tsp. chili powder
3 tsp. salt
2 8-oz. cans kidney beans
1 c. shredded sharp American cheese
½ c. sliced stuffed green olives

Brown meat with 1/2 cup onion. Add catsup, chili powder and salt. Mash beans with bean liquid; add to meat mixture. Garnish with cheese, remaining onion and olives. Place in chafing dish; serve with round corn chips.

Mrs. Barbara Gravelle
Lexington, Kentucky

MEATBALLS

¾ lb. ground lean beef
¼ lb. ground lean pork
¾ c. rolled oats
½ c. milk
¼ c. finely chopped water chestnuts
1 tbsp. Worcestershire sauce
½ tsp. onion salt
½ tsp. garlic salt
Few drops of hot pepper sauce
2 tbsp. butter

Combine all ingredients except butter; mix thoroughly. Shape mixture into 48 small balls. Brown in butter; drain. Add to Sweet-Sour Sauce. Simmer for 30 minutes. Serve hot. Yield: 4 dozen.

SWEET-SOUR SAUCE:

1 c. sugar
¾ c. vinegar
¾ c. water
1 tsp. paprika
½ tsp. salt
2 tbsp. cornstarch

Combine sugar, vinegar, water, paprika and salt. Cook for 5 minutes. Blend cornstarch with 1 tablespoon of cold water; add to hot mixture. Cook until thickened. Serve over meatballs.

Mrs. L. W. Kleppe
Tulsa, Oklahoma

MEAT-FILLED PASTRIES

1 lge. onion, finely chopped
1 tbsp. cooking oil
½ lb. ground round beef
1 tbsp. crushed peanuts
1 tbsp. raisins
2 tbsp. green peas
½ tsp. ginger
½ tsp. turmeric
1 ½ tsp. salt
2 tsp. sugar
1 tbsp. vinegar
1 c. flour
1 tsp. baking powder
4 tsp. shortening
3 tbsp. hot water

Fry onion in oil until light brown. Add ground beef, peanuts, raisins, green peas, ginger, turmeric and 1 teaspoonful salt. Cook until beef is well browned. Add 1/2 cup water; simmer until dry and peas are cooked. Add sugar and vinegar; mix well. Let stand until cool. Mix flour, remaining salt and baking powder; cut shortening into flour. Add hot water; knead well. Make round soft ball; divide dough into eight equal parts. Roll each ball thin; cut each circle into halves. Place filling on each half; fold into triangular shape. Press edges; seal using a drop of water. Fry in deep fat or in a skillet with oil about 1 inch deep, until golden brown. Serve as hor d'oeuvres. Yield: 6-8 servings.

Mrs. D. N. Contractor
Laurel, Maryland

STUFFED GRAPE LEAVES

2 lb. ground beef
1 ½ c. uncooked rice
Salt
1 tsp. pepper
1 tsp. cumin seed
1 tsp. garlic powder
5 med. onions, grated
1 jar grape leaves
2 tbsp. shortening
Juice of ½ lemon
1 ½ c. tomato juice

(Continued on next page)

Mix ground beef with rice, 1 teaspoonful salt, pepper, cumin seed, garlic powder and onions. Let stand for 10 minutes. Rinse grape leaves with water; pat dry with paper towels. Lay smooth side down; place 1 teaspoonful meat filling on each leaf. Roll up; tuck in ends. Place rolls in 3-quart pot in layers. Press down with hand, after each layer. Add shortening and lemon juice. Sprinkle with salt. Add tomato juice. Place in heavy unbreakable dish. Cover; cook over medium heat for 2 hours and 30 minutes.

Mrs. John Solomon
Atlanta, Georgia

SWEDISH MEATBALLS

SAUCE:

- ¾ c. catsup
- 1 ½ tsp. salt
- ½ c. water
- 1 tsp. dry mustard
- ¼ c. vinegar
- ¼ tsp. pepper
- 3 drops of Tabasco sauce
- 2 tbsp. brown sugar
- 1 tbsp. chopped onion
- 2 tsp. Worcestershire sauce

Mix all ingredients in saucepan and simmer for a few minutes.

MEATBALLS:

- ¾ c. dry bread crumbs
- ½ tsp. horseradish
- ¾ lb. ground beef
- 2 eggs, beaten
- ¾ tsp. salt
- 3 drops of Tabasco sauce
- ¼ tsp. pepper
- ½ tsp. monosodium glutamate
- 1 ½ tbsp. chopped onion

Mix bread crumbs with meat in bowl; add remaining ingredients. Mix thoroughly. Shape into miniature meatballs; brown in a skillet. When thoroughly browned, add to sauce. Simmer for 15 minutes. Pour into casserole and refrigerate. Bake at 350 degrees for 2 hours. Stir occasionally. Serve with toothpicks. Yield: 16 servings.

Mrs. Charlotte Shetler
Dover, Delaware

CHEESE AND HAM APPETIZERS

- 2 tbsp. mayonnaise
- 1 pkg. cream cheese
- ½ tsp. mustard
- 2 tbsp. chopped stuffed olives
- 4 thin slices cold boiled ham

Blend mayonnaise, cream cheese and mustard; add olives. Spread mixture about 1/8 inch thick over the ham slices. Roll up ham like a jelly roll; fasten with toothpicks. Chill at least 1 hour. Slice rolls in 1/4-inch slices and serve on small round crackers. Yield: 20-24 servings.

Mrs. J. W. Baldwin
Fort Lauderdale, Florida

BACON APPETIZER

- 1 jar peanut butter
- 1 bottle catsup
- 1 pkg. soda crackers
- 1 pkg. bacon

Mix peanut butter and catsup to a texture for buttering crackers. Use more peanut butter, if necessary, to obtain an easily spreadable mixture. Spread one side of each cracker with mixture. Place crackers on cookie sheet. Place a piece of bacon on each cracker. Broil under low heat until bacon is crisp and browned. Serve hot.

Mrs. A. C. McCoy
High Point, North Carolina

COFFEE BREAK APPETIZER

- 1 pkg. precooked pork link sausage
- 1 pkg. refrigerator butterflake rolls

Cut each sausage in thirds. Peel 2 thin sections off a butterflake roll; wrap around a small piece of sausage. Continue until all sausage is wrapped; place on ungreased cookie sheet. Bake at 450 degrees for 7 to 8 minutes. Serve hot. May be prepared in advance and refrigerated. Yield: 20 rolls.

Mrs. G. M. Clifford
Huntington, West Virginia

KOREAN APPETIZER

- 2 lb. pork, cut in 1-in. cubes
- 2 tbsp. salad oil
- 4 tbsp. sugar
- 4 tbsp. soya sauce
- 4 tbsp. water

Brown pork in salad oil. Combine sugar, soya sauce and water; pour over meat. Stir over medium heat until sauce thickens slightly. Reduce heat and simmer for 10 to 15 minutes.

Mrs. C. D. Harold
Charleston, South Carolina

KRAUT APPETIZERS

3 tbsp. butter or margarine
1 med. onion, finely chopped
1 c. finely chopped cooked ham
1 c. finely chopped cooked corned beef
½ med. clove of garlic, crushed
2 ½ c. plus 6 tbsp. sifted flour
1 egg, beaten
2 c. well-drained sauerkraut, finely chopped
⅛ tsp. seasoned salt
⅛ tsp. monosodium glutamate
⅛ tsp. Worcestershire sauce
1 tbsp. chopped parsley
½ c. beef stock or bouillon
2 c. milk
2 c. fine dry bread crumbs

Melt butter; add onion and cook over low heat for 5 minutes. Add ham, beef and garlic; mix well. Cook for 10 minutes, stirring occasionally. Add 6 tablespoons flour and egg; blend. Add kraut, salt, monosodium glutamate, Worcestershire sauce, parsley and stock; mix well. Cook over low heat until thickened, stirring occasionally. Chill. Shape into 1-inch balls. Combine milk and remaining flour; mix well. Coat balls with flour mixture; roll in bread crumbs. Fry in deep fat at 375 degrees for 2 to 3 minutes or until lightly browned. Drain on absorbent paper; serve on cocktail picks. Yield: 80 balls.

Mrs. T. G. Peters
Houston, Texas

SAUSAGE BALLS

2 lb. hot country sausage or sm. brown and serve hot smoked sausage
½ c. catsup
½ c. wine vinegar
½ c. brown sugar
1 tbsp. soy sauce
½ tsp. ginger

Form sausage into small balls. Fry slowly until well done; drain on paper towels. Combine and heat remaining ingredients; gently add meatballs making certain they are completely covered. Cool; refrigerate for at least 24 hours. Reheat to serve. Will keep well for 4 to 5 days or may be frozen. Yield: 40-50 cocktail servings.

Mrs. L. G. Sheets
Brunswick, Georgia

ROYAL ROMAN DIP

1 c. salad dressing
¼ c. Italian-style dressing
¼ c. grated Parmesan cheese
¼ c. green olives, sliced

Combine all ingredients; mix well. Chill. Serve with raw vegetables, potato chips, corn chips or crackers. Yield: 1 1/2 cups.

Letetia Davis
Goode, Virginia

CLAM CANAPES

1 3-oz. pkg. cream cheese
1 can minced clams, drained
Dash of Worcestershire sauce
Bread slices, cut in fourths
Garlic salt

Combine cream cheese, clams and Worcestershire; mix well. Spread on bread slices. Toast in oven before serving. Sprinkle with garlic salt. Yield: 60 canapes.

Mrs. John H. Tyler
Thomasville, Georgia

CLAMS CASINO

36 cherrystone clams
Rock salt
¼ c. butter
1 tsp. anchovy paste
Juice of ½ lemon
¼ c. finely chopped onion
¼ c. finely chopped green pepper
2 tbsp. diced pimento
Salt and pepper to taste
4 strips bacon, diced

Open and drain clams. Arrange 36 half-shells on bed of rock salt in large, shallow baking tray. Mix butter and anchovy paste; place 1/4 teaspoon in each half shell. Sprinkle lemon juice on clams. Mix onion, green pepper and pimento; distribute over clams. Sprinkle clams with salt and pepper. Top with bacon. Bake at 450 degrees for 15 minutes or until bacon is nicely browned. Rock salt holds clams in place and holds heat. Yield: 8-10 servings.

Mrs. Donald Bertolet
Quincey, Florida

CLAM DIP

½ lb. loaf Velveeta cheese
1 can minced clams, undrained
1 lge. onion, chopped
½ green pepper, chopped
½ tsp. prepared mustard
Dash of Tabasco sauce
1 tsp. Worcestershire sauce
3 tbsp. chili sauce

Melt cheese in top of double boiler. Simmer clams; reduce liquid and add to cheese. Saute onion and green pepper; add with remaining ingredients. Serve warm with crackers.

Mrs. Dana F. Batting
Georgetown, Louisiana

CLAM DIP

2 3-oz. pkg. cream cheese, softened
1 tbsp. salad dressing
1 can minced clams, drained
½ tsp. steak sauce
¼ c. minced onion
Parsley flakes
1 ½ tsp. lemon juice
Dash of salt
Garlic salt to taste

Thoroughly blend all ingredients; chill. Serve with potato chips or crackers.

Mrs. Richard Scribner
Union Grove, North Carolina

CLAM DIP

1 lge. pkg. cream cheese
1 c. fresh minced clams
1 ½ tsp. horseradish
Celery salt to taste
1 tsp. Worcestershire sauce
1 tsp. onion juice
½ tsp. lemon juice
Clam liquid

Combine all ingredients; add reserved clam juice until desired consistency is reached. Mix well. Bake at 450 degrees for 12 to 15 minutes in shells.

Mrs. George R. Andes
Harrisonberg, Va.

CLAM DIP

1 8-oz. pkg. cream cheese
⅓ c. clam juice
1 can clams, drained
1 ½ tsp. lemon juice
½ tsp. salt
Dash of pepper
Garlic powder to taste

Soften cheese; add remaining ingredients. Heat. Serve with crackers, potato chips or corn chips.

Mrs. Frank T. Gamec
Jonesboro, Arkansas

CLAM DIP

½ to 1 c. minced clams
1 8-oz. or 2 3-oz. pkg. cream cheese, softened
½ tsp. salt
1 tsp. lemon juice
1 tsp. Worcestershire sauce
Dash of white or black pepper
1 clove garlic, minced

Drain clams, reserving 1 tablespoonful juice. Blend cream cheese with all ingredients except clams. Mix well; add clams. Chill in covered dish. More juice may be added to make dip softer. One clove cut garlic may be substituted for minced garlic. Rub inside of bowl with cut garlic. Yield: 1 cup.

Mrs. Mary Jane Dean
Charlottesville, Virginia

CLAM HORS D'OEUVRES

1 c. bread crumbs
⅓ c. butter, melted
2 cans minced clams
Salt and pepper to taste
Onion salt to taste

Mix crumbs and butter. Add clams and seasonings. Place in individual buttered shells or in baking dish. Sprinkle with additional crumbs and paprika. Bake at 375 degrees for 30 minutes or until bubbly and brown.

Mrs. H. G. Uphouse
Tulsa, Oklahoma

CLAM SPREAD OR DIP

1 8-oz. pkg. cream cheese
1 10 ½-oz. can minced clams, drained
½ tsp. onion salt or ¼ c. minced onion
⅛ tsp. pepper

Soften cream cheese in small bowl. Drain clams, reserving juice. Add 2 to 4 tablespoonfuls clam juice to cream cheese until mixture is of desired consistency. Add seasonings; beat until smooth and well blended. Stir in clams. Serve with potato chips or crackers. Shrimp, crab, chicken or turkey may be substituted for clams. Yield: 2 cups.

Gayle Chase
Lake Charles, Louisiana

HOT CLAM DIP

1 lge. pkg. cream cheese
1 can clams, partially drained

Whip cream cheese; add clams. Heat at 350 degrees until bubbly. Serve with potato chips.

Mrs. J. Dennis Mock
Athens, Georgia

CAVIAR FORTE

1 4-oz. jar caviar
1 med. onion, finely chopped
3 tbsp. mayonnaise
Juice of 1 lemon

Mix all ingredients; chill. Add more mayonnaise if needed for dipping consistency. Serve with small crackers. Yield: 6 servings.

Helen Iffla Bay
Clearwater, Florida

SPICY CLAM APPETIZER

2 cans refrigerated flaky baking powder biscuits
1 10 ½-oz. can minced clams, drained
¼ c. chili sauce
¼ c. sour cream
Grated process American cheese

Heat oven to 400 degrees. Separate each biscuit into 2 layers. Place on ungreased cookie sheets. Combine minced clams, chili sauce and sour cream. Spread about 2 tablespoons clam mixture on each biscuit half; sprinkle with a little cheese. Bake at 400 degrees 10 to 12 minutes or until golden brown. Serve warm. Yield: 48 halves.

Mrs. James J. Zapalac
Austin County, Texas

CHERRY-O-CRAB DELIGHTS

40 cherry tomatoes
1 6 ½-oz. can crab meat
1 3-oz. pkg. cream cheese, softened
2 tbsp. sour cream
2 tsp. white wine
1 tbsp. minced parsley
½ tsp. salt
½ tsp. celery seed
¼ tsp. seasoned pepper
¼ tsp. seasoned salt
⅛ tsp. onion salt
⅛ tsp. paprika

Wash tomatoes. Remove stem and cut off enough top to make small cap. Scoop out pulp. Drain crab meat thoroughly; crumble into fine shreds. Blend remaining ingredients; add to crab meat. Fill tomatoes with crab meat mixture. Stick toothpick through center of cap and gently stick into stuffed tomato so the two sections hold together. Garnish with tiny sprig of fresh parsley. Yield: 40 servings.

Mrs. Jean Brown
Danville, Kentucky

CRAB DIP

½ c. chili sauce
½ c. mayonnaise
½ tsp. dry mustard
½ tsp. salt
1 tsp. Worcestershire sauce
1 tsp. horseradish
1 can crab meat
2 hard-cooked eggs, finely chopped

Combine all ingredients except crab and eggs; mix well. Add crab and eggs. Mix until well blended. Serve with potato or corn chips.

Arlyne Dees
Knoxville, Tennessee

CRAB MEAT BALLS

½ c. tomato juice
2 eggs
1 c. dry bread crumbs
Dash of salt
Dash of pepper
½ tsp. chopped parsley
½ tsp. chopped celery leaves
1 6 ½-oz. can crab meat, flaked
¾ c. fine dry bread crumbs

Mix tomato juice and 1 well-beaten egg. Add crumbs, seasonings, parsley, celery leaves and crab meat. Mix thoroughly; roll into balls. Dip into remaining slightly beaten egg then into bread crumbs. Fry in deep fat at 370 degrees or until golden. Serve on cocktail picks. Yield: 24 hors d'oeuvres.

Mrs. Lowell Horman
Dayton, Maryland

CRAB MEAT-CHEESE DIP

1 lb. Velveeta cheese
1 stick margarine
1 7-oz. can crab meat, drained

Melt cheese and margarine in top of double boiler, stirring often. When thoroughly melted, add crab meat. Serve with crackers or ruffled potato chips. Keep warm to avoid thickening.

Mrs. Richard Castillo
Cape Kennedy, Florida

CRAB MEAT DIP

2 3-oz. pkg. cream cheese
3 tbsp. milk
1 tbsp. mayonnaise
½ c. finely chopped celery
1 tsp. Worcestershire sauce
2 tsp. lemon juice
1 6-oz. can crab meat

(Continued on next page)

Beat cheese with milk and mayonnaise; add remaining ingredients. Mix well. Refrigerate for 1 hour to blend flavors. Yield: 12 servings.

Mrs. Donald C. Johnson
College Park, Maryland

CRAB MEAT FLIP

1 7 ½-oz. can crab meat
1 hard-cooked egg, chopped
¼ c. finely chopped celery
Mayonnaise

Mix crab meat, egg and celery together; add mayonnaise to moisten. Serve with fancy crackers. Yield: 6 servings.

Irene Loveless
Pecos, Texas

CRAB MEAT SPREAD

1 8-oz. pkg. cream cheese, softened
1 3-oz. can crab meat
1 8-oz. bottle seafood sauce

Spread cream cheese on serving dish. Drain crab meat; flake over cream cheese, pushing meat into cheese. Spread seafood sauce over crab meat. Serve with crackers.

Marge Oberle
Calamine, Arkansas

GOURMET CRAB MEAT CANAPES

1 can refrigerated crescent dinner rolls
1 6 ½-oz. can crab meat, drained and flaked
¼ c. chili sauce
¼ tsp. Worcestershire sauce
⅓ c. sour cream

Separate rolls and cut each triangle into four small triangles. Combine crab meat, chili sauce and Worcestershire sauce. Spread 1 teaspoonful mixture on each triangle. Place on ungreased cookie sheet; top with 1/2 teaspoonful sour cream. Bake at 375 degrees for 10 minutes or until golden brown. Serve warm. Yield: 32 servings.

Mrs. Clifford Seales
Mobile, Alabama

SEAFOOD COCKTAIL

1 pkg. frozen shrimp, cleaned and cooked
1 can crab meat
2 pkg. frozen lobster, cleaned and cooked

Cut seafood in small pieces.

SAUCE:

1 tbsp. prepared mustard
1 tsp. dry mustard
1 tsp. Worcestershire sauce
1 c. chili sauce
1 c. mayonnaise
Salt and pepper to taste
1 sm. onion, grated
Horseradish to taste

Combine ingredients; mix well. Pour over seafood. Yield: 12 servings.

Mrs. Alan Kadet
Southside, Florida

APPETIZER SHRIMP

6 lb. fresh shrimp or 3 1 ½-lb. bags frozen shrimp
¾ c. butter or margarine
¾ c. chopped parsley
2 cloves of garlic, minced
1 ½ tsp. salt
Lemon slices

Wash fresh shrimp; shell and devein. Melt 1/4 cup butter in large frying pan. Stir in one-third each parsley, garlic and salt. Heat stirring constantly, until bubbly. Add one-third shrimp; saute for 6 minutes, turning often until shrimp turns pink and firm. Spoon into chafing dish. Garnish with lemon slices. Repeat as needed. Yield: 25 servings.

Mrs. John Collins
Mesa, Arizona

COPENHAGENS

1 5-oz. can water chestnuts, cut into ⅛ inch thick rounds
1 3-oz. jar cocktail shrimp
¼ c. mayonnaise or salad dressing
1 tbsp. chopped parsley
½ tsp. lemon juice

(Continued on next page)

Drain water chestnuts. Drain shrimp; place in small bowl. Blend mayonnaise, parsley and lemon juice. Place a dab on each water chestnut slice; stand a shrimp on top. Yield: 48 appetizers.

Mrs. Joanna Anderson
Big Bend, Arkansas

FESTIVE SARDINE CANAPES

1 8-oz. pkg. cream cheese, softened
6 drops of Tabasco sauce
¼ c. chili sauce
1 tbsp. lemon juice
1 tsp. olive juice
Small stuffed olives
Dash of garlic salt
Oblong crackers
Sardines

Combine cream cheese, Tabasco sauce, chili sauce, lemon juice, olive juice, 20 chopped olives and garlic salt. Spread on oblong crackers. Top each with 1 whole sardine and thin olive slice.

Mrs. Laura Grenshaw
Lancaster, South Carolina

MARINATED SHRIMP

5 lb. shrimp
1 pt. apple cider vinegar
2 bay leaves
2 med. onions, sliced
1 bottle salad dressing

Boil shrimp in water with 1 tablespoonful vinegar and 2 bay leaves; peel and devein shrimp. Layer shrimp and onions in a large jar; repeat layers until all shrimp are used. Pour salad dressing and remaining vinegar over shrimp and onions. Cover tightly; refrigerate for 3 days, shaking several times. Serve in dish with toothpicks.

Helen T. Renken
Charleston, South Carolina

MARINATED SHRIMP

2 lb. frozen deveined shrimp
1 egg
1 ¼ c. salad oil
Juice of 2 lemons
1 ½-in. square lemon peel
1 sm. onion
12 capers
1 tbsp. juice from capers
1 tbsp. Worcestershire sauce
1 c. chili sauce
1 tsp. salt

Cook shrimp according to package directions; drain. Place egg in blender; add remaining ingredients, one at a time, beating well after each addition. Marinate shrimp in sauce overnight. Drain; place on tray with garnish. Yield: 8-12 servings.

Mrs. S. S. Koru
Gainesville, Florida

MARINATED SHRIMP

2 lb. shrimp
½ c. celery tops
¼ c. mixed pickling spices
1 tbsp. salt
2 med. onions, sliced
7 to 8 bay leaves
1 ¼ c. salad oil
¾ c. white vinegar
2 ½ tbsp. capers and juice
2 ½ tsp. celery seed
1 ½ tsp. salt
Dash of Tabasco sauce
Juice of 1 lemon

Cover shrimp with boiling water; add celery tops, spices and salt. Cook about 10 minutes; drain. Cover with ice; clean and devein. Alternate shrimp, onions and bay leaves in a shallow dish. Combine remaining ingredients; pour over shrimp, onions and bay leaves. Cover; store in refrigerator for at least 12 hours. Serve as cocktail or hors d'oeuvres.

Mrs. E. Kenneth Gavin
Tampa, Florida

PICKLED SHRIMP

1 lb. cooked shrimp
2 med. onions, cut in rings
3 to 4 bay leaves, broken

Place in alternating layers in container.

SAUCE:

1 c. salad oil
2 tsp. sugar
½ tsp. dry mustard
2 tbsp. Worcestershire sauce
⅓ c. catsup
⅓ c. vinegar
1 tsp. salt
Dash of red pepper
Dash of Tabasco sauce
1 clove of garlic, chopped

Mix all ingredients; pour over shrimp and onion mixture. Be sure sauce covers shrimp. Refrigerate for 24 hours.

Mrs. John Sawyer Barr, III
Oak Ridge, Louisiana

SAVORY BITES

1 c. French dressing
1 tbsp. capers and juice
½ tsp. celery seed
4 or 5 drops Tabasco sauce
1 lb. cooked shrimp or 6 frankfurters, cut in 1-inch chunks

Combine dressing and seasonings; pour over shrimp or franks. Refrigerate overnight; drain. Serve with toothpicks on greens. Yield: 10 servings.

Mrs. Terry Kuntz
Rudy, Arkansas

SHRIMP APPETIZER OR DIP

1 lge. pkg. cream cheese
2 tbsp. mayonnaise
¼ tsp. garlic powder
¼ tsp. onion powder
1 lge. or 2 sm. cans shrimp, deveined
1 pt. sour cream

Soften cream cheese at room temperature; add mayonnaise, garlic and onion powders. Mix thoroughly; add finely chopped shrimp. Gently fold in sour cream. Cover; refrigerate until ready to use. Serve with crackers, hot cocktail biscuits or use large whole shrimp to dip. Yield: 12-20 servings.

Roxena Myers
Salem, Florida

SHRIMP DIP

1 8-oz. pkg. cream cheese
3 tbsp. milk or cream
2 tbsp. chopped onion
½ tsp. Worcestershire sauce
1 6-oz. can small shrimp, mashed

Soften cheese with milk or cream; add onion and Worcestershire sauce. Beat. Add shrimp to cheese mixture. Serve with potato chips.

Judi Koehmstedt
Seminole, Florida

SHRIMP DIP APPETIZER

1 c. salad dressing
1 8-oz. pkg. cream cheese
Dash of celery salt
2 tsp. lemon juice
2 tbsp. catsup
1 tbsp. grated onion
1 lb. cleaned boiled shrimp

Mix salad dressing well with softened cream cheese; add other ingredients and mix well. Yield: 2-3 cups.

Mrs. Darrell Methvin
League City, Texas

SHRIMP DIP WITH SOUR CREAM

1 can small shrimp, mashed
1 c. sour cream
¼ c. chili sauce
2 tbsp. lemon juice
½ tsp. salt
⅛ tsp. pepper
2 dashes of Tabasco sauce
Horseradish (opt.)

Mix all ingredients; refrigerate. Yield: 10 servings.

Mrs. Joe Neis
Cypress Gardens, Florida

SHRIMP-PICKLE DIP

4 lb. shrimp
Salt to taste
½ c. diced green pepper
½ c. diced onion
1 ½ c. diced celery
1 c. diced olives
1 c. diced sweet pickles
½ c. diced dill pickles
1 tbsp. (heaping) garlic
2 tbsp. diced parsley
5 tsp. (heaping) horseradish
½ pt. mayonnaise
Black pepper to taste
Red pepper to taste

Boil shrimp with salt. Chop shrimp; add green pepper, onion, celery, olives, pickles, garlic, parsley, horseradish and mayonnaise. Season to taste. Mix thoroughly and serve on crackers.

Mrs. Juanita Jacob
LaPlace, Louisiana

SHRIMP RELISH

1 ½ lb. cleaned large fresh shrimp, cooked
1 c. minced onions
1 c. snipped parsley
⅔ c. salad oil
⅓ c. vinegar
1 clove of garlic, minced
1 ½ tsp. salt
Dash of pepper

(Continued on next page)

Combine shrimp, onions and parsley in a large bowl. Refrigerate for a few hours. Mix salad oil, vinegar, garlic, salt and pepper in a small bowl; beat well. Pour over shrimp. Refrigerate for 1 hour. Heap shrimp in serving dish, placing a few on rim of dish. Spear with colorful picks. Yield: 10 servings.

Mrs. William Duffy
Savannah, Georgia

SHRIMPS DIVINE

1 tbsp. vinegar
3 lb. fresh shrimp
2 onions
½ pt. imported olive oil
Juice of 3 lemons
Freshly ground pepper
Salt to taste
1 clove of garlic

Add vinegar to water; bring to a rolling boil. Boil shrimp with hulls on for 5 minutes. Taste for tenderness. Do not overcook. Cool and peel; place a layer of shrimp and a layer of onions in a shallow dish. Add olive oil, lemon juice, pepper, salt and garlic. Let stand in marinade in refrigerator 8 hours or overnight. Drain and serve in individual cocktail dishes. Yield: 6-8 servings.

Mrs. Douglas Ossenfort
Vero Beach, Florida

TUNA DIP

1 can tuna, flaked
1 tsp. Worcestershire sauce
1 8-oz. pkg. cream cheese
1 tbsp. lemon juice

Combine all ingredients. Thin with milk if needed.

C. A. Lubbes
Bastrop, Louisiana

TUNA DIP

1 can grated tuna
½ c. mayonnaise
1 sm. pkg. cream cheese
Salt and pepper to taste

Mix all ingredients well. Use as a dip with potato chips or crackers.

Mrs. D. W. Hartley
Sanford, Mississippi

SPICED OLIVES

¼ c. lemon juice
1 sliced clove of garlic
1 tsp. basil
1 c. pimento-stuffed olives

Combine lemon juice, garlic, basil and pimento-stuffed olives. Mix well and chill for 4 hours or overnight, stirring occasionally. Drain and remove garlic before serving.

Mrs. Sam P. Arthur
Leesburg, Georgia

BRAUNSCHWEIGER CIRCLES

1 8-oz. pkg. braunschweiger liver sausage
2 tbsp. sweet pickle relish
1 tbsp. hickory-flavored catsup
1 tsp. prepared mustard
1 tsp. Worcestershire sauce
6 to 8 individual French rolls, 2 to 3-in. long

Combine all ingredients except rolls; blend well. Cut ends from rolls; hollow out centers of rolls with a fork or knife to within 1/4 inch from crusts. Fill with sausage mixture, being careful not to leave any air spaces. Wrap rolls securely; chill for at least 2 hours. Cut rolls into slices 1/4 inch thick. Yield: 45 appetizers.

Mrs. R. T. Butler
Pine Bluff, Arkansas

CHEDDAR CHEESE BALLS

1 lb. cheddar cheese
1 tbsp. grated onion
1 tsp. Worcestershire sauce
½ tsp. paprika
Chopped smoked beef, diced
Chopped parsley

Cut cheddar cheese into small pieces; beat at room temperature until smooth and creamy. Add onion, Worcestershire sauce and paprika; beat until well blended. Shape into balls 1 inch in diameter; roll half of balls in beef and half in parsley. Refrigerate; just before serving, spear with wooden picks. Yield: 48 servings.

Mrs. John J. Finley
Jacksonville, Florida

BACON AND CHICKEN LIVER APPETIZER

1 lb. chicken livers
Butter
Salt
½ lb. bacon

(Continued on next page)

Fry chicken livers thoroughly in butter, salting to taste; cool. Lightly fry bacon; cool. Cut liver into bite-sized pieces. Wrap one-half slice bacon around each piece of liver, securing with toothpick. Broil for 10 to 15 minutes or until bacon is thoroughly done. Yield: 20 appetizers.

Mrs. James T. Gaffney
Fairmont, West Virginia

CHOPPED CHICKEN LIVERS

½ c. shortening, oil or rendered chicken fat
2 onions, sliced
1 lb. chicken livers, washed and drained
2 hard-cooked eggs
1 ½ tsp. salt
½ tsp. pepper

Melt 1/4 cup shortening in skillet. Add onions; saute for 10 minutes, stirring frequently. Remove onions; set aside. Melt remaining shortening in the same skillet; saute livers for 10 minutes, stirring occasionally. Grind onions, liver and eggs in a food chopper. Add salt and pepper; mix well. Chill. Spread on crackers or small slices of rye bread. Yield: 6 servings.

Shirley Goldberg
Lakeland, Florida

BACON-WRAPPED CHICKEN LIVERS

1 lb. chicken livers
1 lb. bacon

Clean and cut chicken livers into halves. Cut bacon strips into halves. Wrap bacon around chicken livers; pierce with toothpick. Broil until brown and crisp; turn and brown other side. Drain on paper towel; serve as appetizers. Yield: 6 servings.

Jeanette LeBlanc
Chalmette, Louisiana

RUMAKI

½ lb. chicken livers
2 tbsp. soy sauce
1 sm. can water chestnuts, cut into pieces
1 sm. can pineapple chunks
8 slices bacon, halved

Soak chicken livers in soy sauce for 30 minutes. Cut into pieces. Place a piece of water chestnut on pineapple chunk with a piece of chicken liver in each 1/2 strip bacon. Roll up; fasten with toothpick. Broil, turning frequently, until bacon is done. Yield: 16 servings.

Mrs. G. L. Lawson
Durham, North Carolina

DEVILED CHEESE BITES

1 3-oz. pkg. cream cheese, softened
2 oz. blue cheese, crumbled
1 2 ¼-oz. can deviled ham
¼ c. chopped pecans
Several drops of onion juice
½ c. snipped parsley
Thin pretzel sticks

Blend cream cheese, blue cheese, deviled ham, pecans and onion juice; chill. Shape in small balls; roll in snipped parsley and chill until serving time. Serve with pretzel sticks. Yield: 2 dozen.

Mrs. R. B. Hightower
Leesburg, Georgia

DEVILED HAM CANAPES

2 lge. dill pickles
1 tsp. gelatin
2 tbsp. cold water
½ c. boiling consomme
1 sm. can deviled ham

Hollow out pickles, leaving one solid end. Soften gelatin in cold water. Add heated consomme; stir until dissolved. Add deviled ham. Cool. When it begins to set, pour into pickles. Stand on end in a pan and chill in refrigerator until gelatin has set. Slice in thin slices and place on small round crackers and serve with toothpicks. Yield: 32 canapes.

Mrs. George Scarborough
Dothan, Alabama

DEVILED HAM DIP

1 8-oz. pkg. cream cheese, softened
1 sm. can deviled ham
½ c. mayonnaise
½ tsp. dill seed
½ tsp. chopped parsley
1 tsp. Worcestershire sauce
½ tsp. seasoned salt

(Continued on next page)

Cream the cream cheese and deviled ham with electric mixer. Add mayonnaise, dill seed, parsley, Worcestershire sauce and seasoned salt. Blend. Use as a dip with crackers or potato chips.

Mrs. Virginia Davis
Blountstown, Florida

DEVILED HAM PUFFS

½ lb. pkg. cream cheese
1 tsp. onion juice
½ tsp. baking powder
1 egg yolk
Salt
24 sm. bread rounds
2 2 ¼-oz. cans deviled ham

Combine and blend cheese, onion juice, baking powder, egg yolk and salt to taste. Toast bread rounds on one side. Spread untoasted sides with deviled ham; cover each with a mound of cheese mixture. Place on a cookie sheet. Bake in a 375-degree oven for 10 to 12 minutes or until puffed and brown. Serve hot.

Mrs. J. K. Wilson
Charleston, Virginia

WAFFLE DEVILS

8 bread slices
1 2 ¼-oz. can deviled ham
1 3-oz. pkg. cream cheese
Melted butter or margarine

Spread half of bread slices with deviled ham, and the other half with cheese. Put together sandwich-fashion; brush with butter. Toast in preheated waffle iron until golden brown. Yield: 4 servings.

Mrs. Beaulah Irvin
Vernon Hill, Virginia

CHEESE CHIPPY SPREAD

½ lb. cream cheese
2 tbsp. top milk
Grated onion
Tabasco sauce to taste
Salt and pepper to taste
½ c. finely chopped dried beef

Let cream cheese stand at room temperature until soft enough to beat. Add milk to make a smooth paste; beat in onion and seasonings to taste. Add dried beef, stirring to make the mixture a smooth paste. Rinse bowl or mold with cold water; do not dry. Pack paste firmly into mold. Chill until ready to serve. Yield: 16 servings.

Mrs. John W. Miller
Austin, Texas

CHIPPED BEEF AND CREAM CHEESE CANAPES

1 lge. pkg. cream cheese
Milk
2 spring onions and stalks
¼ lb. chipped dried beef
Crackers or thin bread slices

Soften cream cheese with milk until of spreading consistency. Chop onions and stalks; add to cream cheese. Add minced dried beef. Add more milk if necessary. Spread on crackers or bread.

Mrs. Helen H. Colbert
Alex, Virginia

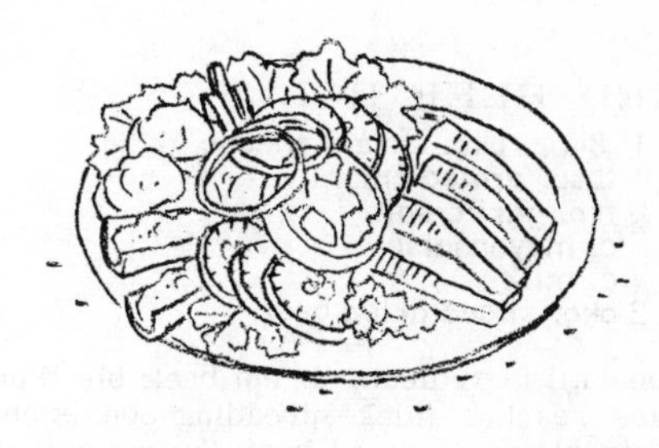

DRIED BEEF APPETIZER BALLS

1 2 ½-oz. jar sliced dried beef
2 3-oz. pkg. cream cheese
¼ c. chopped parsley
1 ½ tbsp. minced onion
1 tsp. prepared mustard

Finely chop dried beef. Mix one-third of beef with the remaining ingredients. Chill mixture for about 1 hour. Form cheese-beef mixture into 1/2-inch balls; roll in the remaining dried beef. Spear with wooden picks. Yield: 50 servings.

Ray Ross
Jacksonville, Florida

DRIED BEEF AND CREAM CHEESE BALLS

1 3-oz. pkg. cream cheese, softened
2 tbsp. horseradish
Dash of onion powder
2 tbsp. cream
3 to 4 oz. sliced dried beef, torn into small pieces

Mash cream cheese with horseradish and onion powder; add enough cream to make creamy. Form into balls; roll in dried beef. Chill until firm. Yield: 8-10 servings.

Mrs. David Christian
Clearwater, Florida

DRIED BEEF PINWHEELS

1 lge. pkg. cream cheese
Garlic salt to taste
½ c. chopped almonds
1 pkg. sliced dried beef

Combine cheese, garlic salt and nuts; spread on beef slices. Roll up and slice to make miniature pinwheels; refrigerate or freeze until ready for use. Yield: 6-8 servings.

Mrs. Clarence Wallner
Jackson, Mississippi

DRIED BEEF ROLLS

1 8-oz. pkg. cream cheese
1 tbsp. grated onion
½ tsp. garlic salt
½ c. mayonnaise
¼ c. milk
2 pkg. sliced dried beef

Combine all ingredients except beef; blend until mixture reaches thick spreading consistency. Separate slices of dried beef. Spread creamed cheese mixture on one end of beef slice; roll up from cheese end.

Mrs. Bernard A. Meyer
Savannah, Georgia

HOT BEEF DIP

¼ c. chopped onion
1 to 2 tbsp. butter or margarine
1 c. milk
1 8-oz. pkg. cream cheese, cubed
1 c. chopped dried beef
1 3-oz. can sliced mushrooms, drained
¼ c. shredded Parmesan cheese
2 tbsp. chopped parsley
Toasted rye bread rounds
Toasted bread sticks

Cook onion in butter until tender. Stir in milk and cream cheese, mixing until well blended. Add remaining ingredients except breads. Serve hot in chafing dish with toasted bread rounds and bread sticks. Yield: 2 cups.

Mrs. W. S. Anderson
Santa Fe, New Mexico

ELLEN'S COCKTAIL LOG

1 4-oz. pkg. dried beef
1 tbsp. minced onion
1 8-oz. pkg. cream cheese
½ pt. sour cream
1 tbsp. prepared horseradish
Crackers

Saute dried beef and onion; set aside. Combine cream cheese, sour cream and horseradish. Spread dried beef and onion on waxed paper. Shape cream cheese mixture into log; roll in dried beef. Spread on crackers. Yield: 30 servings.

Mrs. James W. Turtle
Richmond, Virginia

SNOWBALL PATE

2 tbsp. mayonnaise
2 tbsp. lemon juice
½ lb. liver sausage, cut up
2 green onions, cut up
4 oz. cream cheese, cubed
2 tbsp. milk or cream

Blend first 4 ingredients until smooth. Pack in small bowl and cover; chill for at least 2 hours or overnight. Unmold on serving plate. Blend cream cheese and milk until smooth. Spread over mold and chill until serving time.

Mrs. D. H. Felts
Joiner, Arkansas

YUM-YUMS

½ lb. bacon
½ c. chopped green onions and tops
¼ c. mayonnaise
24 buttered 2-in. toast rounds

Fry bacon until very crisp; drain and crumble. Combine crumbled bacon, chopped onions and mayonnaise; blend. Spread a teaspoonful of mixture on each toast round. Heat in a 350-degree oven for a few minutes. Serve immediately. Melba toast may be substituted for toast rounds, if desired. Yield: 24 appetizers.

Mrs. Earl Ramond
Bay St. Louis, Mississippi

SALAD DRESSINGS

Recipe for Fluffy Date Salad Dressing on Page 48

Dressing Tastefully

Just as homemakers don't overdress, so they should not overdress their salads.

A little salad dressing goes quite a way. The trick is to use just enough to coat the greens lightly without drowning them, or enough to just garnish a salad plate.

Dressings are to add that extra appeal that makes guests want to keep right on eating long after they've taken the first bite.

Add dressing to salad just before serving. This keeps both the salad and the dressing flavors fresh and crisp-tasting.

Try mayonnaise and salad dressing combinations to enhance meat, seafood, egg and molded salads.

Snappy French dressings are especially good for marinating vegetables and tossing with greens. Try French or another tart dressing with fruit salads.

Cooked dressings are the ideal go-with for vegetables and greens. Sour cream dressings add zip to fruit, meat and vegetable salads.

DRESSING DICTIONARY

COOKED DRESSING has a cooked white sauce and egg base. It is fluffy, creamy and has a zippy flavor.

FRENCH DRESSING is a combination of oil and acid (vinegar or lemon juice), plus seasonings such as salt, pepper, paprika and mustard. Clear French dressing separates and must be thoroughly shaken before it is used. Creamy French dressing is homogenized and will stay mixed.

MAYONNAISE is a rich, creamy dressing. It is made by beating vegetable oil very slowly into acid and egg yolk. It is mildly flavored and can be used with additional seasonings.

SALAD DRESSING is similar to mayonnaise but contains less oil, so it costs less.

Fine salad oil is essential to good dressings. Choose corn, olive, peanut or soy oil, or a blend of these. Never use mineral oil; it may rob the body of important vitamins.

For a tangy accent, use lemon juice. Fresh, canned or frozen, it not only adds zip and tartness, but vitamin C as well. Lemon juice is often interchanged with vinegar in dressings.

VINEGAR, a staple for dressings, comes in many exciting flavors:

Basil, Herb and Spice or Mixed Herb—is used lightly in salad dressings or on cooked greens, slaw.

Cider—is made from apples and most often used for salads. It is quite sharp.

Malt—is made from barley and is milder than cider vinegar.

Tarragon—has a distinctive, slightly bitter taste. It is malt vinegar flavored with tarragon, an herb.

White—is distilled and has a medium tang.

Wine—is very mild. It is made from grapes.

ARGYLE DRESSING

1 tsp. butter
1 tsp. salt
1 tbsp. sugar
1 tsp. mustard
4 tbsp. vinegar
4 egg yolks, beaten
8 marshmallows
1 c. whipped cream
1 c. nuts (opt.)

Cream butter, salt and sugar. Dissolve mustard in small amount of the vinegar; add to butter mixture with egg yolks and remaining vinegar. Cook in double boiler. Add marshmallows to hot mixture. Chill; fold in cream and nuts.

Hazel S. Wilkinson
Ozark, Alabama

BUTTERMILK SPECIAL SALAD DRESSING

2 c. salad dressing
1 c. buttermilk
¼ c. catsup
¼ c. sugar
½ tsp. salt
1 tsp. paprika
2 tsp. vinegar
1 clove of garlic, mashed

Combine all ingredients in a 1-quart jar. Shake until thoroughly blended. Refrigerate. Yield: 1 1/2 pints.

Mrs. Charles W. Parton
Plainview, Texas

CENTURY-OLD DRESSING

¼ c. sugar
½ c. water
¼ c. lemon juice
¼ c. vinegar
¼ tsp. salt
¼ tsp. paprika
1 c. salad oil
½ c. catsup
1 sm. onion, grated

Boil sugar with water for 10 minutes. Add lemon juice; simmer for 5 minutes longer. Cool quickly by placing pan in ice water. Add vinegar, salt and paprika to cooled mixture. Beat with rotary beater to blend well. Mix oil, catsup and onion into cold syrup mixture; beat until thickened. Refrigerate. Shake well before serving. Yield: 1 1/2 pints.

Sarah A. McCreight
Morganton, North Carolina

CELERY SEED DRESSING

¾ c. sugar
1 tsp. dry mustard
1 tsp. salt
⅓ c. vinegar
1 ½ tbsp. celery seed
1 tbsp. grated onion
1 c. salad oil

Place all ingredients except oil in a deep bowl. Beat with electric mixer, gradually adding oil till thick. Store in refrigerator. Good with a fruit or vegetable salad.

Mrs. James E. Lamb, Sr.
Laurel Bay, South Carolina

CHILI SAUCE SALAD DRESSING

¾ c. sugar
½ c. water
1 tsp. grated onion
1 tsp. paprika
1 tsp. salt
1 tsp. vinegar
3 tbsp. lemon juice
1 c. chili sauce
1 c. salad oil

Combine sugar and water; cook for 5 minutes. Remove from heat; add all remaining ingredients. Beat well; refrigerate. Yield: 1 pint.

Angie T. Miller
Fredericksburg, Virginia

COOKED SALAD DRESSING

3 tbsp. butter or margarine
3 tbsp. flour
1 c. milk
2 eggs
1 tbsp. sugar
¼ c. vinegar
1 tsp. salt
¼ tsp. mustard
⅛ tsp. paprika

Make thick white sauce in top of double boiler with first 3 ingredients. Beat eggs slightly in mixing bowl; pour in a little of the white sauce, stirring constantly. Add to rest of white sauce in top of double boiler. Add sugar, vinegar, salt, mustard and paprika. Place over boiling water in bottom of double boiler; cook 5 to 10 minutes, stirring constantly, until smooth and thickened. Remove from heat and cool. Store in covered container in refrigerator.

Dianne Woods
Chatham, Virginia

CHINESE SALAD DRESSING

3 tbsp. vinegar or lemon juice
3 tbsp. soy sauce
1 tbsp. sugar
2 tbsp. salad oil
1 tsp. chopped ginger (opt.)

Mix vinegar, soy sauce and sugar; add oil slowly, stirring constantly. Use with cucumbers, cabbage, lettuce, tomatoes or any other vegetables. Add ginger to salad if desired. Delicious on bits of leftover meats. Needs no refrigeration. This is a Queen's Daughters' recipe from the Benedictine Sisters of Peking.

Mary C. DeSpain
Hodgenville, Kentucky

CUCUMBER DRESSING

3 med. cucumbers
3 sm. onions
¼ c. sugar
¼ c. lemon juice
¼ tsp. monosodium glutamate
¼ tsp. garlic powder
2 tbsp. Worcestershire sauce
¼ tsp. green food coloring
1 qt. mayonnaise

Grind cucumbers and onions. Drain well. Add sugar, lemon juice, seasonings, coloring and mayonnaise. Stir until smooth.

Helen Hutchison
Jackson, Tennessee

FLUFFY DATE SALAD DRESSING

1 c. California dates
2 eggs
¼ c. lemon juice
¼ c. sugar
⅛ tsp. salt
1 c. whipping cream
Fresh or canned fruit for salad
Crisp salad greens

Cut dates into wedges. Beat eggs in top of double boiler; blend in lemon juice, sugar and salt. Cook, stirring constantly, until thickened. Remove from heat; cool well. Whip cream; fold in egg mixture and dates. Serve over fruit salads on salad greens. Yield: 3 cups.

Photograph for this recipe on page 45.

BASIC FRENCH DRESSING

⅓ c. corn oil
3 to 4 tbsp. vinegar
1 tbsp. sugar
¾ tsp. salt
¼ tsp. paprika
¼ tsp. dry mustard

Measure all ingredients into a bottle or jar. Cover and shake well. Chill for several hours. Shake well before serving. Yield: 1/4 cup.

Shirley Cotton
Kermit, Texas

CELERY SEED FRENCH DRESSING

½ c. sugar
1 tsp. dry mustard
1 tsp. salt
½ sm. onion, grated
6 tbsp. vinegar
1 c. salad oil
1 tbsp. celery seed

Combine sugar, mustard, salt, onion and half the vinegar. Add oil gradually while beating; beat in remaining vinegar. Add celery seed. Yield: 1 1/2 cups.

Mrs. W. M. Piersall
Tarpon Springs, Florida

FRENCH DRESSING

1 c. salad oil
2 tbsp. (or more) vinegar
1 tbsp. (or more) lemon juice
½ tsp. prepared mustard
1 tsp. sugar
1 tbsp. Worcestershire sauce
3 tbsp. catsup
Salt and pepper to taste
Garlic or onion salt (opt.)
Chopped parsley (opt.)
Mayonnaise (opt.)

Mix all ingredients in jar and shake thoroughly. Place in refrigerator. Shake well before using. Serve with any green salad.

Mrs. Berry Floyd
Canon, Georgia

FRENCH DRESSING

½ c. salad oil
⅓ c. vinegar
1 tsp. salt
⅛ tsp. pepper
¼ tsp. paprika
½ tsp. sugar
Garlic (opt.)

Combine all ingredients in a small bowl. Beat until salad oil is broken into very fine globules and dressing is well blended. If garlic flavor is desired, rub inside bowl with garlic before placing other ingredients in the bowl. Store in glass jar. Shake each time before serving.

Carol Montgomery
Gilmer, Texas

FRENCH DRESSING

1 c. sugar
1 tbsp. (scant) salt
1 tsp. dry mustard
½ c. cider vinegar
½ c. catsup
1 c. oil
1 med. grated onion
1 clove of garlic

Mix in order given and beat with electric mixer or blend in a blender.

Mrs. Earl J. Smith
Calvert City, Kentucky

FRENCH DRESSING

⅓ c. salad oil
2 tbsp. lemon juice
½ tsp. paprika
¼ tsp. salt
Freshly ground pepper

Combine all ingredients in bottle or jar. Cover and shake well. Chill before serving.

Mrs. Janie England
Centertown, Kentucky

HONEY FRENCH DRESSING

1 c. cooking oil
½ c. honey
½ tsp. salt
⅓ c. chili sauce
½ c. vinegar
½ c. finely chopped onion
1 tbsp. Worcestershire sauce

Combine all ingredients in a jar with a tight-fitting cover. Shake vigorously.

Genevieve Inman
Shallotte, North Carolina

RIVIERA FRENCH DRESSING

½ c. salad oil
1 tsp. salt
½ tsp. pepper
¼ c. vinegar
¾ tsp. powdered sugar
1 thin slice onion
2 sprigs parsley
1 whole pimento
1 ¼-in. strip green hot pepper

Put all ingredients in blender and blend thoroughly. Yield: 1 cup.

Mrs. Beulah Gibson
Athens, Alabama

FRUIT MAYONNAISE

1 tsp. butter
2 tsp. flour
1 ½ c. pineapple or grapefruit juice
Juice of 1 lemon
Juice of 1 orange
½ c. sugar
2 eggs, separated
½ c. heavy cream, whipped

Melt butter; blend in flour. Add fruit juices and sugar. Cook over medium heat, stirring constantly, until thickened. Slowly pour over beaten egg yolks; stir vigorously. Cool; fold in stiffly beaten egg whites and whipped cream. Chill and serve over salads.

Grace Strutt
Bessemer City, North Carolina

FRUIT SALAD DRESSING

½ c. sugar
1 tsp. dry mustard
1 tsp. paprika
1 tsp. salt
1 tsp. celery seed
1 tsp. onion juice
1 tsp. lemon juice
1 c. salad oil
¼ c. vinegar

Mix all dry ingredients; add onion and lemon juice. Then add oil and vinegar, drop by drop, beating constantly for dressing to stay thick. The more the dressing is beaten the better it will be.

Mrs. Walter S. Edinger
Louisville, Kentucky

HONEY DRESSING

¼ c. sugar
½ tsp. dry mustard
½ tsp. paprika
¼ tsp. salt
¼ c. strained honey
3 tbsp. vinegar
1 tbsp. lemon juice
½ tsp. grated onion
1 c. salad oil
½ tsp. celery seed

Mix dry ingredients; add honey, vinegar, lemon juice and grated onion. With electric mixer, start pouring in oil slowly, beating continuously. By the time all oil is added dressing will be very thick. Add celery seed and beat just enough to mix. Serve with congealed and fruit salads. Keep refrigerated. Yield: 2 cups.

Marie Mason
Springfield, Tennessee

HONEY-LIME DRESSING

3 tbsp. fresh lime juice
3 tbsp. honey
6 tbsp. salad oil

Combine all ingredients. Beat at medium speed with mixer until mixture looks creamy. Serve on fruit salads. Yield: 6 servings.

Mrs. Doris Dowell
Fort Worth, Texas

ONE-TWO-THREE FRUIT DRESSING

1 egg, well beaten
1 c. sugar
Juice and grated rind of 1 lemon
Juice and grated rind of 1 lime
Juice and grated rind of 1 orange

Combine all ingredients. Cook over medium heat, stirring constantly, for 1 minute. Cool; cover and refrigerate. Yield: 4 servings.

Irina Nikitin
Ramseur, North Carolina

PINEAPPLE DRESSING

Lump butter, size of walnut
1 tbsp. flour
2 eggs, separated
1 c. sugar
1 c. pineapple juice, heated
Whipped cream to taste

Melt butter; add flour and mix. Add well beaten egg yolks, then sugar and cream well. Stir in heated juice and cook in double boiler until thick. When ready to serve add whipped cream to taste.

Mrs. John E. Dail
Blountville, Tennessee

PINEAPPLE DRESSING FOR FRUIT SALAD

Syrup from No. 2 can pineapple
1 tbsp. flour
1 egg yolk

Cook ingredients in top of double boiler until mixture coats a spoon. Cool and use on fruit salads. Do not use pineapple juice.

Mrs. Earl H. Martin
Hendersonville, North Carolina

POPPY SEED DRESSING

¾ c. sugar
1 tsp. salt
1 tsp. dry mustard
1 ½ tbsp. onion juice
⅓ c. vinegar
1 c. salad oil
1 tbsp. poppy seed

Mix sugar, salt, mustard, onion juice and vinegar thoroughly. Add oil gradually, beating constantly with rotary beater or mixer. Add poppy seed. Coconut may be substituted for poppy seed for use on fruit salads.

Marie Krotky
Houston, Texas

SALAD DRESSING

½ c. sugar
2 eggs
Vinegar to taste
Butter, size of an egg

Mix sugar and eggs; beat well. Add vinegar and cook in double boiler till thick. Add the butter. Serve with fruit salads.

Mrs. Arthur D. Brooks
Choudrant, Louisiana

HEALTH DRESSING

⅔ c. salad oil
3 tbsp. sugar
⅓ c. catsup
1 tbsp. lemon juice
½ tsp. grated onion
½ c. vinegar
¾ tsp. salt

Combine all ingredients; shake well. Yield: 1 1/3 cups.

Lydia E. Griffin
Gatesville, North Carolina

HOMEMADE SALAD DRESSING

1 c. catsup
⅔ c. sugar
¾ c. salad oil
¾ c. vinegar
3 tsp. paprika
3 tsp. garlic salt
3 tsp. salt

Mix all ingredients together and refrigerate.

Mrs. William D. Varnell
Rogersville, Alabama

HOT ENDIVE DRESSING

2 tbsp. flour
1 egg
½ c. sugar
⅓ tsp. salt
Vinegar to taste
8 slices bacon

Combine flour, egg, sugar and salt; add vinegar and enough water to obtain smooth mixture. Fry bacon; crumble. Add water to bacon; heat. Stir in flour mixture. Pour over endive. Yield: 4 servings.

Mary E. Ziegler
Sarasota, Florida

LOW-CHOLESTEROL MAYONNAISE

2 egg yolks
¼ tsp. paprika
Dash of cayenne pepper
1 tsp. salt
½ tsp. dry mustard
2 tbsp. vinegar
2 c. corn oil
2 tbsp. lemon juice
1 tbsp. hot water

Bring eggs to room temperature. Combine dry ingredients. Blend in egg yolks. Add vinegar; mix well. Add 1 teaspoon oil at a time, beating at high speed until 1/4 cup has been added. Add remaining oil in increasing amounts, alternating last 1/2 cup with lemon juice. Add an additional tablespoon of lemon juice to vary the flavor. Beat in hot water to take away oily appearance. Yield: 1 pint.

Barbara Waybourn
Afton, Texas

LEMON-LIME DRESSING

4 tsp. lemon juice
2 tsp. lime juice
½ c. mayonnaise or salad dressing
2 tbsp. sugar
½ c. whipping cream

Combine lemon and lime juices, mayonnaise and sugar. Whip cream slightly; fold in. Yield: 1 3/4 cups.

Mrs. Elizabeth Cowley
Saltillo, Mississippi

LIME-MINT DRESSING

¾ c. salad oil
¼ c. lime juice
1 tsp. salt
¼ tsp. white pepper
1 tsp. finely chopped parsley
1 tsp. finely chopped mint
1 tsp. finely chopped chives
1 tsp. prepared mustard

Mix all ingredients; place an ice cube in the dressing and beat until mixture thickens. Serve on tossed green salad or coleslaw.

Sandra England
Centertown, Kentucky

PEACHY-STYLE SALAD DRESSING

2 c. fresh peaches
¼ c. yogurt
1 tbsp. cheese dressing (opt.)

(Continued on next page)

Blend peaches and yogurt on low speed in a blender. Add cheese dressing. Serve on fruit salad. Yield: 1 1/2 cups.

Mrs. John Roberts
Lineville, Alabama

LOW-CALORIE DRESSING

2 c. corn oil
1 c. vinegar
1 tbsp. salt
2 tbsp. sugar
2 tbsp. catsup
1 tsp. mustard
1 clove of garlic, chopped

Blend all ingredients; refrigerate for several hours. Yield: 1 quart.

Helen Hoffman
Lincolnton, North Carolina

LOW-CALORIE PAPRIKA DRESSING

½ med. onion
1 c. vinegar
2 tbsp. paprika
2 tbsp. salt
15 ¼-grain sugar substitute tablets
¼ tsp. dry mustard
3 c. corn oil

Puree onion in blender or chop fine. Add all remaining ingredients except oil. Gradually add oil and continue blending. Shake well before using.

Mrs. Morris M. Campbell
Tavares, Florida

ROQUEFORT DRESSING

2 c. mayonnaise
1 ½ c. buttermilk
½ lb. Roquefort or Danish bleu cheese, crumbled
2 tbsp. Worcestershire sauce
1 tsp. garlic powder

Blend all ingredients thoroughly but gently. Keep in tightly covered jar in refrigerator until ready to serve. Yield: 1 quart.

Mrs. Helen D. Greene
Asheville, North Carolina

SALAD DRESSING

1 c. mayonnaise
¼ c. catsup
¼ c. evaporated milk
2 tbsp. sugar
2 tsp. prepared mustard

Mix all ingredients well and store in refrigerator. Serve on spring greens.

Elsie Harrison
Hatfield, Arkansas

SALAD DRESSING

½ c. vinegar
1 ½ c. water
2 eggs
⅔ c. sugar
1 ½ tsp. dry mustard
4 tbsp. flour
1 tsp. salt
⅛ tsp. pepper

Heat vinegar and water. Beat eggs slightly; add remaining ingredients and mix well. Add egg mixture to vinegar and water, stirring as you pour. If there are any lumps, beat with rotary beater for a minute. Stir constantly over medium heat until mixture thickens.

Mrs. Robert McAllister
Jefferson, Maryland

SALAD DRESSING

⅔ c. sugar
1 egg
2 tbsp. flour
½ tsp. salt
½ tsp. dry mustard
¼ c. vinegar
1 c. hot water
Butter to taste

Combine sugar, egg, flour, salt and mustard; add vinegar and water. Cook until thickened. Add butter. This makes a delicious dressing for potato salad or head lettuce. Yield: 1 1/4 cups.

Mrs. Evelyn Thomas
Miami, Florida

SALAD DRESSING

1 c. sugar
2 tsp. paprika
6 tsp. salt
2 c. oil
2 c. vinegar
2 cans tomato soup
2 sm. onions, chopped fine

(Continued on next page)

Mix dry ingredients; add oil, vinegar, soup and onions. Mix in blender or shake until mixed well. Refrigerate. Yield: 2 quarts.

Mrs. Glenn Gregory
Mooresville, North Carolina

SALAD DRESSING

1 c. sugar
½ c. vinegar
1 can tomato soup
1 soup can oil
⅛ tsp. garlic
1 tbsp. celery seed
1 tbsp. dry mustard
Salt and pepper to taste

Put all ingredients in a large jar. Stir well; shake hard for a few minutes. Keep refrigerated.

Mrs. H. J. McBride
Oakland, Nebraska

SLAW WITH SALAD DRESSING

1 c. vinegar
1 c. sugar
1 tsp. mustard seed
½ tsp. turmeric
½ tsp. salt

Mix all ingredients in saucepan; boil for 2 minutes. Cool; pour over coleslaw and refrigerate.

Mrs. William D. Varnell
Rogersville, Arkansas

BLEU AND COTTAGE CHEESE SALAD DRESSING

1 c. cream-style cottage cheese
½ c. sour cream
½ c. crumbled bleu cheese
2 tbsp. minced onion
2 tbsp. chopped pimento
2 tbsp. Worcestershire sauce
¼ tsp. salt
2 drops Tabasco sauce

Blend cottage cheese and sour cream. Blend all remaining ingredients; combine with cottage cheese mixture. Yield: 2 cups.

Mrs. Mary L. Burleson
Swan Quarter, North Carolina

CREAMY DILL SALAD DRESSING

1 egg
1 tsp. salt
⅛ tsp. pepper
4 tsp. lemon juice
1 tsp. minced onion
¼ tsp. sugar
¼ tsp. dill weed
1 ½ c. sour cream

Beat egg with mixer. Fold in remaining ingredients.

Mrs. Lawrence Dellinger
Cherryville, North Carolina

ROQUEFORT CHEESE DRESSING

½ c. sour cream
¼ tsp. salt
⅛ tsp. garlic powder
¼ tsp. powdered mustard
¼ c. light cream
¼ tsp. mayonnaise
1 tsp. lemon juice
1 3-oz. pkg. cream cheese
⅓ c. Roquefort cheese, crumbled

Stir all ingredients except Roquefort into softened cream cheese. Mix thoroughly. Add Roquefort and blend lightly. Cover and refrigerate.

Mrs. H. H. Dod
Lexington, Virginia

SPINACH DRESSING

1 egg
1 tbsp. (scant) ham drippings
4 tbsp. sour cream
¼ c. vinegar, hot and not too strong
4 tbsp. sugar

Beat whole egg. Mix all ingredients; cook. Serve over spinach. Garnish with hard-cooked eggs.

Mrs. J. A. Cleek
Chattanooga, Tennessee

SPRING GARDEN DRESSING

½ c. mayonnaise
½ c. cottage cheese
3 tbsp. chopped green pepper
1 tsp. salt
Dash of pepper

Combine all ingredients. Chill. Yield: 1 cup.

Ena Mae Jenkins
Elizabethtown, North Carolina

DRESSING FOR SALAD

½ c. cooking oil
¼ c. chili sauce
¼ c. catsup
Juice of 1 onion
1 c. mayonnaise
Dash of paprika
½ tsp. pepper
Dash of salt

Mix together above ingredients. Shake until well blended.

Marie Krotky
Houston, Texas

HEAD LETTUCE DRESSING

1 sm. jar olives
½ lb. cheese
1 sm. onion
1 sm. can pimento
¼ c. chili sauce
Salad dressing

Grind olives, cheese, onion and pimento in food chopper. Add chili sauce and enough salad dressing to thin to desired consistency. Refrigerate. Yield: 1 pint.

Mrs. Jane Thurman
New Castle, Kentucky

KING'S FARE THOUSAND ISLAND DRESSING

1 c. mayonnaise
½ c. chili sauce
1 sm. bottle stuffed olives, diced
½ c. (or more) grated New York State cheese
2 diced, hard-boiled eggs
Juice of ½ lemon

Blend all ingredients and allow to marinate for several hours or overnight before serving. Serve over wedges of crisp lettuce, fruit, salad or as a sauce on seafood cocktail.

Mrs. Charles Snook, Jr.
Birmingham, Alabama

ROTISSERIE DRESSING

2 or 3 cloves of garlic, minced
1 c. mayonnaise
¼ c. chili sauce
¼ c. catsup
1 tsp. Worcestershire sauce
¼ to 1 tsp. pepper
½ c. salad oil
¼ tsp. Tabasco sauce
¼ tsp. paprika
1 sm. onion, grated
2 tbsp. water or juice of 1 lemon plus 1 tsp. water
1 tsp. mustard
Salt to taste

Blend all ingredients well. Keep refrigerated. Yield: 1 pint.

Mrs. Ruth J. Shaw
Umatilla, Florida

THOUSAND ISLAND DRESSING

½ c. oil
½ c. chili sauce
¼ c. vinegar
Paprika, salt, mustard, red pepper
1 grated onion
1 tbsp. sugar
2 hard-boiled eggs, chopped fine
1 stalk celery, cut fine

Mix all ingredients together thoroughly except eggs and celery. Mix eggs and celery with dressing. Serve on lettuce leaves.

Patricia Smallwood
Mariba, Kentucky

TOSS UP SALAD DRESSING

1 tbsp. lemon juice
2 tbsp. vinegar
1 c. evaporated milk
⅓ c. catsup
2 tbsp. sweet pickle relish
1 tsp. Worcestershire sauce
1 tsp. basil
1 tsp. onion salt

Gradually stir lemon juice and vinegar into milk. Add remaining ingredients. Stir well. Place in covered container or jar with lid. Chill well before pouring over salad greens. Yield: 1 1/2 cups.

Diane Jones
Grannis, Arkansas

FRUIT SALADS

Recipe for Fruit Salad in Avocado Boats on Page 78

Choosing Fresh Fruit

FRUIT	HOW TO CHOOSE	STORAGE
APPLES	Avoid those that are soft or have shriveled skin.	Keep in cool place. Can be refrigerated.
BANANAS	Should be plump and firm with a bright yellow skin, or flecked with brown when fully ripe.	Store at room temperature. Refrigerator storage stops ripening, impairs flavor.
BERRIES	Should be bright, clean, plump, and fragrant. Avoid soft berries with leaking juice.	Very perishable. Pick over carefully and spread out before refrigerating. Wash just before using. Use as soon as possible.
CITRUS FRUITS	Should be firm and heavy for their size, with fine-textured skins.	Store in cool, dark, dry place, or refrigerator.
CHERRIES	Should be plump, firm, bright and have stems attached.	Wash and store in refrigerator.
GRAPES	Should be plump, with fresh good color and firmly attached stems.	Store in refrigerator for as short a time as possible.
MELONS	Should have fragrant aroma, be unbruised. A ripe melon will be soft near the stem and will give a little. Thump watermelons. If they give a hollow, not dull, thudding sound, they are ripe.	Store at 70 degrees to ripen. Refrigerate before serving.
PEACHES	Should be plump, firm, smooth-skinned and of good color (whitish or yellowish with a reddish blush).	Very perishable. Handle gently and refrigerate.
PEARS	Should be smooth-surfaced, fragrant, well shaped, firm to fairly firm, but not hard.	Store in cool, dry, dark spot. If hard, ripen at room temperature.
PINEAPPLE	Should be fragrant, dark orange-yellow in color, heavy to feel. To test for ripeness, pull one of the leaves at the top. It should pull out easily.	Keep in cool place.
PLUMS	Choose plump, dark ones that are soft but not mushy. Avoid if shriveled or brownish.	Keep in refrigerator.

Cool Salads

Fruit salads are refreshingly cool and tempting all year. You'll find a palette of colors among fruit, which makes them all the more eye-appealing. Unusual designs make any salad more attractive, but especially fruit salads. Try these tricks for special occasions or even as a family-pleaser at no special time at all.

MELON BALLS

Use a melon ball tool, or scoop fruit out with a teaspoon measuring spoon. Pile mixture of watermelon, canteloupe and honeydew melon balls back into a scooped-out watermelon shell.

CITRUS FRUITS

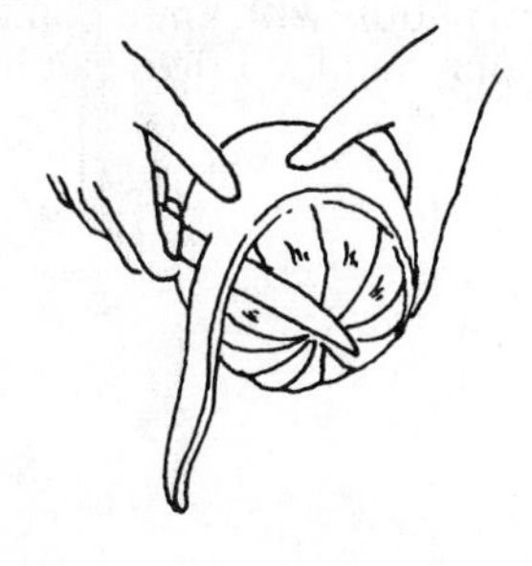

THE 'ROUND AND 'ROUND METHOD—Cut the peel away in a continuing spiral with a slight sawing motion. Don't remove the white inner portion which clings naturally to the meat. It is rich in vitamins and minerals.

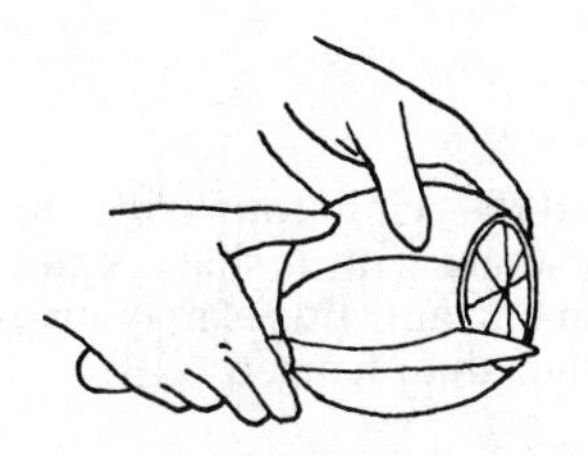

BASKETBALL METHOD—With a sharp knife, slice off the stem end of the fruit. Score the peel with a knife so that it looks like the sections on the outside of a basketball. Don't cut down into the meat. Pull the peel away with your fingers, again leaving the white inner skin which clings to the meat.

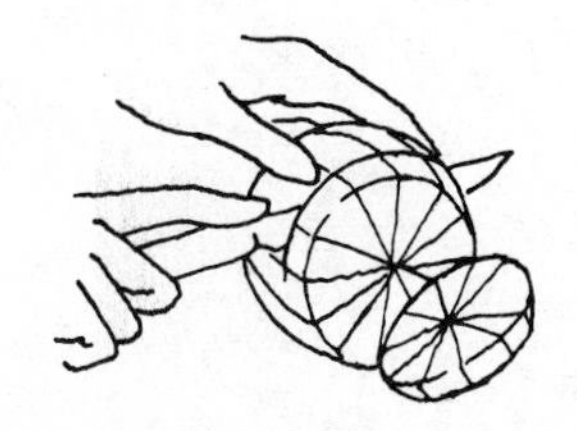

CARTWHEELS—Use them peeled for salads, unpeeled for garnishes. Slice fruit crosswise in desired thickness. For halfwheels, cut cartwheels in two parts.

SECTIONS—Peel fruit. Cut sections half-way between segment walls so that the membrane is in the center of the meat.

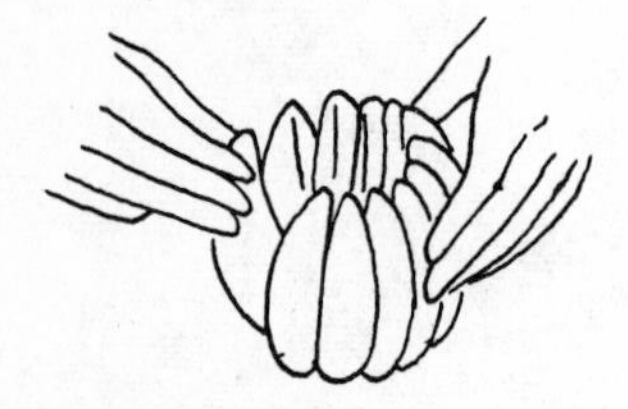

SEGMENTS—Peel fruit, gently separate into natural divisions.

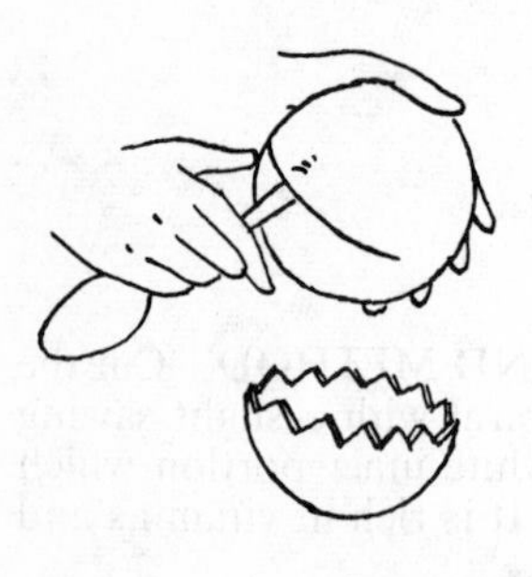

SHELLS—Score fruit around middle with knife point; peel away from fruit with spoon handle. Edges can be notched with scissors.

FANCY CITRUS BASKETS

Cut ¼-inch strip around the top of an orange or grapefruit half, leaving a 1-inch strip on each side uncut. Cut down through membrane to free the strips.

SWIRLING EDGE FRINGE—Cut top edge of orange or grapefruit half at angle with a sharp knife after fruit sections have been cut out. Edges may also be notched with scissors rather than fringed.

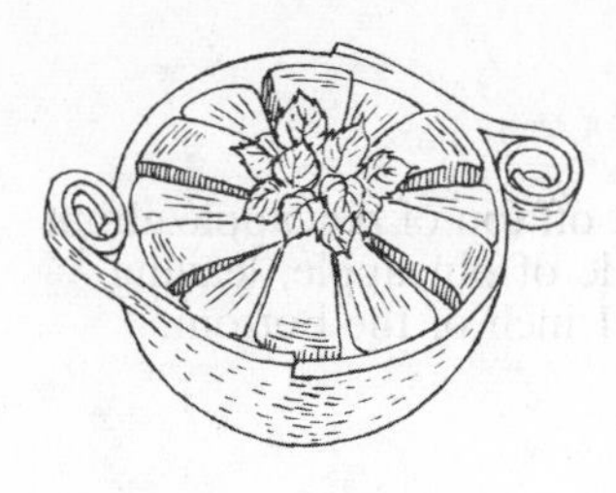

SPIRALS—Cut each strip near attached end. Roll tightly and fasten with toothpicks.

BOW—Cut the ¼-inch strip as directed above. Cut each strip at the center and fold back. Fasten with toothpicks.

HANDLES—Pull together at top the two ¼-inch strips, without further cutting. Fasten with picks.

PINEAPPLE

Use the pineapple as a centerpiece for several days, then put it to use as a salad and the shell as a server.

PINEAPPLE BASKET—At the right of the center of the pineapple, make a vertical cut to the core. Repeat the same cut on the left to form a handle 1 inch wide.

Cut from sides to center to free wedges. Remove the fruit from the cut-out wedges.

Remove fruit from under the handle. Using a grapefruit knife, remove the fruit from the basket. Dice pineapple and mix with other fruits. Pile into pineapple basket for serving.

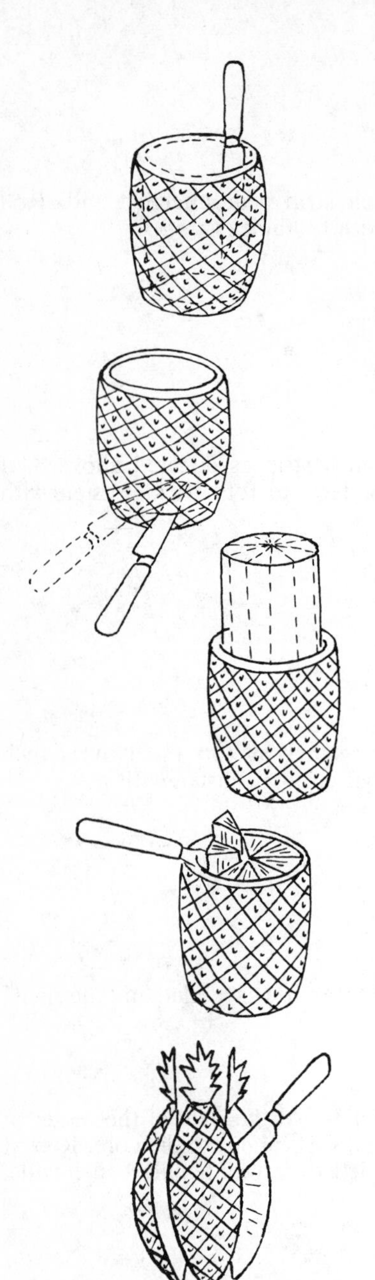

LUAU PINEAPPLE—Cut off top of pineapple about 1½ inches down. Cut inside of pineapple, leaving ½ inch inside rind, to within 1 inch of the bottom.

Insert a knife about 1½ inches up from the bottom, pointing the rind opposite. Draw the knife along the rind to the right. Turn the knife and repeat to sever fruit on the left.

Remove fruit from shell. Cut fruit in wedges or spears and replace in pineapple shell. Or, if desired, cut the hollow shell crosswise to form a bowl that will hold about 2 cups of salad dressing.

Set shell filled with dressing on a large serving plate or tray. Let guests help themselves to the dressing from the pineapple shell.

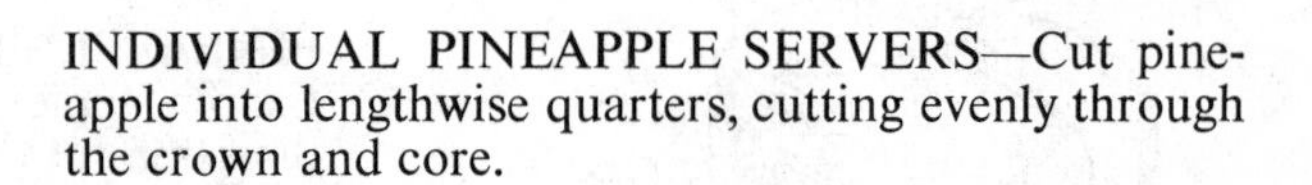

INDIVIDUAL PINEAPPLE SERVERS—Cut pineapple into lengthwise quarters, cutting evenly through the crown and core.

Remove fruit in one piece with curved knife, cutting just under core of each quarter.

Slice fruit. Alternate pieces of fruit under strip of core so they extend alternately. If desired, other fruits may be alternated with the pineapple strips.

CINNAMON-APPLE SALAD

6 firm apples
1 c. cinnamon drops
2 c. sugar
1 c. water
Nuts, chopped
Cream cheese
Mayonnaise

Peel and core apples. Place apples in an open pan on top of the stove. Heat and stir cinnamon drops and sugar in water until dissolved. Pour syrup over apples; cook slowly, turning the apples frequently in the syrup. When apples are done, remove from the syrup with a strainer and cool. Place apples in a crisp lettuce leaf. Fill the centers with mixture of nuts, cream cheese and mayonnaise. Yield: 6 servings.

Mrs. Edward T. Breathitt
Wife of Governor of Kentucky
Frankfort, Kentucky

EVENING SALAD APPETIZER

5 apples, cut in fine cubes
3 tbsp. lemon juice
1 c. pineapple cream dressing
Lettuce
1 c. salted pecans

Mix apples, lemon juice and dressing; place on platter on lettuce. Sprinkle with nuts. Yield: 6 servings.

Blanche Easterlin
Bowman, South Carolina

RED APPLE SALAD

¼ tsp. salt
1 ½ c. sugar
½ c. red cinnamon candies
3 c. water
4 firm tart apples, pared and cored
½ c. cottage cheese, or 3 to 4 ounces cream cheese
¼ c. chopped green peppers

Add salt, sugar and candies to the water. Put over heat and stir until dissolved. Cook apples slowly in syrup in covered pan until just tender, turning occasionally to color evenly. Drain and chill. Mix cheese with green peppers and stuff the apples. Serve on watercress or other dark greens. Yield: 4 servings.

Mrs. Dorothy Patterson
Warner, Oklahoma

WALDORF APPLE SALAD

1 ½ c. chopped apples
1 c. diced celery
½ c. chopped nuts
½ c. diced marshmallows
¼ tsp. salt
2 tbsp. lemon juice
½ c. salad dressing

Chill all the ingredients. Combine and serve on lettuce. Yield: 6 servings.

Mrs. W. A. Gentry
Fletcher, North Carolina

WALDORF SALAD

3 c. diced apples
1 c. celery, cut in pieces
½ c. walnuts, cut in pieces
¾ c. mayonnaise

Mix apples, celery and nuts and moisten with mayonnaise. Arrange on crisp leaves of lettuce and garnish with whole nuts and candied cherries. Yield: 6 servings.

Mrs. Agnes B. Huggins
Boiling Springs, North Carolina

AVOCADO SALAD

1 ripe avocado
¼ green pepper, finely minced
½ stalk celery, finely minced
1 tsp. pimento
½ tsp. salt
1 tbsp. mayonnaise
Lettuce
Sliced stuffed olives

Scoop out avocado; whip pulp until creamy. Add pepper, celery, pimento, salt and mayonnaise. Spoon onto lettuce. Garnish with olive rings. Yield: 6 servings.

Laura Bossier
Convent, Louisiana

CHEESE-AVOCADO SALAD

1 c. sour cream
1 lge. pkg. cream cheese
2 tbsp. finely chopped onion
Salt to taste
2 lge. avocados, peeled and pitted

Mix sour cream, cheese, onion and salt with electric mixer. Add avocados; blend. Serve on lettuce.

Mrs. Lillian S. Ealy
Anthony, New Mexico

GUACAMOLE

1 envelope exotic herbs salad dressing mix
1 to 2 tsp. chili powder
3 tbsp. chili sauce
4 dashes of Tabasco sauce
¼ to ⅓ c. mayonnaise
1 tbsp. lemon juice
1 sm. onion, grated
2 lge. avocados, pureed

Combine all ingredients; mix well. Pour into 1-quart jar; seal tightly. Chill for 1 hour. For an appetizer salad, serve in small mounds on shredded lettuce or romaine. Yield: 8-12 servings.

Mrs. Milton Sanfor
Montross, Virginia

BANANA-COCONUT SALAD

4 bananas
Lemon juice
½ c. mayonnaise
½ c. whipped cream (opt.)
1 c. toasted coconut or chopped nuts

Cut bananas lengthwise into halves and crosswise into halves. To prevent discoloring, prepare just before serving; coat bananas immediately with lemon juice. Combine mayonnaise and whipped cream. Roll bananas in mayonnaise mixture, then in coconut or chopped nuts. Serve on crisp salad greens.

Mrs. Shirley Leslie
Magazine, Arkansas

BANANA-MARSHALLOW AND NUT SALAD

5 bananas
Lemon juice
Lettuce leaves
¼ lb. marshmallows, quartered
¼ c. salad dressing
2 tbsp. cream
½ c. chopped peanuts

Cut bananas in half lengthwise, then in half crosswise. Dip in lemon juice to prevent discoloration. Arrange bananas on lettuce leaves. Fold marshmallows into salad dressing; add cream. Pile lightly on top of bananas. Sprinkle peanuts over top.

Ethel Watkins
Pendleton, South Carolina

BANANA-NUT SALAD

1 c. sugar
2 tbsp. flour
1 egg, well beaten
2 tbsp. butter, melted
¼ c. mild vinegar
¾ c. water
6 or 8 bananas
½ c. chopped nuts

Combine sugar and flour; add egg, mixing thoroughly. Add butter, vinegar and water. Mix thoroughly. Cook over hot water, stirring constantly until thick and smooth. Cool. Dip bananas into dressing; roll in nuts.

Jean Cline
Morehead, Kentucky

BANANA AND PEANUT SALAD

2 bananas
¼ c. peanut butter
¼ c. tart mayonnaise
½ c. finely chopped peanuts

Peel bananas; cut into halves lengthwise. Spread peanut butter between halves of banana sandwich-fashion. Roll in mayonnaise. Roll in chopped nuts. Cut bananas in halves crosswise. Place on lettuce leaves. Yield: 4 servings.

Mrs. A. B. Humphrey
Richlands, North Carolina

BANANA SALAD

5 lge. bananas, sliced
1 5-oz. pkg. miniature marshmallows
3 tbsp. sugar
1 tbsp. mayonnaise
1 pt. heavy cream, lightly whipped
Red pepper
⅔ can peanuts, ground

Arrange layers of bananas and marshmallows in dish. Fold sugar and mayonnaise into cream. Top bananas with mixture. Sprinkle with red pepper and ground peanuts. Repeat layers until all ingredients are used. Yield: 6 servings.

Mrs. Dewey May Skinner
Tishomingo, Mississippi

BANANA SALAD

1 egg
½ c. sugar
Juice of 1 lemon
6 to 8 bananas
1 c. nuts

(Continued on next page)

Combine egg, sugar and lemon juice in a saucepan. Cook until thick, stirring constantly. Cut bananas into medium pieces. Pour dressing over bananas; add nuts. Mix well and chill.

Mrs. Barbara Ward
Neva, Tennessee

ROLLED BANANAS

2 tbsp. mustard
2 ½ tbsp. sugar
½ to ⅔ can sweetened condensed milk
2 tbsp. (rounded) peanut butter
1 pt. cracker crumbs
24 firm ripe bananas

Combine mustard and sugar; add milk, beating slightly. Blend peanut butter and crumbs with fork. Peel bananas; cut into halves crosswise. Dip one piece at a time into milk mixture; roll in crumb mixture. Arrange on tray. Yield: 12-24 servings.

Mrs. Eva Jessup
Glenwood, Arkansas

STUFFED BANANA SALAD

¼ c. peanut butter
2 tbsp. chopped raisins
2 lge. or 4 sm. bananas
Mayonnaise
Lemon juice
Chopped salted peanuts

Mix peanut butter with raisins. Peel and split bananas lengthwise. Fill sandwich-fashion with peanut butter and raisin mixture. Roll in mayonnaise thinned with lemon juice, then in chopped salted peanuts. Serve a half or whole banana on lettuce. Garnish with a red cherry or strawberry.

Mrs. F. D. Canaday
Walterboro, South Carolina

COCONUT-ORANGE SALAD

3 seedless oranges, peeled and sliced
Lettuce or romaine
½ c. coconut
French dressing

Arrange a circle of thick overlapping orange slices on crisp lettuce. Heap coconut in center. Serve with French dressing. Yield: 5 servings.

Loletta Pierce
Cumby, Texas

GREEN GRAPE SALAD

¼ c. mayonnaise
1 4-oz. pkg. cream cheese
Garlic salt to taste
1 lb. seedless green grapes, washed

Whip mayonnaise and cream cheese. Add garlic salt to taste. Fold grapes into cheese mixture. Serve in garnished bowl or as individual servings on salad greens. Yield: 4-6 servings.

Mrs. Emma L. Flake Van Laningham
Walnut Springs, Texas

HOLIDAY SALAD MOLD

1 lb. cranberries
2 c. sugar
1 tbsp. water
1 ½ tsp. grated orange rind
2 c. cottage cheese
½ c. whipping cream, whipped

Chop cranberries fine; add sugar and water. Cover and cook slowly until done. Add grated orange rind; mix well. Turn into ring mold; chill in refrigerator until firm. Unmold on flat plate; fill center with cottage cheese into which has been folded stiffly whipped cream. May be garnished with orange slices. Yield: 8 servings.

Mrs. Otha Nutt
Anson, Texas

FRESH PEACH SALAD

¼ c. sugar
1 c. sour cream
1 tbsp. mayonnaise
8 fresh peaches, peeled and sliced

Mix sugar, sour cream and mayonnaise; pour over peaches. Mix well; chill thoroughly. Serve on lettuce leaves. Yield: 6 servings.

Mrs. Crystal E. Durant
Pensacola, Florida

ELEGANT PEACH SALAD

1 No. 2 ½ can sliced peaches
30 lge. marshmallows, cut in fourths
½ c. chopped celery
½ c. pecans, chopped
½ c. grated American cheese
2 tbsp. red vinegar
2 whole eggs, beaten
¼ tsp. salt
3 tbsp. flour
½ pt. whipping cream

Drain peaches, reserving juice. In a large bowl combine peaches, cut in pieces, quartered marshmallows, chopped celery, pecans and grated cheese. In the top of a double boiler, combine peach juice, vinegar, beaten eggs, salt and flour. Cook, stirring until thick; remove from heat and cool. Whip cream and fold in. Fold the sauce into the fruit mixture. Chill several hours before serving. Serve in lettuce cups.

Mrs. Lillian Herman
Bay City, Texas

PEACH SALAD

1 No. 2 ½ can peaches, well drained
Lettuce
Cool Whip
Cherries

Place peach halves in lettuce cups. Add 1 tablespoon Cool Whip to each peach half. Top with a cherry. Chill.

Mrs. Jack Ramsey
Thomaston, Georgia

SNOWBALL SALAD

10 canned peach halves
2 3-oz. pkg. cream cheese
1 3-oz. can candied fruit and peels
⅓ c. heavy cream, whipped
1 ¼ c. shredded coconut

Drain peaches and dry halves thoroughly. Mash 1 package cream cheese; add candied fruits and peels and mix well. Fill peach halves with mixture and place 2 halves together. Fasten with toothpicks. Add whipped cream to remaining cheese and blend. Roll peaches in mixture until coated; roll in coconut. Chill and serve on crisp lettuce. Yield: 5 servings.

Mrs. Elizabeth R. Whisnaut
Spindale, North Carolina

PEACH SALAD

2 c. dry cooked sweetened peaches
½ pt. cottage cheese
1 tbsp. chopped green pepper
½ tsp. salt
2 drops Tabasco sauce
1 tbsp. mayonnaise

Cut peaches in quarters. Mix with cheese, green pepper, salt, Tabasco sauce and mayonnaise. Serve on crisp lettuce with French dressing.

Mrs. A. H. Henderson, Jr.
Fancy Farm, Kentucky

SUNFLOWER SALAD

¼ pt. cottage cheese
Mayonnaise
Salt to taste
Peaches, fresh or canned slices
Lettuce
½ c. seedless raisins

Make a smooth paste of cottage cheese, mayonnaise and salt. Arrange peach slices on lettuce to resemble petals of sunflower. Place cheese in a mound in center of slices and place raisins to resemble seeds.

Mrs. Clara Seago
Prattville, Alabama

PEANUT-PRUNE SALAD

12 cooked prunes
⅓ c. cottage cheese
1 tsp. grated orange rind
2 tbsp. chopped peanuts
Salt to taste
Mayonniase

Pit and chill prunes. Combine cottage cheese, orange rind, peanuts and salt. Moisten mixture with mayonnaise and stuff into prunes. Serve on salad greens. Yield: 4 servings.

Mrs. Dorothy Patterson
Warner, Oklahoma

BUNNY PEAR SALAD

Mayonnaise
Canned pear halves
Shredded lettuce
Candy cinnamon drops
Marshmallows
Cheese
Parsley

(Continued on next page)

Spread mayonnaise between 2 halves canned pears for each serving. Fasten together with toothpicks and lay on shredded lettuce. Put 2 candy cinnamon drops on either side of stem end for eyes. Cut ears out of marshmallows with damp scissors and fasten above eyes with pieces of toothpick. Use a whole marshmallow for the tail and place a carrot in front of the rabbit made of soft yellow cheese with a sprig of parsley for greens.

Mrs. M. J. Arrington
Roopville, Georgia

CINNAMON-PEAR SALAD

Canned pear halves
Cinnamon candies
Cottage cheese
Lettuce
Salad dressing

Drain pear juice and reserve. Add cinnamon candies to juice; cook until dissolved. Cool syrup. Let pear halves stand in syrup until colored and flavored. Place cottage cheese on lettuce leaves. Cover with cinnamon-pear half, round side up. Serve with salad dressing.

Dianne Woods
Chatham, Virginia

FESTIVE PARTY SALAD

12 canned pear halves
2 pkg. cream cheese
2 tbsp. crystallized ginger, chopped
Mayonnaise

Drain pears; wipe dry. Fill cavities with cream cheese mixed with ginger and mayonnaise. Press 2 halves together. Stand on large end and decorate as desired with softened cream cheese put through a pastry tube. For miniature Christmas trees, spiral the cheese from top to bottom with tiny roses of contrasting colors. Tint pears any desired color by soaking them in their juice to which food coloring has been added. The cream cheese may also be tinted. For a bride's luncheon, decorate pears to resemble wedding bells. Serve on lettuce or in cheese rings.

CHEESE BASE:

1 tbsp. unflavored gelatin
¼ c. cold water
1 c. heavy cream
1 tsp. dry mustard
2 tbsp. pimento, chopped
1 c. cheddar cheese, grated

Soften gelatin in cold water; dissolve over hot water. Mix all ingredients. Pour in individual ring molds. Use as a base for decorated pears if desired.

Mrs. Marie S. Griffin
Thomasville, Alabama

FRESH PEAR SALAD AND DRESSING

DRESSING:

2 tbsp. flour
½ c. sugar
2 tbsp. lemon juice

Mix all ingredients; cook over low heat until flour is cooked and clear. Cool.

SALAD:

1 c. diced celery
2 c. diced or sliced fresh pears
⅓ c. pecans
Salad greens
Maraschino cherries

Mix celery and pears with dressing; add nuts. Serve on salad greens. Garnish with cherries.

Mrs. Margaret Thornton
Thorndale, Texas

PEAR AND CHEESE SALAD

6 halves canned pears
Lettuce
6 tsp. cream or cottage cheese
Mayonnaise

Arrange pears on lettuce leaves. Fill hollow of pears with cheese and top with mayonnaise. If fresh pears are used select the very ripe ones. Sprinkle with lemon juice and sugar; cover and let stand 15 minutes before preparing. Cherries may be used to give color and flavor.

Dena G. Owen
Decatur, Georgia

PEAR SALAD WITH COTTAGE CHEESE

Pear halves
Cottage cheese
Lettuce

Fill pear cavities with cottage cheese. Serve on crisp lettuce leaves.

(Continued on next page)

COTTAGE CHEESE:

Place clabbered milk on stove; heat until whey and clabber separate. Pour into a jelly bag; hang up to drain dry. Season with salt, butter or cream. Mix well.

Frances Jackson
Mill Spring, North Carolina

ANGEL'S DELIGHT SALAD

1 8-oz. pkg. cream cheese
1 8-oz. bottle maraschino cherries
1 No. 2 can sliced pineapple
1 c. pecans
8 c. miniature marshmallows
1 pt. whipping cream

Cream cheese with all the cherry juice. Dice cherries, pineapple and pecans; add with marshmallows to the cream cheese mixture. Whip cream and add to above. Chill until time to serve. Prepare 24 hours before serving. Yield: 12-15 servings.

Mrs. Billy Cook
Hartsville, Tennessee

PINEAPPLE SALAD

1 No. 2 ½ can sliced pineapple, cut into sm. pieces
1 c. chopped English walnuts
2 c. miniature marshmallows
½ pt. whipping cream, unwhipped
1 tbsp. (heaping) sugar
2 egg yolks, beaten

Combine pineapple, nuts and marshmallows. Combine remaining ingredients in saucepan and cook over low heat until mixture thickens. Do not boil. Pour over pineapple mixture and chill.

Mrs. Willard Buchanan
Harrogate, Tennessee

COZETTE SALAD

1 c. almonds, blanched
2 eggs
6 tbsp. vinegar
2 tbsp. sugar
Pinch of mustard
Pinch of salt
1 can pineappple, diced
1 box marshmallows
1 c. whipped cream

Cut almonds into large pieces; do not chop. Cook the eggs, vinegar, sugar, mustard and salt in top of double boiler till coats a spoon; cool. Combine with pineapple, marshmallows and almonds; mix well. Let stand in refrigerator overnight. Combine with whipped cream before serving.

Mrs. B. C. Newman
Hendersonville, Tennessee

EASTER SALAD

4 egg yolks
1 tbsp. butter or margarine
2 ½ tbsp. milk
2 ½ tbsp. vinegar
½ tsp. salt
½ lb. marshmallows
1 c. whipped cream
¼ lb. chopped almonds
1 can crushed pineapple

Cook first 5 ingredients in double boiler until thick. While hot beat in marshmallows; let cool. Add whipped cream, chopped almonds and crushed pineapple. Chill thoroughly and serve on lettuce leaves with a little whipped cream or dressing. Yield: 6-8 servings.

Mrs. Earl L. Faulkenberry
Lancaster, South Carolina

HEAVENLY HASH

1 c. chopped pineapple
1 c. nuts, broken
8 oz. cream cheese
1 can coconut
½ pt. whipping cream, whipped

Mix all ingredients together except cream. Fold in whipped cream. If desired, add red cake coloring and top with maraschino cherries.

Mrs. Jack Kitchens
Salem, Kentucky

PINEAPPLE SALAD

3 c. pineapple, cut into wedges
2 tbsp. cornstarch
2 eggs, well beaten
1 c. sugar
Juice of 2 lemons
1 c. nuts
½ lb. miniature marshmallows

Drain pineapple, reserving 1 cup juice. Combine cornstarch, eggs, pineapple juice and sugar. Cook until thick. Add lemon juice. Cool; add remaining ingredients.

Elizabeth L. Fox
Gustine, Texas

FRUIT SALAD

1 No. 2 can crushed pineapple
¼ c. sugar
½ tsp. salt
2 tbsp. flour
1 egg
2 tbsp. lemon juice
1 tsp. grated lemon peel
¾ c. whipping cream
¼ lb. marshmallows, cut in quarters

Drain crushed pineapple, reserving syrup. Combine sugar, salt and flour in a saucepan. Add egg and blend; stir in pineapple syrup. Cook, stirring until smooth. Remove from heat and add lemon juice and peel. Cover and chill. Whip cream stiff and stir into pineapple mixture. Fold in marshmallows and crushed pineapple. Chill 4 to 6 hours or overnight. Serve in lettuce cups. Garnish with watercress. Yield: 5-6 servings.

Eva Mae Jenkins
Elizabethtown, North Carolina

TWENTY-FOUR HOUR SALAD

24 lge. marshmallows
½ c. chopped pecans
1 c. crushed pineapple
½ pt. whipping cream
2 tbsp. sugar

Chop marshmallows and pecans. Add drained pineapple. Whip the cream; add the sugar. Mix all together. Chill. Serve on lettuce leaf.

Mrs. Elde Remmert
Taylor, Texas

POINSETTIA SALAD

Lettuce
Canned or fresh sliced pineapple
Pimento
Cream cheese
French dressing

Place a lettuce leaf on a salad plate; place pineapple slice in center. Cut a pimento into 1/2-inch strips; place one end in center of pineapple, letting other end extend to the rim. Arrange strips all around like the spokes of a wheel. Mix cream cheese with French dressing to moisten. Place a small ball of mixture in center of pineapple. Serve with French dressing.

Mrs. Walter Liller
Old Town, Florida

WINTER SALAD

1 No. 2½ can crushed or diced pineapple
½ c. sugar
1 egg
2 tbsp. cornstarch
1 10½-oz. pkg. miniature marshmallows
4 slices American cheese, diced
½ c. mayonnaise

Drain pineapple; reserve juice. Mix juice, sugar, egg and cornstarch. Cook until thickened; cool. Add remaining ingredients. Chill. Yield: 8-10 servings.

Mrs. G. P. Wheeler
Mountain Home, Arkansas

RHUBARB SALAD

1 c. rhubarb, fresh or frozen
½ c. water
½ c. sugar
1 pkg. strawberry gelatin
1 sm. can crushed pineapple
1 c. chopped pecans

Heat rhubarb in water. Add sugar; mix gelatin in hot rhubarb. Add pineapple and nuts. Congeal.

Mary Ann Johnston
Jefferson, Georgia

RHUBARB SALAD

2 c. diced rhubarb
1 c. sugar
Juice of 1 lemon (opt.)
1 pkg. strawberry gelatin
1 sm. can crushed pineapple
½ c. broken nuts

Cook rhubarb until tender. Add sugar and lemon juice; stir until thoroughly dissolved. Add gelatin; stir until dissolved. Add pineapple and nuts. Chill until firm. Yield: 6-8 servings.

Mrs. J. B. Henson
Franklin, North Carolina

STRAWBERRY PATCH SALAD

1 ½ c. cottage cheese
3 tbsp. mayonnaise or salad dressing
1 ⅓ c. chopped salted almond nutmeats
¾ c. strawberry halves
Lettuce
Whole strawberries
Mint leaves
Green-tinted citron strips

Combine cottage cheese and mayonnaise. Add nutmeats and strawberry halves. Arrange lettuce in salad bowl or on serving plate; pile cheese mixture on lettuce. Arrange whole berries, mint leaves and citron on cheese mixture in wreath design. Serve with lemon-lime dressing. Yield: 4 servings.

Mrs. Elizabeth Cowley
Saltillo, Mississippi

WHITE GRAPES AND SOUR CREAM SALAD

6 c. seedless white grapes
1 ½ c. sour cream
¾ c. brown sugar

Wash the grapes and dry. Chill for several hours. Sweeten the sour cream with 1/2 cup sugar. Toss with the grapes and serve with remaining brown sugar sprinkled over the top.

Edna Hicken
Springdale, Arkansas

APPLE AND GRAPEFRUIT SALAD

24 grapefruit sections
4 crisp lettuce leaves
16 strips green pepper
4 or 5 sprigs fresh mint
French dressing
3 red eating apples
¼ c. pecan halves
2 or 3 tbsp. mayonnaise

Arrange grapefruit sections on lettuce on 4 chilled plates. Add green pepper, mint leaves and a little French dressing. Wash and core apples. Cut in cubes. Mix with pecans and lightly with mayonnaise. Add generous spoonful to each grapefruit plate. Yield: 4 servings.

Wilma Mansel
West Columbia, Texas

APPLE SALAD

1 egg, beaten
¼ c. cream
1 tsp. butter
1 tsp. flour
¼ c. sugar
¼ tsp. salt
¼ c. vinegar
6 apples, pared and finely chopped
2 stalks celery, finely chopped
½ c. chopped pecans

Combine egg, cream and butter in saucepan. Sift flour, sugar and salt; stir into egg mixture. Add vinegar. Cook slowly, stirring constantly, until thickened. Cool. Mix apples, celery and pecans. Add dressing mixture; mix well. Yield: 12 servings.

Mrs. L. H. DeWolf
Iowa, Louisianna

APPLE SALAD

6 lge. apples, peeled and chopped medium fine
2 c. grapes, seeded and cut
1 sm. can pineapple, chopped
2 celery stalks, chopped fine
½ tsp. salt
3 or 4 tbsp. mayonnaise

(Continued on next page)

Mix all ingredients and toss together lightly. Yield: 8-10 servings.

Mrs. Swanson Vass
Hillsville, Virginia

APPLE SALAD

4 apples, cored, peeled and chopped
2 bananas, sliced
2 tbsp. sugar
1 tbsp. lemon juice
½ c. mayonnaise
½ c. cream, whipped
1 c. chopped pecans
½ c. chopped candied cherries
½ head fresh lettuce

Combine apples and bananas. Sprinkle sugar and lemon juice over fruit. Fold mayonnaise into whipped cream. Add pecans and cherries; mix with spoon. Pour all ingredients in large salad bowl and stir together. Place lettuce leaves on salad plates and spoon mixture on for individual servings. Yield: 6 servings.

Emily Ellis
White Rocks, South Carolina

CINNAMON-APPLE SALAD

1 3-oz. pkg. cream cheese
2 tbsp. milk
1 tsp. lemon juice
¼ c. chopped dates
2 tbsp. chopped celery
2 tbsp. chopped pecans
⅓ c. red cinnamon candies
¼ c. sugar
2 c. water
6 apples, peeled and cored
Lettuce

Combine cream cheese, milk and lemon juice; blend until smooth. Add dates, celery and pecans; mix well. Make syrup of cinnamon candies, sugar and water. Add whole apples; cook slowly until just tender. Drain and chill. For each serving place cinnamon apple on lettuce leaf; fill center with cheese mixture.

Mrs. J. R. Ashworth
Troy, Alabama

COTTAGE WALDORF SALAD

4 med. tart apples, cubed
½ c. raisins
½ c. chopped walnuts
1 tbsp. sugar
1 tbsp. lemon juice
½ c. cottage cheese
½ c. sour cream

Combine apples, raisins and walnuts; sprinkle with sugar and lemon juice. Toss lightly. Blend cottage cheese and sour cream; pour over apples. Mix and toss lightly.

Mrs. E. R. Bobo
Ft. Payne, Alabama

DELIGHTFUL FRUIT SALAD

2 c. tart apples, diced
2 tsp. lemon juice
1 c. seedless green grapes
½ c. mandarin orange sections
1 c. miniature marshmallows
½ c. pecans, coarsely chopped
¼ c. sugar
1 c. whipped cream

Coat apples with lemon juice; mix in grapes, oranges, marshmallows and nuts. Combine sugar and whipped cream. Mix thoroughly. Fold fruit into cream. May be chilled or served immediately.

Ann F. McKinzie
Seagraves, Texas

EASY WALDORF SALAD

8 lge. red apples, unpeeled and cubed
½ c. sour cream or lemon juice
1 c. celery, chopped
1 c. raisins
1 c. English walnuts, chopped
½ c. salad dressing or mayonnaise

Allow apples to stand in sour cream for several minutes. Combine with celery, raisins and walnuts. Add salad dressing; toss lightly.

Mrs. Maria R. Adams
Chatham, Virginia

FRUIT SALAD

1 c. diced apples
1 c. diced pineapple
1 c. orange sections
½ c. chopped nuts
⅓ c. salad dressing

Mix fruit and nuts. Mix in salad dressing. Serve on lettuce or with regular meal. Peaches, pears, or other fresh fruit may be used in place of these.

Mrs. J. C. Boockholdt
Birmingham, Alabama

FRUIT SALAD

3 med. red tart apples, diced
1 c. tiny marshmallows
1 c. coconut
1 c. fresh orange slices
1 sm. can crushed pineapple, drained
1 c. fresh grapes, seeded
1 c. broken pecan halves
1 c. sour cream

Mix all ingredients together several hours before serving. Set in refrigerator to blend and mellow. Serve in lettuce cups.

Mrs. Florence Hudson
Roanoke Rapids, North Carolina

FRUIT SALAD

1 c. sugar
1 ½ c. water
1 tbsp. flour
4 apples, cut into small pieces
4 oranges, cut into small pieces
4 bananas, cut into small pieces
1 c. lge. raisins
1 c. walnuts, chopped
1 whole grated coconut
½ box dry, hard cereal

Combine first 3 ingredients in saucepan. Bring to a boil. Chill. Cut 1 apple, 1 orange and 1 banana into small pieces in a large bowl. Add 1/4 raisins, walnuts, coconut and cereal to fruit layer. Pour some of the dressing over these layers. Continue layering until all ingredients are used. Do not mix or stir layers as dressing runs through salad to moisten.

Mrs. Eva M. Cardwell
Fredericksburg, Texas

NUT SALAD

1 c. nuts
1 c. seedless raisins
2 c. apples, chopped fine

Combine nuts and fruits in one bowl.

DRESSING:

2 egg yolks
1 c. sugar
1 c. sweet milk
3 tsp. flour
⅓ c. vinegar

Combine all ingredients in saucepan; cook dressing till thickens. Stir in fruit and nuts. Cool and serve. Yield: 4 servings.

Patsy Justice
Clinton, Kentucky

FRUIT SALAD

½ c. dark raisins
½ c. chopped nuts
1 c. bananas, cubed
2 c. red apples, diced
½ c. mayonnaise

Mix raisins, nuts, bananas and apples with mayonnaise. Serve on lettuce leaves. Yield: 4 servings.

Mrs. Richard Rutledge
Keysville, Virginia

MOHAVE FRUIT SALAD

1 tsp. grated orange rind
½ c. mayonnaise or salad dressing
2 c. cubed apples
1 c. orange sections
1 ½ c. Cracker Barrel cheese, cubed
½ c. chopped dates
½ c. chopped walnuts

Combine orange rind and salad dressing. Fold gently into apples, orange sections, cheese, dates and walnuts. Yield: 4-6 servings.

Wanda Clement
Claudville, Virginia

OLD-FASHIONED FRUIT SALAD

6 bananas
6 Delicious apples
6 oranges
½ c. pineapple chunks
½ c. pecans or walnuts, chopped
Dressing

Cut all fruit in small pieces and mix together. Combine with nuts and Dressing.

DRESSING:

1 c. sugar
2 egg yolks
1 c. pineapple juice
1 tbsp. cornstarch
1 tbsp. orange juice
1 tbsp. lemon juice

Combine all ingredients. Cook, stirring constantly, until mixture thickens and is a clear color. Remove from heat and let cool. Store in refrigerator for several hours before serving.

Mrs. Lillian Herman
Bay City, Texas

PLAIN FRUIT SALAD

2 apples, peeled and diced
2 oranges, diced
3 bananas, sliced
1 sm. jar maraschino cherries, cut up
1 c. walnuts
1 med. pkg. miniature marshmallows

Put all fruits and nuts in large bowl. Pour cherry juice over the fruit and mix. Add marshmallows and stir. Let stand for 30 minutes before serving. Top with Dream Whip. Cherry juice will sweeten as well as add color. Yield: 6 servings.

Mrs. Elmer Vines
Clarendon, Texas

RAW APPLE AND RAISIN SALAD

5 red tender-skinned apples
½ c. raisins, steamed
⅓ c. mayonnaise
Crisp lettuce

Wash but do not pare apples; core and dice. Combine lightly with steamed raisins and mayonnaise. Pile lightly into lettuce cups on individual salad plates. Yield: 5 servings.

Mary Ann Vess
Tupelo, Mississippi

SEVEN-CUP FRUIT SALAD

1 c. chopped apples
1 c. chopped bananas
1 c. maraschino cherries or fruit cocktail, drained
1 c. miniature marshmallows
1 c. coconut
1 c. chopped nuts
1 c. sour cream

Combine all ingredients and mix well.

Mrs. Radford Chandler
Good Hope, Georgia

SUMMER FRUIT SALAD

1 c. finely chopped apple
1 c. crushed pineapple
½ c. finely chopped celery
¼ c. chopped maraschino cherries
6 lge. pear halves or 12 sm. pear halves
Lettuce

Combine apple, pineapple, celery and maraschino cherries. Place pear half, hollow side up, on a bed of lettuce. Fill center with fruit mixture. Serve with Paprika Dressing.

PAPRIKA DRESSING:

2 tbsp. sugar
¼ tsp. paprika
3 tbsp. lemon juice
3 tbsp. orange juice
3 tbsp. salad oil

Combine all ingredients in a jar or bottle with a tight-fitting cover. Shake vigorously. Chill. Serve on any fruit salad.

Mrs. Robert Spurlock
Parkdale, Arkansas

WALDORF SPIRAL SALAD

6 red apples
⅓ c. lemon juice
4 c. cold water
1 c. celery, diced
⅓ c. seedless raisins
1 c. miniature marshmallows
¼ c. mayonnaise
¼ c. whipped cream
½ c. walnuts, coarsely chopped
6 lettuce cups

Pare apples very thick, being sure each paring is long and unbroken. Add 3 tablespoons of lemon juice to the water; drop parings in to keep color bright. Core pared apples and dice fine; sprinkle with remaining lemon juice. Combine apple cubes, celery, raisins, marshmallows and mayonnaise. Fold in whipped cream. Before serving, add nuts. Curl each paring into cup shape on lettuce. Fill with salad.

Mrs. Shirley Boddie
Calvin, Louisiana

WINTER APPLE SALAD

1 c. golden seedless raisins
Sm. amount orange juice
2 c. diced celery
3 c. diced apples
½ c. seeded grapes
1 c. broken walnuts
1 c. mayonnaise
1 c. sour cream

Place the raisins in a small bowl; and orange juice to cover. Let stand overnight. Drain off remaining juice. Combine raisins, celery, apples, grapes and walnuts. Blend mayonnaise and sour cream. Add to fruit mixture. Mix thoroughly.

Mrs. J. R. Strode
Thompkinsville, Kentucky

TULIP APPLE SALAD

8 red apples
½ c. apple, diced
1 c. canned pears, cubed
¾ c. celery, diced
¾ c. nuts
Mayonnaise
Lettuce

Wash and polish apples. Cut a slice from stem ends; scoop out centers. Cut down in wide points to resemble tulips. Moisten remaining ingredients with mayonnaise. Fill tulips and set in lettuce cups.

Mrs. Mary Ray White
Troup, Texas

APRICOT SALAD

⅔ c. evaporated milk
⅔ c. salad oil
¼ c. vinegar
⅓ c. sugar
1 tsp. prepared mustard
⅛ tsp. salt
1 lge. can apricots, drained
1 med. can pineapple chunks, drained
3 c. miniature marshmallows
¼ lb. American cheese, grated
½ c. chopped pecans

Combine milk, oil, vinegar, sugar, mustard and salt in jar; shake until well mixed. Alternate layers of apricots, pineapple and marshmallows in 8 or 9-inch pan. Cover marshmallows with sauce; top with layers of cheese and pecans. Cover; refrigerate for 24 hours. Yield: 9 servings.

Mrs. Cleo Wheeler
Alvarado, Texas

AVOCADO DELIGHT

2 tbsp. avocados
Lemon juice
24 fresh melon balls or 1 1-lb. pkg. frozen melon balls, partially thawed
Salad greens
Salad dressing

About 10 minutes before serving cut avocados lengthwise and remove seeds. Brush lightly with lemon juice. Fill each avocado half with 6 melon balls; arrange on salad plate. Garnish with greens. Serve with salad dressing. Yield: 4 servings.

June Lunsford
Mena, Arkansas

AVOCADO-FRUIT SALAD

1 sm. jar orange sections
1 sm. jar grapefruit sections
1 ripe avocado
1 sm. head lettuce

Drain fruits. Cut avocado into bite-sized pieces. Tear lettuce into small pieces. Mix.

FRUIT SALAD DRESSING:

½ c. sugar
2 tbsp. vinegar
1 c. salad oil
1 tsp. celery or poppy seed
Paprika (opt.)

Mix all ingredients; combine with lettuce and fruits.

Mrs. L. E. M. Freeman
Raleigh, North Carolina

AVOCADO-ORANGE TOSSED SALAD

Lettuce
Ripe avocado, cut into sm. chunks
1 can mandarin oranges
Bleu cheese dressing
1 can French-fried onion rings

Break lettuce into small pieces; add avocado and oranges. Toss with dressing; top with onion rings.

Dollie S. McCollum
Montgomery, Alabama

AVOCADO SALAD

1 apple, unpeeled
1 banana
½ avocado
1 No. 303 can fruit cocktail, drained
¼ c. chopped nuts (opt.)
1 c. miniature marshmallows
½ c. mayonnaise

Quarter and core apple; cut into small cubes. Slice banana; peel and cube avocado. Add fruit cocktail, nuts and marshmallows; mix well with mayonnaise. Yield: 6-8 servings.

Mrs. Norma Ballard
Sarasota, Florida

BANANA SALAD

1 ½ c. pineapple chunks
2 tbsp. lemon juice
3 oz. cream cheese, mashed
4 bananas
Chicory or lettuce
Lemon French dressing

(Continued on next page)

Drain pineapple, reserving 1/4 cup juice. Add lemon and pineapple juice to cheese gradually. Beat until creamy. Fold in pineapple chunks. Slice bananas lengthwise; arrange on salad greens. Top with cheese mixture. Serve with dressing.

Lavaughn Bouch
Sand Fork, West Virginia

BANANA WALDORF SALAD

1 lge. red apple, unpared and diced
½ c. diced celery
¼ c. salad dressing or mayonnaise
2 ripe bananas, sliced
Lettuce head
¼ c. walnut or pecan halves

Combine apple, celery and salad dressing. Add bananas lightly to apple mixture. Chill for 1 hour. Combine 2 or 3 lettuce leaves to form a cup; arrange on salad plate. Fill cups with fruit mixture; garnish with nuts. Yield 4 - 6 servings.

Mrs. Carlie Brown
Burnsville, Mississippi

CANOE SALAD

4 bananas
1 sm. can crushed pineapple
1 sm. can chopped pecans
Mayonnaise
Candy sticks

Hollow bananas to resemble canoes. Mix pineapple, pecans and mayonnaise with centers of hollowed bananas. Stuff canoes with mixture. Place candy sticks across canoes for paddles.

Patsy Jo Smith
Newark, Arkansas

FRUIT SALAD

2 bananas
1 lge. apple
1 can pineapple chunks
1 stick celery
½ c. pecans
2 to 3 tsp. mayonnaise

Chop first 5 ingredients and toss with mayonnaise.

Mrs. W. David Holmes
Vinemont, Alabama

HEAVENLY HASH

1 sm. can crushed pineapple
4 bananas, sliced
½ bag colored miniature marshmallows
½ c. nuts (English walnuts, black walnuts, or pecan halves)
1 pt. whipped cream

Mix pineapple, bananas, marshmallows and nuts. Whip cream and combine with fruit-nut mixture.

Mrs. Jesse Melton
Erie, Tennessee

CHERRY AND BLACKBERRY SALAD

2 c. lge. cherries
2 c. blackberries
1 c. chopped celery
Lettuce
1 c. nuts
Mayonnaise

Drain fruit well. Arrange cherries, blackberries and celery in heaps on a bed of lettuce. Sprinkle with nuts and serve with mayonnaise.

Mrs. Wilbur Jenkins
Sadieville, Kentucky

WARD-BELMONT FRUIT SALAD

1 pkg. marshmallows, cut in pieces
1 lge. can pineapple, drained and cut in sm. pieces
1 lge. can Royal Anne cherries, drained and halved
1 med. bottle red cherries, drained and halved
1 lge. can peaches, drained and cut in sm. pieces
8 sm. apples, cut in pieces
1 c. pecan or walnut pieces

Soak marshmallows in juice drained from pineapple. Mix well drained fruit with marshmallows and nuts.

(Continued on next page)

DRESSING:

6 tbsp. boiling vinegar plus 2 tbsp. water
4 eggs, beaten
2 tbsp. butter, melted
Salt, sugar and dry mustard to taste
1 pt. whipped cream

Gradually add boiling vinegar and water to eggs. Add butter and cook in double boiler until thick. Cool completely. Season with salt, sugar and dry mustard. Fold in whipped cream. Alternate layers of fruit and dressing in a deep dish, ending with a layer of dressing. Refrigerate overnight.

Mrs. Mary Menking
Hallettsville, Texas

CRANBERRY FLUFF

2 c. raw cranberries, ground
3 c. tiny marshmallows
¾ c. sugar
2 c. diced unpared tart apples
½ c. seedless green grapes
½ c. broken California walnuts
¼ tsp. salt
1 c. heavy cream, whipped

Combine cranberries, marshmallows and sugar. Cover and chill overnight. Add apples, grapes, walnuts and salt. Fold in whipped cream. Chill. Turn into a serving bowl or spoon into individual lettuce cups. Trim with a cluster of additional grapes. Yield: 8-10 servings.

Mrs. R. O. Gilliam
Dallas, Texas

CRANBERRY-PINEAPPLE SALAD

1 can cranberry sauce
Lettuce
1 can pineapple rings, well drained
1 box cottage cheese
8 Maraschino cherries

Place the sliced cranberry sauce on lettuce cups; put a ring of pineapple over the sauce. Place a tablespoon of cottage cheese in the center of the pineapple. Place a cherry on top of cheese.

Mrs. Janice P. Cabler
Nashville, Tennessee

CRANBERRY SALAD

1 qt. cranberries
2 doz. marshmallows
1 c. nuts
1 c. sugar
1 lge. or 2 med. apples
1 lge. or 2 med. oranges

Run all ingredients through coarse blade chopper. Mix and let stand 24 hours.

Mary Louise Lane
San Benito, Texas

CRANBERRY SALAD

1 c. water
2 c. sugar
1 qt. fresh cranberries
2 c. marshmallows, cut into pieces
2 apples, diced
3 bananas, sliced
3 c. orange sections
1 c. pecans, broken

Make a syrup of water and sugar. Add cranberries; cook until skins burst. Remove from heat; let stand, covered, for 10 minutes. Remove lid; cook for 5 minutes longer. Chill. Add marshmallows, apples, bananas, orange sections and pecans. Chill until ready to serve. Salad will keep in refrigerator for several days.

Pat Duncan
Fort Worth, Texas

CRANBERRY SALAD SUPREME

1 c. chopped cranberries
1 c. sugar
2 c. seedless or Tokay grapes, chilled
½ c. canned diced pineapple, chilled (opt.)
½ to 2 c. chopped walnuts or pecans
1 c. whipped cream
½ c. marshmallows, quartered (opt.)

Combine cranberries and sugar. Blend. Refrigerate overnight. Drain liquid. Combine grapes, pineapple, nuts and whipped cream. Fold into cranberry mixture. Add marshmallows; stir until evenly distributed.

Nancy Lee
Cleburne, Texas

RAW CRANBERRY SALAD

1 pkg. raw cranberries
1 ½ c. sugar
1 tall can crushed pineapple, chilled
1 pkg. sm. marshmallows
1 c. chopped nuts
½ pt. heavy cream, whipped

(Continued on next page)

Grind cranberries; add sugar and chill, covered, overnight. Add pineapple, marshmallows and nuts. Fold in unsweetened whipped cream. Chill before serving. Keeps for several days, covered, in refrigerator. Yield: 16-20 servings.

Mrs. Noah McFodden
Paris, Texas

FLAMING CHRISTMAS CANDLE SALAD

1 4-oz. pkg. cream cheese
4 tbsp. pineapple juice
4 bananas
Lettuce
1 8 ½-oz. can sliced pineapple
4 cubes sugar
1 tbsp. lemon flavoring

Soften cream cheese at room temperature; whip until fluffy. Gradually add pineapple juice, continuing to beat until well blended. Cut ends from bananas so that bananas will be straight. Arrange lettuce leaves on four salad plates; place 1 slice pineapple on each lettuce leaf. Stand bananas in center of pineapple rings using cream cheese as support. Top bananas with 1 teaspoon cream cheese. Dip sugar cube into lemon flavoring; place on top cream cheese. Light sugar cube; serve flaming. Cherries may be substituted for flaming sugar cubes. Yield: 4 servings.

Mrs. Robert P. Hunt
Williamsburg, Virginia

FRUIT-CHEESE SALAD

1 No. 2 ½ can fruit salad, well drained
1 8-oz. pkg. cream cheese, softened and creamed

Add fruit salad to cream cheese and mix well. Prepare a day before serving to blend flavors.

Mary Garth Wallace
Fort Worth, Texas

EVERYDAY FRUIT SALAD

1 No. 2 can fruit cocktail, drained
1 orange, sectioned
1 apple, diced
1 banana, diced
¼ c. honey or sugar

Combine fruits; add honey. Refrigerate for 1 hour or more to develop flavor.

Mrs. Joyce Green Harrison
Sebastopol, Mississippi

FAVORITE FRUIT SALAD

1 lge. can fruit cocktail
1 orange, cut into sm. pieces
3 med. apples, unpeeled and cut into sm. pieces
½ c. raisins
½ c. chopped pecans

Mix and put into pretty glass bowl. Chill and serve. Sprinkle coconut and cherries over the top if desired.

Mrs. R. M. English
Pensacola, Florida

FRANCIS' WHIPPED CREAM FRUIT SALAD

1 med. can fruit cocktail
1 sm. can pineapple bits
1 sm. jar maraschino cherries
2 egg yolks
2 tbsp. pineapple juice
2 tbsp. vinegar
2 tbsp. sugar
Dash of salt
2 c. miniature marshmallows
½ c. heavy cream, whipped

Drain fruits reserving pineapple juice. Mix fruits together. Combine egg yolks, pineapple juice, vinegar, sugar and salt. Cook until mixture thickens. Cool. Add to fruit; add marshmallows. Fold in whipped cream.

Mrs. Stanley Hamilton
Lexington, Kentucky

FRUIT COCKTAIL SALAD

1 lge. can fruit cocktail
1 egg
½ c. sugar
1 tbsp. flour
3 or 4 apples, diced
1 bunch grapes
1 c. coconut
1 c. whipping cream

Drain and reserve juice from fruit cocktail. Combine juice from fruit cocktail, egg, sugar and flour. Boil until mixture thickens; Cool. Add all ingredients. Refrigerate until ready to serve.

Mrs. R. M. Martin
Elliston, Virginia

FRUIT COCKTAIL SALAD

24 marshmallows
¼ c. fruit cocktail juice
1 8-oz. pkg. cream cheese
1 No. 303 can fruit cocktail
1 c. pecans

(Continued on next page)

Put marshmallows and fruit cocktail juice in top of double boiler until marshmallows are melted. Add cream cheese; blend well. Remove from stove; add fruit cocktail and nuts. Chill. Yield: 6-8 servings.

Mrs. L. W. Newberry
Pattonville, Texas

FRUIT COCKTAIL SALAD

2 tbsp. butter
4 tbsp. flour
½ c. milk
¼ c. sugar
2 tbsp. lemon juice
1 c. whipping cream
1 lge. can fruit cocktail, drained
1 lge. can chunk pineapple, drained
5 or 6 bananas

Melt butter; add flour and milk. Cook until thick. Stir in sugar and lemon juice. Let cool. Add cream. Stir in fruit. Chill.

Mrs. Dixie Sykes
Dover, Tennessee

FRUIT COCKTAIL SALAD

1 box Dream Whip
½ c. milk
1 tsp. vanilla
1 lge. can fruit cocktail
1 lge. can pineapple chunks
1 c. miniature marshmallows

Place Dream Whip in bowl with 1/2 cup milk. Add vanilla and beat till stiff. Drain fruit cocktail and pineapple. Combine Dream Whip mixture, fruit cocktail, pineapple and marshmallows. Refrigerate till ready to serve.

Mrs. W. A. Thompson
Flemingsburg, Kentucky

FRUIT SALAD

3 med. Winesap apples
3 med. oranges
1 c. pecans
1 No. 2 can fruit cocktail
2 tbsp. sugar
2 tbsp. mayonnaise

Mix all ingredients together and chill.

Mrs. J. A. Whitehead
Sinton, Texas

FRUIT SALAD

1 med. can fruit cocktail
½ c. sugar
1 sm. can crushed pineapple
2 lge. bananas
3 oranges, chopped fine
⅔ c. seeded grapes, chopped
2 apples
1 c. canned peaches, cut up
1 c. canned pears, cut up

Empty the can of fruit cocktail into a large mixing bowl. Add sugar, crushed pineapple, bananas, oranges, grapes, apples, peaches and pears. Mix all together well. Refrigerate until chilled, several hours.

Mrs. G. T. Robinson
Hazel, Kentucky

FRUIT SALAD

1 can fruit cocktail, drained
½ pkg. miniature marshmallows
1 ½ c. sour cream
½ c. seedless raisins
Salad greens

Mix all ingredients except salad greens well. Chill and serve on salad greens. Yield: 4-6 servings.

Mrs. J. R. Cooke
Lawndale, North Carolina

FRUIT SALAD

½ c. cold milk
1 box Whip 'n Chill
½ c. cold water
1 sm. can fruit cocktail, drained
½ c. chopped pecans

In a deep narrow bowl place cold milk with Whip 'n Chill; whip at highest speed of electric mixer for 1 minute. Mixture will be very thick. Blend in cold water and whip at highest speed about 2 minutes. Combine fruit cocktail and chopped nuts. Stir till well mixed. Place in refrigerator until cold, at least 1 hour.

Mrs. Elizabeth Duffy
Loyal, Oklahoma

FRUIT SALAD

1 c. fruit cocktail juice
1 pkg. cream cheese
1 c. miniature marshmallows
2 cans fruit cocktail

Cream juice and cheese; beat till mixed well. Add miniature marshmallows and fruit cocktail.

Mrs. Clara Callan
Clifton, Texas

FRUIT SALAD PARFAIT

¼ c. maraschino cherries
1 c. mandarin oranges
1 lge. can fruit cocktail
1 bag marshmallow bits
½ pt. sour cream

Drain the fruits; slice cherries in small pieces or halves. Add the marshmallows to the fruit. Fold in the sour cream. Chill until firm in a mold.

Mrs. Dorothy Boulter
Rock Hall, Maryland

FRUITY WALDORF SALAD

1 17-oz. can fruit cocktail
¼ c. chopped celery
1 med. apple, chopped
¼ c. chopped nuts
½ c. mayonnaise
Salad greens

Drain chilled fruit cocktail. Combine with celery, chopped apple, nuts and mayonnaise. Spoon into crisp greens. Yield: 6 servings.

Bonnie Butts
San Antonio, Texas

GEM SALAD

4 c. fruit cocktail
1 c. pineapple chunks
1 c. crisp celery, sliced diagonally and very thin
1 c. broken nuts
4 c. miniature marshmallows
1 pt. sour cream
Maraschino cherries

Drain fruits. Mix all ingredients. Garnish with cherries and chill well before serving. Yield: 12-15 servings.

Mrs. T. J. Saunders
Moultrie, Georgia

ICE CREAM SALAD

1 pkg. desired flavor gelatin
1 c. boiling water
1 pt. vanilla ice cream
1 No. 303 can fruit cocktail, well drained

Dissolve gelatin in boiling water. Add ice cream and stir until dissolved. Add fruit cocktail. Chill until firm. Yield: 6 servings.

Mrs. A. R. Walden
Booneville, Mississippi

PARTY FRUIT SALAD

4 bananas
2 oranges
1 lge. apple
½ c. pecans
1 lge. can fruit cocktail
1 lge. can crushed pineapple
1 bottle maraschino cherries
1 pkg. party coconut
1 pkg. dessert topping mix

Cut bananas, oranges, apple and pecans into small pieces. Drain liquids from fruit cocktail, pineapple and cherries. Add to apples, bananas, pecans, oranges and coconut. Beat Dream Whip until thick and fold into fruit mixture. Chill 1 hour. Serve with crackers. Yield: 12 servings.

Mrs. M. B. Wall
Newton County, Mississippi

PHILLY FRUIT SALAD

2 lge. cans fruit cocktail
1 lb. grapes, cut in half and seeded
1 sm. cake cream cheese
⅔ c. chopped nuts
1 lge. can pineapple chunks
½ c. maraschino cherries (opt.)

Drain fruit until very dry, overnight if possible. Thin cream cheese with pineapple juice to consistency of thick salad dressing. Combine nuts and cheese mixture with fruit, stirring carefully so as not to mash the fruit. Chill until firm. Pineapple rings and red and green cherries may be arranged on top for an attractive holiday salad.

Mrs. Grace Gibson
Bruceton Mills, West Virginia

TWENTY-FOUR HOUR SALAD

2 cans fruit cocktail, drained
1 can chunk pineapple, cut and drained
100 miniature marshmallows
2 cartons sour cream

Mix all ingredients. Let stand for 24 hours. Serve on lettuce. Yield: 12 servings.

Mrs. Harold Peele
High Point, North Carolina

SEVEN-CUP SALAD

1 c. fruit cocktail, drained well
1 c. crushed pineapple, drained well
1 c. cottage cheese
1 c. sour cream
1 c. chopped nuts
1 c. miniature marshmallows
1 c. grated coconut

(Continued on next page)

Mix all ingredients well and keep refrigerated until used.

Mrs. R. M. Boyd
Henderson, North Carolina

FRUIT MEDLEY SUPREME

1 No. 2 ½ can fruit cocktail, drained
1 No. 13 ½ oz. can pineapple tidbits, drained
1 No. 16 oz. can mandarin orange sections
1 ½ c. miniature marshmallows
1 8-oz. pkg. Neufchatel cheese
2 tbsp. sour or sweet cream or evaporated milk

Combine fruits and marshmallows. Soften cheese with cream or milk; fold into fruit mixture. Chill.

Jean Beaman Walker
Knoxville, Tennessee

FRUIT PLATE AND DRESSING

Pear halves
Peach halves
Cantaloupe slices
Pineapple rings
Bananas

Arrange fruits on platter.

DRESSING:

2 eggs
3 tbsp. sugar
1 tbsp. cream
3 tsp. dry mustard
½ tsp. salt
3 tbsp. lemon juice
1 pt. whipped cream
1 c. diced marshmallows
1 c. chopped pecans

Combine eggs, sugar, cream, mustard, salt and lemon juice. Cook in double boiler until thick. Cool. Fold in remaining ingredients. Pour over fruit.

Mrs. Frances Morton
Tallulah, Louisiana

FRUIT SALAD

1 med. orange, cut up
1 banana, diced
1 Delicious apple, diced
1 c. miniature marshmallows
½ c. pecans, chopped
Salad dressing or mayonnaise

Combine all ingredients. Serve on individual plates or in a salad bowl.

Mrs. B. D. Vanderbilt
Beedeville, Arkansas

FRUIT SALAD WITH DELIGHTFUL DRESSING

4 oranges
¼ c. sugar
4 bananas, chopped
1 bunch purple grapes, seeded and halved
1 sm. can pineapple chunks, drained
Marshmallows (opt.)

Peel and section oranges; remove all white membrane. Add remaining ingredients. Toss lightly. Add dressing just before serving.

DELIGHTFUL DRESSING:

¼ c. sugar
2 tbsp. flour
1 egg yolk
2 ½ tbsp. lemon juice
½ c. pineapple juice
1 c. whipped cream

Combine sugar, flour and egg yolk; slowly add lemon and pineapple juice. Cook until thick. Cool. Fold in whipped cream.

Mrs. James L. Patton
Lexington, Kentucky

FRUIT SALAD IN AVOCADO BOATS

3 med. ripe avocados
3 tsp. fresh lime juice
1 c. fresh grapefruit sections
1 c. fresh pineapple wedges
¼ c. olive or salad oil
1 tbsp. vinegar
½ tsp. salt
⅛ tsp. ground black pepper
½ tsp. ground cumin seed

(Continued on next page)

Wash avocados; cut in half and remove seeds. Brush with 2 teaspoons lime juice to prevent discoloration. Fill cavities with grapefruit sections and pineapple wedges. Combine remaining ingredients. Beat with a rotary beater and serve over salad. Yield: 6 servings.

Photograph for this recipe on page 55.

FRUIT SALAD GLORY WITH HONEY DRESSING

1 tbsp. sugar
1/8 tsp. cinnamon
Dash of nutmeg
1 3-oz. pkg. cream cheese
1 lge. grapefruit
3 med. bananas, all yellow
1 med. avocado, peeled and sliced
3/4 c. grapes, halved and pitted
3 c. lettuce, shredded

Combine sugar, cinnamon and nutmeg. Shape cream cheese into 8 balls; roll in sugar mixture. Section grapefruit over bowl, reserving 3 tablespoons grapefruit juice. Flute bananas with fork tines; cut into 1/4-inch slices. Sprinkle bananas and avocado with reserved grapefruit juice. Arrange bananas, avocado, grapefruit and grapes on bed of shredded lettuce. Serve with Honey Dressing.

HONEY DRESSING:

1/4 c. salad oil
3 tbsp. honey
1/4 c. vinegar
1/2 tsp. salt
Dash of pepper
1/4 c. water

Shake ingredients together.

Genevieve Miller
St. Petersburg, Florida

GLORIFIED FRUIT SALAD

1 c. grapefruit segments
1 c. orange segments
1/2 c. maraschino cherries
1/2 c. seedless grapes
1 c. canned diced pineapple
10 marshmallows, quartered
1/3 c. mayonnaise
1/3 c. whipped cream

Combine fruits and marshmallows. Chill for 1 hour. Blend mayonnaise and whipped cream together; serve in mounds over fruit mixture.

Meda Long
Franklin, Tennessee

FLOWER BASKET SALAD

2 lge. red apples, halved
1/4 c. orange juice
1/2 c. chopped celery
2 tbsp. chopped walnuts
2 tbsp. mayonnaise or salad dressing
4 walnut meat halves
1 c. white grapes
1 c. red grapes
1/4 c. Fruit Salad Dressing
Romaine

Wash apples; core. Halve crosswise. Partially scoop out centers of apples; flute edges with sharp pointed knife. Dip cut surfaces in orange juice. Chop apple centers and measure 1/4 cup. Combine with celery, chopped nuts and mayonnaise. Fill apple halves with celery mixture; top with walnut halves. Halve grapes; remove seeds. Combine with Fruit Salad Dressing. Arrange romaine on serving dish; place apples on romaine. Place grapes in center of dish; garnish with onion rings.

FRUIT SALAD DRESSING:

1 3-oz. pkg. cream cheese
3 tbsp. cream
Few grains of salt
1 tbsp. mayonnaise or salad dressing
2 tbsp. orange juice
1/2 tsp. grated orange rind

Mash cheese; add cream. Beat until fluffy. Add mayonnaise, salt, orange juice and rind. Combine well.

Paulette Cosby
Stratford, Oklahoma

FRESH GRAPE SALAD

2 tbsp. butter
1 tbsp. flour
1 1/2 c. milk
24 marshmallows
2 lb. fresh green grapes
1 sm. can pineapple
1 c. pecans

Cook butter, flour and milk; cut marshmallows into sauce until melted. Pour sauce over grapes. Add pineapple and nuts; chill.

Mrs. W. B. Harvey
Bryan, Texas

GRAPE, BANANA AND COTTAGE CHEESE SALAD

1/2 c. seedless green grapes, halved
2 bananas, diced
1/2 pt. sm. curd cottage cheese
1/4 c. chopped pecans (opt.)
Maraschino cherries (opt.)

(Continued on next page)

Combine all ingredients. A little cream may be added to make salad creamier. Serve on lettuce leaves; top with maraschino cherries.

Mrs. Irene Miller Byrom
Brenham, Texas

GUMDROP SALAD

- 1 lb. orange and red gumdrops
- 1 lb. marshmallows
- 1 lb. red grapes, seeded and halved
- 1 med. can crushed pineapple, drained
- 1 c. pecans, chopped
- ¾ c. pineapple juice
- ⅔ c. sugar
- 1 tsp. vinegar
- Juice of 1 lemon
- 4 tbsp. flour

Cut gumdrops into fourths. Cut marshmallows in small pieces or use miniature ones. Combine first 5 ingredients. Combine pineapple juice, sugar, vinegar and lemon juice with as much water as lemon juice. Bring to a boil. Thicken with the flour. Pour over salad when cold.

Mrs. Myrle Stickel
Maysville, Kentucky

TASTY SALAD

- 2 c. Concord grapes, halved and seeded
- 2 stalks celery, cut up
- 1 apple, diced
- ¾ c. whipped cream

Mix grapes, celery and apple. Add whipped cream; toss until fruits are coated. Yield: 4 servings.

Mary C. Shaw
Kress, Texas

FAR EAST FRUIT SALAD

- 1 5-oz. can chow mein noodles
- 1 c. canned mandarin orange sections, drained
- 2 c. grapefruit segments, drained
- 1 ½ c. pineapple chunks, drained
- 1 5-oz. can water chestnuts, drained
- ¼ c. French dressing

Make beds of chow mein noodles on 6 individual salad plates. Arrange drained orange sections, grapefruit segments, pineapple chunks and water chestnuts on noodles. Top with French dressing. Yield: 6 servings.

Ann Kirby
San Augustine, Texas

FRUIT FLUFF

- 2 c. miniature marshmallows
- 1 can grapefruit sections, drained
- 1 can pineapple chunks, drained
- 1 c. canned white cherries, pitted and drained
- ¼ c. chopped pecans
- ¼ c. salad dressing
- ½ c. heavy cream, whipped

Combine marshmallows, fruits, nuts and salad dressing; fold in whipped cream. Chill 2 hours or longer. Serve on crisp lettuce. Yield: 8 servings.

Mrs. Lindon Baker
Santa Fe, Tennessee

GRAPEFRUIT-AVOCADO AND CREAM CHEESE SALAD

- 2 grapefruit
- 1 avocado
- ½ c. French dressing
- Lettuce
- 1 3-oz. pkg. cream cheese
- Paprika

Peel whole grapefruit, removing membrane as well as skin; cut into sections. Peel avocado; remove seed and slice thin. Marinate both fruits in the French dressing. Chill thoroughly. Just before serving, arrange drained fruits on lettuce leaves with a ball of cream cheese in the center of each plate. Sprinkle lightly with paprika. Yield: 5 servings.

Mrs. J. E. Wilson
Chidester, Arkansas

GRAPEFRUIT AND NUT SALAD

- 2 ½ c. grapefruit or orange sections
- 1 c. shredded almonds or nuts
- ½ c. chopped dates or chopped apricots
- Honey-Yogurt Fruit Salad Dressing

(Continued on next page)

Combine grapefruit, almonds and dates. Serve in lettuce cups with Honey-Yogurt Fruit Salad Dressing. Yield: 6-8 servings.

Mrs. Al A. Glover
Lynchburg, South Carolina

SUNSHINE SALAD

4 orange sections
4 grapefruit sections
4 slices avocado
3 or 4 leaves romaine
2 strips pimento
Salad Dressing

Arrange orange, grapefruit and avocado on romaine. Garnish with pimento. Serve with salad dressing. Yield: 1 serving.

Martha Hooper
Gray Court, South Carolina

HOT FRUIT SALAD

1 can sliced pineapple
1 can pear halves
1 can peach halves
1 bottle cherries
¼ c. butter, melted
⅓ c. brown sugar (packed)
2 tsp. curry powder

Drain fruit on paper towels. Mix butter, brown sugar and curry powder. Pour over fruit. Bake 1 hour at 325 degrees. Yield: 6 servings.

Mrs. C. L. Broxton
New Brockton, Alabama

CANTALOUPE AND BANANA SALAD

1 cantaloupe, peeled and diced
3 or 4 bananas, sliced
1 c. miniature marshmallows
½ c. pecans
½ c. peach or strawberry ice cream
½ c. mayonnaise
Salad greens

Mix fruits, marshmallows and nuts lightly. Blend ice cream and mayonnaise and stir lightly into fruits. Serve on salad greens. Yield: 6 servings.

Mrs. J. D. Williams
Florence, Alabama

CANTALOUPE AND BLACKBERRY SALAD

1 med. cantaloupe
1 pt. fresh blackberries
Lettuce
Mayonnaise

Cut cantaloupe in wedges or rings; scoop out seeds and fiber from center and peel. Wash and drain blackberries. Arrange wedges of melon on lettuce and fill center with berries. Serve with mayonnaise. Yield: 5 servings.

Mrs. J. E. Wilson
Chidester, Arkansas

CANTALOUPE FRUIT SALAD

1 med. cantaloupe, peeled
Lettuce
3 oranges, peeled and sliced
3 fresh peaches, peeled and sliced
2 nectarines, peeled and sliced
Pineapple slices
1 c. strawberries
1 lge. bunch white grapes

Slice cantaloupe crosswise into five rings. Use pulp to make 1 cup cantaloupe balls. Place rings on lettuce. Arrange orange, peach, nectarine and pineapple slices on top. Add strawberries and cantaloupe balls. Place a small cluster of grapes by each ring.

YOGURT DRESSING:

1 c. yogurt
½ c. mayonnaise
½ c. bleu cheese dressing

Combine ingredients; whip. Chill thoroughly. Serve with cantaloupe rings. Yield: 5 servings.

Helen Sergent
Gate City, Virginia

CANTALOUPE SALAD

1 yellow, firm cantaloupe, diced
6 fresh peaches, diced
1 lb. seedless grapes
1 sm. bag marshmallows, cut in peces
Mayonnaise to taste

Combine fruits and marshmallows. Mix with desired amount of mayonnaise. Chill.

Mrs. A. C. Jones, Jr.
Kingsville, Texas

COLORFUL-QUICK FRUIT AND MELON SALAD

¼ tsp. vanilla flavoring
2 tbsp. sugar
½ c. whipped cream
1 can fruit cocktail, drained
1 cantaloupe or honeydew melon, pared and sliced ½ in. thick
Maraschino cherries

Add vanilla flavoring and sugar to cream. Fold into fruit mixture. Place slice of melon on lettuce leaf. Fill hole with fruit mixture; top with a cherry.

Mrs. Geneva Gill Cooper
Monticello, Kentucky

FRESH FRUIT SALAD

½ lge. cantaloupe, cubed
1 c. fresh peaches, diced
2 or 3 plums, diced

Combine fruit and add Salad Dressing.

SALAD DRESSING:

1 tbsp. sugar
1 tsp. prepared mustard
¼ c. mayonnaise-type salad dressing
Evaporated milk

Mix sugar, mustard and prepared salad dressing. Add evaporated milk to form desired consistency.

Mrs. Frances Hicks
Utopia, Texas

FRESH FRUIT SALAD

Fresh pineapple, cubed
Watermelon balls
Cantaloupe balls or honeydew melon balls
Sliced bananas
White seedless grapes
Cantaloupe or honeydew melon rings
Poppy seed dressing

Prepare above ingredients and serve in cantaloupe rings with poppy seed dressing.

Marie Krotky
Houston, Texas

FRUIT SALAD

Cantaloupe
1 can pineapple chunks
2 c. or 1 can apple or pear pie filling
1 c. miniature marshmallows
1 c. coconut
½ c. sour cream
Salt and sugar to taste

Cut cantaloupe in halves. Combine remaining ingredients. Heap salad mixture in cantaloupe halves. Garnish with cherries.

Mrs. Buck Pruit
Alton, Texas

HAWAIIAN FRUIT SALAD

1 c. fresh cubed pineapple or canned pineapple chunks
1 c. white seedless grapes
1 c. cubed cantaloupe or papaya
1 c. fresh shredded coconut or flaked coconut
½ c. whipped cream

Combine pineapple, grapes, cantaloupe and coconut. Toss lightly with cream.

Mrs. Daisy Massey
Fredericksburg, Texas

HOT SUMMER MELON BOAT SALAD

Pineapple chunks
Fresh strawberries
Melon balls or orange sections
Honeydew melon or cantaloupe, quartered
Honey French Dressing

Combine pineapple, strawberries and melon balls. Spoon fruit mixture into melon quarters. Serve with Honey French Dressing.

HONEY FRENCH DRESSING:

1 tbsp. honey
½ c. basic French dressing

Add honey to French dressing. Shake to mix well.

Mrs. Freddie Gussler
Cherokee, Kentucky

LOW-CALORIE FRUIT SALAD

1 c. cantaloupe balls or cubes
½ c. orange sections, diced
2 bananas, diced
1 c. lettuce, chopped
2 tbsp. low-calorie dressing

Chill all ingredients. Lightly toss together just before serving.

Ruth L. Auge
Belen, New Mexico

RED, YELLOW, BLACK AND WHITE SALAD

8 chunks red watermelon
2 c. chunk pineapple
1 ½ c. cooked prunes
1 c. sm. marshmallows

Chill fruits separately. To serve, place on torn lettuce leaves in individual salad bowls. Place marshmallows and prunes in center of melon, pineapple chunks around the edge with nutmeg sprinkled over all. Serve with pineapple juice or use Honey-Quickie Dressing. Yield: 8 servings.

HONEY-QUICKIE DRESSING:

½ c. honey
1 c. pineapple juice
Dash of salt

Beat all ingredients until completely combined.

Mrs. Lodus Phillips
Baldwyn, Mississippi

SUMMER FRUIT BOWL

1 head lettuce
1 c. cottage cheese
Lemon juice
2 bananas, sliced
1 c. melon balls
1 c. blueberries
1 c. raspberries
1 pear, sliced

Separate lettuce into leaves; arrange on platter. Spoon cottage cheese into center of platter. Sprinkle lemon juice on banana slices. Chill fruit and arrange on lettuce. If desired, serve with mayonnaise thinned with a little fruit juice and seasoned with ginger. Yield: 6 servings.

Nita Carol Sammons
Forest Hills, Kentucky

SUMMERTIME FRUIT SALAD

2 tsp. fresh lemon juice
½ tsp. powdered ginger
1 3-oz. pkg. cream cheese, softened
1 lge. cantaloupe, halved and seeded
1 ½ c. orange sections
1 c. melon balls
1 c. diced pears
1 c. diced pineapple
1 ½ c. seedless grapes
Crisp Bibb lettuce leaves

Combine lemon juice, ginger and cream cheese, mixing until smooth. Spread cheese mixture over outside of cantaloupe halves evenly. Refrigerate covered melon for about 1 hour. Combine remaining fruits. Serve fruits on crisp Bibb lettuce leaves topped with wedges of cantaloupe. Yield: 8 servings.

Mrs. Helen G. Morris
Prescott, Arkansas

WATERMELON BASKET

1 short, plump watermelon, chilled
1 ½ c. fresh or frozen cantaloupe and honeydew melon balls
1 c. whole fresh strawberries, (opt.)
1 sm. can pineapple juice
Few grape leaves or mint, if desired

After watermelon is thoroughly chilled, cut lengthwise, slicing off top third. Use large piece for fruit holder. Scoop out melon balls with melon ball cutter or measuring teaspoon. Scallop top edge of shell. Fill with watermelon, cantaloupe and honeydew melon balls. Add strawberries last. Pour pineapple juice over top. Tuck in grape leaves or mint.

Sharon Klickna
Tularosa, New Mexico

OLD-FASHIONED FRUIT SALAD

1 lge. orange, shredded
1 lge. banana, peeled and sliced
1 lge. apple, peeled and diced
1 c. crushed pineapple, drained
1 c. green grapes, cut in half
6 lge. marshmallows, quartered
¼ c. Fruit Salad Dressing (opt.)

Combine all ingredients. Mix well. Chill. Mold in custard cups.

FRUIT SALAD DRESSING:

Grated rind and juice of 1 lemon
Grated rind and juice of 1 lime
Grated rind and juice of 1 orange
1 egg
1 c. sugar
1 c. whipped cream

Cook all ingredients except whipped cream in a double boiler, stirring constantly, until thickened. Cool. Chill. Fold in whipped cream.

Eleanor M. King
West Monroe, Louisiana

AMBROSIA

8-10 juicy oranges, peeled and diced
1 c. moist coconut
½ c. pecans, chopped
½ c. cherries, halved
¼ c. sugar
1 c. orange juice

Combine all ingredients. Chill. Yield: 4-6 servings.

Laverne Moore
Augusta, Georgia

COCONUT FRUIT BOWL

1 No. 2 can chunk pineapple, drained
1 11-oz. can mandarin oranges, drained
1 c. seedless grapes
1 c. miniature marshmallows
1 3 ½-oz. can flaked coconut
2 c. sour cream
¼ tsp. salt

Combine first 5 ingredients. Stir in sour cream and salt. Chill overnight. Yield: 8 servings.

Mrs. C. F. Young
Rochell, Georgia

FRUIT AND NUT SALAD

2 oranges, peeled and sliced
1 grapefruit, peeled and sliced
1 c. shredded pineapple, fresh or canned
½ c. chopped nuts
1 c. diced fresh peaches or halved strawberries
Whipped cream mayonnaise
Lettuce
Maraschino or mint cherries

Combine oranges and grapefruit with pineapple, nuts and peaches. Moisten with whipped cream mayonnaise. Serve in lettuce-lined bowl topped with additional dressing and garnished with halved cherries. Yield: 6 servings.

Mrs. Mae O. Turner
Maynardville, Tennessee

MANDARIN ORANGE SALAD

2 cans mandarin oranges, drained
1 pkg. miniature marshmallows
1 c. coconut
1 8 ¼-oz. can crushed pineapple
1 carton whipping cream

Mix all ingredients together and store in covered bowl in the refrigerator overnight.

Mrs. Joe Bordonsky
Tioga, Texas

MANDARIN ORANGE SALAD

1 sm. can mandarin oranges, drained
1 c. pineapple chunks, drained
1 c. tiny marshmallows
1 c. flaked coconut
1 sm. carton sour cream
1 c. chopped nuts

Combine all ingredients and mix well. Chill before serving. Yield: 8-10 servings.

Callie Moore
Chatham, Virginia

ORANGE-AVOCADO SALAD BOWL

1 head Boston or leaf lettuce, washed and dried
2 oranges, pared and sectioned
1 avocado, peeled, halved and diced
Oil and vinegar salad dressing

Break lettuce into bite-size pieces; place in salad bowl. Arrange a ring of orange sections on top. Fill center with diced avocado. Just before serving, toss with enough salad dressing to coat greens well.

Mrs. J. R. Mathis
Lometa, Texas

MANDARIN SALAD

1 c. mandarin orange slices
1 c. coconut
1 c. pineapple
1 c. sour cream
1 c. tiny marshmallows

(Continued on next page)

Mix all ingredients together and serve.

Mrs. Charlie Pantan
Milwaukee, North Carolina

ORANGE SALAD

4 c. fresh oranges, diced
1 c. pineapple chunks, drained
1 c. tiny marshmallows
1 c. flaked coconut
1 c. chopped nuts
1 sm. carton sour cream

Combine all ingredients and mix well. Chill before serving. Yield: 18-20 servings.

Mrs. I. B. Sherrill
Atlanta, Georgia

SOUR CREAM SALAD

1 can mandarin orange slices
1 can white grapes, drained well
1 carton sour cream
1 can coconut
2 c. tiny marshmallows

Mix oranges and grapes together. Combine with remaining ingredients.

Mrs. Talmage Griffies
Carrollton, Georgia

TWENTY-FOUR HOUR SALAD

3 egg yolks
2 tbsp. sugar
2 tbsp. vinegar
2 tbsp. pineapple juice
1 tbsp. butter
Dash of salt
1 c. cream, whipped
2 c. drained canned white cherries
2 c. drained pineapple bits
2 c. mandarin oranges
2 c. miniature marshmallows

Cook egg yolks, sugar, vinegar, pineapple juice, butter and salt in double boiler until thick, stirring constantly; cool. Fold in whipped cream, well-drained fruits and marshmallows. Chill for 24 hours. Yield: 8-10 servings.

Mrs. Elzie Sloan
Carlisle, Kentucky

SUMMER SUNSET SALAD

1 sm. head lettuce
1 c. cottage cheese
1 c. blueberries
2 oranges, peeled and sliced
Honey Fruit Salad Dressing

Arrange lettuce leaves on salad plate. Mound cottage cheese in center of each salad plate; surround with circle of blueberries. Edge with half slices of oranges. Serve with Honey Fruit Salad Dressing.

HONEY FRUIT SALAD DRESSING:

1/3 c. salad oil
3 tsp. lemon juice
1/2 tsp. salt
1/3 c. liquid honey

Combine salad oil, lemon juice and salt. Slowly add honey, beating constantly. Chill in tightly covered jar. Mix well before serving. Yield: 4 servings.

Paulette Cosby
Stratford, Oklahoma

WHOLE MEAL FRUIT SALAD

4 to 6 sm. oranges, peeled
3 or 4 avocados peeled and diced
4 to 6 lge. oranges, peeled and sectioned
Cream cheese balls
Walnut halves
Dates
Almonds
Prunes
Peanut butter

Separate the sections of 4 to 6 small oranges to form a cup. Place orange cups in the center of salad plates and fill each with diced avocado. Arrange the large orange sections in 3 groups around each orange cup. Press balls of cream cheese between 2 walnut halves; arrange walnut bonbons in one space around each orange cup. Stuff each date with 3 blanched almonds and arrange in second space around each orange cup. Stuff prunes with peanut butter and place in last space around each orange cup. Garnish fruits with curly endive or crisp lettuce. Serve with French dressing.

FRENCH DRESSING:

1/4 c. lemon juice
1/4 c. salad oil
1/2 tsp. salt
1/2 tsp. paprika
1 tbsp. honey or sugar

Beat all ingredients together until thoroughly combined. Yield: 4-6 servings.

Mrs. J. E. Wilson
Chidester, Arkansas

BUFFET FRUIT SALAD PLATTER

2 c. shredded lettuce
1 ½ c. nuts
Mayonnaise
15 yellow peach halves
15 pear halves
2 c. cottage cheese
15 prunes
6 lge. red apples
Juice of 1 lemon
1 c. cherries

Mix shredded lettuce with 1/2 cup nuts and mayonnaise; stuff peaches. Fill center of pears with cottage cheese and prunes with nuts. Cut apples in sections; sprinkle with lemon juice. Arrange peaches, pears and prunes around edge of platter and heap apple sections in center. Garnish with cherries and serve with mayonnaise. Yield: 15-20 servings.

Mrs. Mary A. Walters
Bonnieville, Kentucky

PEACH, PRUNE AND COTTAGE CHEESE SALAD

¼ lb. dried prunes
1 No. 2 can peach halves
½ lb. cottage cheese
Crisp lettuce or endive

Soak prunes overnight in just enough water to cover; drain. Split on 1 side and remove pits. Drain peaches. Stuff pitted prunes with cottage cheese and arrange in hollows of peach halves on lettuce leaves on individual salad plates. Pile remaining cottage cheese in center of arrangement. Serve with or without mayonnaise.

Mrs. Sida Mae Womark
Lydowice, Georgia

SOUR CREAM SALAD

1 c. mandarin oranges
1 c. crushed pineapple
1 No. 303 can sliced peaches
1 c. miniature marshmallows
1 c. sour cream
½ c. nuts

Put all fruit in colander and drain well. Combine fruit with remaining ingredients. Chill for several hours.

Mrs. F. H. Elms
Monroe, North Carolina

SIX-CUP SALAD

1 c. canned peaches
1 c. canned pears
1 c. pineapple, crushed
1 c. miniature marshmallows
1 c. mayonnaise
1 c. whipping cream

Crush peaches and pears; drain juice. Add to drained pineapple. Add marshmallows. Whip mayonnaise and add. Whip cream and add; mix well. Let stand in refrigerator about 1 hour before serving. Yield: 6 servings.

Mrs. J. A. Plunkett
Nunnelly, Tennessee

FABULOUS FRUIT SALAD

¼ c. cranberry juice
2 tbsp. cider vinegar
tbsp. orange juice
½ tsp. grated orange peel
¼ c. salad oil
⅛ tsp. salt
Dash of pepper
½ tsp. sugar
1 pkg. American blue cheese, crumbled
1 c. fresh peach slices
1 c. seedless green grapes
1 c. fresh pear slices
1 c. apricot halves
1 c. fresh pineapple chunks
6 leaves Boston lettuce
¼ c. slivered toasted almonds

Combine first 9 ingredients in jar with tight-fitting lid; shake well. Refrigerate until ready to serve. Peel and prepare fruit; set aside. Tear greens in bite-sized pieces into large salad bowl. Arrange each fruit in a separate mound on greens. Sprinkle with almond slivers. Shake chilled dressing and pour over salad. Toss and serve at once. Yield: 6-8 servings.

Ann Kirby
San Augustine, Texas

GRAPE CLUSTER SALAD

6 pear halves
Lettuce
1 lge. pkg. cream cheese
¼ c. milk
Seedless white grapes, halved
French or other salad dressing

Place pear half, round side up, on a crisp lettuce leaf or fresh grape leaves. Blend cheese and milk and spread over the pear. Cover the pear half with grape halves to resemble a bunch of grapes. Place a bit of grape stem in the large end of the pear. Serve with French or other salad dressing. Seeded Tokay or Malaga grapes may be used if preferred.

Mrs. Mary A. Carroll
Greenville, Texas

COCONUT-MALLOW SALAD

1 1-lb. 13-oz. can pear halves, drained and cut in fourths
1 1-lb. 14-oz. can pineapple chunks, drained
14 lge. marshmallows, quartered
1 c. flaked coconut
2 c. dairy sour cream

Put fruit in bowl with marshmallows and coconut. Add sour cream and toss lightly to mix well. Cover and chill from 12 to 24 hours before serving. Yield: 8-10 servings.

Mrs. Donald Davis
Erwin, North Carolina

PEAR-AVOCADO SALAD

1 No. 2 ½ can Bartlett pear halves, chilled
2 avocados, peeled and halved
Lettuce
Diced candied ginger

For each serving, arrange 2 pear halves and 1 avocado half on lettuce leaf. Place 2 or 3 pieces of ginger in each pear and avocado half. Serve with poppy seed dressing.

Mildred Williams
El Paso, Texas

STUFFED CRANBERRY-PEAR SALAD

4 c. fresh cranberries
1 whole orange, quartered and seeded
½ sm. grapefruit, sectioned and seeded
2 c. sugar or 1 c. sugar and 1 c. syrup
Pear halves

Put cranberries, orange and grapefruit through food chopper. Add sugar. Mix well. Chill for a few hours before serving. This relish will keep several days in refrigerator. Fill pear halves with mixture at serving time.

Mrs. Zella H. Mills
Sneedville, Tennessee

PEAR-TANGERINE SALAD

1 fresh or canned pear, diced
1 c. seeded grapes
2 tangerines, sectioned
½ grapefruit, sectioned
4 tbsp. olive oil
1 tbsp. lemon juice
1 tbsp. lime juice
1 tsp. salt
Pinch of cayenne
Paprika

Combine pears, grapes, tangerines and grapefruit. Combine oil, lemon juice, lime juice, salt and spices. Pour over mixed fruit and let stand in refrigerator until chilled. Arrange a bed of pale green chicory and dark green watercress in a dish. Place the marinated fruit on greens.

Mrs. Herman Mueck
Cameron, Texas

BUTTERFLY SALAD

Sliced pineapple
Dates
Cream cheese
Stuffed olives
Pimento or green pepper strips
Mayonnaise

For each serving, cut slice of canned pineapple in half. Arrange two halves with cut sides out on lettuce to represent wings. Place a large date, stoned and filled with cream cheese in between wings for body of butterfly. Slice stuffed olives and arrange in pattern on wings. Use strips of pimento for feelers. Serve with mayonnaise. Mayonnaise may be fluted about butterfly with a pastry tube.

Mary S. Shedrick
Edison, Georgia

COTTAGE CHEESE SALAD

1 carton cottage cheese
1 sm. can crushed pineapple
1 ½ c. miniature marshmallows
⅓ c. chopped cherries
¼ c. mayonnaise
½ c. chopped nuts

Mix all ingredients together and chill in refrigerator before serving.

Mrs. J. R. Mathis
Lometa, Texas

FRENCH PINEAPPLE SALAD

1 lge. pineapple
Sugar
1 lge. orange, sectioned and peeled
2 peaches, sliced
1 banana, slant sliced
1 apple, sliced
1 pt. strawberries, hulled and sweetened
1 c. pecan halves

(Continued on next page)

Cut pineapple in half lengthwise; remove fruit and cut into cubes. Dust pineapple cubes lightly with sugar. Combine all ingredients. Chill for 30 minutes. Lightly pile fruit mixture into pineapple shells.

Mrs. Marvel E. Wax
El Paso, Texas

FRUIT CUP

1 med. orange, sectioned
½ apple, quartered
1 med. banana, sliced
½ c. fruit cocktail
1 c. pineapple chunks or seedless grapes

Chill the fruit. Put the orange, apple, drained fruit cocktail and pineapple chunks in a mixing bowl. Mix bananas lightly with the other fruit. Chill, if time permits. Serve in a chilled fruit cup. Yield: 4 servings.

Mrs. Earl Kaiser
Moulton, Texas

FRUIT SALAD WITH DRESSING

1 lge. can pineapple chunks, drained
4 bananas, cut up
1 can mandarin orange sections
¾ c. salad oil
¼ tsp. salt
½ c. apricot pulp, sieved
¼ c. pineapple juice
¼ c. lemon juice

Mix pineapple, bananas and oranges. Mix remaining ingredients. Beat until light and fluffy; pour over fruit mixture.

Mrs. Bill Chase
Follett, Texas

HAWAII SALAD

1 sm. can crushed pineapple, drained
1 tbsp. flour
1 tbsp. butter
1 c. cheese, grated
2 apples, diced
¼ pkg. miniature marshmallows

Combine pineapple juice, flour and butter; cook until thick. Combine remaining ingredients; add to juice mixture. Mix well.

Barbara Pou
Greenville, South Carolina

LUCIOUS DELIGHT

1 lge. can pineapple chunks, drained
1 med. can sweet cherries, drained and pitted
4 oranges, sectioned
1 sm. can grapefruit, drained
1 can fruit cocktail, drained
1 pkg. lge. marshmallows chopped
Nuts, chopped
2 eggs, beaten
2 tbsp. coffee cream
Juice of 1 lemon
1 tbsp. sugar
½ c. whipped cream

Combine fruits, marshmallows and nuts. Mix eggs, coffee cream and lemon juice; cook in double boiler for 1 minute, stirring constantly. Cool. Mix sugar and whipped cream; fold in egg mixture. Pour egg mixture over fruits. Toss gently. Refrigerate overnight.

Mrs. Geraldine Eddleman
Weatherford, Texas

MILLIONAIRE SALAD

5 tbsp. lemon juice
5 tbsp. sugar
2 tbsp. butter
½ lb. marshmallows, cut up
2 eggs
¼ lb. pecans, cut up
1 No. 2 can white Queen Anne cherries, seeded and drained
3 or 4 lge. bananas, sliced
1 No. 2 can pineapple, drained and diced
1 c. whipping cream, whipped

Add lemon juice, sugar, butter and marshmallows to slightly beaten eggs. Cook in double boiler until marshmallows dissolve; cool. Add pecans, cherries, bananas and pineapple. Fold in whipped cream. Pour in ring mold. Refrigerate 12 hours before using.

Lucy Harms
Dover, Arkansas

PARADISE SALAD

1 can pineapple
½ c. sugar
1 tbsp. (heaping) flour
Lump of butter
2 eggs
6 oranges, diced
3 apples, diced
1 lb. Malaga grapes, diced
6 bananas, diced
1 c. cream, whipped
1 c. nutmeats

(Continued on next page)

Drain pineapple, reserving juice. Heat pineapple juice slowly in double boiler. Add sugar, flour, butter and eggs. Cook until thick; cool. Dice the fruits; drain. Add the dressing and let stand several hours. Just before serving, whip cream and mix with salad. Serve in sherbet glasses, garnished with whipped cream and a maraschino cherry in center. Sprinkle with finely chopped nutmeats. Yield: 12 servings.

Eva T. Wightman
Romney, West Virginia

MILLION DOLLAR SALAD

2 egg yolks
2 tbsp. flour
1 c. milk
Juice of 2 lemons
1 pt. whipping cream
1 lb. marshmallows, cut up
1 lge. can sliced pineapple
1 lge. can white cherries

Mix egg yolks and flour. Add milk. Stir in lemon juice very slowly. Cook to consistency as boiled custard. Whip cream and stir dressing into cream. Add marshmallows, drained pineapple and drained cherries. Let stand for 24 hours.

Lurleen B. Wallace
Governor of Alabama
Montgomery, Alabama

MOM'S FRUIT SALAD

2 oranges
2 apples
2 bananas
1 c. nuts
1 can crushed pineapple
2 tangerines
½ lb. grapes
2 c. pineapple juice
Juice of 1 lemon
Pinch of salt
2 tbsp. cornstarch
2 eggs
1 c. sugar
1 tbsp. butter
1 c. whipped cream

Dice oranges, apples, bananas, nuts, pineapple, tangerines and grapes into a large bowl. In a 2-quart saucepan, combine pineapple juice, lemon juice and salt. Bring to a boil. Mix cornstarch with cold water; add to boiling mixture. Stir well. Beat eggs; add a small amount of hot mixture till mixed well. Add to boiling mixture with sugar and butter; cook for 1 minute. Cool. Add diced fruits. Add whipped cream.

Mrs. C. G. Coleman
Elkin, North Carolina

PINEAPPLE-APPLE SALAD

1 No. 2 can sliced pineapple
2 tbsp. flour
⅓ c. sugar
1 whole egg
2 apples
3 slices cheese
½ c. pecans

Drain pineapple reserving juice. Combine flour, sugar, egg and pineapple juice. Cook till thick; set aside until cool. Cut pineapple slices in chunks; peel apples and dice. Cut cheese in chunks and chop nuts. Mix all together. Pour cooked mixture over these ingredients. Refrigerate till ready for use. May be made a day before used.

Mrs. Howard Hollis
McMinnville, Tennessee

PINEAPPLE-DATE SALAD

1 No. 2 can sliced pineapple, drained
1 c. pitted chopped dates
Mayonnaise
Crisp lettuce or endive
Pecan halves

Cut pineapple slices in wedges and mix with dates and mayonnaise. Cover and chill. Serve in lettuce cups. Garnish each salad with a nut. Substitute 1 1/2 cups fresh sugared pineapple when in season for canned. Yield: 5 servings.

Ethel Watkins
Pendleton, South Carolina

PINEAPPLE AND PEANUT BRITTLE SALAD

1 pt. whipping cream
1 sm. can crushed pineapple
1 sm. can white pitted cherries
½ lb. peanut brittle, crushed
12 marshmallows, cut up

Whip cream until fluffy. Add pineapple and drained cherries. Add peanut brittle. Stir in marshmallows; set in cool place for 30 minutes. Add bananas, if desired. Yield: 8 servings.

Mrs. Ruby Jackson
Santa Anna, Texas

PRUNE AMBROSIA SALAD

12 to 16 cooked prunes, drained
1 3-oz. pkg. cream cheese
¼ c. orange peel, grated
2 tbsp. orange juice
Pineapple slices
Salad greens
⅓ c. flaked coconut
French dressing

(Continued on next page)

Slit prunes down one side and remove pits. Soften cheese; blend in peel and juice. Fill prunes with cheese. Arrange drained pineapple slices with stuffed prunes on lettuce. Sprinkle with coconut. Serve with French dressing.

Dorothy Lockamy
Dunn, North Carolina

TWENTY-FOUR HOUR SALAD

3 egg yolks
2 tbsp. sugar
2 tbsp. vinegar
2 tbsp. pineapple juice
1 tbsp. butter or margarine
Dash of salt
1 c. cream, whipped
2 c. pitted white cherries
2 c. drained pineapple tidbits
2 oranges, cut in sections
24 lge. marshmallows, cut in pieces

Mix first 6 ingredients and cook till thick. Add remaining ingredients and mix well. Let stand for 24 hours in refrigerator.

Mrs. Robert J. Brogli
Bondville, Kentucky

PINEAPPLE-RHUBARB RING

1 No. 2 can pineapple tidbits
2 c. 1-in. slices fresh rhubarb
⅓ c. sugar
½ c. water
2 3-oz. pkg. cherry gelatin
1 tbsp. lemon juice
½ c. broken pecans

Drain pineapple, reserving syrup. Combine rhubarb, sugar and water; cover and cook until just tender, about 5 minutes. Drain, reserving syrup. Combine pineapple and rhubarb syrups and add water to make 3 1/2 cups. Heat to boiling; add gelatin and stir until dissolved. Add lemon juice and cool. Chill until partially set; fold in rhubarb, pineapple and nuts. Pour into 6-cup ring mold and chill until firm. Yield: 8-10 servings.

Mrs. Harry P. Clause
Bedford, Virginia

FRUIT DELIGHT

1 pt. sweetened strawberries
1 can mandarin oranges
1 c. pineapple chunks, drained
1 c. miniature marshmallows
1 c. coconut
1 c. dairy sour cream

Combine all ingredients. Chill mixture several hours and spoon onto lettuce leaves for serving. Garnish with additional strawberries.

Mrs. Winnie Vinson
Erin, Tennessee

SUMMER LUNCHEON SALAD

1 lge. cantaloupe, peeled and sliced in 10 crosswise slices
Bibb lettuce, rinsed and chilled
Head lettuce leaves, rinsed and chilled
5 nectarines or peaches, unpeeled
2 bananas, slivered and soaked in lemon juice
5 red or blue plums, unpeeled
10 sm. bunches white, blue or red grapes
30 fresh pineapple spears
Watermelon balls
Honeydew melon wedges
Pineapple sherbet
Orange sherbet
Lime sherbet

Place a cantaloupe slice on alternated Bibb and head lettuce leaves for color. Prop the cantaloupe slice on end with a piece of lettuce heart. Surround front and sides with 1/2 nectarine, a sliver of banana, 1/2 plum, 1 bunch grapes, 3 pineapple spears, watermelon balls and honeydew melon wedges. Top with a scoop of each flavor of sherbet. Add a sprig of fresh mint in center of each sherbet for color and delightful aroma. Serve with cheese straws or grilled cheese sandwiches.

Mary L. Adams
Danville, Kentucky

FRUIT SALAD

1 c. grapefruit sections, drained
1 c. orange sections, drained
2 c. pineapple chunks, drained
2 c. whole strawberries
Lettuce
Cheese-Honey Dressing
½ c. broken, salted pecans

Combine drained, chilled fruits and arrange in 8 lettuce cups. Top with Cheese-Honey Dressing and sprinkle with nuts. Yield: 8 servings.

CHEESE-HONEY DRESSING:

1 tbsp. honey
1 tbsp. lemon juice
1 3-oz. pkg. cream cheese
½ c. heavy cream, whipped

Blend honey, lemon juice and cream cheese. Fold in whipped cream.

Mrs. Ruby Jackson
Santa Anna, Texas

CONGEALED FRUIT SALADS

Recipe for Walnut Jewel Salad on Page 117

The Glamorous Salads

The "glamor gals" among salads are the congealed ones. Even ordinary salads become new and exciting when congealed.

Congealed salads even turn everyday fare into fancy meals. Try them with luncheons and dinners, suppers and snacks.

Special molds are available to make congealed salads in unusual shapes—crescents, rings, stars. There are standard round molds, square, oval and oblong ones.

The ring is probably the most popular mold since the center can be piled with fruits, vegetables, cottage or cream cheese, jelly, a bowl of salad dressing, etc.

And don't overlook the many possibilities of kitchen utensils. Custard cups, cake pans, ice cube trays, muffin tins, even paper cups make excellent molds.

For large groups, paper cups are ideal for molding individual salads. Tear off the cup when the salad is ready to be served.

MOLDING TRICKS

Molding a perfect salad every time is simple if you know the tricks.

Congealed salads are made from three basic steps, using an unflavored gelatin:

1. Soften gelatin by sprinkling it on cold liquid.
2. Dissolve softened gelatin in hot liquid.
3. Chill in refrigerator.

For a quick chill, place gelatin mixture in the freezer compartment for 10 minutes, or set it in a bowl of ice water and stir until it starts to thicken. If mixture becomes too solid, remelt it over boiling water.

To avoid diluting the gelatin mixture, drain frozen or canned fruit before adding it. Or, substitute syrup from the fruit as part of the liquid.

Use concentrated fruit or vegetable juices, condensed soups, etc., for speed in jelling—and for a full, rich flavor.

Before adding solids, chill the gelatin mixture until it thickens to the consistency of unbeaten egg whites. If solids, such as fruits and vegetables, are added to the mixture before it sets, they will settle to the bottom of the mold.

Carefully fold fruits and vegetables into thickened gelatin to distribute them evenly. After filling an undecorated mold, swirl or slice a knife through the mixture several times to release any air bubbles that may be trapped in it. Then refrigerate.

To mold different flavors or colors of gelatin in layers, let each layer set before adding the next one.

To mold fruits, vegetables or meats in a pattern, arrange one layer at a time on thickened gelatin. Chill, add another layer over the set design and chill again.

To keep bubbles in a carbonated beverage that is used as liquid in a gelatin salad, pour the beverage down the side of the bowl. Stir with an up and down motion.

Unmolding Is Easy

Keep gelatin salads chilled until almost time to serve them. When ready, have a plate chilled for the salad, one that is large enough to allow for the salad to be garnished.

There are two ways to proceed with the unmolding.

Moisten the dish slightly. This will prevent the gelatin from sticking and will make it easier to center the mold.

Use a thin knife at several points on the edge to release the vacuum. Then reverse the mold on the plate. If necessary, place a warm damp cloth over the mold for a few seconds. If the gelatin still is not released, shake the mold slightly, bracing it against the serving dish.

The second method is to dip the mold in warm, not hot, water to the depth of the gelatin mixture. Loosen around the edge with the tip of a small knife. Place the serving dish on top of the mold. Hold tightly in place and turn the mold and plate upside down. Shake the mold gently and carefully remove it.

If the gelatin does not unmold rapidly in either case, repeat the process.

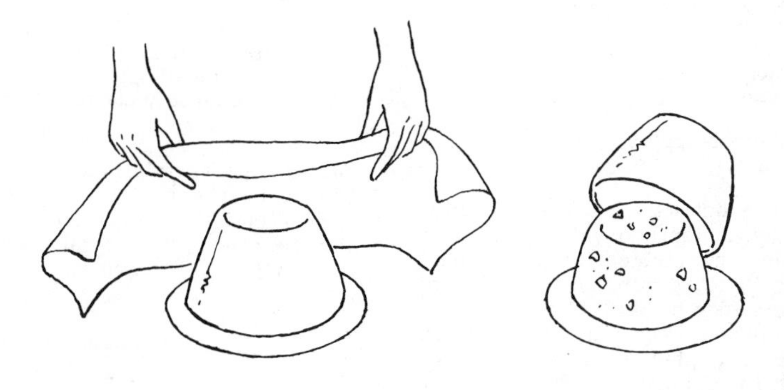

CHILLING GELATIN

Different gelatin recipes call for different degrees of chilling the mixture.

"Chill to unbeaten egg white consistency" means the mixture will pour from the spoon in a slightly thick, unbroken stream. This is the usual consistency required of simple gelatins and chiffons before fruits, vegetables, etc., are added to the mixture.

The mixture will dribble unevenly from a spoon when it is chilled to "slightly thicker than unbeaten egg whites." For whipped cream mixtures, the chilled gelatin should mound slightly when dropped from a spoon.

To set firmly, gelatin requires from two to four hours in the refrigerator. It will congeal much faster in individual molds than in a large one.

If the gelatin salad is a clear one, two hours of chilling should be enough to produce a consistency firm enough to unmold. It will take a full four hours, though, if the gelatin has fruits, nuts, vegetables, etc., added to it.

APPLE-CHEESE SALAD

1 pkg. lemon gelatin
2 c. warm water
1 c. diced apples
1 tsp. sugar
¼ tsp. salt
¼ lb. American cheese
½ c. walnut meats

Dissolve gelatin in warm water; place in refrigerator until firm. Combine apples, sugar, salt, cheese and nut meats. Whip gelatin with beater. Add mixture; pour into ring mold. Place in refrigerator until firmly chilled. Yield: 8 servings.

Mrs. U. G. Richmond
Walnut Grove, Mississippi

APPLE SALAD

1 pkg. lime gelatin
1 c. hot water
½ c. cold water
2 tbsp. lemon juice
½ c. mayonnaise
¼ tsp. salt
1 c. peeled diced apples
¼ c. chopped nuts

Dissolve gelatin in hot water; add cold water, lemon juice, mayonnaise and salt. Blend with rotary beater. Pour in refrigerator tray; quick-chill in freezer 15 to 20 minutes or until firm about 1 inch from edge but soft in center. Turn mixture into bowl and whip with rotary beater until fluffy. Fold in apples and nuts; pour in 1-quart mold. Chill in refrigerator 30 to 60 minutes.

Mrs. Edward N. James
Florence, Alabama

CONGEALED SALAD

3 pkg. apple gelatin
5 c. hot water
Juice of 1 lemon
2 c. chopped celery
2 chopped unpeeled red apples
1 c. broken pecans

Dissolve gelatin in hot water by stirring well. Add other ingredients. Mold in a ring. Serve with cream cheese mixed with mayonnaise and a little lemon juice.

Mrs. Carlie Brown
Burnsville, Mississippi

CONGEALED WALDORF SALAD

1 pkg. lemon gelatin
1 tsp. sugar
2 c. raw apples
1 tbsp. vinegar
3 tbsp. mayonnaise
1 c. cut-up celery
Nuts (opt.)

Prepare gelatin as directed on package. Let set until it begins to thicken. Mix sugar, apples, vinegar, mayonnaise, celery and nuts together and add to gelatin mixture.

Mrs. Louise Gammon
McKenney, Virginia

CRANBERRY WALDORF SALAD

3 3-oz. pkg. peach gelatin
1 ¼ tsp. salt
3 c. boiling water
2 c. cranberry juice cocktail
2 tbsp. lemon juice
1 ½ c. diced apple
½ c. coarsely chopped English walnuts

Dissolve peach gelatin and salt in boiling water. Stir in cranberry juice and lemon juice. Chill until slightly thickened. Fold in apple and English walnuts. Turn into a 2-quart mold and chill until firm. Yield: 6-8 servings.

Jewel H. Wolfe
Winston-Salem, North Carolina

JELLIED FRUIT AND PEANUT SALAD

1 ½ tbsp. gelatin
¼ c. cold water
½ c. boiling water
½ c. sugar
1 c. diced apple
2 c. orange juice
3 tbsp. lemon juice
½ c. roasted peanuts
1 c. whipped cream

Soak gelatin in cold water for 5 minutes. Add boiling water and sugar; stir until dissolved. Add apple, orange, lemon juice and peanuts. Combine all ingredients thoroughly; arrange in 6 molds dipped in cold water. Chill until firm; remove from mold. Arrange on lettuce leaves. Garnish with whipped cream.

Mrs. Alice Benton
Robert Lee, Texas

WALDORF SALAD

1 envelope unflavored gelatin
⅓ c. sugar
½ tsp. salt
1 ½ c. water
¼ c. vinegar or lemon juice
2 c. diced tart apples
½ c. diced celery
¼ c. chopped pecans

Mix gelatin, sugar and salt thoroughly in a small saucepan. Add 1/2 cup water. Place over low heat, stirring constantly, until gelatin is dissolved. Remove from heat and stir in remaining 1 cup water and vinegar. Chill mixture to unbeaten egg white consistency; fold in diced apples, chopped celery and chopped nuts. Turn into a 4-cup mold or individual molds and chill until firm. Unmold by dipping mold in warm water to the depth of the gelatin. Loosen around edge with tip of a paring knife. Place serving dish on mold and turn upside down. Shake, holding serving dish tightly to mold. Lift off mold. Garnish with fruit. Yield: 6 servings.

Mrs. Mildred Epling
Lake City, Florida

SPICY SALAD

2 ¼ c. cold water
1 cinnamon stick
1 3-oz. pkg. pink grapefruit gelatin
½ c. diced apple
½ c. diced celery
¼ c. chopped peanuts

Measure 1 1/4 cups cold water into pan. Add cinnamon stick; bring to boil. Simmer 10 minutes. If needed, add enough water to make 1 cup hot liquid. Add gelatin; stir to dissolve. Blend in rest of cold water. Remove cinnamon stick. Chill until slightly thick. Fold in apple, celery and peanuts. Pour into 3-cup mold. Chill until firm.

Mrs. Edna Chadsey
Corpus Christi, Texas

APPLESAUCE SALAD

1 pkg. lime or lemon gelatin
2 c. applesauce, heated
1 6-oz. bottle Seven-Up or ginger ale
½ c. pecans or walnuts, finely chopped

Dissolve gelatin in hot applesauce. Add remaining ingredients. Chill until firm.

Mrs. Gladys Nichols
Abilene, Texas

APPLESAUCE SALAD

3 tbsp. red cinnamon candies
1 c. hot water
1 pkg. orange gelatin
1 No. 2 can applesauce
½ c. celery, chopped
½ c. pecans, chopped

Melt cinnamon candies in hot water. Pour over gelatin; stir until dissolved. Add applesauce. Cool until mixture thickens. Fold in celery and nuts. Pour into mold; chill until firm.

Mildred C. Fancher
Atmore, Alabama

APPLESAUCE SALAD

1 pkg. lemon gelatin
1 pkg. orange gelatin
2 c. boiling water
2 c. applesauce
1 c. pecans, chopped
½ c. green olives, chopped
1 c. miniature marshmallows

Dissolve gelatin in boiling water. Add applesauce; mix well. Cool until slightly thickened. Add nuts, olives and marshmallows; mix. Chill until firm.

Mrs. Hazel M. Johnson
Fayetteville, Arkansas

APPLESAUCE SALAD

1 pkg. red gelatin
¼ c. red hots
1 c. hot water
1 can applesauce

Put gelatin and red hots in the hot water; stir till red hots are dissolved. Add applesauce. Refrigerate until set.

Mrs. Agnes Scifres
Littlefield, Texas

APPLESAUCE SALAD

⅓ c. cinnamon drops
1 c. hot water
1 pkg. lemon gelatin
1 c. applesauce
1 3-oz. pkg. cream cheese
1 tsp. mayonnaise
3 tbsp. milk

Dissolve cinnamon drops in very hot water; pour over gelatin to dissolve. Add applesauce to the above mixture and chill until it begins to thicken. Add cream cheese to mayonnaise and milk. Mix all ingredients together and place in the refrigerator to congeal. Cut into squares and serve on lettuce leaves with mayonnaise.

Mrs. Edward Kennedy
Hopkinsville, Kentucky

CINNAMON-APPLESAUCE SALAD

1 10-cent pkg. red hots
1 c. boiling water
1 pkg. cherry gelatin
1 No. 2 can applesauce
2 3-oz. pkg. cream cheese
2 tbsp. salad dressing
½ c. chopped nuts

Boil red hots in water until dissolved. Use hot water mixture to dissolve gelatin. Add applesauce; pour half of mixture into dish and let set. Mix cream cheese with salad dressing; add chopped nuts. After gelatin is set spread cheese mixture over it and add remaining gelatin mixture. Yield: 8-10 servings.

Mrs. Ernest Overton
Pond Creek, Oklahoma

HOLIDAY SALAD

½ c. red hots
2 ½ c. boiling water
2 pkg. cherry gelatin
2 No. 2 cans applesauce
Sour cream

Melt red hots in boiling water. Add gelatin and stir in applesauce. Chill until firm in an 8-inch ring mold. Unmold on plate. Fill center hole with sour cream. Yield: 16-18 servings.

Mrs. Edgar T. Milby, Sr.
Campbellsville, Kentucky

MOLDED APPLESAUCE SALAD

1 pkg. lime gelatin
¾ c. boiling water
2 c. sweetened applesauce
½ c. chopped nuts
1 c. chopped celery

Soften gelatin in boiling water. Add applesauce. Cool until mixture thickens. Stir in nuts and celery. Chill in individual molds or a 1-quart mold. Yield: 6 servings.

Mrs. Robert Chapman
Uniontown, Kentucky

APRICOT SALAD

2 pkg. orange gelatin
2 c. boiling water
1 No. 2 can apricots
1 6 ¼-oz. pkg. sm. marshmallows
1 c. whipping cream, whipped

Dissolve gelatin in boiling water and allow to cool and partially set. Beat with electric mixer. Add juice and mashed pulp of apricots. Add marshmallows and beat on low speed. Add cream and beat slowly. Place in refrigerator until congealed. Yield: 12-16 servings.

Mrs. R. L. Roof
Thomas, Oklahoma

AVOCADO MOUSSE

1 tbsp. unflavored gelatin
½ c. cold water
½ c. boiling water
1 tsp. salt
1 tsp. onion juice
2 tsp. Worcestershire sauce
2 tbsp. lemon juice
2 c. avocado, mashed
½ c. heavy cream whipped
½ c. mayonnaise

Soak gelatin in cold water; dissolve in boiling water. Add salt, onion juice, Worcestershire sauce, lemon juice and avocado pulp. Chill until mixture begins to set. Fold in whipped cream and mayonnaise. Turn into an oiled mold or individual molds. Chill until firm.

Mrs. Mary Belle Nutt
Cotulla, Texas

BANANA-PEANUT SALAD

1 3-oz. pkg. strawberry-banana gelatin
1 c. boiling water
1 c. cold water
2 bananas, sliced
2 tbsp. chopped salted peanuts
2 tbsp. mayonnaise

Dissolve gelatin in boiling water; add cold water. Chill until very thick. Pour 1 cup gelatin into mold; arrange banana slices on gelatin. Chill until it begins to set. Take remaining gelatin and blend in peanuts and mayonnaise. Spoon over the bananas. Chill until firm. Yield: 6 servings.

Mildred Gresham
Cadiz, Kentucky

HOLIDAY RIBBON SALAD

1 4 1/2-oz. pkg. lime gelatin
2 bananas, sliced
1 4 1/2-oz. pkg. lemon gelatin
1 8-oz. pkg. cream cheese
1/2 c. chopped pecans
1 4 1/2-oz. pkg. strawberry gelatin

Mix lime gelatin according to directions on box using 1/4 cup less hot water. Add sliced bananas. Pour into container and place in refrigerator until set. Mix lemon gelatin according to directions using 1/4 cup less hot water. Add cream cheese and pecans and set aside to cool. Pour over congealed lime mixture and set in refrigerator to set. Mix strawberry gelatin using 1/4 cup less water and set aside to cool. Pour over congealed lemon mixture and return to refrigerator to set. Slice in squares and serve on lettuce leaf.

Mrs. Georgia P. Crawley
Grand Bay, Alabama

BLACKBERRY DELIGHT

1 pkg. blackberry gelatin
1 c. sugar
1 c. boiling water
1 3-oz. pkg. cream cheese
1 carton frozen blackberries
1/4 c. nuts, chopped

Dissolve gelatin and sugar in boiling water. Soften cheese in 4 tablespoons of the hot mixture. Cool remaining gelatin mixture. Add frozen blackberries, nuts and cheese mixture to cooled gelatin. Refrigerate until firm.

Mrs. Clarice I. Snider
Erwin, Tennessee

CHERRY-COLA SALAD

1 c. chopped maraschino cherries
2 boxes cherry gelatin
1/2 c. sugar
2 bottles cola beverage
1/2 c. chopped pecans

Drain cherries reserving juice; add 1/2 cup water and heat. Dissolve gelatin in hot cherry juice. Add sugar, then cola beverage. Place in the refrigerator until partially set. Add the cherries and nuts; let set until firm.

Mrs. Ivan Gresham
Munday, Texas

CHERRY SALAD

1 lge. can Bing cherries, pitted
2 pkg. cherry gelatin
2 1/2 c. cola beverage
2/3 c. chopped nuts
2/3 c. chopped celery
1 pkg. crumbled cream cheese

Drain juice from cherries and reserve. Heat 1 1/2 cups cherry juice and dissolve gelatin in juice while hot. Add cola beverage immediately and allow to partially jell. Add cherries, nuts, celery and cheese. Chill.

Mrs. Walter McDaniel
Paris, Texas

DARK CHERRY SALAD

1 can dark sweet cherries
1 pkg. cherry gelatin
1/4 c. salad dressing or mayonnaise
1 3-oz. pkg. cream cheese
1/2 c. coconut
6 lge. marshmallows, quartered

Drain cherries, reserving 1 1/2 cups juice. Dissolve gelatin in 1/2 cup hot water and add cherry juice. Refrigerate until slightly set. Cream salad dressing and cream cheese. Add few tablespoons gelatin to thin mixture. Toss coconut, marshmallows and cherries and add to gelatin. After salad has set, serve on lettuce cups with mayonnaise dressing. Yield: 6 servings.

Mrs. J. Cobb
Rosenberg, Texas

COLA CONGEALED SALAD

1 can pitted sweet cherries
1 pkg. cherry gelatin
6-oz. cola drink
½ c. chopped pecans

Drain cherries and heat juice. Dissolve gelatin in hot cherry juice. Set aside to cool. Add cola. When slightly congealed, add cherries and nuts. Pour into mold and let set in refrigerator until firm. Serve on lettuce leaf.

Mrs. Talmage Griffies
Carrolton, Georgia

RASPBERRY-CRANBERRY SALAD

1 box raspberry gelatin
1 8-oz. pkg. cream cheese
1 jar cranberry relish
1 c. miniature marshmallows
1 c. crushed nuts

Mix gelatin according to directions on box. Add cream cheese; stir until dissolved. Chill until it begins to thicken. Stir in relish and sprinkle top with marshmallows and nuts. Refrigerate overnight.

Mrs. Nadean Holley
Eclectic, Alabama

RIBBON SALAD

1 pkg. strawberry or cherry gelatin
1 c. boiling water
1 pt. frozen cranberry sauce or
1 1-lb. can whole cranberries
2 tbsp. lemon juice
1 8-oz. pkg. cream cheese
1 c. whipped cream
½ c. chopped nuts

Dissolve gelatin in boiling water. Add cranberry sauce and lemon juice. Cool. When cooled, pour into square pan. Soften and cream the cheese; fold in whipped cream and chopped nuts. Spoon over gelatin with spatula. Freeze, unwrapped, 3 hours or overnight. Let stand 10 minutes or longer at room temperature before removing from pan. Put waxed paper on bottom.

Mrs. M. K. Ratcliffe, Jr.
Dallas, Texas

GOOSEBERRY SALAD

1 pkg. lemon gelatin
1 c. hot water
1 c. canned gooseberries, drained
⅛ tsp. salt
1 c. marshmallows, cut in pieces
1 orange
1 c. celery, cut in sm. pieces
½ c. chopped nuts

Prepare gelatin with hot water and 1 cup gooseberry juice. Chill until mixture begins to thicken; add salt, marshmallows, well-drained gooseberries, orange cut in small pieces, cubed celery and chopped nuts. Chill until firm. Serve on salad greens with mayonnaise.

Mrs. Velma Trent
Altus, Oklahoma

GRAPEFRUIT SALAD

1 grapefruit
1 pkg. lemon gelatin
½ c. hot water
½ c. cold water

Cut grapefruit in half lengthwise. Remove pulp and juice from the rinds. Strain and reserve 1/2 cup juice and all of the pulp. Dissolve gelatin in hot water; add cold water and grapefruit juice. Add sugar if desired. Chill until mixture starts to thicken. Add grapefruit pulp. Pour mixture into grapefruit shells. Place filled shells in a muffin pan and chill until firm. Cut grapefruit halves in half lengthwise for serving.

SPECIAL DRESSING:

1 3-oz. pkg. cream cheese
1 tbsp. honey
Juice of 1 lime
½ c. whipped cream

Combine ingredients. Refrigerate for 4 hours before serving with grapefruit.

Ruth Averitt
Lexington, Kentucky

ORANGE GELATIN RING

1 6-oz. pkg. orange gelatin
2 c. boiling water
1 pt. orange sherbet
1 11-oz. can mandarin oranges, drained

(Continued on next page)

Dissolve gelatin in water. Immediately add sherbet ; stir until melted. Add oranges. Pour in 1 1/2-quart ring mold; chill until firm. Unmold on greens. Yield: 10-12 servings.

Irene Vanoy
Liberty, Kentucky

ORANGE SALAD

2 c. orange drink
1 pkg. orange gelatin
1 11-oz. can mandarin oranges
1 pkg. dessert topping

Substitute 1 cup hot orange drink and 1 cup cold orange drink for water when dissolving gelatin. Cool; add drained mandarin oranges. Whip dessert topping and mix with gelatin. Pour into mold; chill.

Mrs. William B. Hall
Fayetteville, North Carolina

ORANGE SALAD MOLD

2 pkg. orange gelatin
2 c. hot water
1 c. orange juice
1 ½ c. orange sherbet

Dissolve gelatin in hot water. Add orange juice and mix thoroughly. Fold in sherbet; whip until smooth. Turn into salad mold; chill.

STRAWBERRY DRESSING:

2 c. frozen strawberries, drained
1 ½ c. sour cream

Stir ingredients; serve over molded salad on lettuce leaf. May be garnished with mandarin oranges and pineapple.

Mrs. S. S. Nichols
Meridian. Texas

MOLDED PEACH SALAD

1 No. 2 can peach halves
1 pkg. lemon gelatin
Crisp lettuce or endive
Mayonnaise

Drain peaches and measure peach juice, adding enough water to make 1 3/4 cups liquid. Heat liquid to boiling; add gelatin, stirring until dissolved. Pour layer of gelatin about 1/4 inch thick into a 9 x 5-inch pan. When congealed, place drained peach halves, rounded side down, on firm gelatin. Pour in another thin layer of gelatin, being careful that peaches do not slip around. When this layer is set, pour in remaining gelatin and allow to set. To serve, cut salad into sections, allowing 1 peach half to each serving. Serve on crisp lettuce with mayonnaise. Yield: 5-6 servings.

Mrs. Beulah Harper
Walton, West Virginia

BUFFET PEACH SALAD

1 3-oz. pkg. orange gelatin
1 c. boiling water
¼ c. peach syrup
¼ c. orange juice
½ c. ginger ale or Fresca
1 can peach halves
¼ c. pecan halves
6 drained maraschino cherries

Dissolve orange gelatin in 1 cup boiling water; add peach syrup, orange juice and ginger ale. Chill until slightly thickened. Arrange drained peach halves in shallow serving bowl. Spoon in gelatin. Add pecan halves and maraschino cherries. Chill until firm. Yield: 6-8 servings.

Mrs. Braxton M. Stroud
Nichols, South Carolina

PEACH-GINGER ALE SALAD

1 pkg. strawberry or cherry gelatin
¼ tsp. salt
1 c. hot water
1 c. ginger ale
1 No. 2 ½ can peach halves, drained

Dissolve gelatin and salt in hot water; add ginger ale. Chill until slightly thickened. Place peach halves in 1 8 or 9-inch square pan. Pour slightly thickened gelatin over peaches. Chill until firm. Cut into squares; serve on lettuce leaves with salad dressing and cream cheese balls rolled in chopped nuts. Yield: 4-6 servings.

Mrs. L. D. Grimes
Maud, Texas

PEACH-GRAPE GELATIN

1 tbsp. plain gelatin
¼ c. cold water
¾ c. boiling water
¼ c. sugar
¾ c. grape juice
2 tbsp. lemon juice
¼ tsp. salt
1 c. sliced canned peaches

Combine gelatin and cold water. Let stand 5 minutes. Add boiling water and sugar. Stir until gelatin is dissolved. Add grape juice, lemon juice and salt. Mix thoroughly. Chill until partially set. Arrange peach slices in individual molds; cover with gelatin. Chill until firm. Serve with mayonnaise on crisp lettuce. Yield: 6 servings.

Mrs. Preston Herring
Orrum, North Carolina

PEACH SALAD

2 pkg. orange gelatin
1 lge. can spiced pickled peaches
1 sm. pkg. cream cheese
Mayonnaise to soften cheese
¼ c. finely chopped pecans (opt.)

Add 1 cup boiling water to gelatin and mix well. Add 1 cup peach juice to gelatin. Cool. Remove seed from peaches. Mix cheese and mayonnaise with electric mixer; add peaches and mix until peaches are mashed. Add nuts. Add cooled gelatin to cheese mixture. Place in molds and congeal.

Mrs. Daisy P. Graham
Millpart, Alabama

SLICED PEACH SALAD

1 envelope unflavored gelatin
¼ c. vinegar
1 12-oz. can peach nectar
Cinnamon stick
Dash of ginger
¼ tsp. salt
1 10-oz. pkg. frozen peaches

Sprinkle gelatin on vinegar; add nectar, spices and salt. Stir over low heat until gelatin is dissolved, about 3 minutes. Remove from heat. Discard cinnamon. Stir into frozen fruit. Turn into 1 4-cup mold or individual molds; chill until firm about 30 minutes. Unmold; serve on greens with salad dressing. Yield: 4-6 servings.

Carol Crawford
Haw River, North Carolina

PEACH WHIP SALAD

1 pkg. orange gelatin
1 c. boiling water
1 c. mashed peaches
1 c. peach syrup
1 c. crushed nuts
½ c. whipped cream

Dissolve gelatin in water; chill until slightly thickened. Add remaining ingredients. Pour into mold; chill several hours or until firm.

Mrs. F. E. Corbell
Lockesburg, Arkansas

SPICED PEACH SALAD

1 envelope unflavored gelatin
1 tbsp. sugar
¼ tsp. salt
1 1-lb. can sliced peaches
6 whole cloves
1 stick cinnamon
¼ c. vinegar

Mix gelatin, sugar and salt thoroughly in a saucepan. Drain peaches; add water to peach syrup to make 1 1/4 cups liquid. Add cloves and cinnamon to gelatin; simmer about 10 minutes. Strain; stir in vinegar. Chill to unbeaten egg white consistency. Fold in peaches. Pour into a 2-cup mold or individual molds and chill. Unmold on salad plate garnished with salad greens.

Thelma Farmer
Summers, Arkansas

SPICED PEACH SOUFFLE SALAD

1 1-lb. 14-oz. jar sliced peaches
1 c. peach syrup
1 3-oz. pkg. orange gelatin
1 c. evaporated milk
½ c. chopped celery
½ c. chopped pecans
¼ c. mayonnaise
2 tbsp. lemon juice

Drain peaches, reserving 1 cup syrup. Chop peaches and chill. Heat peach syrup to boiling; remove from heat and add gelatin to dissolve. Pour into a large bowl and chill until the consistency of unbeaten egg white. Chill milk in ice cube tray until partly frozen. When gelatin begins to thicken, stir in chopped peaches, celery, pecans and mayonnaise. Turn partly frozen milk into a small well-chilled bowl. Whip until stiff. Add lemon juice and beat to blend. Fold into gelatin mixture lightly but thoroughly. Spoon into an oiled 6 cup mold. Chill until firm, about 3 hours. Yield: 6-8 servings.

Mrs. Orvil Huskey
Strawberry, Arkansas

PEANUT BUTTER GELATIN SALAD

1 6-oz. pkg. lime gelatin
1 c. peanut butter
1 c. green grapes

Prepare gelatin according to package directions; chill until thickened. Add peanut butter; mix thoroughly. Fold in grapes; chill until set. Serve on crisp lettuce, curly endive, or watercress; garnish each serving with a cluster of additional grapes. Yield: 8-10 servings.

Mary Sue Paddock
San Angelo, Texas

PEAR AND LIME SALAD

¾ c. cottage cheese
1 ½ tbsp. ginger
12 sm. canned pear halves
1 pkg. lime gelatin
2 c. water
Lettuce
Mayonnaise

Mix cottage cheese with finely chopped ginger. Scoop out pear centers; fill with cheese mixture. Place halves together. Dissolve gelatin in boiling water and cool to consistency of thick cream. Pour a small amount of gelatin into molds greased with soft fat and let congeal. Place a pear in center of each mold; cover with gelatin. Chill until congealed. Remove from molds and serve in lettuce cups with mayonnaise.

Mrs. Wilbur Jenkins
Sadieville, Kentucky

PEAR SALAD

¼ c. cold water
1 envelope gelatin
1 tbsp. sugar
¼ tsp. salt
½ c. hot water
2 tbsp. orange juice
1 c. crushed honey pear, drained
⅔ c. grated cheese

Pour cold water in bowl and sprinkle gelatin on top of water; add sugar, salt and hot water. Stir until dissolved. Add orange juice and pear; cool. When mixture begins to thicken, beat in cheese and turn into molds that have been dipped in cold water. Chill. Unmold on crisp lettuce topped with French dressing. Yield: 6 servings.

Malissia Austin
Dermott, Arkansas

SEAFOAM SALAD

1 3-oz. pkg. lime gelatin
1 c. hot pear syrup
2 3-oz. pkg. cream cheese
2 tbsp. salad dressing
1 No. 2 ½ can pears, drained and mashed
1 pkg. plain gelatin
½ pt. whipping cream, whipped

Dissolve lime gelatin in hot pear syrup. Cool. Blend cream cheese with salad dressing. Mash drained pears mixed with gelatin; add to softened cheese. Fold whipped cream into pear-cheese mixture. Fold into gelatin mixture. Pour into molds or square pan; congeal. Serve on lettuce. Yield: 9 servings.

Mrs. Dickson Durden
Twin City, Georgia

UNDER-THE-SEA SALAD

1 pkg. lime gelatin
1 ½ c. boiling water
½ c. canned pear juice
1 tsp. vinegar
¼ tsp. salt
2 pkg. cream cheese
½ tsp. ginger
2 c. canned pears

Dissolve lime gelatin in boiling water; add canned pear juice, vinegar and salt. Pour a thin layer of mixture in a loaf pan or mold; chill until firm. When remaining mixture is cold and syrupy, whip it until fluffy and thick. Combine cream cheese with ground ginger; add to whipped mixture with diced pears. Pour over first layer and chill.

Mrs. L. M. DeShong
Paris, Texas

GREENGAGE PLUM SALAD

1 lge. can greengage plums
1 pkg. lime gelatin
2 pkg. cream cheese, chopped
1 tsp. lemon juice
3 drops Tabasco or 3 dashes cayenne

(Continued on next page)

Drain plums, reserving juice; mix juice and gelatin in saucepan. Bring to boil; remove from heat and cool. Mash plums; add to gelatin. Add remaining ingredients; pour into buttered individual molds. Chill until firm.

Mrs. M. K. Ratcliffe, Jr.
Dallas, Texas

PLUM GOOD SALAD

1 pkg. lime gelatin
½ c. hot water
1 No. 2 can greengage plums
1 sm. pkg. cream cheese, chopped
1 c. pecans, chopped

Dissolve gelatin in hot water. Drain plums, reserving 1 cup liquid; add plum liquid to gelatin. Cool. Mash plums; add to gelatin. Add cream cheese; chill until slightly thickened. Add pecans; turn into mold. Refrigerate for several hours or until firm.

Mrs. Pat Hensley
O'Donnell, Texas

BRIDE'S SALAD

1 pkg. lime gelatin
1 pkg. lemon gelatin
2 ½ c. hot water
⅓ c. mayonnaise
1 c. crushed pineapple
⅓ c. cottage cheese
⅔ c. evaporated milk

Dissolve gelatin in hot water; chill until slightly thickened. Add remaining ingredients; chill for several hours or until firm.

Mrs. Minnie M. Morgan
Fort Smith, Arkansas

CONGEALED ORANGE SALAD

1 c. grated cheese
1 pkg. orange gelatin
1 c. boiling water
1 sm. can crushed pineapple
1 c. mayonnaise
1 sm. can evaporated milk, chilled

Grate cheese; add to gelatin and boiling water. Add pineapple, mayonnaise and whipped milk; chill.

Mrs. E. R. Bobo
Fort Payne, Alabama

CHRISTMAS SALAD

1 pkg. lime gelatin
1 pkg. lemon gelatin
2 c. hot water
1 lb. cottage cheese
1 c. mayonnaise
1 can crushed pineapple
1 c. nuts, chopped
1 can sweetened condensed milk

Dissolve lemon and lime gelatin in hot water; cool. Add remaining ingredients; chill until set.

Mrs. W. A. Copeland
Lindall, Texas

DIFFERENT SALAD

1 pkg. lime gelatin
1 pkg. lemon gelatin
2 c. boiling water
¼ c. green pepper, chopped
1 sm.can crushed pineapple
1 tsp. onion, chopped
½ c. celery, chopped
1 12-oz. pkg. cottage cheese
½ c. mayonnaise

Mix gelatins and water; chill slightly. Fold in all ingredients and chill until firm.

Mrs. S. A. Bone
Des Arc, Arkansas

FALCON'S NEST SALAD

1 pkg. each lemon and lime gelatin
2 c. hot water
1 ¾ c. crushed pineapple
2 tbsp. lemon juice
1 ½ cans evaporated milk, chilled and whipped
2 tsp. horseradish
1 c. tart salad dressing
1 c. nuts
½ lb. cottage cheese

(Continued on next page)

Dissolve lemon and lime gelatin in hot water; fold in remaining ingredients in order given. Mold and chill until firm.

Mrs. Winnie Vinson
Erin, Tennessee

GELATIN SALAD

2 boxes lemon gelatin
4 c. hot water
1 No. 2 can crushed pineapple
1 can sweetened condensed milk
2 boxes cherry gelatin

Dissolve lemon gelatin in 2 cups hot water; let cool. Add crushed pineapple, mixing well. Stir in milk. Pour into 3-quart utility dish; cover with aluminum foil. Chill until firm. Dissolve cherry gelatin in remaining hot water; let cool. Spread over firm layer. Return to refrigerator until ready to serve. Yield: 24 servings.

Mrs. Conley E. Phillips
Cookeville, Tennessee

HEAVENLY CHEESE SALAD

1 c. pineapple juice
1 pkg. lemon gelatin
4 slices pineapple, cut into sm. pieces
1 sm. pkg. cream cheese
½ c. pecans
¼ pt. whipping cream

Bring pineapple juice to boil; pour over lemon gelatin. When cool, add pineapple, cream cheese and nuts; mix well. Whip cream until stiff; fold into mixture. Refrigerate until firm.

Mrs. James Reynolds
Lincoln, Arkansas

HOLIDAY SALAD

1 3-oz. pkg. lemon gelatin
1 c. boiling water
2 tbsp. white vinegar
2 tbsp. sugar
1 c. pineapple juice
1 c. crushed pineapple, drained
1 c. grated cheese
1 c. heavy cream, whipped

Dissolve gelatin in boiling water; add vinegar and sugar. Chill until syrupy. Fold in pineapple juice, pineapple, cheese and whipped cream. Pour into individual bell-shaped molds or 1-quart mold. Chill until thoroughly set; unmold on curly endive or any other greens. Yield: 6-8 servings.

Mrs. Earl L. Faulkenberry
Lancaster, South Carolina

HOLIDAY SALAD

1 pkg. lime gelatin
½ c. boiling water
12 lge. or 1 c. sm. marshmallows
1 sm. pkg. cream cheese
½ c. pineapple juice
1 med. can crushed pineapple, drained
1 c. celery, diced
½ c. chopped nuts
½ pt. whipping cream, whipped or 1 box dessert topping

Combine first 3 ingredients and stir until dissolved. Allow to cool. Cream package of cream cheese with pineapple juice. When gelatin mixture is cool, add cheese mixture, pineapple, celery and nuts. Mix well; allow to set slightly. Fold in whipped cream or dessert topping.

Ida F. Lunerick
Morgantown, West Virginia

JELLED SALAD

1 pkg. strawberry gelatin
1 c. hot water
1 c. sugar
1 c. miniature marshmallows
½ pt. whipping cream, whipped
1 c. cottage cheese
1 8-oz. can crushed pineapple
½ c. chopped pecans
2 tbsp. lemon juice

Mix gelatin, water, sugar and marshmallows; stir until sugar dissolves and marshmallows melt. Add remaining ingredients; chill until ready to serve.

Mrs. Elizabeth Buckler
Paris, Kentucky

LIME-NUT SALAD

1 pkg. lime gelatin
1 c. boiling water
1 sm. can crushed pineapple
½ c. chopped celery
½ c. chopped nuts
1 c. cottage cheese
1 tbsp. chopped pimento

Dissolve gelatin in boiling water. Cool and stir in all other ingredients. Mold in 8 small molds or 8-inch square pan. Yield: 8-9 servings.

Mrs. Joe H. Clark
Winnsboro, South Carolina

LIME SALAD

1 pkg. lime gelatin
1 c. boiling water
1 c. sm. marshmallows
Juice of ½ lemon
¼ c. sugar
1 sm. pkg. cream cheese
1 sm. can crushed pineapple
½ c. chopped nuts
½ pt. whipping cream, whipped

Dissolve gelatin in boiling water; stir in marshmallows, lemon juice and sugar. Add cream cheese; cool. Add pineapple and nuts; fold in whipped cream. Chill until set.

Mrs. Bennie Smith
Olive Hill, Tennessee

LIME-PINEAPPLE SALAD

1 pkg. lime gelatin
12 marshmallows
1 c. hot water
½ c. pineapple juice
1 c. crushed pineapple
1 pkg. cream cheese or cottage cheese
2 tbsp. mayonnaise
1 tsp. unflavored gelatin
Maraschino cherries
1 c. chopped pecans

Dissolve gelatin and marshmallows in hot water; cool. Add pineapple juice and crushed pineapple. Add cream cheese mixed with mayonnaise. Add unflavored gelatin dissolved in cold water. Chop cherries; add with nuts, stirring occasionally, as salad begins to congeal, to bring cherries to top.

Hazel M. Stanberry
Todd, North Carolina

LIME SALAD

1 sm. pkg. lime gelatin
1 No. 2 can crushed pineapple
1 sm jar pimento
Dash of salt
2 sm. pkg. cream cheese, softened
1 pt. whipped cream
1 c. chopped nuts

Place gelatin and pineapple in saucepan; bring to a boil. Remove from heat; cool. Mix pimento, salt and cream cheese until blended. Pour gelatin mixture over cream cheese mixture; mix well. Fold in whipped cream and nuts; pour into mold. Chill until set.

Mrs. Carl Payton
Post, Texas

LIME-PINEAPPLE SALAD

1 sm. can crushed pineapple
1 pkg. lime gelatin
4 oz. cream cheese
⅔ c. walnuts, chopped fine
⅔ c. celery, chopped fine
1 c. (scant) ginger ale
⅔ c. whipping cream

Drain pineapple, reserving juice and combining with water to make 1 cup. Heat juice and water to boiling point and dissolve the gelatin in mixture thoroughly. Add cream cheese, mashing with a fork until dissolved. Add pineapple, walnuts, celery and ginger ale. Refrigerate until mixture becomes thick. Whip cream until stiff; fold in gelatin mixture. Pour into mold and return to refrigerator. Yield: 8-10 servings.

Mrs. Mike Riggs
Laveen, Arizona

MEN-LIKE-IT SALAD

Pineapple juice plus water to equal 1 c. liquid
1 pkg. lemon gelatin
2 3-oz. pkg. cream cheese, softened
1 No. 2 can crushed pineapple, drained
⅔ c. chopped nuts
1 sm. jar pimento, chopped and drained
½ pt. cream, whipped

Bring pineapple juice-water mixture to boil; dissolve gelatin in hot liquid. Mash cream cheese; add pineapple, nuts and pimento. Add gelatin; fold in whipped cream. Chill. Yield: 9 servings.

Mrs. Dickson Durden
Twin City, Georgia

PANAMA SALAD

1 family-sized pkg. lime gelatin
2 c. boiling water
1 lge. can crushed pineapple
1 carton sour cream
1 c. chopped celery
½ c. chopped pecans

Mix gelatin with hot water; let cool. Drain pineapple and mix all ingredients when gelatin is cool. Pour into mold.

Mrs. Joe B. Brown
Mount Airy, North Carolina

ORANGE-PINEAPPLE SALAD

1 sm. pkg. orange-pineapple gelatin, prepared
1 c. cottage cheese, at room temperature
½ wedge bleu cheese, crumbled
1 tbsp. wine vinegar (opt.)

Chill gelatin until partially set. Beat cottage cheese until smooth. Fold cottage cheese, bleu cheese and wine vinegar into congealed mixture; chill until set. Unmold on lettuce leaves; serve with crackers.

Mrs. W. E. Vinson
Greensboro, North Carolina

PINEAPPLE BAVARIAN SALAD

1 pkg. flavored gelatin
1 c. hot water
1 c. pineapple juice
¾ c. sugar
1 c. crushed pineapple
1 c. whipped cream

Dissolve gelatin in hot water. Add pineapple juice and 1/2 cup sugar; mix thoroughly. Place in refrigerator until thickened; add crushed pineapple. Whip cream; gradually add remaining sugar. Fold into gelatin mixture until well blended; chill until firm. Yield: 10 servings.

Mrs. William E. Janata
Houston, Texas

PINEAPPLE DELIGHT

¾ c. evaporated milk
1 pkg. lime gelatin
8 marshmallows, cut fine
1 9-oz. can crushed pineapple, undrained
½ c. broken nuts

Place milk in freezer tray; chill until partially frozen around edges of tray. Dissolve gelatin in 1/2 cup boiling water; add 1/2 cup cold water. Add marshmallows, pineapple and nuts. Whip milk in chilled bowl with chilled beaters until stiff; fold into gelatin mixture. Cover; chill until firm. Garnish with maraschino cherries.

Mrs. George Billingsley
Bowling Green, Kentucky

MOLDED COTTAGE CHEESE AND PINEAPPLE SALAD

1 3-oz. pkg. lemon gelatin
1 pkg. plain or unflavored gelatin
1 c. boiling water
1 c. cream, whipped
1 ½ c. cottage cheese
1 3-oz. pkg. lime gelatin
1 c. pineapple juice
1 c. drained crushed pineapple
⅓ c. sliced, stuffed olives
⅓ c. broken, walnut meats

Dissolve lemon and unflavored gelatin in hot water. Cool slightly; beat with egg beater until light. Add whipped cream and beat. Add cottage cheese. Pour into round mold. Allow to set until quite firm. Dissolve lime gelatin in pineapple juice. Add the pineapple, olives and walnuts. Pour on top of first mold. Allow to set until firm. Unmold on salad plate. Cut like cake. Yield: 12 servings.

Mrs. Jack Henson
Sylva, North Carolina

ORANGE FRUIT SALAD

2 pkg. orange gelatin
1 c. boiling water
1 pt. orange sherbet
1 can crushed pineapple
1 c. miniature marshmallows
1 pkg. dessert topping mix, prepared

Dissolve gelatin in boiling water; let set til mixture begins to jell. Add remaining ingredients, folding in dessert topping last. Chill until firm.

Mrs. Clyde Berkhouse
Spencer, West Virginia

ORANGE-PINEAPPLE SALAD

1 3-oz. pkg. orange gelatin
½ pt. whipping cream
1 c. coconut
1 c. crushed pineapple
1 c. chopped pecans

Dissolve gelatin in 1 cup hot water; add 1 cup cold water. Chill until very firm; whip until fluffy. Whip cream; fold into gelatin. Add coconut, pineapple and pecans; chill until firm. Serve on lettuce leaf.

Mrs. Dale Lawrence
Byers, Texas

PINEAPPLE-CREAM SALAD

2 pkg. lime gelatin
1 c. boiling water
1 pt. thick sour cream
½ tsp. salt
1 No. 2 can crushed pineapple, well drained
½ c. finely chopped blanched almonds

Dissolve gelatin thoroughly in boiling water. Cool until mixture begins to thicken; fold in sour cream, salt, pineapple and nuts. Pour into large mold or individual molds. Chill until firm. Unmold on lettuce. Garnish with desired dressing. Yield: 8 servings.

Mrs. Orby Yarberry
Columbia, Kentucky

PINEAPPLE-SEVEN-UP SALAD

1 pkg. lemon gelatin
1 c. boiling water
1 8-oz. pkg. cream cheese, softened
1 sm. can crushed pineapple, drained
½ c. chopped pecans
1 7-oz. bottle Seven-Up
Few drops green food coloring

Dissolve gelatin in hot water; add cream cheese. Mix well. Add remaining ingredients; chill till firm.

Mrs. Richard McGuire
Bowling Green, Kentucky

RAINBOW PARTY SALAD

1 pkg. lime gelatin
1 pkg. strawberry gelatin
1 c. pineapple juice
½ c. water
¼ c. sugar
Dash of salt
1 pkg. orange gelatin
½ pt. whipped cream

Dissolve lime and strawberry gelatin according to package directions; congeal in separate square cake pans. Cut into cubes. Combine pineapple juice, water, sugar and salt in saucepan; bring to a boil. Add orange gelatin; chill until almost firm. Add whipped cream and gelatin cubes; chill until firm. Yield: 12 servings.

Mrs. Marian E. Causey
Centreville, Mississippi

PINEAPPLE-LIME SALAD

2 pkg. lime gelatin
1 c. boiling water
1 No. 2 can crushed pineapple, undrained
½ c. chopped pecans
1 pt. vanilla ice cream

Add boiling water to gelatin. Stir until dissolved; do not cool. Add pineapple and nuts. Stir in ice cream until melted. Pour in loaf pan. Chill until set.

Mrs. W. Irvin Blythe
Franklin, Virginia

RIBBON SALAD

2 pkg. cherry gelatin
1 pkg. lemon gelatin
1 c. cut marshmallows
1 sm. can crushed pineapple and juice
½ c. mayonnaise
1 sm. pkg. cream cheese, crumbled

Prepare cherry gelatin according to package directions. Pour 1/3 of mixture in 13 x 9 x 2-inch baking dish. Chill until set. Dissolve lemon gelatin in 1 cup boiling water; stir in remaining ingredients. Pour 1/2 of mixture over firm layer of gelatin. Let set until firm. Cover with 1/3 of cherry gelatin mixture. Chill until firm. Cover with remaining cherry gelatin mixture. Chill until firm. Yield: 20 servings.

Maude Childress
Richmond, Virginia

YUM-YUM SALAD

1 envelope unflavored gelatin
½ c. water
1 No. 2 can crushed pineapple, undrained
¾ c. sugar
Juice of 1 lemon
¾ c. grated American cheese
1 c. whipping cream, whipped

Soften gelatin in water for 5 minutes. Place pineapple, sugar and lemon juice in saucepan; bring to a boil. Remove from heat; add gelatin. Cook; add cheese and whipped cream. Pour into molds; chill until firm.

Mrs. Jim McCampbell
Holdenville, Oklahoma

RIBBON SALAD

2 3-oz. pkg. lime gelatin
1 3-oz. pkg. lemon gelatin
½ c. miniature marshmallows, cut into pieces
1 c. pineapple juice
1 8-oz. pkg. cream cheese
1 1-lb. 4-oz. can crushed pineapple, drained
1 c. heavy cream, whipped
1 c. mayonnaise
2 3-oz. pkg. cherry gelatin

Dissolve lime gelatin in 2 cups hot water; add 2 cups cold water. Pour into 14 x 10 x 2-inch pan; chill until partially set. Dissolve lemon gelatin in 1 cup hot water in top of double boiler; add marshmallows and stir to melt. Remove from heat; add pineapple juice and cream cheese. Stir until well blended; stir in pineapple. Cool slightly; fold in whipped cream and mayonnaise. Chill until thickened; pour evenly over lime gelatin. Chill until almost set. Dissolve cherry gelatin in 2 cups hot water; add 2 cups cold water. Chill until syrupy; pour over pineapple layer. Chill until firm. Yield: 24 servings.

Mrs. H. S. McKinney
Chesnee, South Carolina

RASPBERRY BAVARIAN MOLD

1 10-oz. pkg. frozen red raspberries, thawed
1 3-oz. pkg. raspberry or strawberry gelatin
1 c. hot water
1 tbsp. lemon juice
Dash of salt
1 6-oz. can evaporated milk, chilled

Drain raspberries, reserving syrup. Dissolve gelatin in hot water; add reserved raspberry syrup, lemon juice and salt. Chill until partially set; add milk. Beat at high speed on electric mixer until fluffy or until mixture mounds slightly; fold in raspberries. Pour into 1 1/2-quart mold; chill until firm.

Mrs. Lester Burgess
New Braunfels, Texas

STRAWBERRY SALAD

1 lge. pkg. strawberry gelatin
1 sm. pkg. cream cheese, cut up
1 pt. strawberries, crushed
½ c. sugar
½ c. chopped pecans

Prepare gelatin according to package directions; mix in cream cheese. Add strawberries, sugar and pecans; refrigerate until set.

Judy Stanfill
Beech Bluff, Tennessee

APPLE-CHEESE RING

2 pkg. lime gelatin
2 c. boiling water
2 c. cold water
1 3-oz. pkg. cream cheese
¼ c. finely chopped nuts
1 ½ c. diced, unpared, tart red apples
1 c. miniature marshmallows
¾ c. halved, seeded Tokay grapes
¼ c. coarsley broken nuts
Few grains salt

Dissolve gelatin in boiling water. Add cold water. Chill until mixture is consistency of unbeaten egg white. Pour 1 1/2 cups of mixture into bottom of 7-cup ring mold which has been rinsed with cold water; chill until partially set. Shape cream cheese into 7 balls. Roll each ball in finely chopped nuts. Space cheese balls evenly in partly chilled gelatin; chill just until barely firm. Chill remaining gelatin until partially firm. Fold in apples, marshmallows, grapes, nuts and salt. Pour over first layer. Chill until firm. Unmold; garnish and serve with mayonnaise.

Mrs. Harold Fuller
Chapel Hill, Tennessee

APPLE SALAD MEDLEY

2 c. sliced apples, cut fine
1 c. green grapes, halved
1 c. pineapple chunks, drained
½ c. celery, sliced very fine
½ c. plumped raisins, plain or bleached
2 or 3 cherries, cut fine
¾ c. sour cream
2 tbsp. lemon juice
⅓ c. pineapple juice
Dash of mace or nutmeg

Combine first 6 ingredients thoroughly. Mix remaining ingredients well; pour over fruits. Toss lightly.

Mrs. W. H. Phillips
Staunton, Virginia

CHRISTMAS SALAD

1 pkg. lemon gelatin
1 pkg. lime gelatin
2 tbsp. mayonnaise
1 c. chopped apples
1 c. chopped grapes
1 c. chopped nuts
2 tbsp. lemon juice

Make gelatin according to package directions. Chill until partially firm. Add mayonnaise; beat until creamy. Add remaining ingredients. Chill overnight.

Mrs. Connie Hammock
Oneida, Tennessee

COCONUT NESTS WITH SOUR CREAM-FRUIT SALAD

2 c. shredded coconut
½ c. unsifted powdered sugar
2 tsp. green food coloring
½ tsp. water
3 tbsp. butter or margarine, melted
½ c. chopped red apple
½ c. chopped green grapes
½ c. drained pineapple tidbits
½ c. flavored miniature marshmallows
2 tbsp. chopped nuts
2 tbsp. dairy sour cream

Mix coconut and sugar in a 1-quart jar. Combine food coloring and water; sprinkle over coconut. cover jar and shake vigorously to tint coconut. Mix tinted coconut with melted butter. Spoon into a muffin pan and mold to form 6 nests. Refrigerate at least 1 hour. To loosen nests, dip muffin pan into lukewarm water. Lift out nests. Combine remaining ingredients and spoon portion into each coconut nest. Yield: 2 cups.

Mrs. Alvin Reid
Pilot Mountain, North Carolina

CINNAMON-APPLE FLUFF SALAD

½ c. sm. red cinnamon candies
½ c. hot water
1 pkg. lemon gelatin
1 1-lb. can apples
1 9-oz. can crushed pineapple

Combine cinnamon candies with hot water and dissolve over low heat; stir into dry gelatin until dissolved. Blend in applesauce and pineapple. Turn into mold or bowl. Chill till firm.

Mrs. Robert Rector
Millboro, Virginia

ORANGE-APPLE DELIGHT SALAD

1 pkg. orange gelatin
2 c. hot water
¾ c. shredded apple
1 diced banana
¼ c. chopped pecans

Dissolve gelatin in hot water. Cool. When slightly thickened, add apple, banana and pecans. Pour into 6 molds and chill.

Mrs. P. A. Raper
Burgaw, North Carolina

CRUSHED PINEAPPLE 'N' APPLE SALAD

1 pkg. lemon gelatin
2 c. hot water
½ c. crushed pineapple, drained
1 c. diced unpeeled red apples
¼ c. chopped pecans

Dissolve gelatin in hot water. Chill until slightly thickened; fold in crushed pineapple, apples and pecans. Pour into 6 individual molds. Chill until firm; unmold on salad greens. Serve with mayonnaise. Yield: 6 servings.

Bonnie Butts
San Antonio, Texas

APPLESAUCE CONGEALED SALAD

⅓ c. cinnamon-flavored candies
2 regular or 1 family-sized pkg. lemon gelatin
1 can applesauce
1 sm. can crushed pineapple, drained
½ c. diced celery
½ c. chopped pecans

Pour 1/2 cup hot water over cinnamon candies; stir until dissolved. Pour 1 1/2 cups hot water over gelatin; stir until dissolved. Add dissolved candy mixture to gelatin mixture; refrigerate until mixture thickens to consistency of egg whites. Fold in applesauce, pineapple, celery and nuts; return to refrigerator to congeal. Serve with fowl, if desired.

Mrs. G. R. Lindsey
Waco, Texas

WHOOPIE SALAD

½ c. seedless raisins
2 tbsp. red cinnamon candies
1 ½ c. water
1 3-oz. pkg. raspberry gelatin
2 tbsp. lemon juice
1 red apple
¾ c. diced celery
½ c. dairy sour cream

Heat raisins, cinnamon candies and water slowly until candies dissolve. Add gelatin and lemon juice, stirring until gelatin dissolves. Pour thin layer of gelatin in 5-cup mold, arranging some raisins in pattern to fit design of mold. Chill until almost firm. Chill remaining gelatin until it begins to thicken. Fold in diced unpared apple, celery and sour cream. Pour into mold over clear layer. Chill until firm. Unmold and garnish. Yield: 6 servings.

Mrs. Georgie Thorne
Slocomb, Alabama

CINNAMON-APPLE FLUFF

½ c. sm. cinnamon red hot candies
½ c. hot water
1 pkg. lemon gelatin
1 1-lb. can applesauce
1 9-oz. can crushed pineapple
Few drops red food coloring
¼ tsp. nutmeg

Combine cinnamon candies with hot water; dissolve over low heat. Stir in gelatin until dissolved. Blend in applesauce and pineapple. Add red food coloring and nutmeg. Turn into 1-quart mold; chill until firm. Unmold onto chilled plate; For variety, scoop out top of mold; add a fluff of salad dressing, folded into whipped cream. Serve in squares. Nuts may be added.

Mrs. Henry Pratt
Willis, Texas

APRICOT DELIGHT SALAD

1 29-oz. can apricots, drained and finely cut up
1 29-oz. can crushed pineapple, drained
2 pkg. orange gelatin
2 c. hot water
¾ c. miniature marshmallows

Drain fruits and chill, reserving juice. Dissolve gelatin in boiling water; add 1 cup juice. Chill until slightly thickened; add apricots and pineapple. Pour into 11 x 9-inch shallow dish. Chill until firm.

TOPPING:

½ c. sugar
3 tbsp. flour
1 egg, slightly beaten
1 c. pineapple-apricot juice
2 tbsp. butter
1 c. cream, whipped
¾ c. grated American cheese

Combine sugar and flour; blend in beaten egg. Gradually stir in juice. Cook over low heat till thickened, stirring constantly. Remove from heat and stir in butter; cool. Fold in whipped cream and spread mixture over gelatin. Sprinkle with cheese. Chill.

Mrs. Tom Sparkman
Columbia, Tennessee

APRICOT GELATIN SALAD

1 lge. can ripe apricot halves
1 med. can crushed pineapple
2 pkg. orange-pineapple gelatin
2 ripe bananas
½ c. nuts

Drain juice from apricots and pineapple; add enough water to make 3 1/2 cups. Heat 2 cups liquid; dissolve gelatin. Add remaining liquid. Mash bananas and add with remaining fruit to gelatin. Pour into 9 x 13-inch glass dish. Sprinkle top with nuts. Chill and serve in squares.

Marie King
Thomas, Oklahoma

APRICOT SALAD

2 pkg. apricot gelatin
1 lge. can apricots
1 pt. vanilla ice cream
1 can orange slices, diced

Dissolve gelatin in 2 cups boiling water. Drain and reserve 2 cups apricot juice. Add to dissolved gelatin. Add ice cream to warm gelatin. Fold in diced fruits. Pour in a 12 to 13-inch pan. Chill until firm.

Mrs. Blanche Parrish
Worthington, West Virginia

APRICOT GELATIN SALAD

2 boxes orange gelatin
2 c. boiling water
1 lge. can apricots, drained and mashed
1 lge. can crushed pineapple, drained
10 marshmallows, cut up
½ c. sugar
2 tbsp. flour
1 c. whipped cream, whipped

Combine first 5 ingredients, preparing gelatin with boiling water and allowing to cool before adding fruits and marshmallows. Pour into mold; congeal. Combine 1 cup reserved apricot juice with next 2 ingredients. Heat in double boiler, stirring constantly; let cool. Add whipped cream. Pour on top of congealed salad. Serve with grated cheese topping.

Mrs. G. N. Voss
Greenville, Texas

APRICOT-PINEAPPLE CONGEALED SALAD

1 envelope unflavored gelatin
½ c. apricot syrup
½ c. salad dressing
½ c. sour cream
1 17-oz. can apricots, drained and chopped
1 lge. can crushed pineapple
2 pkg. orange gelatin
2 c. hot water
1 c. pineapple juice
1 c. miniature marshmallows

Soften and dissolve unflavored gelatin and syrup over hot water. Combine salad dressing and sour cream; add to gelatin mixture. Pour mixture into a 1 1/2-quart oiled mold. Chill until firm. Chill fruits. Dissolve orange gelatin in hot water; add pineapple juice. Chill until slightly thickened. Fold in fruit and marshmallows. Pour into mold over first gelatin mixture. Chill until firm. Unmold on greens. Orange gelatin may be dissolved in 1 cup hot water with 1 cup ginger ale added when dissolved.

Mrs. Raymond C. Davis
Ellerbe, North Carolina

APRICOT SALAD

2 pkg. orange gelatin
2 c. hot water
1 No. 2 can crushed pineapple, drained
1 No. 2 can apricots, drained and diced
1 c. nuts
1 c. marshmallows

Dissolve gelatin with hot water. Drain fruits; add 1 cup reserved juice to gelatin mixture. Congeal slightly. Add nuts, marshmallows and fruits; congeal.

TOPPING:

½ c. sugar
3 tbsp. flour
1 egg, slightly beaten
1 c. reserved fruit juices
2 tbsp. butter
1 c. whipped cream
¾ c. cheese

Combine sugar, flour, and egg; gradually stir in juice. Cook over low heat, stirring constantly. When thickened, stir in butter and cool completely. Add whipped cream; top with grated cheese. Spoon mixture over congealed salad. Yield: 20 servings.

Mary Ann Johnston
Jefferson, Georgia

APRICOT SALAD

1 lge. can crushed pineapple
1 lge. can apricots
2 pkg. orange gelatin
Miniature marshmallows

Drain fruits well; reserve juice. Dissolve gelatin in 2 cups boiling water; add 1/2 cup reserved apricot juice and 1/2 cup reserved pineapple juice. Cool. Mash apricots with a fork and add with pineapple to gelatin. Pour in dish and top with marshmallows. Chill until firm.

Mrs. Grace Gibson
Bruceton Mills, West Virginia

AUTUMN SALAD

2 3-oz. pkg. orange gelatin
2 c. boiling water
1 No. 2 ½ can apricot halves
1 3-oz. pkg. cream cheese
1 c. green seedless grapes, cut in rounds
½ c. diced toasted almonds
1 ½ c. miniature marshmallows

Dissolve gelatin in boiling water. Measure syrup from drained apricots; add water to make 2 cups. Stir into gelatin; chill to consistency of unbeaten egg white. Soften cream cheese in double boiler; add to beaten apricots. Add grapes, almonds and marshmallows. Fold into gelatin; pour into 1 large mold or 2 small ones. Chill until firm.

Mrs. Leon Alexander
Killen, Alabama

GELATIN FRUIT SALAD

1 envelope gelatin
½ c. cold water
2 tbsp. lemon nectar
3 or 4 drops yellow color
1 ½ c. hot water
⅓ c. sugar
⅛ tsp. salt
1 med. can apricots
1 sm. can pineapple
1 sm. can orange and grapefruit slices
1 sm. can peaches

Soften gelatin in cold water. Add nectar and yellow color. Add hot water, sugar and salt. Let stand in refrigerator until gelatin begins to set. Grease ring mold with small amount of salad oil. Drain apricot halves; arrange in bottom of ring mold with pit side up. Pour part of gelatin over fruit. Drain pineapple slices; cut each slice in half and arrange around edge of mold. Drain orange and grapefruit slices; arrange on next layer. Pour more gelatin over fruit. Arrange drained peaches on next layer; add remaining gelatin. Let stand in refrigerator until firm. Unmold on salad plate with greens; serve with salad dressing. Yield: 10-12 servings.

Alberta Cromer
Townville, South Carolina

FRUIT GELATIN SALAD

1 pkg. lemon gelatin
2 c. boiling water
1 sm. can crushed pineapple
½ c. canned apricots
1 sm. can white cherries
1 grapefruit, sectioned
Paprika

Dissolve gelatin in boiling water. When partially set, add combined fruits which have been drained. Serve with fruit dressing or mayonnaise. Sprinkle with paprika.

Ada McCracken
Jonesboro, Tennessee

ORANGE-APRICOT SALAD

1 12-oz. pkg. dried apricots
1 ½ c. water
2 pkg. orange gelatin
1 c. hot water or fruit juice
1 sm. can crushed pineapple
2 tbsp. lemon juice
1 c. fine slivered almonds

Cook apricots in water until very soft. Stir until almost a pulp. Dissolve gelatin in hot water. Add apricot pulp, crushed pineapple, lemon juice and almonds; stir until well mixed. Congeal. Serve on lettuce leaf and top with mayonnaise.

Mrs. Henry Sherrer
Bay City, Texas

AVOCADO CONGEALED SALAD

1 pkg. lime gelatin
1 c. hot water
1 avocado, mashed
1 tbsp. lemon juice
½ tsp. salt
1 c. grapefruit sections, unsweetened
1 c. cottage cheese
2 c. mayonnaise

Mix all ingredients well. Chill until firm. Serve on lettuce.

Leila Kennedy
Rome, Georgia

AVOCADO SALAD

1 pkg. lime gelatin
1 c. hot water
1 avocado
1 c. cottage cheese
1 tbsp. lemon juice
½ tsp. salt
2 tbsp. mayonnaise
1 diced orange or grapefruit

Dissolve gelatin in hot water; let set till begins to thicken. To partially molded gelatin, add 1/2 avocado, mashed; add cottage cheese, lemon juice, salt and mayonnaise. Beat with egg beater until blended. Add diced orange and remaining half of avocado, sliced. Let mold in refrigerator; serve on lettuce with deviled eggs.

Mrs. Will T. Butts, Jr.
Knoxville, Tennessee

CONGEALED AVOCADO-CHEESE SALAD

1 pkg. lime gelatin
2 c. water and juice from pineapple
1 avocado
1 pkg. cream cheese
1 can crushed pineapple
1 c. nuts

Prepare gelatin as directed on package with water and pineapple juice. Mash avocado and cheese well and mix thoroughly. Add to gelatin with pineapple and nuts; chill until firm.

Mrs. Robert Davis
La Pryor, Texas

FRESH GRAPE AND AVOCADO SALAD

2 envelopes unflavored gelatin
1 c. cold water
1 c. hot water
½ c. sugar
¼ tsp. salt
1 c. fresh orange juice
¼ c. fresh lemon juice
1 ½ c. seeded Tokay grapes
1 c. diced avocados
Salad greens
Mayonnaise (opt.)

Soften gelatin in cold water; stir in hot water. Add sugar and salt and stir until dissolved. Blend in orange and lemon juices; chill until mixture begins to thicken. Fold in grapes and avocados. Turn into an oiled 5-cup mold. Chill until firm and ready to serve. Unmold on a salad plate and garnish with salad greens. Serve with mayonnaise, if desired. Yield: 8-10 servings.

Mrs. Julia Nunley
Bryson, Texas

BLUEBERRY GELATIN SALAD

1 c. pineapple juice
1 can blueberries in heavy syrup
1 lge. pkg. lemon gelatin
1 c. mashed bananas
½ pt. whipping cream, whipped with sugar and vanilla

Heat pineapple juice and drained blueberry juice and dissolve gelatin in the hot juices. Cool. When thick, add bananas and drained blueberries. Chill a little while longer and fold in whipped cream lightly, making a marble effect. Mold in fancy dishes or large serving dish.

Mrs. Velma Hudson
Hereford, Texas

BLUEBERRY SALAD

1 sm. can crushed pineapple
1 can blueberries
2 3-oz. boxes lemon gelatin
3 mashed bananas
½ pt. whipping cream

Drain and reserve pineapple juice and blueberry juice. Bring to boil and add gelatin. Add 1/2 cup cold water. Put blueberries, pineapple and bananas into gelatin mixture and let congeal. Whip the whipping cream and fold into congealed gelatin mixture. Let stand in refrigerator until firm.

Mrs. W. S. Young, Jr.
Hendersonville, Tenn.

BLUEBERRY SALAD

1 No. 3 can pineapple chunks
1 No. 2 can blueberries
2 pkg. raspberry gelatin
½ c. chopped nuts

Drain pineapple and blueberry juices and combine juices. Add enough water to make 3 1/2 cups. Heat 1/2 the liquid and dissolve gelatin in hot liquid. Combine fruits with gelatin; add nuts. Pour into molds or large dish and refrigerate overnight.

Mrs. R. H. Crowder
West Point, Mississippi

CHERRY CHEESE SALAD

4 pkg. cherry gelatin
2 tsp. salt
4 c. boiling water
1 c. cola beverage
½ c. vinegar
1 ½ c. cold water
1 can crushed pineapple, drained
1 can cherries, drained
1 ½ c. diced celery
½ c. pecans, chopped
1 sm. pkg. cream cheese, cubed

Dissolve gelatin and salt in boiling water. Add cola beverage, vinegar and cold water. Chill until slightly thickened. Add remaining ingredients. Chill until firm.

Mrs. W. W. Jackson
Johnston, South Carolina

BING CHERRY MOLD

1 6-oz. pkg. black cherry gelatin
1 c. hot water
1 c. cold water
1 No. 2 ½ can pitted Bing cherries
1 7-oz. can crushed pineapple
1 No. 2 ½ can grapefruit sections

Put gelatin in bowl; add hot water and stir until gelatin dissolves. Add the cold water. Drain fruits; add 2 cups juice to the gelatin. Mix well and add drained fruit. Chill until firm. Serve with mayonnaise or fruit dressing.

Mrs. Holland Ware
Atlanta, Georgia

CHERRY MOLD

1 1-lb. can pitted dark sweet cherries
1 1-lb. can pitted light sweet cherries
1 lge. grapefruit
2 3-oz. pkg. cherry gelatin
2 c. hot apple juice
½ tsp. ground ginger
Dash of salt

Drain cherries, reserving syrup. Peel and section grapefruit, working over bowl to catch juice. Combine cherry and grapefruit juices to measure 1 3/4 cups liquid. Dissolve gelatin in hot apple juice. Add ginger and salt; stir to blend. Stir in fruit juices and chill until slightly thickened. Set aside a few cherries for garnish. Add remaining fruit to thickened gelatin. Pour into 2-quart mold. Chill until firm. Unmold on plate; garnish with dressing, cherries and mint leaves. Yield: 8 servings.

Mrs. Herman Brossmann
Schulenburg, Texas

BING CHERRY SALAD

1 c. juice from cherries and pineapple
1 sm. pkg. cherry gelatin
½ c. cream cheese, diced
¼ c. drained Bing cherries
¼ c. drained chunk pineapple
½ c. pecans, chopped
1 sm. bottle cola beverage
1 c. miniature marshmallows (opt.)

(Continued on next page)

Heat the fruit juices and stir in the gelatin until dissolved. Chill until thickened. Mix in cream cheese, cherries, pineapple, nuts, cola beverage and marshmallows. Stir until completely mixed. Chill until firm. Yield: 10-12 servings.

Mrs. Bill Stout
Piedmont, Oklahoma

CHERRY SALAD

½ c. sugar
1 pkg. cherry gelatin
1 pkg. gelatin, unflavored
1 No. 2 can cherry pie filling
1 No. 2 can crushed pineapple
Rind and juice of 1 orange
Rind and juice of 1 lemon
¼ c. cold water
1 c. pecans, chopped

Mix sugar in cherry gelatin. Measure liquid from cherries and pineapple, orange and lemon juice; add enough water to make 3 cups. Heat to boiling. Dissolve gelatin in cold water; add to hot mixture. Fold in cherries, nuts, pineapple, orange and lemon rind. Congeal and serve in individual molds or in squares. Yield: 10 servings.

Mrs. Ernest Ray
Commerce, Georgia

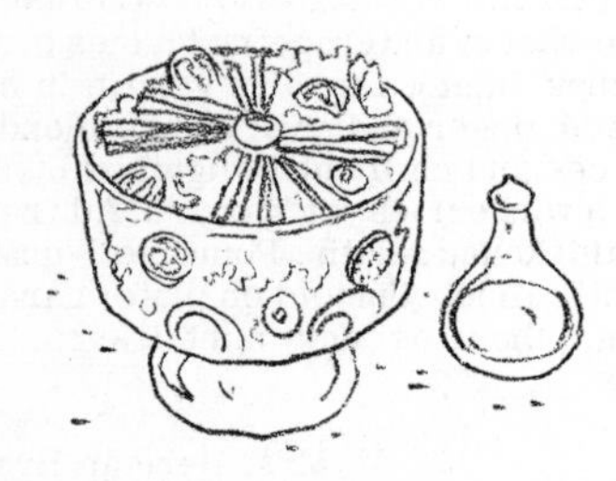

HEAVENLY HASH

1 pkg. cherry gelatin
½ c. whipped cream
1 c. chopped nuts
1 bottle cherries
1 apple, cut up
1 banana, sliced
½ c. marshmallows

Prepare gelatin according to package directions. Chill until begins to thicken. Add whipped cream, beating into gelatin. Add fruits and nuts. Chill until firm.

Mrs. J. T. Vanderford
Piedmont, Alabama

WHITE FRUIT SALAD

2 envelopes gelatin
½ c. cold water
½ c. cherry juice
½ c. pineapple juice
2 tbsp. sugar
1 c. milk
1 No. 2 can seeded white cherries
1 c. crushed pineapple
½ lb. blanched almonds, chopped
1 c. mayonnaise

Soften gelatin in cold water. Combine cherry and pineapple juice and heat to boiling. Pour over softened gelatin and stir until dissolved. Add sugar. Cool and add milk. Chill until mixture begins to thicken. Fold in fruits and nuts. Fold in mayonnaise; beat lightly and transfer to lightly oiled molds. Chill until firm. Turn out on lettuce leaves and serve with mayonnaise or whipped cream.

Mrs. Bernard Lentz
Utica, Mississippi

CONGEALED FRUIT SALAD

3 tbsp. unflavored gelatin
½ c. cold water
⅓ c. sugar
1 c. hot fruit juice
1 c. diced pineapple
2 bananas, diced
1 c. grapefruit pulp
1 c. orange pulp
8 cherries, cut in halves
12 English walnuts

Soak the gelatin in cold water for 5 minutes. Dissolve sugar in hot juice; add gelatin. Set aside to cool. When gelatin begins to set, add the fruits and nuts. Pour into a mold which has been rinsed in cold water; chill. When set, unmold on a bed of lettuce; serve with mayonnaise.

Mrs. Mildred Watford
Abbeville, Alabama

CRANBERRY MOLD

1 pkg. raspberry gelatin
1 ½ c. hot water
½ c. jellied or whole cranberry sauce
1 3-oz. pkg. cream cheese
2 c. drained pineapple and coconut, combined
1 c. chopped pecans

Mix gelatin and boiling water and cool. Mix cranberry sauce with softened cheese. Mix pineapple, coconut and nuts into cream cheese mixture. Add to cool gelatin. Chill until firm in favorite mold or dish. Yield: 8 servings.

Mrs. J. D. Williams
Florence, Alabama

CRANBERRY-CHEESE SALAD

1 sm. pkg. strawberry gelatin
1 c. crushed cranberries
1 c. chopped pecans
1 sm. pkg. lime gelatin
1 lge. can crushed pineapple
1 sm. pkg. lemon gelatin
1 lge. pkg. cream cheese

Prepare strawberry gelatin according to package directions. Add cranberries and pecans. Pour in large mold and chill until firm. Prepare lime gelatin according to package directions. Add crushed pineapple; cool. Pour over first layer and chill until firm. Prepare lemon gelatin according to package directions. Add cream cheese and cool. Pour over second layer and chill until firm.

Mrs. John J. McKeithen
Wife of Governor of Louisiana
Baton Rouge, Louisiana

CRANBERRY MOLD

1 c. ground raw cranberries
1 c. ground unpared raw apple
1 c. sugar
1 pkg. lemon gelatin
1 c. hot water
1 c. pineapple syrup
½ c. seeded Tokay grapes
¼ c. broken walnuts
6 pineapple slices

Combine cranberries, apple and sugar. Dissolve lemon gelatin in hot water; add pineapple syrup. Chill until partially set. Add cranberry-apple mixture, grape halves and walnut meats. Pour into 6 individual molds; chill until firm. Unmold cranberry salads on 6 pineapple slices on crisp lettuce. May be served with mayonnaise.

Mrs. Don Jones
Albany, Georgia

CRANBERRY-CREAM CHEESE

1 sm. pkg. miniature marshmallows
1 lb. fresh cranberries, ground
1 No. 2 can crushed pineapple
1 c. sugar
3 3-oz. pkg. raspberry gelatin
5 c. boiling water
1 pt. cream, whipped
1 c. chopped nuts

Combine marshmallows, cranberries, pineapple and 1/2 cup sugar. Let sit in refrigerator overnight. Dissolve gelatin in boiling water. Let stand until syrupy. Fold in whipped cream sweetened with 1/2 cup sugar. Stir in chopped nuts and cranberry mixture. Stir well and refrigerate until set. Yield: 12-14 servings.

Mrs. Herman W. East
Ajo, Arizona

CRANBERRY SALAD

1 c. hot water
2 pkg. cherry gelatin
1 c. hot water
1 c. sugar
1 tbsp. lemon juice
1 c. pineapple juice
1 c. crushed pineapple
1 c. chopped celery
½ c. pecans
1 c. raw ground cranberries

Dissolve gelatin in hot water. Add sugar, lemon juice and pineapple juice. Chill until partly set. Add remaining ingredients. Chill until firm. Yield: 12 servings.

Mrs. Forrest F. Stevens
Ponchatoula, Louisiana

CRANBERRY SALAD

2 pkg. lemon gelatin
1 lb. cranberries
24 white grapes
½ orange with peel
3 tbsp. crushed pineapple
1 c. sugar

Dissolve gelatin in 2 cups boiling water. Refrigerate to set. Put cranberries, grapes and orange through food chopper. Add pineapple and sugar; mix well. Add mixture to gelatin when partly set. Mix well and chill. Serve on lettuce.

Mrs. James O. Dugger
Butler, Tennessee

MRS. GODWIN'S SALAD MOLD

1 pkg. fresh cranberries
1 orange
2 c. sugar
2 pkg. lemon gelatin
3 c. hot water
1 c. chopped pecans
1 c. chopped celery

Grind cranberries and orange. Add sugar and let stand. Dissolve gelatin in hot water and cool. Combine all ingredients. Put in molds and chill until firm.

Mrs. Mills E. Godwin, Jr.
Wife of Governor of Virginia
Richmond, Virginia

EGGNOG CHRISTMAS SALAD

1 No. 2 can crushed pineapple
1 tbsp. unflavored gelatin
3 tbsp. fresh lime juice
1 ½ c. dairy eggnog
¾ c. finely chopped celery
1 pkg. raspberry gelatin
1 ½ c. boiling water
1 10-oz. pkg. cranberry-orange relish

Drain pineapple syrup into saucepan; soften unflavored gelatin in syrup. Add lime juice; heat until gelatin dissolves. Cool. Add eggnog. Chill until partially set. Fold in pineapple and celery. Turn into a 7-cup salad mold and chill until set. Dissolve raspberry gelatin in boiling water. Add cranberry-orange relish. Chill until partially set. Pour over eggnog layer. Chill. Yield: 8-10 servings.

Mrs. A. B. Dobson
Duncan, South Carolina

MY FAVORITE CRANBERRY SALAD

2 c. cranberries
1 c. sugar
1 c. water
1 pkg. cherry gelatin
2 c. chopped celery
1 c. peeled and chopped apple
24 miniature marshmallows
Nuts (opt.)

Put the first three ingredients in a saucepan and bring to a gentle boil. Cook until the berries start to pop. Add gelatin to the hot juice and dissolve. When cool, add the other ingredients. Refrigerate in individual molds or 1 large dish until well set.

Ruth Baldwin
Oklahoma City, Oklahoma

RED AND GREEN RIBBON RING

1 3-oz. pkg. strawberry gelatin
1 1-lb. can whole cranberry sauce

Dissolve strawberry gelatin in 1 cup boiling water. Add cranberry sauce, mixing well. Chill until partially set. Pour into 8-cup ring mold or two 8 1/2 x 4 1/2 x 2 1/2-inch loaf pans. Chill until almost firm.

CHEESE LAYER:

1 3-oz. pkg. lemon gelatin
1 8-oz. pkg. cream cheese, softened
1 c. crushed pineapple
¼ c. chopped pecans (opt.)
1 3-oz. pkg. lime gelatin
2 tbsp. sugar
2 c. grapefruit sections

Dissolve lemon gelatin in 1 cup boiling water; add cheese, beating smooth with beater or blender. Add pineapple with syrup. Chill until partially set. Stir in pecans. Pour over cranberry layer in mold. Chill until almost firm. Dissolve lime gelatin and sugar in 3/4 cup boiling water. Add grapefruit with syrup. Chill until partially set. Pour over cheese layer. Chill overnight. Unmold. Yield: 10-12 servings.

Mrs. Nettie Searcy
Pleasant Shade, Tennessee

SEVEN-UP HOLIDAY SALAD

1 pt. cranberries
½ c. water
½ c. sugar
1 pkg. lemon gelatin
1 c. hot water
1 c. Seven-Up
¼ tsp. salt
1 c. chopped apple
1 c. chopped celery
1 c. chopped nuts

Boil cranberries in cold water then sieve. Add sugar and heat until dissolved. Cool. Dissolve gelatin in hot water; cool slightly. Add Seven-Up; chill. When partly thickened, add cranberry mixture, salt, apple, celery and nuts. Chill until firm. Serve on lettuce with mayonnaise.

Mrs. Ernest Waddell
Fort Worth, Texas

SPICY PEACH-CRANBERRY RING

1 No. 2 ½ can peach halves
1 tsp. whole cloves
1 3-in. stick cinnamon
¼ c. vinegar
1 pkg. lemon gelatin
1 c. fresh cranberries
½ unpeeled orange
⅓ c. sugar
1 ¾ c. hot water
1 pkg. cherry-flavored gelatin

(Continued on next page)

Drain peaches. Add water to peach syrup to make 1 3/4 cups. Add cloves, cinnamon and vinegar; simmer, uncovered, 10 minutes. Add peaches; heat slowly 5 minutes. Remove peaches; place, with cut sides up, in 3-quart ring mold. Strain peach syrup and measure. Add hot water to make 1 2/3 cups. Add to lemon gelatin, stirring until dissolved; pour over peaches. Refrigerate till almost firm. Put cranberries and orange through food chopper, using medium blade. Stir in sugar. Add hot water to cherry gelatin; stir until dissolved. Cool. Stir in cranberry-orange mixture. Pour over almost firm peach layer. Refrigerate till firm. Unmold; fill center with greens. Serve with Lemon-Cream Mayonnaise. Yield: 10-12 servings.

LEMON-CREAM MAYONNAISE:

3 tbsp. lemon juice
3 tbsp. heavy cream
3 tbsp. confectioners' sugar
Dash of salt

Mix all ingredients well. Omit cream and fold in 1/2 cup heavy cream, whipped, if desired.

Mrs. John D. Thompson
Fort Worth, Texas

RAW CRANBERRY SALAD

2 c. raw cranberries
2 apples
1 peeled orange
1 unpeeled orange
2 c. sugar
½ c. chopped celery
1 c. chopped black walnuts
2 pkg. lemon gelatin
3 c. hot water

Put cranberries, apples and oranges through coarse blade of chopper. Add sugar, celery and nuts. Add gelatin to hot water and let cool until syrupy. Add mixture and refrigerate until firm.

Debbie Hamilton
Hendersonville, North Carolina

WALNUT JEWEL SALAD

1 pkg. pineapple gelatin
1 c. hot water
½ tsp. salt
1 c. cold liquid (drained pineapple juice plus water)
1 c. chopped raw cranberries
½ c. crushed pineapple, drained
½ c. diced celery
½ c. California walnuts, chopped

Dissolve gelatin in hot water. Add salt and cold water-pineapple juice mixture. Chill until slightly thickened. Fold in remaining ingredients. Turn into a 1-quart mold or into 8 individual molds. Chill until firm. Unmold onto bed of crisp lettuce; decorate with additional walnut halves or pieces. Serve with sour cream, Honey-Creme Salad Dressing or dressing of your choice.

HONEY-CREME SALAD DRESSING:

1 3-oz. pkg. cream cheese
¼ tsp. salt
2 tbsp. honey
¼ c. sour cream

In small bowl whip or mash cheese with salt, honey and sour cream. For smoother dressing, whip with beater.

Photograph for this recipe on page 91.

ANGEL FOOD SALAD

1 pkg. lemon gelatin
1 ½ c. boiling water
1 tbsp. unflavored gelatin
1 12-oz. carton cottage cheese
⅛ tsp. salt
½ c. black walnuts, English walnuts or pecans, chopped
1 No. 2 can fruit cocktail, drained
Red and green maraschino cherries
1 No. 2 can crushed pineapple
½ c. flaked coconut
½ c. evaporated milk (opt.)

Dissolve lemon gelatin in boiling water. Dissolve unflavored gelatin in a little cold water. Add to lemon gelatin. Let cool until begins to set. Combine remaining ingredients with gelatin. Chill until firm.

Lois W. King
Rural Retreat, Virginia

COLA SALAD

1 No. 2 can fruit cocktail
1 can crushed pineapple
1 lge. box raspberry gelatin
1 lge. box strawberry gelatin
½ lb. pecans
1 lge. pkg. cream cheese
1 lge. cola beverage

Drain fruits. Put liquid in a small pan; bring to a boil. Pour over gelatins; let cool. Add nuts, fruits, cream cheese and cola beverage. Put in refrigerator to jell.

Mrs. R. L. Crowell
Denver, Tennessee

COTTAGE-FRUIT SALAD

1 pkg. lemon or orange gelatin
1 c. hot water
2 tbsp. lemon juice
1 ½ c. cottage cheese
1 ½ c. well-drained canned fruit cocktail

Dissolve gelatin in hot water; add lemon juice. Chill until syrupy. Beat with egg beater until foamy. Add cheese and continue to beat with egg beater until well-blended. Fold in fruit. Pour into 1-quart mold. Chill until set. Carefully run knife around edge to loosen. Unmold. Garnish with greens and bits of fruit. Yield: 6 servings.

Mrs. George Wheat
Clifton, Tennessee

MILLIONAIRE FRUIT SALAD

2 pkg. orange or lemon gelatin
1 c. boiling water
1 No. 2 can fruit cocktail, drained (saving juice)
1 c. orange slices, cut in pieces
1 pkg. cream cheese, softened with milk
1 sm. can crushed pineapple, drained (saving juice)
1 c. coconut
1 c. chopped pecans
1 c. miniature marshmallows
1 pt. whipping cream, whipped

Dissolve gelatin in boiling water. Add 2 1/2 cups combined reserved juice. Add cold water or orange juice if necessary. Place in refrigerator to jell. Whip congealed gelatin mixture; fold in the drained fruits, softened cream cheese, coconut, chopped pecans, miniature marshmallows and whipped cream. Return to the refrigerator until firm.

Mrs. Larner Davis
Stephenville, Texas

FRUIT GELATIN

1 pkg. strawberry or cherry gelatin
1 c. boiling water
1 doz. lge. or 1 c. small marshmallows
1 c. cold water
1 can fruit cocktail, drained
½ c. shredded coconut
1 c. pecans
3 bananas

Add gelatin to boiling water; add marshmallows. Stir well; add to cold water. Add fruit cocktail, coconut, pecans and bananas; stir. Chill until firm.

Mrs. J. A. Whitehead
Sinton, Texas

QUICK GELATIN SALAD

2 pkg. flavored gelatin
1 pt. ice cream
1 lge. can fruit cocktail

Prepare gelatin according to package directions. Chill until begins to thicken. Add ice cream; mix by hand or with mixer on low speed. Drain fruit cocktail. Stir in, mixing thoroughly. Chill until firm.

Thelma Farmer
Summers, Arkansas

RIBBON SALAD

1 3-oz. pkg. lemon gelatin
1 envelope unflavored gelatin
¼ c. cold water
½ c. fruit cocktail syrup
1 pt. creamed cottage cheese
1 1-lb. can fruit cocktail, drained
1 3-oz. pkg. cherry gelatin

Lightly oil a 9 x 5 x 3-inch loaf pan. Prepare lemon gelatin according to package directions. Pour into pan; chill until firm. Soften unflavored gelatin in cold water. Bring fruit cocktail syrup to a boil. Remove from heat and dissolve unflavored gelatin in hot syrup. Stir into cottage cheese. Add fruit cocktail. Spread evenly over lemon gelatin. Chill until firm. Prepare cherry gelatin according to package directions; chill until mixture mounds when dropped from a spoon. Pour over cheese layer. Chill until firm. Unmold on lettuce.

Mrs. Lewis Mecimore
Taylorsville, North Carolina

FRUIT NECTAR SALAD

1 envelope unflavored gelatin
2 tbsp. sugar
¼ tsp. salt
1 12-oz. can apricot nectar
½ c. water
8 whole cloves
1 tbsp. lemon juice
1 ½ c. drained, diced mixed fruits

(Continued on next page)

Mix gelatin, sugar and salt thoroughly in a small saucepan; add nectar, water and cloves. Place over low heat; stir until gelatin is dissolved. Simmer 5 minutes. Remove from heat; strain to remove cloves. Add lemon juice; chill to unbeaten egg white consistency. Fold in mixed, drained fruits. Turn into a 3-cup mold or individual molds; chill until firm. Unmold on serving platter; garnish with greens and fruit. Serve with salad dressing. If fresh or frozen pineapple is used, boil for 2 minutes before combining with the gelatin. Peach or pear nectar may be substituted for apricot. Yield: 6 servings.

Guadalupe Gonzalez
Alice, Texas

HOLIDAY SALAD

1 pkg. lime gelatin
5 c. hot water
½ c. halved seeded grapes
1 pkg. lemon gelatin
1 c. canned pineapple juice
1 3-oz. pkg. cream cheese
½ c. mayonnaise or salad dressing
1 pkg. strawberry gelatin
1 banana, sliced
Curly endive

Dissolve the lime gelatin in 2 cups hot water. Chill until slightly thickened. Add the grapes. Pour into a 10 x 5 x 3-inch loaf pan. Chill until firm. Dissolve the lemon gelatin in 1 cup hot water. Add the pineapple juice. Gradually add to the cream cheese, blending until smooth. Chill until slightly thickened. Blend into the mayonnaise. Beat until fluffy. Pour on top of the lime gelatin layer. Chill until firm. Dissolve the strawberry gelatin in 2 cups hot water; chill until slightly thickened. Add the sliced banana and pour over the lemon gelatin and cream cheese layer. Chill until firm. Unmold and garnish with endive. Yield: 12-16 servings.

Mrs. Arthur Welchlin
Farmville, Virginia

LIME-CHEESE DELIGHT

1 buffet-sized can crushed pineapple
1 8-oz. can light seedless grapes
1 c. water
1 3-oz. pkg. lime gelatin
1 3-oz. pkg. cream cheese
½ c. chopped nuts
1 c. miniature marshmallows

Drain liquid from pineapple and grapes; heat with 1 cup water. Cream gelatin and cream cheese together until free of lumps. Add boiling water and juice mixture; stir until gelatin is dissolved. Let cool; add pineapple, grapes, nuts, and miniature marshmallows. Refrigerate until firm. Yield: 10 servings.

Mrs. A. L. Douglas
Miles, Texas

LIME RING-MOLD SALAD

1 pkg. lime gelatin
1 c. hot water
1 c. pineapple juice
1 3-oz. pkg. cream cheese, cut in small cubes
1 8-oz. can spiced white grapes, drained
½ c. crushed pineapple, drained
½ c. pecans

Dissolve gelatin in hot water; add pineapple juice. Fold in remaining ingredients. Chill until firm. Yield: 6 servings.

Mrs. Marion E. Causey
Centreville, Mississippi

GRAPEFRUIT SALAD WITH BUTTERCUP DRESSING

1 c. boiling water
1 pkg. lemon or orange gelatin
2 lge. fresh grapefruit, halved
1 No. 2 can crushed pineapple, undrained

Pour boiling water over gelatin. Cool until mixture begins to thicken slightly. Remove all sections from the grapefruit rind. Combine grapefruit sections with crushed pineapple. Add to the gelatin mixture. Pour into hollowed grapefruit halves. Chill until firm. If rind extends too far above the firm gelatin, trim with a knife. When ready to serve, cut grapefruit in half again. Serve plain or with Buttercup Dressing.

BUTTERCUP DRESSING:

½ c. fruit juice
3 tbsp. flour
½ tsp. salt
½ c. sugar
2 eggs, separated
3 marshmallows
¼ c. pecans, chopped (opt.)
⅛ c. lemon juice
½ c. whipped cream

(Continued on next page)

Heat fruit juice. Combine flour, salt and sugar; blend with just enough fruit juice to make a smooth paste. Add to remaining fruit juice and cook for 15-20 minutes or until thickened. Stir in slightly beaten egg yolks and cook for 5 minutes longer. Remove from heat; add marshmallows. Cool. Add nuts and lemon juice. Fold in stiffly beaten egg whites and whipped cream.

Mrs. Mary C. Dyches
Fort Mill, South Carolina

MASHED BANANA SALAD

½ c. crushed pineapple
1 pkg. lime gelatin
1 ¾ c. boiling water
1 lge. or 2 sm. bananas, mashed
½ c. peanuts
1 3-oz. pkg. cream cheese
1 tbsp. mayonnaise

Drain pineapple, reserving 1 tablespoon juice. Dissolve gelatin in boiling water; cool. Fold in bananas, pineapple and peanuts. Pour into mold; let set until congealed. Combine cream cheese, reserved pineapple juice and mayonnaise. Unmold congealed salad on lettuce; serve with cream cheese mixture.

Mrs. Norris Miles
Clarksville, Tennessee

AMBROSIA MOLD

1 c. liquid from oranges and grapes
1 pkg. orange gelatin
1 c. ginger ale
½ tsp. almond flavoring
1 11-oz. can mandarin orange slices, drained
1 8-oz. can seedless white grapes, drained
1 c. coconut, shredded

Bring juices to boil; add gelatin. Stir until dissolved. Add ginger ale and almond flavoring. Chill until slightly firm. Fold in orange slices, grapes and coconut. Chill in individual molds. Serve on lettuce. Sprinkle a little coconut on top. Two or three fresh oranges peeled and sliced may be substituted for mandarin oranges. Add 1 to 2 tablespoonfuls sugar.

Mrs. Mary Sue E. Spencer
Virginia Beach, Virginia

BRAZILIAN FRUIT SALAD

1 11-oz. can mandarin oranges, drained
1 banana, sliced
1 red apple, cored and thinly sliced
¼ c. maraschino cherries
½ c. red grapes
1 c. coarsely chopped celery
2 tbsp. sliced Brazil nuts
¼ tsp. dried mint leaves (opt.)
1 tsp. lemon juice
3 tbsp. mayonnaise or salad dressing
2 tbsp. sour cream
Salad greens

Combine oranges, banana, apple, cherries, grapes, celery and nuts in a bowl. Add dried mint leaves. Sprinkle with lemon juice. Blend mayonnaise and sour cream; combine with fruit mixture or serve dressing separately. Serve on salad greens. Yield: 4-6 servings.

Cindy Mann
Lexington, Mississippi

DAIRY ORANGE SALAD

1 c. boiling water
1 pkg. orange gelatin
2 c. miniature marshmallows
1 sm. can frozen orange juice, undiluted
½ c. sugar
1 sm. pkg. cream cheese
1 sm. can crushed pineapple
1 c. cottage cheese
2 mashed bananas
1 c. mandarin oranges
½ pt. whipped cream
1 pkg. plain gelatin

Pour hot water over gelatin; add marshmallows and stir until gelatin is dissolved. Thaw orange juice and stir in sugar; add to gelatin mixture. Mix cream cheese thoroughly with crushed pineapple; add to gelatin. Add cottage cheese, bananas and orange sections; stir until mixed well. Fold in whipped cream and plain gelatin; mix. Pour in mold and let set for 3 hours.

Martha Lynn Gower
Pleasant View, Tennessee

HEAVENLY ORANGE FLUFF

2 pkg. orange gelatin
2 c. hot water
1 sm. can frozen orange juice, undiluted
2 cans mandarin oranges, drained
1 lge. can crushed pineapple, undrained

(Continued on next page)

Mix gelatin with hot water. Stir in undiluted orange juice; cool. Add mandarin oranges and pineapple to gelatin mixture. Pour in 13x11-inch dish. Congeal.

TOPPING:

1 pkg. instant lemon pudding
1 c. milk
½ pt. whipping cream

Beat pudding with milk until slightly firm. Whip cream; fold into pudding. Spread on gelatin. Cut in squares and serve on lettuce. Yield: 12-15 servings.

Mrs. Sidney G. Ingram
Statesville, North Carolina

MANDARIN ORANGE AND PINEAPPLE SALAD

1 sm. can crushed pineapple, drained
1 can mandarin oranges, drained
1 pkg. orange gelatin
2 tbsp. sugar (opt.)
1 sm. pkg. cream cheese
1 pkg. small marshmallows
½ pt. heavy cream, whipped

Drain pineapple and orange sections; add enough water to make 2 cups liquid. Heat liquid to boiling; pour over gelatin and sugar. Stir to dissolve. Add cream cheese and marshmallows to hot mixture; stir to dissolve. Let cool. Add pineapple and orange sections. Place in refrigerator. When mixture is consistency of syrup, fold in whipped cream; mix well. Pour into mold which has been rinsed with cold water. Refrigerate until firm. Yield: 12-15 servings.

Mrs. Harry Anthony
Hartsville, Tennessee

ORANGE GELATIN

2 pkg. orange gelatin
2 c. hot water
2 c. cold water
1 No. 2 ½ can pears
2 or 3 bananas, sliced

Dissolve gelatin in hot water; add cold water. Chill until consistency of syrup; beat with electric mixer until fluffy. Arrange half of fruit in serving bowl and pour half the gelatin over them. Add remaining fruits and gelatin. Chill until firm.

Mrs. Jack Ramsey
Thomaston, Georgia

MANDARIN ORANGE SALAD

2 3-oz. pkg. orange gelatin
2 c. hot water
1 pt. orange sherbet
1 can mandarin oranges, drained
1 sm. can crushed pineapple
1 egg
½ c. sugar
2 tbsp. lemon juice
1 tbsp. grated orange peel
1 tsp. lemon peel, grated
1 c. whipped cream

Dissolve gelatin in hot water; add sherbet. When mixture begins to congeal, fold in oranges and pineapple; chill until firm. Beat egg in a saucepan; add sugar, lemon juice and grated peels. Cook in double boiler till mixture is thick. When cool, fold in whipped cream. Serve sauce over congealed salad.

Mrs. Daniel Sloan
Nashville, Tennessee

ORANGE MANDARIN SALAD

2 pkg. orange gelatin
1 pkg. unflavored gelatin
2 c. hot water
1 c. fresh or frozen orange juice
1 c. sour cream
2 c. orange sherbet
2 cans mandarin oranges, drained
1 c. pineapple chunks

Dissolve gelatins in hot water. Add orange juice; place in refrigerator until mixture begins to congeal. Mix sour cream and sherbet thoroughly; fold in mandarin oranges and pineapple chunks. Blend into gelatin mixture. Pour into large salad mold; chill.

Mrs. John G. Davis
Conway, North Carolina

ORANGE SALAD

1 pkg. orange gelatin
1 c. boiling water
2 c. miniature marshmallows
1 sm. can frozen orange juice
½ c. sugar
1 sm. pkg. cream cheese
1 sm. can crushed pineapple
1 c. cottage cheese
2 bananas, mashed
1 sm. can mandarin oranges
½ pt. cream, whipped

(Continued on next page)

Dissolve gelatin in boiling water with marshmallows. Add frozen orange juice in which sugar has been dissolved. Soften cream cheese and add to pineapple; add to gelatin mixture. Add cottage cheese, bananas, mandarin oranges and fold in whipped cream. Pour salad in large flat pan or baking dish. Place in refrigerator for at least 3 hours. Yield: 15 servings.

Mrs. A. J. Stafford
Limestone, Tennessee

ORANGE SHERBET SALAD

2 pkg. orange gelatin
2 c. boiling water
1 pt. orange sherbet
1 can mandarin oranges, drained
1 c. crushed pineapple
2 sliced bananas

Dissolve gelatin in boiling water. Add orange sherbet; allow to melt. Add mandarin oranges, pineapple and bananas; chill. Yield: 12-15 servings.

Mrs. Curtis Francis
Canadian, Texas

ORANGE SHERBET SALAD

2 pkg. orange gelatin
2 c. hot water
1 can mandarin orange slices
1 sm. can crushed pineapple
1 pt. orange sherbet

Dissolve gelatin in hot water; drain juices from orange slices and crushed pineapple. Add sherbet to gelatin. When mixture begins to congeal, add fruit. Chill till firm.

Mrs. Gus Fowler
Franklinton, Louisiana

SUNSHINE SALAD

1 pkg. orange gelatin
½ c. sugar
1 c. boiling water
1 sm. can crushed pineapple, drained
1 can mandarin orange slices, drained
½ pt. sour cream

Dissolve gelatin and sugar in hot water; add fruit. Refrigerate until mixture has cooled. Add sour cream, folding in thoroughly. Chill until firm.

Mrs. Marvin C. Grubbs
Griffin, Georgia

GEORGIA PEACH SALAD

2 ¼ c. orange juice
2 3-oz. pkg. orange gelatin
6 tbsp. sugar
1 tsp. lemon rind
2 c. buttermilk
1 c. coarsely chopped fresh peaches
1 c. canned blueberries
Salad greens
1 c. sour cream

Heat 2 cups orange juice to simmering; remove from heat. Add orange gelatin; stir until dissolved. Mix in sugar and lemon rind; chill until gelatin mixture mounds when spooned. Gradually add buttermilk, beating constantly with rotary beater until blended; fold in peaches and blueberries. Pour into a 6-cup mold; chill until set. Unmold on salad greens. Blend sour cream and remaining orange juice together gently; serve over salad. Yield: 8 servings.

Mrs. R. P. Wolfe
Winston-Salem, North Carolina

PEACH GELATIN RING

1 No. 2 ½ can peach halves
½ tsp. whole cloves
1 6-in. stick cinnamon
¼ tsp. salt
2 3-oz. pkg. orange-pineapple gelatin
2 c. orange juice
Unpared apple or plum wedges,
or slices of jellied cranberry
sauce, cut in 3 wedges

Drain peaches, reserving syrup; add water to syrup to make 2 cups. In saucepan, combine syrup mixture, spices and salt; cover and simmer 10 minutes. Remove from heat; add gelatin, stirring to dissolve. Let stand, covered 10 minutes to steep. Strain; add orange juice. Pour about half of the gelatin into a 6 1/2-cup ring mold; chill both portions of gelatin till partially set. When gelatin in mold will support fruit, alternate peach halves and fruit wedges around mold, pushing fruit down into gelatin. Pour remaining gelatin over; chill till firm. Unmold on greens. Yield: 8-10 servings.

Mrs. H. E. Leflett
Rogers, Arkansas

PEACH AND BANANA MOLD

1 pkg. lime, lemon-lime or strawberry gelatin
1 c. boiling water
1 8-oz. can sliced peaches
1 sliced banana

Dissolve gelatin in boiling water. Drain peaches, adding syrup to gelatin; chill until thick. Fold in peaches and banana; pour into 1-quart mold. Chill until firm; unmold. Yield: 6 servings.

Thelma Farmer
Summers, Arkansas

PEACH-CREAM CHEESE LOAF

1 1-lb. 13-oz. can peach slices
1 envelope unflavored gelatin
¼ c. lemon juice
½ c. boiling water
¼ c. sugar
½ tsp. salt
½ tsp. grated lemon rind
2 3-oz. pkg. cream cheese
¼ c. mayonnaise
½ c. orange sections
¼ c. sliced maraschino cherries
Salad greens

Drain peach slices, reserving 3/4 cup syrup. Soften gelatin in lemon juice; dissolve in boiling water. Stir in sugar, salt and grated lemon rind. Add peach syrup to cream cheese gradually; stir in mayonnaise and gelatin mixture. Chill until slightly thickened; fold in 1 1/2 cups chopped peaches, orange sections and maraschino cherries. Turn mixture into an oiled 7 1/2x 3 1/2x3-inch loaf pan; chill until firm. Unmold on crisp salad greens; arrange remaining peach slices on top. Cut in slices to serve. Yield: 6-8 servings.

Mrs. Everette Bruce
Vaiden, Mississippi

PEACH-CREAM SALAD

1 1-lb. can sliced peaches
1 envelope plain gelatin
¼ c. lemon juice
2 tbsp. water
1 3-oz. pkg. cream cheese
2 tbsp. mayonnaise
¼ tsp. salt
¼ tsp. grated onion
1 tsp. horseradish
7 maraschino cherries
½ c. evaporated cream, chilled until icy
1 c. diced celery

Drain peaches; save syrup. Reserve 6 peach slices; dice remainder. Add water to syrup to make 3/4 cup. Soften gelatin in mixture of lemon juice and water. Heat peach syrup; add gelatin mixture and stir to dissolve; cool. Mix softened cream cheese, mayonnaise, salt, onion and horseradish. Stir in gelatin mixture. Chill until slightly thickened. Oil one 6-cup mold; arrange in bottom 6 peach slices with red cherry in each center. Whip evaporated milk in chilled bowl until stiff. Fold into gelatin mixture; fold in diced peaches and celery. Pour just enough in mold to cover all but tips of peach slices. At each tip place a cherry. Chill until partially set. Add remaining mixture. Chill until firm. Unmold and garnish. Serve with mayonnaise blended with whipped milk.

Mrs. Florrie Capo
St. Augustine, Florida

PEACH SALAD

1 pkg. orange gelatin
1 can peaches
1 can mandarin oranges
¼ c. nuts

Prepare gelatin according to directions on package. Drain peaches and oranges; add nuts. Combine with gelatin; chill.

Mrs. Mont McCray
Aline, Oklahoma

WAIKIKI SURPRISE SALAD

1 pkg. lime gelatin
½ c. boiling water
1 c. peach and pineapple juice
1 buffet-sized can drained peaches
1 buffet-sized can drained crushed pineapple
2 bananas, cut up
Salad greens
½ c. grated cheese

Dissolve gelatin in boiling water; cool slightly. Add peach and pineapple juice. Set in pan of ice water; stir until thick. Add drained peaches, crushed pineapple and cut up bananas. Pour into mold; chill until firm. Unmold onto bed of crisp greens; top with grated cheese. Yield: 4 servings.

Mrs. J. D. Williams
Florence, Alabama

STUFFED SPICED PEACH SALAD

1 No. 2 ½ can spiced peaches
1 3-oz. pkg. cream cheese
Thick cream
½ c. nuts, chopped
1 tbsp. candied pineapple, finely diced
Salt to taste
1 pkg. apple gelatin

Remove pits from peaches carefully. Soften cream cheese; blend with sufficient thick cream to make fluffy. Add chopped nuts, diced pineapple and sprinkle of salt; mix. Stuff peach cavities; set aside. Heat juice from spiced peaches, adding enough water to make 1 cup; dissolve gelatin in hot juice. Add 1 cup ice water; refrigerate until mixture begins to set. Rinse square refrigerate dish in cold water; place stuffed peaches in dish. Over the peaches, pour the chilled gelatin. Refrigerate until firm. Cut in squares so that a peach half will be in each serving; place on lettuce. Serve with dabs of mayonnaise and whipped cream blended.

Mrs. Otto Murphy
Springfield, Tennessee

WINONA'S LUCKY SALAD

2 envelopes unflavored gelatin
1 c. warm water
⅓ c. sugar
½ tsp. dry mustard
2 tbsp. lemon juice
½ pt. sour cream
2 3-oz. pkg. cream cheese, at room temperature
1 11-oz. can mandarin oranges, drained
1 1-lb. can sliced peaches, drained
1 1-lb. 14-oz. can pitted, dark sweet cherries, drained
2 c. miniature marshmallows
½ pt. whipping cream, whipped

Soften gelatin in warm water. Combine sugar, mustard, lemon juice, sour cream and cream cheese; beat until well blended. Chill until mixture thickens and begins to set; beat until smooth. Fold in fruit, marshmallows and whipped cream. Pour into round No. 2 or 2 1/2 fruit cans; freeze. To serve, unmold, slice and arrange slices on crisp lettuce leaves. If desired, top with whipped or sour cream. Yield: 8-10 servings.

Winona Kennedy
Niota, Tennessee

SALAD

1 box lemon gelatin
1 c. hot water
1 8-oz. carton sour cream
1 lge. can diced pears
½ c. green grapes, cut in half
1 c. oranges, cut up

Mix gelatin in hot water; refrigerate until thickened. Add sour cream and beat at high speed until foamy, about 5 minutes. Add pears, grapes and oranges. Return to refrigerator until firm. Yield: 10-12 servings.

Mrs. Cleva Harper
Falmouth, Kentucky

VERSATILE SALAD

2 3-oz. pkg. orange gelatin
1 3-oz. pkg. lemon gelatin
3 c. hot water
1 pt. or 1 No. 2 can pears
1 No. 2 can crushed pineapple
¾ c. mayonnaise or salad dressing
4 c. diced celery
½ c. grated coconut
1 c. chopped nuts

Dissolve gelatins in hot water; cool. Drain fruits, reserving juices. Add enough water to juices to make 3 cups; add to cooled gelatin. Congeal mixture to consistency of unbeaten egg whites; fold in mayonnaise. Mix in remaining ingredients evenly. Chill until firm. Yield: 15-20 servings.

Mrs. Dorothy S. Sims
Lamar, South Carolina

APRICOT NECTAR SALAD

1 3-oz. box orange gelatin
1 12-oz. can apricot nectar
1 c. crushed pineapple
2 bananas, chopped
½ c. chopped nuts
½ c. miniature marshmallows

(Continued on next page)

Dissolve gelatin in 1/2 can hot nectar. Add remaining nectar and chill until syrupy. Add pineapple, chopped bananas, nuts and marshmallows. Cover and chill in icebox till firm.

Mrs. Harold Kling
Nardin, Oklahoma

CHEESE-PINEAPPLE SALAD

1 envelope unflavored gelatin
¼ c. cold water
¾ c. sugar
½ c. pineapple juice
1 c. grated cheese
1 c. crushed pineapple, drained
1 c. heavy cream, whipped
1 7-oz. can jellied cranberry sauce, sliced very thin

Soften gelatin in cold water. Dissolve sugar in pineapple juice over low heat. Add softened gelatin and stir until dissolved. Chill until syrupy; fold in cheese, pineapple and whipped cream. Chill in 1 1/2-quart mold until firm. Garnish with fancy shapes cut from canned cranberry sauce slices. Yield: 6-8 servings.

Mrs. Earl L. Faulkenberry
Lancaster, South Carolina

CONGEALED FRUIT SALAD

1 pkg. lemon gelatin
1 c. hot water
½ c. creamy cottage cheese
1 c. heavy cream, whipped
½ c. chopped pecans
½ c. maraschino cherries, quartered
1 c. crushed pineapple, drained

Dissolve gelatin in hot water. Chill until partially set. Fold in remaining ingredients. Pour into 1-quart dish. Chill until firm, about 4 hours. Yield: 8 servings.

Julia Dykes
Bay City, Texas

FROSTED SALAD

2 sm. boxes lemon gelatin
2 c. boiling water
2 c. Seven-Up
1 20-oz. can crushed pineapple
1 c. miniature marshmallows
2 lge. bananas

Dissolve gelatin in water; stir in Seven-Up. Chill until partially set. Drain pineapple, reserving juice for topping. Add to gelatin with bananas and marshmallows. Pour into oblong shallow dish. Let set.

TOPPING:

½ c. sugar
2 tbsp. flour
1 beaten egg
1 c. pineapple juice
2 tbsp. butter
1 c. whipping cream

Mix first 4 ingredients and cook till thick. Add butter and cool. When cold, fold mixture into whipped cream. Spread on gelatin.

Mrs. J. R. Thompson, Jr.
Refugio, Texas

COTTAGE CHEESE SALAD

2 sm. boxes or 1 family size pkg. lime gelatin
2 c. boiling water
1 lb. cottage cheese
1 c. mayonnaise
1 tall can evaporated milk
1 c. pecans
1 c. miniature marshmallows
1 tbsp. sugar
2 c. chopped apples
1 c. crushed pineapple

Dissolve gelatin in boiling water; let cool. Add each of the remaining ingredients one at a time, stirring well after each addition. Chill until firm.

Mrs. Edward K. Caudill
Sparta, North Carolina

FRUIT AND GELATIN SALAD

½ lb. grapes, halved
3 oranges, diced
3 med. red apples, diced
1 can pineapple tidbits
1 c. raisins
1 pkg. each cherry and lime gelatin

Combine grapes, oranges and apples with pineapple and raisins; mix all in a large bowl. Prepare cherry and lime gelatins separately and let set in separate bowls for 2 hours. Cut in chunks and mix with above fruits. Set for 2 to 4 hours in refrigerator.

Mrs. James Wyly
Camden, Tennessee

FRUIT SALAD SQUARES

1 No. 2 can pineapple pieces
1 1-lb. can halved white cherries
½ c. sugar
3 tbsp. cornstarch
1 envelope unflavored gelatin
¼ tsp. salt
½ c. orange juice
¼ c. lemon juice
1 egg, slightly beaten
1 orange, peeled and diced
2 c. tiny marshmallows
½ c. chopped nuts
1 c. heavy cream, whipped

Drain pineapple pieces and white cherries reserving 1/2 cup syrup from each. Combine juice in saucepan with sugar, cornstarch, unflavored gelatin, salt, orange juice and lemon juice. Cook, stirring constantly till mixture thickens; cook 2 minutes. Add small amount to 1 slightly beaten egg. Return to hot mixture and cook 1 minute. Cool to room temperature; fold in diced orange, tiny marshmallows, chopped nuts and whipped cream. Pour into 11x7x2-inch dish. Chill till set. Cut in squares and top with a marachino cherry. Yield: 12 servings.

Mrs. G. C. Holmes
Johnston, South Carolina

GOLDEN DELIGHT

2 pkg. lemon gelatin
2 No. 2 cans diced or crushed pineapple, drained
4 bananas, sliced
½ c. nuts, chopped (opt.)
1 pkg. marshmallows, cut in fourths

Dissolve lemon gelatin according to package directions; cool until partially thickened. Add pineapple and bananas; add nuts and marshmallows. Chill until firm.

TOPPING:

½ c. sugar
¼ tsp. salt (opt.)
2 tbsp. flour
1 c. pineapple juice and water
1 or 2 eggs, well-beaten
1 to 2 tbsp. butter (opt.)
1 envelope unflavored gelatin
¼ c. cold water (opt.)
1 c. whipped cream
1 c. sharp cheese, grated

Mix sugar, salt, flour and juice; stir in eggs. Cook over low heat until thick, stirring constantly. Stir in butter. Soften unflavored gelatin in cold water and dissolve in hot mixture. Chill until partially thickened. Fold in cream; pile on firm lemon gelatin layer. Sprinkle with cheese. Chill until firm. Yield: 15 servings.

Elain Love
Concord, North Carolina

GELATIN SALAD

1 box lime or lemon gelatin
1 c. boiling water
⅔ c. mayonnaise
½ c. water
½ c. chopped nuts
1 sm. jar maraschino cherries
1 c. crushed pineapple
3 medium bananas
3 stalks celery, chopped
1 ¼ c. sm. marshmallows

Dissolve gelatin in boiling water; cool. Mix mayonnaise with 1/2 cup water; add to other ingredients. Chill until firm.

Mrs. Grace Gibson
Bruceton Mills, West Virginia

HOLIDAY SALAD

¾ c. boiling water
1 3-oz. pkg. lime gelatin
15 lge. marshmallows
1 3-oz. pkg. cream cheese
½ c. mayonnaise
1 ½ to 2 c. crushed drained pineapple
1 c. mashed bananas
½ c. chopped pecans
½ c. milk

Add boiling water to gelatin. Add marshmallows and cream cheese and cook over low heat until dissolved. Cool, then add remaining ingredients. Refrigerate until congealed.

Mrs. Olen Ariail
Carnesville, Georgia

MOLDED COLA SALAD

2 boxes cherry gelatin
1 No. 2 can crushed pineapple, drained
1 sm. bottle maraschino cherries, drained
3 6-oz. bottles cola beverage
2 3-oz. pkg. cream cheese
1 c. finely chopped celery
¼ tsp. salt
1 ½ c. chopped nuts

Dissolve gelatin in heated juice from pineapple and cherries. Add cola. Cream the cheese and slowly add gelatin mixture. Mix well. Chill until almost set; add remaining ingredients. Pour into bowl and chill in refrigerator until firm.

Mrs. J. A. Whitehead
Sinton, Texas

IMITATION CRANBERRY SALAD

1 pkg. cherry gelatin
1 hot cola
1 cold cola
1 c. chopped nuts
1 lge. can pineapple, drained
1 orange, peeled and grated
1 apple, peeled and grated

Mix gelatin with boiling cola; add ice cold cola. Add nuts, pineapple, grated orange and apple. Place in refrigerator until firm.

Mrs. Roy Linker
Harrisburg, North Carolina

MOTHER'S DAY SALAD

1 pt. hot water
2 pkg. orange gelatin
½ c. miniature marshmallows
1 No. 2 can crushed pineapple
1 11-oz. can mandarin oranges
1 c. coconut
1 c. cottage cheese
Chopped nuts (opt.)
1 pkg. dessert topping

Pour hot water over gelatin and marshmallows. Stir until well dissolved and marshmallows are melted. Drain juice from pineapple and orange sections; add enough water to make pint of liquid. Add to gelatin mixture and set in refrigerator until not too firm. Add pineapple, oranges, coconut, cottage cheese and nuts. Add dessert topping prepared by directions on package. Mix and let set until firm. A few nuts sprinkled on top makes a nicer looking salad.

Mrs. Miller Stewart
Lebanon, Tennessee

PINEAPPLE-CHEESE SALAD

2 pkg. unflavored gelatin
1 c. water
1 8-oz. pkg. cream cheese, softened
¾ c. mayonnaise
1 ⅓ c. evaporated milk
1 6-oz. jar maraschino cherries and juice
1 16-oz. can crushed pineapple and juice
1 c. chopped nuts
1 10 ½-oz. pkg. miniature marshmallows

Mix unflavored gelatin in water. Mix with other ingredients and cool. Chill several hours before serving.

Mrs. Anthony Jilek
Gainesville, Florida

PINEAPPLE-CHEESE SALAD

2 3-oz. pkg. lemon gelatin
2 c. hot water
½ c. cold water
¼ c. lemon juice
1 14 ½-oz. can crushed pineapple, undrained
1 c. halved seedless green grapes
2 c. finely grated American cheese
1 c. chopped nuts

Dissolve gelatin in hot water; add cold water and lemon juice. Chill until syrupy. Fold in remaining ingredients; pour into a mold. Refrigerate until firm.

Mrs. Bob McCain
Maben, Mississippi

PINEAPPLE-CHEESE SALAD

2 pkg. lemon gelatin
2 c. boiling water
2 c. cold water
6 bananas, peeled and sliced
2 c. miniature marshmallows
½ c. sugar
3 tbsp. cornstarch
2 8 ½-oz. cans crushed pineapple, undrained
1 c. heavy cream
1 c. shredded cheddar cheese

Dissolve gelatin in boiling water; add cold water. Chill until syrupy. Stir in sliced bananas and marshmallows. Pour into a 9x13x2-inch pan. Chill until set. Mix sugar and cornstarch; add to undrained pineapple. Cook over medium heat, stirring constantly until thickened. Cool. Whip cream and fold into pineapple mixture along with half the shredded cheese. Spread mixture on congealed lemon gelatin. Sprinkle remaining cheese over top. Chill overnight. Cut in squares. Yield: 12-15 servings.

Mrs. A. D. Jenkins
Warsaw, Virginia

SEVEN-UP SALAD

1 box lemon gelatin
1 c. hot water
1 tsp. sugar
1 8-oz. pkg. cream cheese, softened
¼ c. pecans, chopped
1 tsp. vanilla
¼ c. cherries, chopped
1 sm. can crushed pineapple, drained
1 bottle Seven-Up

(Continued on next page)

Dissolve gelatin in hot water; add sugar. Chill until slightly thickened. Beat cream cheese until very creamy; gradually add gelatin. Beat constantly. Add remaining ingredients. Chill until firm.

Mrs. Gus Fowler
Franklinton, Louisiana

SEVEN-UP SALAD

2 pkg. lemon gelatin
2 c. hot water
2 c. Seven-Up
1 lge. can crushed pineapple, drained
1 c. sm. marshmallows
2 bananas
2 tbsp. butter
½ c. sugar
1 c. pineapple juice
2 tbsp. flour
1 egg
1 c. whipping cream
Cheddar cheese

Dissolve gelatin in hot water. Let cool and add Seven-Up, pineapple, marshmallows and bananas. Place in refrigerator and let jell. Cook the butter, sugar, pineapple juice, flour and egg as a pudding. When mixture cools, fold in the whipping cream. Spread over the jelled mixture and cover with cheese. Chill and serve. Yield: 10-12 servings.

Mrs. James E. Conrad
Owenton, Kentucky

PINEAPPLE FLOWER POT SALAD

1 1-lb. 4 ½-oz. can crushed pineapple
1 3-oz. pkg. lime gelatin
½ c. half and half
1 8-oz. pkg. cream cheese
2 tbsp. lemon juice
¼ c. mayonnaise
1 11-oz. can mandarin oranges, drained
¾ c. sliced celery
½ c. chopped walnuts

Heat undrained pineapple to boiling. Add gelatin stirring until dissolved; cool. Stir in half and half; chill until slightly thickened. Combine softened cream cheese with lemon juice and mayonnaise. Blend into thickened gelatin. Fold well-drained oranges, celery and walnuts into gelatin. Turn into 1 1/2-quart mold. Chill until firm; unmold. Decorate as desired with pineapple slices and tidbits, ripe olives or mandarin oranges. Yield: 8 servings.

Mrs. F. J. Turner
Smithfield, Virginia

BLUE PLUM SALAD DELIGHT

2 pkg. pineapple gelatin
1 ½ c. boiling water
½ c. plum juice
1 tbsp. unflavored gelatin
1 No. 2 can crushed pineapple
1 lge. can blue plums, diced
½ pt. sour cream

Dissolve pineapple gelatin in boiling water. Pour the plum juice over the unflavored gelatin and let set until juice is absorbed or 5 minutes. Add to dissolved pineapple gelatin and mix well. Add the crushed pineapple and remaining plum juice. Refrigerate until begins to congeal. Fold in the plums and sour cream. Pour into a mold. May be served plain, with sour cream, whipped cream or mayonnaise.

Mrs. Lillian Herman
Bay City, Texas

GREENGAGE PLUM SALAD

2 3-oz. pkg. lime gelatin
1 c. boiling water
1 pt. lime sherbet
1 8 ½-oz. can crushed pineapple
1 c. miniature marshmallows
1 1-lb. 14-oz. can greengage plums, drained and chopped
½ pt. whipping cream, whipped

Dissolve gelatin in boiling water. Add lime sherbet. When partially set, add other ingredients. Fold in the whipped cream last. Chill until firm.

Mrs. Kendrick Mullins
Sparta, Tennessee

PRUNE SALAD

1 pkg. raspberry gelatin
Prune juice
1 c. chopped prunes
1 sm. can crushed pineapple, drained
½ c. chopped pecans
Whipped cream
Honey

Prepare gelatin according to directions on package, using prune juice for water. Chill until mixture begins to thicken. Fold in prunes, pineapple and nuts. Chill until firm. Mix whipped cream and small amount of mayonnaise; sweeten with a little honey. Serve over salad.

Mrs. L. E. Terry
Cookeville, Tennessee

RASPBERRY SALAD

1 pkg. raspberry gelatin
1 c. boiling water
1 tsp. lemon juice
1/8 tsp. salt
Sprinkle of red pepper
1 box frozen raspberries, thawed
2/3 c. applesauce

Dissolve gelatin in 1 cup boiling water. Add seasonings and raspberries; allow to jell slightly. Fold in applesauce; chill. Serve with dressing of equal parts mayonnaise and whipped cream.

Mrs. Daisy P. Graham
Millport, Alabama

FRUIT SALAD

2 c. diced rhubarb
1/2 c. sugar
2 tbsp. unflavored gelatin
1/2 c. water
2 c. frozen strawberries
1 c. ginger ale
Red food coloring

Cook diced rhubarb and sugar. Soften unflavored gelatin in water. Add hot rhubarb; stir well. Cool slightly. Add strawberries, ginger ale and red food coloring to color.

Viola L. Heinrichs
Corn, Oklahoma

RHUBARB SALAD

1 pkg. raspberry gelatin
1 c. hot, sweetened rhubarb
1 c. crushed pineapple
1/2 c. pineapple juice
1 c. diced raw apple

Mix gelatin with rhubarb while hot. Add other ingredients. Pour into mold and chill until firm.

Mrs. Harold F. Nichols
Bluff City, Tennessee

RHUBARB SALAD

2 c. boiling rhubarb sauce
2 pkg. raspberry gelatin
1/2 c. boiling water
2 c. cold water or pineapple juice
1 c. chopped pineapple
1 c. chopped nuts
1 c. diced celery

Boil rhubarb sauce; dissolve gelatin in 1/2 cup boiling water. Mix all ingredients and place in pan to chill.

Mrs. Earl Caston
Wewaka, Oklahoma

RHUBARB SALAD

1 pkg. strawberry gelatin
1 c. boiling hot rhubarb sauce
1 c. cold water or pineapple juice
1 c. chopped apples
1 c. chopped walnuts or pecans

Dissolve gelatin in hot sauce. Add juice and cool. Add apples and nuts; pour into individual molds. Serve with cream cheese or cottage cheese dressing.

Mrs. H. A. Henderson
Florence, Alabama

SPICY RAISIN SALAD

1 13 1/2-oz. can pineapple, crushed or tidbits
1 c. raisins
1 pkg. lemon gelatin
1/2 tsp. (or more) whole cloves
1/4 tsp. ground cinnamon

Drain pineapple and divide into 8 individual molds. Add enough water to juice to make 2 cups liquid. Add raisins and spices; bring to a boil. Skim out cloves; add gelatin. Stir until dissolved; pour into molds. Chill. Serve topped with sour cream or any fruit dressing.

Ida F. Limerick
Morgantown, West Virginia

FRESH STRAWBERRY SALAD

3 pkg. strawberry gelatin
3 c. hot water
1 lge. can crushed pineapple
2 medium bananas, cut in pieces
2 sm. pkg. frozen strawberries, thawed
1 c. sour cream
1 sm. pkg. softened cream cheese (opt.)

Dissolve gelatin in hot water; mix together pineapple, bananas and strawberries. Pour into gelatin mixture. Chill until firm. Combine sour cream and cream cheese. Ice congealed salad with sour cream mixture.

Mrs. J. C. McElroy, Jr.
Cuba, Alabama

FRUIT SALAD WITH SWEET DRESSING

2 pkg. raspberry gelatin
3 c. boiling water
1 sm. pkg. frozen strawberries
1 No. 2 can crushed pineapple

Dissolve gelatin in boiling water. Let set until begins to thicken. When mixture thickens, add partially thawed strawberries and crushed pineapple. Pour into mold to set.

DRESSING:

1 egg
¼ c. honey
1 tbsp. lemon juice
Dash of salt
4 marshmallows, diced
¼ c. whipping cream

Beat egg; add honey, lemon juice and salt. Cook until thickened. Add marshmallows. Cool. Add cream and serve with salad.

Chlois McInnish
Talladega, Alabama

STRAWBERRY-NUT SALAD

1 sm. pkg. strawberry gelatin
½ c. boiling water
1 10-oz. pkg. frozen strawberries, thawed, not drained
1 8-oz. can crushed pineapple
½ c. chopped pecans
½ pt. sour cream

Combine gelatin with boiling water; stir until dissolved. Fold strawberries, pineapple and pecans into gelatin. Turn 1/2 mixture into rectangular dish; refrigerate until firm. Spread with sour cream. Gently spoon remaining strawberry mixture over sour cream. Chill until firm.

Mrs. Douglas Wright
Ramseur, North Carolina

STRAWBERRY SALAD

2 pkg. strawberry gelatin
1 ½ c. boiling water
1 No. 303 can pineapple
1 pkg. frozen strawberries

Dissolve gelatin in boiling water; add fruits. Pour into ring mold and congeal.

TOPPING:

8 to 10 marshmallows
1 c. sour cream

Combine marshmallows with sour cream. Chill overnight. Unmold salad onto plate. Place topping in center and garnish with a few whole strawberries.

Mrs. John Meadows, Jr.
Columbia, Alabama

STRAWBERRY SALAD

2 pkg. strawberry gelatin
1 c. boiling water
1 No. 2 can crushed pineapple
½ bag miniature marshmallows
1 pt. frozen strawberries
1 pkg. dessert topping
1 3-oz. pkg. cream cheese
Nuts, finely chopped

Dissolve gelatin in boiling water. Add pineapple, marshmallows and strawberries. Place in refrigerator and chill until set. Prepare dessert topping according to directions on package. Combine with cream cheese. Spread over top of first layer. Sprinkle nuts over all.

Barbara Smalling
Tellico Plains, Tennessee

STRAWBERRY SALAD

1 3-oz. pkg. strawberry gelatin
2 ½ c. boiling water
1 10-oz. pkg. frozen strawberries
1 pkg. lemon gelatin
½ c. pineapple juice
1 3-oz. pkg. cream cheese
½ c. drained crushed pineapple
1 c. heavy cream, whipped

Dissolve strawberry gelatin in 1 1/2 cups boiling water. Add strawberries and stir until berries are completely thawed. Pour into a flat dish and chill until firm. Dissolve lemon gelatin in 1 cup boiling water. Add pineapple juice and cool. Blend in softened cream cheese and crushed pineapple and chill until slightly thickened. Fold in whipped cream and pour lemon mixture over firm strawberry mixture. Chill until firm. Yield: 10-12 servings.

Mable Carpenter
Mercer County, Kentucky

VEGETABLE SALADS

Recipe for Caesar Salad on Page 142

ASPARAGUS-RADISH SALADS

3 tbsp. olive oil
1 tbsp. vinegar
1 tsp. salt
Freshly ground pepper
1 sm. clove of garlic, crushed
20 to 25 radishes, thinly sliced
Green asparagus, cooked and chilled
Salad greens

Mix oil, vinegar, salt, pepper and garlic. Add radishes; marinate for 2 to 3 hours. Place asparagus on salad greens. Arrange the radishes on top. Pour remaining marinade over radishes. Yield: 4 servings.

Mrs. Aussie A. Miller
Newton, Texas

GREEN ASPARAGUS SALAD

3 cans whole green asparagus
1 tsp. dried tarragon leaves
Fresh ground black pepper
1 tsp. garlic salt
1 bottle Italian dressing
½ c. tarragon vinegar

Drain asparagus well. Place in layers on shallow pan; sprinkle each layer with a little dry tarragon, ground black pepper and garlic salt. Cover with salad dressing and vinegar; let stand overnight at room temperature. Chill and serve on lettuce leaves. Top with mayonnaise flavored with a little of the marinade.

Mrs. Winthrop Rockefeller
Wife of the Governor of Arkansas
Little Rock, Arkansas

CREAMY GREEN BEAN SALAD

1 can French-style green beans
½ tsp. finely chopped garlic
¾ tsp. salt
Dash of pepper
2 tbsp. vinegar
3 tbsp. salad oil
2 tbsp. evaporated milk
¼ c. thinly sliced onion

Drain beans well; cover and chill. Place garlic on waxed paper; add salt and mash with flat of knife. Combine pepper, vinegar, oil, milk and garlic in a jar; shake well. Pour over beans and onion; mix. Serve on bed of lettuce.

Mrs. J. D. Williams
Florence, Alabama

FAVORITE RED BEAN SALAD

1 1-lb. can red beans
3 hard-boiled eggs
½ c. chopped sweet pickle
⅓ c. mayonnaise
1 tsp. prepared mustard
1 tsp. lemon juice

Combine beans, eggs and pickle. Mix mayonnaise, mustard and lemon juice; add to bean mixture carefully. Yield: 4 servings.

Mrs. Robert Chapman
Uniontown, Kentucky

GREEN BEAN SALAD

1 lb. green beans, cut
1 red pepper
2 lge. white onions
1 c. sugar
¾ c. vinegar
¾ c. water
4 tbsp. vegetable oil
2 cloves of garlic

Cook beans and red pepper in salted water until tender. Slice onions over beans; set aside. Mix sugar, vinegar, water, oil and garlic; pour over beans and chill for 12 hours. Serve on bed of watercress; decorate with quarters of pickled beets.

Mrs. Estelle Shalla
Bay City, Texas

GREEN BEAN SALAD

1 can green beans
1 can wax beans
1 can kidney beans
½ c. chopped sweet peppers
¾ c. sugar
1 sliced onion
⅔ c. vinegar
½ c. salad oil
1 tsp. salt
Black pepper to taste

Drain all beans well. Mix all ingredients and let stand overnight.

Hazel M. Stanberry
Todd, North Carolina

FIVE-BEAN SALAD

½ c. wine vinegar
½ c. sugar
½ c. oil
Salt and pepper to taste
1 can each garbanza, green, kidney, baby lima and yellow wax beans
1 green pepper, sliced
1 onion, sliced

Heat vinegar, sugar, oil and seasoning; pour over beans, pepper and onion. Stir and mix well. Let stand overnight.

Ethel Reed
Oklahoma City, Oklahoma

KIDNEY BEAN SALAD

1 15-oz. can red kidney beans, drained
½ c. diced celery
2 tbsp. dill pickle, chopped
2 tbsp. minced onion
¼ tsp. salt
Dash of pepper
1 tbsp. salad oil
1 tbsp. mild vinegar

Combine all ingredients; toss together lightly. Chill well. Heap into bowl. Garnish with onion rings or hard-cooked eggs. Yield: 4-5 servings.

Blanford T. Anderson
Chatham, Virginia

GARDEN PATCH SALAD

1 can French-style green beans, drained
1 ½ c. finely chopped celery
1 c. chopped onion
1 c. sweet green and red peppers
3 tbsp. Italian dressing
½ c. sugar
½ c. white vinegar

Mix first 4 ingredients together. Combine remaining ingredients; mix well and pour over vegetables. Chill for 24 hours.

Mrs. John Lambright
Springlake, Texas

STRING BEAN AND BACON SALAD

1 tsp. salt
Dash of pepper
½ tsp. sugar
⅓ c. salad oil
2 tbsp. vinegar
3 tbsp. catsup
2 c. cooked green beans or 1 can French-style green beans
Salad greens
3 slices cooked bacon, crumbled

Combine first 6 ingredients; beat well. Toss beans with dressing. Arrange salad greens on plate; top with beans and bacon. Garnish with radish roses. Yield: 6 servings.

Mrs. J. D. Williams
Florence, Alabama

GREEN BEAN SALAD

1 can cut green beans, drained
1 can cut wax beans, drained
1 can kidney beans
½ c. diced onions
½ c diced celery
½ c. pimento
¼ c. sliced green pepper
½ c. vinegar
½ c. sugar
⅓ cup oil
Salt and pepper to taste

Mix all ingredients and let stand overnight for best flavor. Adjust sugar and oil measurement to taste.

Ida F. Simerick
Morgantown, West Virginia

SOUTHERN BEAN SALAD

½ tsp. prepared mustard
⅛ tsp. salt
½ c. mayonnaise
¼ c. vinegar
1 tbsp. minced onion
2 tbsp. minced sweet pickles
2 c. baked beans
Lettuce

Mix first 6 ingredients together thoroughly. Add beans and mix lightly. Serve on lettuce. Yield: 6 servings.

Mrs. Mary P. Murray
De Funiak Springs, Florida

PORK AND BEAN SALAD

2 regular cans pork and beans
1 diced sweet pickle
3 hard-cooked eggs, chopped
½ sm. onion, diced fine
1 tbsp. vinegar
¼ c. mayonnaise

Combine pork and beans, pickle, eggs, onion and vinegar in bowl. Stir in mayonnaise. Yield: 6-8 servings.

Mrs. Beth Trent
Childress, Texas

THREE-BEAN SALAD

2 c. lima beans
2 c. kidney beans
2 c. cooked green beans
1 c. chopped tomato
1 c. sliced celery
½ c. chopped sweet pickles
French dressing

Combine all ingredients except dressing. Add dressing and toss lightly. For better flavor let stand overnight.

Mrs. Ruby Jackson
Santa Anna, Texas

SWEET-SOUR BEAN SALAD

1 No. 2 can green snap beans
1 No. 2 can yellow wax beans
Mild vinegar
Sugar
1 No. 2 can kidney beans
1 med. onion, sliced thin

Drain green and yellow beans, reserving liquid. Measure reserved liquid; add vinegar and sugar in proportionate amounts. Mix all the ingredients together in glass bowl. Cover. Allow to stand overnight. Drain and serve.

Eva Reese
Durham, North Carolina

ZIPPY RED-BEAN SALAD

1 can red kidney beans, drained
6 slices crisply fried bacon, crumbled
1 c. diced celery
½ c. diced dill pickle
2 hard-cooked eggs, diced
⅓ c. mayonnaise
2 tbsp. lemon juice
1 tbsp. minced onion
Salt and pepper to taste

Combine beans, bacon, celery, pickle and eggs in large bowl. Blend mayonnaise with lemon juice, onion, salt and pepper. Pour over salad ingredients and toss lightly. Cover and chill thoroughly. Serve in lettuce-lined bowl. Yield: 6 servings.

Mrs. Q. A. Bradley
Taft, Texas

TRIPLE-BEAN SALAD

½ c. sugar
½ c. salad oil
¾ c. cider vinegar
1 can wax beans
1 can green beans
1 can lge. kidney beans
½ c. chopped celery
1 med. green pepper, cut in strips
1 med. purple onion, sliced into thin rings

Drain beans; toss with celery, green pepper and onion in large bowl. Thoroughly mix sugar, oil and vinegar; pour over vegetables, tossing with a fork to coat evenly. Cover and set in refrigerator at least 8 hours, tossing several times. Baby green limas may be substituted for green beans.

Mrs. G. N. Voss
Greenville, Texas

BEET SALAD

1 can beets, diced or 2 c. fresh cooked beets
1 stalk celery, diced
1 med. onion, chopped fine
2 hard-boiled eggs, diced
Mayonnaise to taste
Salt and pepper to taste
Pinch of sugar (opt.)

Combine beets, celery, onion and eggs in a bowl. Add mayonnaise, salt and pepper. Add a pinch of sugar. Mix all ingredients; chill a few minutes before serving. Yield: 6-8 servings.

Mrs. Kenneth Austin
Gladys, Virginia

PEANUT-BEET SALAD

1 ½ c. diced sweet pickled beets
2 slices crisp fried bacon, crumbled
1 tsp. minced onion
½ c. finely crushed salted peanuts
¼ c. mayonnaise

Combine first 4 ingredients. Toss together with mayonnaise. Chill until ready to serve. Serve on lettuce leaves or layers of watercress.

Mrs. J. C. Biddy
Blair, Oklahoma

BROCCOLI SALAD

1 ½ lb. broccoli spears
6 tbsp. cider vinegar
¼ c. water
½ c. apple juice
Salt and pepper to taste
2 hard-cooked eggs, chopped

Cook broccoli until tender; cool. Mix with next 4 ingredients. Sprinkle eggs over top.

Mrs. Emma Craig
Rowlesburg, West Virginia

CABBAGE RELISH SALAD

3 c. shredded cabbage
½ cucumber, diced
⅓ c. diced celery
½ green pepper, shredded
1 tbsp. minced onion
¾ tsp. salt
½ c. vinegar
⅛ tsp. pepper
½ c. cream

Crisp cabbage, cucumber and celery in iced water. Drain and dry. Blend all other ingredients together except cream and chill in refrigerator. Just before serving stir in cream.

Mrs. O. J. Porter
Centertown, Kentucky

CABBAGE AND PEANUT SALAD

3 c. finely shredded cabbage
1 tsp. salt
¾ c. chopped peanuts
Salad dressing or mayonnaise
Paprika
1 pimento

Crisp cabbage in ice water. Drain well and combine with salt and peanuts. Add salad dressing; garnish with paprika and strips of pimento.

Clara Burton
Chandlerville, Kentucky

CABBAGE SLAW

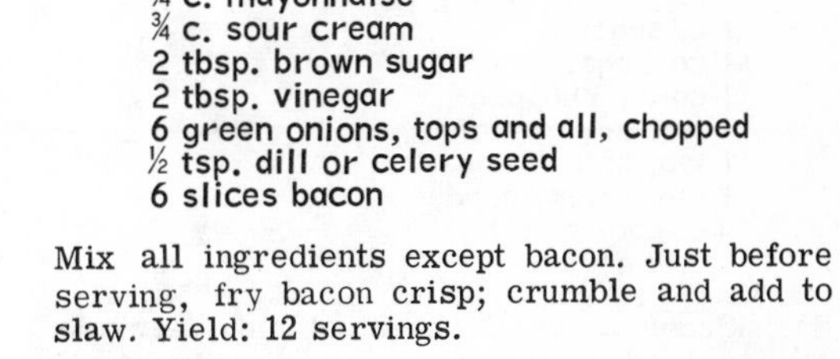

1 lge. head cabbage, shredded
Salt and pepper to taste
¾ c. mayonnaise
¾ c. sour cream
2 tbsp. brown sugar
2 tbsp. vinegar
6 green onions, tops and all, chopped
½ tsp. dill or celery seed
6 slices bacon

Mix all ingredients except bacon. Just before serving, fry bacon crisp; crumble and add to slaw. Yield: 12 servings.

Mrs. O. F. Crider
Leander, Texas

CREAM COLESLAW

4 c. shredded cabbage
½ c. finely sliced celery
¼ c. finely sliced green pepper
2 tbsp. finely sliced green onion
¼ c. finely sliced sweet red pepper or carrots
¾ c. sour cream
3 tbsp. vinegar
3 tbsp. sugar
1 tsp. salt
⅛ tsp. white pepper
1 tbsp. celery seed

Combine cabbage, celery, pepper and onion. Combine remaining ingredients; pour over cabbage mixture. Mix lightly. Yield: 6 servings.

Charlotte B. Love
Bells, Tennessee

COLESLAW

1 med. firm cabbage, shredded
1 c. toasted almonds, sliced
½ c. sliced stuffed green olives
1 c. mayonnaise
½ c. sour cream
⅓ c. wine vinegar
1 tbsp. chopped parsley
1 clove garlic, chopped fine
Salt and red and black pepper to taste

Mix all ingredients. Chill for 2 hours before serving.

Margaret Carre'
New Orleans, Louisiana

GERMAN SLAW

1 c. sugar
1 cabbage, chopped
1 onion, chopped
1 tsp. dry mustard
1 tsp. salt
1 tsp. celery seed
¾ c. cooking oil
1 c. vinegar

Sprinkle sugar over cabbage and onion; set aside. Mix mustard, salt, celery seed, oil and vinegar; bring to boil. Pour over cabbage and onion, while hot. Cool and refrigerate.

Tim Williams
Cleburne, Texas

GERMAN SLAW

¾ c. chopped bacon
2 tbsp. lemon juice
½ tsp. mustard
1 tsp. salt
½ c. mayonnaise
4 tbsp. chopped green pepper
2 c. cabbage, chopped
2 tbsp. parsley
1 onion, chopped

Place bacon in frying pan and cook to golden color. Add lemon juice, mustard and salt. Stir well and mix with mayonnaise. Toss chopped vegetables together with mixed dressing.

Mrs. H. A. Henderson
Florence, Alabama

CREAM COLESLAW

½ med. head cabbage
½ c. sour cream
2 tbsp. vinegar
½ tsp. salt
⅛ tsp. pepper
2 tbsp. sugar

Chill cabbage thoroughly; shred fine. Measure 4 cups. Combine remaining ingredients; pour over cabbage.

Mrs. Ruby Beckler
Beton, Tennessee

DEVILED CABBAGE

2 eggs, hard-cooked and chopped
½ c. salad dressing
¼ c. sweet pickle relish
¼ c. mustard
¼ c. sugar
¼ tsp. salt
½ c. pimento red pepper
2 lb. cabbage, shredded

Combine all ingredients except cabbage. Mix with cabbage just before serving.

Mrs. Jane Nobles
Tulsa, Oklahoma

MAKE-AHEAD SLAW

1 lge. head cabbage, shredded
2 lge. onions, shredded
2 c. sugar
1 c. vinegar
¾ c. salad oil
1 tbsp. celery seed
1 tbsp. dry mustard
1 tbsp. salt

Put cabbage and onions in large bowl. Add sugar; do not stir. Bring all the other ingredients to a boil. Pour over slaw. Do not stir. Refrigerate at least 4 hours. May be kept 3 weeks or longer. Will stay crisp indefinitely.

Mrs. Leo Bruns
Conehatta, Mississippi

PEANUT CRUNCH SLAW

4 c. shredded cabbage
1 c. finely cut celery
½ c. sour cream
½ c. mayonnaise
1 tsp. salt
¼ c. chopped green onions
¼ c. chopped green pepper
½ c. chopped cucumber
1 tbsp. butter
½ c. salted peanuts, coarsely chopped
2 tbsp. Parmesan cheese

Toss cabbage and celery together. Chill. Mix sour cream, mayonnaise, salt, onions, green pepper and cucumber; chill. Just before serving, melt butter in small skillet; add peanuts and heat until lightly browned. Immediately stir in cheese. Toss chilled vegetables with dressing. Sprinkle peanut mixture on top. Yield: 6-8 servings.

Wilma Mansel
West Columbia, Texas

SASSY SLAW

1 lge. head red cabbage
½ c. salad dressing
1 c. shredded green cabbage
¼ c. dairy sour cream
Salt and pepper to taste

Shred the red cabbage to measure 2 cups, reserving outer leaves. Mix the salad dressing with the red and green cabbage and sour cream tossing lightly. Season to taste. Serve in a bowl lined with red cabbage leaves. Yield: 4 servings.

Louise Phillips
Morven, North Carolina

KRAUT SALAD

1 sm. can chopped kraut
1 c. chopped onion
1 c. chopped celery
1 sm. can pimentos, chopped fine
¾ c. sugar

Drain kraut. Mix with all ingredients. Let stand in refrigerator 24 hours. Yield: 6-8 servings.

Mrs. J. D. Williams
Florence, Alabama

RED AND GREEN SALAD

1 lge. can kraut or 1 qt. home-canned kraut
1 lge. red onion
1 lge. bell or sweet pepper
1 lge. jar pimento
1 med. jar chopped sweet relish
½ c. sugar
½ c. apple cider vinegar

Chop the kraut, onion, pepper and pimento; mix well. Add the relish and stir well. Pour sugar into vinegar and stir to dissolve. Pour over salad mixture.

Mildred L. Gates
Memphis, Tennessee

SAUERKRAUT SALAD

1 10-oz. can sauerkraut
½ c. diced celery
½ c. chopped white onion
½ c. chopped green pepper
1 2-oz. jar pimentos, drained
½ c. sugar
Dash of black pepper

Drain sauerkraut; toss until well separated. Add remaining ingredients; toss lightly until well mixed. Cover. Refrigerate several hours or overnight. Yield: 10-12 servings.

Mrs. J. E. Finley
Fort Worth, Texas

SAUERKRAUT SALAD

1 can sauerkraut, drained
1 c. finely cut celery
1 c. finely cut green pepper
1 c. finely cut onion
1 ½ c. sugar
½ c. vinegar
½ c. salad oil

Combine vegetables; add remaining ingredients. Chill 2 hours and serve.

Mrs. J. H. Mitchell
Upper Marlboro, Maryland

SAUERKRAUT SLAW

1 10-oz. can sauerkraut, drained
2 tbsp. chopped pepper
1 tbsp. chopped pimento
⅓ c. sour cream

(Continued on next page)

Combine sauerkraut, pepper and pimento. Add sour cream and mix well. Chill. Serve on lettuce. Yield: 4 servings.

Mrs. J. D. Williams
Florence, Alabama

SAUERKRAUT SALAD

1 No. 303 can sauerkraut
2 c. celery, chopped
1 sm. can pimento
1 green pepper
2 tbsp. chopped onion
¾ c. sugar
½ c. vinegar

Mix all ingredients well; chill until serving time.

Mrs. Pearl E. Wright
Arkinda, Arkansas

SAUERKRAUT SALAD

1 No. 303 can sauerkraut, drained
1 med. onion, chopped
1 med. green pepper, chopped
1 sm. can pimentos, chopped
1 c. chopped celery
½ c. vinegar
¾ c. sugar

Combine first 6 ingredients; set aside. Mix vinegar and sugar together; pour over combined vegetables and mix well. Let stand a few hours.

Mrs. Ray Perkins
Celeste, Texas

SKILLET SALAD

4 slices bacon
¼ c. vinegar
1 tbsp. brown sugar
1 tsp. salt
1 tbsp. finely chopped onion
4 c. shredded cabbage
½ c. chopped parsley

Cook bacon till crisp; remove from skillet and crumble. Add vinegar, sugar, salt and onion to bacon fat in skillet. Add crumbled bacon. Heat thoroughly; take from range and toss cabbage and parsley in hot dressing.

Mrs. Ernest Storek
Seymour, Texas

CARROT SALAD MEAL

3 lge. carrots, shredded
4 strips bacon, cooked and diced
3 hard-cooked eggs
¼ c. salad dressing
¼ tsp. salt
½ c. grated cheese
¼ tsp. pepper

Combine all ingredients; mix thoroughly. Serve on lettuce. Yield: 4 servings.

Mildred Ellis
Newport News, Virginia

LEMONED CARROTS

12 sm. carrots, peeled
1 6-oz. can frozen lemonade, undiluted
6 whole cloves
Lettuce

Boil carrots in small amount of water until tender. Drain. Add lemonade and cloves; simmer gently for 5 minutes. Cool. Chill thoroughly. Drain. Serve on lettuce.

Mrs. Doveta Hunt
Pecos, Texas

PEANUT AND CARROT SALAD

2 c. grated carrots
1 c. ground peanuts
1 tbsp. grated onion
½ tsp. salt
½ c. mayonnaise
Lettuce
1 tomato, cut into wedges

(Continued on next page)

Combine carrots, peanuts, onion, salt and mayonnaise; mix. Serve on lettuce. Garnish with tomato wedges.

Mrs. Bill Lauring
Hickory, North Carolina

VITAMIN CARROT SALAD

2 c. grated carrots
2 tbsp. lemon juice
1 c. diced celery
¼ c. finely chopped nuts
Salad dressing

Lightly toss all ingredients with salad dressing. Chill. Serve on salad greens.

Mrs. Carolyn W. Yeatts
Farmville, Virginia

CAULIFLOWER SALAD

1 med. head cauliflower
½ c. grated American or cheddar cheese
½ c. French dressing
½ tsp. salt

Wash cauliflower thoroughly; break into flowerettes and slice each about 1/8 to 1/4 inch thick. Sprinkle with grated cheese. Pour French dressing over all. Season with salt. May be served in a bowl or on lettuce leaves for individual servings.

Mrs. Charles B. King
Decatur, Tennessee

GOOD CAULIFLOWER SALAD

¼ c. minced green onions
½ c. minced celery leaves
1 c. sour cream
½ c. French dressing
2 tsp. caraway seed (opt.)
Salt to taste
1 cauliflower, diced

Combine onions, celery leaves, sour cream, French dressing, caraway seed and salt. Dip cauliflower tidbits into dressing. Yield: 8 servings.

Mrs. Dwight R. Mann
Levelland, Texas

CELERY RINGS

3 tbsp. butter
1 3-oz. pkg. cream cheese
3 tbsp. tomato paste
Salt and red pepper to taste
1 bunch celery

Cream butter; add cheese and tomato paste. Mix well. Add salt and red pepper. Stuff celery stalks with mixture. Put celery hearts together; place remaining pieces of celery around to make the stalk into its original shape. Wrap in waxed paper; chill. Slice into rings.

Evelyn Ford
Berryville, Virginia

CELERY ROOT SALAD

2 c. cooked celery roots
4 slices bacon, diced
1 tbsp. onion, cut fine
1 tsp. all-purpose flour
½ c. water
½ c. vinegar
2 tsp. sugar
1 tsp. salt
Dash of pepper

Cook celery roots in salted water until tender. Dice celery; set aside. Fry bacon and onion together until light brown. Blend in flour; add water, vinegar, sugar, salt and pepper. Cook for 1 minute. Pour over celery roots; mix and set in a warm place for a few minutes to season. Yield: 6 servings.

Sara Ward
Carson, Mississippi

CORN SALAD

1 No. 2 can whole kernel corn, drained
1 pimento, chopped
1 sm. onion, chopped
1 sm. green pepper, chopped
1 sm. cucumber, chopped
½ c. French dressing

Combine all ingredients. Serve on lettuce cups. Mayonnaise may be substituted for French dressing. Yield: 4 servings.

Mrs. Judy Brumley
Kyle, Texas

CUCUMBER COOLER

¼ c. vinegar
1 tbsp. lemon juice
1 tsp. celery seed
2 tbsp. sugar
1 tsp. salt
⅛ tsp. pepper
¼ tsp. Accent
¼ c. onion, chopped
2 tbsp. parsley, chopped
3 med. cucumbers, thinly sliced

Mix all ingredients except cucumbers in jar or plastic container. Add cucumbers; toss to coat with dressing. Chill thoroughly. Turn or shake container several times while chilling.

Mrs. Emely Sundbeck
Manor, Texas

EL TANGO SALAD

1 12-oz. can Mexicorn, drained
2 c. lge. curd cottage cheese
2 green onions with tops, minced
¾ c. lightly crushed corn chips

Combine corn, cheese and onions. Chill thoroughly. Toss with corn chips just before serving.

DRESSING:

¾ c. sour cream
½ c. salad mustard
Dash of hot sauce

Combine ingredients; whip thoroughly. Pour over salad. Serve on crisp lettuce leaves, if desired. Yield: 6-8 servings.

Mrs. Carl R. Payne
Denison, Texas

CUCUMBER MARINADE

5 med. cucumbers
1 c. vinegar
2 tbsp. water
1 tbsp. salad oil
1 tbsp. sugar
1 tsp. salt
½ tsp. pepper
1 tsp. dried parsley flakes
½ tsp. dill seed
1 lge. onion, coarsely chopped

Peel and thinly slice cucumbers. Mix remaining ingredients except onion; pour over cucumbers and onion. Marinate at least 3 hours in refrigerator before serving. Yield: 8 servings.

Mrs. Bernard Lewis
Cleveland, Texas

COTTAGE CHEESE-CUCUMBER SALAD

2 tbsp. white vinegar
2 tbsp. sugar
½ tsp. each poppy and celery seed
½ c. creamed cottage cheese
Salad greens
20 slices unpeeled cucumber

Heat vinegar, sugar and poppy and celery seed to boiling. Pile cheese on greens. Arrange cucumber slices diagonally in cheese. Pour dressing over top. Chill until ready to serve. Yield: 4 servings.

Mrs. D. B. Pierce
Yuma, Arizona

SOUR CREAM-CUCUMBER SALAD

⅓ c. sour cream
1 tsp. finely minced onion
1 tsp. cider vinegar
Salt
1 lge. cucumber, thinly sliced

Put sour cream, onion and vinegar in a mixing bowl and mix well. Lightly salt cucumber; add to sour cream mixture. Toss until each slice of cucumber is thoroughly coated. Cover bowl and refrigerate for 30 to 40 minutes. Serve on lettuce.

Mrs. Eulalie Woods
Gainesville, Texas

SLICED RAW CUCUMBER SALAD

2 cucumbers
1 tbsp. salt
½ c. ice water
¾ c. vinegar
¼ c. water
4 tsp. sugar
½ tsp. pepper
1 sm. onion, sliced

Peel and slice cucumbers 1/8 inch thick. Mix in salt and pour ice water over cucumbers in dish. Place in refrigerator to chill for about 1 hour. Drain off liquid. Mix vinegar, water, sugar and pepper together. Pour over cucumbers and add sliced onion.

Mrs. Russell A. Bauer, Sr.
Andrews, South Carolina

CUCUMBER SALAD

2 med. cucumbers, diced
1 med. onion, chopped
1 tbsp. (or more) mayonnaise
½ tsp. sugar
Salt and pepper to taste

Mix all ingredients together and serve.

Mrs. Jon La Baume
Wellington, Texas

YOGURT-CUCUMBER SALAD

4 cucumbers, peeled and thinly sliced
1 ½ tsp. salt
1 clove of garlic, minced
2 tbsp. lemon juice
2 c. yogurt
1 tbsp. finely chopped dill
¼ c. olive oil
2 tsp. chopped fresh mint

Sprinkle cucumbers with salt; set aside for 15 minutes. Mix garlic, lemon juice, yogurt and dill; add drained cucumbers. Cover with oil; sprinkle with mint. Yield: 8 servings.

Evelyn Ann Farris
Beckley, West Virginia

SOUR CREAM-CUCUMBER SALAD

2 lge. cucumbers, pared and sliced
1 thinly sliced Bermuda onion or Italian red onion
1 tbsp. sugar
1 tsp. salt
1 thinly sliced celery heart
1 c. sour cream
1 tbsp. vinegar
Black pepper

Combine first 4 ingredients and mix well. Refrigerate for 1 hour. Drain. Stir in celery, sour cream and vinegar. Sprinkle generously with black pepper. Serve in salad bowl with lettuce around the sides.

Mabel Burkhalter
Cedar Bluff, Alabama

GREEN MUSTARD SALAD

2 c. finely chopped mustard greens
1 hard-boiled egg, cut fine
½ tsp. salt
¼ tsp. black pepper
½ tsp. sugar
1 tbsp. mayonnaise
1 tsp. sweetened vinegar

Wash and drain mustard; mix all ingredients together in bowl well. Cover and set in refrigerator for 15 minutes before serving.

Mrs. H. D. Nelms
Glenwood, Georgia

INDIAN SALAD

1 No. 2 can hominy
3 tbsp. catsup
1 tbsp. chopped onion
1 tbsp. chopped pimento
2 tbsp. chopped dill pickle
2 tbsp. coarsely grated carrot
3 tbsp. mayonnaise
1 c. cottage cheese
Salt to taste

Simmer hominy in saucepan for 10 minutes. Drain; add catsup, onion and pimento while still hot. Let cool. Add remaining ingredients.

Mrs. Henry J. Pohl
Hallettsville, Texas

CAESAR SALAD

½ c. salad oil
½ clove of garlic, crushed
1 ½ c. sm. white bread cubes
1 lge. head romaine
½ clove garlic
1 egg
2 tbsp. lemon juice
½ tsp. salt
⅛ tsp. pepper
6 anchovy fillets, chopped
2 oz. blue cheese, crumbled
¼ c. grated Parmesan cheese

Slowly heat 1/4 cup oil and crushed garlic in medium skillet. Add bread cubes; saute over medium heat, stirring occasionally until bread cubes are golden. Remove from heat; discard garlic. Set croutons aside until ready to use. Wash romaine; dry very well. Store in crisper until ready to use. Just before serving, rub large wooden salad bowl with cut side of 1/2 clove garlic. Into bowl, tear romaine into bite-sized pieces. Pour 1/4 cup salad oil over romaine; toss to coat leaves evenly. In small bowl, beat egg, lemon juice, salt, pepper, and anchovies to combine. Toss with romaine. Add cheeses and garlic croutons. Toss again. Serve the salad at once. Yield: 6-8 servings.

Evelyn Marie Frasier
Wadmalaw Island, South Carolina

CAESAR SALAD

1 lge. head romaine
1 lge. head lettuce
¼ c. grated Parmesan cheese
¾ c. Basic French Dressing
1 egg
2 c. Garlic-Flavored Croutons

Tear romaine and lettuce into bite-sized pieces into salad bowl. Sprinkle with Parmesan cheese. Add Basic French Dressing and toss lightly. Break raw egg into greens; toss lightly until egg particles disappear. Add croutons; toss. Yield: 6 servings.

GARLIC FLAVORED CROUTONS:

2 tbsp. salad dressing
1 clove of garlic, minced
2 c. bread crumbs

Heat salad oil in skillet with minced garlic. Add bread cubes and heat until lightly browned.

BASIC FRENCH DRESSING:

1 tsp. salt
1 tsp. sugar
1 tsp. dry mustard
1 tsp. paprika
1 c. salad oil
½ tsp. Tabasco sauce
1 c. vinegar

Mix dry ingredients thoroughly; add oil and Tabasco. Stir until well blended. Add vinegar and beat or shake well. Beat or shake well again before serving. Serve with mixed greens. Yield: 2 cups.

Photograph for this recipe on page 131.

DELICIOUS LETTUCE SLAW

1 c. mayonnaise
¼ c. chili sauce
¼ c. creamed cottage cheese
2 tbsp. chopped green pepper
1 tbsp. chopped onion
1 tbsp. finely chopped pimento
1 head of lettuce, shredded

Combine first 6 ingredients and chill. Shred lettuce and toss with dressing. Yield: 8 servings.

Mrs. J. D. Williams
Florence, Alabama

GALA GREENS

6 heads Belgium endive
1 bunch romaine
1 1-lb. jar sliced papaya
1 2-oz. can rolled fillets of anchovies
French dressing

Chill greens and papaya. Arrange in a bowl; add anchovies and French dressing. Sprinkle with croutons. Makes 4-6 servings.

Naomi Bourne
House, New Mexico

MEDITERRANEAN SALAD

1 head lettuce, torn to bite-sized pieces
6 green sm. young onions, thinly sliced
½ c. diced celery
2 tbsp. snipped parsley
¾ c. shredded sharp natural cheddar cheese
½ c. salad oil
¼ c. lemon juice
½ tsp. dried dillweed
½ tsp. salt
¼ tsp. freshly ground pepper

(Continued on next page)

In salad bowl, combine lettuce, onions, celery, and parsley. Add cheese. Combine remaining ingredients; add to salad for dressing. Toss lightly.

Mrs. Desola Little
Taylorsville, North Carolina

STUFFED LETTUCE

1 head lettuce
2 c. grated American cheese
¼ c. chopped pimento
2 tbsp. chopped green pepper
2 tsp. lemon juice
1 tbsp. sugar
Mayonnaise or salad dressing

Clean lettuce; cut out about 1/4 of the inside. Place in a plastic bag; refrigerate for 3 to 4 hours. Combine remaining ingredients with enough mayonnaise or salad dressing to moisten. Stuff filling into lettuce; chill. To serve, cut head into quarters. Yield: 4-6 servings.

Mrs. Doris J. Combs
Woodstock, Virginia

STUFFED LETTUCE SALAD

1 lge. head lettuce
1 3-oz. pkg. cream cheese
2 tbsp. crumbled bleu cheese
2 tbsp. grated carrot
1 tbsp. minced green pepper
½ med. tomato, chopped
1 tbsp. minced pimento
1 tbsp. minced chives or onion
3 tbsp. mayonnaise
Dash of salt, pepper and paprika

Cut out center from head of lettuce. Combine remaining ingredients and thoroughly blend. Pack into hollowed out lettuce head. Wrap in damp cloth. Place in refrigerator to chill for several hours. Slice crosswise for individual servings. Serve with mayonnaise or salad dressing. Yield: 4-6 servings.

Mrs. James Price
Alexandria, Virginia

LETTUCE SALAD

2 hard-boiled eggs, chopped
1 tsp. sugar
2 tsp. butter
Pepper
½ tsp. salt
½ tsp. mustard
4 tbsp. vinegar
2 heads lettuce

Rub egg yolks to powder; add sugar, chopped egg whites, butter, pepper, salt and mustard. Let stand 5 minutes; beat in vinegar. Cut lettuce with knife and fork. Serve with dressing.

Eva T. Wightman
Romney, West Virginia

WILTED LETTUCE

1 head lettuce, torn into bite-sized pieces, or a large bowl of leaf lettuce
4 tbsp. minced onion
6 bacon slices, diced
¼ c. vinegar
1 tsp. dry mustard
Dash of garlic salt
2 tsp. sugar
¼ tsp. salt
¼ tsp. pepper

In salad bowl, combine lettuce and onion. Fry bacon until crisp, pouring off fat as it cooks. Drain bacon; add to salad bowl. Return 1/4 cup fat to skillet; add rest of ingredients. Bring to boil, stirring constantly. Pour over salad; toss. Serve salad immediately. Yield: 4 servings.

Mrs. Charles B. King
Decatur, Tennessee

WILTED LETTUCE

1 head shredded lettuce
½ c. crisp crumbled bacon
2 tbsp. bacon drippings
2 tbsp. vinegar
2 tbsp. sugar
¼ tsp. black pepper
¼ tsp. salt

(Continued on next page)

Toss lettuce and bacon in bowl. In skillet, reserve 2 tablespoons bacon drippings; add vinegar, sugar, pepper and salt. Heat to boiling. Pour over lettuce and toss again. Serve at once.

Mrs. Lorane Fite
Paden, Oklahoma

WILTED LETTUCE SALAD

½ lb. leaf lettuce, shredded
½ c. radishes, sliced
2 tbsp. onion, chopped
3 slices bacon, cut in small pieces
1 tbsp. flour
½ c. vinegar
¾ c. water
½ tsp. salt
1 ½ tbsp. sugar

Combine lettuce, radishes and onion; set aside. Saute bacon pieces until brown. Blend flour with drippings. Add vinegar and water. Cook, stirring constantly, until slightly thickened and smooth. Stir in salt and sugar; cook 2 minutes larger. Remove from heat; add vegetables. Toss lightly. Serve immediately while salad is still warm. Yield: 4 servings.

Mrs M. E. Causey
Centreville, Mississippi

MUSHROOM RIO SALAD

1 lb. fresh mushrooms
1 c. tender celery, chopped
2 pimentos
1 c. shredded lettuce
1 hard-cooked egg
2 tbsp. minced chives or green onions
1 c. French dressing
2 dashes salt and black pepper

Dice mushrooms, celery and pimentos very thinly. In salad bowl, toss ingredients with lettuce and crumbled egg and onions. Serve on crisp lettuce leaves and lightly pour on French dressing. Top with dash of salt and pepper. Yield: 6 servings.

Mrs. S. B. Goodwin
Tombstone, Arizona

GREEN PEA SALAD

1 can small green peas, drained
1 sm. bottle olives, cut up
3 stalks celery, cut up
2 boiled eggs, cut up
Salt and pepper to taste
Mayonnaise

Put peas in a bowl. Add olives, celery and eggs. Season with salt and pepper. Mix mayonnaise with all ingredients. Serve on lettuce leaves. Yield: 4 servings.

Mrs. R. P. Wolfe
Winston-Salem, North Carolina

ENGLISH PEA SALAD

1 sm. onion, diced
1 sm. green pepper, diced
¼ c. celery, diced
¼ c. pickles, diced
2 hard-boiled eggs, diced
1 can English peas
2 tbsp. mayonnaise

Mix first 5 ingredients. Add peas and mayonnaise. Chill.

Mrs. Clara Seago
Prattville, Alabama

ENGLISH PEA SALAD

½ lb. American cheese, cut up
Pimentos, cut up
2 hard-boiled eggs, cut up
1 can English peas, drained
1 pkg. salted peanuts
2 tbsp. mayonnaise

Combine cheese, pimentos and eggs with peas. Mix in peanuts and mayonnaise last. Chill slightly. Yield: 6 servings.

Mrs. Charles Knight
Saltillo, Mississippi

ENGLISH PEA SALAD

1 can English peas, drained
1 tbsp. finely chopped onion
½ c. pecan pieces
¾ c. cheddar cheese, diced
⅓ c. mayonnaise
Salt and pepper to taste

(Continued on next page)

Combine peas, onion, pecans and cheese. Add mayonnaise, salt and pepper. Mix lightly so as not to mash peas. Yield: 4-6 servings.

Mrs. Edward Rather
Holly Springs, Mississippi

PEA AND CHEESE SALAD

2 c. peas
1 c. celery, diced
1 tsp. onion, grated
½ c. sweet pickles, chopped
½ c. mayonnaise
¼ lb. sharp cheese, diced
Salt
Pepper
Salad greens

Chill and drain peas. Combine with next 5 ingredients and toss lightly. Season to taste with salt and pepper. Serve on salad greens. Yield: 6 servings.

Marilyn Berousek
Maysville, Oklahoma

BAKED POTATO SALAD

6 med. potatoes, peeled and sliced thin
3 tbsp. bread crumbs
1 c. sour cream
1 c. mayonnaise
2 tbsp. flour
2 tbsp. minced green onions
Salt to taste
6 hard-cooked eggs, sliced
¼ c. melted butter

Cook potatoes in small amount of water until tender. Drain. In greased 2-quart casserole, sprinkle 1 tablespoon bread crumbs over bottom. Combine sour cream, mayonnaise, flour and onions. Place layer of potatoes in casserole; salt to taste. Add layer of egg slices. Spread 1/2 creamy mixture over eggs. Repeat layers. Sprinkle 2 tablespoons bread crumbs on top. Drizzle melted butter over top. Bake at 350 degrees for 25 minutes. Yield: 6-8 servings.

Mrs. Velma Winslow
Hartshorne, Oklahoma

CREAMY POTATO SALAD

7 c. sliced warm boiled potatoes
⅓ c. chopped chives
1 teaspoon salt
⅛ tsp. pepper
1 tbsp. grated onion
1 c. garlic salad dressing
½ c. chopped celery
½ c. diced cucumber
½ c. sour cream
½ c. mayonnaise

Combine potatoes, chives, salt, pepper, onion and 1/2 cup garlic salad dressing. Stir well; chill. Combine celery, cucumber, sour cream and mayonnaise. Stir in the remaining 1/2 cup salad dressing. Chill. Just before serving time, combine the potato mixture with the mayonnaise mixture. Garnish with salad greens, parsley, radishes and additional chives, if desired. Yield: 8 servings.

Martha Hooper
Gray Court, South Carolina

CURRIED POTATO SALAD

3 c. water
1 ½ tsp. curry powder
2 ½ tsp. salt
4 c. diced Irish potatoes
3 tbsp. French dressing
2 tbsp. lemon juice
2 tbsp. grated onion
¼ tsp. black pepper
¼ tsp. garlic powder
1 ½ c. diced celery
½ c. diced green pepper
3 hard-cooked eggs, diced
¾ c. mayonnaise

Combine water, curry powder and 1 teaspoon salt. Add potatoes and cook covered, until tender. Drain. Combine French dressing, lemon juice, onion, 1 1/2 teaspoons salt, pepper and garlic powder. Mix lightly with potatoes and let stand for 30 minutes. Add celery, green pepper and eggs. Mix; blend in mayonnaise. Yield: 6 servings.

Mrs. R. B. Elliott
Livingston, Alabama

FAVORITE POTATO SALAD

3 c. diced hot potatoes
3 hard-boiled eggs, chopped
½ c. diced cucumbers
⅓ c. diced celery
2 tbsp. minced onion
1 tsp. salt
2 tbsp. sugar
2 tbsp. vinegar
½ c. mayonnaise

(Continued on next page)

Mix all ingredients together thoroughly and chill. Yield: 6 servings.

Mrs. J. C. Murphy
Carthage, Mississippi

GOURMET POTATO SALAD

1 c. creamed cottage cheese
1 c. sour cream
2 tsp. seasoned salt
2 tsp. prepared mustard
4 c. diced cooked potatoes
1 c. diced green onions with tops
1 c. diced celery
½ c. diced green pepper
3 hard-cooked eggs, coarsley chopped
1 1-oz. pkg. bleu cheese, crumbled

Combine cottage cheese, sour cream, salt and mustard. Pour over potatoes, onions, celery, green pepper and eggs. Mix carefully. Chill several hours to blend flavors. Fold in bleu cheese just before serving. Yield: 6-8 servings.

Wanda Clement
Claudville, Virginia

HOT GERMAN POTATO SALAD

6 to 8 slices bacon, chopped
¼ c. chopped onion
1 tbsp. flour
1 tbsp. sugar
Salt
Dash of pepper
⅓ c. vinegar
¼ c. water
3 tbsp. salad dressing
4 c. diced cooked potatoes
2 hard-cooked eggs
1 tbsp. minced parsley
½ tsp. celery seed

Cook bacon till crisp; add onion and cook till tender but not brown. Blend in flour, sugar, 1 1/2 teaspoons salt and pepper. Add vinegar and water. Cook, stirring constantly, till thick. Remove from heat and stir in salad dressing. Sprinkle potatoes with 3/4 teaspoon salt; pour dressing over and toss lightly. Bake in 350-degree oven for 20 minutes or till thoroughly heated. Top with eggs and sprinkle with parsley and celery seed. Serve while hot. Yield: 8 servings.

Mrs. Ben T. Jacob
Georgetown, Texas

HEARTY SALAD

6 cold cooked potatoes, diced or sliced thin
3 eggs, hard-cooked
1 tsp. dry mustard
1 c. sour cream
Paprika or dash of cayenne pepper
Salt to taste
Pickled beets, canned pimentos or allspice

Mix potatoes with chopped whites of eggs. Mix the yolks with dry mustard; stir into thick sour cream. Add a little paprika or dash of cayenne pepper and salt to taste. Pour the dressing over potatoes and stir gently. Cut red hearts from pickled beets or canned pimentos. Sprinkle over top of salad. Serve each portion of salad on a leaf of lettuce or the white leaf inside of cabbage.

Eva T. Wightman
Romney, West Virginia

HOT GERMAN POTATO SALAD

6 med. potatoes
1 tsp. salt
⅛ tsp. pepper
2 tbsp. chopped parsley
1 sm. onion

Scrub potatoes and cook in boiling salted water. Peel, cube, and season with salt and pepper. Keep hot. Add parsley and onion to potatoes.

HOT DRESSING:

6 slices bacon
1 tbsp. flour
½ c. hot water
½ c. hot vinegar
1 tbsp. sugar

Cut up bacon in small pieces and fry until crisp and brown. Pour off all fat except 2 tablespoons. Stir in flour and cook, stirring constantly, for 2 minutes. Add hot water, vinegar and sugar. Bring to a boil, stirring occasionally. Pour dressing over potatoes and toss gently. Yield: 4 servings.

Mrs. Stanley Short, Jr.
Dover, Delaware

OUR FAVORITE POTATO SALAD

4 lge. potatoes
2 eggs, hard-cooked, cut fine
1 c. celery, cut very fine
½ c. onion, cut fine
¼ c. green pepper (opt.)

(Continued on next page)

DRESSING:

½ c. vinegar
½ c. evaporated milk
¼ c. sugar
Salt and pepper
1 tbsp. prepared mustard

Combine all vegetables. Mix dressing ingredients, blending well. Combine with vegetables.

Mrs. W. H. Phillips
Staunton, Virginia

HOT POTATO-DANDELION SALAD

6 med. potatoes
1 c. finely chopped raw dandelion leaves
1 carrot, cut fine
1 med. onion, minced
4 tbsp. vinegar
1 tsp. sugar
1 tsp. salt
Pepper to taste
1 tsp. prepared mustard
3 slices bacon, diced and fried crisp
3 tbsp. hot bacon fat

Cook potatoes tender without paring. Peel and dice potatoes. Add remaining ingredients, mixing lightly. Cover tightly and keep in a warm place about 30 minutes or until serving time.

Mrs. Walter Black
Catlettsburg, Kentucky

HOT POTATO SALAD

3 tbsp. fat
¼ c. finely chopped onion
1 tbsp. flour
1 ½ tsp. salt
1 tbsp. sugar
¼ tsp. dry mustard
3 tbsp. vinegar
3 tbsp. water
2 tbsp. sweet pickle relish
⅓ c. diced celery
2 tbsp. chopped green pepper
2 ½ c. diced cooked potatoes

Heat the fat and brown the onion lightly. Mix flour, salt, sugar, and mustard with onion. Add vinegar and water slowly, stirring constantly; cook until thick. Mix pickle relish, celery and green pepper with potatoes; add the hot dressing and mix thoroughly. Turn into baking dish; cover, and heat in oven at 350 degrees about 20 minutes.

Mrs. Iva Moore
Ringgold, Louisiana

MASHED POTATO SALAD

4 c. unseasoned mashed hot potatoes
⅓ c. mayonnaise or salad dressing
1 tbsp. vinegar
1 tsp. salt
1 ½ tbsp. chopped green pepper
1 ½ tbsp. finely chopped pimento
¾ c. finely chopped celery
¾ c. finely chopped green onions

Toss all ingredients together. Serve hot or cold. Yield: 6 servings.

Mrs. Lanier Calvert
Buckeye, Arizona

MUSTARD-POTATO SALAD

6 med. potatoes, cooked in jackets
1 c. diced celery
½ c. chopped onion
½ c. chopped sweet pickles
3 hard-cooked eggs, diced
Salt to taste
Pepper to taste
¼ tsp. onion seasoning
⅛ tsp. celery salt
1 tbsp. prepared mustard
½ c. sweet pickle vinegar
½ c. mayonnaise

Peel and dice potatoes. Add celery, onion, sweet pickles, eggs and seasonings. Pour mustard, pickle vinegar and mayonnaise over potatoes while still hot. Refrigerate overnight. More dressing may be added if salad becomes too dry. Yield: 6 servings.

Mrs. C. Hallum
Burneyville, Oklahoma

PARSLEY-POTATO SALAD RING

3 qts. cubed cooked potatoes
2 c. sliced celery
1 c. chopped onion
¾ c. sliced stuffed olives
¾ c. chopped parsley
Salad dressing
Salt and pepper
Cherry tomato halves

Combine potatoes, celery, onion, olives, 1/4 cup parsley, and enough salad dressing to moisten; mix lightly. Season to taste. Pack into 9 or 10-inch tube pan; chill. Invert on serving plate. Sprinkle sides with parsley; garnish top with additional parsley and tomatoes. Yield: 10-15 servings.

Mrs. James Clay
Carthage, Tennessee

PEPPY POTATO SALAD

1 ½ tsp. mustard seed
1 tsp. dillseed
2 tbsp. vinegar
1 ½ tsp. salt
5 c. diced cooked potatoes
⅓ c. sliced green onions
¼ c. thinly sliced celery
¾ c. dressing

Combine mustard seed and dillseed with vinegar; add salt. Mix potatoes, onions and celery lightly with 3/4 cup dressing. Combine with vinegar mixture. Toss to coat well. Chill thoroughly. Garnish with radish roses.

DRESSING:

2 tbsp. all-purpose flour
2 tbsp. sugar
1 tsp. salt
1 tsp. dry mustard
Dash of cayenne
2 slightly beaten egg yolks
¾ c. milk
¼ c. vinegar
1 ½ tsp. butter or margarine

Mix dry ingredients in small saucepan. Gradually stir in egg yolks and milk. Cook and stir over medium heat till mixture thickens and boils. Remove from heat; stir in vinegar and butter. Mix. Cover and cool. Yield: 1 cup.

Judy Dunn
Bulan, Kentucky

SPRING VEGETABLE SALAD

1 qt. cold boiled new potatoes
1 tsp. salt
½ tsp. pepper
Cucumber
1 bunch red radishes, unpeeled
1 bunch green onions
½ c. sweet cream
1 c. Boiled Salad Dressing

Mix vegetables, salt and pepper with Boiled Salad Dressing. Pour cream over salad. Serve cold.

BOILED SALAD DRESSING:

2 eggs
2 tbsp. sugar
1 tsp. mustard
¼ tsp. pepper
¼ tsp. salt
1 c. vinegar
1 tbsp. butter

Beat eggs; add sugar, seasonings, vinegar and butter. Cook in double boiler until thick, like custard.

Mrs. George Scarborough
Dothan, Alabama

QUICK POTATO SALAD

1 envelope instant potatoes
3 tbsp. mayonnaise
2 hard-cooked eggs, chopped
4 tbsp. sweet or dill pickles, cubed
2 stalks celery, chopped
1 sm. onion, chopped
2 tbsp. pimento, chopped
Salt and pepper

Prepare potatoes according to package directions using 1/4 cup less liquid than called for. Add mayonnaise until desired consistency is reached. Add remaining ingredients. Salad will mold well if packed in an oiled container. If sour taste is desired, use vinegar as part of liquid in preparing potatoes.

Mrs. Betty G. Lawrence
Mooresville, North Carolina

POTATO SALAD

7 med. potatoes, cooked in jackets, peeled and sliced
¾ c. sliced celery
⅓ c. sliced green onions, with tops
¼ c. pickles, chopped
1 cucumber, peeled and sliced
½ green pepper, sliced
Salt
Paprika
Cayenne pepper
Salad dressing, mayonnaise or sour cream
4 hard-cooked eggs, sliced

Chill sliced, cooked potatoes 2 hours. Add celery onion, pickles, cucumber and green pepper. Add salt, paprika and cayenne pepper. Mix in dressing and part of hard-cooked eggs, reserving some for garnish. Chill for 2 hours or overnight. Celery seed may be added for extra flavor. Garnish with reserved eggs and cherry tomatoes.

Mrs. Ernest Ray
Commerce, Georgia

POTATO SALAD

5 lge. potatoes, diced and cooked
3 hard-boiled eggs, chopped
1 c. celery, chopped
1 sm. onion, chopped
½ tsp. garlic salt
3 tbsp. sweet pepper relish, drained
Salt and pepper to taste
Salad dressing

Combine all ingredients with enough salad dressing for desired consistency.

Mrs. Hazel Bush
Atwood, Tennessee

PROSPERITY SALAD

2 No. 2 cans cooked dried black-eyed peas or red kidney beans, drained
1 c. salad oil
¼ c. wine vinegar
1 clove of garlic
¼ c. onion, thinly sliced
½ tsp. salt
Freshly ground pepper to taste

Combine all ingredients. Mix thoroughly. Refrigerate. Remove garlic bud from salad after 2 days. For improved flavor store at least 2 days or as long as 2 weeks before serving.

Mrs. Georgia Waters Scott
Clarksville, Texas

FRESH SPINACH WITH CHEESE SALAD

2 slices bacon, dried and crumbled
1 8-oz. pkg. cream cheese
1 med. onion, grated
1 8-oz. bottle French dressing
¼ c. vinegar
2 pkg. fresh spinach

Combine bacon, bacon drippings and cream cheese; mix well. Add onion, French dressing and vinegar; stir thoroughly. Just before serving, pour mixture over spinach.

Mrs. Frances Baker Bishop
Denton, Texas

FRESH SPINACH SALAD

1 lb. fresh spinach
4 hard-cooked eggs, chopped
8 slices bacon, fried and crumbled
¼ c. green onions, chopped
½ c. Italian salad dressing
Salt to taste

Remove large veins from spinach and tear into small pieces. Combine spinach, eggs and bacon. Add onions; toss lightly. Just before serving add dressing and salt.

Mrs. Jane Davis
Corpus Christi, Texas

FRESH SPINACH SALAD

½ lb. washed dried spinach, torn into bite-sized pieces
1 sm. Bermuda onion, sliced
¼ c. diced celery
4 hard-cooked eggs, sliced
Classic French Dressing

Toss first 4 ingredients together lightly; chill. Before serving, toss lightly with French Dressing. Yield: 8 servings.

CLASSIC FRENCH DRESSING:

¼ c. olive oil or half vegetable oil
2 tbsp. wine or tarragon vinegar
1 ½ tsp. salt
1 sm. clove garlic, put through press or minced
⅛ to ¼ tsp. fresh ground black pepper
⅛ to ¼ tsp. monosodium glutamate

(Continued on next page)

Combine all ingredients; mix well.

Wilma Mansel
West Columbia, Texas

Combine sugar, vinegar and bacon fat; bring to a boil. Add bacon. Pour over salad. Serve immediately. Yield: 8 servings.

Mary Martin
Cleburne, Texas

POPEYE SALAD

1 lb. washed spinach
1 tbsp. grated onion
½ tsp. salt
2 hard-boiled eggs, chopped
4 slices diced bacon, fried crisp
4 tbsp. vinegar
2 tsp. sugar

Chop spinach fine; add onion and salt. Toss lightly with eggs and bacon. Mix vinegar and sugar well; pour over prepared salad. Pickled beets may be added for color if desired. Yield: 4 servings.

Mrs. A. C. Vance
Woodland, Mississippi

SPINACH SALAD

2 qt. fresh spinach, cut or chopped
3 hard-boiled eggs, chopped
3 green onions, cut fine
1 tbsp. vinegar
¼ c. salad oil

Combine all ingredients; mix and serve.

Mrs. J. W. Reyenga
Emmet, Arkansas

SPINACH SALAD

½ lb. spinach, shredded
1 med. onion, finely chopped
4 tbsp. diced celery
6 to 8 radishes, chopped
4 hard-cooked eggs, chopped
½ tsp. salt

Combine all ingredients. Toss and chill.

HOT FRENCH DRESSING:

1 tbsp. sugar
¼ c. vinegar
4 tbsp. bacon fat
2 slices bacon, fried crisp and chopped

SPRING SALAD

2 ⅔ c. cottage cheese
½ c. skim milk
2 tsp. lemon juice
¾ tsp. salt
1 c. chopped green pepper
1 c. chopped celery
1 c. chopped radishes
½ c. chopped scallions or green onions

Blend first 4 ingredients in container until smooth. Pour over chilled chopped vegetables in a bowl and serve. Yield: 4 servings.

Mrs. P. R. Reese
Tucson, Arizona

STUFFED GREEN PEPPERS

2 lge. bell peppers
2 3-oz. pkg. cream cheese, mashed
½ c. mayonnaise
¼ c. chopped olives
½ tsp. salt
Dash of black pepper

Cut top from peppers; set aside. Clean peppers. Chop reserved tops; add remaining ingredients and mix thoroughly. Pack cheese mixture firmly into peppers. Chill 3 to 4 hours or overnight. Slice thin and serve with French dressing.

Mrs. T. R. Baddley
Water Valley, Mississippi

SWEET POTATO SALAD

2 c. diced cold sweet potatoes
1 c. chopped celery
1 tbsp. chopped bell pepper
1 tbsp. chopped onion
1 tbsp. chopped parsley
½ c. French dressing

Mix all ingredients well; chill. Yield: 6 servings.

Mrs. Ernest Waddell
Ft. Worth, Texas

SWEET POTATO SALAD

2 c. diced, cold, boiled sweet potatoes
1 c. chopped celery
1 tbsp. chopped bell pepper
1 tbsp. chopped onion
1 tbsp. chopped parsley
½ c. French dressing

Mix all ingredients thoroughly. Chill. Yield: 6 servings.

FRENCH DRESSING:

1 c. olive oil
3 tbsp. vinegar
1 tsp. salt
1 tsp. sugar
⅛ tsp. pepper
⅛ tsp. paprika

Combine all ingredients and beat or shake until thoroughly mixed.

Mrs. Eddie Withrow
Owingsville, Kentucky

SWEET POTATO SALAD

1 lge. can sweet potatoes
½ stick butter
2 tbsp. sugar
⅛ tsp. salt
½ tsp. allspice
½ c. cream or milk
¾ c. pecans, chopped
Miniature marshmallows

Cook potatoes until soft; mash thoroughly. Cream all ingredients until well blended. Top with marshmallows.

Mrs. Ola Belle Roebuck
Longview, Texas

SWEET POTATO SALAD

1 No. 2 ½ can sweet potatoes or
3 med. sweet potatoes
1 c. diced celery
1 apple, cubed
½ tsp. grated onion
¼ c. French dressing
1 tbsp. honey or corn syrup
1 tbsp. lemon juice

Boil fresh potatoes or drain canned potatoes. Chill and cube. Add celery, apple and onion. Mix French dressing with honey or syrup and lemon juice. Pour over salad mixture. Mix carefully. Let stand at least 1 hour in refrigerator.

Mrs. Henry J. Pohl
Hallettsville, Texas

CANNED TOMATO SALAD

1 can tomatoes, well-drained
3 hard-boiled eggs, chopped
1 c. chopped celery
Mayonnaise and salt to taste
1 tsp. grated onion
2 c. coarsely crumbled
crackers

Mix all ingredients except cracker crumbs, adding these just before serving.

Mary Ann Johnston
Jefferson, Georgia

CUCUMBER-STUFFED TOMATO SALAD

6 ripe tomatoes
4 sm. cucumbers
Boiled salad dressing
Salt and pepper
Lettuce
1 tsp. chopped parsley

Scald and peel tomatoes; cut a slice from top of each and with spoon remove pulp and seeds. Peel, dice and moisten cucumber with dressing. Chill and stuff tomatoes. Sprinkle with salt and pepper; place on lettuce, garnishing with additional dressing and dusting with parsley.

Glenda Jackson
Adarville, West Virginia

HASTY SALAD

½ sm. head lettuce
Cottage cheese
2 sm. or 1 lge. tomato
French dressing

Chop lettuce into very shallow serving dish. Mound a cup or 1 1/2 cups of cottage cheese in center of lettuce. Quarter tomatoes and place around cheese. Pour salad dressing in wagon wheel fashion with cottage cheese as hub and lettuce as rim.

Mrs. J. T. Springer
Lenorah, Texas

RED CROSS SALAD

4 med. tomatoes
½ lb. cottage cheese
2 tbsp. cream
Dash of white pepper
¼ tsp. paprika
¼ tsp. salt

Remove skins from tomatoes and chill; cut into quarters, leaving stem end whole. Combine cottage cheese with cream and seasonings. Shape into balls and place in center of tomato. Arrange on a crisp lettuce leaf. Serve with mayonnaise. Yield: 4 servings.

Sara Ward
Carson, Mississippi

PLANTATION TOMATO SALAD

3 med. tomatoes, peeled, sliced
1 onion, cut in rings
Salad greens
⅓ c. French dressing
¾ tsp. celery seed
¼ c. pickle relish
6 slices crisp-cooked bacon, crumbled
3 hard-cooked eggs, quartered

Arrange tomato slices with onion rings on salad greens. Mix dressing, celery seed and pickle relish; pour over tomatoes and onions. Sprinkle bacon on top; garnish with egg sections.

Virginia Redden
McCool, Mississippi

STUFFED TOMATO SALAD

4 med. tomatoes
1 ½ c. cottage cheese
2 tsp. minced onion
1 tbsp. chopped parsley
2 tbsp. chopped pimento
Salad greens
Low-calorie dressing

Wash and peel tomatoes; cut out stems. Hollow out centers. Mix cottage cheese, minced onion parsley and pimento in mixing bowl thoroughly. Fill centers of tomatoes with mixture; chill. Place tomatoes on lettuce greens. Add dressing. Yield: 4 servings.

Mrs. J. D. Long
Mesa, Arizona

SUNBURST SALAD

5 firm tomatoes
Lettuce
5 hard-boiled eggs
5 tbsp. mayonnaise
¼ c. finely chopped celery
2 tbsp. finely chopped green pepper
¼ tsp. salt
Dash of pepper
Paprika

Peel tomatoes; cut each into 5 sections, leaving whole at the stem end. Place on lettuce-lined salad plates. Chop eggs; mix with mayonnaise, celery, green pepper, salt and a dash of pepper. Blend egg salad thoroughly; stuff tomatoes. Serve with a sprinkling of paprika and additional mayonnaise.

Mrs. W. A. Gentry
Fletcher, North Carolina

TOMATO-ANCHOVY APPETIZER SALAD

2 tomatoes
Lettuce or watercress
1 sm. onion, sliced thin
6 rolled anchovies
1 tsp. lemon juice
1 hard-cooked egg yolk
French dressing

Peel tomatoes and cut into thick slices; chill. Arrange lettuce on 6 salad plates; place tomato slice on each. Cover with onion slice and top with anchovy. Sprinkle with lemon juice and garnish with sieved egg yolk. Serve with French dressing. Yield: 6 servings.

Mrs. Q. A. Bradley
Taft, Texas

TOMATO DELIGHT

4 tomatoes
1 c. cream cheese
2 tbsp. mayonnaise
1 tsp. salt
Pepper (opt.)
1 stalk celery, diced
4 stuffed olives, diced
4 lettuce leaves

Peel tomatoes; remove pulp. Mix remaining ingredients with pulp till well blended. Return to tomato shells; place on lettuce leaves and chill. May be garnished with extra olives.

Mrs. W. A. Carlos
Jackson, Louisiana

TOMATO AND PEPPER SURPRISE SALAD

2 lge. tomatoes, diced
1 lge. bell pepper, diced
1 med. onion, diced
¼ lge. box soda crackers, crumbled
2 tbsp. (heaping) mayonnaise
Salt and pepper to taste

Combine all ingredients. Toss lightly. Yield: 6 servings.

M. Jean Blackwood
Jonesville, South Carolina

TOMATO ROSE SALAD

Firm small tomatoes
Cream cheese
Milk
Hard-cooked egg yolk
Watercress or lettuce
French dressing or mayonnaise

Peel tomatoes and chill them. Slightly soften cream cheese with milk. Form two rows of petals on each tomato by pressing level teaspoons of the softened cheese against the side of the tomato, then drawing the teaspoon down with a curving motion. Sprinkle center of each tomato with hard-cooked egg yolk pressed through a strainer. Serve on watercress with dressing.

Mrs. Howard L. Briggs
Reidsville, North Carolina

VEGETABLE DINNER SALAD

Tomatoes, uniform size
Cottage cheese
Chopped chives (opt.)
Paprika (opt.)
Sliced celery (opt.)
Shredded cabbage (opt.)
Mayonnaise (opt.)

Scald tomatoes; remove skins. Chill. Just before serving, cut each tomato into 4 to 5 sections without severing at stem end. Fill center with cottage cheese. Decorate salad with 1 or more of the remaining ingredients.

Mrs. M. J. Arrington
Roopville, Georgia

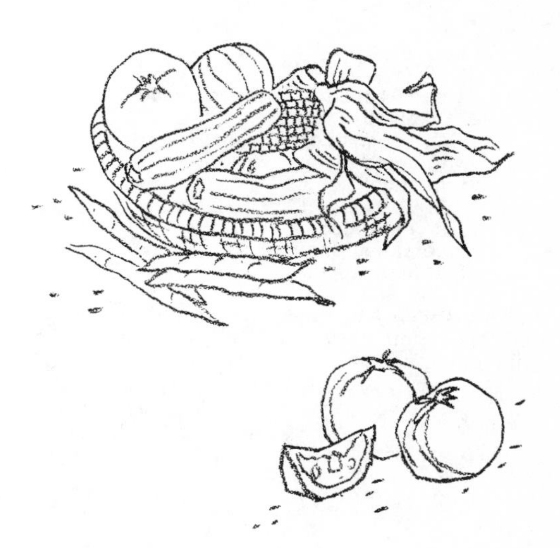

WATERCRESS A LA DENNIS

2 eggs, beaten
2 c. salad oil
2 tbsp. horseradish
¼ c. catsup
¼ lge. onion, grated
1 tbsp. salt
⅓ c. vinegar
2 tbsp. paprika
Dash of pepper
1 tbsp. Worcestershire sauce
1 slice bacon per serving, crisply fried
Watercress

Thoroughly mix all ingredients except bacon and watercress. Toss watercress with bacon. Serve with dressing.

Mrs. J. D. Wigley
Huntsville, Alabama

ASPARAGUS SALAD

20 spears cooked asparagus
½ c. celery
½ sm. onion, sliced thin
½ c. raw cabbage
5 slices tomatoes
½ c. whole olives
Mayonnaise

Arrange asparagus like the spokes of a wheel and fill in between the spokes with the above vegetables. Top with the mayonnaise and serve.

Mrs. Lorane Fite
Paden, Oklahoma

BAVARIAN SALAD

1 can French-style green beans, drained
1 can sugar peas, drained
½ c. salad oil
¾ c. sugar
1 c. vinegar
1 onion, diced
2 celery stalks, cut
Salt and pepper

Drain beans and peas. Mix together oil, sugar, vinegar, onion, celery, salt and pepper. Pour mixture over vegetables; let stand overnight.

Mrs. J. L. Sellers
Kings, North Carolina

BEAN-PEA SALAD

1 bunch celery, chopped fine
1 med. onion, chopped
1 green pepper
1 ½ c. chopped pimento
1 can French green beans, cut up
1 can tiny English peas
⅓ c. salad oil
1 c. sugar
½ c. vinegar
4 tbsp. water
½ tsp. paprika
Salt to taste

Combine vegetables and pour dressing over top. Chill at least 24 hours in refrigerator; drain.

Mrs. Robert H. Parker
Nashville, Tennessee

BEAN SALAD

1 bunch green onions
4 carrots
1 bottle stuffed olives
4 stalks celery
2 No. 2 cans French beans
1 No. 2 can small peas
¼ lb. or 1 5-oz. can slivered almonds
2 c. cooking oil
½ c. vinegar
1 tsp. Worcestershire sauce
¾ tsp. paprika
Juice of 1 ½ oranges
Juice of 1 ½ lemons
¾ c. powdered sugar
1 tsp. salt
½ tsp. dry mustard
2 cloves garlic, sliced thin

Dice onions, carrots and olives. Slice celery very thin; combine first 7 ingredients and mix thoroughly. Mix remaining ingredients together and pour over vegetables. Let stand from 4 hours to overnight.

Mrs. Tate Jennings
Jonesboro, Tennessee

BEAN SALAD

1 can cut green beans
1 can small peas
1 green pepper, chopped
1 2-oz. jar pimentos, chopped
4 ribs of celery, chopped
1 onion, sliced thin
¾ c. sugar
½ c. vinegar
½ c. salad oil
3 tbsp. wine vinegar
1 tsp. salt
Dash of pepper

Cook green beans 5 minutes. Drain beans and peas. Combine vegetables. Combine remaining ingredients; bring to boil and pour over vegetables. Refrigerate for 24 hours. Pour off liquid when ready to serve.

Mrs. Gus Fowler
Franklinton, Louisiana

GREEN BEAN AND BEET SALAD

1 can green beans, drained
1 can cut beets, drained
½ med. sweet onion, sliced in rings and separated
Oil and vinegar

(Continued on next page)

Combine all vegetables; toss with oil and vinegar. Season to taste. Yield: 4-6 servings.

Ruth A. Fanelli
Riverview, Florida

BEAN SALAD

2 No. 2 cans green beans
1 No. 2 can carrots, diced
½ c. sugar
¼ c. vinegar
¾ c. salad oil
Salt to taste
1 onion, sliced thinly
1 No. 2 can English peas
½ c. finely cut celery
½ bell pepper
Mayonnaise and paprika to taste

Night before, drain beans and carrots. In saucepan, mix and heat sugar, vinegar, salad oil and salt to taste. Add onion to beans and carrots; add hot liquid. Weight down and let set overnight. Next morning, drain; add English peas, celery, pepper, mayonnaise and paprika.

Mary Ann Johnston
Jefferson, Georgia

GREEN AND RED VEGETABLE SALAD

1 No. 303 can tiny peas
1 No. 303 can French-style green beans
1 4-oz. can pimentos
1 green pepper, chopped
1 c. celery, sliced extra thin
1 med. onion, chopped
¾ c. sugar
¼ c. oil
½ c. vinegar
1 tsp. salt
½ tsp. paprika
1 tbsp. water

Drain liquid from first 3 ingredients. Add pepper, celery and onion. Mix remaining ingredients and pour over vegetables. Marinate in refrigerator for at least 2 to 3 hours. Yield: 12 servings.

Mrs. Dean Bixler
Alva, Oklahoma

BEAN SALAD

1 sm. can yellow wax beans
1 sm. can green beans
1 sm. can red kidney beans
1 sm. can white beans
1 sm. can crowder peas
1 lge. onion, chopped
1 lge. green pepper, chopped
1 ½ c. white vinegar
1 ½ c. water
1 ½ c. cooking oil

Combine beans, peas, onion and pepper; pour a mixture of remaining ingredients over vegetables.

Mrs. Pearl Higgins
Henryetta, Oklahoma

BEAN SALAD

2 c. vinegar
2 c. sugar
1 can French green beans, drained
1 can kidney beans, drained
1 can wax beans, drained
1 can lima beans, drained
1 ½ c. cauliflower, cut up in small pieces
1 c. celery, cut up
2 sm. onions, sliced
1 tbsp. salt

Boil vinegar and sugar. Combine vegetables; pour liquid over all. Season.

Mrs. Thelma Duck
Asheville, North Carolina

GREEN BEAN SALAD

1 qt. green beans, cooked in salted water and drained
1 c. diced cooked potatoes
2 hard-boiled eggs
½ c. chopped sweet pickles
1 sm. chopped onion
Salt and pepper
Mayonnaise to moisten
1 lge. firm tomato, chopped

Mix all ingredients except tomato together thoroughly. Fold in tomato; serve.

Mrs. Dulane O. Holt
Sanford, North Carolina

MERRY MARINATED SALAD

1 c. French-style green beans
1 c. English peas
2 pimentos, chopped
1 c. whole kernel corn
2 ½ c. celery
Salt, pepper and paprika to taste
½ c. sugar
½ c. vinegar
¼ c. salad oil

Drain vegetables thoroughly. Season. Dissolve sugar in vinegar; add oil. Pour over salad and toss. Marinate in refrigerator overnight. Drain salad before serving.

Mrs. Haywood B. Smith
Norwood, North Carolina

PATIO SALAD

1 28-oz. can pork and beans
1 c. chopped celery
1 c. thinly sliced cucumber
½ c. chopped green pepper
1 tbsp. vinegar
1 tsp. salt
Dash of pepper

Lightly mix all ingredients; chill. Serve on crisp greens. Yield: 6-8 servings.

Mrs. Pat Fortier
Fort Fisher, North Carolina

PATIO SALAD

1 1-lb. can kidney beans, rinsed and drained
2 med. tomatoes, seeded and coarsely chopped
1 c. chopped celery
½ c. chopped green pepper
¼ c. thinly sliced green onions
2 c. diced sharp cheddar cheese
1 tsp. prepared mustard
½ tsp. salt
Dash of pepper
1 tbsp. sugar
1 tbsp. flour
1 tbsp. salad oil
1 egg, beaten
¼ c. vinegar
½ c. evaporated milk

Combine kidney beans, tomatoes, celery, green pepper, onions and cheese. Cover and chill while preparing dressing. Combine mustard, salt, pepper, sugar and flour in a small saucepan. Blend in salad oil, egg and 2 tablespoons vinegar. Cook and stir over low heat until thickened. Remove from heat; stir in remaining vinegar and evaporated milk. Beat until smooth. Cool. Mix lightly but thoroughly throughout salad mixture. Chill before serving. Yield: 6-8 servings.

Mrs. Thomas J. Holbrooks
Pendleton, South Carolina

SCANDINAVIAN SALAD

1 No. 2 can English peas, drained
1 No. 2 can French green beans, drained
1 sm. can chopped pimento
4 lge. stalks celery, chopped
1 onion, chopped
½ c. salad oil
1 c. red vinegar
1 tbsp. salt
1 c. sugar
1 tsp. paprika

To peas and beans, add pimento, celery and onion. Mix together. Combine remaining ingredients. Pour over vegetables. Let stand in refrigerator for 24 hours. Drain and serve.

Mrs. W. C. Thomas
Nashville, Tennessee

SPLIT BEAN SALAD

1 No. 303 can French-style green beans, drained
1 sm. can English peas, drained
1 sm. can pimento, cut into strips and drained
4 stalks celery, cut into rings
1 lge. bell pepper, diced
1 med. onion
½ c. salad oil
½ c. vinegar
⅓ c. sugar
1 tsp. salt

Mix vegetables; blend remaining ingredients and pour over vegetables. Refrigerate overnight. Yield: 12 servings.

Mrs. Addie Lancaster
Gordo, Alabama

PICKLED SNAP BEAN AND ONION SALAD

1 ¼ c. vinegar
¾ c. sugar
2 tbsp. pickling spices
1 sm. can whole beets, drained
1 can snap beans, drained
1 ½ c. sm. onion rings

Combine vinegar, sugar and pickling spices; bring to a boil. Combine beets, snap beans and onion rings. Cover with dressing. Let stand in refrigerator for 2 to 3 days before serving.

Mrs. Herman Lynch
Harlingen, Texas

STRING BEAN SALAD

½ c. salad oil
½ c. vinegar
1 c. sugar
⅛ tsp. salt
1 can French-style green beans
1 sm. can English peas
1 c. chopped celery
1 lge. onion, sliced
1 sm. carrot, grated
3 tbsp. canned pimento

Mix oil, vinegar, sugar and salt. Add to vegetables and mix. Chill several hours or overnight.

Mrs. Gladys Cooper
Tifton, Georgia

THREE-WAY BEAN SALAD

½ c. wine vinegar
½ c. sugar
½ c. cooking oil
½ c. onion rings
1 c. chopped celery
1 green pepper, cut in rings
1 1-lb. chick peas, drained
1 1-lb. red kidney beans, rinsed with cold water, then drained
1 1-lb green string beans, drained
1 1-lb. can yellow wax beans, drained
Salt to taste

Bring vinegar to a simmer; add sugar and oil. Let cool; pour over vegetables. Let marinate about 24 hours.

Mrs. Hanley Rexroad
Ireland, West Virginia

AUTUMN GARDEN SALAD

3 c. shredded cabbage
1 c. cherry tomato halves
2 med. carrots, cut in strips
1 sm. red onion, thinly sliced
¼ c. sliced radishes
½ c. dairy sour cream
1 tsp. curry powder
½ tsp. salt
4 slices drained fried bacon

Toss vegetables together lightly. Combine sour cream, curry powder and salt; pour over vegetables. Toss lightly. Crumble bacon over salad. Serve immediately. Yield: 6 servings.

Mrs. Hoyte Young
Portland, Tennessee

BEET SLAW

½ head cabbage, finely shredded
1 sm. can beets, drained and diced
1 tsp. sugar
3 tbsp. vinegar
1 tbsp. oil
½ tsp. salt
¼ tsp. pepper

Combine all ingredients; toss lightly. Chill and serve. Yield: 8 servings.

Mrs. Caroline Libersky
Chestertown, Maryland

CALICO SALAD

1 tsp. salt
¼ tsp. pepper
½ tsp. dry mustard
2 tbsp. sugar
2 tbsp. salad oil
½ tsp. grated onion
⅓ c. vinegar
5 c. shredded cabbage
¼ c. chopped green pepper
¼ c. grated carrots

Mix salt, pepper, mustard, sugar, salad oil, onion and vinegar in mixing bowl. Add cabbage, green pepper and carrots; toss lightly with fork and spoon. Serve immediately.

Mrs. Vernon Benner
Gatesville, Texas

CALICO SALAD

3 c. shredded green cabbage
3 c. shredded purple cabbage
1 green pepper, chopped
½ c. shredded carrots
⅓ c. wine vinegar
2 tbsp. oil
½ tsp. dry mustard
1 tsp. salt
½ tsp. grated onion
2 tbsp. sugar

To cabbage add green pepper and shredded carrots. Mix vinegar, oil, dry mustard, salt, grated onion and sugar to make dressing. Toss vegetables; pour dressing over salad. Serve immediately. Yield: 5-6 servings.

Mrs. Lewis Pierce
Leakesville, Mississippi

CARROT, CABBAGE AND RAISIN SALAD

½ c. raisins
2 c. shredded chilled cabbage
2 lge. carrots, shredded and chilled
1 tsp. salt
1 tsp. sugar
2 tsp. lemon juice
½ c. mayonnaise

Put raisins in boiling water; let set 10 minutes. Drain raisins; chill. Toss raisins with all remaining ingredients. Yield: 6-8 servings.

Mrs. M. A. Landermilk
Baton Rouge, Louisiana

CARROT AND CABBAGE SALAD

Shredded cabbage
Carrots
French dressing

Combine equal parts shredded cabbage and raw carrots with enough French dressing to moisten; serve on lettuce. A small amount finely cut green pepper may be added, if desired.

Mrs. M. J. Arrington
Roopville, Georgia

CONFETTI COLESLAW

1 med. head cabbage
3 stalks celery, chopped
2 carrots, chopped
1 onion, chopped
1 med. green pepper
⅓ c. honey
⅓ c. oil
⅔ c. vinegar
2 tsp. salt
1 tsp. celery seed
½ tsp. mustard seed

Chop cabbage in blender with enough water to cover; drain in a colander. Squeeze cabbage to remove any water remaining. Combine with remaining vegetables. Combine honey, oil, vinegar, salt, celery seed and mustard seed in a small saucepan and bring to a boil. Pour over the vegetables; stir well. Refrigerate for at least 2 hours. One half green pepper and 1/2 red pepper may be used, if desired. Onion may be blended with cabbage.

Mrs. S. P. Baker
Comstock, Texas

EGG SLAW

4 hard-cooked eggs, diced
½ c. chopped celery
2 c. shredded cabbage
½ c. firm tomatoes, diced
½ c. green bell pepper, chopped fine
1 tbsp. grated onion
2 tbsp. sweet or dill pickle, chopped fine
½ c. salad dressing
1 tsp. salt
Dash of pepper

Combine all ingredients; let set for 2 to 3 hours before serving.

Mrs. J. R. Cain
Abbeville, Mississippi

GARDEN VEGETABLE SLAW

1 No. 303 can mixed garden vegetables
2 c. finely shredded cabbage
1 tbsp. grated onion
¼. c finely chopped green pepper
Mayonnaise

Chill and drain mixed vegetables. Add cabbage, onion, green pepper and mayonnaise to moisten.

Ena Mae Jenkins
Elizabethtown, North Carolina

HARLEQUIN SALAD

1 c. each red and white cabbage, shredded
1 c. cooked peas
½ c. diced cooked beets
½ c. shredded raw carrots
1 onion, chopped
Salt and pepper
French dressing or mayonnaise

Combine all vegetables; season highly. Marinate with French dressing. Chill thoroughly.

Glenda Jackson
Cedarville, West Virginia

HOT VEGETABLE SALAD

½ cabbage
1 green pepper
1 sm. bunch green onions
8 to 10 red radishes
4 or 5 carrots
1 tbsp cooking oil

Slice all vegetables into long thin strips. Place in hot oil; cook over low heat until thoroughly heated. Do not saute. Vegetables should be tender yet crisp. Serve hot. Yield: 4-6 servings.

Carolyn Belanger
Tomball, Texas

ONION-LOVER SALAD

2 c. finely chopped cooked beets
1 c. finley chopped sweet onions
2 c. finely shredded cabbage
½ c. mayonnaise or salad dressing
Salt and pepper to taste
Lettuce

Combine the beets, onions and cabbage. Add mayonnaise and toss until well blended. Season to taste. Serve on crisp lettuce. Yield: 6 servings.

Mrs. Elizabeth Cowley
Saltillo, Mississippi

KRAUT SALAD

1 c. sugar
¼ c. vinegar
¼ c. vegetable oil
1 tsp. caraway seed
1 lge. can chopped sauerkraut
1 med.
1 ½ c. diced celery
1 sm. can chopped pimento
1 med. onion, chopped
1 diced carrot

Mix sugar, vinegar, oil and seed until dissolved; add all vegetables. Stir well. Let stand at least overnight, unrefrigerated.

Mrs. C. Floyd Lewis
Greensboro, North Carolina

KRAUT SALAD

1 sm. can chopped sauerkraut
½ c. sugar
½ c. celery, chopped
½ c. chopped onion
½ c. chopped carrot
½ c. sweet pepper, chopped
½ c. vinegar
¼ c. cooking oil

Mix all ingredients. Let stand several hours or 2 to 3 days.

Mrs. J. B. Spakes
Sparta, Tennessee

KRAUT SALAD

2 c. sauerkraut
⅓ c. sugar
½ c. chopped celery
½ c. chopped green pepper
½ c. shredded carrots
¼ c. chopped onion

(Continued on next page)

Cut sauerkraut with scissors. Stir in sugar and let stand while preparing vegetables. Add remaining ingredients. Chill before serving.

Mary Sue Paddock
San Angelo, Tex.

Toss all ingredients together lightly and serve cold with your favorite salad dressing.

Mrs. C. V. Jackson
Bastrop, Louisiana

SAUERKRAUT SALAD

1 lge. can sauerkraut, well drained
1 c. celery
1 medium onion
1 green pepper, diced real fine
½ c. shredded carrot or red pepper
1 c. sugar
½ c. vegetable oil
¼ c. vinegar

Combine vegetables; blend remaining ingredients. Pour dressing over vegetables. Serve.

Karin L. Durst
Grantsville, Maryland

SAUERKRAUT SALAD

1 c. sauerkraut
1 c. diced carrots
½ c. diced onions
½ c. celery, cut fine
½ c. bell pepper, cut fine
1 c. sugar

Mix all ingredients well; let stand overnight in icebox.

Mrs. U. L. Lafon
McKinney, Texas

SUMMER SALAD

2 c. shredded cabbage
⅔ c. grated carrots
⅔ c. chopped celery
⅓ c. green pepper, cut fine
⅓ c. radishes, sliced
¼ c. onions, chopped fine
¼ c. thin slices cucumbers

SHREDDED VEGETABLE SALAD

2 tbsp. chopped onion
2 c. shredded cabbage
1 ½ c. shredded raw carrots
1 c. shredded raw turnips
¼ c. finely chopped parsley
French dressing

Mix onion and shredded cabbage together and arrange on platter. Place shredded carrots and turnips in heaps on the cabbage. Sprinkle with parsley and serve with French dressing. Celery, raw cauliflower, spinach or beets may be substituted for carrots and turnips.

Mrs. Mary A. Walters
Bonnieville, Kentucky

VITAMIN SALAD

1 c. celery, diced
1 c. carrots, cooked and diced
½ green pepper, diced fine
2 c. cottage cheese
½ c. Cheese Dressing
2 c. cabbage, shredded

Mix celery, carrots, green pepper and cottage cheese with 1/4 cup Cheese Dressing. Place a generous amount of cabbage on a plate and mound a portion of cottage cheese mixture on the cabbage. Serve with crisp crackers and Cheese Dressing.

CHEESE DRESSING:

1 c. evaporated milk, undiluted
1 c. soft cheese
Salt to taste

Mix ingredients thoroughly; chill. For variation, soft cheese may be combined with mayonnaise for cheese dressing. Yield: 6 servings.

Blanford T. Anderson
Chatham, Virginia

SLAW

1 med. head cabbage, shredded
1 green pepper, chopped fine
1 red pepper, chopped fine (opt.)
1 sm. onion, chopped fine
1 carrot, shredded fine
1 c. sugar
1 c. vinegar
½ tsp. salt
½ tsp. celery seed
½ tsp. turmeric

Combine first 5 ingredients. Mix together sugar, vinegar, salt, celery seed and turmeric. Bring to a boil; boil 3 minutes. Pour over the vegetable mixture and stir well. Chill several hours or overnight. Will keep several days in refrigerator.

Mrs. Lawrence Hinton
Hopkinsville, Kentucky

CALICO SALAD BOWL

1 c. diced, cooked potatoes
1 c. diced, cooked carrots
1 c. cooked green peas
1 can pimento, chopped
2 tbsp. chopped onion
2 tbsp. chopped parsley
¼ c. French dressing
½ head lettuce
Mayonnaise

Combine all ingredients except lettuce and mayonnaise; chill for 1 hour. Break lettuce in bite-sized pieces; add vegetables and toss lightly. Serve with mayonnaise. Yield: 6 servings.

Mrs. Jimmie G. Gregory
Carlisle, South Carolina

DELUXE VEGETABLE SALAD

⅓ c. vinegar
¼ c. cooking oil
2 tbsp. sugar
Salt and pepper to taste
Dash of garlic powder
1 box cauliflower, cooked and cut into bite-sized pieces
1 can yellow string beans, cut up
1 cucumber, sliced thin
1 sm. onion, in rings

Combine first 5 ingredients and heat. Pour over vegetables. Let stand for several hours.

Mrs. W. H. Phillips
Staunton, Virginia

RAINBOW SALAD

Leaf lettuce
1 c. cooked green peas
1 ½ c. raw cauliflower, broken into flowerets
6 green olives, cut in ½-in. pieces
1 c. grated raw carrots
Salt and pepper
½ c. cubed cheddar cheese
⅔ c. mayonnaise

Arrange lettuce on salad plate. Put peas in center; circle with cauliflower, olives and carrots. Sprinkle with salt and pepper. Mix cheese and mayonnaise; pile in center. Serve at once. Yield: 5 servings.

Mrs. Clara Comer
Florence, Alabama

CORN SALAD

1 No. 2 can whole kernel corn, drained
1 pimento, chopped
1 sm. onion, chopped
1 sm. green pepper, chopped
1 sm. cucumber, chopped
½ c. French dressing

Combine all ingredients. Serve on lettuce cups. Mayonnaise may be substituted for French dressing and salad used for stuffing tomatoes. Yield: 4 servings.

Mrs. Judy Brumley
Kyle, Texas

MIXED SALAD

1 c. cucumbers, chopped
1 med. onion, chopped
1 green pepper, chopped
1 stalk celery, chopped
½ c. carrots, chopped
Mayonnaise

(Continued on next page)

Combine cucumbers, onion, green pepper, celery and carrots. Serve with mayonnaise on lettuce leaves. Garnish with beets.

Mrs. Frances Jackson
Mill Spring, North Carolina

CUCUMBER SALAD

3 or 4 lge. cucumbers, sliced
2 lge. tomatoes, cubed
1 pkg. Swiss cheese, diced
1 lge. onion, chopped
2 No. 303 cans mixed carrots and peas, drained
¾ bottle Italian dressing
⅔ c. milk
⅔ c. sugar
1 pt. mayonnaise
Garlic salt to taste
1 to 2 c. cooked shrimp or ham diced (opt.)

Combine cucumbers, tomatoes, cheese, onion, carrots and peas. Combine Italian dressing and milk; add sugar. Cook and stir over low heat until sugar is dissolved. Cool. Add mayonnaise and garlic salt; blend thoroughly. Add to vegetable mixture. Add shrimp or ham, if desired.

Mrs. Ella Jo Adams
Allen, Texas

STUFFED CUCUMBER SALAD

3 med. cucumbers
2 tomatoes
½ c. diced celery
½ tsp. salt
⅛ tsp. pepper
1 tbsp. chopped onion
Mayonnaise

Chill cucumbers and tomatoes. Peel cucumbers and cut in halves lengthwise. Remove pulp from the centers, being careful not to break the outside. Peel tomatoes; cut in small pieces and drain off juice. Mix cucumber pulp, tomato, celery, salt, pepper and onion with mayonnaise to moisten. Fill cucumber halves with mixture and arrange on crisp lettuce leaves. Chill. Garnish with green pepper rings, radishes or parsley.

Mrs. Woodrow Worrell
Hillsville, Virginia

FOO YUNG TOSS

1 head romaine lettuce, bite-sized pieces
1 1-lb. can bean sprouts, drained
1 5-oz. can water chestnuts, sliced (opt.)
5 slices bacon, fried crisp, crumbled
2 hard-cooked eggs, sliced
Salt and pepper to taste
1 c. salad oil
½ c. sugar
⅓ c. catsup
¼ c. vinegar
2 tbsp. grated onion
2 tsp. Worcestershire sauce

In salad bowl combine romaine, bean sprouts, water chestnuts, bacon and eggs. Sprinkle lightly with salt and pepper. Combine remaining ingredients. Blend on electric blender or shake well in a screw-top jar until well mixed. Add to salad; toss lightly.

Mrs. Desola Little
Taylorsville, North Carolina

GOOD EARTH SALAD

2 c. shredded raw carrots
1 c. sauerkraut
Mayonnaise
Sliced olives

Mix carrots with sauerkraut; add mayonnaise to moisten. Pack into a mold and chill. Unmold to serve, garnishing with sliced olives.

Elsie Harrison
Hatfield, Arkansas

CHEESE AND PEAS SALAD

1 No. 303 can peas, drained
1 c. diced celery
1 c. diced cheese
½ c. chopped sweet pickles
1 tbsp. grated onion
½ c. mayonnaise
Salt and pepper to taste
Lettuce

Chill peas. Combine celery, cheese, pickles and onion; add to drained peas and mix lightly. Add mayonnaise to moisten. Season with salt and pepper to taste. Serve on lettuce. Yield: 6 servings.

Mrs. Lindon Baker
Santa Fe, Tennessee

CHEESE-PEA SALAD

1 med. head lettuce
1 c. cooked English peas
½ lb. American cheese, cut in ¼-in. cubes
1 c. celery
½ c. sweet pickles, cut in slices
¼ c. chopped green onions
½ c. mayonnaise
2 tbsp. chili sauce
¾ tsp. salt
2 lge. tomatoes, sliced ½ in. thick

Trim lettuce, core, wash and drain; chill. Measure next 5 ingredients into bowl. Add combined mayonnaise, chili sauce and salt. Toss just to mix well. Cover and chill for 30 minutes. Place a leaf of lettuce on each of 6 individual salad plates. Arrange salted tomato slices on each. Break remaining lettuce into bite-sized pieces; toss with marinated vegetables. Heap on tomato slices. Yield: 6 servings.

Mrs. B. H. Gregory, Sr.
Carlisle, South Carolina

GREEN PEA GARDEN SALAD

1 can peas, drained
1 lge. carrot, cut up
1 sm. onion, cut up
2 hard-boiled eggs
Cut-up celery, to taste
2 tbsp. chopped sweet pickles

Place peas in a bowl; add chopped eggs. Mix remaining ingredients except mayonnaise with peas. Sprinkle with a little salt and pepper. Mix with enough mayonnaise for right consistency. Chill before serving on lettuce.

Mrs. Annie R. Davis
Statesboro, Georgia

NEW PEA SALAD

1 c. new peas, cooked and drained
1 qt. lettuce, cut or broken in pieces
3 or 4 green onions, cut up
3 or 4 radishes, sliced
1 carrot, grated
Salt and pepper to taste

Mix all ingredients with salad dressing, tossing to mix well.

Mrs. Allen Gregory
Hopkinsville, Kentucky

ONE-BOWL SALAD

2 heads lettuce
3 eggs, hard cooked
2 tomatoes, sliced
1 c. peas, cooked
Spinach leaves

Tear lettuce into small pieces. Cut eggs in half lengthwise. Slice tomatoes. Place the lettuce into a small bowl; add one row sliced tomatoes down the center with halved eggs on other side. In each corner place a cup-like leaf of lettuce, filling with peas. Trim outer edge of dish with darker spinach leaves. Yield: 8 servings.

Jean A. Cary
Burkesville, Kentucky

LAZY-DAY SALAD

1 c. uncooked peas
1 c. uncooked corn
1 c. diced firm ripe tomatoes
1 c. lettuce, chopped fine
½ c. cauliflower, finely chopped
½ c. fine chopped carrots
2 stalks celery, chopped fine
1 minced garlic bulb
1 tbsp. each parsley, dill and basil, minced
4 tbsp. corn oil
4 tbsp. pure apple cider vinegar

Toss enough to mix and serve.

Mrs. Walter Chenault
Pine Ridge, Kentucky

EASY TOSS SALAD

1 med. head lettuce
2 long tender carrots
6 med. radishes, chopped
⅓ med. bottle French dressing
Pinch of salt
1 tbsp. vinegar

(Continued on next page)

Chop the lettuce coarsely into a mixing bowl. Add the carrots and radishes. Add the French dressing, salt and vinegar. Toss lightly together and chill a short time before serving.

Mrs. G. T. Robinson
Hazel, Kentucky

CAESAR SALAD

1 clove of garlic
½ c. salad oil
½ head lettuce
½ bunch curly endive
1 c. croutons
1 2-oz. can anchovy fillets
3 or 4 tomatoes, diced
1 beaten egg
1 tsp. Worcestershire sauce
¼ c. lemon juice
½ tsp. pepper
½ tsp. salt
½ c. grated Parmesan cheese

Mash garlic; add to salad oil and let stand. Break lettuce in bowl. Tear endive. Add croutons, anchovies and tomatoes. Strain salad oil to remove garlic. Pour over vegetables. Combine remaining ingredients; beat well. Pour over salad and toss lightly. Garnish with sliced tomatoes.

Thelma Zeiler
Paris, Arkansas

FOURTH-OF-JULY PICNIC SALAD

½ doz. lge. leaves curly mustard
1 head lettuce
1 doz. sprigs parsley
1 sm. red sweet pepper or a piece of red sweet pickled pepper
Liquid from a jar of spicy sweet cucumber or mixed pickles
Salt to taste

Trim off about 1 1/2 inches of each mustard leaf and save for lining the edge or rim of the salad bowl. Cut up finely the rest of the mustard, all of the lettuce, parsley and red pepper. Mix together using the pickle liquid for dressing. Salt to taste. Place the mixture in an attractive salad bowl and arrange the curly mustard trimmings around the edge.

Mrs. L. L. James
Grandview, Tennessee

GOURMET SALAD

2 c. coarsely chopped lettuce
1 ½ c. coarsely chopped cabbage
¾ c. coarsely chopped watercress
¾ c. coarsely chopped raw spinach
⅓ c. chives
2 tbsp. chopped anchovy
2 tbsp. crumbled bleu cheese
6 tbsp. bleu cheese salad dressing

Combine all ingredients and toss lightly. Yield: 8 servings.

Mary K. Witmer
Sabillasville, Maryland

GREEK SALAD PLATTER

1 head Boston lettuce
2 carrots, pared and coarsely grated
2 tomatoes, sliced
1 med. cucumber, pared and sliced
½ c. thinly sliced radishes
12 pitted ripe olives
½ tsp. dried oregano leaves
½ c. bottled Italian-style salad dressing

Line salad bowl or rectangular serving dish with outside leaves of lettuce. Break remaining lettuce into bite-sized pieces into bowl. Add carrot, tomato, cucumber, radishes and olives. Sprinkle with oregano. Pour dressing over all; toss until vegetables are well coated. Yield: 6 servings.

Kathy Mashburn
Powhatan, Arkansas

SPRING SALAD BOWL

½ head lettuce
¼ bunch curly endive
½ bunch watercress
2 tomatoes, cut in wedges
2 stalks celery, cut in sticks
6 radishes, sliced
3 green onions, chopped
½ green pepper, sliced in rings
½ c. dressing

Break lettuce in bowl; tear endive and watercress in small pieces. Arrange tomatoes, celery, radishes, onions and green pepper over top of greens. Pour dressing over vegetables and toss lightly. Serve immediately.

(Continued on next page)

DRESSING:

½ c. mayonnaise
½ c. sour cream
Dash of garlic salt

Mix ingredients well and pour over vegetables. Toss lightly and serve. Yield: 6 servings.

Mrs. Lewis Pierce
Leakesville, Mississippi

HOLLAND HOT SALAD

4 c. crisp lettuce
⅛ lb. bacon or salt pork, finely cut
3 tbsp. cider vinegar
1 tsp. salt
2 tbsp. sugar
1 c. hot mashed potatoes
3 hard-cooked eggs, sliced
12 red radishes
12 green onions

Chill lettuce in salad bowl. Slowly fry bacon in skillet until crisp. Drain and crumble. Sprinkle over lettuce. Add vinegar, salt and sugar to bacon fat in skillet. Heat through. Pour over crisp lettuce and bacon, tossing lightly. Carefully fold in hot mashed potatoes and hard-cooked eggs. Garnish with crisp red radishes and scallions. Serve immediately. Yield: 6 servings.

Rhonda Awtrey
Ulysses, Kansas

SPRING GARDEN SALAD

1 lge. head lettuce
6 sm. spring onions
1 cucumber
8 radishes

Tear lettuce in bite-sized pieces. Slice onions, cucumber and radishes in thin slices. Be sure all vegetables are very crisp. Just before serving toss with the following dressing.

GRANDMOTHER'S DRESSING:

1 tsp. sugar
1 tbsp. flour
2 eggs
1 tsp. mustard
1 c. cold water
Pinch of salt and pepper
½ c. vinegar
1 tbsp. butter
½ c. sweet cream

Mix sugar and flour; add beaten eggs, mustard, water, salt, pepper and vinegar and boil until thick. Add the butter while boiling. When this is cold, add the cream.
PERSONAL COMMENT: My grandmother Aumack did mostly plain cooking but in the spring when there was a supply of new baby onions and fresh leaf lettuce, she would make the most wonderful dressing to go with these. She died when I was ten years old and I never found a recipe that made dressing that tasted exactly as hers. Something always seemed to be lacking. We moved to a new home last fall and while going through some old trunks I found an old cookbook and there in it, in her own handwriting, was the recipe! It had been lost to me for over thirty years. I might add she only used onions and lettuce but I suppose that was because that was all that was available at that time. I added the radishes and cucumbers. Others may want to add tomatoes, celery, etc.

Mrs. Henry C. Fitzhugh
Gordonsville, Virginia

TOSSED GARDEN SALAD FOR 50

8 med. heads lettuce, torn in pieces
2 med. heads cabbage, coarsely cut
4 med. carrots, finely diced or coarsely grated
6 bunches radishes, thinly sliced
6 bunches celery, diced
2 med. green peppers, diced or 1 red and 1 green
1 c. chopped onions
12 med. tomatoes, diced
2 tbsp. salt
French dressing

Combine all ingredients except dressing and chill. Add 2 1/2 to 3 cups French dressing just before serving.

Mrs. L. M. Nafzinger
Earleville, Maryland

TOSSED GREEN SALAD

1 sm. head lettuce
¼ lb. uncooked spinach
⅛ lb. chicory
1 bunch watercress
2 scallions, minced
Garlic clove
¼ c. French dressing
Salt and pepper

(Continued on next page)

Wash greens well; drain and chill for 30 minutes. Dry greens by wrapping in towel. Rub salad bowl with cut clove of garlic, letting tiny shreds remain in bowl. Tear or cut small pieces of greens into salad bowl; add French dressing and season with salt and pepper. Toss lightly with 2 forks until greens are coated with dressing. Serve in bowl or individual salad plates. Yield: 4 servings.

Dianne Woods
Chatham, Virginia

TOSSED SALAD

1 clove garlic
1 tsp. salt
2 tbsp. lemon juice
¼ tsp. sugar
¼ tsp. pepper
½ tsp. celery seed
½ tsp. paprika
¾ tsp. dry mustard
1 med. head lettuce
1 bunch endive
1 avocado
¾ c. raw cauliflower
1 or 2 firm ripe tomatoes
1 c. freshly roasted peanuts
1 c. sharp coarsely grated cheese

Place garlic and salt in small bowl; mash with a spoon. Add lemon juice, sugar, pepper, celery seed, paprika and dry mustard. Blend seasonings well; add salad oil. Pour dressing into small jar with cover and shake well to blend. Rub peeled garlic over salad bowl. Tear or cut the remaining ingredients into bowl. Add dressing and toss well, about 10 or 12 times.

Mrs. Hunter Daughtrey
Carrsville, Virginia

MARINATED OKRA SALAD

1 pkg. whole okra
Juice of 1 lemon
½ c. salad oil
2 tbsp. horseradish
½ c. paper-thin onion slices
2 med. peeled sliced tomatoes

Prepare okra according to package directions. Boil in salted water for 15 minutes. Drain and chill thoroughly. Combine lemon juice, salad oil and horseradish. Marinate chilled okra, onion and tomato slices with dressing.

Mrs. Reps O. Brown
Pegram, Tennessee

MARINATED VEGETABLE PLATTER

1 med. head cauliflower
Salt to taste
1 1-lb. can whole green beans, drained
1 envelope onion salad dressing mix
⅔ c. salad oil
⅓ c. vinegar
Lettuce cups

Separate cauliflower into small flowerets. Cook, covered, in small amount boiling water, adding salt to taste, just until tender, about 10 minutes. Drain well. Place hot cauliflower and beans in medium bowl. In a screw-type jar combine salad dressing mix, oil and vinegar; cover tightly and shake well. Pour dressing over vegetables. Chill several hours or overnight, turning vegetables once or twice. Drain. Arrange vegetables on lettuce. Yield: 4-6 servings.

H. S. Dobbs
Blytheville, Arkansas

ORIENTAL SALAD

1 can bean sprouts, drained
1 can mixed Chinese vegetables, drained
1 sm. can bamboo shoots, drained
1 sm. can water chestnuts, diced
1 canned pimento, diced
½ c. diced onion
½ c. diced green pepper
½ c. diced celery
8 slices bacon, chopped and fried
Bottled Italian dressing

Mix all ingredients except dressing in deep bowl. Cover with Italian dressing. Cover bowl tightly; refrigerate for 1 hour or more. Yield: 6-8 servings.

Mrs. Harry Earle
Middlesboro, Kentucky

POTATO SALAD SPECIAL

3 c. diced cooked potatoes
1 ½ c. sliced raw cauliflower
1 c. diced celery
2 hard-cooked eggs, chopped
¼ c. chopped onion
6 slices crisp bacon, crumbled
1 c. mayonnaise or salad dressing
1 tbsp. bacon fat
2 tsp. caraway seed (opt.)

(Continued on next page)

Combine potatoes, cauliflower, celery, eggs, onion and bacon. Mix mayonnaise, bacon fat and caraway seed. Pour over salad; toss lightly. Salt to taste. Chill. Yield: 5-6 servings.

Mrs. R. T. Darrell
Morristown, Tennessee

POTATO-VEGETABLE SALAD

3 lge. potatoes, boiled and peeled
Vinegar
Mayonnaise
2 raw carrots, shredded
1 sm. bunch radishes, shredded
3 sweet pickles, chopped
1 sm. raw onion, chopped
3 hard-boiled eggs, chopped
Salt and pepper
Paprika
Dry mustard

Marinate potatoes in vinegar for 30 minutes. Fold in enough mayonnaise to moisten all vegetables. Add eggs, salt and pepper to taste. Sprinkle paprika and few grains of dry mustard on top. Olives or pimentos may be added if desired.

Mrs. W. U. Adams
Stratford, Oklahoma

KOREAN SALAD

1 bag washed and stemmed spinach
1 can water chestnuts, drained and sliced
2 hard-cooked eggs, sliced
5 strips bacon, crumbled
1 can bean sprouts, drained

Mix all ingredients together; chill.

DRESSING:

¾ c. sugar
1 c. salad oil
⅓ c. catsup
¼ c. vinegar
3 tbsp. Worcestershire sauce
1 grated onion
Salt to taste

Mix all ingredients together; blend well. Pour over salad just before serving.

Mrs. J. J. Crayton
Arlington, Texas

SPINACH-LETTUCE-BACON SALAD

6 strips bacon, diced
4 c. bite-sized pieces raw spinach
2 c. bite-sized pieces lettuce
2 hard-cooked eggs, finely chopped
⅓ c. salad dressing

Fry bacon until crisp; drain. Place spinach and lettuce in a bowl. Sprinkle bacon and eggs over the greens. Add salad dressing and toss lightly. Yield: 8 servings.

Martha Hooper
Gray Court, South Carolina

SPINACH SALAD

¼ lb. spinach, chopped
2 carrots, shredded
½ head cabbage, shredded
French dressing

Combine all ingredients. Toss. Serve on lettuce leaves.

Anita Smith
Edinburg, Texas

HOT ORIENTAL SALAD

2 lge. onions, cut up
3 tbsp. oil
4 ripe tomatoes, cut up
2 green peppers, cut up
1 tbsp. brown sugar
1 tbsp. cornstarch
1 tbsp. soy sauce
½ c. water

Cook onions in oil 5 minutes. Add tomatoes and peppers. Mix remaining ingredients and add to vegetables. Cover. Cook 15 to 20 minutes until tender-crisp. Turn frequently but carefully.

Mrs. L. E. M. Freeman
Raleigh, North Carolina

A-1 SALAD

Lettuce
½ c. celery
⅓ c. radishes
2 or 3 tomatoes, quartered
½ c. diced cucumber sweet pickles
2 tsp. chopped green pepper
½ c. canned artichoke hearts
½ c. French dressing
Onion seasoning
Celery salt

Into mixing bowl, place 6 or 8 leaves of shredded lettuce. Crisp diced celery, sliced radishes, diced cucumbers and chopped green pepper in ice water. Add tomatoes and French dressing. Toss all together until well mixed. Two tablespoons Roquefort cheese and 1/2 cup grated carrot may be added.

Mrs. J. C. Murphy
Carthage, Mississippi

RUSSIAN SALAD

8 lge. tomatoes, quartered
2 lge. red onions, sliced into rings
6 ribs of celery, diced
1 green pepper, diced
2 tsp. salt
¼ tsp. pepper
1 clove of garlic, minced (opt.)
¼ tsp. (scant) cayenne pepper
½ c. sugar
Juice of 2 lemons
¾ c. olive oil
¼ c. cider vinegar

In large bowl with tight cover blend all ingredients. Cover and refrigerate at least 6 to 8 hours. Shake bowl several times. Will keep several days. Yield: 15 servings.

Mrs. Ben Lowe
Bowling Green, Kentucky

TUBOOLI SALAD

1 c. cracked wheat seed
½ c. olive oil
Juice of 3 or 4 lemons
1 tsp. salt
4 finely chopped tomatoes
2 finely chopped cucumbers
1 lge. onion, chopped
½ bunch parsley, chopped

Soak the wheat seed in warm water; drain. Mix with the olive oil, lemon juice and salt. Pour over chopped tomatoes, cucumbers and onion. Refrigerate several hours before serving. Garnish with chopped parsley.

Mrs. Hoyal Sloan
Pryor, Oklahoma

TOSSED VEGETABLE SALAD

2 c. shredded spinach
2 c. shredded lettuce
6 green onions, sliced thin
12 sm. radishes, sliced

Tear spinach and lettuce in manageable pieces. Mix all ingredients and store in refrigerator until just before serving. Blend with Bacon Dressing and serve.

BACON DRESSING:

6 slices bacon
¼ c. bacon fat
3 tbsp. vinegar
2 hard-cooked eggs

Cook bacon until crisp and break into small pieces. Drain fat and measure 1/4 cup; put fat into skillet and reheat. Take skillet from stove; add vinegar and chopped eggs. Yield: 6-8 servings.

Mrs. Elbert Hodge
Marion, Kentucky

VEGETABLE SALAD

2 8-oz. cans diced carrots
2 8-oz. cans diced beets
2 8-oz. cans party peas
2 8-oz. cans green beans
2 lge. onions, sliced thin
1 8-oz. bottle Italian salad dressing

Open, drain and arrange layers of vegetables in a bowl, then onion rings, alternating. Pour on salad dressing. Cover tightly and refrigerate 12 to 24 hours.

Mrs. A. J. Stafford
Limestone, Tennessee

VEGETABLE SALAD

1 c. chopped lettuce
1 c. chopped mustard greens
1 c. chopped radishes
1 c. chopped sweet cucumber pickles
½ c. chopped carrots
1 tsp. salt
½ c. bacon grease
1 onion, size of an egg, chopped
2 hard-boiled eggs
Salt and pepper to taste
2 tbsp. vinegar
Bologna

Put first 5 ingredients in mixing bowl. Add salt, bacon grease and onion; mix well. Put chopped eggs in another bowl with salt, pepper and vinegar; mix well. Add chopped bologna; mix well. Add to vegetables. Serve with any kind of beans.

Mrs. Roy Livingston
Piedmont, Alabama

CONGEALED VEGETABLE SALADS

Recipe for Tomato-Sour Cream Ring on Page 187

GOURMET SALAD

- 1 pkg. Italian salad dressing mix
- 1 9-oz. pkg. frozen artichoke hearts
- 1 c. thinly sliced fresh mushrooms
- 1 3-oz. pkg. Italian-flavor salad gelatin
- 1 c. boiling water
- 2 tsp. vinegar
- 7 ice cubes
- 1 tbsp. diced pimento
- 1 c. mayonnaise or salad dressing

Prepare salad dressing according to package directions. Cook artichokes according to package directions; drain and cool. Cut into halves. Marinate artichokes and mushrooms in dressing for 1 hour; drain, reserving dressing. Refrigerate dressing. Dissolve gelatin in boiling water. Add vinegar and ice cubes. Stir until slightly thickened. Drain artichokes and mushrooms again; fold into gelatin with pimento. Turn into 1-quart mold; cover and chill overnight. Beat mayonnaise until smooth with refrigerated Italian dressing. Dip mold quickly in and out of hot water; place on serving plate. Serve with seasoned mayonnaise. Yield: 4-6 servings.

Mrs. F. G. Young
Memphis, Tennessee

JELLIED ARTICHOKE SALAD

- 1 can consomme
- 1 envelope unflavored gelatin
- ⅓ c. water
- 1 tsp. lemon juice
- ⅛ tsp. salt
- 1 box frozen artichoke hearts, cooked
- ½ pt. sour cream

Heat consomme. Soak gelatin in water; add consomme, lemon juice and salt. Quarter artichoke hearts; arrange around sides of 8 small cup salad molds. Fill 3/4 full with gelatin mixture. Chill until almost set. Fill each mold with sour cream. Chill until firm. Invert on lettuce leaf and top with dab of mayonnaise, if desired. Yield: 8 servings.

Mrs. R. T. Cook
Baltimore, Maryland

ASPARAGUS SALAD

- 1 pkg. lemon gelatin
- 1 ¾ c. hot water or asparagus liquid
- 2 tbsp. sugar
- 1 tsp. salt
- 3 tbsp. vinegar
- 1 c. chopped celery
- 1 c. chopped asparagus
- 2 tbsp. chopped onion
- 1 tbsp. chopped pimento (opt.)

Dissolve gelatin in hot water; add sugar, salt and vinegar. Chill until slightly thickened; add remaining ingredients. Chill until firm.

Mrs. Lloyd Dunn
Ponca City, Oklahoma

ASPARAGUS MOLD

- 1 pkg. unflavored gelatin
- ¼ c. cold water
- 1 c. hot asparagus liquid
- ½ c. mayonnaise
- ½ c. cream, whipped
- 1 tsp. salt
- 2 tbsp. lemon juice
- 1 can asparagus or 2 pkg. frozen asparagus
- 1 c. blanched almonds, cut in small pieces

Dissolve gelatin in water; stir in asparagus liquid. Let partially set. Fold in mayonnaise, cream, salt and lemon juice. Add asparagus and almonds. Pour in mold; congeal. Serve with mayonnaise whipped with a small amount of lemon juice.

Mrs. L. M. DeShong
Paris, Texas

ASPARAGUS SALAD

- ¾ c. sugar
- Pinch of salt
- ½ c. vinegar
- 1 c. cold water
- 2 envelopes unflavored gelatin
- ½ c. hot water
- 1 c. chopped celery
- ½ c. chopped toasted pecans
- 1 can asparagus, cut into bite-sized pieces
- 1 can pimento, cut into strips
- Juice of ½ lemon
- 1 tbsp. onion, scraped

Combine sugar, salt, vinegar and cold water; bring to a boil. Continue boiling for 5 minutes. Dissolve gelatin in hot water. Remove boiling mixture from heat; add gelatin. Cool. Combine remaining ingredients; add to liquid mixture. Chill until firm.

Mrs. Mary J. Higgins
Marietta, Georgia

ASPARAGUS SALAD

1 envelope unflavored gelatin
¼ c. cold water
1 c. hot asparagus juice
½ c. sour cream
½ c. mayonnaise
1 tsp. salt
½ c. toasted almonds
2 tbsp. lemon juice
1 lge. can asparagus, drained

Dissolve gelatin in water; stir in asparagus juice. Beat in sour cream and mayonnaise until well blended. Add salt, almonds, lemon juice and asparagus. Congeal in mold; serve on lettuce.

Mrs. W. M. Cavin
Stanley, North Carolina

COTTAGE CHEESE ASPARAGUS MOUSSE

1 1-lb. can green asparagus or
2 9-oz. pkg. frozen asparagus, cooked
1 tbsp. unflavored gelatin
¼ c. water
1 ½ c. cottage cheese
2 tbsp. lemon juice
½ tsp. prepared mustard
½ tsp. salt
1 c. blanched almonds, slivered or chopped

Drain asparagus, reserving liquid. Sprinkle gelatin over water to soften. Add enough water to asparagus liquid to give 1 cup; heat to boiling. Stir in softened gelatin until dissolved; chill until jelly consistency. Sieve cottage cheese or blend in blender until smooth and creamy; combine with lemon juice, mustard and salt. Dice asparagus; fold into gelatin along with cottage cheese mixture and almonds. Turn into 1-quart mold; chill until firm. Unmold on salad greens.

Alberta Cramer
Townville, South Carolina

CONGEALED ASPARAGUS SALAD

1 box lime gelatin
1 c. boiling water
1 c. mayonnaise
½ c. milk
¼ tsp. salt
½ c. grated cheese
1 tbsp. grated onion
1 tbsp. vinegar
Dash of red pepper or a few drops Tabasco sauce
1 No. 300 can green cut asparagus, drained

Dissolve gelatin in boiling water. Cool until syrupy. Mix mayonnaise, milk, salt, cheese, onion, vinegar and pepper. Fold into thickened gelatin. Add asparagus. Turn into oiled molds. Congeal.

Elizabeth Heard
Jackson, Mississippi

EGG AND ASPARAGUS SALAD

2 envelopes unflavored gelatin
¼ c. cold water
½ c. whipping cream
1 c. asparagus
3 hard-cooked eggs, chopped
⅔ c. of pimento
½ tsp. salt
¼ c. mayonnaise or salad dressing
Lettuce

Soften gelatin in cold water; dissolve over hot water. Whip cream; add gelatin. Fold in asparagus, eggs, pimento, salt and mayonnaise. Pour into individual molds; chill until firm. Unmold on lettuce.

Mrs. Alice Vincent
Itta Bena, Mississippi

JELLIED ASPARAGUS SALAD

¾ c. sugar
1 ½ c. water
½ c. white vinegar
2 pkg. gelatin
Cold water
½ tsp. salt
2 pimentos, chopped
1 sm. can asparagus tips
Juice of ½ lemon
2 tsp. grated onion
1 c. chopped celery

Mix sugar, 1 cup water and vinegar; bring to a boil. Dissolve gelatin in remaining water; add to hot mixture. Cool; add remaining ingredients. Congeal.

DRESSING:

1 c. sour cream
¼ c. lemon juice
2 tbsp. sugar
1 tsp. salt
Cayenne pepper
½ tsp. celery salt (opt.)
½ tsp. paprika (opt.)
1 tsp. dry mustard (opt.)
¼ tsp. garlic salt (opt.)

Combine all ingredients; blend with rotary beater until smooth and thick. Serve with salad. Yield: 6-8 servings.

Jimmie Garvin Harris
Aiken, South Carolina

TOMATO-ASPARAGUS SALAD

2 c. canned tomatoes or tomato juice
1 tsp. salt
Dash of pepper
1 sm. bay leaf
3 whole cloves
3 tbsp. minced onion
1 pkg. lemon gelatin
1 tbsp. vinegar
2 tbsp. cold water
1 ¼ c. cottage cheese
2 tbsp. minced green pepper
½ c. diced celery
1 c. cooked asparagus, cooled
Salt to taste
⅓ c. mayonnaise or salad dressing

Combine tomatoes, salt, pepper, bay leaf, cloves and onion. Cook gently for 20 minutes. Remove bay leaf after 10 minutes of cooking. Force mixture through sieve. Measure; add hot water to make 1 1/2 cups. Dissolve gelatin in hot tomato mixture. Add vinegar. Measure 1/2 cup mixture; add cold water. Turn into ring mold or individual molds. Chill until firm. Chill remaining gelatin mixture until slightly thickened. Combine cottage cheese with remaining ingredients; fold into thickened gelatin mixture. Turn into mold over firm gelatin layer. Chill until firm. Unmold onto crisp lettuce. Yield: 8 servings.

Mrs. T. J. Ware
Panama City, Florida

BEET JELLY SALAD

1 envelope gelatin
½ c. cold water
⅓ c. sugar
½ tsp. salt
1 c. hot beet juice
¼ c. mild vinegar or lemon juice
1 c. chopped cooked beets
1 c. chopped celery
4 tbsp. horseradish

Sprinkle gelatin over cold water; add sugar, salt and hot beet juice. Stir until dissolved. Add vinegar; mix well. Chill until thickened; add beets, celery and horseradish. Pour into ring mold that has been rinsed in cold water. Chill until firm. Yield: 8 servings.

Mrs. S. B. West
Hagerstown, Maryland

BEET-RASPBERRY SALAD

1 pkg. raspberry gelatin
2 c. cooked shoestring beets
½ c. finely chopped celery

Prepare gelatin according to package directions. Let partially thicken. Add remaining ingredients. Chill. Yield: 6 servings.

Hilma R. Davis
Pittsburg, Kansas

BEET SALAD

1 No. 2 can beets, drained and chopped
2 tbsp. vinegar
½ tsp. celery salt
2 tsp. salt
2 tbsp. grated onion
2 pkg. lemon gelatin
Whipped cream
Mayonnaise
Grated unpeeled cucumber

Combine beets, vinegar, salts, onion and horseradish. Prepare gelatin according to package directions, using only 3 cups water. Chill until gelatin begins to set; add beet mixture. Pour into 8-inch ring mold. Chill until set. Mix equal portions of whipped cream, mayonnaise and cucumber; serve over salad. Yield: 8 servings.

Mrs. P. T. Martin
Columbia, South Carolina

BEET SALAD

1 3-oz. pkg. lemon gelatin or mixed vegetable gelatin
1 c. boiling water
¾ c. pickled beet liquid
¾ tsp. salt
1 tsp. prepared horseradish
2 tsp. grated onion
Dash of pepper
¾ c. diced celery
¾ c. pickled beets, drained and diced

(Continued on next page)

Dissolve gelatin in boiling water; add beet liquid, salt, horseradish, onion and pepper. Chill until consistency of egg white. Fold in celery and beets. Spoon into 1-quart mold; chill until firm. Yield: 6 servings.

Marietta Smith
Barmsdall, Oklahoma

BEET SALAD RING

1 pkg. lemon gelatin
1 c. hot water
1 c. cold water
1 lge. stalk celery, chopped
1 can shoestring beets, drained
⅓ c. horseradish
1 ¼ tsp. salt
Few grains of pepper

Dissolve gelatin in hot water; add cold water. Chill until thick. Combine celery, beets, horseradish, salt and pepper. Stir vegetable mixture into gelatin; pour into 5 1/2-cup ring mold. Chill until firm. Yield: 4-6 servings.

Mrs. H. S. King
Hyattsville, Maryland

BEET SALAD RING

1 1-qt. can beets, diced
2 pkg. lemon gelatin
⅓ c. vinegar
2 tbsp. horseradish
1 tsp. grated onion
1 c. chopped celery

Drain liquid from beets; measure and add water to make 3 cups. Heat to boiling; add gelatin, stirring until dissolved. Add vinegar, horseradish and onion; chill until slightly thickened. Add beets and celery; pour into 9-inch ring mold or individual molds. Chill until firm. Pickled beets may be used by omitting vinegar and using unflavored gelatin.

Mrs. Noah Elam
Index, Kentucky

BEET SALAD RING

1 1-qt. can beets
2 pkg. lemon gelatin
⅓ c. vinegar
1 tsp. grated onion
2 tbsp. grated horseradish

Drain liquid from beets. Measure liquid; add water to make 3 cups. Heat to boiling; add gelatin, stirring until dissolved. Add vinegar, onion and horseradish. Chill until mixture begins to thicken. Dice beets. Add beets and celery. Pour into 9-inch ring mold or into individual molds; chill until firm. Unmold on platter; surround with salad greens.

Alice Cox
Vanceburg, Kentucky

MOLDED BEET SALAD

1 pkg. lemon gelatin
1 c. boiling water
1 No. 2 can beets, sieved
1 c. sour cream
1 tbsp. lemon juice
1 tsp. minced onion
Salt and pepper to taste

Dissolve gelatin in boiling water; stir in beets. Cool until mixture begins to thicken; fold in sour cream, lemon juice, onion, salt and pepper. Fill six individual molds or one large mold; chill until firm. Unmold on crisp lettuce; serve with salad dressing. Yield: 6 servings.

Mrs. Linden Baker
Santa Fe, Tennessee

VEGETABLE SALAD ITALIAN

1 3-oz. pkg. Italian salad-flavored gelatin
1 c. hot water
¼ c. cold water
1 ½ tsp. vinegar
1 c. diced red beets, drained
½ c. thinly sliced celery
¼ c. finely chopped green pepper
1 tbsp. grated onion
¼ tsp. seasoned salt
½ c. evaporated milk, undiluted
1 tbsp. lemon juice

Dissolve gelatin in hot water; add cold water, vinegar, beets, celery, green pepper, onion and seasoned salt. Chill milk in refrigerator tray 10 to 15 minutes; whip until stiff. Add lemon juice; whip very stiff. Fold into gelatin mixture; pour into 5-cup mold. Chill 2 hours or until firm.

Mrs. Joe Wiles
Moreland, Georgia

BROCCOLI SALAD

1 envelope unflavored gelatin
2 c. hot beef consomme
2 pkg. broccoli, cooked and mashed
4 hard-cooked eggs, chopped
½ c. mayonnaise
Dash of Tabasco and Worcestershire sauce

Dissolve gelatin in hot consomme. Cool slightly. Add remaining ingredients. Pour into oiled molds; chill.

Mrs. K. D. Phillips
Hyattsville, Maryland

SURPRISE BROCCOLI MOLD

2 pkg. frozen broccoli
3 c. water
1 envelope unflavored gelatin
1 can consomme
½ sm. onion, grated
2 hard-cooked eggs, finely chopped
1 tbsp. lemon juice
1 c. mayonnaise
Salt and pepper to taste
Sliced avocado (opt.)
Olives (opt.)
Shrimp (opt.)

Cook broccoli in 2 1/2 cups salted water for 20 minutes or until well done. Soften gelatin in remaining cold water. Heat consomme to a boil; stir in softened gelatin. Mash broccoli until smooth. Add consomme; cool. Add onion, eggs, lemon juice, mayonnaise, salt and pepper; pour into ring mold. Refrigerate for 2 to 3 hours or until firm. Carefully unmold and garnish with avocado, olives and shrimp. Yield: 6-8 servings.

Mrs. R. D. Gregory
Baton Rouge, Louisiana

COLESLAW SALAD

1 pkg. lemon gelatin
1 c. hot water
½ c. mayonnaise
½ c. cold water
2 tbsp. vinegar
¼ tsp. salt
1 ½ c. finely shredded cabbage
½ c. radish slices
½ c. diced celery
2 to 4 tbsp. diced green pepper
1 tbsp. diced onion

Dissolve gelatin in hot water. Blend in mayonnaise, cold water, vinegar and salt. Chill mixture until partially set. Beat till fluffy. Add cabbage, radish slices, celery, green pepper and onion. Pour into individual molds or one 1-quart mold. Chill until set. Small amounts of cucumber and carrots may be added for extra flavor if desired.

Mrs. C. C. Sanders
Mt. Pleasant, Tennessee

COLESLAW SOUFFLE SALAD

1 pkg. lemon gelatin
1 c. hot water
½ c. mayonnaise
½ c. cold water
2 tbsp. vinegar
1 tbsp. diced onion
¼ tsp. salt
1 ½ c. finely shredded cabbage
½ c. sliced radishes
½ c. diced celery
2 tbsp. diced green pepper

Dissolve gelatin in hot water; blend in mayonnaise, cold water, vinegar and salt. Chill until partially set. Beat till fluffy; add remaining ingredients. Pour into individual molds or one 1-quart mold; chill.

Mrs. William E. Marter
Morehead City, North Carolina

EASY PERFECTION SALAD

2 3-oz. pkg. vegetable-flavored gelatin
2 c. boiling water
1 tbsp. vinegar
12 ice cubes
½ c. chopped onion
1 pimento, chopped
1 1-lb. can sauerkraut, chopped
1 tsp. horseradish
1 c. mayonnaise

Dissolve gelatin in water in 8 1/4 x 4 1/2-inch loaf pan. Add vinegar and ice cubes; stir until gelatin begins to thicken. Remove any unmelted ice. Stir in onion, pimento and sauerkraut. Stir gently to distribute vegetables; chill until set. Unmold on crisp greens. Combine horseradish with mayonnaise; serve with salad.

Mrs. Jessie I. Strauss
Collinsville, Alabama

OLD-FASHIONED PERFECTION SALAD

2 envelopes unflavored gelatin
½ c. sugar
1 tsp. salt
1 ½ c. boiling water
1 ½ c. cold water
½ c. vinegar
2 tbsp. lemon juice
2 c. finely shredded cabbage
1 c. chopped celery
½ c. chopped green pepper
¼ c. diced pimento
⅓ c. sliced stuffed green olives

Combine gelatin, sugar and salt; dissolve in boiling water. Add cold water, vinegar and lemon juice; chill until partially set. Add remaining ingredients; pour into loaf pan. Chill until firm. Unmold salad; garnish with carrot curls and ripe olives.

Mrs. Horace Bertraud
Crowley, Louisiana

PERFECTION SALAD

1 tbsp. gelatin
2 tbsp. cold water
1 c. boiling water
2 tsp. sugar
½ tsp. salt
¾ c. canned pineapple juice
¼ c. white wine vinegar
1 c. shredded cabbage
¾ c. diced celery
2 tbsp. chopped green pepper
¼ c. sliced stuffed olives

Soften gelatin in cold water for 5 minutes. Add boiling water; stir until dissolved. Add sugar, salt and pineapple juice; chill until syrupy. Add vinegar and vegetables; pour into eight molds or an 8 x 8-inch square glass pan. Chill until set. Yield: 8 servings.

Mrs. D. E. Morris
Alexandria, Louisiana

SEAFOAM COLESLAW

1 pkg. lime gelatin
1 c. hot water
¾ c. cold water
¾ tsp. salt
2 tbsp. vinegar
⅔ c. salad dressing
Dash of pepper
¾ tsp. celery seed
1 tbsp. onion, grated
2 c. cabbage, finely grated

Dissolve gelatin in hot water; add cold water, salt and vinegar. Let set until partially congealed; add salad dressing, pepper, celery seed, onion and cabbage. Mold and chill until firm.

Mrs. A. H. Martin
Pensacola, Florida

PERFECTION SALAD

1 envelope unflavored gelatin
¼ c. sugar
½ tsp. salt
1 ¼ c. water
¼ c. vinegar
1 tbsp. lemon juice
½ c. finely shredded cabbage
1 c. chopped celery
1 pimento, cut in small pieces or
2 tbsp. chopped sweet red or green pepper

Combine gelatin, sugar and salt thoroughly in a small saucepan. Add 1/2 cup water; place over low heat stirring constantly until gelatin dissolves. Remove from heat; stir in remaining water, vinegar and lemon juice. Chill mixture to unbeaten egg white consistency. Fold in cabbage, celery and pimento. Turn into individual molds; chill until firm. Unmold; garnish with salad greens. Serve with salad dressing.

Mrs. Algier Vaiden
Hernando, Mississippi

TANGY CABBAGE SALAD

1 3-oz. pkg. salad gelatin
½ tsp. salt
1 c. boiling water
1 ½ c. cold water
2 tsp. vinegar
2 tbsp. horseradish
½ c. chopped celery
1 tbsp. chopped pimento
1 ½ c. shredded cabbage
¼ c. chopped dill pickles
3 drops Tabasco sauce

Dissolve gelatin and salt in boiling water; add cold water and vinegar. Chill until slightly thickened. Add remaining ingredients. Pour into bowl or muffin tins. Chill until firm. Serve with beef, if desired. Yield: 8 servings.

Mrs. C. D. Thames
Waco, Texas

VEGETABLE-GELATIN SALAD

1 pkg. unflavored gelatin
1 ½ c. boiling water
1 ½ c. cold water
2 c. shredded cabbage
1 c. finely chopped celery
¼ c. finely chopped green pepper
¼ c. chopped pimento
⅓ c. chopped stuffed olives
2 tbsp. lemon juice
½ c. vinegar

Dissolve gelatin in boiling water; add cold water. Combine cabbage, celery, green pepper, pimento and olives. Add lemon juice and vinegar to gelatin; pour over vegetable mixture. Let jell. Serve on lettuce cups.

Nita Carol Sammons
Forrest Hills, Kentucky

GELATIN WHIP SALAD

1 pkg. lemon gelatin
2 c. boiling water
¾ c. Velveeta cheese
¾ c. finely chopped celery
¾ c. grated carrots
6 lge. marshmallows, chopped
Chopped maraschino cherries (opt.)
2 c. heavy cream, whipped

Dissolve gelatin in boiling water. Add cheese to hot water; cool. Combine all ingredients except cream; chill until thickened. Fold in whipped cream; chill until firm.

Mrs. E. S. Edwards
Hattiesburg, Mississippi

JADE RING SALAD

1 pkg. lime-flavored gelatin
2 c. hot water
1 tbsp. vinegar
1 c. cottage cheese
¼ c. salad dressing or mayonnaise
⅓ c. green pepper strips
½ c. cooked diced carrot
½ tsp. grated onion
1 ½ tsp. salt
⅛ tsp. pepper

Dissolve gelatin in hot water; add vinegar. Pour thin layer into ring mold and chill until firm. Chill remaining gelatin until slightly thickened. Place in bowl of chipped ice and whip with rotary beater until fluffy and thick. Combine cheese, salad dressing, green pepper, carrots, onion, salt and pepper. Fold into whipped gelatin. Turn onto firm gelatin in mold. Chill.

Chlois McInnish
Talladega, Alabama

LIME GELATIN SALAD

2 pkg. lime gelatin
2 c. hot water
1 c. cold water
2 tbsp. vinegar
¾ c. salad dressing
½ tsp. salt
½ c. cottage cheese
½ c. chopped pecans
½ c. grated carrots

Dissolve gelatin in hot water; add cold water, vinegar, salad dressing and salt. Blend with an electric mixer. Pour into freezing tray; chill 15 minutes or until firm around edges. Whip with electric mixer until fluffy. Add cottage cheese, pecans and carrots. Pour into mold; chill until firm.

Mrs. Boyd W. Clanton
Obion, Tennessee

CELERY-PEPPER CONGEALED SALAD

1 pkg. lemon gelatin
1 c. hot water
1 c. mayonnaise
1 c. cottage cheese
Pinch of salt
1 c. chopped celery
2 tbsp. finely chopped onion
¼ c. chopped green pepper
Green food coloring (opt.)
Chopped pimento (opt.)

Dissolve gelatin in hot water. Let cool. Stir in mayonnaise, cottage cheese and salt. Add remaining ingredients. Let set for several hours. Yield: 6-8 servings.

Virginia L. Langston
Baton Rouge, Louisiana

CHICORY CROWN SALAD

1 clove of garlic
3 3-oz. pkg. plain cream cheese or with chives
½ to 1 tsp. salt
2 c. drained grated cucumbers
1 c. mayonnaise
¼ to ½ c. minced onion
¼ c. minced parsley
1 tbsp. unflavored gelatin
¼ c. cold water
1 head chicory (opt.)
2 hard-cooked eggs, sieved

(Continued on next page)

Rub salad bowl with garlic. Combine cheese, salt, cucumbers, mayonnaise, onion and parsley in salad bowl. Soften gelatin in cold water; dissolve over hot water. Cool to lukewarm; combine with cheese mixture. Pour into mold; chill until firm. Arrange on chicory; garnish with sieved eggs. One-half teaspoon of garlic powder may by used in salad instead of rubbing bowl with garlic clove.

Mrs. R. T. Key
Baton Rouge, Louisiana

CUCUMBER ASPIC SALAD

1 pkg. lime gelatin
1 c. boiling water
1 cucumber, peeled and grated
1 tsp. minced onion
1 tbsp. cider vinegar
1 c. sour cream

Dissolve gelatin in boiling water. Add cucumber, onion and vinegar to sour cream. Pour hot gelatin very slowly into sour cream, stirring constantly to avoid curdling. Mold. Yield: 6 servings.

Mrs. J. H. Green
Tallahassee, Florida

COTTAGE CHEESE CUCUMBER SALAD

1 ½ c. hot water
1 pkg. lemon gelatin
2 ½ tbsp. vinegar
¾ tsp. salt
½ c. mayonnaise
¼ tsp. paprika
1 tbsp. minced onion
½ c. milk
½ c. cottage cheese
½ c. diced cucumber
2 tbsp. diced green pepper
2 tbsp. sliced stuffed olives

Pour hot water over gelatin, add vinegar and salt. Combine mayonnaise, paprika, onion and milk; add to gelatin. Beat with rotary beater until mixed. Chill until slightly thickened; whip until light and fluffy. Add remaining ingredients. Pour into mold. Chill until firm.

Mrs. M. D. Bell
Meridian, Mississippi

CREME DE CUCUMBER SALAD

2 c. boiling water
1 lge. pkg. lime gelatin
1 tbsp. vinegar
1 c. mayonnaise
1 c. grated cucumbers
1 tbsp. grated onion
1 tbsp. horseradish

Pour boiling water over gelatin. Add vinegar and a small portion of mayonnaise. Add remaining ingredients. Chill in mold. If desired, cooled gelatin may be whipped before remaining ingredients are added.

Mrs. R. W. Thomas
Thomasville, Georgia

CUCUMBER CREAM CHEESE RING

2 tbsp. unflavored gelatin
¼ c. cold water
½ to ¾ c. boiling water
2 to 4 tbsp. sugar
½ tsp. salt
2 to 3 tbsp. lemon juice
1 tsp. onion, grated
1 c. cucumber, grated and drained
2 to 3 3-oz. pkg. cream cheese
Canned pears, drained
¼ lb. red cinnamon candies
Lettuce

Soften gelatin in cold water; dissolve in boiling water. Add sugar; cool. Add salt, lemon juice, onion and cucumber. Soften cream cheese with 1/4 cup gelatin mixture. Chill remaining gelatin until partially thickened. Beat chilled mixture with an egg beater until foamy. Combine with cheese-gelatin mixture. Pour into a ring mold and chill until firm. Heat pear juice and candy until candy is dissolved. Add pears and let stand for 1 hour in the candy syrup. Unmold the cucumber ring on a cold plate; fill the center with lettuce and garnish with pears in crisp lettuce cups.

Mrs. C. C. Wells
Meridian, Mississippi

CUCUMBER-CREAM SALAD

1 pkg. lime gelatin
1 tsp. salt
1 c. hot water
2 tbsp. vinegar
1 tsp. onion juice (opt.)
½ c. mayonnaise
1 c. heavy sour cream
2 c. finely chopped drained cucumbers

(Continued on next page)

Dissolve gelatin and salt in hot water; add vinegar and onion juice. Allow to thicken slightly. Fold in mayonnaise; blend thoroughly. Fold in sour cream and cucumbers; blend thoroughly. Chill overnight or until firm. Sour cream may be whipped before adding, if desired. Yield: 8 servings.

Mrs. J. M. Rogers
Cleveland, Tennessee

CUCUMBER MOLD

- 1 ½ pkg. lemon gelatin
- ½ c. boiling water
- 1 tbsp. vinegar
- 1 pt. cottage cheese
- ½ c. mayonnaise
- 1 med. unpeeled cucumber, ground
- 1 sm. onion, ground
- ¼ c. heavy cream

Dissolve gelatin in boiling water; add vinegar. Chill until partially set. Add cottage cheese, mayonnaise, cucumber and onion. Add whipped cream. Pour into mold; chill until firm. Yield: 4-6 servings.

Mrs. C. H. Dobbs
Chandler, Arizona

CUCUMBER MOLD

- 3 boxes apple or lime gelatin
- 1 tbsp. salt
- 2 c. boiling water
- ⅓ c. vinegar
- 1 tbsp. grated onion
- 1 ½ pt. sour cream
- ¾ c. mayonnaise
- 2 c. drained, pared, finely chopped cucumbers
- 2 cucumbers, fluted and sliced
- Watercress

Place gelatin and salt in large bowl; add boiling water, stirring until gelatin is dissolved. Stir in vinegar and onion. Chill to consistency of syrup. Beat in sour cream and mayonnaise, then chopped cucumbers with rotary beater. Pour into 2 1/2-quart tube mold. Refrigerate until firm. Arrange fluted sliced cucumbers around base; place watercress in center of mold. Yield: 10-12 servings.

Mrs. F. G. Norris
Las Vegas, New Mexico

CUCUMBER MOLD

- 1 3-oz. pkg. lime gelatin
- 1 c. hot water
- 1 tbsp. vinegar
- 1 c. grated cucumber
- 1 tsp. salt
- 1 tbsp. chopped onion
- 1 sm. carton sour cream
- ¼ c. mayonnaise

Dissolve gelatin in hot water; add vinegar. Chill until thickened. Fold in remaining ingredients. Pour into one medium mold or six individual molds. Chill until firm. Yield: 6 servings.

Mrs. C. C. Harris
Covington, Kentucky

CUCUMBER MOLDED SALAD

- 1 pkg. lime gelatin
- ½ tsp. salt
- 1 c. boiling water
- 1 c. diced cucumbers
- ¼ c. chopped onion
- ¾ c. salad dressing
- 1 c. cottage cheese

Dissolve gelatin and salt in boiling water. Cool until thickened; add remaining ingredients. Pour into molds; chill until firm. Yield: 6 servings.

Mrs. S. G. Fox
Augusta, Georgia

CUCUMBER SALAD

- Salt
- 1 c. diced cucumbers
- ⅓ c. diced onions
- 1 pkg. lime gelatin
- 1 ½ c. boiling water
- 1 c. salad dressing
- ½ c. diced celery
- 1 sm. jar olives, diced
- 1 tbsp. horseradish
- 2 tbsp. vinegar

Salt cucumbers and onions; set aside. Dissolve gelatin in bowling water; cool slightly. Spoon salad dressing into large jar. Add gelatin to salad dressing while still warm; shake well. Cool. Combine cucumbers, onions, olives, horseradish and vinegar with gelatin mixture; pour into 9 x 12-inch baking dish. Chill until firm. Serve on lettuce. Yield: 15 servings.

Mrs. H. Lancaster
Florala, Alabama

CUCUMBER SALAD

1 lge. unpeeled cucumber, grated
1 sm. onion, grated
1 pt. cottage cheese, small curd
1 pkg. lemon gelatin
½ c. hot water
1 tbsp. vinegar
½ c. mayonnaise
½ c. pecans

Combine cucumber, onion and cottage cheese; drain. Dissolve gelatin in water. Stir vinegar and gelatin into mayonnaise; add to cucumber mixture. Add pecans; pour into molds. Chill for several hours before serving.

Mrs. R. C. Hicks
Paris, Texas

CUCUMBER RING

1 pkg. lemon gelatin
1 pkg. lime gelatin
2 c. boiling water
½ c. cold water
1 ½ tbsp. vinegar
½ tsp. salt
2 c. seeded, unpeeled finely chopped cucumber

Dissolve gelatin in boiling water; add cold water, vinegar and salt, mixing well. Chill until slightly thickened; stir in cucumber. Pour into 1 1/4-quart mold; chill until firm.

Alice Cox
Vanceburg, Kentucky

GREEN FROST SALAD

6 envelopes lime gelatin
1 ½ c. boiling water
1 lb. dry cottage cheese
1 pt. buttermilk
1 tbsp. chopped onion
1 tbsp. white vinegar
½ tsp. pepper
½ tsp. paprika
½ c. chopped cucumber, drained
½ c. finely chopped celery
1 c. thinly sliced radishes

Dissolve lime gelatin in boiling water; cool. Beat cottage cheese and buttermilk in blender until almost smooth. Add cheese mixture to cooled gelatin; mix well. Chill until slightly thickened. Combine remaining ingredients and fold into gelatin mixture. Pour into mold; chill until firm.

Mrs. Wanda Kyles
Cleveland, North Carolina

SPRING SONG SALAD

1 pkg. lemon gelatin
1 ½ c. hot water
1 tbsp. lemon juice
1 tbsp. vinegar
1 tsp. salt
1 c. chopped cucumber
1 c. chopped celery
½ c. sliced green onion
½ c. sliced radishes

Dissolve gelatin in hot water; add lemon juice, vinegar and salt. Chill till thick. Add remaining ingredients. Pour into molds. Chill till firm. Serve topped with mayonnaise.

Mrs. R. L. Hamilton
Hillsboro, Kentucky

ZIPPY CUCUMBER SALAD

2 pkg. lemon gelatin
2 c. boiling water
2 tsp. unflavored gelatin
¼ c. cold water
1 tsp. salt
Few drops of green food coloring
¼ c. vinegar
2 tbsp. grated onion
¼ c. horseradish
2 c. unpared grated cucumbers or 2 med. cucumbers, grated

Dissolve lemon gelatin in boiling water. Mix unflavored gelatin in cold water; let stand until thick. Mix gelatins; cool. Add remaining ingredients. Mix well; chill for 10 to 12 minutes.

DRESSING: (opt.)

½ c. mayonnaise
1 tsp. horseradish
1 c. sour cream
½ tsp. salt
1 tsp. dry mustard
Green food coloring

Combine all ingredients, mixing well. Serve with salad. Yield: 8 servings.

Mrs. P. A. Fleming
Ashland, Kentucky

GREEN PEA SALAD

1 10-oz. pkg. frozen green peas
1 sm. onion, diced
4-oz. mild cheddar cheese, diced
2 tbsp. mayonnaise or salad dressing
1 tbsp. prepared mustard
1 tbsp. horseradish

Cook green peas according to package directions. Chill; stir in onion and cheese. Blend salad dressing, mustard and horseradish; combine with peas, onion and cheese. Serve chilled. Yield: 4-6 servings.

Mrs. N. K. Crook
Little Rock, Arkansas

HORSERADISH MOLD

1 pkg. lemon gelatin
½ c. boiling water
1 envelope unflavored gelatin
1 5-oz. jar horseradish
1 c. mayonnaise
1 c. sour cream

Dissolve lemon gelatin in 1/2 cup boiling water. Dissolve unflavored gelatin in 2 tablespoons cold water; add to lemon gelatin. Stir in horseradish, mayonnaise and sour cream; pour mixture into ring mold. Chill until firm. May be served with ham or beef. Yield: 8 servings.

Mrs. N. O. Drawin
Arkadelphia, Arkansas

HORSERADISH MOLD

1 pkg. lemon gelatin
1 c. boiling water
½ c. cold water
½ c. mayonnaise
Dash of salt
1 5-oz. jar horseradish
½ c. heavy cream, whipped

Dissolve lemon gelatin in boiling water; add cold water. Chill until partially set. Fold in mayonnaise, salt, horseradish and whipped cream; whip until smooth. Place in mold. Chill until set. Unmold; garnish and serve. Yield: 8-10 servings.

Mrs. C. P. Land
Valdosta, Georgia

HORSERADISH MOLD

⅔ c. prepared horseradish
1 pkg. lemon gelatin
1 c. boiling water
½ tsp. salt
½ pt. heavy cream, whipped

Drain horseradish, reserving vinegar. Dissolve gelatin in boiling water. Add drained vinegar and salt; cool. Add horseradish; fold in whipped cream. Pour into ring mold and chill. Unmold; fill center with coleslaw. Yield: 6-8 servings.

Mrs. W. B. Warner
Clearwater, Florida

MOLDED HORSERADISH RING

1 envelope unflavored gelatin
¾ c. cold water
½ c. mayonnaise-type salad dressing
⅓ c. cream-style horseradish
¼ tsp. salt
1 c. heavy cream, whipped

Soften gelatin in cold water; heat over low heat, stirring until dissolved. Combine salad dressing, horseradish and salt; stir in gelatin. Fold in whipped cream; pour into 1-quart mold. Chill until firm.

Pearl Scott
Gainesville, Florida

LIME CONGEALED SALAD

2 c. boiling water
1 pkg. lime gelatin
1 pkg. lemon gelatin
1 c. cottage cheese or cream cheese
½ c. celery
¼ c. chopped bell pepper
1 tsp. grated onion

Pour boiling water over gelatins. Let cool; stir in remaining ingredients. Turn into salad mold; congeal.

Mrs. L. E. Strickland
Athens, Georgia

LETTUCE-LIME SALAD

1 6-oz. pkg. lime gelatin
2 c. boiling water
2 c. cold water
1 head lettuce

(Continued on next page)

Dissolve gelatin in boiling water in 1-quart ring mold; add cold water. Cool. Shred lettuce into liquid until it is fairly solid. Chill until set. Unmold on lettuce leaves. Yield: 6-8 servings.

Mrs. T. I. Parks
Bisbee, Arizona

MOLDED RELISH SALAD

1 pkg. lime gelatin
1 pkg. lemon gelatin
3 c. boiling water
1 c. chopped celery
½ to 1 c. chopped nuts
1 green pepper, chopped
4 tbsp. chili sauce
4 tbsp. India relish
1 sm. bottle olives, chopped
1 sm. can pimento, chopped
Pinch of salt

Dissolve gelatins in boiling water. Chill until partially set. Combine remaining ingredients; fold into gelatin mixture. Chill until firm.

Virginia C. Lee
Memphis, Tennessee

AUNT NELL'S ONION SALAD

1 pkg. lemon gelatin
1 c. boiling water
10 ice cubes
1 c. cottage cheese
1 c. mayonnaise
1 c. finely chopped onions

Dissolve gelatin in boiling water; add 10 ice cubes. Chill for 5 minutes. Fold in remaining ingredients. Pour into mold. Chill until set. Unmold on bed of lettuce and garnish with strips of pimento and green pepper. Yield: 8 servings.

Mrs. M. J. Boswell
Highpoint, North Carolina

GREEN ONION SALAD

1 pkg. lemon gelatin
1 c. hot water
1 c. cottage cheese
1 c. chopped celery
4 sm. whole green onions, chopped
⅔ c. salad dressing

Dissolve gelatin in hot water; set aside to cool. Combine all ingredients; pour in 9 x 9-inch dish. Chill until firm. Cut in squares; serve on lettuce leaves. Yield: 6 servings.

Mrs. R. G. Gipson
Perkinston, Mississippi

POTATO SALAD MOLD

1 envelope unflavored gelatin
2 tbsp. sugar
1 tsp. salt
1 ¼ c. boiling water
¼ c. lemon juice
8 stuffed green olives, sliced
Green pepper strips
3 hard-cooked eggs, chopped
4 c. diced cooked potatoes
¼ c. chopped parsley
¼ c. chopped green onions
¼ c. diced celery
¼ c. diced green pepper
¼ c. diced pimento
1 ½ tsp. salt
1 c. mayonnaise
½ c. heavy cream, whipped

Mix gelatin, sugar and salt thoroughly; add boiling water and stir to dissolve. Add lemon juice. Pour thin layer of mixture into 1 1/2-quart ring mold; chill until almost firm. Make flower design on gelatin, using olive slices and green pepper strips. Add remaining ingredients to remaining gelatin mixture. Spoon over gelatin in ring mold. Chill until firm. Yield: 8 servings.

Bernice Morgan
Jacksonville, Alabama

SOUFFLE POTATO SALAD

2 c. diced boiled potatoes
5 ½ tbsp. vinegar
⅓ c. chopped dill pickles
1 tsp. salt
⅛ tsp. pepper
½ tsp. dried dill
2 tbsp. sliced scallions or green onion
1 pkg. lemon gelatin
1 c. hot water
½ c. cold water
½ c. mayonnaise
1 tsp. prepared mustard
2 hard-cooked eggs, sliced

(Continued on next page)

Combine potatoes with 2 1/2 tablespoons vinegar, dill pickles, salt, pepper, dried dill and scallions. Dissolve gelatin in hot water. Add cold water, 3 tablespoons vinegar and mayonnaise, blended with mustard; beat with rotary beater until smooth. Pour into refrigerator tray; chill in freezing unit until mixture is firm 1-inch from edge, but soft in center. Turn into bowl; beat with rotary beater or electric mixer until fluffy. Fold in potato mixture and eggs. Pour into 1-quart ring mold; chill until firm. Unmold; serve on salad greens. Yield: 6 servings.

Mrs. E. D. Volmar
Beaumont, Texas

SOUR CREAM MUSHROOM MOLD

1 3-oz. pkg. Italian, celery, or mixed vegetable-flavored salad gelatin
1 tsp. salt
1 c. boiling water
¾ c. cold water
2 tbsp. chopped scallions
1 tbsp. chopped parsley
2 tsp. wine vinegar
⅛ tsp. black pepper, coarsely ground
1 c. sour cream
½ lb. or 2 ½ c. mushrooms, chopped

Dissolve gelatin and salt in boiling water; add cold water. Stir in scallions, parsley, vinegar, and pepper; chill until very thick. Blend in sour cream; stir in mushrooms. Pour into 1-quart mold; chill until firm or about 4 hours. Unmold; Garnish with romaine, black olives and cherry tomato halves. Yield: 8-12 servings.

Mrs. Estell Shalla
Bay City, Texas

MOLDED SPINACH SALAD

1 3-oz. pkg. celery or vegetable gelatin
1 c. boiling water
½ c. cold water
2 tbsp. cider vinegar
½ c. mayonnaise or salad dressing
4 tsp. grated onion
½ tsp. salt
Dash of pepper
1 8-oz. carton cream-style cottage cheese
⅓ c. chopped celery
1 c. raw chopped spinach

Dissolve gelatin in boiling water. Add cold water, vinegar, mayonnaise, onion, salt and pepper. Beat slightly to blend. Chill until mixture begins to jell. Fold in cottage cheese, celery and spinach. Pour into 1-quart mold or 6 5-ounce molds. Chill about 2 hours or until firm. Serve with salad greens. Yield: 6 servings.

Mrs. Dean Collins
Parrottsville, Tennessee

SPINACH COTTAGE CHEESE SALAD

1 pkg. lemon gelatin
1 c. hot water
½ c. cold water
1 ½ tsp. vinegar
½ c. mayonnaise
Salt and pepper
1 c. raw chopped spinach
¾ c. cottage cheese
⅓ c. diced celery
1 tbsp. finely chopped onion

Dissolve gelatin in hot water; add cold water, vinegar, mayonnaise, salt and pepper. Blend well with rotary beater. Pour into refrigerator tray; chill in freezing unit 15 to 20 minutes or until firm 1-inch from edge but soft in center. Place in bowl; whip with rotary beater until fluffy. Fold in spinach, cottage cheese, celery and onion. Pour into mold.

Mrs. Ernest Stouk
Seymour, Texas

SPINACH SALAD MOLD

2 pkg. frozen spinach
2 pkg. gelatin
1 can consomme
4 hard-cooked eggs, diced
¾ c. mayonnaise
1 ¾ tsp. salt
2 tbsp. lemon juice
2 tbsp. Worcestershire sauce
Dash of Tabasco sauce

Cook spinach, without water, until done. Drain. Soften gelatin in 1/2 cup cold consomme; heat remaining consomme. Add to gelatin mixture. Cool until partially congealed. Add eggs, mayonnaise and seasonings to spinach; fold into gelatin mixture. Pour into 13 x 9 x 2-inch pan; chill until set.

Mrs. T. S. Fulton
Panama City, Florida

THOUSAND ISLAND RING

2 envelopes unflavored gelatin
½ c. cold water
1 c. chili sauce
½ c. catsup
1 ½ c. mayonnaise
¾ tsp. salt
1 ½ tsp. sugar
Dash of Tabasco sauce
1 c. thinly sliced celery
3 to 6 hard-cooked eggs, sliced
½ c. pitted olives

Soften gelatin in cold water; let stand. Melt over hot water. Mix chili sauce, catsup and mayonnaise; add seasonings. Stir in gelatin. Add celery, eggs and olives; blend well. Pour into ring mold; chill until firm. Unmold onto lettuce. Fill center with shrimp, crab, lobster, tuna or salmon salad.

Mrs. G. C. Hall
Beaumont, Texas

ASHVILLE SALAD

1 can tomato soup
3 sm. pkg. cream cheese
2 tbsp. unflavored gelatin
½ c. cold water
1 ½ c. chopped celery
1 onion, chopped
1 green pepper, chopped
1 cucumber, chopped
1 c. mayonnaise

Heat soup; stir in cream cheese until thoroughly blended. Dissolve gelatin in cold water. Add to soup; partially cool. Fold in vegetables; chill until firm. Whip mayonnaise into this mixture. Pour into individual molds or 8-inch square pan. Chill. Yield: 8 servings.

Mrs. J. H. Garson
Albuquerque, New Mexico

ASPIC RING SALAD

2 envelopes plus 2 tsp. unflavored gelatin
1 qt. tomato juice, chilled
½ tsp. onion juice
Salt and pepper to taste
¼ c. cold water
½ c. salad dressing
1 ½-lb. pkg. cream cheese
1 c. chopped celery
1 tbsp. chopped pimento
1 tbsp. chopped green pepper
½ c. chopped pecans
1 tsp. lemon juice

Soften 2 envelopes of gelatin in 1 cup cold tomato juice; dissolve over hot water. Add dissolved gelatin to remaining cold tomato juice with onion juice and seasonings. Pour one-half of mixture into 2-quart ring mold. Chill until firm. Soften remaining gelatin in cold water; dissolve over hot water. Blend salad dressing into cream cheese; add celery, pimento, green pepper, pecans, lemon juice and gelatin. Spread over firm gelatin mixture. Chill until firm. Pour remaining aspic over cream cheese layer. Chill again. Unmold on lettuce and place ripe olives in center of ring. Yield: 11-12 servings.

Mrs. C. D. Barnes
Las Vegas, New Mexico

ASPIC SALAD PIE

1 pkg. frozen mixed vegetables, cooked and drained
¼ c. French or oil and vinegar dressing
2 pkg. lemon gelatin
2 c. hot water
1 tsp. salt
Dash of pepper
2 tbsp. vinegar
½ c. cold water
1 8-oz. can tomato sauce
1 c. lge. curd cottage cheese
1 9-in. pie shell, baked

Marinate vegetables in dressing for 2 hours; drain. Dissolve gelatin in hot water; add salt, pepper and vinegar, stirring to blend. Divide mixture in half. Add cold water to first half and tomato sauce to remaining half. Chill each until slightly thickened. Combine cottage cheese and vegetables; fold into clear gelatin mixture, reserving 1 cup of mixture for top. Spoon into pie shell. Chill until set, but sticky. Top with tomato sauce mixture. Chill for 2 hours. Garnish with remaining cottage cheese-vegetable mixture. Yield: 6-8 servings.

Mrs. S. T. Jones
Jacksonville, Florida

BARBECUE SALAD

2 sm. pkg. lemon gelatin
2 ½ c. hot water
2 8-oz. cans tomato sauce
3 tbsp. vinegar
1 tsp. salt
Pepper to taste

Dissolve gelatin in hot water. Add remaining ingredients. Chill until firm. Yield: 8-10 servings.

Mrs. L. E. M. Freeman
Raleigh, North Carolina

JELLIED TOMATO SALAD

2 tbsp. gelatin
½ c. cold water
1 pt. boiling water
½ c. vinegar
½ c. sugar
½ tsp. salt
1 tbsp. Worcestershire sauce
½ onion, diced
1 c. tomato soup

Soak gelatin in cold water for 5 minutes; dissolve in boiling water. Add vinegar, sugar, salt, Worcestershire sauce, onion and soup. Pour into mold which has been rinsed in cold water. Chill until set. Serve on lettuce with mayonnaise, if desired. Yield: 10 servings.

Mrs. T. B. Goodwin
Port Arthur, Texas

JELLIED TOMATO SALAD

1 tbsp. unflavored gelatin
¼ c. cold water
1 ¾ c. tomato juice
¾ c. shredded cabbage
½ c. chopped celery
¼ c. chopped green pepper
2 tbsp. chopped olives
1 tbsp. onion juice
1 tsp. salt

Soften gelatin in cold water. Heat tomato juice; add gelatin, stirring until dissolved. Cool; add remaining ingredients. Pour into mold; chill until firm. Yield: 4-6 servings.

Mrs. W. I. Charles
New Orleans, Louisiana

JELLIED TOMATO SALAD

1 tbsp. unflavored gelatin
1 ¾ c. tomato juice
¼ c. finely chopped watercress
1 tbsp. finely chopped chives
½ tsp. salt
1 tbsp. lemon juice
Few drops Worcestershire sauce
1 tsp. sugar
2 hard-cooked eggs
Mayonnaise
Watercress

Soften gelatin in 1/2 cup tomato juice. Place cup in pan of boiling water and stir until gelatin has dissolved. Add gelatin to remaining tomato juice. Chill until slightly thickened; stir in watercress, chives, salt, lemon juice, Worcestershire sauce and sugar. Turn into 4 molds. Cut eggs in half. Press an egg half into center of each mold. Chill until firm. Unmold on crisp lettuce. Garnish with mayonnaise and watercress. Yield: 4 servings.

Mrs. Mary P. Murray
De Funiak Springs, Florida

HORSERADISH-TOMATO ASPIC

1 pkg. lemon gelatin
1 c. hot tomato juice
2 tsp. prepared horseradish
1 c. cold tomato juice
2 tsp. grated onion
1 ½ tsp. salt
Dash of cayenne

Dissolve gelatin in hot tomato juice; add remaining ingredients. Pour into shallow pan, 1/2-inch deep. Chill until firm. Cut into 1/2-inch cubes.

CHILI-CREAM DRESSING:

½ c. mayonnaise
½ c. sour cream
¼ c. chili sauce

Combine all ingredients; chill. Serve over salad. Yield: 4-6 servings.

Mrs. B. C. Goins
Chattanooga, Tennessee

PRIZE TOMATO-CHEESE SALAD

1 can tomato soup
3 sm. pkg. cream cheese
2 tbsp. unflavored gelatin
½ c. cold water
1 c. mayonnaise
¼ c. chopped onion
¼ c. chopped pimento
¼ c. chopped green pepper
¾ c. chopped celery

(Continued on next page)

Bring tomato soup to a boil; add cheese. Beat with rotary beater until smooth. Soften gelatin in cold water; add to hot tomato-cheese mixture. Cool. Add remaining ingredients. Chill until firm. Yield: 10 servings.

Mrs. K. L. Barnes
Nashville, Tennessee

QUICK TOMATO MOLD

1 3-oz. pkg. lemon gelatin
1 1pt. 2-oz. can tomato juice
1 ½ tbsp. lemon juice or vinegar
½ tsp. salt
Dash of pepper

Dissolve gelatin in 1 cup boiling tomato juice; pour into juice can with remaining juice. Blend; add remaining ingredients. Chill until firm. Puncture bottom of can; dip in warm water to unmold. Serve on relish dish or as side salad.

Mrs. Joe Wiles
Moreland, Georgia

SURPRISE SALAD

3 pkg. raspberry gelatin
1 ¼ c. hot water
3 1-lb. cans tomatoes, broken slightly
4 drops Tabasco sauce
1 pt. cottage cheese
1 tbsp. horseradish
½ tsp. salt
½ tsp. sugar

Dissolve gelatin in hot water; add tomatoes. Add Tabasco sauce. Pour into 12-cup mold; chill until firm. Beat cottage cheese until smooth; add horseradish, salt and sugar. Chill few hours to mellow.

Mrs. S. P. Baker
Comstock, Texas

SURPRISE SALAD

3 envelopes unflavored gelatin, dissolved in a little cold water
1 lge pkg. cream cheese
1 can tomato soup
1 c. mayonnaise
1 c. blanched, chopped almonds

Combine cheese and soup; heat stirring until the cheese melts. Add gelatin; stir until dissolved. Cool and add mayonnaise; add almonds. Put in individual molds and let congeal. Serve on lettuce with a dab of mayonnaise and a stuffed olive.

Mrs. Russell O. Behrens
Apalachicola, Florida

TOMATO ASPIC

1 pkg. unflavored gelatin
2 ½ c. tomato juice
1 tbsp. chopped onion
1 bay leaf
3 peppercorns
Leaves of 1 stalk of celery
¾ tsp. salt
1 tsp. vinegar or lemon juice
1 tsp. sugar
¼ tsp. Worchestershire sauce

Soften gelatin in 1/2 cup tomato juice. Add onion, bay leaf, peppercorns and celery leaves to remaining tomato juice; bring slowly to boil. Simmer for 5 minutes; strain. Add softened gelatin; stir until dissolved. Add remaining ingredients. Pour into molds; chill until firm.

Lola A. Harris
Shelbyville, Kentucky

TOMATO ASPIC

4 c. tomato juice
⅓ c. chopped onion
¼ c. celery leaves
2 tbsp. brown sugar
1 tsp. salt
2 sm. bay leaves
4 whole cloves
2 envelopes unflavored gelatin
3 tbsp. lemon juice
1 c. finely chopped celery

Mix 2 cups tomato juice with next 6 ingredients. Simmer, uncovered, 5 minutes; strain. Soften gelatin in 1 cup cold tomato juice and lemon juice. Chill until partially set; add celery. Pour into 5-cup ring mold; chill till firm. Unmold on crisp lettuce or other mixed crisp greens. Yield: 8-10 servings.

Mrs. Harold L. Presley
Coldwater, Mississippi

TOMATO ASPIC WITH CREAM CHEESE

2 tbsp. unflavored gelatin
¼ c. cold water
1 can tomato soup
2 pkg. cream cheese
1 c. chopped celery
1 lge. bottle stuffed olives, sliced
¼ tsp. Worcestershire sauce
¼ tsp. pepper
2 tbsp. tarragon vinegar
1 c. finely chopped nuts (opt.)

Dissolve gelatin in water. Heat soup to boiling; add cream cheese, stirring until dissolved. Add gelatin; let stand until slightly congealed. Add remaining ingredients; pour into individual molds. Chill overnight. Yield: 8 servings.

Mrs. Alpine Redmond
Swansea, South Carolina

TOMATO ASPIC WITH ONION SOUR CREAM DRESSING

1 No. 2 can tomatoes or tomato juice
1 tbsp. unflavored gelatin
½ c. cold water
1 tsp. scraped onion
½ tsp. salt
¼ tsp. celery salt
1 tsp. sugar
2 tbsp. vinegar

Bring tomatoes to a boil; press through sieve. Soften gelatin in cold water; dissolve in hot tomato juice. Add remaining ingredients; pour into 6 small molds. Chill until set.

ONION SOUR-CREAM DRESSING:

1 tbsp. mayonnaise
¼ c. chopped onion
1 c. sour cream
Dash of parsley
Salt to taste

Combine all ingredients; serve with salad. Yield: 6 servings.

Mrs. J. B. Roberts
Perry, Florida

TOMATO ASPIC SALAD

1 pkg. lemon gelatin
1 ¼ c. hot water
1 c. tomato sauce
1 ½ tbsp. vinegar
½ tsp. salt
Dash of pepper

Dissolve gelatin in water. Blend in tomato sauce, vinegar, salt, and pepper. Chill until firm in individual molds or ice cube tray. Serve on bed of lettuce.

Mrs. A. J. Neal, Jr.
Tucson, Arizona

TOMATO ASPIC SALAD

2 1-lb. cans tomatoes
2 3-oz. pkg. strawberry gelatin
1 tsp. salt
2 tsp. lemon juice

Heat tomatoes to boiling; remove from heat. Immediately add gelatin, salt and lemon juice, stirring until dissolved. Pour into mold; chill until firm. Serve on salad greens.

Mrs. Myrle Strickle
Maysville, Kentucky

TOMATO ASPIC SALAD

3 c. tomato juice
1 stalk celery
1 sm. onion, sliced
2 lemon slices
1 bay leaf
1 tsp. salt
2 envelopes unflavored gelatin
⅔ c. cold tomato juice
2 tbsp. vinegar
1 sm. jar stuffed olives (opt.)
Cottage cheese (opt.)

Combine tomato juice, celery, onion, lemon slices, bay leaf and salt. Simmer, uncovered, 10 minutes; strain. Sprinkle gelatin over cold tomato juice; add vinegar, stirring into hot mixture until dissolved. Let partially set; stir in olives. Chill in individual molds; unmold on lettuce leaves.

Mrs. W. E. Vinson
Greensboro, North Carolina

TOMATO-VEGETABLE ASPIC

1 envelope unflavored gelatin
¼ c. cold tomato juice
1 tbsp. grated onion
1 tsp. salt
1 ¾ c. boiling tomato juice
¾ c. finely shredded cabbage
¼ c. chopped celery

(Continued on next page)

Soften gelatin in cold tomato juice. Add gelatin, onion and salt to boiling tomato juice; stir. Chill until slightly thickened. Fold in cabbage and celery. Chill until firm. Yield: 5-6 servings.

Mrs. Frances Chappell
Apel, North Carolina

TOMATO ASPIC WITH SAUERKRAUT

½ No. 303 can sauerkraut, finely chopped
3 tbsp. gelatin
3 c. tomato juice
½ tsp. thyme
Salt and pepper
1 tsp. onion salt
¼ c. vinegar
1 tsp. sugar
⅓ c. finely chopped green pepper
Stuffed olives (opt.)

Drain sauerkraut, reserving 3/4 cup liquid; soften gelatin in sauerkraut liquid. Heat tomato juice; add gelatin, seasonings, vinegar and sugar. Chill until partially thickened; fold in green pepper, sauerkraut and olives. Chill until set. Yield: 6-8 servings.

Mrs. T. B. Hill
Nashville, Tennessee

TOMATO-SOUR CREAM RING

1 ¼ c. tomato juice
1 c. water
2 pkg. lemon gelatin
1 c. sour cream
1 c. mayonnaise or salad dressing
3 tbsp. vinegar
1 tbsp. prepared horseradish
1 tsp. onion salt
4 drops of Tabasco sauce

Heat tomato juice and water to boiling. Pour over gelatin, stirring to dissolve. Cool until syrupy but not set. Add remaining ingredients and beat until smooth. Pour into 5-cup ring mold. Chill until firm. Unmold on crisp salad greens. Fill center with sliced cucumbers and onions which have marinated for 1 hour in 1 cup vinegar and 1/4 cup sugar. Drain before putting on salad. Circle mold with chilled, cooked and deveined shrimp. Yield: 6 servings.

Photograph for this recipe on page 169.

TOMATO SOUP SALAD

1 pkg. lemon gelatin
1 c. boiling water
1 c. tomato soup
4 tbsp. lemon juice
Salt to taste
1 c. finely chopped celery
¼ c. finely chopped green peppers
¼ c. chopped onions
1 pkg. slivered toasted almonds

Dissolve gelatin in boiling water; add tomato soup, lemon juice and salt. Chill until almost congealed. Add remaining ingredients; chill until firm.

Lola A. Harris
Shelbyville, Kentucky

TOMATO SOUP SALAD

1 can condensed tomato soup
2 pkg. cream cheese
2 tbsp. unflavored gelatin
¼ c. cold water
Pinch of salt
½ c. mayonnaise
1 c. chopped celery
1 c. chopped green and red peppers
1 sm. onion, chopped
1 cucumber, chopped
1 c. chopped nuts

Heat soup; beat in cream cheese. Soften gelatin in water; beat into soup mixture and cool. Add remaining ingredients. Turn into mold; chill until firm. Yield: 10 servings.

Mrs. Lee Houser
Mooresboro, North Carolina

V-8 ASPIC

1 can V-8 juice
1 pkg. lemon gelatin
2 tbsp. vinegar
½ c. diced celery and onion

Heat 1 cup V-8 juice; add gelatin, stirring until dissolved. Add remaining V-8 juice and vinegar. Chill until mixture begins to thicken; add celery and onion. Chill in mold until firm. Yield: 6-8 servings.

Mrs. O. B. Bancroft
Lexington, Kentucky

ZIPPY TOMATO-CHEESE MOLD

2 envelopes unflavored gelatin
½ c. cold water
1 pkg. cream cheese
1 can tomato soup
1 c. mayonnaise
1 tsp. horseradish
1 ½ c. chopped celery
½ c. chopped pepper
½ c. diced onion

Soften gelatin in cold water. Combine with cheese and soup. Simmer over low heat until gelatin is dissolved. Remove from heat; cool. Stir in mayonnaise, horseradish, celery, green pepper and onion. Chill until firm. Yield: 8 servings.

Mrs. T. D. Arnold
Tucson, Arizona

BEET-CABBAGE SOUFFLE

1 pkg. lemon gelatin
1 ¼ c. hot water
¼ c. beet juice
1 tbsp. vinegar
½ c. mayonnaise
¼ tsp. salt
Dash of pepper
1 c. beets, drained and diced
1 c. cabbage, shredded
1 tbsp. onion, finely chopped

Dissolve gelatin in hot water. Add beet juice, vinegar, mayonnaise, salt and pepper. Blend well with rotary beater. Pour into refrigerator freezing tray. Quick-chill in freezing unit for 15 to 20 minutes or until firm about 1 inch from edge but soft in center. Whip with rotary beater until fluffy. Fold in beets, cabbage and onion. Chill for 30 to 60 minutes.

Mrs. S. B. Monroe
Paducah, Kentucky

CONGEALED SALAD

1 ½ tbsp. gelatin
½ c. hot water
½ c. cold water
½ c. sugar
½ c. vinegar
Salt to taste
3 tbsp. lemon juice
3 tbsp. pimento
1 ½ c. chopped celery
1 ½ c. shredded cabbage
½ c. shredded carrots

Dissolve gelatin in hot water; add cold water. Add sugar, vinegar, salt and lemon juice. Add remaining ingredients; pour into mold. Chill until firm.

Mrs. Minnie Trosper
Covington, Tennessee

CONGEALED SPRING SALAD

2 pkg. lemon gelatin
1 ¾ c. boiling water
2 c. cold water
1 tbsp. salt
3 tbsp. vinegar
1 ½ c. finely chopped carrots
1 ¾ c. finely chopped cabbage
1 ½ c. finely chopped spinach
1 tsp. finely chopped onion

Dissolve gelatin in boiling water; add cold water, salt and vinegar. Divide mixture into 3 parts, chilling each part separately until slightly thickened. Add carrots to first part; pour into an oiled loaf mold. Chill until firm. Add cabbage to second part; pour onto firm layer in mold. Chill until firm. Add spinach and onion to third part; pour onto firm gelatin. Chill until firm. Unmold on salad greens. Yield: 12 servings.

Darlene Thomas
Dunnville, Kentucky

CORNFLOWER SALAD

2 No. 2 cans cream corn
1 tsp. onion, grated
1 tsp. salt
Pepper to taste
2 tbsp. sugar
3 envelopes unflavored gelatin
½ c. water
6 med. green peppers, hollowed
6 cooked carrots

Blend corn, onion, salt, pepper and sugar. Soften gelatin in water; dissolve over hot water. Add to corn mixture. Put a piece of carrot in each hollowed out pepper and fill with corn mixture. Set peppers in muffin pan to steady them while chilling. Slice and serve on salad greens with dressing.

Mrs. D. C. Craig
Tullahoma, Tennessee

COTTAGE CHEESE AND KIDNEY BEAN SALAD

1 ½ c. cottage cheese
1 envelope unflavored gelatin
1 c. milk
⅔ c. French dressing
1 tbsp. minced onion
Dash of pepper
1 c. canned kidney beans, drained
1 c. shredded cabbage

Sieve or beat cheese on high speed of electric mixer 3 minutes. Stir gelatin into 1/2 cup milk to soften; place over low heat stirring constantly until gelatin dissolves. Remove from heat; stir in remaining milk, French dressing, onion, pepper and cottage cheese. Place pan in bowl of ice water or chill in refrigerator to unbeaten egg white consistency. Fold in kidney beans and cabbage. Turn into a 4-cup mold; chill until firm. Turn out on a dish; garnish with greens and cucumbers. Yield: 6-8 servings.

Mrs. Algier Vaiden
Hernando, Mississippi

COTTAGE CHEESE-VEGETABLE RING

2 envelopes unflavored gelatin
½ c. cold water
1 ½ c. creamed cottage cheese
1 ¼ c. salad dressing or mayonnaise
¾ c. whipped cream
2 tbsp. chopped parsley
2 tbsp. chopped pimento
2 tbsp. chopped onion
1 tbsp. lemon juice
½ tsp. Worcestershire sauce
Dash of Tabasco sauce
½ tsp. monosodium glutamate
Salt to taste

Sprinkle gelatin over cold water; dissolve over hot water. Cool slightly. Combine cottage cheese and salad dressing. Stir in dissolved gelatin. Fold in whipped cream. Add remaining ingredients. Turn into oiled 5-cup ring mold. Chill until firm. Unmold onto large platter.

VEGETABLE SALAD MEDLEY:

½ c. salad oil
2 tbsp. vinegar
½ tsp. garlic salt
Dash of Tabasco sauce
½ tsp. paprika
2 1-lb. cans mixed vegetables or
 2 12-oz. pkg. frozen mixed
 vegetables, cooked and cooled

Combine salad oil, vinegar, garlic salt, Tabasco sauce and paprika. Beat with rotary beater. Pour over mixed vegetables. Chill. Fill center of mold with vegetable medley. Yield: 8 servings.

Mrs. Buford N. Irwin
Knoxville, Tennessee

CUCUMBER-CABBAGE MOLD

2 3-oz. pkg. lime gelatin
2 c. boiling water
1 ¾ c. cold water
2 tbsp. vinegar
1 tsp. horseradish
½ tsp. salt
10 to 15 paper-thin cucumber slices
1 c. diced cucumber
1 c. chopped cabbage

Dissolve gelatin in boiling water; add cold water, vinegar, horseradish and salt. Chill until mixture is partially set. Pour 1/2 cup gelatin mixture into 5-cup ring mold. Arrange cucumber slices in gelatin mold; chill until almost set. Add remaining ingredients to remaining gelatin; spoon over cucumber slices. Chill until firm. Serve on crisp green lettuce.

Mrs. Desola Little
Taylorsville, North Carolina

FRESH VEGETABLE SALAD

2 c. water
¼ c. vinegar
¼ c. sugar
¼ tsp. salt
1 pkg. lemon gelatin
1 c. grated carrots
1 c. shredded cabbage
½ c. chopped celery
¼ c. chopped bell pepper

Combine water, vinegar, sugar and salt; add gelatin. Chill until slightly thickened; add remaining ingredients. Chill until firm.

Mrs. G. E. Brown
Oneonta, Alabama

GARDEN PATCH SALAD

1 envelope unflavored gelatin
¼ c. sugar
½ tsp. salt
1 ½ c. water
¼ c. lemon juice
2 c. mixed vegetables

(Continued on next page)

Mix gelatin, sugar and salt thoroughly in small saucepan; add 1/2 cup water. Place over low heat, stirring constantly until gelatin dissolves. Remove from heat; stir in remaining water and lemon juice. Chill mixture to the consistency of unbeaten egg white. Fold in mixed vegetables. Turn into 3-cup mold or individual molds; chill till firm. Unmold; garnish with salad greens, onions, radishes and cucumbers. Yield: 6 servings.

Mrs. Joe R. Jackson
Cave City, Kentucky

GARDEN COTTAGE CHEESE MOLD

- 1 tbsp. unflavored gelatin
- 1 c. milk
- 2/3 c. French dressing
- 1 12-oz. carton cottage cheese
- 1/2 c. chopped celery
- 1/4 c. green pepper strips
- 1/4 c. thin radish slices
- 1/4 c. shredded carrot
- 1/4 c. shaved or thinly sliced cucumber
- 2 tbsp. minced onion

Soften gelatin in 1/4 cup cold milk. Heat remaining milk to lukewarm. Dissolve gelatin over hot water in saucepan or top of double boiler. Add gelatin to warm milk. Stir in French dressing and cottage cheese. Cool mixture until thickened. Fold in vegetables; pour into well oiled 1-quart ring mold. Chill until firm. Unmold on crisp lettuce; garnish with relishes. Serve plain or with salad dressing. Yield: 4-6 servings.

Anita June Story
Pikeville, Tennessee

GELATIN SLAW

- 1 pkg. orange or lime gelatin
- 1 c. shredded cabbage
- 1 med. onion, finely chopped
- 2 carrots, shredded
- 8 to 10 radishes, finely sliced
- 1/3 cucumber, finely sliced
- 1/8 tsp. salt
- 1/8 tsp. garlic salt
- 1/8 tsp. celery salt or seed
- Dash of pepper

Mix gelatin according to package directions; refrigerate. Mix all vegetables; add seasonings. Stir vegetable mixture into gelatin; chill until firm. Yield: 8 servings.

Mrs. A. G. Frost
Amarillo, Texas

GARDEN SLAW

- 8 c. shredded cabbage
- 2 shredded carrots
- 1 green pepper, cut in strips
- 1/2 c. chopped onions
- 1 envelope unflavored gelatin
- 2/3 c. sugar
- 2/3 c. vinegar
- 2 tsp. celery seed
- 1 1/2 tsp. salt
- 1/4 tsp. pepper
- 2/3 c. salad oil

Combine cabbage, carrots, green pepper and onions. Sprinkle with 1/2 cup cold water. Chill. Soften gelatin in 1/4 cup cold water. Mix sugar, vinegar, celery seed, salt and pepper together in a saucepan; bring to a boil. Stir in gelatin. Cool until slightly thickened. Beat well. Gradually add salad oil. Drain vegetables; pour dressing over top. Mix lightly until all vegetables are coated with dressing. Serve immediately or store in refrigerator.

Mrs. L. B. Gunn
Leachville, Alabama

GELATIN SALAD

- 2 boxes lime gelatin
- 2 to 3 carrots, shredded
- 1/4 c. finely chopped celery
- 1/4 c. shredded cabbage

Prepare gelatin according to package directions; add remaining ingredients. Chill until firm. Serve on crisp lettuce leaf and top with mayonnaise or favorite topping, if desired. Yield: 8 servings.

Mrs. T. E. Graves
Decatur, Georgia

JELLIED VEGETABLE SALAD

- 3 tbsp. unflavored gelatin
- 1/2 c. cold water
- 1 c. boiling vegetable liquid
- 1 c. cooked cubed carrots
- 1 c. cooked cubed potatoes
- 1 c. cooked peas
- 1 green pepper, finely chopped
- 2 stalks celery, finely chopped
- 1 tbsp. vinegar
- Onion juice
- Salt, pepper and paprika

Soften gelatin in cold water; add vegetable liquid, stirring until dissolved. Cool. Add vegetables, vinegar, onion juice and seasonings; mix thoroughly. Pour into mold; chill until firm. Serve on crisp lettuce with mayonnaise; garnish with paprika. Yield: 8 servings.

Betty Hicks
Athens, Texas

GREEN SALAD MOLD

1 envelope unflavored gelatin
1 tbsp. sugar
1 tsp. salt
1/8 tsp. pepper
1 3/4 c. water
1/4 c. vinegar
1 tbsp. lemon juice
1/4 c. chopped scallions
1 c. shredded raw spinach
1 c. chopped celery
1/4 c. shredded raw carrots

Mix gelatin, sugar, salt and pepper thoroughly in small saucepan. Add 1/2 cup water; place over low heat, stirring until gelatin dissolves. Remove from heat; stir in remaining water, vinegar and lemon juice. Chill to unbeaten egg white consistency. Fold in scallions, spinach, celery and carrots. Turn into 3-cup mold or individual molds; chill until firm. Unmold; serve with mayonnaise or salad dressing. Garnish with tomatoes and olives. One cup shredded lettuce may be substituted for spinach; add 1/4 cup chopped mushrooms and 1/4 cup chopped green pepper. Yield: 6 servings.

Guadalupe Gonzalez
Alice, Texas

MOLDED GARDEN SALAD

2 pkg. lemon gelatin
2 tbsp. lemon juice
1/2 c. finely sliced green onions
3/4 c. diced cucumbers
1/2 c. thinly sliced radishes
1/2 c. thinly sliced celery
1/2 c. uncooked caulifowerets
1 tsp. salt

Prepare gelatin according to package directions. Chill until partially set. Add remaining ingredients. Chill until firm. Yield: 4-6 servings.

Mrs. R. P. Watson
Hagerstown, Maryland

ITALIAN SALAD

1 pkg. Italian gelatin
1 c. chopped celery
1 c. grated cabbage
1/2 c. grated carrots
1/4 tsp. salt
1 tbsp. tarragon vinegar

Prepare gelatin according to directions; let chill slightly. Add remaining ingredients.

Mrs. H. C. Raynor
Henderson, North Carolina

JELLIED VEGETABLE SALAD

Salt to taste
1 tsp. allspice
1 1/3 c. hot water
1 envelope unflavored gelatin
1/4 c. cold water
1/3 c. vinegar
1/2 c. chopped cabbage
1/2 c. chopped celery
1/4 c. fresh green peas
1/4 c. cubed fresh beets

Add salt and allspice to hot water; bring to boil. Soften gelatin in cold water; dissolve in hot mixture. Add vinegar; strain and set aside to cool. When gelatin is nearly set, stir in the vegetables. Pour into mold; chill until firm. Unmold on lettuce.

Mrs. J. K. Galbraith
Arkadelphia, Arkansas

PEA SALAD

1 pkg. lemon gelatin
1/2 tsp. salt
1 c. hot water
1 c. cold water
1 tbsp. vinegar
1 tsp. grated onion
1/2 c. chopped celery
1 No. 2 can peas, drained
1 No. 2 can julienne beets, drained

Dissolve gelatin and salt in hot water; add cold water, vinegar, onion and horseradish. Chill until slightly thickened; add celery. Divide mixture into 2 equal parts. Add peas to one part; turn into 4 or 6 individual molds. Chill about 30 minutes. Add beets to remaining half; pour over pea layers. Chill until firm. Yield: 4-6 servings.

Mrs. L. D. Grimes
Maud, Texas

PERFECTION SOUFFLE

2 pkg. Italian-flavored gelatin
2 c. hot water
1 c. cold water
4 tbsp. vinegar
1 c. mayonnaise
1/2 tsp. salt
1/8 tsp. pepper
3 c. shredded cabbage
1 c. thinly sliced radishes
1/4 c. thinly sliced celery
1/4 c. shredded carrots

Dissolve gelatin in hot water. Add cold water, vinegar, mayonnaise, salt and pepper; blend well. Pour into bowl; chill until thickened, 15 to 20 minutes. Remove from refrigerator; whip until fluffy. Fold in cabbage, radishes, celery and carrots. Pour into 2-quart mold; chill until firm. Yield: 10 servings.

Mrs. H. T. Scott
Kingsport, Tennessee

PIQUANT SALAD

2 tbsp. unflavored gelatin
½ c. cold water
½ c. red cider vinegar
2 tbsp. lemon juice
2 tsp. Worcestershire sauce
2 c. boiling water
½ c. sugar
1 tsp. salt
⅛ tsp. Tabasco sauce
1 ½ c. shredded cabbage
1 c. diced celery
¼ c. chopped pimento
1 c.tiny green peas
1 c. green beans

Soak gelatin in cold water for 5 minutes; add vinegar, lemon juice, Worcestershire sauce, boiling water, sugar, salt and Tabasco. Chill until mixture begins to thicken. Add remaining ingredients. Turn into mold and chill until firm. Yield: 10 to 12 servings.

Mrs. Henry Sherrer
Bay City, Texas

SUMMERTIME SALAD

1 3-oz. pkg. lemon or lemon-lime gelatin
1 c. water
¾ tsp. onion salt
2 tbsp. vinegar
2 c. chopped mixed tomatoes, cucumbers, celery, onions, radishes and green peppers

Dissolve gelatin in boiling water; add onion salt and vinegar. Chill until slightly thickened. Fold in salad ingredients. Pour into mold; chill until firm. Unmold on lettuce. Serve with mayonnaise, if desired. Yield: 6 servings.

Mrs. B. J. Patterson
Austin, Texas

VEGETABLE SALAD

2 envelopes unflavored gelatin
1 ¾ c. cold water
1 tsp. salt
¾ c. sugar
½ c. vinegar
2 c. finely chopped celery
1 ½ c. grated carrots
1 ½ c. grated cabbage
1 sm. can chopped pimento
1 8 ½-oz. can small, green party peas

Dissolve gelatin in 1-cup cold water; set aside. Mix 3/4-cup cold water, salt, sugar and vinegar; heat to a boil. Remove from heat; stir in gelatin. Add remaining ingredients; mix well. Pour into lightly oiled 2-quart mold. Chill 4 hours before serving.

Mrs. C. M. Roberts
Lithonia, Georgia

VEGETABLE MOLD

1 pkg. frozen or 1 16-oz. can asparagus
1 pkg. frozen or 1 16-oz. can mixed vegetables
1 pkg. lemon gelatin
1 12-oz. can vegetable juice cocktail
3 tbsp. vinegar
¼ tsp. salt
Pepper to taste
¼ c. chopped pimento

Cook frozen asparagus and mixed vegetables according to package directions; drain. Dissolve gelatin in 1 cup hot vegetable juice cocktail; add remaining cold vegetable juice, vinegar, salt, pepper, pimento and drained vegetables. Pour into 1 1/2-quart mold. Chill until firm. Unmold and serve on salad greens with mayonnaise or salad dressing, if desired. Yield: 4-6 servings.

Mrs. S. D. Bledsoe
Arlington, Virginia

VEGETABLE SALAD

1 pkg. lemon or lime gelatin
¼ c. hot water
½ c. hot pea liquid
1 tsp. vinegar
1 tsp. salt
1 tbsp. minced onion
1 tsp. prepared mustard
1 c. mayonnaise
2 c. small green peas
1 c. chopped celery
1 c. cooked chopped carrots
1 tbsp. green pepper, finely cut

Dissolve gelatin in water and pea liquid; cool slightly. Add remaining ingredients; congeal in mold. Serve on lettuce leaf. Yield: 8 servings.

Mrs. Oder Scott
Crossville, Alabama

VEGETABLE SALAD DELIGHT

1 pkg. lemon gelatin
½ c. boiling water
¼ c. vegetable liquid
4 tbsp. vinegar
1 tbsp. chopped onion
1 tsp. prepared mustard
1 tbsp. chopped green pepper
1 tsp. salt
1 c. celery, finely cut
1 c. salad dressing
2 c. cooked English peas
1 c. cooked carrots, finely cut

Add boiling water to gelatin; stir until dissolved. Stir in vegetable liquid, vinegar, seasonings and salad dressing. Add vegetables. Refrigerate to chill.

Mrs. J. R. Jackson
Marion, South Carolina

MIXED FRUIT AND VEGETABLE SALADS

Recipe for Green and Gold Salad on Page 203

ARKANSAS SALAD

1 med. head lettuce, chopped fine
6 green onions, chopped fine
4 lge. tomatoes, chopped fine
2 ripe apples, chopped fine
2 tbsp. apple vinegar
1 c. sour cream or cream
4 hard-boiled eggs
1 tsp. salt

Combine first 6 ingredients thoroughly. Arrange eggs on top; season. Chill 1 hour.

Mrs. M. M. Fox
Magazine, Arkansas

APPLE-FIG-CARROT SALAD

1 c. dried figs
2 c. red apples, unpeeled, diced
1 c. celery, diced
1 c. carrots, finely chopped

Pour boiling water over figs; let stand 5 minutes. Drain and cut in chunks. Combine all ingredients. Toss with Peanut Butter Dressing.

PEANUT BUTTER DRESSING:

4 tbsp. peanut butter
4 tbsp. lemon juice
½ c. mayonnaise

Blend peanut butter and lemon juice. Fold into mayonnaise.

Mrs. Jessie I. Strauss
Collinsville, Alabama

ONE-TWO-THREE SALAD

1 sm. onion, diced
2 sweet pickles, chopped
3 apples, diced
Mayonnaise

Combine all ingredients. Yield: 4 servings.

Mrs. A. S. Starr
Biloxi, Mississippi

RED APPLE SALAD

3 c. shredded red cabbage
2 c. sliced unpeeled red apples
½ c. golden raisins
½ c. mayonnaise
½ c. sour cream

Combine cabbage, apples and raisins. Combine mayonnaise and sour cream; add to mixture. Toss until well blended. Yield: 6 servings.

Mrs. Mary Alice Campbell
Raleigh, North Carolina

SEPTEMBER APPLE SALAD

2 c. diced unpeeled apples
2 c. diced peeled cucumbers
½ tsp. salt
¼ c. lemon juice
½ c. salad dressing
¼ c. chopped nuts
Lettuce leaves

Toss apples and cucumbers with salt; sprinkle with lemon juice. Mix in salad dressing and nuts. Serve chilled on lettuce. Yield: 6 servings.

Rhonda Awtrey
Ulysses, Kansas

APPLE-POTATO SALAD

6 c. sliced cooked potatoes
1 c. diced celery
½ c. diced green pepper
2 c. thinly sliced unpeeled red apples
¼ c. minced onion
1 c. mayonnaise
1 tbsp. vinegar
1 tbsp. sugar
½ tsp. salt
Pepper

Combine potatoes, celery, green pepper, apples and onion. Combine mayonnaise, vinegar, sugar, salt and pepper; add to mixture. Mix well. Arrange on salad greens. Yield: 6 servings.

Mrs. E. F. Falkner
Paducah, Kentucky

ARTICHOKE-GRAPEFRUIT SALAD

1 head crisp green lettuce
1 bunch endive
1 can artichoke hearts
2 onions, sliced and separated into rings
2 grapefruit, sectioned
Garlic French dressing or Roquefort dressing

(Continued on next page)

Make a nest of lettuce and endive. Place artichoke hearts, onion rings and grapefruit sections on nest. Season with dressing. Yield: 6 servings.

Monna S. Ray
Alexandria, Virginia

AVOCADO SALAD

2 tbsp. finely chopped dill pickle
2 tbsp. finely chopped sour pickle
¼ c. chopped onion
1 hot green chili pepper, seeded and chopped
1 tomato, diced
2 ripe avocados, diced
Dash of salt
2 tbsp. mayonnaise
Shredded lettuce
Sliced stuffed olives

Combine pickles and onion. Blend in pepper. Add tomato, avocados and salt. Toss lightly with mayonnaise. Serve on lettuce. Garnish with olives. Yield: 6 servings.

Mrs. Homer D. Shurbet
Katy, Texas

AVOCADO SALAD

2 ripe avocados
½ head cauliflower
¼ head lettuce
½ c. salad dressing
Dash of salt
1 c. cottage cheese
⅛ tsp. garlic salt

Mash avocados. Grate cauliflower and chop lettuce. Mix all ingredients except lettuce together. Add lettuce just before serving.

Thelma Farmer
Summers, Arkansas

AVOCADO SALAD

3 avocados
1 ripe tomato
1 c. chopped celery (opt.)
1 tbsp. minced peeled green chili
Ripe olives
1 tbsp. red chili puree
1 tbsp. finely chopped onion
½ tsp. salt

Mash peeled and seeded avocados in red chili puree; add remaining ingredients. Serve on lettuce leaves with French dressing, corn chips, additional tomato wedges and ripe olives.

Joyce Stockstill
Picayune, Mississippi

CHILI-Y AVOCADO SALAD

2 sm tomatoes, cubed
2 sm. tomatoes, cubed
1 sm. onion, cubed
Shredded lettuce
3 tbsp. mayonnaise
2 tsp. chili powder
1 tbsp. oil
2 tsp. sugar
Salt and pepper

Mix tomatoes, avocados and onion. Put mixture in nests of lettuce in individual bowls. Combine remaining ingredients; pour over salads. Chill for 30 minutes. Yield: 4 servings.

Mrs. S. E. Bryan
Las Vegas, New Mexico

GUACAMOLE SALAD

½ to 1 tbsp. onion juice
Juice of 1 lemon
½ tsp. salt
⅛ tsp. pepper
¼ c. chopped pimento
2 sm. avocados, pared and mashed
Lettuce
2 tomatoes, quartered
Paprika

(Continued on next page)

Add onion and lemon juices, salt, pepper and pimento to mashed avocados; blend well. Mound mixture on individual salad plates in lettuce cups. Garnish with quartered tomatoes; sprinkle with paprika. Yield: 4 servings.

Mrs. Robert Davis
La Pryor, Texas

MEXICAN-STYLE AVOCADO SALAD

4 or 5 ripe avocados, peeled and mashed
4 tbsp. mayonnaise or salad dressing
4 sm. diced onions
4 tomatoes, peeled and chopped
Dash of cayenne pepper
1 finely chopped bell pepper
¼ tsp. paprika
1 tsp. salt
1 tsp. lemon juice

Mix all ingredients in order given. Place in individual molds. Chill and serve on lettuce leaves. Yield: 8 servings.

Mrs. Leonard Gibbs
Sonora, Texas

SPANISH SALAD

2 avocados
2 hard-cooked eggs
3 sm. tomatoes
1 garlic pod
2 onions
6 stuffed olives
1 sweet pickle
Salt to taste
½ tsp. lemon juice
½ tsp. chili powder
French dressing

Chop avocados, eggs, tomatoes, garlic, onions, olives and pickle fine. Season with salt, lemon juice and chili powder. Mix with French dressing to moisten. Serve on crisp, cold lettuce leaves.

Mrs. Estelle Shalla
Bay City, Texas

PEDRO'S SALAD

2 avocados
2 lge. tomatoes
2 Spanish onions, cut into rings
6 leaves lettuce
French or Russian dressing
1 c. corn chips

Remove seed from avocados; cut into halves. Lay each half on cutting board, cut-side down; slice crosswise, straight through to cutting board. Slice tomatoes from top to stem. Alternate slices of avocado, tomato and onion on lettuce leaves. Serve with French or Russian dressing; garnish with corn chips. Yield: 6 servings.

Mrs. P. E. Moore
Tampa, Florida

WEST INDIAN SALAD

2 avocados, halved and pared
Shredded lettuce
1 cucumber, coarsely grated
Juice of 1 lemon
Salt and pepper to taste
1 tbsp. olive oil

Place avocados on shredded lettuce. Season cucumber with lemon juice, salt, pepper and olive oil. Fill avocados with cucumber mixture. Yield: 4 servings.

Mrs. B. S. Brown
Knoxville, Tennessee

RED BEAN SALAD

1 1-lb. can red beans, drained
½ c. diced celery
1 c. diced apple
1 tbsp. lemon juice
3 hard-boiled eggs, chopped
1 sm. onion, chopped
1 tsp. salt
Dash of pepper
¼ c. salad dressing
1 tsp. sugar

Mix all ingredients thoroughly and chill well. Yield: 4 servings.

Mrs. Robert Chapman
Uniontown, Kentucky

TYROLESE SALAD

1 8-oz. can cut green beans, drained
1 c. drained, sliced pickled beets
½ sm. onion, sliced paper thin and separated into rings
2 med. apples, pared and cut into thin strips
French dressing
Lettuce
2 hard-cooked eggs

Mix beans, beets, onion and apples with enough French dressing to flavor. Arrange mixture on lettuce. Garnish with sliced eggs. Yield: 6 servings.

Mrs. John Fathergill, Jr.
Brooksville, Kentucky

BLACK-EYED PEA SALAD

1 can black-eyed peas
2 med. raw apples
2 raw carrots
2 stalks celery
1 med. onion
½ c. diced sweet pickles
½ tsp. prepared mustard
½ c. French dressing

Drain peas; chop apples, carrots, celery and onion. Add diced pickles and mustard; mix. Pour French dressing over mixture. Yield: 5-6 servings.

Mrs. Esta Mae Tackett,
East Point, Kentucky

CABBAGE, APPLE AND PRUNE SALAD

3 lge. red apples
4 c. shredded cabbage
1 tsp. dry mustard
¼ tsp. salt
1 ½ tsp. brown sugar
2 tbsp. flour
1 c. water
¼ c. vinegar
2 egg yolks
1 tbsp. butter
⅓ c. whipped cream
2 c. cooked pitted prunes

Dice apples; toss with cabbage. Mix mustard, salt, brown sugar and flour; add water and vinegar. Cook mixture until thick; pour slowly over well-beaten egg yolks. Cook 2 minutes longer and add butter. Chill. Serve dressing over cabbage-apple mixture with whipped cream and pitted prune garnish.

Mrs. Ed Hulette
Paint Lick, Kentucky

APPLE-SOUR CREAM SLAW

1 c. sour cream
2 tbsp. lemon juice
2 tbsp. vinegar
2 tbsp. sugar
1 tsp. salt
¼ tsp. pepper
1 tbsp. dry mustard
1 c. sliced celery
2 c. shredded cabbage
1 c. shredded carrots
2 lge. apples, chopped
⅓ c. raisins

Combine sour cream, lemon juice, vinegar, sugar, salt, pepper and dry mustard; beat until smooth. Mix celery, cabbage, carrots, apples and raisins; toss with sour cream mixture. Yield: 8 servings.

Mrs. J. F. Crenshaw
New Orleans, Louisiana

CABBAGE-BANANA-APPLE SALAD

2 ½ c. finely shredded cabbage
1 tsp. salt
Salad dressing thinned with cream
1 c. red apples, cut up
½ c. bananas, cut up
¼ c. salted peanuts
Maraschino cherries

Soak cabbage in ice water; drain and chill until crisp. Add salt and moisten with cooked salad dressing and cream. Add apples, bananas and salted peanuts. Garnish with cherries. Yield: 6 servings.

Mrs. Milford Jenkins
Glenwood, West Virginia

CABBAGE SALAD

1 sm. head crisp cabbage
1 c. chopped dates
1 can pineapple tidbits
1 c. pecans
2 lge. apples, chopped
1 c. miniature marshmallows
Mayonnaise

Mix all ingredients well with mayonnaise to moisten. Yield: 8 servings.

Mrs. Truman Dowdy
Mayfield, Kentucky

CABBAGE SALAD

2 c. shredded cabbage
½ c. celery, grated
½ c. carrot, grated
1 avocado, peeled and cubed
1 apple, unpared and grated
1 tsp. salt
Pinch of paprika or pepper
1 tbsp. salad dressing

Mix all ingredients together; toss lightly. Serve.

Mrs. Bernice Gawlik
Falls City, Texas

CABBAGE SALAD

3 c. shredded cabbage
1 c. sliced pineapple
1 c. sliced apples
1 c. miniature marshmallows
½ c. sliced celery
½ c. salad dressing

Mix all ingredients except salad dressing. Refrigerate. Mix in salad dressing just before serving. Yield: 8 servings.

Mrs. R. G. Gipson
Perkenston, Mississippi

CABBAGE SLAW

1 firm head cabbage, chopped fine
1 onion, chopped fine
1 lge. or 2 sm. apples, chopped
Salt and pepper to taste
Sugar
1 to 2 tbsp. butter, melted
¼ c. white vinegar

Mix first 5 ingredients together thoroughly. Pour butter and vinegar over cabbage mixture. Mix well; serve cold.

Frances E. Jackson
Mill Spring, North Carolina

COLESLAW

1 head cabbage
1 onion
1 sm. can pineapple
1 c. sour cream
1 c. mayonnaise
1 tbsp. sugar
1 tsp. salt

Shred cabbage; chop onion. Drain pineapple; add to cabbage mixture. Mix pineapple juice, sour cream, mayonnaise, sugar and salt. Add to cabbage mixture. Refrigerate 30 minutes.

Mrs. Alma Weishuhn
Ledbetter, Texas

CABBAGE SLAW

2 c. shredded cabbage
¼ c. minced onion
½ c. pineapple chunks
⅛ c. chopped pimento
¼ c. sliced stuffed olives
½ c. shredded cheddar cheese
¼ c. mayonnaise
1 tbsp. lemon juice
Dash of salt and pepper
¼ c. heavy cream, whipped

Toss cabbage, onion, pineapple, pimento, olives and cheese. Refrigerate for 30 minutes. In large bowl, mix mayonnaise, lemon juice, salt and pepper until smooth. Fold cream into mayonnaise mixture. Pour over salad; toss well. Yield: 4 servings.

Mrs. S. J. Blum
Amarillo, Texas

COLESLAW WITH GRAPEFRUIT

1 sm. head cabbage
1 c. thick sour cream
1 ½ tbsp. lemon juice
1 tsp. salt
1 tsp. dry mustard
1 8-oz. can grapefruit segments

Shred cabbage. Mix sour cream, lemon juice, salt and mustard until well blended. Combine cabbage and sour cream dressing with chilled grapefruit segments. Toss gently and serve. Yield: 4 servings.

Mrs. Harry H. Holmes
Woodward, Oklahoma

FOUR-STAR COLESLAW

4 c. finely shredded cabbage
1 c. seedless green grapes
½ tsp. salt
½ tsp. sugar
½ to 1 tsp. dry mustard
1 tsp. cider vinegar
½ tsp. grated fresh onion with juice
½ c. blanched almonds, halved and toasted
Mayonnaise to taste

(Continued on next page)

Allow cabbage to crisp in ice water in refrigerator. Drain well; dry with a terry towel. Place in a chilled bowl; add grapes, salt, sugar, mustard, vinegar and onion juice. Toss thoroughly; add almonds and mayonnaise. Toss well; season to taste. Chill; serve cold. Yield: 6 servings.

Mrs. D. P. Scott
Raleigh, North Carolina

DELICATE COLESLAW

¾ c. mayonnaise
¼ c. vinegar
2 tsp. sugar
1 tsp. salt
¼ tsp. pepper
3 qt. finely shredded cabbage
1 11-oz. can mandarin orange sections, drained
1 6-oz. can cranberry sauce, chilled and cubed

Mix first 5 ingredients well and chill. Just before serving, add cabbage, orange sections and cranberry sauce. Toss lightly. Yield: 6-8 servings.

Mrs. G. W. Pradmore
Pahuska, Oklahoma

FRUITED CABBAGE SALAD

1 c. chopped fresh cranberries
¼ c. sugar
2 c. finely shredded cabbage
½ c. orange juice
¼ c. finely diced celery
¼ c. diced green pepper
1 c. green or red grapes
¼ tsp. salt
¼ c. mayonnaise thinned with milk or cream

Mix cranberries with sugar. Moisten cabbage with orange juice. Add sugared cranberries, celery, green pepper and seeded grapes to cabbage. When ready to serve, add salt and toss lightly with mayonnaise. Yield: 4 servings.

Mrs. Mary P. Murray
Defuniak Springs, Florida

DELICIOUS SALAD

1 med. head cabbage
1 No. 2 can crushed pineapple, drained
1 10-oz. bag marshmallows, chopped
½ c. pecans, chopped
Salt to taste
Mayonnaise

Grate cabbage fine; add pineapple, marshmallows and pecans. Add salt to taste and enough mayonnaise to moisten mixture. Place in refrigerator to chill. Serve on lettuce leaves.

Mrs. Clara Seago
Prattville, Alabama

FRUIT-VEGETABLE SALAD

2 c. shredded cabbage
1 c. diced celery
1 c. peeled diced apple
1 c. white seedless grapes
¼ to ½ c. mayonnaise
Lettuce

Combine cabbage, celery, apple and washed, stemmed grapes; mix lightly with mayonnaise. Heap mixture on lettuce leaves; serve on salad plates. Yield: 5-6 servings.

Mrs. J. E. Wilson
Chidester, Arkansas

GARDEN GREEN SALAD

1 bunch watercress
1 stalk celery
1 med. white radish
2 green onions
1 sm. green apple
1 green pimento pepper
1 med. green cucumber
1 med. yellow tomato
2 c. shredded green cabbage
1 c. lemon juice
¼ tsp. black pepper
¼ tsp. salt
1 c. sweet cucumber relish

Shred or chop all vegetables and fruits. Toss together lightly; refrigerate to crisp. Mix remaining ingredients; toss into salad mixture until well coated. Yield: 6 servings.

Mrs. Eula A. Wright
Buffalo, Kentucky

HEALTH SALAD

1 c. grated raw carrots
2 c. finely shredded raw cabbage
1 c. chopped celery
2 tbsp. lemon juice
1 diced apple
¼ c. minced green pepper
1 tsp. salt
Mayonnaise

Combine all ingredients except mayonnaise. Add enough mayonnaise to moisten. Serve on small leaves of lettuce. Yield: 8 servings.

Alice Cox
Vanceburg, Kentucky

MY BEST SLAW

4 c. chopped cabbage
2 tbsp. sugar
1 tsp. salt
1 tsp. celery seed
1 c. chopped apples
½ c. raisins
3 tbsp. vinegar
½ c. mayonnaise

Mix all ingredients thoroughly and serve.

Mrs. Harvey Grace
Kingsport, Tennessee

PINEAPPLE, CABBAGE AND DATE SALAD

1 9-oz. can crushed pineapple, drained
3 c. shredded cabbage
½ c. pitted dates, chopped
½ c. mayonnaise
Crisp lettuce or endive

Combine pineapple, cabbage, dates and mayonnaise. Toss together gently until mayonnaise coats all ingredients. Heap lightly into lettuce cups. Yield: 5 servings.

Mrs. Woodrow Holland
Holland, Virginia

ROYAL SLAW

¼ c. French dressing
½ c. sliced peeled apple
1 banana
2 c. shredded red cabbage
½ c. diced celery

Combine dressing and apple slices. Slice banana; add to apple mixture. Combine with cabbage and celery.

FRENCH DRESSING

1 c. salad oil
⅓ c. vinegar
1 ½ tsp. salt
2 tsp. sugar
½ tsp. dry mustard
1 tsp. paprika
Few grains pepper

Beat all ingredients with rotary beater until well mixed. Chill in tightly covered jar. Mix well before serving.

Paulette Cosby
Stratford, Oklahoma

SUN-GOLD COLESLAW

1 sm. head cabbage, finely shredded
3 carrots, scraped or peeled and shredded
1 9-oz. can pineapple tidbits, drained
2 tbsp. sugar
½ tsp. salt
½ c. mayonnaise
1 tbsp. bottled lime juice
1 tsp. celery seed
¼ tsp. dry mustard

Mix cabbage, carrots and pineapple tidbits in large bowl; sprinkle with sugar and salt. Chill at least 30 minutes or until serving time. Blend mayonnaise, lime juice, celery seed and mustard in cup; pour over cabbage mixture. Toss lightly with fork to coat well. Yield: 6-8 servings.

Mrs. B. W. Collins
Hopewell, Virginia

TASTY SUMMER SLAW

2 c. shredded cabbage
⅓ c. thinly sliced radishes
1 can grapefruit sections, well drained
1 tbsp. sugar
Dash of salt
Dash of pepper
2 c. cottage cheese
Salad greens

Combine cabbage, radishes, grapefruit sections, sugar, salt and pepper; add cottage cheese. Fold in lightly; serve on salad greens. Yield: 6 servings.

Mrs. Eugene Behanon
Lafayette, Tennessee

TOSSED APPLE-CABBAGE BOWL

2 apples, cut into sm. wedges
2 oranges, peeled and sectioned
¼ c. chopped peanuts
2 tsp. minced onion
2 c. finely shredded green cabbage
¼ c. French dressing

Place all ingredients except dressing in salad bowl. Add dressing before serving and toss well. Yield: 4 servings.

Mrs. R. P. Samson
Morgantown, West Virginia

WHITE RAISIN SLAW

3 c. fine, knife-shredded, firmly packed green cabbage
¼ c. light raisins, rinsed in hot water and drained
¼ c. mayonnaise
¼ c. milk
1 tbsp. sugar
1 tbsp. lemon juice
½ tsp. salt
Salad greens (opt.)
Paprika (opt.)

Toss together cabbage and raisins. Mix together mayonnaise, milk, sugar, lemon juice and salt; mix well with cabbage and raisins. Serve at once for crisp salad; if refrigerated overnight, salad will be less crisp. Garnish with salad greens and paprika just before serving. Yield: 4 servings.

Mrs. C. W. Gilmore
Stanton, Texas

CARROT SALAD

½ tsp. lemon juice
½ c. sour cream, whipped
2 c. cottage cheese
½ c. grated carrots
½ c. diced peaches
½ c. pineapple, grated

Add lemon juice to sour cream; whip and mix with cottage cheese. Add grated carrots, peaches and pineapple. Mold; place in icebox overnight. Unmold on plate; garnish with lettuce and radish roses.

Nancy Merritt
Germanton, North Carolina

CARROT DESSERT SALAD

1 12-oz. bag marshmallows, cut up
7 c. shredded carrots or 1 2-lb. bag carrots
1 c. seedless raisins
1 No. 2 can crushed pineapple, drained
⅔ c. mayonnaise
½ c. sugar

Mix all ingredients together. Yield: 10 servings.

Mrs. H. A. House
West Columbia, South Carolina

CARROT SALAD

2 c. grated carrots
1 c. chopped celery
2 c. chopped apples
1 c. raisins
½ c. mayonnaise

Mix all ingredients together and chill.

Lydia Tidwell
Haleyville, Alabama

CARROT AND RAISIN SALAD

½ c. raisins
½ c. mayonnaise
1 tbsp. orange juice
1 tsp. lemon juice
1 tsp. grated orange peel
3 c. grated carrots

Soak raisins in warm water until plump. Drain. Mix mayonnaise with fruit juices and orange peel. Add to carrots; toss lightly with fork. Serve on salad greens. Yield: 6 servings.

Mrs. T. O. Todd
Greenville, Mississippi

CARROT SALAD

1 ½ c. grated carrot
1 sm. can crushed pineapple
1 apple, peeled and diced
2 or 3 tbsp. (heaping) salad dressing

Mix all ingredients together; serve.

Mrs. L. A. Moore
Alexander City, Alabama

EASY SALAD

1 med. can fruit cocktail, drained
1 c. grated carrots
1 c. flake coconut
½ c. sour cream

Mix ingredients all together. Chill overnight; serve on lettuce. Yield: 6 servings.

Mrs. J. H. Foster
Florence, Alabama

FAMILY-FAVORITE SALAD

1 12-oz. carton cream-style cottage cheese
1 9-oz. can drained crushed pineapple
1 c. grated carrots
12 marshmallows, cut in eighths
½ c. salad dressing
1 tbsp. lemon juice
2 tbsp. sugar
½ tsp. salt

Combine cottage cheese, pineapple, grated carrots, marshmallows, salad dressing, lemon juice, sugar and salt. Chill at least 6 hours; serve in crisp lettuce cups. Yield: 6 servings.

Mrs. Ruby Jackson
Santa Anna, Texas

HEALTH SALAD

2 c. carrots, ground or grated
1 lemon, ground or grated
½ tsp. salt
¼ c. sugar
6 halves canned peaches, pears or apple slices
Salad dressing (opt.)

Grind carrots and lemon including rind in food chopper. Add salt and sugar. Let stand 5 minutes. Put a large spoonful of carrot mixture in center of each piece of fruit placed on lettuce. Top with salad dressing. Yield: 6 servings.

Mrs. Daisy W. Smith
Seven Springs, North Carolina

PARADISE SALAD

3 c. grated or ground carrots
1 c. raisins
½ c. salad dressing

Mix carrots, raisins and dressing together with a fork. Chill thoroughly. Yield: 4-6 servings.

Mrs. Helen Stokes
Immokalee, Florida

RAW CARROT SALAD

6 carrots, grated
3 or 4 bananas, sliced
3 or 4 tbsp. mayonnaise
¼ to ½ c. sugar
Dash of salt

Mix all ingredients together; refrigerate until mixture is chilled. Yield: 4-6 servings.

Mrs. Leon Weatherford
Darlington, South Carolina

CAULIFLOWER AND APPLE SALAD

1 sm. cauliflower, thinly sliced
3 apples, diced
1 c. sliced celery
4 sm. green onions, sliced
½ c. chopped parsley
¼ c. red wine vinegar
¼ c. olive or salad oil
½ tsp. salt
Dash of white pepper
1 bunch watercress

Chill cauliflower, apples, celery, onions and parsley. Shake vinegar, oil, salt and pepper in a tightly covered jar. Pour over salad; toss lightly. Garnish with watercress. Yield: 6 servings.

Mrs. J. W. Bowen
Marianna, Florida

HERBED CAULIFLOWER-GRAPEFRUIT SALAD

1 cauliflower
1 3-oz. pkg. cream cheese
½ c. sour cream
1 tsp. dill weed
1 tbsp. parsley
1 tsp. basil
½ tsp. oregano
Bibb lettuce
1 or 2 cans grapefruit segments
1 or 2 avocados, sliced

(Continued on next page)

Wash cauliflower and break into small flowerets. Combine cream cheese, sour cream, dill, parsley, basil and oregano. Place cauliflower on 4 or 5 full leaves of lettuce on individual plates. Circle lettuce with alternate pieces of grapefruit and avocado. Pour dressing over cauliflower. Yield: 6 servings.

Mrs. R. A. Blue
Pine Bluff, Arkansas

COMBINATION SALAD

1 c. minced celery
1 c. boiled potatoes, cut small
1 c. chopped red apple, unpared
3 med. carrots, coarsely grated
1 sm. jar red pimento and liquid
1 green pepper, shaved thin
1 tsp. minced onion (opt.)
1 tsp. sugar
½ tsp. salt
1 c. salad dressing

Mix all ingredients thoroughly with fork. Serve on lettuce leaves decorated with olive halves and bits of lettuce heart.

Mrs. Emma F. Overby
Blackstone, Virginia

CORN SALAD

1 tbsp. salt
12 ears corn, cut off whole kernel
1 lge. head cabbage, chopped fine
3 hot peppers, chopped
3 sweet peppers, chopped
12 lge. apples, chopped
6 onions, chopped fine
1 qt. green tomatoes, chopped fine
2 c. sugar
3 pt. vinegar

Combine all ingredients and cook 15 minutes. Can and seal in pint jars.

Mrs. Donald Warder
Wallingford, Kentucky

GREEN GODDESS SALAD

Romaine lettuce
Head lettuce
Spinach leaves
Avocado wedges
Grapefruit sections
Whole white seedless grapes

Toss crisp greens and fruits.

DRESSING:

1 c. salad dressing
½ c. sour cream
1 clove of garlic, crushed
4 anchovies, chopped
4 tbsp. parsley, chopped
3 tbsp. chives or green onions, chopped
1 tbsp. lemon juice
1 tbsp. tarragon vinegar
½ tsp. salt
Dash of pepper

Combine all ingredients; pour over salad. Toss gently. Yield: 8 servings.

Mrs. P. A. Patton
Jackson, Mississippi

GREEN AND GOLD SALAD

½ c. olive oil
2 tbsp. vinegar
1 tbsp. lemon juice
1 clove garlic, halved
1 tbsp. chopped parsley
1 tsp. each dry mustard and salt
Freshly ground pepper
2 ripe California avocados
6 c. torn lettuce
4 c. torn spinach
1 c. sliced pimento-stuffed olives
2 lge. oranges, sectioned
½ red onion, thinly sliced

Combine oil, vinegar, lemon juice, garlic, parsley, dry mustard, salt and pepper; chill. At serving time, halve avocados lengthwise, twisting gently to separate halves. Whack a sharp knife directly into seed and twist to lift out. Peel avocado; place cavity-side down and slice. Arrange avocado and remaining ingredients in salad bowl and toss with dressing. Yield: 6-8 servings.

Photograph for this recipe on page 193.

LETTUCE-AVOCADO DELIGHT

3 to 4 heads Bibb lettuce, torn into bite-sized pieces
½ head iceberg lettuce, torn into bite-sized pieces
2 sm. ripe avocados, sliced
3 hard-cooked eggs, sliced
½ lb. bacon, crisply fried and crumbled
1 can mandarin oranges, drained
½ c. slivered almonds
1 envelope bleu cheese dressing mix

Combine greens, avocados, eggs, bacon, oranges and almonds. Chill. Just before serving, toss thoroughly with bleu cheese dressing prepared according to package directions. Yield: 6-8 servings.

Mrs. B. A. Griffin
Atlanta, Georgia

MANDARIN ORANGE TOSSED SALAD

1 tsp. sugar
½ tsp. salt
½ tsp. dry mustard
½ tsp. paprika
Dash of Tabasco sauce
2 tbsp. lemon juice
2 tbsp. vinegar
½ c. salad oil
1 11-oz. can mandarin oranges, drained
4 green spring onions, chopped
½ head lettuce
2 tbsp. mayonnaise

Mix all ingredients except oranges, onions, lettuce and mayonnaise. Pour dressing over oranges. Refrigerate overnight. Drain dressing from oranges. Combine all ingredients. Toss lightly. Yield: 6 servings.

Mrs. S. W. Dalton
Lake Charles, Louisiana

MIXED GREENS WITH ORANGE AND AVOCADO

¼ c. vinegar
2 tsp. grated orange peel
½ c. orange juice
Juice of 1 lge. lemon
¼ c. sugar
½ tsp. dry mustard
½ tsp. salt
1 c. salad oil
3 lge. oranges, peeled and sliced
2 lge. avocados, peeled and cubed
2 med. sweet onions, thinly sliced
2 heads romaine
1 head leaf lettuce
1 head iceberg lettuce

Combine vinegar, orange peel, orange juice, lemon juice, sugar, mustard, salt and salad oil in quart jar. Cover and shake well; refrigerate. Cut each orange slice into 2 or 3 pieces. Combine oranges, avocados and onions; cover with part of the dressing. Cover and refrigerate for several hours. Just before serving, tear crisp greens; place in large salad bowl. Add oranges, avocados, onions and remaining dressing; mix gently. Yield: 12 servings.

Mrs. H. B. Rosefield
Jackson, Mississippi

LETTUCE AND TOMATO SALAD

1 sm. head lettuce, diced
2 med. tomatoes, diced
1 apple, diced
1 tbsp. vinegar
2 tbsp. salad dressing

Mix all ingredients well and serve.

Mrs. Arthur Davis
Mt. View, Oklahoma

ORANGE-OLIVE SALAD PLATE

Crisp salad greens
6 chilled oranges, peeled and cut into thin crosswise slices
⅔ c. chopped ripe olives
⅓ c. finely chopped leeks
Whole ripe olives
½ c. olive oil
2 tbsp. red wine vinegar
1 tsp. ground coriander
¼ tsp. salt
¼ tsp. pepper
¼ tsp. sugar
¼ tsp. dry mustard

Line chilled salad platter with greens. Arrange orange slices on greens. Sprinkle with chopped olives and leeks. Garnish with whole olives. Shake olive oil, vinegar, coriander, salt, pepper, sugar and mustard in covered jar. Pour over oranges. Yield: 6 servings.

Mrs. N. W. Crawford
Scotsdale, Arizona

ORANGE AND TOMATO TOSSED SALAD

½ head iceberg lettuce
1 head romaine
2 tomatoes
1 sm. can mandarin oranges, drained
½ Bermuda onion, thinly sliced

Break lettuce and romaine into large salad bowl. Slice tomatoes lengthwise into eight sections. Add tomatoes and oranges to lettuce. Arrange onion slices on top. Serve with choice of dressing. Yield: 6 servings.

Mrs. R. C. Phillips
Newland, North Carolina

GOLD AND WHITE SALAD

1 c. peeled grated raw parsnips
⅔ c. diced orange sections
½ c. shredded tart apples
2 tbsp. lemon juice
½ c. mayonnaise

Combine parsnips, orange and apples. Chill. Add lemon juice and mayonnaise to parsnip mixture just before serving.

Mrs. Herman Mueck
Cameron, Texas

RAW PARSNIP SALAD

2 to 4 raw parsnips, finely grated
⅓ c. crushed pineapple
½ c. marshmallows
⅓ c. salad dressing
1 tbsp. sugar
⅓ c. pineapple juice

Mix parsnips, pineapple and marshmallows. Mix salad dressing, sugar and pineapple juice. Pour dressing over parsnip mixture; blend. Chill. Yield: 4 servings.

Colleen Stevenson
Ripley, Oklahoma

PEA SALAD

1 can English peas
1 c. chopped apples
½ c. grated sweet peppers
2 chopped pickles
¼ c. pimento
½ c. chopped celery
¾ c. grated cheese
Salt and pepper
Mayonnaise

Mix first 7 ingredients together; salt and pepper to taste. Mix with mayonnaise or salad dressing to taste.

Mrs. L. D. Grimes
Maud, Texas

ENGLISH PEA SALAD

2 c. peas
2 chopped apples
1 med. sour pickle
⅓ c. chopped pimentos
¼ c. chopped nuts
2 tbsp. mayonnaise
½ tsp. sugar
½ tsp. salt

Mix all ingredients together and serve on crisp lettuce leaves.

Mrs. J. L. Thompson
Powderly, Texas

HOLIDAY SALAD

4 pear halves
4 or 5 med. green onions, chopped fine
4 stalks celery, chopped fine
5 or 6 stuffed olives, chopped fine
½ tsp. garlic powder
Mayonnaise

(Continued on next page)

Fill pear halves with combination of next 4 ingredients. Top with mayonnaise and serve on beds of lettuce.

Mrs. P. R. DeLoach
Del Rio, Texas

PEAR AND CARROT SALAD

1 can pear halves, drained
Lettuce
½ c. grated raw carrots
1 tbsp. seeded raisins, chopped
1 tbsp. nuts (opt.)
Mayonnaise

Chill and drain pears; arrange on lettuce leaves. Combine carrots, raisins and nuts. Mix with enough mayonnaise to moisten. Fill pear cavities with carrot mixture.

Mrs. Joe Bordovsky
Tioga, Texas

PINEAPPLE AND TOMATO SALAD

1 med. head lettuce
1 9-oz. can crushed pineapple, drained
1 firm tomato, diced
¼ c. mayonnaise
Strips of pimento

Arrange lettuce on salad plates. Combine pineapple, tomato and mayonnaise; toss together very gently. Heap lightly in lettuce cup. Garnish with pimento. Yield: 5 servings.

Mrs. Woodrow Holland
Holland, Virginia

SOONER'S PINEAPPLE SALAD

8 slices canned pineapple
Lettuce
1 c. diced cucumber
¼ c. mayonnaise
Canned pimentos or green pepper

Lay 1 slice pineapple on each individual serving of lettuce. Fill cavity of each slice of pineapple with spoonful of diced cucumber mixed with mayonnaise. Cross 2 narrow strips of pimentos over center of each slice of pineapple. Serve with additional mayonnaise dressing. Yield: 8 servings.

Sherri Hitchcock
Maud, Oklahoma

SALAD OF THE ISLANDS

Lettuce
4 c. cubed fresh pineapple
2 c. cubed tomatoes
1 tbsp. grated onion
3 tbsp. lemon juice
3 tbsp. catsup
½ c. light cream
Salt and pepper to taste

Line salad bowl with lettuce. Add pineapple and tomatoes. Sprinkle with grated onion. Combine remaining ingredients. Mix well. Pour over salad. Yield: 6 servings.

Mrs. C. V. Camden
Blytheville, Arkansas

POLYNESIAN SALAD

2 tbsp. sesame seed
1 head romaine
3 tomatoes
1 ripe avocado
6 tbsp. salad oil
2 tbsp. wine vinegar
2 tbsp. chutney juice
2 tsp. finely minced chutney
Salt and pepper to taste

Toast sesame seed at 300 degrees until golden brown, about 20 minutes. Tear lettuce into bite-sized pieces. Cut tomatoes into 6 sections each. Chill lettuce and tomatoes in a covered container for 1 hour. Combine remaining ingredients except salt and pepper. Place lettuce and tomatoes in salad bowl. Slice avocado into bowl; salt and pepper to taste. Add sesame seed and salad dressing; toss gently. Yield: 6 servings.

Mrs. G. M. Voltz
Lexington, Kentucky

SPINACH-GRAPEFRUIT SALAD

1 Bermuda onion, thinly sliced
1 bag fresh spinach, torn into bite-size pieces
2 slices pimento, cut into strips
1 grapefruit, sectioned

(Continued on next page)

Divide onion slices into rings. Lightly toss onion rings, spinach and pimento strips with dressing, saving 1 tablespoon of dressing. Add grapefruit sections to spinach mixture; pour remaining dressing over fruit. Yield: 8 servings.

DRESSING:

Dash of cayenne pepper
Dash of black pepper
½ tsp. salt
Pinch of sugar
Pinch of oregano
1 tbsp. olive oil
1 tbsp. vinegar
1 tbsp. lemon juice
1 tbsp. grapefruit juice

Mix dry ingredients with a fork in a wooden bowl. Add olive oil alternately with vinegar, lemon juice and grapefruit juice.

Mrs. G. D. Richards
Huntington, West Virginia

SPINACH-AVOCADO SALAD

1 10-oz. pkg. frozen spinach
2 med. onions, chopped
2 tbsp. butter
1 hard-cooked egg, chopped
1 ripe avocado, chopped
Salt and pepper to taste
Vinaigrette or French dressing
Crumbled bacon
Croutons

Cook spinach according to package directions. Drain well. Saute onions in butter until golden. Add onions to spinach; chop well. Add egg and avocado. Season to taste; serve with vinaigrette or French dressing. Crisp crumbled bacon or croutons may be sprinkled on top. Yield: 4-6 servings.

Mrs. C. D. Cameron
Raleigh, North Carolina

SESAME-SPINACH SALAD

1 2-lb. pkg. fresh spinach
1 head Boston lettuce
1 bunch watercress
1 cucumber, thinly sliced
1 sm. head iceberg lettuce (opt.)
1 10-oz. jar mandarin oranges, drained
1 avocado, sliced

SESAME DRESSING:

⅓ c. salad oil
2 ½ tbsp. cider vinegar
1 ¼ tbsp. sugar
2 tsp. soy sauce
1 ½ tsp. sesame seed

Combine all ingredients in a jar; shake well. Pour over salad. Yield: 6-8 servings.

Mrs. V. L. Matthews
Hattiesburg, Mississippi

TOSSED MANDARIN ORANGE-AVOCADO SALAD

2 heads Boston lettuce
2 green onions
1 can mandarin oranges, drained
1 ripe avocado, sliced
½ c. red wine vinegar
1 c. oil
1 onion or 2 tbsp. dry onion
½ tsp. celery seed
1 tsp. dry mustard
1 tsp. salt
½ c. sugar

Break lettuce into bite-sized pieces. Chop onions, using the green part. Add oranges and avocado. Combine remaining ingredients. Pour over salad. Dressing is better if made a day ahead. Yield: 6 servings.

Mrs. B. C. Wade
Beaumont, Texas

WATERCRESS-ORANGE SALAD

2 bunches watercress
3 heads Belgian endive, cut into ¼-in. slices
2 oranges, peeled and sectioned
2 shallots, finely chopped
⅓ c. olive oil
2 tbsp. lemon juice
Salt and pepper to taste

Wash, trim and cut watercress into small pieces. Place in a large bowl. Add endive and orange sections. Combine remaining ingredients; pour over salad. Toss gently. Yield: 6-8 servings.

Mrs. L. C. Smith
San Antonio, Texas

TURNIP SALAD

1 1-lb. each white and yellow turnips
2 apples
1 c. raisins
1 tbsp. sugar
½ tsp. salt
2 tbsp. lemon juice
½ c. mayonnaise

(Continued on next page)

Pare and grate turnips and apples. Toss with next 4 ingredients; chill 1 hour. Drain; stir in mayonnaise.

Mrs. Dude Fryar
Alice, Texas

WILTED LETTUCE AND FRESH ORANGE SALAD

2 heads lettuce
6 green onions, thinly sliced
1/4 c. sugar
1/4 tsp. seasoned salt
1/8 tsp. pepper
1/4 c. fresh lemon juice
2 oranges, cut into bite-sized pieces
6 slices bacon

Tear lettuce into bite-sized pieces; add onions. Sprinkle with sugar, seasoned salt and pepper. Add lemon juice and orange pieces. Dice bacon and fry until crisp. Pour hot bacon and drippings over salad; toss lightly. Yield: 6 servings.

Mrs. M. F. Kelley
Tampa, Florida

YAM-FRUIT SALAD

3 med. yams, cooked or 1 sm. can yams
2 firm bananas
2 red apples
2 c. seedless grapes
1 c. mayonnaise
1 tbsp. honey
1 tbsp. lemon juice

Peel and cube the cooked or drain the canned yams. Cube bananas; dice the unpared apples. Combine yams with fruits; toss together lightly. Mix together remaining ingredients. Serve vegetables-fruit mixture on crisp lettuce with honey dressing.

Mrs. Clara Seago
Prattville, Alabama

YOUNGBLOOD SALAD

1 lge. head lettuce, cut fine
1 med. red apple, chopped unpared
3 celery stalks
1 med. tomato
2 sm. cucumber pickles, cut fine
1 sm. can English peas, drained
2 tbsp. salad dressing

Combine all ingredients thoroughly; refrigerate until ready to serve.

Mrs. Myrtle Youngblood
Como, Texas

APPLE-CHEESE SALAD

1 envelope unflavored gelatin
2 c. apple juice
1/2 c. sour cream
3/4 tsp. salt
1/2 c. diced cucumber
1/2 c. diced celery
1 c. shredded cheddar cheese
1 tsp. grated onion
1/2 c. shredded cabbage
1/2 c. chopped unpared red apple

Soften gelatin in 1/2 cup juice. Heat remaining juice to boiling and stir into softened gelatin until dissolved. Chill until mixture begins to set. Fold in sour cream, salt, cucumber, celery, cheddar cheese, onion, cabbage and apple. Pour into 1-quart mold which has been rinsed in cold water. Chill until firm. Unmold on salad greens and garnish with apple slices which have been dipped in fruit juice to prevent discoloring.

Alberta Cromer
Townville, South Carolina

APPLE DESSERT SALAD

3 eggs, slightly beaten
1/2 c. sugar
1/3 c. lemon juice
1/4 tsp. salt
Drained pineapple liquid
1 can crushed pineapple, drained
1/2 c. shredded carrots
1/2 c. chopped walnuts
1 c. finely chopped celery
2 envelopes unflavored gelatin
1/2 c. water
2 c. canned applesauce
1 c. sour cream

Combine eggs, sugar, lemon juice, salt and pineapple liquid. Stir while heating over low heat until thick; cool. Add pineapple, carrots, nuts and celery. Soften gelatin in water; dissolve over low heat. Fold in applesauce and sour cream. Combine with pineapple mixture. Chill until firm. Yield: 8-10 servings.

Mrs. S. M. Harris
Charlottesville, Virginia

FLORIDA MOLDED SALAD

Tomato juice
1 sm. bay leaf
3 or 4 whole cloves
2 slices onion
Salt and pepper to taste
1 tsp. lemon juice
1 pkg. lemon gelatin
1 c. finely cut celery
Salad greens
½ c. grapefruit segments, diced
Sugar
Lemon juice
Mayonnaise
Paprika

Simmer 2 cups tomato juice, bay leaf, cloves and onion for 15 minutes. Strain; add salt, pepper and lemon juice. Measure liquid; if needed, add additional hot tomato juice to make 2 cups. Pour over lemon gelatin; stir until dissolved. Chill until partially set. Fold in celery; turn into 7-inch ring mold. Chill until firm. Unmold onto large platter. Garnish with greens. Fill center with grapefruit segments seasoned with salt, pepper, sugar, lemon juice and mayonnaise to moisten. Sprinkle generously with paprika. Yield: 4-6 servings.

Mrs. A. U. Kessler
Beaufort, South Carolina

GREEN SALAD WITH ASPIC CUBES

1 pkg. lemon gelatin
½ tsp. salt
¾ c. hot water
Dash of pepper
1 8-oz. tomato sauce
1 ½ tbsp. vinegar
½ c. bleu cheese, crumbled
6 c. mixed salad greens
½ c. small sprigs watercress
¼ c. scallions, sliced
¼ c. olives, sliced
1 c. grapefruit sections
Garlic salad dressing

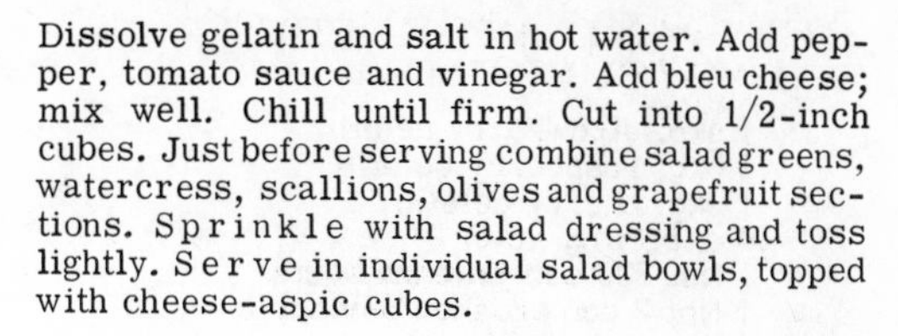

Dissolve gelatin and salt in hot water. Add pepper, tomato sauce and vinegar. Add bleu cheese; mix well. Chill until firm. Cut into 1/2-inch cubes. Just before serving combine salad greens, watercress, scallions, olives and grapefruit sections. Sprinkle with salad dressing and toss lightly. Serve in individual salad bowls, topped with cheese-aspic cubes.

Mrs. L. M. Newman
Chattanooga, Tennessee

AVOCADO-GELATIN SALAD

1 pkg. lemon or lime gelatin
1 c. boiling water
½ c. mayonnaise
1 3-oz. pkg. cream cheese
¼ c. chopped onion
½ c. chopped celery
¼ c. chopped green pepper
1 ripe avocado
1 tsp. chopped parsley
Juice of ½ lemon

Dissolve gelatin in boiling water; cool. Place remaining ingredients in electric blender; blend for 1 to 2 minutes or until mixture is fairly smooth. Add to cooled gelatin; chill until set. Yield: 4-5 servings.

Mrs. C. E. Gibson
Daytona, Florida

BEET AND NUT SALAD

1 No. 303 can julienne beets
1 No. 2 can crushed pineapple
3 tbsp. lemon juice
¼ c.water
¼ c. white vinegar
1 tbsp. sugar
1 to 2 pkg. raspberry gelatin
½ c. chopped walnuts

Drain liquid from beets and pineapple; heat drained liquids with lemon juice, water, vinegar and sugar. Dissolve gelatin in hot liquid. Chill until syrupy. Stir in beets, pineapple and nuts. Pour into a 1-quart mold or individual molds. Chill until firm. Serve with sour cream or a dressing of equal parts of whipped cream and salad dressing or mayonnaise. Yield: 10-12 servings.

Mrs. P. R. Norris
Atlanta, Georgia

BEET AND PINEAPPLE SALAD SUPREME

1 pkg. strawberry gelatin
1 pkg. raspberry gelatin
1 pkg. cherry gelatin
4 c. boiling water
1 No. 303 can julienne beets
1 No. 2 can crushed pineapple
½ c. sweet pickle juice

Dissolve all gelatins in boiling water. Drain beets and pineapple, reserving liquid. Add drained liquid and pickle juice to gelatin; chill until syrupy. Stir in beets and pineapple. Pour into a 3-quart mold; chill until firm. Yield: 16-18 servings.

Mrs. W. B. Murray
Clarksburg, West Virginia

BEET-RASPBERRY SALAD

1 sm. can crushed pineapple
1 c. diced beets
⅛ tsp. salt
⅛ tsp. cinnamon
1 tbsp. vinegar
1 tbsp. sugar
1 pkg. black raspberry gelatin
1 c. hot water

Drain pineapple and beets, reserving juices. Combine pineapple and beet juice; add enough water to make 1 cup liquid. Add salt, cinnamon, vinegar and sugar. Heat liquid; add gelatin. Add hot water; stir until dissolved. Cool until gelatin begins to set; add pineapple and beets. Chill until firm.

Mrs. I. G. Engel
Covington, Kentucky

GOLDEN SALAD

1 pkg. lemon gelatin
1 c. finely shredded carrots
1 c. crushed pineapple
1 tbsp. vinegar
1 c. finely shredded cabbage
Salt to taste

Prepare gelatin according to package directions; chill until partially set. Add remaining ingredients. Pour into mold; chill until firm. Serve on crisp lettuce; garnish with mayonnaise. Yield: 6 servings.

Mrs. Marvin N. Tunning
Valley Bend, West Virginia

CABBAGE SALAD

3 c. shredded cabbage
2 pkg. lemon gelatin
3 ¾ c. boiling water
1 c. chopped celery
1 c. chopped, unpeeled red apples
2 tbsp. lemon juice

Chill cabbage in cold water before shredding. Dissolve gelatin in boiling water; chill until slightly thickened. Add celery to gelatin. Cover apple pieces with lemon juice. Add apples to cabbage; add to gelatin mixture. Chill until firm.

Mrs. Grace Gibson
Bruceton Mills, West Virginia

CARROTS-PINEAPPLE SALAD

2 pkg. orange gelatin
2 c. hot water
Drained pineapple liquid
1 sm. can crushed pineapple
2 c. grated carrots

Dissolve gelatin in hot water. Add water to pineapple liquid to make 2 cups; add to gelatin. Chill until partially set; add pineapple and carrots. Chill until firm.

Mrs. Keith Carlton
Warsaw, North Carolina

CONGEALED SALAD

2 pkg. lime gelatin
2 c. hot water
2 c. cold water
1 tsp. unflavored gelatin
2 carrots, grated
2 apples, unpeeled and finely cut
3 pieces celery, finely cut
½ c. pineapple, drained

Dissolve lime gelatin in hot water; add cold water. Add remaining ingredients; chill until firm. Yield: 10 servings.

Mrs. Travis Cockrell
Carthage, Texas

CREAMY CARROT-NUT MOLD

1 6-oz. pkg. orange gelatin
2 c. hot water
1 c. sour cream
1 ⅔ c. crushed pineapple with juice
2 c. grated carrots
½ c. chopped walnuts

(Continued on next page)

Dissolve gelatin in hot water. Gradually add gelatin to sour cream, stirring until well blended; chill until mixture begins to set. Stir in pineapple, carrots and nuts. Pour into mold; chill until firm. Yield: 8-10 servings.

Mrs. W. S. Arnold
Richmond, Virginia

PINEAPPLE-CARROT SALAD

1 pkg. orange gelatin
¾ c. hot pineapple juice
¼ c. vinegar
¼ tsp. salt
1 c. shredded carrots
1 c. drained crushed pineapple

Dissolve gelatin in pineapple juice; add vinegar. Add salt to carrots. Add carrots and pineapple to gelatin mixture. Pour into mold; chill until firm. Garnish with pineapple slices halved and maraschino cherries; place on lettuce leaves.

Mrs. Beulah Higgs
Caneyville, Kentucky

CHEESE 'N' VEGETABLE SALAD

3 ½ c. hot water
2 pkg. lime gelatin
1 c. cabbage, shredded
½ c.celery, diced
1 c. sharp cheese, coarsely grated
6 pear halves
6 apricot halves

Pour hot water over gelatin; stir until dissolved. Chill until mixture reaches the consistency of unbeaten egg whites; stir occasionally. Add cabbage, celery and cheese. Chill until firm. Top with pear and apricot halves.

Mrs. G. E. Vines
Waco, Texas

GRAPEFRUIT-CUCUMBER MOLD

1 envelope unflavored gelatin
1 tbsp. sugar
¼ tsp. salt
1 1-lb. can grapefruit sections
1 tbsp. vinegar
1 c. diced cucumbers
Salad greens

Mix gelatin, sugar and salt thoroughly in saucepan. Drain grapefruit, reserving juice. Add water to juice to make 1 3/4 cups. Add juice to gelatin. Place over low heat; stir until gelatin is dissolved. Remove from heat; stir in vinegar. Chill to unbeaten egg white consistency. Fold in drained grapefruit sections and cucumbers. Turn into a 3-cup mold. Chill until firm. Unmold onto serving plate; garnish with salad greens. Yield: 6 servings.

Mrs. M. N. Duncan
Tucson, Arizona

COLORFUL SALAD

2 c. boiling water
4 3-oz. pkg. pineapple-orange gelatin
4 c. cranberry cocktail juice
½ c. lemon juice
1 tsp. salt
3 c. fresh cranberries, ground
3 c. cooked or canned sliced carrots, drained
2 c. minced celery

Add boiling water to gelatin; stir until dissolved. Add cranberry juice, lemon juice and salt. Chill until slightly thickened. Fold in remaining ingredients. Pour mixture into 3-quart mold. Chill until firm. Unmold; garnish with whole fresh cranberries. Yield: 12-14 servings.

Justine Mobley
Robeson County, North Carolina

OLIVE GREEN SALAD

2 pkg. lime gelatin
2 c. hot water
2 c. ginger ale
1 med. apple, diced
½ c. diced celery
½ c. chopped green pepper
½ c. sliced olives
1 c. tiny English peas
½ c. broken pecans

Dissolve gelatin in hot water; cool. Add ginger ale; refrigerate until partially set. Add remaining ingredients. Pour into mold; chill until set. For a more attractive salad, slice olives in bottom of mold before pouring in gelatin mixture. Yield: 8-10 servings.

Mrs. A. M. Greene
Shreveport, Louisiana

HOLLAND APPLE-VEGETABLE SALAD

1 envelope unflavored gelatin
¼ c. cold water
½ c. hot orange juice
24 drops of liquid sugar substitute or
  ¼ c. sugar
½ tsp. salt
1 c. cold orange juice
¼ c. lemon juice
½ c. chopped apple
1 c. shredded cabbage
½ c. chopped celery
½ c. shredded carrot
Chicory
Apple slices
Mayonnaise

Sprinkle gelatin on cold water. Dissolve in hot juice. Stir in sugar substitute and salt. Add cold juice; chill until syrupy. Sprinkle lemon juice over apple to prevent discoloration. Spoon a small amount of gelatin into mold. Add a few apple pieces to form design. Chill until set. Add alternate layers of gelatin, apple and vegetables until all is used. Chill until firm. Unmold onto chicory. Dip apple slices in lemon juice. Garnish salad with apple slices and mayonnaise. Yield: 6 servings.

Mrs. D. T. James
Winston-Salem, North Carolina

SWEET PICKLE SALAD

1 3-oz. pkg. lime gelatin
1 ½ c. boiling water
1 c. chopped sweet pickles
¾ c. chopped nuts
1 pimento, chopped
6 marshmallows, cut in eighths
¼ c. diced American cheese
½ c. diced celery
1 c. pineapple tidbits, drained

Dissolve gelatin in boiling water; cool until partially set. Add remaining ingredients; pour into mold. Chill until firm.

Mrs. Robert Kuhl
Taylor, Texas

VEGETABLE SALAD

2 envelopes unflavored gelatin
1 c. cold water
1 c. sugar
½ c. pineapple juice
½ c. lemon juice
½ c. olive juice
½ c. pickle juice
½ c. crushed pineapple
2 lge. pickles, chopped
1 c. chopped nuts
½ c. olives, cut up

Dissolve gelatin in cold water. Let set until partially thickened. Bring sugar, pineapple juice, lemon juice, olive juice and pickle juice to a boil. When boiling add gelatin, stirring until smoothly dissolved. Cool in refrigerator until begins to thicken. Add crushed pineapple, pickles, nuts and olives. Let set until firm. Serve with favorite dressing or mayonnaise.

Mrs. Frank Groessel
Clint, Texas

CARROT AND PINEAPPLE SALAD

1 pkg. orange gelatin
1 ½ c. boiling water
1 c. grated carrots
1 sm. can crushed pineapple

Dissolve gelatin in boiling water; stir until completely dissolved. Set aside until partially congealed. Add carrots and pineapple. Pour into casserole dish or individual dishes. Chill until firm. Turn out on lettuce leaves; serve with mayonnaise, if desired. Yield: 7 servings.

Mrs. Lucian E. Wood
Rudy, Arkansas

CARROT SALAD

1 pkg. orange gelatin
1 c. cold water
1 c. pineapple juice
1 c. pineapple chunks
1 c. sugar
1 c. grated carrots
1 orange, sectioned

Dissolve gelatin in cold water. Heat pineapple juice to boiling; pour over gelatin. Combine remaining ingredients; add to gelatin. Chill until firm. Yield: 6 servings.

Mrs. Noah McTodden
Paris, Texas

CRUSHED PINEAPPLE-CARROT MOLD

1 20-oz. can crushed pineapple
1 pkg. lemon gelatin
½ c. sugar
¼ tsp. salt
4 tbsp. lemon juice
1 c. finely grated carrots
1 c. evaporated milk

(Continued on next page)

Drain pineapple, reserving syrup. Add enough water to syrup to make 1 1/2 cups; heat to a boil. Add gelatin; stir until dissolved. Add sugar, salt and 2 tablespoons lemon juice; chill until slightly thickened. Add pineapple and carrots. Whip evaporated milk, adding 2 tablespoons lemon juice; fold into gelatin mixture. Pour into an 8-inch ring mold; chill until firm. Yield: 10-12 servings.

Mrs. G. I. Loeb
Nashville, Tennessee

COTTAGE CHEESE-VEGETABLE SALAD

1 pkg. lime gelatin
1 ½ c. boiling water
⅓ c. carrots, shredded
¼ c. pepper, chopped
1 tbsp. onion, minced
½ c. celery, cut
1 c. dry cottage cheese
½ c. crushed pineapple
½ tsp. salt
¼ c. whipping cream
½ c. salad dressing

Dissolve gelatin in boiling water; chill until partially set. Add vegetables, cottage cheese, pineapple and salt. Blend cream and salad dressing together; add to gelatin mixture. Chill.

Mrs. F. J. Boyd
Meridian, Mississippi

CUCUMBER SALAD

1 pkg. lime gelatin
1 c. boiling water
1 No. 2 can crushed pineapple
½ c. pineapple juice
1 tsp. salt
1 tsp. grated onion
½ c. finely chopped cucumbers
½ c. mayonnaise
2 tbsp. vinegar

Dissolve gelatin in boiling water. When cool, add remaining ingredients. Pour in molds; chill until firm. Yield: 8 servings.

Mrs. Robert E. McNair
Wife of Governor of South Carolina
Columbia, South Carolina

DIAMOND SPRING GARDEN SALAD

2 pkg. apple-flavored gelatin
3 c. boiling water
Drained pineapple liquid
1 13 ½-oz. can pineapple chunks
10 maraschino cherries, halved
½ c. chopped walnuts
1 c. shredded carrot
¼ c. chopped green pepper

Dissolve gelatin in boiling water; cool until slightly thickened. Add pineapple juice to gelatin. Divide gelatin mixture in half. Add pineapple, cherries and walnuts to one half; pour into 6-cup mold and chill. Add remaining ingredients to second half; pour over first layer. Chill until firm. Unmold on lettuce; garnish with mayonnaise and walnut halves.

Mrs. Ruedell Harvill
Alamo, Georgia

GOLDEN SALAD

1 envelope unflavored gelatin
¼ c. sugar
¼ tsp. salt
¾ c. canned pineapple syrup
¼ c. orange juice
¼ c. vinegar
1 c. well-drained, diced, canned pineapple
½ c. drained orange sections, cut in small pieces
½ c. coarsely grated raw carrots

Mix gelatin, sugar and salt thoroughly in small saucepan. Add pineapple syrup; heat over low heat, stirring constantly until gelatin dissolves. Remove from heat; stir in orange juice and vinegar; chill to unbeaten egg white consistency. Fold in pineapple, orange sections and carrots. Turn into 3-cup mold or individual molds; chill until firm. Unmold by dipping mold in warm water to depth of gelatin; loosen edges with knife tip. Place on serving dish. Garnish with salad greens; serve with salad dressing. Yield: 6-8 servings.

Mrs. Algier Vaiden
Hernando, Mississippi

JEWEL'S BEST SALAD

1 pkg. lemon gelatin
1 c. boiling water
1 No. 2 can crushed pineapple
1 3-oz. pkg. cream cheese, softened
⅓ c. mayonnaise
1 lge. carrot, grated
1 c. finely chopped celery
½ c. chopped pecans

(Continued on next page)

Dissolve gelatin in boiling water. Drain pineapple; measure juice. Add water to make 1 cup; add to gelatin. Chill until partially set. Add creamed cheese and mayonnaise to gelatin; stir well. Add carrot, celery and pecans; mix well. Pour into mold; chill until firm. Yield: 10 servings.

Jewel H. Wolfe
Winston-Salem, North Carolina

LIME SALAD

2 pkg. lime gelatin
3 c. water
1 sm. can crushed pineapple, drained
1 sm. onion, finely chopped
½ c. chopped nuts
1 c. cottage cheese
½ cucumber, finely chopped
1 8-oz. pkg. cream cheese (opt.)

Dissolve gelatin in water; add remaining ingredients, mixing well. Chill until firm. Before serving, spread with cream cheese.

Grace Leslie
Dacoma, Oklahoma

PINEAPPLE GELATIN SALAD

2 pkg. lemon gelatin
1 c. hot water
Drained pineapple liquid
1 tbsp. vinegar
¼ tsp. salt
2 ½ c. drained crushed pineapple
1 c. grated carrots, salted

Dissolve gelatin in hot water. Add water to pineapple liquid to make 1 1/2 cups. Add pineapple liquid, vinegar and salt to gelatin; chill until slightly thickened. Add pineapple to carrots; fold into gelatin mixture. Chill until firm; cut in squares. Serve on lettuce leaf.

Mrs. L. E. Jamieson
Ripley, Mississippi

ROQUEFORT AND CHEESE CREAM SALAD

2 3-oz. pkg. lime gelatin
2 sm. wedges Roquefort cheese
2 3-oz. pkg. cream cheese
1 tbsp. cider vinegar
1 No. 2 can crushed pineapple, well drained
1 c. whipped cream
1 c. blanched almonds
Grapefruit sections
Sliced cucumbers
French dressing

Pour 2 cups boiling water over gelatin. Stir until dissolved. Add 2 cups cold water. Cream the cheeses and vinegar; add to warm gelatin mixture. Beat until smooth. Fold in drained pineapple, whipped cream and almonds. Pour into oiled ring mold; chill until firm. Unmold on a round tray; fill the center with grapefruit sections and slices of cucumbers which have been marinated in French dressing. Serve with mayonnaise.

Mrs. J. L. Stringfield, Sr.
Cottageville, South Carolina

RAINBOW SALAD

1 pkg. lemon gelatin
3 c. boiling water
1 c. pineapple juice
1 c. crushed pineapple
1 pkg. lime gelatin
1 c. cold water
2 3-oz. pkg. cream cheese, room temperature
1 c. mayonnaise
1 pkg. orange gelatin
1 c. orange juice
1 c. grated carrots

Dissolve lemon gelatin in 1 cup boiling water; cool slightly. Add pineapple juice and pineapple; pour into mold. Chill until firm. Dissolve lime gelatin in 1 cup boiling water; add cold water. Add cream cheese, mixing well. Add mayonnaise. Pour onto congealed lemon mixture. Chill until firm. Dissolve orange gelatin in 1 cup boiling water; cool slightly. Add orange juice and carrots; pour over top of lime mixture. Chill until firm. Unmold and slice.

Mrs. John R. Hughes
Chattanooga, Tennessee

SUNSHINE SALAD

1 pkg. lemon gelatin
1 c. hot water
1 No. 2 can crushed pineapple
1 tbsp. vinegar
½ tsp. salt
1 c. grated carrots
⅓ c. chopped pecans

Dissolve gelatin in water. Drain pineapple; add juice to gelatin. Add vinegar and salt. Chill until partially set. Fold in carrots, pineapple and nuts. Pour into mold; chill until firm. Yield: 6 servings.

Betsy Brown
Ruffin, North Carolina

FROZEN SALADS

Recipe for Frozen Citrus Salad on Page 217

APPLE-ORANGE FROST

1 No. 2 can applesauce
1 sm. can orange juice
2 or 3 tbsp. lemon juice
Artificial sweetener equivalent to
3 tbsp. sugar
3 egg whites, stiffly beaten

Combine applesauce, orange juice, lemon juice and sweetener. Fold in egg whites. Freeze until firm. Salad will keep from 2 to 4 weeks in freezer.

Mrs. B. A. Jones
San Antonio, Tex.

AVOCADO SALAD

4 peeled diced tomatoes
1 tbsp. diced onion
1 c. mayonnaise
1/8 tsp. salt
Dash of pepper
3 lge. avocados, cut lengthwise

Combine tomatoes, onion, mayonnaise, salt and pepper; place in ice tray. Freeze. Serve frozen mixture in center of avocados. Decorate with minced parsley, if desired. Yield: 6 servings.

Mrs. R. P. Hilton
Durham, North Carolina

COMPLEXION SALAD

1 pkg. orange gelatin
1 can pineapple
4 carrots, grated
1/3 cabbage head, shredded

Prepare gelatin according to package directions. Add remaining ingredients, mixing well. Freeze.

Wanda Cherry
Mars, Tennessee

FESTIVE SALAD

1 can whole cranberries
Sugar to taste
1 pt. heavy cream, whipped
1 can pecans, chopped

Spoon cranberries into 6 small paper cups until half full. Whip sugar into whipped cream. Fold in pecans. Fill remaining portion of paper cups with whipped cream mixture; freeze. Dip cups into hot water to loosen; unmold onto lettuce. Yield: 6 servings.

Mrs. L. T. Thomas
Jacksonville, Florida

FROSTY CRANBERRY TIP-TOP

1 1-lb. can jellied cranberry sauce
3 tbsp. lemon juice
1 c. whipped cream
1 3-oz. pkg. cream cheese, whipped
1/4 c. mayonnaise
1/4 c. sifted powdered sugar
1 c. chopped English walnuts

Mix cranberry sauce with lemon juice; place in greased ice cube tray. Combine remaining ingredients; spread over cranberry sauce. Freeze; unmold onto lettuce, if desired. Yield: 12 servings.

Mrs. R. J. Burton
Baton Rouge, Louisiana

FROZEN CRANBERRY SALAD

1 16-oz. can jellied cranberry
sauce
3 tbsp. lemon juice
1 c. heavy cream, whipped
1/4 c. mayonnaise
1/2 c. confectioners' sugar
1 c. chopped nuts

Crush cranberry sauce with a fork. Add lemon juice; pour into paper cups or refrigerator tray. Combine remaining ingredients; spread over cranberry mixture. Freeze firm; unmold on lettuce. Serve with nuts. Yield: 8 servings.

Mrs. J. T. Teas
Haleyville, Alabama

ROSY-PINK SALADS

1 c. whipping cream
1/4 c. sugar
Dash of salt
2 tbsp. mayonnaise
1 1-lb. can whole cranberry
sauce, diced
1/2 6-oz. can frozen orange
juice concentrate, thawed
1 c. miniature marshmallows

(Continued on next page)

Whip cream, sugar and salt to soft peaks. Stir in mayonnaise. Mix well. Fold in cranberry sauce, orange concentrate and marshmallows. Line muffin tins with paper baking cups. Fill with cranberry mixture. Freeze. Remove to refrigerator about 10 minutes before serving time. Peel off paper cups. Unmold onto salad greens and garnish with a pickled peach, a spiced crab apple or orange sections.

Mrs. W. H. Ross
Morton, Mississippi

FROZEN BANANA SALAD

- 4 med. bananas, mashed
- 2 tbsp. lemon juice
- ½ c. sugar
- ¼ c. mayonnaise
- ½ c. chopped maraschino cherries
- ½ c. chopped walnuts
- ¾ c. heavy cream, whipped

Blend bananas with lemon juice, sugar, mayonnaise, cherries and nuts. Fold in whipped cream; place in freezing tray. Freeze. May be served on lettuce leaves and garnished with walnuts. Yield: 8 servings.

Mrs. G. C. Carter
Chattanooga, Tennessee

FROZEN CITRUS SALAD

- 1 c. California orange pieces
- 1 c. miniature marshmallows
- ¼ c. sliced red or green maraschino cherries
- ½ c. shredded coconut
- 1 3-oz. pkg. cream cheese
- ¼ c. mayonnaise
- ¼ tsp. salt

Mix orange pieces, marshmallows, cherries and coconut together lightly. Cream the cheese at room temperature until soft. Add mayonnaise and salt; blend with the fruit mixture. Pour into refrigerator tray and freeze. Serve on lettuce leaf. Yield: 6-8 servings.

Photograph for this recipe on page 215 .

FROZEN DELIGHT FRUIT SALAD

- ½ c. salad dressing
- ½ c. whipped cream
- ½ c. maraschino cherries, chopped
- 1 ½ c. fresh orange chunks
- ½ c. pecans, chopped
- ½ c. celery, diced
- 1 c. miniature marshmallows

Fold salad dressing into whipped cream. Gradually fold in remaining ingredients. Freeze until firm.

Mrs. Mary A. Campbell
Fort Necessity, Louisiana

FROZEN TOMATO SALAD

- 1 tbsp. unflavored gelatin
- ¼ c. cold water
- 2 c. tomato juice
- 1 sm. can crushed pineapple, drained
- ½ c. mayonnaise
- 1 ½ tsp. salt
- 1 carton sour cream
- ⅛ tsp. dry mustard
- ¼ tsp. dry ginger
- Dash of red pepper
- 1 tsp. onion juice
- Tabasco sauce to taste

Soak gelatin in cold water; dissolve in a little hot tomato juice. Add remaining ingredients, mixing well. Freeze in ice cream freezer or an ice tray. Stir 3 times at 30 minute intervals to prevent flaking. Yield: 8 servings.

Mrs. H. C. Hammond
Paducah, Kentucky

FROZEN TUNA SALAD

- 2 tsp. unflavored gelatin
- 2 tbsp. cold water
- ⅔ c. catsup
- 2 tbsp. lemon juice
- 3 tbsp. vinegar
- ½ c. mayonnaise or salad dressing
- 1 tsp. Worcestershire sauce
- 2 c. flaked tuna
- 1 tsp. prepared mustard
- 1 tsp. prepared horseradish
- ¾ tsp. salt

Soften gelatin in cold water; dissolve over hot water. Add remaining ingredients; mix thorouthly. Freeze. Unmold; slice. Serve on crisp lettuce with mayonnaise or salad dressing. Garnish with tomato wedges.

Mrs. A. T. Blackwell
Bentley, Louisiana

FROZEN PEACH AND PECAN SALAD

8 peach halves
1 c. cream cheese
1 c. mayonnaise
1 c. chopped pecans
1 c. heavy cream, whipped

Arrange peach halves hollow side up in refrigerator tray. Mix cream cheese, mayonnaise, pecans and whipped cream together. Pour over peach halves. Freeze 3 to 4 hours. Cut into 8 pieces. Serve on crisp salad greens.

Priscilla Childers
Cullman, Alabama

FROZEN PEACH SALAD

1 lge. pkg. cream cheese
1 No. 2 ½ can sliced peaches

Soften cream cheese to thick paste with little peach juice. Add remaining peach juice; stir until smooth. Add peaches. Pour into shallow pan or refrigerator tray; freeze slightly. Cut into squares; serve on lettuce leaves. Yield: 6-8 servings.

Mrs. Sol G. Jones
Beltore, Texas

FROZEN SPICED PEACH SALAD

1 1-lb. 13-oz. can spiced peaches
1 3-oz. pkg. cream cheese
¼ c. sugar
⅓ c. evaporated milk
1 c. miniature marshmallows
½ c. chopped pecans
⅔ c. evaporated milk, partially frozen
1 tbsp. lemon juice
Yellow food coloring

Drain peaches, reserving 1/2 cup juice. Chop peaches. Blend cream cheese with sugar until smooth; slowly add evaporated milk and peach juice. Stir in peaches, marshmallows and pecans. Whip partially frozen evaporated milk until very stiff; beat in lemon juice. Fold into cheese mixture. Add enough yellow food coloring to obtain a light yellow shade. Pour into 2-quart freezer carton; freeze. Slice; serve on lettuce leaf. Yield: 10-12 servings.

Mrs. Alvie Carter
Wichita Falls, Texas

FROZEN PEAR AND CREAM CHEESE SALAD

1 1-lb. can pears
2 3-oz. pkg. cream cheese
6 tbsp. French dressing
Salad greens
Mayonnaise

Drain juice from pears, reserving juice. Cut pears into thin lengthwise slices. Mash the cream cheese; add pear juice and 6 tablespoons French dressing. Beat with a hand or electric beater until smooth. Arrange pear slices in refrigerator tray. Pour cheese mixture over pears. Freeze until firm enough to slice into squares. Arrange on salad greens; serve with mayonnaise or additional French dressing. Yield: 8-10 servings.

Mrs. E. N. Cross
Johnson City, Tennessee

FROZEN PEAR SALAD

1 No. 3 can pears, diced
1 pkg. lime or cherry gelatin
Juice of ½ lemon
2 3-oz. pkg. cream cheese
½ c. almonds, slivered (opt.)
½ pt. whipped cream

Drain pears, reserving 1 3/4 cups juice. Heat pear juice. Add gelatin, stirring to dissolve. Add lemon juice and cream cheese; mix well. Chill. Add pears, nuts and whipped cream. Pour into 9 x 9-inch pan. Freeze, stirring once or twice.

Mrs. F. I. Fisher
Meridian, Mississippi

FROZEN DESSERT SALAD

1 pt. sour cream
Juice of ½ lemon
¾ c. sugar
⅛ tsp. salt
1 9-oz. can crushed pineapple, drained
¼ c. chopped maraschino cherries

Mix first 4 ingredients; fold in fruits. Pour into refrigerator tray; freeze until firm. Cut in squares; arrange on fresh lettuce leaves. Yield: 6 servings.

Alfreda Mudd
Millwood, Kentucky

FROZEN MINT SALAD

12 marshmallows
4 tbsp. pineapple juice
3 or 4 drops green food coloring
3 or 4 drops mint flavoring
1 c. drained crushed pineapple
¼ c. mayonnaise
¼ c. heavy cream, whipped

Melt marshmallows in pineapple juice in double boiler; add food coloring. Cool; add flavoring, pineapple and mayonnaise. Fold in whipped cream; pour into individual molds. Freeze. Remove from molds quickly; wrap in waxed paper. Place in plastic bag; store in freezer. Yield: 6 servings.

Mrs. F. H. Forester
Charleston, West Virginia

FROZEN PEPPERMINT DESSERT SALAD

1 No. 2 can crushed pineapple
1 pkg. strawberry gelatin
¼ c. cinnamon candies
1 10 ½-oz. pkg. miniature marshmallows
2 c. heavy cream
¼ lb. soft butter mints, crushed

Combine pineapple, gelatin, candies and marshmallows; mix well. Chill overnight. Set refrigerator control at lowest temperature. Beat cream, 1 cup at a time, in chilled bowl with chilled beaters until cream piles softly. Pour cream and mints into chilled pineapple mixture. Fold together thoroughly; pour into refrigerator trays. Freeze for 2 to 3 hours or until firm.

Mrs. C. T. Ball
Columbia, South Carolina

FROZEN PINEAPPLE SALAD

2 c. sour cream
1 tbsp. lemon juice
¾ c. sugar
1 c. drained sweetened crushed pineapple
¼ c. chopped maraschino cherries

Mix sour cream, lemon juice and sugar; fold in pineapple and cherries. Pour into freezing tray; freeze. Cut into squares; serve on lettuce. Yield: 6 servings.

Mrs. S. B. Ridge
Greenville, South Carolina

FROZEN PINEAPPLE SALAD

2 sm. pkg. cream cheese
1 c. salad dressing
1 can crushed pineapple
2 sm. jars maraschino cherries
1 lb. marshmallows
1 c. finely chopped pecans
1 c. whipping cream, whipped

Combine cream cheese, salad dressing, pineapple, cherries and marshmallows; whip. Add pecans. Pour whipped cream over top; place in freezer. Freeze. Slice with knife to serve.

Mrs. Leonard Gibbs
Sonora, Texas

FROZEN SALAD

1 pkg. orange gelatin
1 ½ c. hot water
¾ c. sugar
2 eggs, separated
1 tsp. vanilla
10 marshmallows, quartered
½ c. chopped pecans
2 c. crushed pineapple with syrup
1 sm. bottle maraschino cherries with syrup
Salt to taste
1 c. whipping cream, whipped

Dissolve gelatin in hot water; add sugar. Chill until slightly thickened. Beat with rotary beater or electric mixer until double in bulk. Beat egg yolks; add to gelatin with vanilla, marshmallows, pecans, pineapple, cherries and salt. Beat egg whites until fluffy, but not dry. Add whipped cream. Freeze.

Mrs. M. S. Strader
Ruffin, North Carolina

RASPBERRY SALAD

2 c. red raspberries
Juice of 1 lemon
1 c. sugar
1 c. whole milk
1 c. whipped cream
½ c. salted pecans, coarsely chopped

Rub raspberries through a sieve. Measure 1 cup of the pulp. Add lemon juice, sugar and milk. Fold in whipped cream. Fold in pecans. Stir once while salad is freezing.

Mrs. Mildred Rivers
Charlotte, North Carolina

FROZEN STRAWBERRY SALAD

2 c. sour cream
¾ c. sugar
1 tbsp. lemon juice
1 c. crushed fresh strawberries, lightly sweetened or 1 pkg. frozen sliced strawberries

Combine all ingredients. Place in freezer tray; freeze until firm. Cut into servings. Yield: 4 servings.

Mrs. G. W. Reynolds
Flagstaff, Arizona

STRAWBERRY-CHEESE SALAD

1 pt. strawberries
2 tbsp. sugar
2 3-oz. pkg. cream cheese
2 tsp. lemon juice
½ c. whipped cream

Crush strawberries with sugar. Mix with cream cheese and lemon juice. Fold in whipped cream. Freeze.

Mrs. S. F. Barnes
Oklahoma City, Oklahoma

STRAWBERRY SALAD

2 pkg. strawberry gelatin
1 c. hot water
1 c. cold water
2 10-oz. pkg. frozen strawberries, thawed
1 envelope dessert topping mix, whipped
2 tbsp. sugar
1 3-oz. pkg. cream cheese, softened

Dissolve gelatin in hot water; stir in cold water. Add 2 ice cubes; chill. Add strawberries. Pour half of mixture in oblong glass baking dish. Freeze. Chill remaining half of mixture until nearly set. Combine dessert topping mix, sugar and cream cheese. Beat until smooth. Spread dessert topping mixture on top of frozen layer; top with chilled gelatin. Chill for several hours.

Mrs. Fayma Drummond
Petersburg, Texas

APPLE-CREAM SALAD

½ c. crushed pineapple, drained
3 eggs, beaten
½ c. sugar
⅓ c. lemon juice
¼ tsp. salt
½ c. shredded carrots
½ c. walnuts or pecans
½ c. diced celery
2 c. chilled applesauce
1 c. sour cream

Drain pineapple; reserve juice. Combine eggs, sugar, lemon juice, salt and pineapple juice; cook over slow heat until mixture coats spoon. Cool slightly; add all remaining ingredients. Pour into individual molds. Freeze for about 4 hours. Salad will keep in freezer for 1 month. Yield: 12 servings.

Mrs. L. S. Davis
Houston, Texas

FROZEN PARTY SALAD

1 c. salad dressing
2 tbsp. confectioners' sugar
1 8-oz. pkg. cream cheese, room temperature
1 c. pineapple tidbits
1 c. chopped canned apricots
½ c. chopped maraschino cherries
Red food coloring
2 c. miniature marshmallows
1 c. heavy cream, whipped

Gradually add salad dressing and confectioners' sugar, cream cheese, mixing until well blended. Add pineapple, cherries and a few drops of red food coloring. Fold in marshmallows and whipped cream. Pour into 9 x 5-inch pan; freeze. Allow at least 3 hours for freezing, overnight being best. Unmold; serve.

Mrs. Orby Yarberry
Columbia, Kentucky

GRACE'S ROYAL SALAD

1 8-oz. pkg. cream cheese
1 c. sour cream
¼ c. sugar
¼ tsp. salt
1 ½ c. pitted, halved Bing cherries
1 1-lb. can unpeeled apricot halves, drained and sliced
2 c. miniature marshmallows
Few drops of red food coloring

Let cheese stand at room temperature to soften; beat thoroughly. Stir in sour cream, sugar and salt. Stir in fruits and marshmallows. Add few drops red food coloring. Pour mixture into 8 1/2 x 4 1/2 x 2 1/2-inch loaf pan. Freeze 6 hours or overnight. To serve, let stand at room temperature for a few minutes; remove from pan. Slice and place on crisp greens. Trim with pitted cherries and peach slices. Yield: 8 servings.

Mrs. Raymond Williams
Morrison, Tennessee

BANANA-SOUR CREAM JUBILEE

2 c. sour cream
¾ c. sugar
2 tbsp. lemon juice
1 sm. can crushed pineapple
Salt to taste (opt.)
2 to 4 tbsp. maraschino cherries, chopped
½ c. miniature marshmallows (opt.)
1 to 2 bananas, crushed
¼ to ½ c. nuts, chopped

Combine all ingredients in order; mix. Pour into paper baking cups; freeze. Serve on lettuce. Garnish with additional maraschino cherries, or nuts, lemon twists, mint leaves, or orange slices.

Mrs. L. G. Crane
Biloxi, Mississippi

FROZEN BANANA SALAD

2 3-oz. pkg. cream cheese
1 tsp. salt
½ c. mayonnaise
Juice of 1 lemon
½ c. crushed pineapple
2 med. bananas
½ c. walnuts
1 c. whipping cream
Crisp lettuce leaves

Mix cream cheese with salt, mayonnaise and lemon juice; add pineapple, sliced bananas and nuts. Fold in whipped cream and pour into freezing tray. When frozen, serve in slices on crisp lettuce leaves. Garnish with fresh fruit. Yield: 6-8 servings.

Mrs. Ola Noe
London, Kentucky

FROZEN BANANA-STRAWBERRY SALAD

2 c. miniature marshmallows
1 No. 2 ½ can crushed pineapple
½ c. whipped cream
1 c. fresh or canned peaches, diced
1 c. strawberries, sliced
4 bananas, sliced
½ c. salad dressing

Heat marshmallows and pineapple together until marshmallows are melted. Cool until slightly thickened. Fold in whipped cream, fruit and salad dressing. Freeze.

Mrs. Marjorie Stewart
Hartford, Kentucky

FROZEN FRUIT SALAD

2 lge. ripe bananas
¾ c. granulated sugar
1 sm. can crushed pineapple, drained well
2 tbsp. chopped maraschino cherries
2 c. sour cream
½ c. chopped pecans

Mash bananas gently with fork. Blend in other ingredients. Stir well. Pour into salad mold or 9 x 5 x 3-inch loaf pan. Freeze until firm at least 3 to 4 hours. Yield: 6-8 servings.

Mrs. Philip Johle
Burton, Texas

FROZEN SALAD

5 bananas
2 tbsp. lemon juice
¾ c. sugar
1 sm. can pineapple
1 sm. jar maraschino cherries
1 c. nuts
½ pt. sour cream

(Continued on next page)

Mash bananas; pour lemon juice and sugar over fruit. Mix with remaining ingredients and freeze.

Mrs. S. H. Manuel
Wellington, Texas

FROZEN SALAD

1 c. whipped cream
½ c. sugar
½ c. cooked salad dressing
2 tbsp. lemon juice
⅔ c. banana pulp
½ c. orange pulp
½ c. strawberry or peach pulp
½ c. Royal Anne cherries or grapes, seeded

Whip cream and fold in sugar, salad dressing, lemon juice and fruit. Pour in molds; place in mixture of 1 part salt to 3 parts ice or freeze in refrigerator trays. Serve with a small amount of salad dressing mixed with whipped cream and fruit juice.

Mrs. Hattie Gallaher
Beech Grove, Tennessee

FRUIT SALAD FREEZE

2 lge. ripe bananas
1 sm. can crushed pineapple, well drained
2 tbsp. chopped maraschino cherries
¾ c. sugar
2 c. sour cream
2 tbsp. lemon juice
½ c. chopped pecans

Mash bananas gently with fork; blend in remaining ingredients. Stir well; pour into ice tray or mold. Place in freezing compartment of refrigerator; freeze until firm. Cut into slices; serve on lettuce, if desired. Yield: 6 servings.

Mrs. H. J. Perry
Pine Bluff, Arkansas

BERRY-ICE CREAM SALAD

1 qt. vanilla ice cream
½ c. mayonnaise
1 c. canned pineapple, drained
1 c. drained blueberries
2 c. raspberries or strawberries

Soften ice cream; quickly blend in mayonnaise. Add fruit; mix. Freeze for 2 to 3 hours or until firm.

Mrs. J. K. Moore
Jackson, Mississippi

COTTAGE CHEESE SALAD

2 c. sm. curd cottage cheese, sieved
1 c. sour cream
3 tbsp. confectioners' sugar
¾ tsp. salt
1 c. pineapple tidbits, drained
1 c. orange, diced
1 c. cooked prunes, pitted and chopped
1 lge. banana, sliced
½ c. maraschino cherries, drained and sliced
½ c. blanched almonds, chopped
1 c. sour cream
2 tbsp. maraschino cherry juice

Combine all ingredients except sour cream and cherry juice. Pour into trays rinsed in cold water. Freeze. Let stand at room temperature for a few minutes before serving. Serve with a mixture of sour cream and cherry juice.

Mrs. Trudy Fulmer
Springfield, South Carolina

CRANBERRY AND APPLE SALAD

2 med. red apples
1 can jellied cranberry sauce
½ pt. heavy cream
¼ c. powdered sugar
1 tsp. vanilla
½ c. chopped nuts

Coarsely grate unpared apples. Mash cranberry sauce with a fork; mix with apples. Whip cream, adding sugar and vanilla gradually; fold in nuts. Pour apple mixture into a refrigerator tray; spread whipped cream over top. Freeze until firm; serve in squares. Yield: 8 servings.

Mrs. L. D. Riggs
Tucson, Arizona

CRANBERRY SALAD

1 c. well-drained crushed pineapple
1 can whole cranberry sauce
1 c. pecans
1 c. sour cream

(Continued on next page)

Combine all ingredients. Freeze for 8 hours in rectangular pan or ring mold. May be served as a salad or dessert. Yield: 12 servings.

Mrs. M. A. Pierce
Little Rock, Arkansas

FROZEN CRANBERRY-PINEAPPLE SALAD

1 1-lb. 13-oz. can crushed pineapple, drained
½ pt. sour cream
1 1-lb. can whole cranberries
½ c. chopped pecans
2 tsp. grated orange peel (opt.)

Combine all ingredients, mixing well. Place in an oiled 8 x 8-inch pan; freeze. Yield: 16 servings.

Mrs. P. G. Garrett
Austin, Texas

FROZEN CRANBERRY SALAD

1 can whole cranberries
1 lge. can crushed pineapple, drained
2 3-oz. pkg. cream cheese
4 tbsp. salad dressing
½ c. chopped nuts
1 pkg. dessert topping mix

Mix cranberries, pineapple, cream cheese, salad dressing and chopped nuts well. Fold in dessert topping mix; pour into 2 single ice trays and freeze until firm. Cut in squares and place on lettuce leaves to serve. Yield: 10-12 servings.

Mrs. H. M. Thomason
Rochester, Texas

FROZEN CRANBERRY WALDORF

1 lb. raw cranberries
3 unpeeled red apples, cored
1 c. sugar
1 c. chopped pecans
1 pkg. miniature marshmallows
1 c. cream, whipped

Wash and drain cranberries. Grind berries and apples together. Stir in sugar; let stand for 1/2 hour. Fold in pecans, marshmallows and cream. Freeze. For salad of less tartness add 2 cups sugar.

Mrs. Ernest Stoaek
Seymour, Texas

FROZEN FRUIT SALAD

3 bananas, mashed
2 tbsp. sugar
1 sm. can crushed pineapple
2 c. cranberry sauce
1 lge. pkg. small marshmallows
1 c. nuts
1 c. whipped cream

Mix all ingredients. Place in 1-quart ice cream carton and freeze. Cut both ends out of carton; push out salad. Slice and serve. Yield: 20 servings.

Mrs. Mary Chandler
Marquez, Texas

PINK ARCTIC FREEZE

2 3-oz. pkg. cream cheese
2 tbsp. mayonnaise or salad dressing
3 tbsp. sugar
1 1-lb. can whole cranberry sauce
1 9-oz. can crushed pineapple or pineapple chunks, drained
½ c. chopped walnuts or pecans
1 c. heavy cream, whipped

Soften cheese; blend in mayonnaise and sugar. Add fruits and nuts. Fold in whipped cream. Pour into 8 1/2 x 4 1/2 x 2 1/2-inch loaf pan. Freeze for 6 hours or overnight. Let stand at room temperature for 15 minutes before serving; slice. Serve on lettuce, if desired. Yield: 8-10 servings.

Mrs. M. L. Polk
Phoenix, Arizona

WALNUT-CRANBERRY RIBBON LOAF

1 1-lb. can cranberry sauce
¾ c. grated apple
½ pt. whipped cream
¼ c. confectioners' sugar
1 tsp. vanilla flavoring
½ c. chopped English walnuts or pecans

Crush cranberry sauce with fork; stir in apple. Pour into freezing tray. Mix whipped cream, sugar, vanilla flavoring and 1/3 cup nuts. Spoon over cranberry layer; sprinkle with remaining nuts. Freeze until firm.

Mrs. H. V. Hill
Tampa, Florida

DATE-CHEESE SALAD

1 sm. can evaporated milk, chilled
¼ c. lemon juice
2 pkg. cream cheese, softened
½ c. mayonnaise
½ c. pecans, chopped
½ c. almonds, slivered
1 c. dates, chopped
1 8 ½-oz. can crushed pineapple

Whip the milk; gradually add lemon juice as it begins to thicken. Blend cheese and mayonnaise together; blend into milk mixture. Fold in remaining ingredients. Freeze.

Carolyn Lutkemeier
Frankfort, Kentucky

FROZEN CHEESE AND DATE SALAD

½ c. evaporated milk
2 tbsp. lemon juice
1 3-oz. pkg. cream cheese, softened
¼ c. mayonnaise
¼ c. dates, sliced
¼ c. ripe olives, diced
¼ c. maraschino cherries, halved
¼ c. crushed pineapple

Chill milk in refrigerator until ice crystals form. Place in a chilled bowl; whip. Add lemon juice; beat until stiff. Blend cheese with mayonnaise; fold into whipped milk. Add dates, olives, cherries and pineapple. Pour into a tray lined with waxed paper. Freeze until firm.

Mrs. Hazel B. Walker
Chattanooga, Tennessee

FROZEN FRENCH FRUIT SALAD

1 tbsp. lemon juice
2 bananas, diced
¾ c. pineapple, diced
12 red maraschino cherries, chopped
⅓ c. French dressing
1 c. whipped cream
½ c. mayonnaise
⅛ tsp. salt
2 tbsp. confectioners' sugar

Pour lemon juice over bananas; add pineapple, cherries and French dressing. Chill for 2 hours. Drain. Fold whipped cream into mayonnaise; add salt and sugar. Fold in fruit mixture. Freeze, do not stir.

Mrs. Ray Sartor
Ripley, Mississippi

FROZEN FRUIT AND CHEESE SALAD

2 c. sm. curd cottage cheese
1 c. sour cream
3 tbsp. confectioners' sugar
¾ tsp. salt
1 c. pineapple chunks, drained
1 c. diced orange sections
1 c. pitted cooked dates, chopped (opt.)
1 lge. banana, sliced
½ c. maraschino cherries
½ c. blanched chopped almonds

Blend all ingredients; pour into refrigerator trays that have been rinsed in cold water. Freeze until firm. Allow to stand a few minutes before cutting into serving pieces. Serve on lettuce.

TOPPING:

1 c. sour cream
2 tbsp. maraschino cherry juice
Red or green cherries
Orange sections

Combine sour cream with juice; pour over salad. Garnish with cherries and oranges. Yield: 6-8 servings.

Mrs. W. S. Baker
Atlanta, Georgia

FROZEN FRUIT SALAD

1 envelope unflavored gelatin
1 c. cold water
⅓ c. mayonnaise
1 c. whipped cream
1 c. canned pineapple chunks, drained
1 c. orange, diced
½ c. maraschino cherry halves, dates, nuts, or a combination
1 c. bananas, sliced
2 tbsp. lemon juice

Soften gelatin in cold water; dissolve over hot water. Blend into mayonnaise and whipped cream. Fold in remaining ingredients. Freeze until firm.

Mrs. K. G. Hallins
Winston-Salem, North Carolina

FROZEN FRUIT-DRESSING SALAD

3 ripe bananas, mashed
1 c. canned pineapple, diced
1 c. canned pears
12 maraschino cherries, thinly sliced
1 c. Fruit Salad Dressing
1 c. whipped cream

(Continued on next page)

Combine bananas, pineapple, pears and cherries. Add Fruit Salad Dressing and whipped cream. Freeze until firm.

FRUIT SALAD DRESSING:

½ c. sugar
1 tsp. salt
3 tbsp. flour
2 eggs
4 tbsp. vinegar
1 ½ c. pineapple juice

Mix ingredients in order given, stirring well. Cook over low heat until thick and smooth, stirring constantly. Chill. Yield: 2 cups.

Mrs. LaVerne Kennedy
Rotan, Texas

FROZEN FRUIT SALAD

1 tsp. gelatin
2 tbsp. cold water
1 c. mayonnaise
3 c. diced fruit
2 tbsp. powdered sugar
1 c. cream, whipped
Pinch of Salt
Lemon juice

Add gelatin to cold water; let stand 5 minutes. Soften over steam and beat into mayonnaise. Mix mayonnaise with diced fruit. Add sugar to whipped cream and fold into fruit mixture with salt and lemon juice. Freeze before serving.

Mrs. L. E. Stickland
Athens, Georgia

FROZEN FRUIT SALAD

1 c. cream, whipped
1 3-oz. pkg. cream cheese
⅓ c. salad dressing
2 ½ c. mixed canned fruit
¼ c. chopped maraschino cherries
¼ c. chopped nuts
¼ c. marshmallows
1 banana diced

Combine first 3 ingredients; add remaining ingredients. Mix well; pour in tray and freeze. Cut in squares; serve on crisp lettuce. Yield: 8 servings.

Mrs. H. E. Pennington
Paris, Kentucky

FROZEN FRUIT SALAD

5 oranges
5 bananas
1 sm. can pineapple
1 c. whipped cream
1 sm. bottle maraschino cherries
1 c. cooked salad dressing

Blend all ingredients; turn into mold and chill several hours. Serve on crisp lettuce.

Mrs. H. B. Ladd
Lena, Mississippi

FROZEN FRUIT SALAD

1 pt. whipping cream, whipped
2 3-oz. pkg. cream cheese
3 tbsp. mayonnaise
24 marshmallows
3 tbsp. pineapple juice
2 c. white grapes, cut in halves and seeded
1 c. pineapple tidbits

Whip cream. Blend cream cheese, mayonnaise, marshmallows and pineapple juice; fold in grapes, pineapple tidbits and whipped cream. Place in mold and freeze.

Mrs. R. E. Hayes
Louisburg, North Carolina

FROZEN GINGER ALE SALAD

1 ½ tsp. unflavored gelatin
2 tbsp. orange juice
1 tbsp. lemon juice
2 tbsp. sugar
½ c. pale dry ginger ale
¼ c. canned crushed pineapple, drained
⅓ c. diced canned pears
¼ c. halved strawberries
⅓ c. chopped nuts (opt.)
⅓ c. mayonnaise or salad dressing
½ c. heavy cream, whipped

Soak gelatin in orange juice for 5 minutes; add lemon juice. Place over boiling water; stir until gelatin is dissolved. Add sugar and ginger ale; stir until sugar is dissolved. Add fruits and nuts. Mix thoroughly. Fold in mayonnaise and whipped cream. Pour mixture into small freezing tray. Freeze until mixture is firm. Yield: 6 servings.

Mrs. S. A. Haynes
Monroe, Louisiana

FROZEN FRUIT SALAD DELIGHT

1 3-oz. pkg. cream cheese
½ c. mayonnaise
½ c. heavy cream, whipped
¼ lb. marshmallows
1 c. diced peaches
1 c. pineapple
½ c. chopped walnuts

Whip cheese until light; mix in mayonnaise. Fold in whipped cream. Add marshmallows, fruits and nuts; spoon into refrigerator tray. Freeze at coldest setting until firm. Yield: 6 servings.

Mrs. G. C. Elliott
Annapolis, Maryland

FROZEN GOLDEN FRUIT SALAD

½ c. oranges, drained and diced
⅓ c. pineapple, drained and diced
¾ c. Royal Anne cherries, pitted
¼ c. maraschino cherries, drained
¾ c. bananas, diced
1 c. Golden Fruit Dressing

Combine all ingredients; mix thoroughly. Freeze. May be kept in freezer for as long as 2 months.

GOLDEN FRUIT DRESSING:

1 tbsp. butter
¼ c. orange juice
¼ c. pineapple juice
1 tsp. lemon juice
¼ c. sugar
3 egg yolks
½ c. whipped cream

Combine all ingredients, folding in whipped cream last.

Mrs. R. A. Dixon
Nashville, Tennessee

FROZEN GRAPEFRUIT-AVOCADO SALAD

1 8-oz. pkg. cream cheese, softened
1 c. sour cream
¼ tsp. salt
½ c. sugar
1 grapefruit, sectioned
1 avocado, diced
1 c. halved seedless white grapes
½ c. broken pecans

Blend cream cheese and sour cream; add salt and sugar. Stir until well blended. Add grapefruit sections, avocado, grapes and pecans. Pour into 9 x 5-inch loaf pan; freeze until firm. Slice and serve on salad greens with French dressing, if desired. Yield: 6-8 servings.

Mrs. D. S. Callahan
Bradenton, Florida

FROZEN MIXED FRUIT SALAD

1 pkg. unflavored gelatin
¼ c. cold water
1 3-oz. pkg. cream cheese
½ c. salad dressing
1 No. 2 can apricots, drained
1 No. 2 can pineapple
1 No. 2 can sliced peaches, drained
1 sm. jar maraschino cherries
½ c. sugar
1 c. strawberry ice cream or whipped cream

Combine gelatin and cold water; set in a pan of warm water until gelatin dissolves. Blend cream cheese and salad dressing; add all remaining ingredients. Place in paper-lined muffin tins. Freeze. Let stand at room temperature for 10 minutes before serving.

Mrs. Billie Nowlin
Rising Star, Texas

FROZEN PRUNE SALAD

1 c. chopped cooked prunes
½ c. drained crushed pineapple
½ c. halved maraschino cherries
1 banana
1 tbsp. lemon juice
1 3-oz. pkg. cream cheese
¼ c. mayonnaise
1 c. heavy cream
Salad greens

Combine prunes, pineapple and cherries. Mash banana; mix with lemon juice. Soften cheese; add banana and mayonnaise. Whip cream until barely stiff; fold into fruits. Turn into refrigerator tray. Freeze until barely firm. Serve on greens. Yield: 6-8 servings.

Mrs. M. O. Prentiss
Raleigh, North Carolina

FROZEN SALAD

3 bananas, mashed
1 c. crushed pineapple
1 c. pears, chopped
12 maraschino cherries
½ c. sugar
1 ½ tbsp. flour
1 egg
½ tsp. salt
2 tbsp. vinegar
¾ c. pineapple juice
1 c. whipped cream

Combine first 4 ingredients. Cook 1/4 cup sugar, flour, egg, salt, vinegar and pineapple juice until thick; cool. Fold in whipped cream to which remaining sugar has been added. Mix dressing with fruits; pour in mold and freeze.

Mrs. Opal Shoemaker
Hazel, Kentucky

FROZEN FRUIT-HONEY SALAD

2 tbsp. sugar
1 tbsp. flour
½ c. honey
1 egg
⅓ c. lemon juice
2 c. drained fruit cocktail
1 c. sliced bananas
⅓ c. diced orange slices
¼ c. maraschino or Bing cherries, pitted and quartered
1 c. whipped cream

Combine sugar, flour and honey. Bring to a boil; cook for 1 minute, stirring constantly. Beat egg; gradually add lemon juice. Add a small amount of honey mixture to egg; mix well. Return mixture to heat; bring to a boil, stirring constantly. Remove from heat; cool. Combine fruits; add to honey mixture. Fold in whipped cream. Freeze.

Mrs. B. K. Norris
Lexington, Kentucky

FROZEN WALDORF SALAD

3 eggs
½ c. sugar
½ c. pineapple juice
¼ c. lemon juice
Pinch of salt
½ c. chopped celery
½ c. crushed pineapple
½ c. chopped nuts
½ c. fresh red grapes (opt.)
2 apples, cored and chopped
1 c. heavy cream, whipped

Beat eggs; add sugar, juices and salt. Cook until thick; cool. Add remaining ingredients. Turn into 9 x 9-inch pan. Freeze. Yield: 12 servings.

Mrs. D. F. Walker
Oklahoma City, Oklahoma

FROZEN FRUIT SALAD

1 No. 303 can fruit cocktail
1 tbsp. flour
2 tbsp. sugar
8 lge. marshmallows
1 sm. can chilled evaporated milk
4 tbsp. lemon juice
2 tbsp. mayonnaise

Drain juice from fruit cocktail. Add flour and sugar to juice and blend well. Cook mixture until thickened. Add marshmallows; stir until melted. Chill. Add whipped milk, lemon juice, mayonnaise and fruit to cooked mixture, stirring. Pour salad into individual molds or into 1 large mold and freeze.

Betty P. Simpson
Dobson, North Carolina

FROZEN FRUIT SALAD

1 13-oz. can evaporated milk, chilled
1 No. 2 ½ can fruit cocktail, drained
¼ c. halved green maraschino cherries, drained
3 tbsp. lemon juice
16 marshmallows, cut into eighths
½ c. chopped walnuts
½ c. mayonnaise

Whip chilled evaporated milk until very stiff; fold in fruits, cherries, lemon juice, marshmallows, nuts and mayonnaise. Freeze in molds or in ice cube trays. Serve on lettuce and garnish with mayonnaise or whipped cream, if desired. Yield: 6-8 servings.

Mrs. R. S. Woods
Asheville, North Carolina

FROZEN FRUIT SALAD

1 pkg. lemon gelatin
Dash of salt
1 c. hot water
¼ c. fruit juice
¼ c. lemon juice
⅓ c. mayonnaise
2 c. drained canned fruit cocktail
¼ c. diced maraschino cherries
½ c. whipping cream

Dissolve gelatin and salt in hot water. Add fruit juice and lemon juice. Stir in mayonnaise until well blended. Chill until slightly thickened. Fold in fruits. Whip cream; fold in gelatin mixture. Pour into freezing tray and set control for coldest freezing temperature. Freeze about 4 hours or until firm. Cut into slices or squares. Serve on crisp lettuce. Yield: 8-10 servings.

Mrs. Algier Vaiden
Hernando, Mississippi

FROZEN LEMON-COCKTAIL SALAD

1 pkg. lemon pie filling
1 lge. can fruit cocktail, drained
1 lge. can evaporated milk
2 sm. oranges, peeled and diced
1 c. miniature marshmallows
1 c. pecans, chopped

Prepare pie filling according to instructions on package, substituting juice from fruit cocktail for part of the liquid. Cool. Chill milk until it is frozen around the edges; whip. Fold milk into pie filling. Fold in remaining ingredients. Freeze.

Mrs. Margaret W. Cyrus
Herndon, Virginia

FROZEN FRUIT SALAD

1 can fruit cocktail, drained
1 sm. can pineapple, drained
1 pkg. lemon gelatin
1 ½ c. miniature marshmallows
1 ½ c. sugar
¼ c. mayonnaise
1 tbsp. lemon juice
½ c. nuts
1 can chilled evaporated milk, whipped

Heat drained juice from cocktail and pineapple until boiling. Add gelatin and stir until dissolved. Add marshmallows and sugar; chill. Add fruit, mayonnaise, lemon juice, nuts and whipped milk. Pour into square pan. Cover and freeze. Cut into squares to serve. Yield: 12 servings.

Nelda L. Saenz
Mission, Texas

FROZEN SALAD

2 eggs
2 tbsp. vinegar
2 tbsp. sugar
4 tbsp. pineapple juice
2 c. miniature marshmallows
1 can pineapple, crushed and drained
1 can fruit cocktail, drained
½ pt. whipping cream

Cook first 4 ingredients in double boiler until thick. Mix all remaining ingredients together; stir in dressing. Freeze mixture. Cherries and nuts may be added.

Mrs. H. S. Rainey
Cooper, Texas

FROZEN SALAD DELIGHT

1 can fruit cocktail
1 pkg. cream cheese
1 c. mayonnaise
1 c. cherries
2 c. miniature marshmallows
½ pt. whipping cream
Red food coloring

Pour fruit cocktail into Pyrex dish. Mix cream cheese, mayonnaise, cherries and marshmallows well. Mix remaining ingredients with fruit cocktail. Whip cream; add food coloring to desired shade. Pour over above mixture and freeze. Yield: 8 servings.

Mrs. Avis Graham
Dublin, Georgia

FROZEN SALAD

1 3-oz. pkg. cream cheese
1 tbsp. mayonnaise
½ pt. whipping cream
2 c. drained fruit cocktail

Beat cheese until soft; add mayonnaise and cream. Whip until it forms peaks; add the fruit. Freeze in ice trays or a mold.

Mrs. J. T. Barnes
Monette, Arkansas

FROZEN SALAD LOAF

1 1-lb. 1-oz. can fruit cocktail, drained
2 c. sour cream
3 c. miniature marshmallows
2 tbsp. fresh lemon juice
¼ tsp. salt
1 or 2 drops of red food coloring

Place 1/2 cup fruit cocktail in bottom of 5-cup mold. Combine sour cream, marshmallows, lemon juice, salt and enough food coloring to tint very light pink. Add remaining fruit cocktail; mix lightly. Spoon into mold over fruit. Freeze until firm. Unmold; cut into slices to serve. Yield: 8 servings.

Mrs. C. F. Clifton
Charleston, South Carolina

FROZEN WHIPPED SALAD

1 sm. can fruit cocktail
20 lge. marshmallows
1 can evaporated milk
½ c. mayonnaise
½ c. chopped nuts

Drain fruit cocktail, reserving 1/4 cup of juice. Place marshmallows and fruit juice in top of double boiler. Heat over hot water until marshmallows are melted. Chill milk, but do not freeze. Whip milk until thick. Combine all ingredients. Pour into 8 x 12 x 1 1/2-inch pan. Freeze for at least 12 hours. Remove from freezer until easy to cut. Yield: 8 servings.

Mrs. O. J. West
Shreveport, Louisiana

FRUIT COCKTAIL SALAD

1 lge. can fruit cocktail
8 marshmallows
2 pkg. cream cheese
2 tbsp. salad dressing
½ c. chopped pecans
¼ c. chopped celery

Drain juice from fruit. Chop marshmallows into small pieces and mix with fruit. Cream cheese with milk enough to mix to a soft consistency. Add salad dressing and remaining ingredients; freeze. Serve on lettuce cups.

Mrs. Hollis Cook
Elba, Alabama

FROZEN FRUIT COCKTAIL SALAD

1 tbsp. unflavored gelatin
¼ c. cold water
1 No. 1 can fruit cocktail
½ c. mayonnaise
1 c. heavy cream, whipped
⅓ c. maraschino cherries

Soften gelatin in cold water. Dissolve over hot water; cool slightly. Add fruit cocktail with syrup. Fold in mayonnaise and whipped cream. Pour into refrigerator tray. Dot with cut cherries. Freeze till just firm. Yield: 6 servings.

Mrs. Jimmie G. Gregory
Carlisle, South Carolina

FRUIT SALAD FREEZE

1 lge. can fruit cocktail
1 pkg. miniature marshmallows
1 c. pecans
3 bananas, sliced
1 pt. whipping cream, whipped
Lemon juice

Drain cocktail and reserve liquid. Pour liquid over marshmallows; let stand 1 hour. Drain juice from marshmallows; add cocktail, pecans, bananas and whipped cream to marshmallows. Pour mixture in a mold and freeze.

Mrs. J. W. McKnight
Jackson, Tennessee

ICY SALAD ROUNDS

1 can fruit cocktail
Lettuce
Mayonnaise
Salted slivered almonds

Slip can of fruit cocktail into freezing compartment and leave overnight. When ready to serve, open can at both ends and push out frozen fruit cocktail. Slice. Serve on crisp lettuce with mayonnaise and salted slivered almonds.

Mrs. Earl J. Moone
Birmingham, Alabama

LEMON-LIME SHERBET

1 tbsp. gelatin
¼ c. water
⅓ c. sugar
1 c. fruit cocktail
Juice of 2 lemons
2 bottles Seven-Up
2 egg whites, stiffly beaten

Soften gelatin in water for 5 minutes; dissolve over hot water. Stir sugar into fruit cocktail until dissolved. Add gelatin, lemon juice and Seven-Up. Freeze in a refrigerator tray until mushy. Remove to a bowl. Beat for a few seconds. Add stiffly beaten egg whites; beat again for a second. Return to tray; freeze. Cut into squares; serve on lettuce, if desired. Yield: 6 servings.

Mrs. T. L. Gray
Pensacola, Florida

FROZEN FRUIT SALAD

1 1-qt. can fruits for salad, diced
3 tbsp. flour
3 tbsp. sugar
¼ c. mayonnaise
2 tbsp. lemon juice
1 c. heavy cream

Drain fruits, reserving juice. Bring juice to a boil. Combine flour and sugar; stir into hot juice. Cook until clear; cool. Mix with fruit; add mayonnaise, lemon juice and cream. Freeze. Serve on lettuce leaves, if desired.

Mrs. B. C. Curtis
Hyattsville, Maryland

GINGER-FRUIT FREEZE

1 3-oz. pkg. cream cheese
3 tbsp. mayonnaise
1 tbsp. lemon juice
¼ tsp. salt
½ c. chopped preserved kumquats
½ c. dates, cut up
¼ c. quartered maraschino cherries
1 9-oz. can crushed pineapple, drained
2 tbsp. finely chopped candied ginger
1 c. heavy cream, whipped
¼ c. toasted slivered almonds

Soften cream cheese; blend in mayonnaise, lemon juice and salt. Stir in fruits and ginger; fold in whipped cream. Pour into 1-quart freezer tray; sprinkle with nuts. Freeze until firm. Yield: 6-8 servings.

Mrs. S. C. Jordan
Norfolk, Virginia

MOLDED FRUIT SALAD

1 med. can pineapple
1 tbsp. gelatin soaked in ¼ c. cold water
½ c. whipped cream
1 c. boiled dressing
1 No. 2 can white cherries
1 sm. bottle maraschino cherries
1 c. chopped nuts
1 No. 2 can pears
1 grapefruit, sectioned

Heat pineapple juice and add 1 cup to gelatin. Mix cream and dressing together; pour in cooled gelatin gradually. Chop pineapple, white and red cherries; drain and dry. Add nuts. Sprinkle with salt; fold lightly into dressing with pears and grapefruit sections. Pour into mold and pack with ice several hours. Yield: 12-14 servings.

Fern Draughn
Dobson, North Carolina

FROZEN FRUIT SALAD

1 tbsp. gelatin
1 c. cold water
1 c. mayonnaise
1 c. whipped cream
1 c. orange sections
1 c. diced pineapple
½ c. seeded and halved white grapes
½ c. chopped maraschino cherries
Fruit Salad Dressing

Soften gelatin in cold water; dissolve over hot water. Add mayonnaise; mix thoroughly. Fold in cream and fruits. Pour into mold; cover tightly. Pack in ice and salt; let stand 4 hours. Unmold. Serve slices on crisp lettuce with fruit salad dressing.

FRUIT SALAD DRESSING:

½ c. syrup from frozen or canned peaches
2 egg yolks, well beaten
1 tbsp. sugar
⅛ tsp. salt
⅛ tsp. paprika
1 ½ tsp. lemon juice

Heat peach syrup. Combine egg yolks, sugar, salt and paprika; add syrup slowly, stirring constantly. Cook over hot water until thick and smooth. Remove from heat; add lemon juice slowly. Mix thoroughly and chill. Other fruit juices may be substituted for peach juice. Yield: 6 servings.

Goldie Hall
Olive Hill, Kentucky

FROZEN FRUIT SALAD

2 tsp. gelatin, soaked in 3 tbsp. water
1 c. cream, whipped
1 c. mayonnaise
1 c. oranges, cut up
1 c. bananas, cut up
1 c. shredded pineapple

Dissolve soaked gelatin over hot water. Add to cream. Mix mayonnaise and cream with fruit. Pour mixture into freezing tray. Freeze. Remove from tray; slice and serve on lettuce leaves with salad dressing. Yield: 12 servings.

Mrs. Stanley Short, Jr.
Dover, Delaware

FROZEN FRUIT SALAD

1 tbsp. gelatin
¼ c. cold water
1 c. mayonnaise
1 c. whipped cream
1 c. diced pineapple
1 c. orange sections
½ c. seeded and halved white grapes
½ c. chopped maraschino cherries

Soften gelatin in cold water. Dissolve over hot water. Add mayonnaise. Mix thoroughly; fold in cream. Fold in fruits. Pour into mold. Cover tightly. Pack in ice and salt. Let stand 4 hours; unmold. Slice. Serve on crisp lettuce. Serve with fruit salad dressing. Yield: 6 servings.

Mrs. Earl LaFon
Grand Prairie, Texas

FROZEN ORANGE SALAD

1 pkg. lime gelatin
1 c. hot water
½ c. cold water
½ c. sugar
2 c. orange slices, drained
1 c. maraschino cherries
1 tbsp. lemon juice
⅓ c. mayonnaise
1 c. cottage cheese
1 c. whipping cream

Dissolve gelatin in hot water; add cold water. Chill until slightly thickened. Add sugar to drained orange slices, cherries and lemon juice. Add mayonnaise, cottage cheese and whipping cream to fruit mixture. Combine all ingredients; let congeal.

Mrs. L. E. Strickland
Athens, Georgia

FROZEN ORANGE BASKETS

4 oranges, cut into halves
1 c. drained fruit cocktail
¼ c. chopped blanched almonds
2 3-oz. pkg. cream cheese
¼ c. mayonnaise
1 tbsp. vinegar
¼ tsp. prepared mustard
⅛ tsp. salt
½ c. heavy cream, whipped
Orange sherbet

Carefully remove pulp from orange shells, leaving shell unbroken. Combine 1 cup chopped orange sections, fruit cocktail and almonds. Blend in cream cheese, mayonnaise, vinegar, mustard and salt. Fold in whipped cream. Heap mixture into orange shells; freeze. To keep for a longer time, wrap in airtight, moisture-proof paper. Let stand a few minutes before serving; top with a scoop of orange sherbet. Yield: 8 servings.

Mrs. Joseph W. Morel
West Palm Beach, Florida

FROZEN SALAD IN ORANGE SHELLS

4 oranges
2 3-oz. pkg. cream cheese, softened
¼ c. mayonnaise
1 tbsp. vinegar
¼ tsp. mustard
1 ½ c. diced fresh fruit
¼ c. slivered almonds
½ c. heavy cream, whipped

Cut oranges into halves; scoop out centers, reserving one-half of the orange pulp. Dice reserved orange pulp. Blend cheese with mayonnaise, vinegar and mustard; combine with orange pulp, diced fruit and nuts. Gently fold in whipped cream. Heap into orange shells; freeze until firm. Let shells stand at room temperature 10 minutes before serving. Yield: 8 servings.

Mrs. C. R. Boyd
New Orleans, Louisiana

FROSTY FRUIT SALAD

½ c. mayonnaise-type salad dressing
1 8-oz. pkg. cream cheese
2 c. softened vanilla ice cream
1 10-oz. pkg. frozen raspberries, drained
1 1-lb. can sliced peaches, drained

(Continued on next page)

Gradually add salad dressing to cream cheese, mixing until well blended. Stir in ice cream. Fold in fruits; pour into 6-cup ring mold or individual molds. Freeze until firm. Unmold on lettuce; garnish with raspberries and mint. Yield: 6-8 servings.

Carolyn Jennings
Afton, Tennessee

FROZEN PEACH SALAD

1 pkg. cherry gelatin
1 c. hot water
1 15-oz. can sliced peaches, drained
1 13 ½-oz. can crushed pineapple, drained
1 1-lb. can pears, drained and diced
½ c. miniature marshmallows
½ c. chopped nuts
1 c. heavy cream, whipped
¼ c. sugar
1 3-oz. pkg. cream cheese, softened
½ c. mayonnaise

Dissolve gelatin in hot water; chill. Add fruits with marshmallows and nuts to gelatin; chill. Combine whipped cream with sugar, cream cheese and mayonnaise; add to gelatin as soon as it begins to congeal. Pour into molds and freeze. Remove from freezer 10 minutes before serving. Yield: 16-18 servings.

Mrs. R. M. Scott
Baltimore, Maryland

GOLDEN PEACH FROZEN SALAD

2 3-oz. pkg. cream cheese
1 c. heavy cream
⅓ c. mayonnaise
2 tbsp. lemon juice
1 c. miniature marshmallows
1 10-oz. pkg. frozen sliced peaches, thawed and drained
1 1-lb. 15-oz. can crushed pineapple, drained
Few drops yellow food coloring

Whip cheese; slowly add cream. Beat until thick. Fold in other ingredients. Pour into muffin-cup pans lined with cupcake papers. Garnish with nuts and maraschino cherries. Place in freezer; when frozen remove from pans. Put in plastic bags; return to freezer. To serve, remove from freezer in the quantity desired; remove paper cups. Place on crisp greens. Yield: 18 servings.

Mrs. Richard Claycomb
Guston, Kentucky

FROZEN PEACH-PINEAPPLE SALAD

1 3-oz. pkg. cream cheese
¼ c. mayonnaise
1 No. 2 can crushed pineapple, drained
¼ lb. marshmallows, chopped
½ c. chopped pecans
1 c. diced, drained canned peaches
¼ c. maraschino cherries, chopped
1 c. diced bananas
1 c. heavy cream, whipped

Stir cream cheese until soft; blend in mayonnaise. Add pineapple, marshmallows, nuts, peaches, cherries and bananas; mix well. Fold whipped cream into fruit mixture. Spoon into two 1 1/2-pint waxed paper containers. Place in freezer. Will keep for several months in freezer.

Mrs. C. P. Todd
Enid, Oklahoma

FROSTY HALF AND HALF SALAD

2 3-oz. pkg. cream cheese, softened
2 tbsp. cream
¼ tsp. paprika
Dash of salt
½ c. chopped pecans
1 No. 2 ½ can peach halves, drained
1 No. 2 ½ can pear halves, drained

Combine cream cheese, cream, paprika, salt and pecans; fill centers of peach halves. Top each peach half with pear half; press together. Wrap separately in waxed paper; place in refrigerator trays. Freeze until slightly firm. Yield: 8 servings.

Edna Mae Basden
Rienzi, Mississippi

DELICIOUS FROZEN FRUIT SALAD

2-oz. cream cheese
2 tbsp. cream
⅓ c. mayonnaise (opt.)
1 c. drained crushed pineapple
½ c. maraschino cherries, drained
½ c. orange sections
½ c. banana

Blend cream cheese with cream; add mayonnaise, whipping until smooth. Fold in fruits. Pour into refrigerator tray; freeze until firm. Cut; serve on lettuce.

Mrs. L. M. Nafzinger
Earleville, Maryland

FROZEN CHERRY-PINEAPPLE SALAD

1 pt. pineapple juice
2 3-oz. pkg. lemon gelatin
1 8-oz. pkg. cream cheese, softened
1 4-oz. can red cherries
1 4-oz. can green cherries
1 c. broken pecans
8 slices pineapple, cubed
1 pt. heavy cream
Lettuce

Heat pineapple juice to boiling; dissolve gelatin in hot juice. Cool in refrigerator. Add cream cheese, cherries, pecans and pineapple. Whip cream; fold into mixture. Turn into refrigerator trays; freeze overnight. Serve on lettuce. Yield: 8 servings.

Mrs. S. K. Engel
Yuma, Arizona

FROZEN FRUIT-CHEESE SALAD

2 3-oz. pkg. cream cheese
2 tbsp. lemon juice
1/3 c. mayonnaise
3/4 c. pineapple tidbits, drained
1/2 c. orange segments, diced
1/4 c. maraschino cherries, chopped
1/2 c. candied ginger, chopped
1 c. whipped cream

Blend cream cheese, lemon juice and mayonnaise. Fold in remaining ingredients in order. Freeze.

Mrs. E. G. Gates
Oak Ridge, Tennessee

FROZEN FRUITED CHEESE SALAD

4 tbsp. mayonnaise
2 tsp. lemon juice
1/8 tsp. salt
1 3-oz. pkg. cream cheese, softened
2 tbsp. chopped maraschino cherries
1 13-oz. can pineapple chunks, drained
1 c. diced bananas
1/2 c. chopped walnuts
1/2 c. heavy cream, whipped

Add mayonnaise, lemon juice and salt to cream cheese, mixing well. Add fruits and nuts. Fold in whipped cream. Pour into refrigerator tray; freeze until firm.

Mrs. Lanier Calvert
Buckeye, Arizona

FROZEN FRUIT-NUT SALAD

1 No. 2 1/2 can pineapple chunks
1 lb. marshmallows
1 lb. pecans
1 jar cherries
8 egg yolks, beaten
8 tsp. sugar
8 tsp. tarragon vinegar
1 qt. heavy cream, whipped

Cut pineapple, marshmallows, pecans and cherries into small pieces. Add egg yolks, sugar and vinegar. Fold in whipped cream. Pour into refrigerator trays; freeze for 4 hours. Yield: 24 servings.

Mrs. O. R. Hunter
Richmond, Virginia

FROZEN FRUIT SALAD

1 3-oz. pkg. mixed fruit or lemon gelatin
Dash of salt
1 c. boiling water
1 8 3/4-oz. can pineapple tidbits
1/4 c. lemon juice
1/3 c. mayonnaise
1 c. heavy cream
1 med. banana, diced
1/2 c. seeded grapes, halved
1/4 c. diced maraschino cherries
1/4 c. chopped nuts

Dissolve gelatin and salt in boiling water. Drain pineapple, measuring syrup; add water to make 1/2 cup. Stir into gelatin with lemon juice. Blend in mayonnaise; chill until very thick. Whip cream; fold into gelatin with fruits and nuts. Pour into 9 x 5-inch loaf pan. Freeze until firm, at least 3 to 4 hours. Cut in squares. Yield: 8 servings.

Shirlynn Roberts
Dike, Texas

FROZEN FRUIT SALAD

4 1-lb. 4-oz. cans crushed pineapple
2 1-lb. cans sliced peaches
2 c. fresh white seedless grapes, halved
1 1/2 c. chopped maraschino cherries
1/2 lb. or 30 marshmallows, quartered
2 tsp. finely chopped crystallized ginger
1 envelope unflavored gelatin
1/4 c. cold water
1 c. orange juice
1/4 c. lemon juice
2 1/2 c. sugar
1/2 tsp. salt
2 c. coarsely chopped pecans
2 qt. heavy cream, whipped
3 c. mayonnaise

(Continued on next page)

Drain fruit; save 1 1/2 cups pineapple juice. Cut peaches in 1/2-inch cubes. Combine fruit, marshmallows and ginger. Soften gelatin in cold water. Heat pineapple juice to boiling. Add gelatin; stir to dissolve. Add orange and lemon juice, sugar and salt; stir to dissolve. Chill. When mixture starts to thicken, add fruit mixture and nuts. Fold in whipped cream and mayonnaise. Dessert topping may be substituted for whipped cream. Spoon into quart cylinder cartons. Cover; freeze. Remove from freezer; thaw enough to slip out of carton. Cut in 1-inch slices. Serve salad on lettuce; garnish with cherries. Yield: 9 quarts.

Mrs. Fletcher Peterson
Loretto, Kentucky

FROZEN SALAD

1 lb. grapes, halved and seeded
1 lge. can pineapple, drained and diced
1 lge. pkg. marshmallows, chopped
½ c. chopped pecans
1 tsp. cornstarch
2 eggs, beaten
½ c. milk
Juice of 1 lemon
½ pt. cream, whipped

Combine first 4 ingredients. Add cornstarch to eggs with milk. Add lemon slowly, so not to curdle milk. Heat until smooth; cool. Add whipped cream to egg mixture. Pour over fruit mixture; freeze.

Mrs. William Mathis
Shelbyville, Kentucky

FROZEN PINK SALAD

4 tbsp. butter
2 tbsp. flour
2 tbsp. sugar
1 No. 2 can crushed pineapple
Small bottle red cherries
1 egg
15 marshmallows
3 oranges, peeled and diced
¾ c. pecans
Pinch of salt
1 pt. whipping cream

Cream butter, flour and sugar. Add juice from crushed pineapple and cherries. Cook over low heat a few minutes. Beat egg and add to mixture. Cook a little longer. Add marshmallows and cook slowly until melted. Add oranges, cherries, nuts, pineapple and salt. Cool. Whip cream and add. Freeze in a 9 x 14-inch container. Cut in squares or in round cylinders.

Mrs. B. C. Freeman
Caledonia, Mississippi

FROZEN SOUR CREAM-FRUIT SALAD

1 c. crushed pineapple, drained
¼ c. sugar
1 med. banana, chopped
⅓ c. maraschino cherries, chopped
⅓ c. pecans, chopped
1 c. sour cream

Combine pineapple and sugar; mix well. Combine banana, cherries and pecans. Add to pineapple mixture. Add sour cream; blend. Freeze.

Kittye Maggard
Bowling Green, Kentucky

FROZEN SALAD

2 3-oz. pkg. cream cheese
1 c. mayonnaise
½ c. red maraschino cherries, quartered
½ c. green maraschino cherries
1 No. 2 can pineapple, drained
2 ½ c. miniature marshmallows
½ c. pecans
1 c. cream, whipped

Beat cream cheese and mayonnaise; add maraschino cherries, pineapple, marshmallows and pecans. Fold in whipped cream. Freeze until firm.

Zera L. Greene
Deep Gap, North Carolina

JIFFY FROZEN SALAD

2 c. sour cream
¾ c. sugar
2 tbsp. lemon juice
1 lge. can crushed pineapple, well drained
½ c. maraschino cherries cut and drained
1 banana, thinly sliced
½ c. chopped pecans

Mix sour cream, sugar and lemon juice well; add fruit and nuts. Pour into 9 x 9-inch casserole. Salad should be 1 to 1 1/2 inches thick. Freeze until solid, 3 to 4 hours or overnight. Thaw slightly, 1/2 to 1 hour, before serving. Cut into squares.

Mrs. Robert Mc Allister
Jefferson, Maryland

PINK FROZEN FRUIT SALAD

2 3-oz. pkg. cream cheese, softened
1 8 ½-oz. can crushed pineapple
1 c. finely chopped dates
¼ c. maraschino cherries plus 3 tbsp. cherry syrup
⅛ tsp. salt
½ c. whipping cream, whipped
¼ c. chopped nuts

Blend cheese and undrained pineapple. Add remaining ingredients. Pour into individual molds. Freeze overnight or until firm. Remove from freezer 20 to 30 minutes before serving. Unmold and garnish with additional cherries. Yield: 6-8 servings.

Wilma Mansel
West Columbia, Texas

RAINBOW FROZEN FRUIT SALAD

16 marshmallows, whole
1 c. canned crushed pineapple
½ c. mayonnaise
½ pt. heavy cream, whipped
6 marshmallows, quartered
3 bananas, sliced
1 c. diced peaches
1 c. raspberries

Heat whole marshmallows with pineapple until marshmallows are melted. Cool until slightly thickened. Add mayonnaise, whipped cream, quartered marshmallows and fruits. Pour into trays; freeze without stirring. Slice and serve on crisp lettuce. Yield: 8 servings.

Mrs. J. H. Martin
Louisville, Kentucky

RARE DELIGHT

½ cantaloupe, diced
4 ripe red plums, diced
1 c. halved fresh red cherries
1 c. halved white grapes
1 can frozen orange juice, slightly thawed

Lightly mix fruits. Place in ice cube tray or similar tin. Pour orange juice over all; freeze only until ice chips begin to form or freeze completely until needed, but serve in ice chip state. Yield: 4 servings.

Mrs. G. D. Kelley
Newport, Kentucky

FROZEN FRUIT SALAD

1 c. crushed strawberries
1 banana, diced
1 sm. can crushed pineapple
¼ c. chopped walnuts
1 c. sugar
3 egg whites, stiffly beaten
¼ tsp. salt
1 c. heavy cream, whipped

Combine fruits with nuts and sugar; freeze until mushy. Fold in egg whites, salt and whipped cream; freeze. Yield: 10 servings.

Mrs. W. C. Bowman
Kingsport, Tennessee

FROZEN FRUIT SALAD

2 3-oz. pkg. cream cheese
½ c. mayonnaise
Pinch of salt
1 c. quartered strawberries, fresh or frozen
½ c. cubed canned pineapple, well drained
½ c. orange pieces
⅓ c. chopped toasted nuts
½ c. cream, whipped

Blend cream cheese, mayonnaise and salt. Add fruit and nuts. Fold in whipped cream. Freeze in mold.

Mrs. Mildred Watford
Abbeville, Alabama

FROZEN STRAWBERRY SALAD

1 pt. frozen sweetened strawberries
1 c. crushed pineapple, drained
½ c. pecans, chopped
½ lb. miniature marshmallows
1 c. whipped cream
1 c. salad dressing
1 3-oz. pkg. cream cheese

Combine strawberries, pineapple, pecans and marshmallows. Combine remaining ingredients; beat until smooth. Add to fruit mixture; mix well. Freeze.

Mrs. H. R. Woodall
Augusta, Georgia

FROZEN STRAWBERRY-PINEAPPLE SALAD

1 envelope unflavored gelatin
2 tbsp. cold water
½ c. sugar
1 c. fruit juice
1 8-oz. can crushed pineapple
1 c. sliced drained strawberries
8 marshmallows, cut in pieces
¼ c. broken pecans
1 c. whipped cream
½ c. mayonnaise

Put gelatin in a cup; add water and let stand. Heat sugar and fruit juice; remove from heat and add gelatin. Stir. Let cool. Combine pineapple, strawberries, marshmallows and nuts. Fold whipped cream and mayonnaise into fruit-nut mixture. Add gelatin mixture; pour in molds and freeze.

Miss Lila Mae Jordan
Conway, South Carolina

FROZEN STRAWBERRY SALAD

16 lge. marshmallows
2 tbsp. strawberry juice
1 c. strawberries, drained and sliced
½ to 1 c. crushed pineapple, drained
1 3-oz. pkg. cream cheese
½ c. mayonnaise
1 c. whipped cream
½ tsp. vanilla (opt.)

Melt marshmallows in strawberry juice in double boiler. Cool. Add strawberries and pineapple. Cream the cheese until smooth; add mayonnaise. Combine whipped cream and vanilla; add to strawberry mixture. Freeze until firm.

Mrs. I. H. Mosley
Little Rock, Arkansas

STRAWBERRY FROZEN SALAD

2 3-oz. pkg. cream cheese
2 tbsp. mayonnaise
2 tbsp. sugar
2 c. frozen strawberries
1 9-oz. can crushed pineapple
½ c. English walnuts, chopped
1 c. whipping cream, whipped stiff

Soften cream cheese. Add mayonnaise and sugar; blend. Add strawberries and pineapple. Add nuts. Fold in whipped cream and freeze. Take out at least 15 minutes before serving. Put on lettuce leaves, and serve with crackers. Yield: 8 servings.

Jewel H. Wolfe
Winston-Salem, North Carolina

STRAWBERRY-PINEAPPLE CUPS

1 9-oz. can pineapple chunks
1 c. drained sliced strawberries
1 c. miniature marshmallows
¼ c. broken pecans
1 envelope unflavored gelatin
¼ c. mayonnaise
1 c. heavy cream, whipped

Drain pineapple, reserving syrup. Combine pineapple, strawberries, marshmallows and nuts. Soften gelatin in 3 tablespoons of reserved syrup. Heat remaining syrup just to boiling. Add to gelatin; stir to dissolve. Add to fruits. Fold mayonnaise into whipped cream; fold into fruit mixture. Fill paper baking cups with mixture; place in muffin pans. Freeze until firm. Yield: 16 servings.

Mrs. A. M. Sherman
Baton Rouge, Louisiana

STRAWBERRY SALAD SUPERB

2 3-oz. pkg. cream cheese
2 tbsp. honey
1 c. sweetened strawberries, crushed
½ c. canned pineapple, diced
¼ c. lemon juice

Blend cheese with honey; add strawberries, pineapple and lemon juice. Freeze.

Mrs. P. T. Pitts
Winston-Salem, North Carolina

MEAT SALADS

Recipe for Knockwurst and Kraut Salad on Page 264

BEEF SALAD

1 lb. boneless stew meat, seasoned and boiled
6 hard-boiled eggs
1 stalk celery
Pickles to taste
Green onions to taste
½ c. mayonnaise
Salt and pepper

Grind cooked meat, eggs, celery, pickles and onions. Blend in mayonnaise. Add salt and pepper to taste.

Mrs. Delia G. Sanson
Wildsville, Louisiana

BEEF SALAD

1 3-lb. lean beef roast or boiling beef
1 c. chopped pickles
6 hard-cooked eggs, chopped
1 sm. can pimento, chopped
1 pt. salad dressing
Broth

Cook beef in moderate amount of water until very tender; cool. Remove fat and bones; grind in food chopper using fine plate. Mix pickles, eggs and pimento with ground meat, adding salad dressing and enough meat broth to make a moist mixture. Place in mold or serving dish; refrigerate until ready to serve. Yield: 12 servings.

Mrs. Max L. Suess
Booker, Texas

CAPRI BEEF SALAD

2 lb. round steak, cut in strips
1 8-oz. bottle Italian dressing
2 c. sliced carrots, cooked
2 c. lima beans, drained
1 c. chopped green peppers
½ c. pimento strips
1 c. red onion rings
1 head lettuce, cut in 2-in. chunks

Brown meat in small amount of Italian dressing. Combine meat with carrots, lima beans, green peppers, pimento strips, onion rings and remaining dressing. Chill. Add lettuce; toss lightly. Yield: 6 servings.

Mrs. H. M. Polk
Abilene, Texas

CHEF'S SPECIAL SALAD BOWL

1 head romaine
1 bunch chicory
1 bunch escarole
Thin ham strips
Roast beef
Swiss cheese
Dressing
Tomatoes
Halved hard-cooked eggs

Tear greens into bite-sized pieces; add thin strips of ham, roast beef and Swiss cheese. Toss well with dressing. Garnish with peeled and quartered tomatoes and eggs.

DRESSING:

1 c. olive oil
1 c. wine vinegar
1 c. catsup
1 c. chili sauce
1 tbsp. grated onion
½ dill pickle, diced
1 clove of garlic, mashed
1 tbsp. parsley
½ tsp. salt
½ tsp. sugar
Ground pepper

Mix all ingredients well. Yield: 1 quart.

Mrs. W. A. Giberson
Brunswick, Georgia

COLD MEAT SALAD

2 c. leftover roast, diced
1 c. celery, diced
1 c. tart apple, pared and diced
¼ c. mayonnaise
1 tbsp. prepared mustard
½ tsp. salt

Combine meat, celery and apple; mix with remaining ingredients. Toss lightly until well coated. Serve on lettuce leaves.

Mrs. Willie T. Rogers
Smartt, Tennessee

JELLIED MEAT LOAF

1 envelope unflavored gelatin
¼ c. cold water
¾ c. boiling tomato juice or water
¼ c. vinegar
½ tsp. salt
½ c. mayonnaise
2 c. finely diced cooked beef
¼ c. diced celery
¼ c. chopped pimento
¼ c. chopped green pepper
¼ c. minced onion
2 hard-cooked eggs, sliced

(Continued on next page)

Soften gelatin in cold water; dissolve in hot liquid. Stir in vinegar and salt; chill until syrupy. Combine remaining ingredients except eggs. Arrange egg slices along bottom and sides of loaf pan. Combine gelatin-meat mixture; mix thoroughly. Turn into loaf pan; chill until firm. Serve cold on shredded lettuce. Yield: 6 servings.

Mrs. Miles Nelson
Bryson, Texas

MAIN DISH SALAD

2 c. julienne cooked beef or pork
1 No. 2 can red kidney beans, drained
1 c. chopped celery
¼ c. chopped onion
2 hard-cooked eggs, chopped
2 tbsp. sliced sweet pickle
¼ c. mayonnaise
1 tbsp. chili sauce
1 tsp. salt
1 head lettuce

Chill all ingredients. Combine meat, beans, celery, onion, eggs, pickle, mayonnaise, chili sauce and salt. Toss lightly; chill in covered bowl for 30 minutes. Serve in lettuce cups. Yield: 4-6 servings.

Mrs. Aline Wilson
Ringgold, Louisiana

MEAT SALAD

1 12-oz. can roast beef
1 can sm. lima beans
4 hard-boiled eggs
1 c. celery
1 c. (about) pecans
Onion and olives to taste
Mayonnaise

Mix all ingredients together. Serve at room temperature.

Mrs. Herman Cates
Madras, Georgia

MEAT SALAD

1 lb. boneless stew meat
1 tsp. salt
3 hard-cooked eggs
1 onion or onion flakes
1 clove of garlic or garlic flakes
½ c. chopped celery
¼ tsp. pepper
½ c. mayonnaise
6 lettuce leaves

Boil stew meat in salted water until tender; drain and cool. Place meat in food grinder; grind with eggs, onion, garlic and celery. Add pepper and mayonnaise; mix well. Serve on lettuce or in sandwiches. Yield: 6 servings.

Mrs. T. P. Ferguson
Biloxi, Mississippi

RASSOLJE

DRESSING:

1 ½ c. sour cream
Mustard
Vinegar
Sugar
Salt and pepper to taste

SALAD:

2 or 3 pickled beets, diced
1 herring, diced
5 or 6 cooked potatoes, diced
2 pickled cucumbers, diced
1 med. apple, diced
1 or 2 hard-cooked eggs, diced
¾ lb. cold roast. diced
½ raw carrot, diced
½ onion, diced

Mix all ingredients; add dressing, mixing lightly. Garnish with finely diced egg yolks, egg whites and cooked beets. Yield: 6 servings.

Mrs. R. B. Phillips
Tubac, Arizona

HOT MEAT SALAD

½ head lettuce
1 tomato, diced
1 onion, chopped
1 lb. ground beef
1 8-oz. can tomato sauce
2 tbsp. chili powder
Salt and pepper to taste
1 med. pkg. corn chips

(Continued on next page)

Combine lettuce, tomato and onion. Brown meat. Add tomato sauce, chili powder, salt and pepper; cook until blended. Pour meat mixture over salad; toss. Add corn chips; toss lightly. Serve immediately. Yield: 6 servings.

Mrs. Allen Daggett
Houston, Texas

MEAT SALAD

1 lb. ground chuck
3 c. water
1 tsp. salt
½ tsp. pepper
1 sm. onion, finely chopped
1 ½ c. chopped lettuce
1 sm. tomato, cut into small pieces
¼ c. salad oil or dressing

Grind meat twice. Place meat in saucepan with water, salt and pepper; cook until done. Drain meat and place in large salad dish. Add onion, lettuce and tomato. Pour salad oil or dressing over salad; mix well. Yield: 8 servings.

Mrs.W. W. Thorne
Jewett, Texas

SALAD CON CARNE

1 lb. ground beef
¼ c. chopped onion
1 tbsp. beef-flavor gravy base
6 to 8 drops hot pepper sauce
1 tsp. cornstarch
1 med. head lettuce torn in bite-sized pieces
1 lge. tomato, cut in wedges
½ sm. onion, thinly sliced and separated into rings
¼ c. green pepper, cut in strips
½ c. sliced ripe olives
4 oz. shredded sharp natural cheddar cheese
1 6-oz. pkg. corn chips, coarsely crushed

In skillet, brown ground beef; add chopped onion, gravy base and hot pepper sauce. Stir in the 3/4 cup water. Simmer, uncovered, 10 minutes, stirring frequently. Combine cornstarch and 1 tablespoon water; stir into meat mixture. Cook and stir until mixture thickens and boils. In salad bowl, combine lettuce, tomato, sliced onion, green pepper, olives and cheese; toss well. Spoon on meat; top with corn chips. Yield: 4-6 servings.

Judy Dunn
Bulane, Kentucky

MEXICAN SALAD

1 lb. ground beef
¼ c. chopped onion
2 c. drained kidney beans
½ c. bottled French dressing
½ c. water
1 tbsp. chili powder
4 c. shredded lettuce
½ c. sliced green onions
8 oz. sharp cheddar cheese, shredded

Brown meat; add onion and cook until tender. Stir in beans, French dressing, water and chili powder. Simmer for 15 minutes. Combine lettuce and green onions. Add meat sauce and 1 1/2 cups cheese; toss lightly. Sprinkle with remaining cheese. Serve with crisp tortillas. Yield: 4-6 servings.

Mrs. J. B. Garner
Anderson, South Carolina

ROAST BEEF SALAD OR SANDWICH

3 c. ground leftover pot roast
4 hard-cooked eggs
¾ c. chopped pickles or pickle relish
1 sm. onion, chopped (opt.)
1 c. salad dressing

Combine all ingredients; chill. Serve on lettuce leaves, if desired. Yield: 6-8 servings.

Mrs. Joe Ramsey
Whitesburg, Kentucky

TACO SALAD

1 lb. hamburger
1 can solid-pack tomatoes
1 c. shredded Velveeta cheese
2 heads lettuce, shredded
½ c. chopped green onions
½ tsp. Tabasco sauce
½ 15-oz. can refried beans
6 oz. corn chips
Salt and pepper to taste

Fry hamburger; drain, reserving grease. Drain tomatoes, reserving juice; cut up tomatoes. Add with cheese, lettuce and onions to beef. Heat grease, tomato juice, Tabasco sauce and refried beans; add to hamburger mixture. Toss. Add corn chips; season to taste. Yield: 12 servings.

Mrs. D. T. Kirkland
Baton Rouge, Louisiana

TACO SALAD

1 ½ lb. ground beef
1 ½ c. diced onions
3 cloves of garlic, diced
Salt to taste
Chili powder to taste
Cumin to taste
1 lb. Velveeta cheese
1 can tomatoes with chilies
1 lge. head lettuce, coarsely chopped
2 lge. firm ripe tomatoes, diced
1 lge. pkg. corn chips

Brown beef in small amount of oil. Saute onions and garlic until soft but not brown. Add to meat; simmer for a few minutes. Season with salt, chili powder and cumin. In top of double boiler, melt cheese; add tomatoes with chilies. Place lettuce and tomatoes in large salad bowl; add meat and vegetables. Mix lightly; top with hot cheese mixture. Sprinkle with corn chips. Serve immediately. Yield: 6-8 servings.

Mrs. O. G. Charles
Columbia, South Carolina

CHOPPED HAM SALAD MOLD

½ c. cucumber
1 tbsp. unflavored gelatin
¼ c. cold water
1 ½ c. tomato juice, heated
1 tsp. lemon juice
½ tsp. salt
1 c. cooked ham, chopped
3 hard-cooked eggs, chopped
1 c. celery, chopped
½ c. bell pepper, chopped
1 tbsp. onion, chopped
½ c. mayonnaise

Soak cucumber in salted water. Drain and chop. Soften gelatin in cold water. Add hot tomato juice; stir until gelatin is dissolved. Add lemon juice and salt. Chill until partially set. Combine remaining ingredients; fold into thickened gelatin. Pour into mold; chill until firm.

Daphne Smith
Winnsboro, Texas

CONGEALED HAM SALAD

1 tbsp. unflavored gelatin
¼ c. cold water
¾ c. boiling water
¼ c. vinegar
½ tsp. salt
½ c. chopped pimento
½ c. chopped celery
1 tbsp. minced onion
½ c. mayonnaise
1 ¼ c. ground cooked ham
2 hard-cooked eggs, sliced

Soak gelatin in cool water for 5 minutes; dissolve in hot water. Stir in vinegar and salt; let cool until slightly thickened. Fold in remaining ingredients except eggs. Chill mold by dipping into cold water. Arrange egg slices on bottom and sides of mold. Turn salad into mold. Press back into place with a knife the egg slices floating out of place.

Mrs. Kenneth Brett
Emporia, Virginia

CRUNCHY BAKED HAM SALAD

3 c. cooked diced ham
1 c. diced celery
½ c. chopped stuffed green olives
4 hard-cooked eggs, diced
¼ c. chopped onion
1 tbsp. lemon juice
1 tbsp. prepared mustard
Dash of pepper
¾ c. mayonnaise or salad dressing
1 c. crushed potato chips

Combine all ingredients except potato chips. Place in 8 x 2-inch round baking dish; sprinkle with potato chips. Bake at 400 degrees for 20 to 25 minutes.

Kasie Hope
Shelby, North Carolina

EASY HAM SALAD

2 c. cooked ground ham
2 or 3 hard-cooked eggs, chopped
2 tsp. ground onion
2 stalks celery, chopped
¾ c. ground sweet pickles
½ c. ground peanuts (opt.)
Mayonnaise to taste

Thoroughly blend all ingredients. Yield: 6 servings.

Mrs. William L. Jones
Ozona, Florida

HAM AND APPLE SALAD

1 ½ c. diced apples
½ c. chopped celery
1 ½ c. diced ham
Lettuce, shredded

(Continued on next page)

Combine all ingredients; toss with sweet and sour dressing. Pile onto shredded lettuce or individual lettuce cups; serve.

Mrs. Hazel Tilghman
Kinston, North Carolina

HAM AND CUCUMBER

2 3-oz. pkg. lemon-lime gelatin
1 tsp. salt
2 c. boiling water
1 ½ c. cold water
¼ c. vinegar
1 c. slivered cooked ham
1 c. sliced celery
1 9-oz. can drained pineapple chunks
½ c. thinly sliced quartered cucumber
¾ tsp. grated onion
3 tbsp. prepared horseradish

Dissolve gelatin and salt in boiling water. Add cold water and vinegar. Chill until thick. Fold in remaining ingredients. Pour into 1-quart ring mold. Chill until firm. Yield: 8 servings.

Mrs. H. M. Callaway
Lexington, Georgia

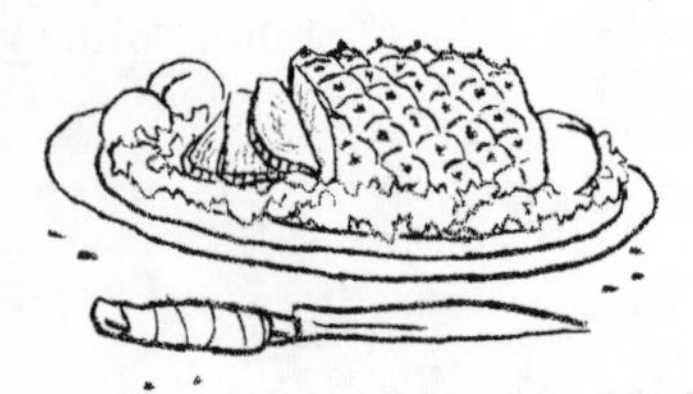

MANDARIN-HAM SALAD

3 c. cooked ham, cut in ¾-in. squares
1 13 ½-oz. can pineapple chunks, well drained
1 16-oz. can Bing cherries, drained
1 11-oz. can mandarin oranges, drained
1 ½ c. miniature marshmallows
1 c. sour cream
½ c. mayonnaise
2 c. cooked rice
Lettuce
Toasted coconut or toasted slivered almonds

Combine ham, pineapple, cherries, oranges and marshmallows. Mix sour cream, mayonnaise and rice. Toss with fruit mixture. Serve on individual lettuce cups. Sprinkle with coconut. Yield: 6 servings.

Mrs. James W. Cullings
Knoxville, Tennessee

APPLE BALL AND HAM SALAD

8 tart apples, pared
2 tbsp. lemon juice
2 c. cubed cooked ham
1 c. diced celery
¼ c. mayonnaise
¼ c. light cream
2 oz. blue cheese, crumbled

Cut balls from apples, using melon ball cutter or measuring spoon; sprinkle with lemon juice. Add to ham and celery. Blend mayonnaise and cream; add to apple mixture and toss. Sprinkle with blue cheese. Garnish with apple wedges and parsley. Yield: 6-8 servings.

Mrs. Sanders Cox
Oklahoma City, Oklahoma

HAM 'N' ORANGE SALAD

1 clove of garlic (opt.)
2 c. cooked cubed ham
1 ½ c. orange sections
1 c. chopped celery
½ c. chopped nuts
⅓ c. minced onion (opt.)
½ c. mayonnaise
2 tbsp. cream
1 tbsp. vinegar
Dash of pepper

Rub salad bowl with garlic. Mix ham, orange sections, celery, nuts and onion in bowl. Combine remaining ingredients; add to ham mixture and toss. Yield: 6-8 servings.

Mrs. Delmer Shugart
Granbury, Texas

HAM AND CHEESE SALAD

6 slices boiled ham, chopped
4 hard-cooked eggs, chopped
4 slices Swiss cheese, chopped
Lettuce
Salt and pepper
French dressing

Combine ham, eggs and cheese; toss with lettuce, salt and pepper. Sprinkle French dressing on salad; serve. Yield: 4 servings.

Mrs. Robert H. Cornell
Winston-Salem, North Carolina

HAM MOUSSE

1 tbsp. gelatin
¼ c. cold water or chicken stock
¼ tsp. salt
2 ½ c. chopped ham or chicken
⅛ tsp. paprika
¾ c. sweet cream, stiffly beaten

Soak gelatin in cold water for 5 minutes; dissolve over boiling water. Mix salt, meat and paprika with gelatin. Fold in cream. Pour into molds which have been dipped in cold water. Chill. Turn out on bed of crisp lettuce; garnish with pimento. Serve with mayonnaise dressing. Salt may be left out if ham is used.

Mrs. Ruby Itz
Doss, Texas

HAM MOUSSE

2 c. finely chopped boiled ham
2 tsp. prepared mustard
1 tsp. horseradish
1 c. heavy cream
4 tbsp. mayonnaise
2 tbsp. unflavored gelatin
½ c. cold water

Put ham through meat chopper twice; mix well with mustard and horseradish. Whip cream until stiff; add to mayonnaise. Soften gelatin in cold water; dissolve over hot water. Cool a few minutes; strain into cream. Refrigerate for 15 minutes. Fold in ham. Mix thoroughly and pour into cold mold. Set on ice for several hours. Turn out on serving dish; garnish with lettuce hearts and potato roses. Yield: 6 servings.

Mrs. H. L. Cockrum
Houston, Texas

HAM SALAD

½ c. cubed cooked ham
½ c. diced Swiss cheese
2 hard-cooked eggs, chopped
1 c. diced celery
Salt and pepper to taste
2 tbsp. chopped sweet pickle
2 tbsp. minced green onion and tops
2 tbsp. chopped pimento
⅓ c. mixed salad dressing and mayonnaise
Lettuce

Combine all ingredients except lettuce; toss lightly. Refrigerate until ready to serve. Add lettuce and more salad dressing if needed; toss lightly to combine. Garnish with slices of tomato if desired. Yield: 6 servings.

Ruth Gurr
Mobile, Alabama

HAM SALAD

1 ½ c. diced ham
6 hard-cooked eggs, coarsely diced
½ c. diced celery
½ c. sliced gherkins
⅓ c. salad dressing
2 tbsp. prepared mustard
1 tbsp. lemon juice
Salt and pepper to taste

Combine ham, eggs, celery and gherkins. Blend salad dressing, mustard and lemon juice. Add to ham mixture; toss lightly. Season to taste. Garnish with additional salad dressing or mayonnaise; sprinkle with paprika. Serve on lettuce. Yield: 6 servings.

Mrs. Donald Warder
Wallingford, Kentucky

HAM SALAD

1 3-oz. pkg. lemon gelatin
1 c. boiling water
½ tsp. salt
¾ c. cold water
2 tbsp. vinegar
⅓ c. whipping cream
⅓ c. mayonnaise
2 c. chopped ham
½ c. chopped celery
½ c. chopped sweet pickles
1 tsp. grated onion
½ tsp. Worcestershire sauce

Dissolve gelatin in boiling water; stir in salt. Add cold water and vinegar. Chill until very thick. Whip cream. Fold cream and mayonnaise into gelatin, blending well. Add remaining ingredients. Pour into 1-quart mold and chill until firm. Yield: 6 servings.

Mildred Gresham
Cadiz, Kentucky

HAM SALAD

2 c. diced cold cooked ham
1 tsp. chopped onion
1 tbsp. chopped parsley
1 tbsp. chopped pickle
2 hard-cooked eggs, chopped
French dressing

Mix ingredients except dressing; marinate in dressing. Chill. Serve with mayonnaise. One cup shredded cabbage may be added. Yield: 4 servings.

Mrs. Ellie Hayes
Benson, North Carolina

HAM SALAD SANDWICH FILLING

2 c. ground ham
2 hard-cooked eggs, ground
4 tbsp. ground green pepper
4 tbsp. ground sweet pickles
¼ c. mayonnaise
2 tbsp. horseradish seasoning sauce
¼ tsp. onion seasoning
Dash of pepper

Combine ham, eggs, green pepper and pickles; add mayonnaise, horseradish seasoning sauce, onion seasoning and pepper. Mix well with fork. Chill several hours or overnight. Yield: 3 cups.

Rebecca Clements
Chatham, Virginia

HAM SALAD MOLD

3 c. finely chopped cooked ham
¾ c. diced celery
¼ c. diced green pepper
¼ c. chopped ripe olives
½ tsp. salt
2 tbsp. unflavored gelatin
½ c. cold water
1 c. pineapple juice, heated
1 tsp. mustard
1 tsp. horseradish
Juice of 1 lemon
1 c. evaporated milk, chilled

Mix ham, celery, green pepper, olives and salt. Soak gelatin in cold water for about 5 minutes; combine with hot pineapple juice. Stir in mustard, horseradish and lemon juice. Cool. Beat chilled milk until peaks form; slowly add cooled gelatin mixture, beating continuously. Fold in ham mixture. Pour into greased 9 x 5-inch pan. Chill until firm. Unmold and slice. Yield: 6-8 servings.

Mrs. Betty Lou James
Russiaville, Indiana

HAM SALAD SUPREME

2 c. ground boiled ham
4 hard-boiled eggs, ground
1 c. ground sweet cucumber pickles
½ c. mayonnaise or salad dressing

Mix all ingredients; chill.

Mrs. Henry Hunt
Jewell Ridge, Virginia

HEARTY TOSSED SALAD

1 med. onion, thinly sliced
1 8-oz. pkg. boiled ham, chopped
1 8-oz. pkg. Swiss cheese, chopped
4 tbsp. diced green pepper
1 lge. head lettuce, shredded
⅓ c. salad oil
3 tbsp. vinegar
¼ tsp. pepper
⅓ tsp. salt

Soak onion in ice water for 30 minutes. Combine onion, ham, cheese, pepper and lettuce; toss until mixed. Place in salad bowl. Mix remaining ingredients; pour over salad. Toss and serve. Yield: 6 servings.

Mrs. Ken Rogers
Indianola, Iowa

HOT BAKED HAM SALAD

3 c. diced cooked ham
1 c. diced celery
½ c. chopped stuffed olives
2 hard-cooked eggs, diced
2 tsp. diced onion
1 tbsp. lemon juice
2 tbsp. prepared mustard
⅛ tsp. pepper
¾ c. mayonnaise
1 c. crushed potato chips

Combine all ingredients except potato chips; place in greased 8 x 8-inch square pan. Sprinkle with potato chips. Bake at 400 degrees for 20 minutes. Yield: 6 servings.

Mrs. Pershing Kettleson
Albion, Nebraska

HOT HAM SALAD

4 c. cooked cubed ham
1 c. finely chopped ripe olives
3 hard-cooked eggs, chopped
½ c. finely chopped celery
¼ c. finely chopped onion
½ c. chopped almonds (opt.)
½ c. mayonnaise
½ c. sour cream
Salt and pepper to taste
Italian herb seasonings
½ c. grated sharp cheddar cheese
½ c. ground potato or corn chips

Combine all ingredients except cheese and potato or corn chips. Place in greased loaf pan; sprinkle with cheese and chips. Bake in preheated 350-degree oven for 30 minutes. Yield: 10 servings.

Mrs. K. H. Wilson
Meridian, Mississippi

HAM-MACARONI SALAD

1 8-oz. pkg. elbow or lge. short-cut macaroni
½ c. mayonnaise
½ c. or less finely chopped sweet cucumber pickles
¼ c. chopped pimento
1 tbsp. mustard
1 tsp. celery seed
½ c. chopped apple
2 tbsp. chopped onion
2 boiled eggs, chopped fine
¾ c. cooked, finely chopped ham
Salt and pepper to taste

Cook macaroni according to package directions; drain in colander. Rinse with cold water; drain. Chill. Mix all ingredients; toss well. Chill. Serve on lettuce leaf; garnish with cherry tomatoes. Yield: 6-8 servings.

Mrs. Guyton H. McGee
Kosciusko, Mississippi

HAM-MACARONI SALAD

½ lb. boiled or baked ham, cubed
½ c. diced yellow cheese
2 c. cooked elbow macaroni
1 c. chopped celery
1 sm. onion, chopped
½ c. diced dill pickles
½ c. mayonnaise
2 tsp. mustard
6 hard-cooked eggs, sliced
3 tomatoes, cut into quarters

Combine ham, cheese, macaroni, celery, onion and pickles. Mix mayonnaise and mustard; stir into macaroni mixture, mixing well. Chill until ready to serve. Heap salad on lettuce leaves. Garnish with eggs and tomatoes. Yield: 6 servings.

Mrs. B. G. Lawton
Tucson, Arizona

HAM AND MACARONI SALAD

1 pkg. elbow macaroni
¼ c. vinegar
2 c. cooked cubed ham
½ tsp. pepper
2 tsp. salt
½ c. mayonnaise
¼ c. grated onion
1 c. chopped celery
¼ c. chopped pimento
1 head lettuce
4 tomatoes, quartered

Boil macaroni in salted water until tender; drain. Pour vinegar over macaroni; allow to stand 10 minutes. Add remaining ingredients except lettuce and tomatoes; toss lightly. Serve on lettuce; garnish with tomato sections.

Mrs. Bertha Pippin
Malvern, Alabama

HAM AND MACARONI SALAD

1 can cream of chicken soup
¼ c. chopped celery
¼ c. chopped onion
2 tbsp. chopped green pepper
½ tsp. mustard
Dash of Tabasco sauce
Dash of pepper
2 c. cooked macaroni
1 c. diced cooked ham

Mix soup, celery, onion, green pepper, mustard, Tabasco sauce and pepper. Stir in macaroni and ham. Chill. Yield: 4-6 servings.

Mrs. James L. Fothergill
Miami, Florida

SUPREME SALAD

2 ½ c. cooked elbow macaroni
½ c. mayonnaise
3 tbsp. minced onion
1 tbsp. sweet pickle juice
2 c. diced celery
1 ½ c. diced cooked ham
1 ½ c. diced cheddar cheese
¾ c. diced ripe olives
¼ c. diced green olives
¼ c. diced sweet pickles
¼ tsp. salt
½ head lettuce

Cook macaroni in water; drain and cool. Combine mayonnaise, onion, pickle juice, celery, ham, cheese, olives, pickles and salt; add macaroni. Mix lightly; serve on lettuce. Keep refrigerated. Yield: 10 servings.

Mrs. Norman May
Paducah, Kentucky

MAC'S CHEF SALAD

1 head lettuce, torn into bite-sized pieces
1 lge. onion, chopped
3 stalks celery, chopped
1 tomato, chopped
1 cucumber, chopped
1 hard-cooked egg, chopped
¼ lb. cooked ham, chopped
¼ lb. sharp cheese, grated
4 tbsp. grated Parmesan cheese
1 oz. vinegar with garlic
1 oz. salad oil
1 oz. olive oil
Lemon juice to taste
8 ripe pitted olives
8 green olives
Pinch of salt
Pepper
Oregano

Place lettuce, onion, celery, tomato, cucumber, egg and ham in salad bowl. Add cheeses. Mix vinegar, salad oil, olive oil and lemon juice in small jar; shake well. Add olives, salt, pepper and oregano; toss all ingredients. Yield: 4-8 servings.

Mrs. P. O. Alson
Orlando, Florida

MEAL-IN-ONE SALAD

6 c. shredded lettuce
4 ripe tomatoes
3 lge. green peppers
1 lge. onion, thinly sliced
1 c. diced cheese
1 c. diced celery
6 radishes, thinly sliced
1 c. diced cucumbers
1 c. cooked diced ham or chicken

Combine; toss lightly.

DRESSING:

¾ c. salad oil
⅓ c. vinegar
1 tsp. salt
1 tsp. pepper
1 tsp. sugar
1 tsp. catsup
1 tsp. onion powder
½ tsp. garlic powder

Combine all ingredients in fruit jar; shake well. Pour over salad and toss. Garnish with ripe olives. Serve with hot biscuits or crackers. Yield: 8 servings.

Mrs. F. H. Frazier
Louisville, Kentucky

PARTY HAM RING

1 envelope unflavored gelatin
¼ c. cold water
1 c. sour cream
½ c. mayonnaise
3 tbsp. vinegar
¼ tsp. salt
Pepper to taste
1 ½ c. diced cooked ham
1 c. sliced celery
¼ c. chopped parsley
3 tbsp. chopped green onion

(Continued on next page)

Soften gelatin in water; bring to a boil. Blend in sour cream, mayonnaise, vinegar, salt and pepper. Chill until thickened; whip until fluffy. Fold in remaining ingredients; pour into five 1/2-cup ring mold. Chill until firm. Yield: 6 servings.

Mrs. Jerry M. Daily
Prestwick AFB, Scotland

SUPER CHEF SALAD

1 head lettuce, chopped
1 c. ham or desired meat, slivered or diced
½ c. dry packaged dressing
French dressing

Combine ingredients in order, adding French dressing, just before serving.

Catherine H. Maeder
Alva, Florida

HAM AND CABBAGE SALAD

1 sm. cabbage, shredded
2 c. cooked diced ham
½ onion, chopped
1 sweet red pepper, chopped
1 green pepper, chopped
1 c. mayonnaise
Salt to taste

Combine cabbage, ham, onion and peppers; blend with mayonnaise. Salt to taste. Yield: 8 servings.

Mrs. M. D. Dawson
Charleston, South Carolina

SUNDAY SUPPER SALAD

½ lb. cooked or canned ham, cut into strips
½ lb. American cheese, cut in strips
1 sm. head cabbage, shredded
1 green pepper, thinly sliced
1 Bermuda onion, thinly sliced
Olive French Dressing

Combine ingredients, except dressing; chill. Toss lightly with dressing.

OLIVE FRENCH DRESSING:

1 c. salad oil
⅓ c. vinegar
1 ½ tsp. salt
Pepper to taste
2 tsp. sugar
1 ½ tsp. dry mustard
1 tsp. paprika
½ c. chopped olives

Combine all ingredients; beat with rotary beater until well mixed. Chill in covered jar. Mix well before serving; add olives.

Paulette Cosby
Stratford, Oklahoma

HAM-SLAW SALAD

2 eggs
½ tsp. salt
½ tsp. pepper
3 tbsp. sugar
⅓ c. vinegar
⅓ c. water
2 to 3 c. cooked diced ham
3 c. coarsely chopped cabbage
1 med. carrot, thinly sliced
¼ c. chopped green pepper
¼ c. chopped onion

Beat eggs; add salt, pepper, sugar, vinegar and water. Cook slowly until thickened about 3 minutes, stirring well. Chill. Combine ham, cabbage, carrot, green pepper and onion. Add desired dressing; toss well. Serve in cabbage or lettuce-lined bowl.

Mrs. Vada Goode
Esmont, Virginia

KID'S SALAD

½ head lettuce, broken in pieces
4 c. halved tomatoes
2 c. fresh green onions and tops, sliced
1 c. chopped celery
2 c. cubed cheese
4 c. cubed cooked ham
1 c. quartered radishes
¼ to ½ c. shredded purple cabbage

Combine all ingredients. Serve with favorite salad dressing.

Mrs. Edwin Paul Schaefer
Cisco, Texas

IMPERIAL SALAD

1 lge. pimento pepper
6 lb. cabbage
1 med. onion
3 lge. cucumbers
3 green sweet peppers
2 red sweet peppers
1 11-oz. jar sweet pickles
2 lb. cooked ham
1 pt. mayonnaise
Salt and pepper

Wash pimento with a fork. Put next 7 ingredients through a food chopper; add mayonnaise. Salt and pepper to taste. Mix all ingredients well. Yield: 4 quarts.

Mrs. J. C. Holt
Zebulon, North Carolina

MAIN-DISH SLAW

1 sm. head cabbage, shredded
1 c. ham, diced
1 c. cheddar cheese, cubed
¼ c. chopped sweet pickle
½ tsp. sugar
¾ tsp. salt
½ tsp. celery seed
¼ tsp. pepper
Mayonnaise or sour cream to taste
1 hard-cooked egg, sliced

Combine first 8 ingredients; toss lightly with mayonnaise. Garnish with egg. Yield: 6-8 servings.

Mrs. Fitchett Ober
Richmond, Virginia

COLD MEAT IN ASPIC

1 pkg. unflavored gelatin
¼ c. cold water
1 ½ c. heated highly seasoned consomme
½ c. cooked peas
1 hard-cooked egg, sliced
1 c. cooked sliced beets
Cubed ham, chicken or veal

Soften gelatin in cold water; stir into hot consomme. Pour a thin layer into greased pan; chill until thickened. Arrange peas, egg and beets on gelatin. Cover with another layer of gelatin; chill. Mix meat with remaining gelatin mixture; pour over cooled layer. Serve on lettuce garnished with radish roses. Yield: 6 servings.

Mrs. L. K. Hilton
Knoxville, Tennessee

KIDNEY BEAN SALAD

1 1-lb. can kidney beans
½ to 1 c. cubed, cooked ham
½ c. chopped celery
¼ c. mayonnaise or salad dressing
¼ c. pickle relish
¼ c. minced onion
1 tsp. prepared mustard
¼ tsp. Worcestershire sauce
1 tsp. celery seed
¼ tsp. salt

Combine first 3 ingredients, mixing well. Set aside. Combine remaining ingredients; add to first mixture. Mix lightly until blended. Chill. Serve on lettuce. Yield: 4 servings.

Mrs. Orby Yarberry
Columbia, Kentucky

MAIN DISH KIDNEY BEAN SALAD

1 can kidney beans, drained
½ c. celery, chopped
½ c. green pepper, diced
1 onion, cut in circles
½ c. pickles, chopped
½ lb. cheese, chopped
1 lb. ham, cut in strips
2 eggs, sliced
Mayonnaise

Combine and toss all ingredients except mayonnaise. Chill. Just before serving, add mayonnaise and mix carefully. Place in lettuce cups and serve with hot bread or crackers.

Mrs. Mary Ann Lea
Vilonia, Arkansas

HAM AND PEA SALAD

1 can peas, drained
1 c. cooked diced ham
½ c. diced cheese
1 tsp. salt
½ tsp. pepper
2 tbsp. salad dressing
½ c. chopped pickles
½ sm. onion, chopped

Combine all ingredients; mix well. Chill and serve. Yield: 6 servings.

Dorothy J. Kimball
Raleigh, North Carolina

HAM SALAD

2 c. diced cooked ham
¾ c. cooked peas
3 tbsp. chowchow

Mix well; chill. Arrange on crisp lettuce leaves; garnish with hard-cooked egg slices.

Frances Jackson
Mill Spring, North Carolina

HAM SALAD MOUNDS

3 lb. cubed ham
¼ lb. longhorn cheese, cubed
⅓ pkg. circle noodles, cooked
2 hard-cooked eggs, cubed
2 sticks celery, finely cut
Finely chopped onion to taste
⅓ can pimento, finely cut
1 qt. salad dressing
1 16-oz. can evaporated milk, chilled and whipped
4 tbsp. mustard
1 c. honey
Juice of 1 lemon
1 can peas, drained

Combine ham, cheese, noodles, eggs, celery, onion and pimento. Whip remaining ingredients except peas to make a dressing. Add as much dressing as needed to ham mixture. Add peas. Serve in mounds on lettuce; garnish top with a slice of olive. Yield: 30 servings.

Mrs. E. P. Patterson
Beaumont, Texas

HAM SALAD DELUXE

2 pkg. unflavored gelatin
½ tsp. salt
¼ tsp. onion salt
2 c. boiling water
1 ½ c. cold water
2 tbsp. vinegar
1 ½ c. diced cooked ham
1 c. cooked peas
½ c. sliced celery

Dissolve gelatin and salts in boiling water; add cold water and vinegar. Chill until thick; add ham, peas and celery. Pour into 1 1/2-quart mold. Chill until firm. Unmold. Yield: 5 servings.

Mrs. K. E. Davis
Albuquerque, New Mexico

PATIO CHEF'S SALAD

1 ⅓ c. instant rice
1 ⅓ c. boiling salted water
½ c. chopped dill pickle
1 tsp. grated onion
Dash of pepper
1 10-oz. pkg. frozen green peas
1 c. thin strips cooked ham
1 c. thin strips Swiss cheese
¾ c. mayonnaise or salad dressing

Pour rice into boiling liquid. Cover; remove from heat. Let stand 5 minutes. Fluff with a fork; cool. Combine rice with remaining ingredients except dressing; chill. Add mayonnaise; mix lightly with a fork. Serve on greens. Yield: 6 servings.

Mrs. Bettie K. Littig
Albuquerque, New Mexico

PATIO SALAD WITH HAM

1 pkg. frozen green peas
½ tsp. salt
1 ½ c. boiling water
1 ⅓ c. instant rice
¾ c. mayonnaise
½ c. chopped dill pickles
1 tsp. grated onion
¼ tsp. pepper
1 c. cooked ham strips
1 c. Swiss cheese strips

Add frozen peas and salt to water; boil for 2 minutes. Add rice; stir to moisten. Cover; remove from heat. Let stand for 5 minutes. Stir in mayonnaise, pickles, onion and pepper. Mix lightly with fork; chill. Add ham and cheese; mix lightly. May be served on crisp salad greens and garnished with tomato wedges. Yield: 6 servings.

Betty McDonald
Marion, South Carolina

PEA SALAD

1 can English peas, drained
1 c. chopped cheddar cheese
1 c. chopped ham
Mayonnaise

(Continued on next page)

Combine peas, cheese and ham. Add mayonnaise to desired consistency.

Joyce Barker
Winslow, Arkansas

YUMMY HAM SALAD

1 c. cooked ham, cut in thin strips
1 c. cheese, cut in thin strips
1 c. canned peas, drained
½ onion, chopped
2 hard-cooked eggs, chopped
½ head lettuce, shredded
Mayonnaise

Combine all ingredients, adding enough mayonnaise to moisten. Serve on lettuce. Yield: 4 servings.

Mrs. Herbert Strand
Jackson, Mississippi

PICNIC NOODLE SALAD

Salt
3 qt. boiling water
8 oz. med. egg noodles
1 ½ c. mayonnaise
1 tsp. caraway seed
⅛ tsp. pepper
1 1-lb. can ham, cubed
½ lb. Swiss cheese, cubed
½ c. sliced olives
½ c. chopped celery
Crisp chicory

Add 1 tablespoonful salt to rapidly boiling water. Gradually add noodles so water continues to boil. Cook, uncovered, stirring occasionally until tender. Drain in colander. Rinse with cold water; drain again. Combine mayonnaise, caraway seed, 1 teaspoonful salt and pepper. Toss dressing in large bowl with cooked noodles, ham, cheese, olives and celery; chill. Garnish with chicory, just before serving. Yield: 6 servings.

Oceale Bishop
Mt. Airy, North Carolina

ALL-IN-ONE SALAD

1 head lettuce
1 ½ c. cooked cubed beans
2 c. cooked cubed potatoes
3 tomatoes, cubed
1 c. ham, beef or chicken cubed
3 hard-cooked eggs
½ c. cubed cucumber pickles

Break lettuce into bowl. Add other ingredients in layers. When ready to serve, add dressing. Toss lightly with two forks and serve.

DRESSING:

¾ c. salad oil
¼ c. vinegar
¼ tsp. mustard
¼ tsp. paprika
¼ tsp. pepper
¼ tsp. salt

Shake all ingredients well before adding to salad.

Mrs. Dorsie Harrell
Meadows of Dan, Virginia

HAM AND POTATO SALAD

1 c. diced cooked ham
2 c. diced cooked potatoes
1 c. diced celery
3 hard-cooked eggs, diced
1 pimento or mango, chopped
½ c. mayonnaise
¼ c. prepared mustard
Salt and pepper to taste

Combine all ingredients; serve on lettuce. If desired, garnish with additional pimento, olives or eggs.

Mrs. W. U. Adams
Stratford, Oklahoma

INDEPENDENCE DAY SALAD

2 c. cooked chopped ham
4 c. cooked cubed potatoes
2 c. diced celery
1 c. torn lettuce
¼ c. finely diced pickles
¼ c. minced green pepper
4 hard-cooked eggs, sliced
1 tsp. salt
Dash of pepper
1 tsp. prepared mustard
¼ c. sour cream
1 c. mayonnaise
Watercress
Ripe olives

Combine ham, potatoes, celery, lettuce, pickles, green pepper and 2 eggs. Mix seasonings, cream and mayonnaise. Blend into ham mixture. Pile onto bed of lettuce. Garnish with sprigs of watercress, remaining eggs and ripe olives, if desired. Yield: 8-10 servings.

Mrs. K. H. Moore
Flagstaff, Arizona

EGG CROWNED SUPPER MOLD

4 hard-cooked eggs
1 envelope unflavored gelatin
1 ¾ c. chicken broth
3 tbsp. prepared mustard
3 tbsp. sweet pickle relish
3 tbsp. diced green pepper
2 tbsp. instant minced onion
1 tsp. sugar
½ tsp. celery salt
2 ½ c. finely diced cooked potatoes
2 c. diced baked ham
Freshly ground pepper
½ c. mayonnaise

Cut egg in half crosswise; cut each piece in half so that egg is in four pieces. Set aside for later. Soften gelatin in 1/4 cup chicken broth. Heat remaining broth; add gelatin mixture and stir to dissolve. Float a 6-cup ring mold in a pan of ice and water. Using 1/2 cup gelatin-broth mixture, pour 2 to 3 tablespoons mixture into bottom of mold; rotate to coat bottom of pan. Stand egg pieces on end, in a circle, on congealed gelatin. Spoon remaining part of the 1/2 cup gelatin mixture around egg pieces. Let stand until set. Combine mustard, pickle relish, green pepper, onion, sugar and celery salt; add remaining broth. Add potatoes, ham and any remaining pieces of egg. Season with pepper. Place pan in ice and water; when liquid begins to thicken, fold in mayonnaise. Spoon mixture over eggs in mold. Chill for several hours or until firm. Unmold on platter; fill center and around mold with lettuce. Garnish with stuffed olives. Yield: 6 servings.

Mrs. B. R. Rawlings
Shreveport, Louisiana

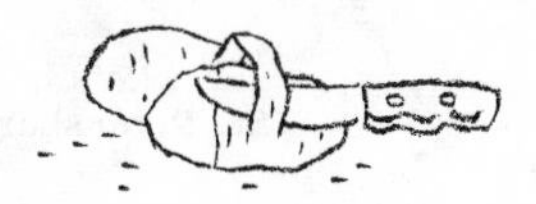

MEAL-IN-ONE SALAD

1 head lettuce, broken in pieces
2 tomatoes, cubed
1 cucumber, sliced
1 green pepper, chopped
1 can shoestring potatoes
1 can minced ham or luncheon meat, cubed
½ c. salad dressing
¼ c. cream
1 tbsp. vinegar
Salt and pepper to taste

Chill lettuce in ice water; drain well. Add tomatoes, cucumber, green pepper, potatoes and ham. Combine remaining ingredients in a covered jar; shake well. Pour dressing over salad and toss. Yield: 4-6 servings.

Mrs. James A. Mock
Tampa, Florida

LEFTOVER HAM SALAD

2 c. diced cooked ham or lamb
1 c. diced cooked potatoes, carrots, peas or beets
2 hard-cooked eggs, chopped
1 med. onion, minced
½ c. diced celery
Salt and pepper to taste
½ c. mayonnaise

Combine meat, vegetables, eggs, onion and celery; mix lightly with 2 forks. Add seasonings and mayonnaise. Serve on lettuce; garnish with paprika. Yield: 6 servings.

Mrs. M. W. Tunning
Valley Bend, West Virginia

WHITE SALAD

¼ c. chopped celery
¼ c. chopped green pepper
¼ c. chopped sweet pickles
¼ c. minced onion
1 tbsp. salt
1 6-oz. can pimento
1 tbsp. mustard
4 boiled eggs, chopped
3 slices ham, bologna or salami, chopped
1 c. mayonnaise

Combine all ingredients; mix well. Garnish with lettuce. Yield: 6-8 servings.

Louise Fox
Lecompte, Louisiana

SWEET POTATO SALAD

2 c. cooked sweet potatoes
¼ c. French dressing
1 c. chopped celery
2 c. diced ham
½ c. mayonnaise

Boil potatoes with jackets; peel and slice while hot. Marinate in French dressing. Blend all ingredients and serve on crisp lettuce garnished with deviled eggs.

Mrs. Annie G. Blanchard
Heth, Arkansas

NEW ENGLAND SAUSAGE SALAD

2 ½ lb. pkg. sausage links
7 oz. shell macaroni, cooked
½ c. shredded cheddar cheese
½ c. sliced celery
¼ c. chopped green pepper
¼ c. chopped sweet pickle
½ c. mayonnaise
½ c. sour cream
1 tsp. lemon juice
½ tsp. onion salt

Cut meat into small pieces; combine with macaroni, cheese, celery, green pepper and pickle in large bowl. Blend mayonnaise, sour cream, lemon juice and onion salt; toss with meat mixture.

Mrs. A. M. Carpenter
Savannah, Georgia

MOCK CHICKEN SALAD

2 c. cooked cubed roast pork
1 c. diced celery
4 olives, chopped
½ red pepper, cooked and diced
Mayonnaise

Combine all ingredients; chill. Serve garnished with strips of celery and red pepper. Yield: 4 servings.

Mrs. T. C. Daniels
West Point, Mississippi

ANTARCTIC SALAD

¾ c. oil
⅛ c. cider vinegar
⅛ c. lemon juice
1 clove garlic, skewered on toothpick
½ tsp. soy sauce
1 tsp. salt
Few grains cayenne pepper
½ tsp. curry powder
2 crushed juniper berries, threaded on toothpick
2 c. lean roast pork, diced
2 tbsp. unflavored gelatin
1 ½ c. hot chicken broth or chicken bouillon cubes dissolved in water
Juice of 1 lge. lemon
Celery crescents
Capers
Green pepper
Cooked mushrooms, cooled
Cucumbers
Radish roses
Carrots
Baby lima beans
Peas
Onions

Make a marinade of oil, vinegar, lemon juice, garlic, soy sauce, salt, cayenne pepper, curry powder and juniper berries. Add meat; let stand at least 4 hours or overnight. Stir occasionally. Soak gelatin in 1/2 cup chicken broth; dissolve in remaining 1 cup hot broth. Add lemon juice. Remove meat, garlic and juniper berries from marinade. Drain meat. Oil a tall mold for a mountain. When gelatin begins to thicken, pour a small amount in the mold, turning to coat the inside of the mold with a layer of gelatin. Refrigerate mold. Keep remaining gelatin at room temperature. Use any desired combination of vegetables, neatly cut into thin, varied shapes. If desired, vegetables may be gently folded into the drained meat or layers of vegetables, meat and gelatin may be alternated in the mold. Chill until firm.

PENGUINS:

8 hard-cooked eggs, halved lengthwise
32 lge. black olives, pitted
Mayonnaise
4 almonds, blanched and halved lengthwise
1 sm. head red cabbage, chilled and finely shredded

Remove yolks from eggs; mash and season to taste. Moisten with a little mayonnaise. Stuff eggs with yolk mixture; fit halves together firmly. Wrap each egg in waxed paper. Twist ends of paper to hold eggs firmly together. Place olives in oil so they will be shiny. Fasten olives in half lengthwise. Use 4 halves for the wings and back of the penguins, placing large ends toward the head. Use two halves for feet. Arrange finely shredded cabbage on serving platter. Unmold the gelatin mountain on the bed of cabbage. Arrange penguins around the mountain, serving 1 penguin per person. Serve with Russian or Thousand Island dressing.

Mrs. J. L. Dixson
St. Petersburg, Florida

PORK AND APPLE SALAD

2 c. diced cooked pork
2 c. diced unpeeled red apples
1 c. diced celery
¼ c. India or sweet relish
1 tbsp. lemon juice
¼ tsp. onion juice
Dash of salt
⅓ c. mayonnaise

Combine all ingredients; chill. Serve on lettuce. Yield: 4 servings.

Mrs. W. C. Dobbs
Arlington, Virginia

PORK AND APPLE SALAD

1 ½ c. diced cooked pork
2 c. diced apples
1 c. diced celery
½ c. chopped pecans
⅓ c. salad dressing
1 tsp. salt

Combine pork, apples, celery and pecans in bowl. Add salad dressing and salt; mix and chill. Serve in lettuce cups. Yield: 6 servings.

Mrs. William Gilbert
Nashville, Tennessee

PORK CHOP SALAD

1 lb. pork chops
1 tbsp. salt
1 sm. onion, diced
½ bell pepper, diced
1 c. celery, diced
½ c. mayonnaise
1 tbsp. prepared mustard
1 hard-boiled egg, diced
½ c. olives, diced
½ c. sweet cucumber pickles, diced

Sprinkle salt on pork chops; let stand 12 hours in refrigerator. Rinse chops and boil until tender in enough water to cover. Remove fat and dice. Mix pork with remaining ingredients and serve on lettuce leaves. Yield: 6 servings.

Mrs. R. L. Patrick
Engelhard, North Carolina

PORK SALAD

2 envelopes unflavored gelatin
2 ½ c. milk
¼ c. butter
3 tbsp. flour
1 ½ c. salad dressing
½ tsp. salt
½ c. diced unpeeled apple
Dash of pepper
Dash of monosodium glutamate
½ tsp. grated onion
3 c. diced, cooked and seasoned fresh pork
1 c. thinly sliced celery
½ c. sliced stuffed olives
½ c. slivered blanched almonds
¾ c. heavy cream, whipped

Soften gelatin in 1/2 cup cold milk. Melt butter over low heat; blend in flour. Add remaining milk; cook until smooth and creamy. Add gelatin mixture. Blend in salad dressing; cool. Carefully fold in remaining ingredients. Pour into ring mold; refrigerate for at least 2 hours. Yield: 6-8 servings.

Mrs. W. G. Grove
New Orleans, Louisiana

TENDERLOIN SALAD

1 lb. lean tenderloin
1 lb. lean veal
1 c. diced celery
¼ c. diced olives
¾ lb. brick cheese, diced
Mayonnaise

Boil meats; cool and dice. Combine all ingredients; use only enough mayonnaise to moisten. Serve on lettuce. Yield: 12 servings.

Mrs. Russell Blankenship
Huntington, West Virginia

ANTIPASTO SALAD

1 head romaine, washed and chilled
1 head lettuce, washed and chilled
6 oz. sliced mozzarella cheese
6 oz. sliced salami
1 7-oz. can tuna
½ c. sliced green onions
½ c. sliced radishes
6 cherry tomatoes
6 ripe olives

Line a large salad bowl with romaine. Pull lettuce into bite-sized pieces; place in bowl. Cut cheese and salami into 1/2-inch strips. Drain tuna; break into chunks with a fork. Arrange cheese, salami, tuna, green onions and radishes in rows on top of greens. Arrange tomatoes and olives around side of salad bowl for garnish. Serve with chilled Anchovy Salad Dressing.

ANCHOVY SALAD DRESSING:

1 c. evaporated milk
½ c. salad oil
¼ c. wine vinegar
1 tsp. salt
¼ tsp. pepper
Dash of garlic powder
¼ c. chopped parsley
2 2-oz. cans flat fillets of anchovies

(Continued on next page)

Place all ingredients in container of electric blender. Cover; blend for a few seconds or until smooth. Chill; serve with salad. Yield: 4-6 servings.

Mrs. G. P. Lawson
Pensacola, Florida

A-LOTTA BOLOGNA SALAD

2 envelopes unflavored gelatin
2 ½ c. water
½ tsp. salt
½ c. vinegar
½ c. diced sweet pickles
2 c. diced bologna
2 c. grated American cheese
½ c. diced celery

Soften gelatin in 1-cup cold water in saucepan. Place over low heat, stirring constantly, until gelatin dissolves. Remove from heat; add remaining water, salt and vinegar. Chill until mixture is consistency of unbeaten egg whites. Fold in remaining ingredients. Pour into 6-cup mold. Chill until firm. Unmold on watercress; serve with mayonnaise thinned with sour cream. Surround mold with tomato slices, topped by green pepper rings and minced onion.

Mrs. Boyd Call
Heddenite, North Carolina

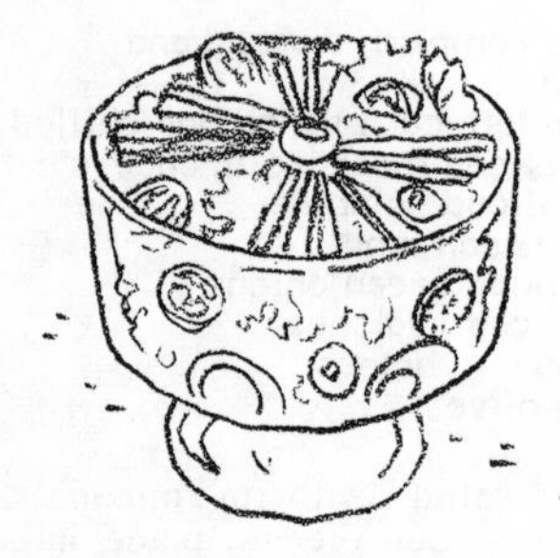

COMBINATION MEAT SALAD

2 lb. all meat bologna
½ lb. pimento cheese
4 eggs, hard-boiled
8 to 10 lge. sweet pickles
1 sm. onion
1 sm. jar chopped pimento
¼ tsp. pepper
¾ tsp. celery seeds
¼ c. sweet pickle vinegar
2 tbsp. prepared mustard
Salad dressing

Grind bologna, cheese, eggs, pickles, onion and pimento in food grinder. Mix in pepper and celery seed. Add vinegar and mustard. Add desired amount of salad dressing.

Nita Carol Sammons
Forest Hills, Kentucky

CREAMY DILL SALAD

2 pkg. lemon gelatin
2 c. hot water
4 c. cream cottage cheese
½ c. chopped bologna
¾ c. chopped dill pickles
Dill pickle slices
Radish slices

Add gelatin to hot water; stir until dissolved. Add cheese, bologna and chopped pickles. Chill until slightly thickened; turn into 8-inch springform pan. Chill until firm; unmold. Garnish with dill pickle and radish slices. Yield: 4-6 servings.

Mrs. Dean Collins
Parrottsville, Tennessee

MEAT AND POTATO SALAD

1 c. mayonnaise
¼ c. French dressing
1 tbsp. prepared mustard
2 tbsp. lemon juice
2 tbsp. Worcestershire sauce
2 tbsp. minced onion
¼ tsp. salt
¼ tsp. paprika
¼ tsp. pepper
2 lb. cooked, cold potatoes, cut in ¼-inch cubes
½ lb. Swiss cheese, cubed
3 c. cooked, drained green peas
18 thin slices bologna
18 pickled cucumber slices
3 hard-cooked eggs, sliced
2 2-oz. can anchovies, drained

Blend mayonnaise, French dressing, mustard, lemon juice, Worcestershire sauce, onion, salt, paprika and pepper. Fold in potatoes, cheese and peas. Arrange salad on lettuce leaves. Fold each bologna slice into a cone shape; place pickle slice in cone. Arrange cones around salad. Arrange egg slices alternating with rolled anchovy slices.

Mrs. Dellar B. Ellis
Independence, Virginia

MOCK HAM SALAD

½ c. sugar
1 tbsp. (heaping) flour
Salt to taste
1 egg
½ c. vinegar
⅔ c. water
1 lb. bologna, ground
6 sweet pickles, ground
1 sm. onion, ground

Combine sugar, flour and salt in saucepan; mix well. Mix in egg. Add vinegar and water, mixing well. Cook over low heat, stirring constantly, until mixture is consistency of salad dressing. Cool. Add remaining ingredients.

Mrs. Martin Huebner
Covington, Kentucky

ALL-IN-ONE SALAD

2 c. cooked cubed meat
¼ c. French dressing
1 c. diced celery
2 hard-cooked eggs
2 tbsp. chopped pimento
2 tbsp. chopped green onions
2 tbsp. chopped green pepper
Salt and pepper to taste
½ c. mayonnaise

Marinate meat in French dressing for 15 minutes; drain. Combine with all remaining ingredients. Place on lettuce leaves and serve chilled. Yield: 4 servings.

Mrs. Glenn E. Lemon
Navasota, Texas

BASIC MEAT SALAD

2 c. cubed cooked or canned meat
1 c. diced celery
1 tsp. Worcestershire sauce
⅓ c. mayonnaise or salad dressing
Salt and pepper to taste
Lettuce

Combine meat, celery, Worcestershire sauce and mayonnaise. Season with salt and pepper. Serve on lettuce. Garnish with tomato wedges and mayonnaise. Yield: 4 servings.

Mrs. Elizabeth Cowley
Saltillo, Mississippi

BASIC MEAT SALAD

2 c. cubed cooked meat
1 c. diced celery
1 tsp. salt
3 hard-cooked eggs, chopped
¼ c. chopped pickles
Mayonnaise

Combine all ingredients, moistening with mayonnaise. Toss lightly with two forks. Chill and serve. Yield: 6-8 servings.

Ethel Downs
Guntersville, Alabama

CHEF MEAT SALAD BOWL

2 c.diced cooked meat
2 hard-cooked eggs, diced
1 c. diced sharp cheddar cheese
4 c. chopped mixed greens
2 tbsp. grated onion
1 c. finely diced celery
2 tomatoes, cut into wedges
½ tsp. salt
¼ clove of garlic, crushed
Pepper to taste
Salad dressing

Place all ingredients except dressing in mixing bowl in order given. Toss lightly with dressing just before serving; serve cold. Garnish with watercress or parsley. Yield: 4-6 servings.

Mrs. Buena B. Hedden
Hayesville, North Carolina

CHEF'S SALAD

1 head lettuce
1 cucumber, thinly sliced
3 stalks celery, diced
2 c. leftover meat slices or sliced ham
3 slices cheddar cheese
3 slices crisp bacon
3 lge. ripe tomatoes, cut into wedges
French dressing
3 hard-cooked eggs, quartered

Tear lettuce into a large salad bowl; add cucumber and celery. Cut meat and cheese into 1/4 x 3-inch strips; add to lettuce. Crumble bacon over all; add tomato wedges and enough French dressing to moisten. Toss; garnish with eggs.

J. C. Smith
Tampa, Florida

DICED MEAT SALAD

1 ½ c. diced leftover meat
1 c. chopped celery
½ c. chopped green pepper
½ c. chopped or grated onion
¼ c. diced longhorn cheese
1 med. head lettuce, shredded
1 pt. mayonnaise
8 tomatoes
4 hard-cooked eggs, quartered

Mix meat, celery, pepper, onion, cheese and lettuce with enough mayonnaise to moisten. Cut each tomato lengthwise onto 6 wedges almost to the bottom; spread open. Fill with salad; serve with 2 egg wedges. Top with mayonnaise. Yield: 8 servings.

Mrs. H. W. Patterson
Huntington, West Virginia

COLD MEAT SALAD

2 c. cooked diced meat
1 c. sliced pascal celery
1 c. pared diced tart apple
¼ c. mayonnaise
1 tbsp. prepared mustard
½ tsp. salt
Crisp lettuce

Combine meat, celery and apple. Mix mayonnaise thoroughly with mustard and salt; add to meat mixture. Toss lightly until all pieces are well coated with dressing. Serve in lettuce cups. Yield: 5 servings.

Lula M. McKoy
Maxton, North Carolina

MEAT SALAD

2 c. cooked chopped meat
2 hard boiled eggs, chopped
½ c. sweet cucumber
pickle, finely chopped
¾ c. finely cut celery
½ c. chopped pecans
1 lge. apple, pared and diced
¾ c. mayonnaise
½ tsp. salt

Combine all ingredients.

Mrs. Annie R. Davis
Statesboro, Georgia

CRANBERRY MEAT SALAD

3 ½ tbsp. unflavored gelatin
¾ c. plus 7 tbsp. cold water
2 c. hot meat broth
1 tbsp. grated onion
Salt and pepper to taste
1 c. finely chopped celery
2 c. minced cooked meat
1 ½ c. sugar
4 c. cranberries
1 stick cinnamon, 2-inches long
6 whole cloves
Grated rind of 1 orange
½ c. finely diced apples
½ c. chopped nuts

Soften 2 tablespoons gelatin in 4 tablespoons cold water; dissolve in hot meat broth. Add onion, salt and pepper; cool until slightly thickened. Fold in celery and meat; fill large oiled mold half full. Chill until firm. Dissolve sugar in 3/4 cup water. Bring to boiling point; add cranberries, spices and orange rind. Cook slowly until cranberries pop open. Put through a fine sieve. Soften 1 1/2 tablespoons gelatin in 3 tablespoons cold water; dissolve in hot cranberry mixture. Cool until slightly thickened; fold in apples and nuts. Pour in mold over congealed meat mixture. Chill until firm. Unmold on lettuce; serve with mayonnaise blended with whipped cream. Chicken, duck, turkey or pork tenderloin may be used. Yield: 12-15 servings.

Mrs. Sue Hester
Tuscumbia, Alabama

MEAT SALAD

2 c. cooked cubed meat
1 c. diced celery
1 tsp. salt
3 hard-cooked eggs, chopped
3 pickles, chopped
Mayonnaise

Combine all ingredients; moisten with mayonnaise. Toss lightly with two forks.

Mrs. Mildred Watford
Abbeville, Alabama

SOUP MEAT SALAD

2 c. cooked soup meat
2 onions, sliced
1 clove garlic, finely chopped
1 c. celery, chopped
1 c. green pepper, chopped
½ c. French dressing

(Continued on next page)

Cut cold meat from bones. Combine meat, onions, garlic, celery and green pepper. Marinate in French dressing. Place on lettuce.

Mrs. Lucille R. Boyter
St. Bernard, Louisiana

ASPARAGUS-MEAT MOLD

- 2 tsp. unflavored gelatin
- ¼ c. cold water
- 1 c. hot meat broth
- 2 c. chopped cooked meat
- 1 c. asparagus tips
- ¼ c. chopped green pepper
- ½ c. chopped celery
- ½ tsp. salt
- Mayonnaise
- Stuffed olives

Soften gelatin in cold water; add hot meat broth. Stir until dissolved. Chill until partially set. Arrange meat, asparagus, pepper and celery in a mold; season with salt. Add gelatin. Chill until firm. Turn out on a bed of crisp lettuce. Garnish with mayonnaise and olives. Yield: 6 servings.

Mrs. C. R. Ledbetter
Black Rock, Arkansas

COUNTRY CLUB SALAD

- 1 ½ to 2 c. chopped meat
- 1 c. thinly sliced cooked carrots
- 1 c. cooked English peas
- ¼ c. chopped bell pepper
- ¼ c. chopped onion
- ½ c. chopped celery
- 3 boiled eggs, sliced
- ½ c. mayonnaise or salad dressing
- Salt and pepper to taste

Mix all ingredients; toss. Yield: 6-8 servings.

Mrs. W. F. Barganier
Ft. Deposit, Alabama

JEAN LAFITTE SALAD

- 2 c. cooked diced meat
- ¾ c. cooked diced potatoes
- ¾ c. cooked diced carrots
- ¾ c. string beans, cooked
- 1 c. French dressing
- 4 sweet pickles, chopped
- 2 hard-boiled eggs, chopped
- 1 c. mayonnaise

Mix meat and vegetables with dressing. Let stand for 1 hour; add pickles, eggs and mayonnaise. Chill; serve on lettuce leaf. Yield: 8 servings.

Mrs. Earl Moeller
San Antonio, Texas

JELLIED MEAT MAIN DISH SALAD

- 1 ½ tbsp. unflavored gelatin
- ¼ c. water
- 1 c. meat or poultry broth or consomme, heated
- 1 tbsp. chopped onion
- Salt to taste
- 1 tbsp. vinegar or lemon juice
- 1 c. chopped cooked meat or poultry
- 1 c. cooked peas
- 2 tbsp. chopped celery
- 2 tbsp. sliced cucumber pickle

Soften gelatin in cold water; dissolve in hot broth. Add onion, salt, vinegar or lemon juice and other seasonings to taste. Chill until thickened. Stir in meat, peas, celery and pickle. Pour into individual molds; chill until firm. Serve on lettuce. Yield: 4-6 servings.

Mrs. D. O. Jones
Tulsa, Oklahoma

JELLIED MEAT SALAD

- 3 ½ tsp. gelatin
- 3 tbsp. cold water
- 1 c. hot broth
- 1 tsp. onion juice
- Salt to taste
- 1 tbsp. vinegar or lemon juice
- 1 c. chopped cooked meat or poultry
- ¼ c. cooked or canned peas
- 2 tbsp. chopped celery
- 2 tbsp. sliced pimento

Sprinkle gelatin over water; soak for few minutes. Dissolve in hot broth. Add onion juice, salt and vinegar; chill until thick enough to hold solid food in place. Stir in remaining ingredients. Pour in small loaf pan or individual molds; chill until firm. Yield: 4 servings.

Mrs. Lois Sells
Monroe, Tennessee

JELLIED MEAT SALAD

2 tbsp. gelatin
¼ c. cold water
2 c. hot broth or bouillon
2 tbsp. grated onion
Salt to taste
2 tbsp. vinegar or lemon juice
2 c. chopped cooked meat
½ c. cooked peas
¼ c. chopped celery

Soften gelatin in water; dissolve in hot broth. Add onion, salt and vinegar. Chill until thickened. Stir in meat, peas and celery. Pour into small loaf pan or individual molds; chill until firm. Yield: 6 servings.

Mrs. A. C. Watson
Johnson City, Tennessee

LEFTOVER MEAT SALAD

½ head lettuce
2 tomatoes, quartered
Cooked vegetables
Cooked cubed meat
Salt and pepper to taste
Vinegar and oil dressing

Cut lettuce into small pieces; add tomatoes, leftover vegetables and meat. Add dressing just before serving. Yield: 4 servings.

Mrs. R. S. Hill
Valdosta, Georgia

MEAT-POTATO SALAD

1 qt. cubed cooked meat, chilled
Salad dressing
4 cooked cold potatoes, diced
1 sm. onion, chopped
1 c. diced celery
½ c. slivered green or red pepper
6 hard-cooked eggs, chopped
Salt to taste

Marinate meat in salad dressing for 1 hour; drain well. Mix meat with vegetables, eggs and salt; toss with Oil Dressing.

OIL DRESSING:

⅔ c. vinegar
¾ c. sugar
⅓ c. salad oil
1 tsp. salt
1 tsp. celery seed

Combine ingredients in jar. Cover; shake a few times. Do not stir. Yield: 8-10 servings.

Mrs. C. S. May
Atlanta, Georgia

MEAT SALAD

2 c. cooked diced meat
1 c. cooked diced potatoes, carrots, peas, beans or beets
2 hard-cooked eggs, diced
1 med. onion, minced
½ c. chopped sweet pickles
½ c. mayonnaise dressing
Salt and pepper to taste

Combine meat, vegetables, eggs, onion and pickles. Moisten with mayonnaise; add seasonings. Mix lightly with 2 forks. Serve on crisp lettuce; garnish with paprika. Yield: 6 servings.

Mrs. Goldie Hall
Olive Hill, Kentucky

SALMAGUNDI SALAD

1 c. boiled diced potatoes
2 c. cooked diced meat
½ c. cooked peas
2 pimentos, chopped
½ c. diced celery
2 sweet pickles, finely diced
½ c. mayonnaise
Salt to taste

Toss ingredients together lightly. Meat may be ham, pork, veal, beef or combinations. Garnish with hard-cooked eggs and more mayonnaise, if desired. Yield: 8 servings.

Mrs. Clint Blevins
Crumpler, North Carolina

ROAST MEAT SALAD

1 head lettuce
2 c. diced, cooked, cold, lean meat
1 c. boiled diced potato
1 onion, chopped
½ c. diced celery
2 hard-cooked eggs, diced
2 sweet pickles, chopped
2 tomatoes
1 green pepper, cut in strips
⅔ c. mayonnaise
½ tbsp. catsup
⅛ tsp. pepper
2 tsp. prepared mustard

(Continued on next page)

Line salad bowl with lettuce leaves. Mix meat, potato, celery, eggs and pickles. Place mixture in bowl in layers separated by green pepper strips. Garnish with quartered tomatoes. Salt to taste. Mix mayonnaise, catsup, pepper and mustard; spread over salad top. Chill. Yield: 6 servings.

Mrs. Eva Wiggins
Monroeville, Alabama

CONGEALED MEAT SALAD

1 can beef consomme
1 pkg. lemon gelatin
1 can corned beef, chopped
1 c. salad dressing or mayonnaise
1 c. chopped celery
1 sm. onion, chopped
2 tbsp. chopped pimento (opt.)
3 hard-cooked eggs, chopped

Add enough water to consomme to make 2 cups liquid; pour into saucepan. Bring to a boil; stir in gelatin until dissolved. Chill until thickened. Fold in corned beef, salad dressing, celery, onion, pimento and eggs. Pour into mold; chill until firm. Yield: 8 servings.

Mrs.F. L. Blair
Asheville, North Carolina

CORNED BEEF-EGG SALAD

1 can corned beef
2 c. diced celery
⅔ c. diced cucumber
3 hard-cooked eggs, diced
½ c. diced olives
Diced onion
Diced sweet pickle
Diced green pepper
1 pkg. lemon gelatin
¾ c. boiling water
1 c. salad dressing
½ pt. heavy cream, whipped

Combine corned beef, celery, cucumber, eggs, olives, onion, pickle and green pepper. Dissolve gelatin in boiling water; cool. Combine with meat mixture, salad dressing and whipped cream. Pour into dish; refrigerate. Yield: 8-12 servings.

Mrs. R. S. Johns
Beaumont, Texas

CORNED BEEF-BOUILLON SALAD

2 envelopes unflavored gelatin
1 c. cold water
1 c. beef bouillon
1 c. salad dressing
1 can chilled corned beef, ground or finely cut
1 sm. green pepper, chopped
1 sm. can pimento, chopped
½ c. chopped celery
3 hard-cooked eggs, chopped

Soften gelatin in cold water. Bring bouillon to a boil; pour over gelatin. Mix salad dressing and beef. Add green pepper, pimento, celery and eggs. Mix with gelatin mixture; chill until firm. Yield: 12 servings.

Mrs. R. B. Stewart
Atlanta, Georgia

CORNED BEEF-GELATIN SALAD

2 3-oz. pkg. lemon gelatin
1 qt. hot water
4 tbsp. vinegar
1 c. mayonnaise
1 can corned beef, broken
2 c. chopped celery
4 tbsp. minced onion
1 green pepper, finely chopped
6 hard-cooked eggs, chopped

Dissolve gelatin in hot water and vinegar. Chill until partially set; fold in mayonnaise and all remaining ingredients. Chill until firm. Yield: 10 servings.

Mrs. R. I. Cochran
Paducah, Kentucky

CORNED BEEF-GELATIN SALAD

1 pkg. lemon gelatin
1 c. hot water
1 can corned beef, shredded
1 ½ tsp. salt
½ onion, grated
5 hard-cooked eggs, chopped
1 c. chopped celery
1 c. mayonnaise

Dissolve gelatin in water; add all remaining ingredients. Pour into oblong pan; chill until firm. Yield: 8-10 servings.

Mrs. W. S. Howard
Augusta, Georgia

CORNED BEEF-GELATIN SALAD

2 sm. pkg. lemon gelatin
3 c. boiling water
1 sm. green pepper, thinly sliced
1 sm. onion, diced
1 c. diced celery
1 tbsp. vinegar
1 pt. salad dressing
1 can corned beef, separated into small pieces

Dissolve gelatin in boiling water. Chill slightly. Mix remaining ingredients; add to gelatin mixture. Pour into square or oblong pan; store in refrigerator for 12 hours. To serve, cut into squares; serve on salad greens with additional salad dressing, if desired. Canned, cubed luncheon meat may be substituted for the corned beef. Yield: 12 servings.

Mrs. M. G. Craig
Albuquerque, New Mexico

CORNED BEEF HASH SALAD

1 can corned beef hash
1 c. diced cheese
1 c. pecans
¼ c. chopped pimento
¼ c. chopped celery
¼ c. chopped onion
½ c. chopped sweet pickles
2 hard-boiled eggs, sliced
3 tbsp. mayonnaise
3 tbsp. sweet pickle vinegar
1 tsp. salt
Dash of pepper

Combine all ingredients.

Ethel Wheat
Rogers, Arkansas

CORNED BEEF AND POTATO SALAD

4 med. potatoes, cooked and diced
2 tbsp. chopped onions
2 tbsp. chopped pickles
¾ c. mayonnaise
1 12-oz. can corned beef, diced

Combine potatoes, onions, pickles and mayonnaise. Add corned beef to potatoes. Mix all together lightly. Cover; chill in refrigerator 2 or 3 hours until flavors are well blended. Serve on crisp lettuce leaves.

Mrs. Barbara Ward
Neva, Tennessee

CORNED BEEF LOAF

1 pkg. lemon gelatin
1 c. boiling water
1 c. meat stock or 1 c. water plus 4 bouillon cubes
1 tbsp. Worcestershire sauce
¼ tsp. paprika
3 c. canned corned beef, ground
1 tbsp. grated onion
1 tbsp. prepared mustard

Dissolve gelatin in boiling water. Add meat stock, Worcestershire sauce and paprika; chill until firm. Unmold; slice and serve on crisp lettuce. Garnish with egg slices and tomato wedges; Yield: 10 servings.

Mrs. T. R. Parkerson
Raleigh, North Carolina

CORNED BEEF WITH MACARONI SALAD

4 oz. ring macaroni
1 pkg. lemon gelatin
1 ½ c. hot water
1 ½ c. celery, finely diced
1 c. salad dressing
1 tbsp. onion, chopped
½ green pepper, finely chopped
3 hard-cooked eggs, chopped
1 can corned beef, shredded
2 tbsp. vinegar

Cook macaroni according to package directions. Dissolve gelatin in hot water. Chill until slightly congealed. Gently fold in remaining ingredients. Refrigerate until firm.

Mrs. B. A. Cole
Houston, Texas

CORNED BEEF SALAD

1 ½ c. V-8 juice
½ c. water
1 pkg. lemon gelatin
1 can corned beef, shredded
2 hard-cooked eggs, chopped
1 ½ c. chopped celery
2 tbsp. chopped green pepper
½ sm. onion, finely minced
1 c. salad dressing

Heat V-8 juice and water; dissolve gelatin in mixture. Cool. Add remaining ingredients. Pour into 8 x 8-inch pan; refrigerate overnight. Cut into squares for serving. Yield: 6-8 servings.

Mrs. Donald Hawks
Baton Rouge, Louisiana

CORNED BEEF MOLDED SALAD

2 pkg. lemon gelatin
2 cans corned beef
3 hard-cooked eggs, chopped
3 c. chopped celery
½ c. chopped cucumber
½ c. chopped onion
½ tsp. salt
2 tbsp. horseradish
1 c. sour cream

Dissolve gelatin in 3 1/2 cups hot water. Chill until slightly thickened. Mix remaining ingredients; pour into 10 x 13-inch pan. Pour gelatin over mixture. Refrigerate until set. Yield: 12-16 servings.

Mrs. E. V. Harold
Valdosta, Georgia

CORNED BEEF SALAD

½ envelope unflavored gelatin
¼ c. cold water
1 can beef bouillon
1 can water
1 pkg. lemon gelatin
1 can corned beef, broken in pieces
1 c. diced celery
3 eggs, chopped
1 sm. onion, grated
½ pepper, diced
¾ c. mayonnaise
½ c. finely chopped pickle (opt.)

Soften unflavored gelatin in 1/4 cup cold water. Combine bouillon and remaining water; heat. Pour over combined lemon gelatin and unflavored gelatin, stirring until dissolved. Add corned beef; cool. Add remaining ingredients. Pour into 5-cup mold; refrigerate. Stir several times while congealing.

Mrs. Harry P. Clause
Bedford, Virginia

CORNED BEEF SALAD

1 pkg. lemon gelatin
1 c. hot water
1 c. cold water
½ c. finely chopped celery
½ c. finely chopped cucumber
¼ c. minced onion
½ can corned beef
2 hard-boiled eggs, chopped
½ c. mayonnaise
1 hard-boiled egg, sliced

Dissolve gelatin in hot water; add cold water and cool. Add remaining ingredients except for egg slices, mixing well. Chill. Use last egg to garnish with before serving.

Mrs. M. E. Miles
Van Buren, Arkansas

HE-MAN SALAD

1 8-oz. pkg. elbow macaroni
¾ c. mayonnaise or salad dressing
¼ c. pickle relish
¼ tsp. salt
1 12-oz. can corned beef, chopped
1 1-lb. 1-oz. can peas, drained
1 c. cubed Swiss cheese
½ c. chopped celery

Cook macaroni according to package directions. Drain; rinse with cold water and drain again. Add mayonnaise, pickle relish and salt to macaroni, mixing well. Add remaining ingredients; toss together lightly until blended. Chill until ready to serve. Yield: 6-8 servings.

Mrs. Orby Yarberry
Columbia, Kentucky

IRISH TURKEY

1 pkg. unflavored gelatin
1 c. cold water
1 can corned beef, minced
1 c. mayonnaise
2 tbsp. finely chopped green pepper
2 tbsp. finely chopped onion
1 c. finely chopped celery
3 hard-cooked eggs, grated

(Continued on next page)

Soften gelatin in cold water; dissolve over hot water. Set aside until thick. Whip gelatin until very stiff; add remaining ingredients except eggs. Place one-half the mixture in a waxed paper-lined loaf pan; spread grated eggs over gelatin. Spread remaining gelatin mixture over eggs. Refrigerate overnight. Unmold and slice; serve on lettuce. Yield: 8 servings.

Mrs. W. V. Edgar
Pikesville, Kentucky

CORNED BEEF AND SLAW SALAD

- 2 envelopes unflavored gelatin
- 2 tbsp. sugar
- ¾ tsp. salt
- 1 ¾ c. water
- 4 tbsp. lemon juice
- ¼ c. vinegar
- 2 tbsp. chopped green pepper
- 2 c. finely shredded cabbage
- ¾ c. mayonnaise
- 1 12-oz. can corned beef, finely chopped
- ½ c. diced celery
- ½ c. chopped sweet pickle
- ¼ c. minced onion

Mix 1 envelope gelatin, sugar and 1/2 teaspoon salt thoroughly in small saucepan; add 1/2 cup water. Place over low heat, stirring constantly, until gelatin dissolves. Remove from heat; stir in 3/4 cup water, 2 tablespoons lemon juice and vinegar. Chill mixture to unbeaten egg white consistency. Fold in green pepper and cabbage. Turn into 8-inch square pan; chill until almost firm. Soften remaining gelatin over remaining water; place over low heat, stirring until gelatin dissolves. Remove from heat; stir in remaining lemon juice and salt. Cool. Gradually add mayonnaise; mix in remaining ingredients. Turn on top of slightly firm first layer; chill until firm. Unmold; cut into squares. Serve with mayonnaise.

Mrs. L. D. Lee
Moss Point, Mississippi

MOLDED CORNED BEEF SALAD

- 1 box lemon gelatin
- 1 c. boiling water
- 1 c. corned beef
- 2 c. celery, chopped
- ½ onion, diced
- ¾ c. green pepper, chopped
- 1 c. mayonnaise

Dissolve gelatin in boiling water. Cool. Add corned beef, celery, onion and green pepper. Stir in mayonnaise; mix well. Pour into a large mold or individual molds. When set, serve on lettuce leaves.

Mrs. W. R. Maynard
Tucson, Arizona

MOLDED MEAT SALAD

- 1 pkg. lemon gelatin
- 1 ½ c. hot water
- ¼ c. vinegar
- 1 c. mayonnaise
- 1 med. onion, finely chopped
- 1 c. finely chopped celery
- 1 c. chopped cucumbers
- 1 can corned beef, shredded
- 2 hard-cooked eggs, chopped

Combine gelatin, water and vinegar; cool. Add remaining ingredients; mix well. Pour into large loaf pan; chill until firm. Yield: 8 servings.

Mrs. B. J. Boyd
Prescott, Arizona

SALAD SUPREME

- 4 beef bouillon cubes
- 2 c. boiling water
- 2 envelopes unflavored gelatin
- ½ c. cold water
- 1 c. diced cucumbers
- 2 c. diced celery
- 1 c. salad dressing
- 1 can corned deef, diced
- 3 hard-cooked eggs, diced
- 1 tbsp. diced onion
- 1 tbsp. vinegar

Dissolve bouillon cubes in boiling water. Soak gelatin in cold water. Dissolve in hot liquid. Chill until mixture is slightly thickened. Add remaining ingredients. Pour into 9 x 13-inch pan. Chill until set.

Mrs. M. H. Sidney
Arkadelphia, Arkansas

DEVILED TOMATOES

- 4 med. tomatoes
- 1 4 ½-oz. can deviled ham
- ¼ c. chopped green pepper
- ¼ c. chopped celery

(Continued on next page)

Halve tomatoes; scoop out pulp. Blend ham with green pepper and celery. Refill tomato halves; put back together. Yield: 4 servings.

Mrs. W. A. Gentry
Fletcher, North Carolina

HAM LOAF

2 envelopes unflavored gelatin
¼ c. cold water
1 c. boiling water
2 chicken bouillon cubes
2 tbsp. tomato puree
2 4 ½-oz. cans deviled ham
1 c. cream, whipped

Soften gelatin in cold water; dissolve in boiling water with bouillon cubes. Chill until slightly thickened; fold in remaining ingredients. Fill mold with mixture; chill until firm. Unmold; garnish with grapes and fruit slices. Yield: 8 servings.

Rita Cook
Rogers, Texas

FRANKFURTER-POTATO SALAD

8 skinless frankfurters
6 lge. potatoes
½ c. heavy cream, whipped
1 c. mayonnaise
2 tsp. prepared mustard
Snipped scallions
Bottled capers
1 ½ tsp. salt
⅛ tsp. pepper
12 to 16 hard, thin, skinless salami slices
Parsley sprigs

Simmer frankfurters for 5 minutes; drain. Cover and refrigerate overnight. Cook potatoes; cool and dice potatoes. Cover and refrigerate overnight. Slice frankfurters into 3/4-inch slices. Combine whipped cream, mayonnaise, mustard, 1/3 cup snipped scallions, 1 1/2 tablespoons capers, salt and pepper. Fold in potatoes and all but 10 frankfurter slices. Mound into 1-quart salad bowl. Decorate with 10 frankfurter slices, scallions and capers. Make salami roses from salami and parsley. Tuck around edges. Yield: 8 servings.

Mrs. G. B. Jackson
Columbia, South Carolina

HOT POTATO-FRANK SALAD

6 strips bacon, chopped
1 tbsp. flour
½ c. chopped green onions with tops
¼ c. vinegar
1 ½ tsp. salt
½ tsp. pepper
1 tbsp. sugar
½ c. water
1 lb. wieners, sliced
1 qt. sliced cooked potatoes, hot

Fry bacon until crisp. Blend in flour until smooth. Add onions, vinegar, seasonings, water and wieners; cook for 5 minutes. Pour over hot potatoes; mix lightly. Yield: 6 servings.

Mrs. George L. Walker
Haines City, Florida

LETTUCE AND TOMATO SALAD

2 tomatoes
¼ head lettuce
4 frankfurters, cut in ¼-inch slices
2 sweet pickles, chopped
¼ c. mayonnaise
Salt and pepper to taste

Cut up tomatoes and lettuce; add frankfurters. Add pickles and mayonnaise; mix well. Season to taste.

Mrs. S. M. Harris
Charlottesville, Virginia

POTATO-HOT DOG SALAD

6 med. potatoes, cooked and diced
3 hard-boiled eggs, diced
1 lb. frankfurters, cut in pieces
½ c. diced sweet pickles
½ c. chopped green pepper
½ c. finely chopped celery
⅓ c. chopped pimento, well drained
Creamy salad dressing

Mix all ingredients except dressing. Pour dressing over salad in desired amount; toss lightly. Chill 2 to 3 hours or longer; toss lightly before serving.

CREAMY DRESSING:

½ c. mayonnaise
½ c. mustard
¼ c. sweet pickle juice

(Continued on next page)

Blend all ingredients together; pour over salad.

Mrs. Glenn Driver
Middlesex, North Carolina

MACARONI-FRANK SALAD BOWL

4 oz. macaroni
1 sm. clove of garlic
1 sm. onion
1 c. thick sour cream
¼ c. French dressing
½ tsp. salt
2 med. tomatoes
2 c. torn curly endive
1 c. diced celery
¼ c. thinly sliced radishes
¼ c. sliced green onions
4 frankfurters, sliced

Cook macaroni in boiling, salted water with garlic and onion until tender; drain. Remove and discard garlic and onion. Blend hot macaroni, sour cream, French dressing and salt. Chill thoroughly. Peel and cut tomatoes into wedges; chill. Place endive, celery, radishes, green onions and frankfurters in large salad bowl; add macaroni mixture and tomato wedges. Toss lightly to mix thoroughly. Yield: 6 servings.

Carolyn Kinard
Norphlet, Arkansas

WIENER SALAD BAKE

3 tbsp. butter or margarine
3 tbsp. flour
1 tsp. salt
¼ tsp. pepper
¾ tsp. dry mustard
1 ½ c. milk
¾ c. mayonnaise or salad dressing
4 med. potatoes, cooked and diced
1 can cut green beans, drained
1 med. onion chopped
6 wieners, cut into diagonal slices
1 c. buttered bread crumbs

Melt butter in saucepan; remove from heat. Blend in flour, salt, pepper and mustard; slowly stir in milk. Cook over medium heat, stirring constantly, until mixture thickens and boils 1 minute. Remove from heat; blend in mayonnaise. Reserve three-fourths cup of sauce. Fold potatoes, green beans, onion and three-fourths of wiener slices into remaining sauce; spoon into baking dish. Arrange remaining wieners on top; spoon reserved sauce over wieners. Sprinkle with buttered bread crumbs. Bake at 350 degrees for 45 minutes or until bubbly hot. Yield: 5-6 servings.

Mrs. O. P. Smith
Gainesville, Florida

WIENER SALAD

8 to 10 lge. wieners
Chopped pickles
Chopped onions
3 hard-boiled eggs, diced
Mayonnaise

Boil wieners; peel and mash. Add pickles and onions as desired. Add eggs. Add mayonnaise to desired consistency. Chill; slice.

Geraldine Grimes
Dalton, Kentucky

KNOCKWURST AND KRAUT SALAD

1 lb. knackwurst, cut in bite-sized pieces
1 16-oz. can sauerkraut, drained and chopped
2 tbsp. chopped onion
½ c. chopped celery
¼ c. chopped green pepper
½ c. vinegar
¼ c. salad oil
½ c. sugar

Combine meat, sauerkraut, onion, celery and green pepper. Chill. Mix vinegar, oil and sugar. Just before serving, pour dressing over salad mixture; toss lightly. Yield: 4 servings.

Photograph for this recipe on page 237.

LIVER SALAD

1 1-lb. beef or pork liver
1 ½ c. water
½ tsp. salt
3 c. grated cabbage
1 tbsp. grated onion (opt.)
¾ c. salad dressing
⅛ tsp. pepper
1 tsp. celery seed
1 tsp. caraway seed
2 tbsp. vinegar
1 tbsp. sugar
2 tbsp. catsup
1 tsp. Worcestershire sauce

Boil liver in salted water for 10 minutes; drain. Grind liver; add cabbage and onion. Combine remaining ingredients; add to liver mixture. Chill and serve. Yield: 6 servings.

Mrs. L. J. Wallace
Riverdale, Maryland

CHOPPED LIVER

1 lb. liver
2 med. onions, sliced or chopped
Cooking oil
2 hard-cooked eggs, chilled
Salt and pepper to taste

Broil liver until done; chill. Brown onions in oil until soft. Alternate layers of liver, eggs and hot onions with oil in meat grinder or chopper; grind. Toss well; season to taste. Serve cold as a salad on lettuce leaves or as an appetizer on crackers. Yield: 6-8 servings.

Mrs. Selma Geiger
Houma, Louisiana

HAWAIIAN SALAD

1 12-oz. can luncheon meat, cut in thin strips
1 tbsp. vinegar
1 tsp. horseradish
1 c. mayonnaise
2 c. shredded cabbage
2 c. coarsely diced celery
¼ c. green pepper
1 c. shredded lettuce
2 c. cubed pineapple

Mix meat and vinegar. Combine remaining ingredients; toss lightly with meat.

Mrs. Lydia Roddy
Pyote, Texas

ITALIAN SALAD

2 c. finely chopped various luncheon meats
½ c. chopped pickles
1 tsp. vinegar
Salt and pepper to taste
Few drops Tabasco (opt.)
Mayonnaise

Combine all ingredients; cover with mayonnaise.

Mrs. Lily Smith
Plainville, Georgia

HEARTY SUPPER SALAD

1 c. rice, cooked
2 c. luncheon meat, chopped
1 ½ c. chopped cheese
1 onion, chopped
¼ c. mayonnaise

Combine all ingredients, except mayonnaise. Add mayonnaise just before serving. Yield: 6-8 servings.

Mrs. J. B. Henson
Franklin, North Carolina

MACARONI LUNCHEON

1 can luncheon meat
5 stalks celery, chopped
⅓ c. pickle relish
¼ c. chopped onion
3 hard-cooked eggs, chopped
½ c. grated longhorn cheese
½ c. mayonnaise
2 tbsp. mustard
1 tsp. salt
1 tsp. pepper
1 lb. macaroni, cooked and drained

Grate luncheon meat; add celery, relish, onion, eggs, cheese, mayonnaise, mustard, salt and pepper. Mix with macaroni in large mixing or serving bowl. Chill or serve immediately. Yield: 12 servings.

Mrs. Sue Shaw
Kingman, Arizona

MEAT SALAD

1 can luncheon meat or bologna, ground or grated
2 hard-cooked eggs
1 lge. dill pickle
2 tbsp. finely chopped olives
1 sour apple, finely chopped
½ c. chopped celery
1 tbsp. chopped pimento
Salt and pepper to taste
3 tbsp. salad dressing

(Continued on next page)

Combine all ingredients; chill for 2 hours. Yield: 6-8 servings.

Lynda Freeman
Mesquite, Texas

QUICK POTATO SALAD

1 lb. frozen French fries
1 green pepper, sliced
2 green onions, diced
1 can luncheon meat, cubed
¼ c. French dressing
Salt to taste
1 ½ c. diced American cheese
Cucumber slices (opt.)

Brown French fries in electric skillet; drain off excess fat. Add remaining ingredients except cheese and cucumbers; simmer until meat browns lightly. Top with cheese. Garnish with cucumber slices. Yield: 6 servings.

Mrs. B. S. Tyler
Atlanta, Georgia

SOUR CREAM-POTATO SALAD

3 c. chopped cooked cold potatoes
½ c. diced canned luncheon meat
2 hard-cooked eggs, chopped
½ tsp. pepper
2 tsp. salt
½ c. chopped pickles
⅓ c. chopped onion
1 tbsp. vinegar
1 tbsp. prepared mustard
1 c. sour cream

Combine potatoes, luncheon meat, eggs, pepper, salt, pickles and onion; mix well. Add vinegar, mustard and cream. Chill. Serve on leaf lettuce.

Mrs. S. B. Sanford
Abilene, Texas

SPAM 'N' CHEESE RIBBON LOAF

1 can Spam, cut in 8 slices
1 3-oz. pkg. cream cheese
Milk
1 tsp. lemon juice
1 tbsp. grated onion
1 tbsp. minced parsley
¼ tsp. salt

Soften cream cheese with little milk; add remaining ingredients except Spam. Spread mixture between Spam slices. Chill for 4 hours or overnight if desired. Slice; serve.

Mrs. Sidney Darden
Farmville, North Carolina

SUMMER SUPPER SALAD

1 can luncheon meat, cut in bite-size pieces
1 can English peas, drained
6 slices cheddar cheese, cut in 1-inch squares
¼ c. sliced celery
1 sm. green pepper, thinly sliced
2 ripe firm tomatoes, quartered
¼ c. French garlic dressing

Combine meat, vegetables and cheese; add salad dressing; toss lightly.

Oleta Morris
Bonham, Texas

WEDDING RING SALAD

2 lb. ring macaroni
2 cans peas
1 green pepper
1 can pimento
1 onion
2 lge. bunches celery
12 hard-cooked eggs, finely diced
2 cans luncheon meat, finely diced
1 pt. mayonnaise
1 pt. salad dressing
Salt

Cook macaroni in salted water until tender. Rinse with cold water. Refrigerate. Finely dice vegetables. Add eggs and meat. Combine with macaroni; mix with mayonnaise and dressing. Salt to taste; refrigerate until ready to serve. Yield: 50 servings.

Mrs. L. L. Thomas
Lancaster, South Carolina

PARTY PORK CROWN

1 3-oz. pkg. celery flavored gelatin
1 c. hot water
½ c. cold water
1 tbsp. cider vinegar
½ c. mayonnaise or salad dressing
½ tsp. prepared mustard
¼ tsp. salt
1 12-oz. can pork luncheon meat, diced
1 8-oz. can peas, drained
Romaine leaves

(Continued on next page)

Dissolve gelatin in hot water; stir in cold water and vinegar. Beat in mayonnaise, mustard and salt; pour into a shallow pan. Freeze for 20 minutes. Spoon into medium bowl; beat until light. Fold in meat and peas; spoon into 4-cup ring mold. Chill until firm. Unmold onto serving plate; garnish with romaine leaves. Yield: 4-6 servings.

Mrs. R. H. Fulton
Austin, Texas

PEPPERONI AND ONION SALAD

1 head iceberg lettuce, torn
1 long link pepperoni, chopped
1 med. onion, chopped
2 sm. tomatoes, chopped
1 cucumber, chopped
Salt to taste
Vinegar and oil dressing
Parmesan cheese
Toast

Place lettuce, pepperoni, onion, tomatoes and cucumber in salad bowl. Salt to taste; toss. Pour vinegar and oil dressing over salad; toss again. Sprinkle with Parmesan cheese. Serve with crisp dry toast. Yield: 4 servings.

Mrs. E. W. Daniels
College Park, Maryland

SPANISH SALAD

1 slice bacon
½ head romaine lettuce
2 green onions, sliced
¼ c. celery, chopped
1 tbsp. green pepper
⅛ c. cheese, sliced
¼ c. salami, sliced in 1-inch strips
¼ c. cucumbers, sliced in 1-inch strips
1 med. tomato, quartered

Fry bacon until crisp; drain and crumble. Combine all ingredients; toss lightly.

DRESSING:

½ c. hot bacon drippings
¼ c. hot wine vinegar
1 tsp. garlic salt
¼ tsp. pepper
¼ c. black olives
1 hard-cooked egg, sliced

Combine bacon drippings, vinegar, garlic salt and pepper; pour over salad. Garnish with olives and egg slices.

Mrs. Penny Winchester
Munday, Texas

VEGETABLE-SALAMI SALAD

1 qt. potatoes, cooked and cubed
2 c. cubed salami
2 tbsp. vinegar
2 c. lge. cooked or canned peas
1 c. chopped celery
1 pimento, chopped
8 sweet pickles, chopped
4 hard-cooked eggs, sliced
Mayonnaise
Salt and pepper to taste

Combine all ingredients. Heap in a large shallow bowl lined with crisp lettuce and garnish with slices of hard-cooked egg, adding parsley if desired. Yield: 6 servings.

Mrs. E. B. Ellison
New Orleans, Louisiana

SUNGLOW MEAT SALAD

6 oz. sliced salami, cut in strips
6 oz. sliced cooked tongue, cut in strips
2 c. cauliflower pieces
1 greenpepper, cut in strips
1 tsp. grated onion
½ c. French dressing
1 c. orange sections
Lettuce

Combine salami, tongue, cauliflower, green pepper, onion and dressing. Toss lightly and marinate in the refrigerator 3 to 4 hours. Add orange sections; toss lightly. Serve in lettuce-lined bowl. Yield: 5-6 servings.

Mrs. R. H. Jacobs
Atlanta, Georgia

BEEF TONGUE SALAD

1 lge. beef tongue
1 c. diced celery
½ c. diced apple
¼ c. chopped pecans
4 hard-cooked eggs, chopped
¼ c. diced sweet pickles
Salad dressing

Steam or boil tongue until tender; remove skin and roots. Finely chop or put tongue through food chopper. Add remaining ingredients, using enough salad dressing to moisten. Yield: 10 servings.

Mrs. B. A. Harvey
West Point, Mississippi

MEAL-IN-ONE SALAD

6 slivered slices tongue, corned beef or luncheon meat
¼ lb. slivered Swiss cheese
2 hard-cooked eggs
1 cucumber, chopped
1 green pepper, chopped
1 carrot, chopped
2 tomatoes, chopped
1 tsp. minced onion
1 tsp. vinegar
4 tbsp. mayonnaise
3 tbsp. milk or cream
Sharp cream dressing

Combine all ingredients except cream dressing. Serve with sharp cream dressing. Yield: 6 servings.

Mrs. C. R. Webster
Jackson, Mississippi

TROPICAL LAMB SALAD

2 bananas, sliced
2 tbsp. lemon juice
¾ c. sliced celery
2 c. cooked diced lamb
1 ½ tsp. prepared mustard
¼ c. mayonnaise
¼ c. whole stuffed olives
¼ c. salted almonds
½ tsp. salt
Boston lettuce
Watercress

Toss bananas with lemon juice. Add celery and lamb. Combine mustard and mayonnaise; pour over meat mixture. Add olives, nuts and salt; toss. Refrigerate for 30 minutes. Serve with lettuce and watercress. Yield: 4 servings.

Mrs. M. S. Nichok
Murfreesboro, Tennessee

FRUITED MEAT SALAD

2 c. cubed cooked veal
1 c. cubed pineapple
½ c. red grapes halved and seeded
½ c. chopped celery
⅓ c. chopped pecans
3 tbsp. mayonnaise
2 tbsp. pineapple juice

Mix veal, pineapple, grapes, celery and pecans. Combine mayonnaise and pineapple juice; add to veal mixture. Toss lightly; chill. Serve in lettuce cups. Yield: 4-6 servings.

Mrs. V. A. Pearson
Daytona, Florida

JELLIED VEAL

2 tbsp. unflavored gelatin
2 c. beef consomme or meat juice
3 c. diced veal or chicken
1 ½ tsp. salt
½ c. finely diced carrots
1 c. diced celery
Tomato slices

Dissolve gelatin in heated consomme. Add remaining ingredients except tomatoes and peas. Arrange tomatoes and peas in bottom of individual dishes. Add gelatin mixture. Chill until firm. Serve on lettuce leaf and garnish.

Mrs. N. J. Bell
Louisville, Kentucky

TENDERLOIN-VEAL SALAD

1 lb. lean tenderloin
1 lb. lean veal
1 c. diced celery
¼ c. diced olives
¾ lb. brick cheese, diced
Mayonnaise to taste

Combine all ingredients; serve with jellied veal. Yield: 12 servings.

Mrs. R. B. Boswell
Jackson, Mississippi

TOWER VEAL SALAD

1 c. veal broth
2 cubes beef bouillon
2 pkg. unflavored gelatin
½ c. cold water
2 tbsp. lemon juice
1 c. mayonnaise
1 c. diced celery
1 c. green grapes
2 lb. cooked cubed veal
Salt to taste
½ c. toasted slivered almonds

Heat veal broth; add bouillon. Stir until dissolved. Soften gelatin in water; dissolve in bouillon mixture. Chill until thickened. Fold in all ingredients except almonds; mix well. Place in a 1 1/2-quart mold; chill until firm. Sprinkle salad with almonds. May be garnished with chilled cranberry sauce, sliced avocado strips, salad fruits and pineapple chunks. Yield: 8 servings.

Jessie Mae Jacobs
Apoka, Florida

POULTRY SALADS

Recipe for Royal Coach Chicken Salad on Page 283

AUNTIE BESS'S SOUTHERN CHICKEN SALAD

1 5-lb. hen
Celery
1 tbsp. salt
½ onion
1 pt. mayonnaise
1 jar mustard chow-chow pickles, diced
Monosodium glutamate
Tabasco sauce to taste

Boil hen in water with 2 stalks celery, salt and onion until meat falls from bones. Cut meat and celery into small pieces. Combine 2 cups chicken and 1 cup celery at a time. Continue until all are used. Add remaining ingredients; mix. Salad is better if prepared a day in advance of serving. Yield: 12-16 servings.

Mrs. T. A. Burke
Oklahoma City, Oklahoma

BREAST OF CHICKEN SALAD

3 c. cooked, coarsely chopped chicken breast
2 c. coarsely chopped celery
2 tbsp. cream
¾ c. mayonnaise
1 tbsp. lemon juice
Salt and pepper to taste

Combine all ingredients. Use enough mayonnaise to moisten. Garnish with olives and parsley.

Lillie Mae Edgeston
Ripley, Mississippi

CHICKEN BUFFET MOLDS

1 envelope unflavored gelatin
½ c. cold water
1 c. mayonnaise or salad dressing
1 ½ c. diced, cooked or canned chicken
½ c. unpared chopped cucumber
⅓ c. diced celery
3 tbsp. minced onion
3 tbsp. chopped green olives
1 tbsp. chopped pimento
2 tbsp. lemon juice
½ tsp. salt
¼ tsp. paprika
1 c. heavy cream, whipped

Soften gelatin in cold water; dissolve over hot water. Add all remaining ingredients folding in whipped cream last. Pour into individual molds. Chill until firm. Yield: 8 servings.

Mrs. L. M. Dawson
Tampa, Florida

CHICKEN-COTTAGE CHEESE SALAD

1 pkg. lime gelatin
1 c. hot water
½ c. cold water
2 tbsp. lemon juice
½ tsp. salt
½ c. mayonnaise
1 c. creamed cottage cheese
½ c. diced celery
1 c. diced cooked chicken
½ c. finely chopped pickles

Dissolve gelatin in hot water; add cold water, lemon juice, salt and mayonnaise. Blend well; chill until partially set. Whip with beater until light and fluffy. Fold in remaining ingredients. Chill until firm. Unmold. Serve on lettuce leaves if desired. Yield: 6-8 servings.

Elizabeth Heard
Jackson, Mississippi

CHICKEN MOUSSE

2 tbsp. gelatin, soaked in ¼ c. cold water
1 c. mayonnaise
2 c. cooked chicken, cut up
4 hard-cooked eggs, mashed
½ c. celery
8 pickle chips, cut fine
Salt and pepper to taste
Dash Worcestershire sauce
Dash of red pepper
1 small pimento, cut up
Juice of ½ lemon

Dissolve gelatin in cold water; then add 1/2 cup boiling water. Stir until gelatin is melted. Let cool and add mayonnaise and remaining ingredients. Congeal in loaf pan and serve in slices. Yield: 8 servings.

Elizabeth Heard
Jackson, Mississippi

CHICKEN-PECAN SALAD

2 pkg. lime gelatin
2 c. hot water
1 c. cooked diced chicken
1 c. chopped pecans
1 c. celery, chopped
1 c. cottage cheese
1 c. mayonnaise

Dissolve gelatin in hot water. Cool until partially set. Add remaining ingredients and mix well. Pour into 8 x 12-inch pan. Cool. Yield: 12 servings.

Mrs. Dean Gillham
Richmond, Virginia

CHICKEN MOUSSE SPECIAL

1 4 to 5-lb. hen
2 c. water
Salt and pepper
Onion, sliced
Celery, diced
1 can cream of celery soup
1 8-oz. pkg. cream cheese
1 ½ pkg. unflavored gelatin
Chicken stock
¾ c. diced green pepper
2 tbsp. diced green onion

Cook hen in water seasoned with salt, pepper, onion and desired amount of celery for flavor until tender. Cut meat from bone. Reserve strained stock. Heat soup and cream cheese in top of double boiler. Stir occasionally until hot and well blended. Add gelatin and 1 1/2 cups of cold stock. Add stock mixture to cheese mixture; heat until gelatin is dissolved. Remove from heat; cool slightly. Add 3/4 cups celery, green pepper, green onion and chicken. Put in lightly greased ring mold; chill at least 4 hours. Serve with mayonnaise or salad dressing.

Dr. Mary E. Dichmann
Lafayette, Louisiana

CHICKEN SALAD

2 c. diced chicken
1 c. diced celery
6 chopped green olives, pitted
1 sweet red pepper or canned pimento
Salt to taste
½ c. mayonnaise

Mix chicken, celery, olives and 1/2 pepper, parboiled and cut in pieces. Salt to taste; moisten with mayonnaise. Serve in mounds, decorated with remaining pepper, cut in strips. Two or 3 diced hard-cooked eggs and 1/4 to 1/2 cups cooked peas may be used instead of olives. For mock chicken salad, use lean veal or pork. Yield: 6-8 servings.

Mrs. Frank Keister, Jr.
Morristown, Tennessee

CHICKEN SALAD

Chicken, cooked, boned and diced
1 c. diced celery
1 c. chopped nuts
Salt to taste
Mayonnaise

Combine chicken, celery, nuts and salt. Add enough mayonnaise to moisten. Chill; serve on crisp lettuce.

Mrs. T. W. Taylor
Abbeville, South Carolina

CHICKEN SALAD

1 frying-size chicken, salted
1 c. water
2 hard-boiled eggs
5 to 6 sweet pickles

Cook chicken on rack in pressure saucepan with water for 30 minutes at 10 pounds pressure. When cool, remove meat from bones. Chop fine in blender. Chop eggs and pickles in blender. Mix together.

DRESSING:

½ c. mayonnaise
2 tbsp. sour cream
2 tsp. vinegar
½ tsp. salt
¼ tsp. pepper
¼ tsp. paprika
¼ tsp. onion salt (opt.)
½ c. chicken broth

Mix together thoroughly; pour over chopped chicken mixture. Blend thoroughly. Add more broth, if needed.

Mrs. Howard Burchette
Thurmond, North Carolina

CHICKEN SALAD

1 chicken, cooked, boned and chopped
6 hard-boiled eggs, chopped
1 ½ c. diced celery
1 onion, chopped
Salt and pepper to taste
½ c. chopped pickles
1 ½ c. cream, whipped
1 c. mayonnaise

Combine all ingredients except cream and mayonnaise. Blend cream and mayonnaise; combine with chicken mixture. Serve on lettuce leaf.

Mrs. Susie Bowlin
Carnegie, Oklahoma

CHICKEN SALAD

1 hen, boiled, boned and finely chopped
6 hard-cooked eggs, sieved
Cucumber pickles, finely chopped
6 tbsp. salad dressing
1 ½ c. ground pecans

Combine all ingredients; serve.

Mrs. Hollis Cook
Elba, Alabama

CHICKEN SALAD

1 lge. hen
3 lb. lean pork
12 hard-cooked eggs, chopped
2 bunches celery, chopped
12 sweet pickles, chopped
½ lb. blanched almonds, finely chopped (opt.)

Cook chicken and pork together until tender. Put all meat through food chopper. Add eggs, celery, pickles and nuts. Mix together with mayonnaise or Cooked Dressing.

COOKED DRESSING:

4 egg yolks
1 c. sugar
1 tsp. salt
3 tsp. melted butter
3 tsp. flour
Dash of cayenne pepper
2 c. hot milk
1 c. vinegar
1 tsp. dry mustard
Juice of 1 lemon

Beat egg yolks until thick; add sugar and salt. Mix butter, flour and pepper in top of double boiler. Add milk and egg mixture. Put over hot water; when hot add vinegar into which mustard has been dissolved. Cook until thick. Remove from stove; beat until fluffy. When cold, add lemon juice. Yield: 20 servings.

Mrs. Raymond Combs
Bradenton, Florida

CHICKEN SALAD WITH EGG DRESSING

2 c. chopped cooked chicken, chilled
1 c. diced celery tips
1 raw egg
3 hard-cooked eggs
½ c. olive oil
4 tbsp. vinegar
1 tsp. salt
½ tsp. pepper
6 stuffed green olives

Mix chicken and celery together; place in refrigerator while preparing dressing. Add yolk of raw egg to yolks of hard-cooked eggs. Slowly add olive oil, beating until thick. Beat in vinegar; add salt and pepper. Finely chop hard-cooked egg whites; add to egg yolk mixture, mixing well. Pour over chicken and celery mixture; garnish with olives and celery tips before serving.

Mrs. Estelle Shalla
Bay City, Texas

CHICKEN SALAD DELUXE

¼ c. chicken broth
¾ c. mayonnaise
2 ½ c. cooked diced chicken
¼ c. broken pecans
1 ½ c. diced celery
¼ c. sliced stuffed olives
¾ tsp. salt
¼ tsp. pepper
4 lge. tomatoes
4 lettuce leaves

Blend chicken broth and mayonnaise. Toss with chicken, pecans, celery, olives and seasonings. Peel tomatoes; cut into 5 sections almost to stem end. Place on lettuce leaves; press sections apart. Fill with chicken salad. Garnish with mayonnaise or parsley. Yield: 4 servings.

Mrs. George McCullough
Tulsa, Oklahoma

CHICKEN SALAD MOLD

4 tbsp. unflavored gelatin
¾ c. cold chicken broth
2 ¾ c. hot chicken broth
Juice of 1 lemon
4 c. cubed chicken
3 c. chopped celery
1 6-oz. jar stuffed olives, sliced
1 ½ c. cream
1 ½ c. salad dressing
Salt and pepper to taste

Dissolve gelatin in cold chicken broth; add hot broth and lemon juice. Let cool until mixture begins to thicken. Mix chicken, celery and olives. Whip cream. Add salad dressing, then chicken mixture. Fold mixture into jelled broth. Add salt and pepper. Pour into 10 x 15-inch pan greased with salad oil. Chill until firm. Yield: 10 servings.

Mrs. T. B. Hall
Richmond, Virginia

CHICKEN SALAD WITH PECANS

4 c. diced cooked chicken
2 c. diced celery
1 4-oz. can button mushrooms, drained
½ c. toasted pecans
4 slices crisp fried bacon, crumbled
1 c. mayonnaise or salad dressing
1 c. sour cream
2 tbsp. lemon juice
1 ½ tsp. salt

Combine chicken, celery, mushrooms, pecans and crumbled bacon in large bowl. Blend mayonnaise with sour cream, lemon juice and salt. Add chicken mixture, tossing lightly until mixed. Chill thoroughly. Serve in crisp lettuce cups; garnish with watercress. Toast pecans by placing in shallow baking pan for 15 minutes at 350 degrees. Yield: 6-8 servings.

Mrs. Ernest Senkel
Cameron, Texas

CHICKEN SALAD SUPREME

4 c. (packed) diced cooked chicken
4 c. finely diced celery
2 c. sliced ripe olives
½ c. minced onion
2 c. finely chopped green peppers
½ c. finely chopped pimento
½ c. lemon juice
1 ¾ c. mayonnaise
1 ½ c. heavy cream, whipped

Combine chicken, celery, olives, onion, green peppers, pimento and lemon juice; toss to mix. Fold mayonnaise into whipped cream; add to chicken mixture, folding in carefully. Chill for several hours. Yield: 15-20 servings.

Mrs. M. J. Oliver
Roswell, New Mexico

CHICKEN SOUP SALAD

1 envelope unflavored gelatin
¼ c. water
1 can cream of chicken soup, heated
1 3-oz. pkg. cream cheese
½ c. mayonnaise
Juice of 1 lemon
½ tsp. grated onion
1 carrot, grated
2 hard-cooked eggs, grated
½ c. diced celery
¼ tsp. salt
1 c. diced cooked chicken

Soften gelatin in water; pour hot chicken soup over gelatin and cool. Mix cream cheese, mayonnaise and lemon juice; add to gelatin mixture. Add remaining ingredients; chill. Yield: 6 servings.

Mrs. H. B. Newton
Hollandale, Mississippi

CHICKEN SALAD TULIP CUPS

PASTRY TULIP CUPS:

½ c. enriched cornmeal
1 ½ c. sifted enriched flour
1 tsp. salt
½ c. shortening
4 to 6 tbsp. cold water

Preheat oven to 450 degrees. Sift together cornmeal, flour and salt; cut in shortening until mixture resembles coarse crumbles. Add water gradually, mixing with a fork until pastry will just hold together. Divide pastry into 2 parts. On a floured board, roll each part to form a 9-inch square. Cut each into four 4 1/2-inch squares. Shape each square over bottom of custard cup; pleat edges, leaving corners to give tulip effect. Prick surface of each with fork; place on cookie sheet. Bake for 12 to 15 minutes. Cool 10 minutes; remove from custard cups. Fill tulip cups with chicken salad.

CHICKEN SALAD:

2 c. cooked, chopped chicken
1 c. finely chopped celery
2 hard-cooked eggs, diced
1 tsp. salt
¼ tsp. pepper
1 tbsp. grated onion
½ c. mayonnaise

Combine chicken, celery and eggs. Blend salt, pepper, onion and mayonnaise. Lightly stir into chicken mixture. Chill. Fill tulip cups. Yield: 8 servings.

Mrs. Jiles Vestal
Abingdon, Virginia

CHICKEN AND TONGUE IN ASPIC

2 envelopes plus 2 tbsp. unflavored gelatin
¼ c. cold water
4 c. cold concentrated chicken broth
1 ½ to 1 ¾-lb. can tongue, thinly sliced
1 4-lb. stewing chicken
2 hard-cooked eggs, sliced
2 tomatoes, cut in wedges
Mayonnaise
Chili sauce or cream

(Continued on next page)

Soften gelatin in water for 5 minutes. Skim off fat from cold broth. Heat broth to boiling; add gelatin, stirring until dissolved. Pour 1-cup gelatin into 6 or 7-cup mold. Set mold in ice water, tilting mold until inside surface is covered with a thin layer of congealed aspic. Slice chicken thinly. Arrange shapeliest pieces of tongue and chicken alternately around sides and bottom of mold. Place egg slices near top all around mold. Combine remaining aspic with remaining chicken, tongue and egg; carefully spoon into mold. Press down gently to displace any air bubbles, making a smooth surface on top. Chill until firm. Unmold on flat serving dish; garnish with tomato wedges. Serve with mayonnaise blended with chili sauce or cream of desired consistency.

James T. Harris
South Hill, Virginia

CONGEALED CHICKEN SALAD

2 tbsp. unflavored gelatin
¼ c. cold water
2 c. hot clear chicken broth
1 ½ c. chopped cooked chicken
1 c. finely cut celery
2 tbsp. chopped pimento
½ tsp. grated onion
4 tbsp. lemon juice
Salt
2 hard-cooked eggs, sliced

Soak gelatin in cold water; add to hot broth to dissolve. Chill until almost set. Fold in chicken, celery, pimento, onion and lemon juice. Season to taste with salt. Line mold with hard-cooked egg slices. Pour chicken mixture over egg slices. Chill until firm.

Mrs. Ed. Glasgow
Phil Campbell, Alabama

CUCUMBER AND CHICKEN SALAD

4 c. cold diced chicken
1 ½ c. celery, chopped
½ c. sliced cucumber
¼ c. French dressing
3 hard-cooked eggs
1 tbsp. shredded pimento
1 tsp. salt
¼ c. parsley

Mix chicken, celery and cucumbers together carefully; marinate with French dressing. Chill thoroughly. Add remaining ingredients; mix well. Serve on lettuce with boiled dressing.

Mrs. Mary A. Walters
Bonnieville, Kentucky

CURRIED CHICKEN SALAD

3 c. cubed cooked chicken
1 ½ c. sliced celery
½ c. mayonnaise
¼ c. sour cream
1 tsp. salt
⅛ tsp. onion salt
Juice of 1 lemon
1 to 3 tbsp. curry powder

Combine chicken and celery; add mixture of remaining ingredients. Serve on salad greens with a sprinkling of toasted almonds; garnish with slices of avocado, sweet red pepper and a wedge of lime, if desired. Yield: 4 servings.

Mrs. L. P. Ramage
Richmond, Virginia

EASY-AS-PIE CHICKEN SALAD

2 envelopes unflavored gelatin
1 ½ c. cold water
1 can beef broth
1 c. salad dressing
2 tbsp. chopped onion
1 tsp. salt
2 tbsp. lemon juice
2 tbsp. chopped pimento
1 c. diced celery
2 c. diced cooked chicken
1 9-in. pie shell, baked

Sprinkle gelatin on water in 2 1/2-quart saucepan to soften; place over moderate heat. Stir constantly until gelatin is dissolved, about 3 minutes. Remove from heat; stir in beef broth, salad dressing, onion, salt, lemon juice and pimento. Beat with rotary beater until smooth. Chill, stirring occasionally, until mixture mounds slightly when dropped from a spoon. Add celery and chicken. Turn into pie shell; chill until firm. Garnish with wreath of green pepper and pimento, if desired. Two cups of cut corned beef, turkey or cooked seafood may be used for chicken. Yield: 6 servings.

Mrs. Don A. McKnight
Tampa, Florida

CHICKEN SALAD

Juice of 1 lemon
2 c. diced cooked chicken
½ c. diced apple
1 c. diced celery
2 hard-cooked eggs, chopped
½ c. chopped toasted almonds
⅓ c. mayonnaise
½ tsp. salt
Dash of pepper
¼ c. minced onion

(Continued on next page)

Sprinkle lemon juice over chicken and apple; toss lightly. Add celery, eggs and almonds to chicken. Blend mayonnaise with seasonings and onion; fold into chicken. Garnish with apple wedges and parsley. Yield: 8 servings.

Mrs. J. W. Slay
Texarkana, Texas

CHICKEN-APPLE SALAD

- 4 c. diced cold cooked chicken
- 2 c. diced apples
- 1 c. diced celery
- 1 c. diced pineapple
- 1 c. chopped nuts
- Mayonnaise

Combine chicken, apples, celery, pineapple and nuts; add enough mayonnaise to moisten. Mix lightly with two forks. Serve on crisp lettuce, if desired. Yield: 12 servings.

Mrs. James Pennington
Macon, Georgia

CHICKEN SALAD

DRESSING:

- 2 eggs
- ½ c. sugar
- 1 tbsp. flour
- 1 tsp. mustard
- ½ c. vinegar
- 1 c. boiling water
- Pinch of salt
- 1 tbsp. butter

Combine eggs, sugar, flour and mustard; beat until smooth. Add vinegar, water and salt. Cook in double boiler until thickened. Remove from heat and beat in butter. Cool.

SALAD:

- 6 c. diced cubed chicken
- 2 c. diced celery
- 1 c. chopped nuts
- 6 hard-cooked eggs, chopped
- 1 c. diced apples
- 1 sm. can diced pimento
- ½ c. diced sweet pickle
- Mayonnaise

Combine all ingredients except mayonnaise; mix well. Mix equal parts of dressing and mayonnaise. Blend dressing into salad; chill. Yield: 10 servings.

Mrs. Ruth Reams
Greenville, Florida

CHICKEN SALAD

- 1 c. cooked chopped chicken
- 1 c. chopped apple
- 3 tbsp. lemon juice
- ½ c. chopped celery
- 3 tbsp. mayonnaise
- Salad greens

Mix first 5 ingredients lightly. Chill. Serve on salad greens.

Dianne Woods
Chatham, Virginia

NAUGHTY RAISIN SALAD

- 1 lge. red apple
- ¾ c. seedless raisins
- 1 ½ c. cooked diced chicken
- 1 ½ c. sliced celery
- ⅓ c. mayonnaise
- 1 ½ tbsp. lemon juice

Dice unpeeled apple. Combine with raisins, chicken and celery. Blend mayonnaise and lemon juice. Blend lightly with salad mixture. Yield: 5 servings.

Mrs. Georgie Thorne
Slocomb, Alabama

AVOCADO CHICKEN-APPLE SALAD

- 2 lge. apples, cubed
- 1 ripe avocado, cubed
- 2 tbsp. lemon juice
- ½ c. mayonnaise
- ¼ c. cream
- 1 tsp. minced onion
- ¼ c. crumbled bleu cheese
- 2 c. cubed cooked chicken

Sprinkle apples and avocado with lemon juice. Combine mayonnaise and cream; add onion. Toss avocado, apples, cheese and chicken with cream dressing. Serve on lettuce leaves.

Mrs. Katherine S. Hunter
Irving, Texas

AVOCADO LUNCHEON SALAD

- 2 avocados
- 1 c. cooked, diced chicken or crab meat
- ¾ c. diced celery
- ½ c. diced cucumber
- ½ c. mayonnaise
- Lettuce or watercress
- 4 lemons, quartered

(Continued on next page)

Cut avocados in half lengthwise; remove seeds. Combine chicken, celery, cucumber, and mayonnaise. Mix lightly. Heap in avocado halves. Place on lettuce leaf; garnish with lemon. Yield: 4 servings.

Wilma Mansel
West Columbia, Texas

AVOCADO-CHICKEN SALAD WITH ALMONDS

2 ½ lb. chicken breasts
Chicken broth
1 tbsp. lemon juice
⅓ c. French dressing
¼ tsp. dry mustard
1 tsp. salt
½ tsp. celery salt
⅛ tsp. white pepper
1 c. celery, cut into ¼-in. pieces
1 c. diced avocados
1 tbsp. capers
Mayonnaise
¼ c. salted blanched almonds

Cook chicken in a small amount of well-seasoned chicken broth until tender; cool thoroughly in broth. Remove bones and chop meat. Sprinkle lemon juice, French dressing, mustard and seasonings over chicken; toss lightly. Chill for at least 1 hour. Add celery, avocados, capers and enough mayonnaise to lightly bind; mix very gently. Season to taste. Sprinkle with almonds. Garnish with ripe olives and watercress, if desired. Yield: 6 servings.

Mrs. James. K. Dowling
Tucson, Arizona

CHICKEN-AVOCADO-RICE SALAD

2 tbsp. lemon juice
1 ½ c. cubed avocado
1 c. cubed chicken
1 c. cooked rice
½ c. finely chopped celery
½ tsp. finely chopped green onion
1 tsp. salt
2 tbsp. sour cream
2 tbsp. mayonnaise

Pour lemon juice over avocado. Combine remaining ingredients; add avocado mixture. Toss lightly; chill. Serve on crisp lettuce leaves. Yield: 6 servings.

Mrs. Hubert Adami
Alice, Texas

CHICKEN AND AVOCADO SALAD

3 envelopes unflavored gelatin
¾ c. cold water
2 c. chicken stock, heated
2 tbsp. fresh lemon juice
1 ½ tsp. grated onion
2 tsp. salt
¼ tsp. white pepper
2 c. ripe avocado pulp, sieved
½ c. mayonnaise
3 c. cooked diced chicken
Salad greens
Cantaloupe balls

Soften gelatin in cold water; stir in hot stock. Add remaining ingredients except salad greens and cantaloupe balls, folding in chicken last. Turn into a lightly oiled 2-quart mold. Chill until firm. Serve garnished with salad greens and cantaloupe balls. Yield: 10-12 servings.

Mrs. Lucy Coggins
Oakwood, Georgia

CHICKEN CONDIMENT SALAD

1 ½ c. mayonnaise
¾ to 1 c. raisins
¾ to 1 c. salted peanuts
1 c. slivered mango chutney
1 c. shredded coconut
2 lb. chicken, cooked and chopped
1 c. finely diced celery
Sliced bananas
Salt and pepper to taste
Salad greens
Avocado slices
Lemon juice

Mix mayonnaise with raisins, peanuts, chutney and coconut; toss with chicken and celery. Gently combine with 2 cups diagonally sliced bananas; season with salt and pepper. Mound in large salad bowl or on platter lined with shredded lettuce and lettuce leaves. Garnish with slices of avocado and banana which have been dipped in lemon juice. Yield: 12 servings.

Mrs. Okey W. Snodgrass
Laredo, Texas

COBB SALAD

1 lge. head lettuce
1 bunch watercress
3 hard-cooked eggs
12 slices bacon
4 med. tomatoes
2 med. avocados
2 chicken breasts, cooked and boned
1 tbsp. chopped chives
⅓ c. crumbled bleu or Roquefort cheese
French dressing

(Continued on next page)

Coarsely chop lettuce, watercress and eggs. Cook bacon until crisp; crumble to make 1 cup. Coarsely cut tomatoes, avocados and chicken. Combine lettuce, watercress, eggs, bacon, tomatoes, avocados, chicken, chives and cheese; mix lightly with French dressing. Yield: 10 servings.

Mrs. L. F. Sugnet
Nashville, Tennessee

COBB SALAD

½ head lettuce, shredded
2 chicken breasts, cooked and diced
2 tomatoes, diced
3 hard-cooked eggs, chopped
6 slices bacon, cooked and crumbled
¾ c. crumbled Roquefort cheese
2 med. avocados, cut into wedges
1 tbsp. cut chives
½ c. Brown Derby Dressing

Place lettuce in salad bowl. Arrange chicken, tomatoes, eggs, bacon and cheese over lettuce. Add avocado wedges; sprinkle with chives. Toss with Brown Derby Dressing. Yield: 6-8 servings.

BROWN DERBY DRESSING:

½ c. wine vinegar
½ c. water
1 tbsp. lemon juice
1 ½ tsp. Worcestershire sauce
1 tsp. salt
1 ½ tsp. pepper
½ tsp. sugar
½ tsp. dry mustard
1 clove of garlic
1 ½ c. salad oil
½ c. olive oil

Blend all ingredients except salad and olive oil; simmer for 15 minutes. Cool; add oil. Shake well. Yield: 2 cups.

Mrs. R. E. Goggin
Key West, Florida

BANANA-CHICKEN SALAD

1 c. sliced bananas
½ c. diced pineapple
1 ½ c. diced cooked chicken
½ c. diced celery
¼ c. sliced olives
1 ½ tsp. salt
2 tbsp. mayonnaise
Lettuce

Combine bananas and pineapple. Add chicken, celery, olives, salt and mayonnaise; mix lightly. Serve in lettuce cups. Yield: 4-6 servings.

Mrs. G. S. Tramn
Orlando, Florida

BIRD OF PARADISE

3 c. cubed cooked chicken
1 ½ c. diced celery
1 tsp. salt
3 hard-cooked eggs, chopped
3 sweet pickles, chopped
Mayonnaise
1 fresh pineapple
1 apple
Maraschino cherries
Lettuce
1 tomato, sliced

Combine chicken, celery, salt, eggs and pickles; moisten with mayonnaise. Slice pineapple in half. Scoop out meat; cut into cubes. Place back in shells. Place chicken salad on pineapple cubes to form body of birds. Slice apple in half; attach an apple half to each pineapple half with toothpick, forming head of bird. Attach cherries to apple for eyes. Place on platter of lettuce; garnish with tomato slices and additional eggs. Form tail of bird with straws. Yield: 2 servings.

Mrs. Richard L. Smith
Tucson, Arizona

CHICKEN-ALMOND SALAD

3 c. diced cooked chicken
1 ½ c. diced celery
3 tbsp. lemon juice
½ unpeeled apple, diced
½ c. drained pineapple chunks
1 c. toasted almonds
1 ½ tsp. salt
1 tsp. dry mustard
Pinch of pepper
¼ c. light cream
1 c. mayonnaise

(Continued on next page)

Combine chicken, celery and lemon juice; chill for 1 hour. Add apple, pineapple and almonds. Combine remaining ingredients; toss lightly with chicken mixture. Arrange salad on pineapple and lettuce leaves, if desired. One cup seedless green grapes may be added. Yield: 8 servings.

Mrs. M. C. Chandler
Shreveport, Louisiana

CHICKEN AND FRUIT SALAD

1 5-lb. roasting chicken
¾ c. diced celery
1 c. seedless white grapes, halved
1 c. mandarin orange sections, drained
½ c. mayonnaise
½ c. sour cream
2 tbsp. finely minced onion
Parsley
1 tbsp. lemon juice
½ tsp. salt
½ tsp. pepper
½ tsp. pkg. herb salad dressing mix
Lettuce and watercress
¼ c. toasted slivered almonds

Steam chicken until tender, being careful not to let it boil. Cool; remove skin. Bone meat; cut into large pieces. Mix chicken lightly with celery, grapes and oranges. Chill. Mix mayonnaise, sour cream, onion, parsley, lemon juice and seasonings; pour over chicken. Mix well; cover and chill several hours. Serve on chilled lettuce; sprinkle with almonds. Garnish with watercress, clusters of additional grapes and oranges.

Mrs. Maude Pomine
Tempe, Arizona

CHICKEN AND FRUIT SALAD

2 c. chopped, cooked chicken breasts
1 orange, sectioned
¼ c. halved seeded grapes
¼ c. halved salted almonds
1 banana, sliced
¾ c. mayonnaise

Combine all ingredients in chilled bowl; mix lightly. Serve on fresh pineapple slices and garnish with watercress, if desired. Yield: 8 servings.

Mrs. Thomas H. Beeson
Panama City, Florida

CHICKEN-FRUIT SALAD

2 c. diced cooked chicken
½ c. pitted white cherries
½ c. diced pineapple
1 pared orange, sliced
½ c. chopped nuts
1 c. mayonnaise

Combine all ingredients; mix well. Chill. Serve on lettuce. Yield: 6 servings.

Eugah Pearl Webster
Winfield, Alabama

CHICKEN-FRUIT SALAD

½ c. whipped cream
1 c. mayonnaise
3 c. diced cooked chicken
1 c. seedless grapes
1 c. diced apples
1 tbsp. lemon juice
½ tsp. salt
¼ tsp. paprika
3 c. diced celery

Combine whipped cream and mayonnaise. Combine remaining chilled ingredients. Mix in one-half of whipped cream mixture. Top salad with remaining mixture. Yield: 12-14 servings.

Mrs. G. P. Stark
Foreman, Arkansas

CHICKEN LUNCHEON SALAD

4 c. cooked diced chicken
2 c. chopped celery
1 c. chopped apples
1 c. pineapple chunks, drained
½ tsp. salt
1 tbsp. curry powder
½ c. chopped toasted almonds
1 c. mayonnaise
2 tbsp. lemon juice

Combine all ingredients; serve on crisp lettuce. Yield: 10 servings.

Mrs. John I. Loy
Parris Island, South Carolina

CHICKEN-CRANBERRY MOLD

1 pkg. lemon gelatin
1 ½ c. hot water
2 c. cooked cubed chicken
1 hard-cooked egg, chopped
¼ c. chopped celery
⅓ c. salad dressing
1 can cranberry jelly
2 tbsp. orange juice

(Continued on next page)

Dissolve gelatin in hot water. Combine chicken, egg, celery and salad dressing with 1/2 cup gelatin. Chill in 8-inch square pan. Beat cranberry jelly until smooth; add orange juice and pour over chilled gelatin. Cut into squares and serve on lettuce. Yield: 9 servings.

Mrs. M. L. Hostetter
Huntington, West Virginia

CHICKEN-CRANBERRY PARTY SALAD

3 envelopes unflavored gelatin
½ c. cold water
2 cans cream of chicken soup
¼ c. mayonnaise
½ c. whipped cream
1 c. diced cooked chicken
½ c. slivered almonds
½ c. chopped celery
1 1-lb. can jellied cranberry sauce
1 tsp. grated orange or lemon peel
1 tbsp. lemon juice

Soften 2 envelopes gelatin in 1/4 cup water. Heat 1/4 cup soup; add to gelatin. Stir until dissolved; add to remaining soup. Cool. Fold in mayonnaise, whipped cream, chicken, almonds and celery. Pour into greased molds; chill until firm. Crush cranberry sauce with fork. Soften remaining gelatin in remaining water. Set in pan of boiling water; stir until gelatin dissolves. Mix gelatin, cranberry sauce, orange peel and lemon juice. Pour over chilled layer. Chill until cranberry layer is firm. Serve on crisp salad greens. Yield: 6-8 servings.

Mrs. J. M. Christian
Dublin, Georgia

CHICKEN-CRANBERRY SALAD

CHICKEN LAYER:

2 envelopes unflavored gelatin
½ c. cold water
2 cans condensed cream of chicken soup
¼ c. mayonnaise
1 tbsp. minced parsley

Soften gelatin in cold water. Place over boiling water; stir until dissolved. Blend in remaining ingredients. Pour into 1 1/2-quart mold. Chill until firm.

CRANBERRY LAYER:

1 envelope unflavored gelatin
½ c. cold water
1 1-lb. can cranberry sauce

Soften gelatin in cold water. Place over boiling water; stir until dissolved. Stir in cranberry sauce. Pour on top of firm chicken layer; chill until cranberry layer is firm. Unmold; serve on crisp salad greens. One cup drained, crushed pineapple or 1 cup diced, cooked chicken may be added to the chicken layer. Yield: 6 servings.

Mrs. Robert Chapman
Uniontown, Kentucky

CHICKEN-CRANBERRY SALAD

2 c. whole cranberry sauce
2 c. crushed pineapple
⅓ c. chopped pecans or walnuts
4 envelopes unflavored gelatin
1 c. cold water
2 c. (heaping) chicken
¾ c. finely chopped celery
3 tbsp. chopped parsley
1 ½ c. mayonnaise
¾ c. evaporated milk
Monosodium glutamate, salt, rosemary and lemon juice to taste

Blend cranberry sauce, pineapple and pecans; Soften 2 envelopes gelatin in 1/2 cup water; dissolve over hot water. Add to cranberry mixture; chill until partially set. Combine chicken, celery and parsley. Soften remaining gelatin in remaining water; dissolve over hot water. Combine mayonnaise, milk and seasonings; blend in gelatin. Add to chicken mixture. Cover cranberry layer. Chill. Yield: 8 servings.

Mrs. Curtis E. Conner
Daingerfield, Texas

CHICKEN-CRANBERRY SALAD

2 c. cooked coarsely chopped chicken
1 c. celery, cut into ½-in. pieces
1 tbsp. lemon juice
Salt and pepper to taste
½ c. mayonnaise
2 c. cubed cranberry jelly

Toss chicken with celery, lemon juice, salt and pepper; mix in mayonnaise. Carefully fold in jelly. Chill thoroughly. Arrange a mound of salad in lettuce cup and garnish with olives or sweet pickles and parsley, if desired. Yield: 6 servings.

Mrs. John M. Wypick
Dallas, Texas

CHICKEN-CRANBERRY SALAD

2 envelopes unflavored gelatin
1 c. water
2 c. whole cranberry sauce
1 c. crushed pineapple
½ c. broken walnuts
4 tsp. lemon juice
1 c. mayonnaise
½ c. water
¾ tsp. salt
2 c. diced chicken breasts
½ c. diced celery
2 tsp. chopped parsley

Soften 1 envelope gelatin in 1/4 cup water; dissolve over hot water. Add cranberry sauce, pineapple, walnuts and 1 teaspoon lemon juice. Pour into 6 x 10-inch dish; chill until firm. Soften remaining gelatin in 1/4 cup water; dissolve over hot water. Blend mayonnaise with remaining water, remaining lemon juice and salt. Add remaining ingredients. Pour over first layer; chill until firm. Cut in squares, garnish with mayonnaise and a walnut half.

Mrs. R. P. Smith
Victoria, Virginia

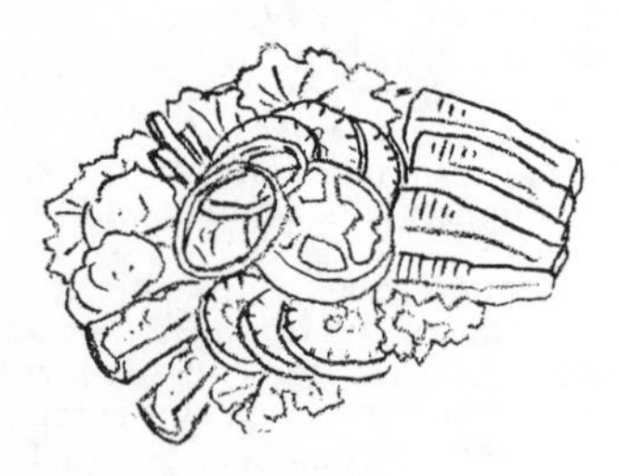

CHICKEN SALAD WITH CRANBERRY TOPPING

1 5-lb. hen, cooked and cut up
1 lge. onion, chopped
3 stalks celery, chopped
12 pieces pickle, chopped
4 hard-cooked eggs, chopped
3 c. mayonnaise
4 tbsp. Durkee's dressing
2 c. white grapes, halved
½ lb. almonds, sliced
1 tsp. salt
Pepper to taste
Pineapple slices

Combine all ingredients except pineapple. Serve on pineapple slices.

TOPPING:

½ c. heavy cream, whipped
½ c. mayonnaise
⅓ c. cranberry sauce

Combine all ingredients. Chill. Serve over chicken salad. Yield: 15 servings.

Mrs. Ernest S. Gibson
Centenary, South Carolina

LUNCHEON CHICKEN SALAD

1 3-oz. pkg. softened cream cheese
½ c. sour cream
Dash of salt
1 c. drained pineapple chunks
¾ c. chopped celery
¼ c. chopped green pepper
½ c. English walnuts
1 ½ c. cubed cooked chicken
1 c. cranberry sauce, chilled and cubed

Blend cheese, sour cream and salt. Add pineapple, celery, green pepper and nuts. Mix well. Fold in chicken and cranberry cubes. Serve in lettuce cups. Garnish with additional cranberry cubes. Serve with hot rolls. Cranberry sauce and nuts may be omitted and salad served in tomato roses. Yield: 4-6 servings.

Mrs. William Burns
Marysville, Ohio

MOLDED CHICKEN SALAD

1 envelope unflavored gelatin
1 c. cold water
1 can condensed cream of chicken soup
Few drops of Tabasco sauce
2 tbsp. lemon juice
¼ c. mayonnaise
1 5-oz. can boned chicken, diced
1 5-oz. can water chestnuts, drained and chopped
⅓ c. chopped, toasted salted almonds
1 1-lb. can jellied cranberry sauce, sliced

Soften gelatin in 1/2 cup cold water. Place over low heat; stir until gelatin dissolves. Blend together remaining water and soup; stir in gelatin, Tabasco, lemon juice and mayonnaise. Chill mixture until the consistency of unbeaten egg whites. Fold in remaining ingredients. Turn into a 3-cup mold. Chill until firm or about 1 hour and 30 minutes. Unmold; garnish with cranberry sauce slices. Yield: 4 servings.

Jean A. Cary
Burkesville, Kentucky

MRS. EISENHOWER'S CHICKEN JEWEL RING SALAD

2 envelopes unflavored gelatin
1 c. cranberry juice cocktail
1 1-lb. can whole cranberry sauce
2 tbsp. lemon juice
¾ c. cold water
1 tbsp. soy sauce
1 c. mayonnaise
1 ½ c. diced cooked chicken
½ c. diced celery
¼ c. coarsely chopped toasted almonds

(Continued on next page)

Sprinkle 1 envelope unflavored gelatin on cranberry juice cocktail in saucepan to soften. Dissolve gelatin over low heat, stirring constantly. Break up cranberry sauce; stir into gelatin mixture with lemon juice. Pour into 6-cup ring mold; chill until almost firm. Sprinkle remaining gelatin on cold water in saucepan to soften. Dissolve over low heat, stirring constantly. Remove from heat; stir in soy sauce. Cool. Gradually stir gelatin mixture into mayonnaise until blended. Mix in remaining ingredients. Spoon over chilled cranberry layer. Chill until firm. Unmold onto salad greens. Yield: 8 servings.

Mrs. Cecil Day
Stuttgart, Arkansas

FRUIT AND CHICKEN SALAD SUPREME

2 c. cubed cooked chicken
2 tbsp. chopped green olives
¾ c. chopped celery
½ c. toasted almonds
1 c. chopped raw apple
2 tbsp. chopped ripe olives
2 tbsp. chopped sweet pickle
2 hard-cooked eggs, diced
1 c. diced pineapple
½ c. raisins
¾ c. mayonnaise
1 c. crushed potato chips

Combine ingredients except potato chips; toss lightly. Serve on lettuce and garnish with spiced apple rings, ripe olives and watercress. Just before serving, crush 1 cup of potato chips over the top. Yield: 8 servings.

Mrs. P. G. Garrison
Roanoke, Virginia

CURRIED CHICKEN SALAD

2 lb. chicken, cooked and diced
1 apple, peeled and diced
1 c. diced fresh pineapple
¼ c. white raisins
⅓ c. diced dates
2 tbsp. undrained chopped chutney
½ c. shredded coconut
½ tsp. salt
1 tbsp. curry powder
2 tbsp. chicken consomme
1 c. mayonnaise

Combine chicken, apple, pineapple, raisins, dates, chutney and coconut; sprinkle with salt. Mix curry powder and chicken consomme; cook until thickened, stirring constantly. Add curry paste to mayonnaise; stir into salad mixture. Yield: 4-6 servings.

Mrs. Gustavo O. Benavides
Knoxville, Tennessee

CHICKEN SALAD

3 c. cooked cubed chicken
1 ½ c. diced celery
1 sm. diced apple
¾ c. chopped, green seedless grapes
3 sweet gherkins, diced
1 tsp. salt
Mayonnaise

Combine all ingredients; moisten with mayonnaise. Serve on lettuce leaves; garnish with olives.

Mrs. E. F. Mulvehill
Morris, Alabama

CHICKEN-FRUIT SALAD

2 to 2 ½ c. cut-up cooked chicken
1 c. diced celery
1 c. green seedless grapes
1 tbsp. lemon juice (opt.)
½ to 1 c. mayonnaise
Lettuce

Combine chicken, celery, grapes and lemon juice; chill. Fold in mayonnaise just before serving. Serve on lettuce. Garnish with slices of chicken, olives and parsley, if desired. Yield: 6-8 servings.

Mrs. W. B. McDonald
Fort Worth, Texas

CHICKEN SALAD

2 c. coarsely diced chicken
2 tbsp. lemon juice
½ tsp. salt
1 c. diced celery
1 c. seedless white grapes
2 hard-cooked eggs, chilled and cut
½ c. mayonnaise
¼ c. slivered, blanched and toasted almonds

Sprinkle chicken with lemon juice and salt. Chill several hours. Add celery, grapes, chopped eggs, mayonnaise and almonds. Toss lightly. Season with salt to taste. Serve on lettuce cups. Yield: 4-5 servings.

Mrs. M. G. Moss
Fairmont, West Virginia

CHICKEN SALAD

1 ½ c. cooked diced chicken
1 c. chopped celery
¾ c. white seeded grape halves
⅓ c. mayonnaise

Combine all ingredients; serve on lettuce.

Mrs. F. G. Thames
Beaumont, Texas

CHICKEN SALAD

1 c. chopped seeded white grapes
¼ c. chopped celery leaves
1 c. finely chopped celery
¼ c. mayonnaise or salad dressing
2 c. chopped white chicken meat

Combine ingredients; arrange on lettuce. Garnish with almonds.

Mrs. John C. Hardin
Moulton, Alabama

CHICKEN SALAD

2 c. diced chicken
1 c. diced celery
3 hard-boiled eggs, diced
1 c. broken pecans
½ c. seeded Tokay grapes
¼ c. drained crushed pineapple
¾ tsp. salt
⅛ tsp. pepper
1 c. salad dressing

Mix all ingredients except dressing together. Add the salad dressing last. Serve very cold on salad greens. Salad dressing may be combined with 1/2 cup whipped cream, if desired. Yield: 6 servings.

Mrs. H. W. Jackson
Mesa, Arizona

CHICKEN SALAD DELUXE

2 ½ c. cooked diced chicken
1 c. finely chopped celery
1 c. white grapes (opt.)
1 c. shredded almonds
2 tbsp. minced parsley (opt.)
1 tsp. minced onion (opt.)
1 tsp. salt
1 c. mayonnaise or salad dressing
½ c. heavy cream, whipped

Combine all ingredients. Chill. Yield: 5-8 servings.

Mrs. J. C. Keleher
Panhandle, Texas

CHICKEN SALAD SUPREME

2 ½ c. cooked diced cold chicken
1 c. finely chopped celery
1 c. white grapes, sliced
½ c. slivered toasted almonds
1 to 2 tbsp. minced parsley
1 tsp. salt
½ c. whipped cream
¾ to 1 c. mayonnaise

Combine ingredients in order. Serve on lettuce or scooped-out tomatoes well drained. Chill thoroughly before serving time. Yield: 8 servings.

Mrs. W. C. Pittman
Pineville, Louisiana

CRUNCHY CHICKEN SALAD

2 c. green grapes
3 c. diced cooked chicken
1 c. cashews
⅔ c. sesame seed
1 tbsp. butter
1 c. sour cream
½ c. mayonnaise
1 tbsp. tarragon vinegar
1 tbsp. sugar
1 tsp. salt
White pepper to taste

Mix grapes with chicken and cashews. Saute sesame seed in butter until brown; add remaining ingredients. Pour over chicken. Yield: 10 servings.

Mrs. Howard Boydstun
Hot Springs, Arkansas

CURRIED CHICKEN AND GRAPE SALAD

3 c. cooked diced chicken
1 ½ c. thinly sliced celery
1 c. green seedless grapes
2 tbsp. lemon juice
1 ¼ tsp. salt
¼ tsp. pepper, freshly ground
1 ½ tsp. curry powder
6 tbsp. mayonnaise
3 tbsp. toasted slivered almonds

(Continued on next page)

Combine all ingredients; toss lightly. Chill. Serve on lettuce; garnish with almonds.

Lois Pullen
Baton Rouge, Louisiana

HEARTY VEGETABLE AND CHICKEN SALAD

2 c. sliced celery
1 c. green seedless grapes
4 c. cubed cooked chicken
1 ¼ tsp. salt
¼ tsp. ground black pepper
1 tbsp. fresh lemon juice
1 tsp. finely chopped fresh onion
⅓ c. mayonnaise
Head lettuce
Hard-cooked eggs, sliced
Radish roses

Combine celery, grapes, chicken, salt, black pepper, lemon juice, onion and mayonnaise. Toss lightly and serve on lettuce. Garnish with sliced hard-cooked egg and radish roses. Yield: 6 servings.

Photograph for this recipe on cover.

SALADE DE POULET

1 tbsp. unflavored gelatin
½ c. cold water
1 10 ½-oz. can cream of chicken soup
½ c. mayonnaise
2 tbsp. prepared horseradish
1 c. diced cooked chicken, chilled
3 hard-cooked eggs, chopped
½ c. chopped celery
½ c. chopped cucumber
½ c. sliced seeded grapes
½ c. salted pecan halves

Sprinkle gelatin evenly over cold water; let stand for 5 minutes. Stir dissolved gelatin into mixture of soup, mayonnaise and horseradish. Chill until thick. Mix remaining ingredients; blend into gelatin mixture. Pour into oiled mold. Chill for 4 hours. Yield: 12 servings.

Mrs. Vernelle K. Byrd
Clarkton, North Carolina

ROYAL COACH CHICKEN SALAD

3 c. diced cooked chicken
2 lge. unpeeled apples, diced
1 ½ c. sm. seedless white grapes
½ c. diced celery
⅔ c. salad dressing
Salad greens
½ c. toasted slivered almonds

Combine chicken, apples, grapes and celery in a bowl. Add salad dressing and toss to mix well. Chill. At serving time, turn into bowl lined with salad greens and pile almonds in center. Yield: 6 servings.

Photograph for this recipe on page 269.

LUNCHEON CHICKEN SALAD

3 c. cooked diced chicken
1 c. diced celery
1 c. diced pineapple
1 c. mandarin oranges
½ c. chopped walnuts
2 tbsp. salad oil
2 tbsp. orange juice
2 tbsp. vinegar
Dash of marjoram
Dash of salt
Dash of rosemary
Dash of thyme
½ c. mayonnaise

Combine chicken, celery, fruits and nuts. Blend oil, orange juice, vinegar and seasonings. Add to chicken mixture; let stand for 1 hour. Drain. Add mayonnaise and toss lightly. Yield: 8-10 servings.

Empo Henry
Stillwater, Oklahoma

CHICKEN AND FRUIT SALAD

1 5-lb. roasting chicken
¾ c. diced celery
1 c. seedless white grapes
1 c. mandarin orange sections, drained
½ c. mayonnaise
½ c. sour cream
2 tbsp. finely chopped parsley
2 tbsp. finely minced onion
1 tbsp. lemon juice
½ tsp. salt
½ tsp. pepper
½ tsp. herb salad dressing mix
Lettuce
¼ c. slivered almonds, toasted

(Continued on next page)

Steam chicken until tender, being careful not to boil. Cool; remove skin. Remove meat from bones; cut into bite-sized pieces. Place in bowl; add celery, grapes and orange sections. Chill. Mix mayonnaise, sour cream, parsley, onion, lemon juice, salt, pepper and dressing mix; pour over chicken mixture. Mix well. Cover; chill for several hours. Serve over lettuce; garnish with almonds. Yield: 10 servings.

Mrs. Ed Barnett
Waco, Texas

CHICKEN-FRUIT SALAD

3 c. diced cooked chicken
1 c. diced celery
1 can mandarin oranges, drained
1 can pineapple chunks, drained
Sliced ripe olives (opt.)
2 tbsp. salad oil
2 tbsp. wine vinegar
2 tbsp. frozen orange juice concentrate
½ c. mayonnaise
½ c. slivered almonds

Combine chicken, celery, oranges, pineapple and olives. Blend oil, vinegar and orange juice. Marinate chicken mixture in vinegar mixture for 1 hour or overnight. Add mayonnaise and almonds before serving. Yield: 8 servings.

Mrs. Frank Kiddoo
Waco, Texas

CHICKEN SALAD

3 c. diced chicken
1 c. diced celery
1 c. mandarin oranges
or 1 can drained
1 9-oz. can pineapple tidbits
½ c. slivered almonds
2 tbsp. salad oil
2 tbsp. orange juice
2 tbsp. vinegar
½ tsp. salt
Dash of marjoram
½ c. mayonnaise-type salad
dressing

Combine first 4 ingredients. Combine remaining ingredients except salad dressing; add to first mixture. Marinate for 1 hour; drain. Beat salad dressing until slightly fluffy; add to salad. Yield: 6 servings.

Mrs. Ben T. Jacob
Georgetown, Texas

LUNCHEON CHICKEN SALAD

2 c. cooked cubed chicken or canned
white meat
1 c. orange sections
¼ to ½ c. grapes, seeded and halved
¼ to ½ c. slivered toasted or salted
almonds or pecans
1 or 2 bananas, sliced
¾ to 1 c. mayonnaise or salad
dressing

Chill ingredients. Combine all ingredients, using enough mayonnaise to moisten. Serve on crisp lettuce or pineapple slices with watercress garnish. Salad may be garnished with whole strawberries if desired.

Elizabeth Chenoweth
Corpus Christi, Texas

MANDARIN CHICKEN SALAD

3 c. chopped cooked chicken
1 tbsp. minced onion
1 tsp. salt
2 tbsp. fresh lemon juice
1 c. thinly sliced celery
1 c. seedless grapes
⅓ c. mayonnaise or cooked salad
dressing
1 11-oz. can mandarin orange sections
or 1 c. tangerine sections, drained
½ c. slivered almonds, toasted
6 to 8 lettuce leaves
6 pitted ripe olives

Combine chicken, onion, salt, lemon juice and celery; refrigerate for several hours. Toss chicken mixture lightly with grapes, mayonnaise, orange sections and almonds, reserving a few orange sections and almonds for garnish. Line salad bowl with lettuce leaves; fill with chicken mixture. Garnish with reserved orange sections, almonds and ripe olives. Yield: 6 servings.

Mrs. Donald H. Swan
Clearwater, Florida

ORIENTAL CHICKEN SALAD

3 c. cubed cooked chicken
1 c. canned mandarin oranges,
drained
1 c. chopped celery
⅛ tsp. ginger
1 tbsp. soy sauce
Mayonnaise
Salt and pepper to taste
2 c. chow mein noodles

(Continued on next page)

Combine chicken, orange slices, celery, ginger and soy sauce. Add enough mayonnaise to moisten well; season to taste. Chill thoroughly. Serve on a bed of crisp noodles. Yield: 4 servings.

Mrs. S. P. Gordan
Memphis, Tennessee

CABOOM MESS

- 1 ½ c. diced chicken
- ¾ c. drained crushed pineapple
- ½ c. chopped pecans
- 1 c. mayonnaise
- 1 c. heavy cream, whipped

Combine chicken, pineapple, pecans and mayonnaise in a large mixing bowl; mix well. Gradually fold whipped cream into mixture. Pour into 1 1/2-quart rectangular dish; freeze for 2 to 3 hours. Divide into eight servings; place on lettuce leaves just before serving. Yield: 8 servings.

Mrs. James D. Nally
Little Rock, Arkansas

CHICKEN-COTTAGE CHEESE SALAD

- 1 pkg. lemon gelatin
- 1 c. hot water
- ½ c. pineapple juice
- 1 to 2 tbsp. lemon juice or vinegar
- ½ c. mayonnaise
- ¼ tsp. salt
- ¾ c. diced celery
- 1 ½ c. cubed cooked chicken
- ½ c. crushed pineapple
- 1 c. cottage cheese

Dissolve gelatin in hot water; add pineapple juice and lemon juice. Let set until thick. Add mayonnaise and salt; whip until fluffy. Fold in celery, chicken, pineapple and cottage cheese. Chill until set.

Mrs. F. G. Trenton
Flagstaff, Arizona

CHICKEN SALAD

- 1 pkg. lemon gelatin
- 1 ½ c. water
- 1 lge. pkg. cream cheese, softened
- ¾ c. salad dressing
- ½ pt. whipped cream
- 3 tbsp. sugar
- ¾ c. grated carrots
- ¾ c. chopped celery
- 1 No. 2 can crushed pineapple, drained
- 2 cans boned chicken or tuna

Prepare gelatin with water; whip when congealed. Mix cream cheese with salad dressing and whipped cream. Add sugar, carrots, celery and pineapple; add chicken. Mix well; place in 9 x 13-inch pan. Refrigerate for several hours. Yield: 12-15 servings.

Mrs. E. H. Patterson
Atlanta, Georgia

CHICKEN HAWAIIAN SALAD

- 1 lb. chicken breasts
- 3 to 4 celery tops
- ½ onion, chopped
- Salt and pepper to taste
- ⅔ c. instant rice
- ½ c. flaked coconut
- 1 tsp. grated onion
- 1 c. mayonnaise
- 1 tbsp. lemon juice
- ½ to 1 tsp. curry powder
- 1 c. finely chopped celery
- 1 13-oz. can pineapple chunks

Cook chicken with celery tops, chopped onion, salt and pepper to taste in 1/2 cup water until tender. Remove bones from chicken. Cook rice and salt to taste in 2/3 cup water. Combine all ingredients. Let set for 24 hours. Serve in lettuce cups, if desired. Yield: 8 servings.

Mrs. William Wilcox
Fort Worth, Texas

CHICKEN SALAD

- 2 c. diced cooked chicken
- 2 c. diced celery
- 3 oz. blanched almonds
- Dash of onion juice
- Dash of Tabasco sauce
- Dash of lemon juice
- Mayonnaise
- Pineapple rings
- Lettuce

Mix chicken, celery, almonds and seasonings; moisten with mayonnaise. Serve on slice of pineapple on lettuce leaf.

Mrs. D. E. Rushton
Macon, Georgia

CHICKEN SALAD

5 c. cooked diced chicken
1 ½ c. diced celery
4 hard-cooked eggs, chopped
1 sm. can crushed pineapple, drained
Salt to taste
⅛ tsp. pepper
1 c. sliced sweet pickles
2 c. mayonnaise

Combine all ingredients; toss lightly. Serve on lettuce leaf. Yield: 6-8 servings.

Jo Ann Carter
Folkston, Georgia

CHICKEN SALAD PIE

2 c. diced cooked chicken
¾ c. shredded American cheese
½ c. diced celery
½ c. well-drained crushed pineapple
⅓ c. chopped walnuts
½ tsp. paprika
½ tsp. salt
¾ c. mayonnaise
1 pie shell, baked
½ c. heavy cream
Grated cheese

Combine chicken, American cheese, celery, pineapple, walnuts, paprika, salt and 1/2 cup mayonnaise; turn into cooled pie shell. Whip cream until thick and stiff; carefully fold in remaining mayonnaise. Spread mixture over salad in pie shell. Garnish with additional grated cheese. Chill for at least 30 minutes. Yield: 6 servings.

Mrs. Dale Kinney
Greenville, Florida

CHICKEN SALAD SURPRISE

1 pkg. lemon gelatin
1 tsp. garlic salt
¾ c. boiling water
1 ½ tsp. grated onion
Dash of pepper
1 tbsp. vinegar
1 c. sour cream or mayonnaise
¼ c. chopped pecans
2 c. cooked diced chicken
½ c. diced celery
4 qt. torn salad greens
⅓ c. sliced ripe olives
½ c. drained canned pineapple tidbits
2 med. tomatoes, diced

Dissolve gelatin and garlic salt in boiling water; add onion, pepper and vinegar. Cool. Blend in sour cream; chill until very thick. Fold in pecans, chicken and celery. Pour into 9-inch square pan. Chill until firm. Cut into cubes. Combine remaining ingredients; toss lightly with salad dressing.

Mrs. Walter Sherron
Bethpage, Tennessee

CHICKEN SURPRISE SALAD

1 3-oz. pkg. lemon or orange gelatin
1 tsp. garlic salt
¾ c. boiling water
1 ½ tsp. grated onion
Dash of pepper
1 tbsp. wine vinegar
1 c. sour cream or mayonnaise
¼ c. chopped pecans
2 c. cooked diced chicken
½ c. diced celery
4 qt. torn salad greens
⅓ c. sliced ripe olives
½ c. drained, canned pineapple tidbits
2 med. tomatoes, diced

Dissolve gelatin and garlic salt in boiling water. Add onion, pepper and vinegar; cool. Blend in sour cream; chill until very thick. Fold in pecans, chicken and celery. Pour into 9-inch square pan; chill until firm. Cut into cubes. Toss remaining ingredients lightly with salad dressing, if desired; place in salad bowls. Arrange cubes on salads; do not toss. Yield: 6 servings.

Mrs. Peggy Shomaker
Lenoir, North Carolina

DOVER CHICKEN SALAD

1 8-oz. can pineapple chunks
3 c. cooked diced chicken
1 c. diced celery
½ c. sliced ripe olives
½ c. slivered almonds

Drain pineapple; reserve juice. Marinate all remaining ingredients in pineapple juice for 1 hour. Drain off juice; arrange salad on a bed of endive and top with mayonnaise. Yield: 6-8 servings.

Mrs. Jean Forsgren
Cheraw, South Carolina

FRUITED CHICKEN SALAD

2 c. diced cooked chicken
White pepper to taste
1 c. pineapple chunks
½ c. grapes, halved and seeded
2 med. bananas, diced
¼ c. chopped pecans
1 c. mayonnaise

Combine all ingredients; toss lightly to mix. Chill. Serve on lettuce or pineapple rings. Yield: 8 servings.

Mrs. William Collman
Homestead, Florida

HOLIDAY CHICKEN SALAD

2 tbsp. gelatin
¼ c. cold water
3 c. hot chicken broth
1 to 2 tsp. onion juice
½ tsp. salt
1 c. mayonnaise
2 c. cubed chicken
½ c. chopped cooked ham
½ c. celery

Soak gelatin in cold water for 5 minutes; add to broth, stirring until dissolved. Add onion juice, salt and mayonnaise. Beat until well blended. Chill until thickened. Stir in chicken, ham and celery. Place in 9-inch bread pan; chill until firm. Serve on shredded lettuce or cabbage with mayonnaise.

Mrs. M. J. Arrington
Roopville, Georgia

HAWAIIAN CHICKEN SALAD

2 ½ c. cooked chicken, cubed
1 14-oz. can pineapple chunks, drained
1 c. celery, chopped
3 tbsp. salad oil
2 tbsp. lemon juice
¼ tsp. salt
5 tbsp. mayonnaise
¼ c. slivered almonds

Combine chicken, pineapple and celery. Mix salad oil, lemon juice and salt. Pour over chicken mixture; marinate for 1 hour. Add mayonnaise; mix well. Serve on bed of greens; sprinkle almonds over top. Yield: 6 servings.

Danita Degraw
Leesburg, Florida

BAKED CHICKEN SALAD

2 c. boned chicken
1 c. cream of chicken soup
1 c. diced celery
3 tbsp. minced onion
½ tsp. salt
¼ tsp. pepper
1 tbsp. lemon juice
1 to 3 c. mayonnaise
3 hard-boiled eggs, sliced
Potato chips, crumbled

Combine all ingredients except potato chips. Sprinkle potato chips over top. Bake at 350 degrees for 15 to 20 minutes. Yield: 4-6 servings.

Mrs. Thomas Hudson
Roanoke Rapids, North Carolina

BAKED CHICKEN SALAD

2 c. diced cooled chicken
2 c. diced celery
3 tbsp. lemon juice
3 tbsp. minced onion
⅔ c. mayonnaise
½ c. almonds
Salt and pepper to taste
1 can cream of chicken soup
1 c. crushed potato chips

Combine all ingredients except soup and potato chips; mix well. Pour soup over salad; top with potato chips. Bake at 325 degrees for 30 minutes.

Mrs. J. M. Thornton
Lewisburg, Tennessee

HOT CHICKEN-NUT SALAD

2 c. stewed chicken
1 c. diced celery
3 hard-cooked eggs, diced
1 c. mayonnaise
1 tbsp. lemon juice
1 can cream of chicken soup
1 can water chestnuts or ⅓ c. almonds, slivered
Salt and pepper to taste
Potato chips, crushed

Mix all ingredients except potato chips. Cover with crushed potato chips. Bake at 400 degrees for 20 minutes.

Margaret Hefner Peden
Raeford, North Carolina

HOT CHICKEN SALAD

⅔ c. mayonnaise or salad dressing
2 tsp. cider vinegar
1 tsp. salt
¼ tsp. celery seed
⅛ tsp. pepper
2 c. diced, cooked chicken
1 c. diced celery
¼ c. blanched, slivered almonds
¼ c. chopped sweet pickles
2 tsp. chopped onion
1 c. crushed potato chips or 1 c. grated process American cheese

Heat oven to 350 degrees. Blend mayonnaise with next 4 ingredients. Combine chicken with next 4 ingredients; toss with mayonnaise mixture. Place in 10 x 6 x 2-inch baking dish or individual casseroles. Sprinkle with potato chips. Bake for 20 minutes or until cheese is melted. Garnish with parsley or pickle fans. Yield: 6 servings.

Mrs. Robert Chapman
Uniontown, Kentucky

HOT CHICKEN SALAD

2 c. chicken, boiled and diced
2 c. finely cut celery
½ c. toasted almonds, chopped
½ tsp. salt
2 tsp. grated onion
2 tbsp. lemon juice
1 c. mayonnaise
Grated cheese
1 c. potato chip crumbs

Mix all ingredients. Top with grated cheese and potato chip crumbs. Bake in buttered casserole at 450 degrees for 10 to 15 minutes. Yield: 3-4 servings.

Mrs. Stanley Short, Jr.
Dover, Delaware

HOT CHICKEN SALAD

1 ½ c. cooked diced chicken
1 c. chopped celery
2 tbsp. chopped onion
½ c. pecan pieces
2 tbsp. lemon juice
½ c. mayonnaise
½ tsp. salt
¼ tsp. pepper
1 10 ½-oz. can cream of chicken soup
6 saltine crackers, crushed

Combine all ingredients except chicken soup and saltines; pour into buttered baking dish. Pour soup over top; sprinkle with crushed saltines. Bake at 450 degrees for 20 minutes. Yield: 6 servings.

Martha Lewis
Douglasville, Georgia

HOT CHICKEN SALAD

2 c. cooked chopped chicken
2 c. chopped celery
½ c. minced green pepper
2 tbsp. pimento
1 tbsp. minced onion
1 tbsp. Worcestershire sauce
2 tbsp. lemon juice
½ c. mayonnaise
1 can cream of chicken soup
Crushed potato chips
Grated cheese
Almonds

Combine all ingredients except last 3 ingredients. Top with potato chips, cheese and almonds. Bake at 350 degrees for 25 minutes. Yield: 6-8 servings.

Mrs. Hoyt Clark
Angelus, South Carolina

HOT CHICKEN SALAD

1 c. chopped celery
¼ c. margarine
1 can mushrooom soup
1 5-oz. can boned chicken
¼ tsp. mayonnaise
3 hard-boiled eggs, sliced
¼ c. cracker crumbs

Saute celery in margarine. Mix with remaining ingredients except crumbs. Pour mixture into baking dish; sprinkle crumbs over top. Bake 20 minutes at 350 degrees. Yield: 6 servings.

Mrs. Hollis Jones
Liberty, Mississippi

HOT CHICKEN SALAD EN CASSEROLE

2 c. diced cooked chicken
2 c. chopped celery
½ c. slivered toasted almonds
2 tbsp. chopped pimento
2 tbsp. minced onion
½ tsp. salt
⅓ c. chopped green pepper
2 tbsp. lemon juice
¾ c. mayonnaise
½ c. grated Swiss or sharp cheese
1 ½ c. crushed potato chips

Mix all ingredients except cheese and potato chips. Turn into buttered 1 1/2-quart casserole. Top with cheese and potato chips. Bake in 350-degree oven for 25 minutes or until cheese is melted. Yield: 6 servings.

Mrs. E. S. Davis
Jacksonville, Florida

HOT CHICKEN-SPAGHETTI SALAD

½ lb. spaghetti
Chicken broth
Salt
1 onion, chopped
1 green pepper, chopped
¼ lb. butter or margarine
1 c. milk
2 tbsp. flour
1 4 to 5-lb. hen, cooked and diced
½ lb. Old English cheese
½ lb. American cheese
1 can mushrooms

Cook spaghetti in broth; drain, reserving broth. Add 2 tablespoonfuls salt. Cook onion and pepper in butter. Add milk to reserved broth with flour and 2 teaspoonfuls salt. Combine chicken, cheeses and white sauce; cook slowly until cheeses are melted. Combine all ingredients. Place in baking dish. Top with buttered crumbs if desired. Bake at 350 degrees for 30 minutes. Yield: 8-10 servings.

Mrs. Louis Montague
Oakland, Tennessee

JELLIED CHICKEN SALAD

2 tbsp. gelatin
2 tbsp. cold water
½ c. mayonnaise
½ c. cream, whipped
¾ tbsp. lemon juice
1 ½ c. finely cut chicken
¼ c. minced olives

Dissolve gelatin in cold water; let stand 5 minutes. Set dish in hot water until gelatin dissolves completely. Add mayonnaise to gelatin; fold into whipped cream. Add lemon juice, chicken and olives. Chill for 2 hours. Serve on lettuce. Yield: 8 servings.

Mrs. Charles V. Haston
Sparta, Tennessee

JELLIED CHICKEN SALAD

1 envelope gelatin
¼ c. cold water
1 chicken bouillon cube
1 c. hot chicken broth
1 tbsp. lemon juice
½ tsp. salt
2 hard-cooked eggs, chopped
6 or 8 stuffed olives, sliced
1 pimento, chopped
½ c. chopped celery
1 ½ c. diced chicken
½ c. mayonnaise

Dissolve gelatin in cold water. Dissolve bouillon cube in hot chicken broth; add gelatin mixture, dissolving thoroughly. Allow to cool slightly. Add lemon juice and salt. Mix eggs, olives, pimento, celery, chicken and mayonnaise. Add to gelatin mixture, combining ingredients thoroughly. Pour into mold; chill overnight. Yield: 6 servings.

Mrs. Edward Rather
Holly Springs, Mississippi

JERRY'S CHICKEN SALAD

2 c. cooked chopped chicken
¾ c. chopped celery
2 tbsp. green olives
2 tbsp. ripe olives
2 hard-cooked eggs
2 tbsp. pickle
¾ c. mayonnaise
½ c. almonds (opt.)

Combine chicken, celery, olives, eggs and pickle; add mayonnaise. Add almonds when ready to serve. Serve on crisp lettuce leaf, if desired.

Mrs. Jerry Kasten
Tulsa, Oklahoma

CHICKEN-FRUIT SALAD

2 c. canned chicken
1 tbsp. minced onion
1 tsp. salt
1 c. grapes
1 c. chopped celery
1 c. mandarin oranges
½ c. slivered almonds
1 c. raw macaroni rings, cooked
1 c. salad dressing
1 c. whipped cream

Combine chicken, onion and salt; refrigerate for several hours. Mix remaining ingredients except salad dressing and whipped cream. Fold in salad dressing and whipped cream. Yield: 6 servings.

Mrs. W. T. Westmore
Roanoke, Virginia

CHICKEN-MACARONI SALAD

1 5-oz. can boned chicken
3 hard-cooked eggs
1 c. cooked macaroni
2 tbsp. sweet pickle relish
1 tbsp. mustard
1 tsp. salt
1 tbsp. minced onion
Pimento (opt.)
Salad dressing to taste

Chop chicken and eggs; combine with macaroni. Add all remaining ingredients. Yield: 6 servings.

Mrs. N. F. Williams
Sarasota, Florida

CHICKEN-MACARONI SALAD

3 ½ qt. cooked elbow macaroni
1 ¾ qt. diced celery
1 qt. cooked diced chicken
2 c. diced green pepper
2 c. chopped pimento
2 c. mayonnaise or salad dressing
4 tsp. salt
1 tsp. pepper

Combine all ingredients; chill. Yield: 30-35 servings.

Mrs. O. F. Green
Tulsa, Oklahoma

CHICKEN-MACARONI SALAD

1 chicken, cooked and chopped
1 pkg. frozen peas and carrots, cooked
¼ c. chopped green pepper
1 c. chopped celery
1 tbsp. chopped dill pickle
6 hard-cooked eggs, diced
6 oz. macaroni, cooked
¾ c. heavy cream, whipped
1 ½ c. salad dressing
2 tsp. parsley
Salt and pepper to taste
Garlic salt

Combine chicken, vegetables, pickle, eggs and macaroni. Combine whipped cream and salad dressing; fold into chicken mixture. Add parsley; season to taste. Garnish with tomato slices, olives and parsley, if desired. Yield: 12-15 servings.

Mrs. C. A. Davis
Charleston, South Carolina

MACARONI SALAD

2 c. macaroni, cooked
2 c. diced cooked chicken or ham
1 lge. cucumber, finely chopped
1 c. mayonnaise
2 pimentos, chopped

(Continued on next page)

Combine all ingredients; toss lightly. Yield: 8-10 servings.

Mrs. F. E. Parker
Meridian, Mississippi

MACARONI-CHICKEN SALAD

1 chicken, stewed
1 14-oz. pkg. shell macaroni, cooked and cooled
Onion
Salt and pepper
1 can peas
1 c. diced celery

Remove chicken from bones; break into small pieces. Combine remaining ingredients. Add chicken.

DRESSING:

½ c. sugar
1 tsp. salt
1 tbsp. flour
½ tsp. dry mustard
¼ c. vinegar
¼ c. water
1 egg, beaten
Salad dressing
Cream

Combine all ingredients except egg, dressing and cream. Mix well; add egg. Boil until thickened. Add a small amount of salad dressing and cream just before serving. Chill. Mix with chicken salad. Yield: 4 servings.

Mrs. N. P. Tucker
Charleston, West Virginia

MY FAVORITE CHICKEN-MACARONI SALAD

4 oz. salad macaroni
1 c. chopped chicken
1 c. chopped apples
1 c. chopped celery
¾ c. chopped nuts
1 green pepper, chopped
3 green onions, chopped
¼ c. chopped sweet pickle
Salt and pepper to taste
Mayonnaise
1 tbsp. lemon juice
Pimento strips

Cook macaroni until tender; drain. Combine macaroni, chicken, apples, celery, nuts, green pepper, onions and pickle. Season with salt and pepper; moisten with mayonnaise and lemon juice. Serve on lettuce leaves, if desired, and garnish with pimento strips. Yield: 8-10 servings.

Mrs. K. L. Wilson
Jackson, Mississippi

MAIN DISH SALAD

1 4-oz. pkg. elbow macaroni
1 c. cooked chopped chicken, turkey or tuna
2 hard-cooked eggs, diced
½ c. crushed pineapple, drained
¼ c. sliced radishes
¼ c. chopped nuts
1 tbsp. chopped onion
⅓ c. mayonnaise
1 ½ tbsp. pineapple juice
¼ tsp. celery seed
¼ tsp. salt
Dash of pepper

Cook macaroni as directed on package. Combine meat, eggs, pineapple, radishes, nuts and onion. Add macaroni; toss lightly. Combine mayonnaise and pineapple juice; mix until smooth. Stir in celery seed, salt and pepper. Pour over macaroni mixture. Toss until well blended. Chill. Serve on salad greens. Yield: 4 servings.

Mrs. Ruth A. Blomgren
Silver Springs, Maryland

TALK-OF-THE-TOWN SALAD

1 sm. head lettuce, torn
2 tomatoes, cut as desired
¼ c. diced celery
1 4-oz. can mushrooms
⅛ c. Velveeta cheese, diced
2 tbsp. bleu cheese, diced
⅔ c. canned peas or French-cut beans
8 stuffed olives, sliced
½ tsp. onion salt
Dash of garlic salt
1 ½ c. chicken, crab, lobster, shrimp or combination
French dressing
Salt and pepper to taste
1 c. cooked macaroni (opt.)

Toss all ingredients in a large salad bowl. If seafood is used, sprinkle with 1 teaspoonful lemon juice. Yield: 4 servings.

Mrs. O. H. Parsons
Johnson City, Tennessee

SUNSHINE SALAD

1 pkg. lemon gelatin
1 tsp. salt
1 c. boiling water
½ c. salad dressing
3 c. cooked macaroni
1 c. diced cooked chicken
1 c. cooked peas
2 tbsp. sweet pickle
2 tbsp. chopped onion
½ c. diced cheese

(Continued on next page)

Mix gelatin, salt and boiling water; cool. Blend in salad dressing; chill until slightly thickened. Whip gelatin mixture. Combine remaining ingredients; fold in gelatin mixture. Chill well. Yield: 12 servings.

Mrs. William Block
Columbia, South Carolina

MOLDED CHICKEN SALAD

1 tbsp. gelatin
¼ c. cold water
1 c. mayonnaise
2 c. cooked chicken, cut in small pieces
½ c. chopped celery
¼ c. chopped pimento

Soak gelatin in cold water; dissolve over boiling water. Add mayonnaise; fold in chicken, celery, pimento, and more mayonnaise if necessary. Turn into large mold; chill until firm. Unmold on crisp lettuce; garnish with pickles, stuffed olives or radish roses.

Mrs. Virginia Calhoun
Baston, Kentucky

PERFECT CHICKEN SALAD

1 5 to 6-lb. chicken, quartered
Salt
1 onion, sliced
2 cloves
1 stalk celery
Sprig parsley
Pepper
Mayonnaise
Lettuce
Cucumber
Capers
Toasted walnut halves

Cook chicken in salted water to cover with salt, onion, cloves, celery and parsley. The white meat should take one third less time to cook than the dark; remove it when tender, leaving the dark meat for an additional period. Cool the chicken and remove skin. Cut the white meat in long pieces; dice dark meat. Season to taste. Toss chicken with mayonnaise. Arrange on salad plate with lettuce on one end and cucumber on other. Garnish with capers and walnuts. Yield: 4 servings.

Mrs. P. R. Bowman
Houston, Texas

MOLDED CHICKEN SALAD

2 pkg. unflavored gelatin
¼ c. cold water
1 c. cream of chicken soup, heated
2 3-oz. pkg. cream cheese
1 c. mayonnaise
½ c. grated onion
1 c. diced onion
2 tbsp. Worcestershire sauce
3 hard-boiled eggs, chopped
2 c. chopped chicken
1 tbsp. chopped sweet pickle
1 tbsp. chopped pimento

Soften gelatin in cold water. Combine soup and cream cheese; add gelatin and cool. Fold in remaining ingredients. Pour into mold; chill. Garnish with canned cranberry jelly slices.

Mrs. Ben W. Musick
Kingfisher, Oklahoma

PRESSED CHICKEN

3 pkg. unflavored gelatin
½ c. cold water
4 c. chicken broth
1 lge. hen, cooked and cubed
1 c. finely chopped celery
½ c. chopped sweet pepper
½ c. chopped pecans
6 hard-cooked eggs, chopped
1 or 2 slices pimento, chopped
Juice of 1 lemon
Salt and pepper to taste

Soak gelatin in cold water; add to hot chicken broth. Simmer until dissolved. Add remaining ingredients. Pour in mold and congeal. Yield: 24 servings.

Mrs. Robert W. Davis
Laurens, South Carolina

PRESSED CHICKEN MOLD

2 chickens, cut up
1 c. broth
¼ lb. butter
¼ tsp. (heaping) pepper
⅓ tsp. allspice
1 egg, beaten

Cook chicken slowly until tender. Remove chicken from broth; chop. Boil chicken broth until evaporated to 1 cup; add butter, pepper, allspice and egg. Mix thoroughly; add chicken. Press into mold; chill. Slice and serve with hard-cooked eggs on lettuce leaves with dressing. Yield: 6-8 servings.

Mrs. Ruth Edwards
Cullman, Alabama

CHICKEN AND RICE SALAD

1 ½ c. diced cooked chicken
1 c. cold cooked rice
¾ c. chopped celery
2 tbsp. chopped green pepper
1 tbsp. chopped sour pickle
6 stuffed olives, chopped
12 pecan halves, chopped
½ tbsp. chopped parsley
⅔ c. mayonnaise
⅔ c. whipped cream
1 tbsp. unflavored gelatin
2 c. cold water
½ tsp. salt
Dash of black pepper
Dash of red pepper
Dash of paprika

Combine chicken, rice, celery, green pepper, sour pickle, olives, pecans, parsley, mayonnaise and whipped cream. Soften gelatin in cold water for 5 minutes; dissolve over hot water. Stir into chicken mixture. Cool. Add salt, pepper and paprika. Pour into mold; chill until firm. Yield: 8 servings.

Mrs. P. D. Abner
High Point, North Carolina

BUDGET CHICKEN SALAD

⅔ c. mayonnaise
⅓ c. French dressing
1 tsp. salt
⅛ tsp. pepper
2 c. diced cooked chicken
1 c. diced celery
1 c. drained crushed pineapple
2 c. cold cooked rice

Combine all ingredients. Chill in a greased ring mold. Unmold onto platter. Fill center of ring with stuffed olives. Garnish with sliced tomatoes and cucumbers, if desired. Yield: 8 servings.

Mrs. W. T. Doyel
Portsmouth, Virginia

SESAME-CHICKEN SALAD

1 chicken, cooked, boned and diced
½ c. soy sauce
¼ c. corn oil
3 or 4 green onions, chopped
Salt and pepper to taste
¼ c. roasted sesame seed

Combine chicken, soy sauce and oil; cool. Add green onions and seasonings; mix well. Cover and let stand for 1 hour. Add sesame seed, just before serving; mix well. Shredded lettuce may be added, if desired. Yield: 12 servings.

Mrs. William K. Toy
Phoenix, Arizona

SILHOUETTE SALAD

1 envelope unflavored gelatin
1 c. water
1 10 ½-oz. can condensed cream of chicken or mushroom soup
1 tbsp. lemon juice
Dash of pepper
1 5-oz. can boned chicken or turkey diced or leftovers
½ c. chopped celery

Soften gelatin in 1/2 cup of water. Place over low heat; stir until gelatin dissolves. Remove from heat; blend in soup until smooth. Add remaining water, lemon juice and pepper. Chill to consistency of unbeaten egg white. Fold in chicken, celery, green pepper, pimento and onion. Turn into a 3-cup mold or individual molds; chill until firm. Unmold on serving plate; garnish with salad greens. Yield: 4 servings.

Guadalupe Gonzalez
Alice, Texas

BEANS, BACON AND CHICKEN

4 tbsp. catsup
½ c. mayonnaise
2 tbsp. vinegar
½ tsp. salt
⅛ tsp. pepper
2 c. cooked string beans
4 tomatoes, diced
1 head lettuce, chunks
2 c. cooked cubed chicken
5 slices bacon, fried and crumbled
1 c. grated Swiss cheese

Combine catsup, mayonnaise, vinegar, salt and pepper. Pour over beans, tomatoes, lettuce and chicken. Toss lightly and chill. Garnish with bacon and cheese. Yield: 4 servings.

Mrs. W. M. Sawyer
Hot Springs, Arkansas

CHICKEN SALAD

4 c. cooked cubed chicken
1 c. chopped celery
1 c. grated carrots
1 tbsp. chopped onion
1 c. heavy cream, whipped
1 c. salad dressing
1 6 or 8-oz. can shoestring potatoes

Combine all ingredients except potatoes in a bowl; just before serving, add potatoes. If added too soon, potatoes will loose crispness. Yield: 8 servings.

Mrs. C. A. Jones
Memphis, Tennessee

CHICKEN SALAD

1 stewing hen
Salt
½ c. cubed celery
2 hard-cooked eggs
½ c. diced sweet pickles
¼ c. diced stuffed olives
1 carrot, grated
½ c. salad dressing

Partially cover hen with water. Add 1 tablespoonful salt; boil slowly until tender. Remove meat from bones and dice. Add remaining ingredients; season to taste. Mix lightly, but well. Serve on lettuce leaves. Yield: 6 servings.

Mrs. C. S. Tatum
Cameron, Oklahoma

CHICKEN-CAULIFLOWER SALAD

1 cauliflower
1 onion
1 tbsp. salt
1 tbsp. vinegar
1 cooked chicken, cubed
Celery, cubed
6 hard-cooked eggs
Slivered almonds
Pimento
Salad dressing
Lettuce, shredded

Cut cauliflower and onion in small pieces; cover with boiling water which contains salt and vinegar. Let stand until cool; pour off water. Combine all ingredients. Yield: 12 servings.

Mrs. B. I. Winters
Tallahassee, Florida

CURRIED CHICKEN SALAD

1 tbsp. salt
4 qt. boiling water
1 16-oz. pkg. rice
6 to 7 c. cooked coarsely chopped chicken or turkey
1 c. raw cauliflower, cut into ¼-in. slices
8 oz. creamy French dressing
1 c. mayonnaise or salad dressing
1 tbsp. curry powder
1 tbsp. salt
½ tsp. pepper
½ c. milk
1 c. thin strips green pepper
1 c. diced celery
1 c. thinly sliced red Italian onions
1 head romaine

Add salt to boiling water; add rice. Cook, covered, over low heat until rice is tender. Drain if necessary; place in a bowl. Cool; cover and refrigerate. Chill meat. Toss cold rice with cauliflower and French dressing; cover and refrigerate for at least 2 hours. Combine mayonnaise, curry powder, salt and pepper; slowly stir in milk. Add chicken; toss. Cover and refrigerate for at least 2 hours. Just before serving, combine rice and chicken mixtures; add green pepper, celery and onions. Turn out on romaine leaves. Serve with following curry accompaniments: flaked coconut, canned French-fried onions, salted peanuts, canned pineapple cubes, currant jelly, tomato wedges, chutney, raisins, snipped parsley, crisp bacon bits, chopped hard-cooked eggs, sweet or sour pickles, sliced avocados and grated orange rind. Yield: 12 servings.

Mrs. B. J. Tourville
Ft. McPherson, Georgia

CHICKEN AND ARTICHOKE DELIGHT

2 c. chilled cooked chicken, cut into ¾-in. pieces
1 qt. (lightly packed) torn romaine
1 6-oz. jar marinated artichoke hearts
12 pitted, whole ripe olives
Olive oil
Wine vinegar
Seasoned salt and pepper to taste

Toss chicken with lettuce, undrained artichoke hearts and olives; add oil, vinegar, salt and pepper. Yield: 4 servings.

Mrs. G. T. Olson
Nashville, Tennessee

CHICKEN SALAD MANDALAY

3 c. chopped cooked chicken
½ c. slivered almonds
1 sm. cabbage, shredded
1 green pepper, seeded and shredded
1 whole pimento, chopped
3 stalks celery, diagonally sliced
1 sm. can pineapple chunks, drained
1 c. mayonnaise
3 tbsp. chopped candied ginger
Juice of ½ lemon
1 tsp. monosodium glutamate
1 tsp. salt
2 tbsp. curry powder
Dash of cayenne pepper
Lettuce leaves

(Continued on next page)

Combine chicken, almonds, cabbage, green pepper, pimento, celery and pineapple in wooden salad bowl. Combine remaining ingredients except lettuce; blend well. Mix with chicken mixture. Serve on lettuce-lined plates. Yield: 6 servings.

Mrs. E. B. Jarman
Paducah, Kentucky

CHICKEN-ASPARAGUS SALAD

1 ½ c. cooked diced chicken
1 c. asparagus tips
2 tbsp. minced green pepper
¼ c. shredded cabbage
¾ c. mayonnaise

Thoroughly blend all ingredients; serve. Yield: 6 servings.

Mrs. R. B. Gilbert
Lincolnton, North Carolina

CHICKEN SALAD MOLD

1 pkg. lemon gelatin
2 c. hot chicken stock
½ c. cooked peas
½ c. grated carrots
½ c. chopped celery
1 ½ c. diced cooked chicken

Dissolve lemon gelatin in chicken stock; chill until consistency of egg whites. Fold in remaining ingredients. Pour into mold; chill until set. Serve with mayonnaise on salad greens. Yield: 6 servings.

Mrs. E. C. Bailey
Moulton, Alabama

CHICKEN MAYONNAISE

2 envelopes gelatin
1 c. hot stock
1 tsp. prepared mustard
Salt and pepper
2 c. diced celery
2 tsp. chopped olives
2 tsp. chow-chow
3 sour pickles, chopped
1 can English peas, drained
1 c. pecans
1 pt. salad dressing
1 hen, boiled and cut fine

Dissolve gelatin in hot stock. Cool and add remaining ingredients. Mix well; chill and put in a 9 x 13 x 2-inch Pyrex dish. When set, cut in squares and serve on lettuce leaf.

Mrs. Chloe Thorp
Abilene, Texas

CHICKEN MAYONNAISE

2 envelopes gelatin
½ c. cold water
2 c. hot chicken broth
1 cooked chicken, cut finely
1 c. nuts, chopped
1 No. 2 can English peas, drained
1 pt. salad dressing
2 c. diced celery
3 hard-cooked eggs, sliced
Salt and pepper to taste

Dissolve gelatin in cold water; add hot chicken broth. Let cool, then add other ingredients to gelatin mixture. Let stand overnight in refrigerator. Cut in squares and serve on lettuce leaves. Pimentos, garlic salt, red pepper and paprika may be added to taste.

Essie L. Stanley
Saltillo, Texas

CHICKEN MAYONNAISE

1 3 ½ to 4-lb. hen or 2 fryers
1 c. almonds, toasted and chopped
1 ½ c. chopped celery
1 lge. can small peas
4 hard-cooked eggs, finely chopped
½ pt. mayonnaise
5 tbsp. relish
1 envelope unflavored gelatin
¼ c. cold water
1 c. hot chicken stock

(Continued on next page)

Stew chicken; chop finely. Mix with almonds, celery, peas and liquid, eggs, mayonnaise and relish. Soften gelatin in cold water; dissolve in hot stock. Pour over remaining ingredients; pour into serving dish or mold. Chill until firm. Serve on lettuce leaves. Yield: 10-12 servings.

Mrs. Orrissa P. Simpson
Knoxville, Tennessee

CHICKEN SALAD

1 3-oz. pkg. lemon gelatin
2 c. hot chicken broth
2 tbsp. vinegar
½ tsp. salt
1 c. diced cooked chicken
1 c. cooked peas, drained
½ c. celery
½ c. seedless or Tokay grapes
2 pimentos, cut up

Dissolve gelatin in chicken broth. Add vinegar and salt. Chill until thickened. Add remaining ingredients. Chill in individual serving molds or a large mold. Unmold on lettuce leaf; garnish with mayonnaise, if desired. Yield: 12 servings.

Mrs. J. W. Dyer
Stillwater, Oklahoma

DELUXE CHICKEN SALAD

2 3-oz. pkg. lime gelatin
½ tsp. salt
¼ tsp. onion salt
2 c. boiling water
1 ½ c. cold water
2 tbsp. vinegar
2 c. cooked diced chicken
1 c. cooked green peas
½ c. chopped celery

Dissolve gelatin, salt and onion salt in boiling water. Add cold water and vinegar; chill until very thick. Add chicken, peas and celery; pour into 1 1/2-quart mold. Chill until firm. Yield: 6 servings.

Mildred Gresham
Cadiz, Kentucky

PRESSED CHICKEN SPECIAL

1 ½ c. cold chicken broth
2 envelopes unflavored gelatin
2 c. cooked diced chicken
2 c. cooked peas
½ c. blanched chopped almonds
2 tbsp. pickle relish
1 c. mayonnaise

Skim fat from cold chicken broth; sprinkle gelatin over broth to soften. Dissolve over hot water; cool slightly. Stir in chicken and all remaining ingredients. Pour into 2-quart mold or 10 x 5 x 3-inch loaf pan. Chill until set. Remove from mold; slice and serve on greens. Turkey may be substituted for chicken. Yield: 10 servings.

Mrs. B. P. Peterson
Little Rock, Arkansas

PICNIC CHICKEN SALAD

1 c. mayonnaise or salad dressing
1 ½ tsp. lemon juice
1 ½ tbsp. diced pimento (opt.)
¼ tsp. pepper
1 tsp. salt
1 ½ c. cooked rice
1 ½ c. cooked or canned peas
1 ½ c. cooked chicken, cut in small pieces
1 ½ c. finely diced celery

Mix together mayonnaise, lemon juice, pimento and seasonings. Add remaining ingredients; toss all together lightly. Chill for 10 to 15 minutes before serving. Serve in lettuce cups; garnish with tomato wedges. Yield: 8-10 servings.

Cora Lee Ramsey
McCall, South Carolina

SPECIAL CHICKEN MAYONNAISE

2 envelopes unflavored gelatin
1 c. hot stock
1 hen, cooked and finely chopped
1 tsp. mustard
Salt and pepper
2 c. diced celery
2 tsp. chopped olives
2 tsp. chow chow
3 sour pickles, chopped
1 can English peas, drained
1 c. pecans
1 pt. salad dressing

Dissolve gelatin in 1 cup hot stock. Cool; add all remaining ingredients. Mix well; place in 9 x 13 x 2-inch dish. Chill until firm; cut into squares. Serve on lettuce leaf. Yield: 20 servings.

Mrs. Chloe Thorp
Abilene, Texas

EASY CHICKEN SALAD

1 c. shredded carrots
1 c. diced celery
2 tbsp. minced onion
1 can boned chicken or tuna
½ c. salad dressing
2 tbsp. cream
Pinch of dry mustard (opt.)
1 No.2 ½ can shoestring potatoes

Combine carrots, celery, onion and chicken. Combine dressing, cream and mustard; add to vegetable mixture. Refrigerate; add potatoes before serving. Yield: 6 servings.

Mrs. S. M. Bower
New Orleans, Louisiana

CHICKEN SHOESTRING SALAD

1 ½ c. chopped celery
2 tbsp. chopped onion
2 apples, unpeeled and chopped
2 c. grated carrots
1 chicken, cooked and finely chopped
½ c. mayonnaise
1 tbsp. mustard
1 tbsp. sugar
½ tsp. salt
1 c. light cream
1 can shoestring potatoes

Combine celery, onion, apples, carrots and chicken; chill. Combine remaining ingredients except potatoes. Stir dressing and potatoes into chicken mixture. Yield: 10 servings.

Mrs. Harold Trolson
Baton Rouge, Louisiana

CRUNCHY CHICKEN SALAD

1 c. diced chicken
1 c. shredded carrots
2 tbsp. minced onion
½ c. diced celery
½ c. salad dressing
¼ tsp. prepared mustard
1 tbsp. cream or milk
1 can shoestring potatoes

Combine all ingredients, except potatoes; chill. Add potatoes when ready to serve. Yield: 4 servings.

Mrs. A. C. Hoppe
Valdosta, Georgia

POTATO SALAD A LA CHICKEN AND HAM

2 chicken breasts, cooked
4 slices boiled ham, ½ in. thick
2 tbsp. salad oil
2 tbsp. lemon juice
8 med. boiled potatoes, diced
¼ c. chopped onion
½ c. chopped celery
3 hard-cooked eggs, diced
Mayonnaise

Cut chicken and ham into 36 1/2-inch wide strips each. Pour salad oil and lemon juice over meat strips; toss lightly with a fork. Cover and refrigerate overnight. Combine any meat scraps, potatoes, onion and celery. Two hours before serving, add eggs and enough mayonnaise to moisten. Place 12 individual servings of potato salad in lettuce cups. Top with 2 sticks each of chicken and ham. Garnish with mayonnaise and a stuffed olive. Yield: 12 servings.

Mrs. E. G. Rice
Covington, Kentucky

SHOESTRING POTATO SALAD

1 c. finely cut celery
1 tsp. grated onion
1 c. salad dressing
2 sm. cans boneless chicken
1 c. raw grated carrots
1 can shoestring potatoes

Combine all ingredients except potatoes. Add potatoes at serving time.

Mrs. Juanita Watson
Paris, Tennessee

SHOESTRING SALAD

½ c. salad dressing
Cream
Vinegar (opt.)
Sugar (opt.)
1 c. shredded carrots
¼ c. minced onion
1 c. diced chicken or tuna
1 c. diced celery
1 can shoestring potatoes

Thin salad dressing with cream; add a small amount of vinegar and sugar. Combine all ingredients except potatoes; chill. Add potatoes just before serving. Serve on lettuce leaves if desired. If tuna is used, pour hot water over tuna, then drain. Yield: 5-6 servings.

Mrs. C. R. Pierce
Somerset, Kentucky

STUFFED ARTICHOKE SALAD

2 c. cooked cubed chicken
¼ c. finely diced celery
1 6-oz. can water chestnuts, cut into strips
¾ c. tart mayonnaise
4 artichokes
1 tbsp. salt
2 tbsp. salad oil
½ lemon, cut up
1 clove of garlic
12 stuffed olives
1 tbsp. capers

Mix chicken, celery, water chestnuts and mayonnaise. Toss lightly with fork. Refrigerate for several hours. Cut stems from artichokes. Cook about 1 hour in boiling water with salt, oil, lemon and garlic. Drain; cool and refrigerate for several hours. Carefully spread leafy spines of cooled artichokes from tip so the inner leaves can be removed. Use a spoon to remove the heart. Fill cavity with chilled chicken salad. Garnish with olives and sprinkle with capers. Yield: 4 servings.

Margaret Lopp
Chandler, Arizona

STUFFED TOMATOES IN ASPIC

¾ c. diced celery
1 ¼ c. chopped chicken
⅓ c. mayonnaise
½ tsp. salt
⅛ tsp. pepper
⅛ tsp. celery salt
6 sm. tomatoes
3 c. aspic jelly
1 green pepper, sliced
Stuffed olives, sliced

Mix celery, meat, mayonnaise, salt, pepper and celery salt. Stuff tomatoes with mixture. Chill. Cover bottom of individual molds with aspic. Place green pepper and olives in bottom of mold; let set. Carefully place tomatoes in molds, upside down; add more aspic to cover. Unmold on lettuce leaf; serve with sharp dressing. Yield: 6 servings.

Mrs. R. B. Jones
Louisville, Kentucky

TOMATO STUFFED WITH CHICKEN SALAD

1 c. diced, cooked chicken
⅔ c. diced celery
3 tbsp. diced cucumber
3 tbsp. French dressing
Mayonnaise
8 med. tomatoes

Mix all ingredients except tomatoes, adding enough mayonnaise to moisten. Chill 30 minutes. Wash and peel tomatoes; cut out blossom end. Cut tomatoes from top to within a quarter inch of bottom into 4 or 6 wedge-shaped sections. Salt and chill. Pull wedges apart to resemble petals of a flower; fill with salad which has been mixed with additional mayonnaise. For variety, use crab meat, tuna or salmon for the chicken. Add 1 cup cooked peas. Add 6 stuffed olives, sliced or chopped; also 3 hard-cooked eggs, chopped, may be added. Yield: 8 servings.

Mrs. T. F. Sherman
Richmond, Virginia

TOMATOES STUFFED WITH CORN AND TURKEY SALAD

6 lge. tomatoes
1 ½ c. cooked diced turkey
½ c. sliced black olives
½ c. mayonnaise
1 tbsp. steak sauce
1 c. cooked whole kernel corn
Salt to taste
2 tbsp. butter or margarine

Cut off tomato tops; scoop out pulp, reserving for other use. Turn tomatoes upside down; drain while preparing salad. Mix remaining ingredients, except butter. Fill tomatoes with mixture; dot with butter. Put under broiler about 8 inches from unit; broil until lightly browned on top. Yield: 6 servings.

Patricia Williams
Jacksonville, North Carolina

CRANBERRY-TURKEY MOLD

2 tbsp. unflavored gelatin
4 tbsp. cold water
2 c. hot turkey broth
1 tsp. grated onion
Salt and pepper to taste
1 c. finely diced celery
2 c. diced cold turkey
2 pimentos, chopped
1 ½ c. sugar
¾ c. hot water
4 c. cranberries
1 stick cinnamon
6 cloves
Grated rind of 1 orange
½ c. finely diced apple
½ c. chopped nuts

(Continued on next page)

Soften 1 tablespoonful gelatin in 2 tablespoonfuls cold water; dissolve in hot turkey broth. Add onion and seasoning to taste. Cool until slightly thickened. Fold in celery, turkey and pimentos. Pour into a fancy mold; chill until almost firm. Boil sugar and water; add cranberries, spices and orange rind. Cook until cranberry skins pop. Put through fine sieve. Soften remaining gelatin in remaining cold water; dissolve in hot cranberry mixture. Cool until thickened; add apple and nuts. Pour over firm gelatin in mold. Chill until firm. Unmold onto lettuce and garnish with mayonnaise if desired. Yield: 6-8 servings.

Mrs. J. B. Nash
Laurel, Mississippi

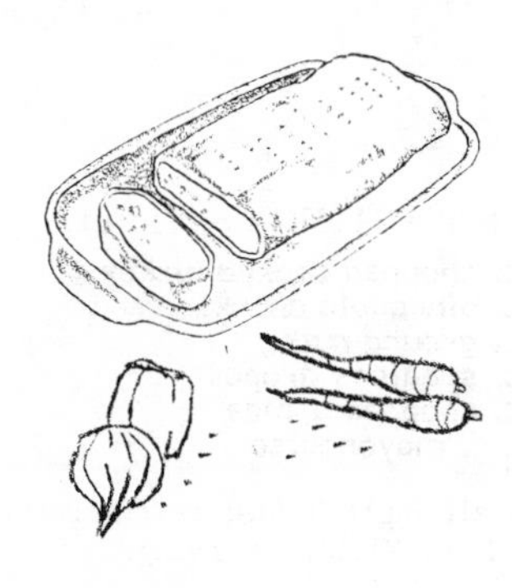

CRANBERRY-TURKEY SALAD LOAF

2 envelopes unflavored gelatin
2 ¼ c. turkey or chicken bouillon or broth
1 tsp. salt
1 tsp. onion juice
2 c. diced turkey
1 c. chopped celery
2 tbsp. chopped green pepper
2 c. cranberries
1 ¼ c. water
¾ c. sugar
1 tbsp. lemon juice
½ tsp. salt
½ c. chopped apple
¼ c. chopped nuts

Soften 1 envelope gelatin in 1/4 cup cold broth. Heat remaining broth; add 1/2 teaspoonful salt, onion juice and softened gelatin. Remove from heat; stir until dissolved. Cool. Chill until mixture begins to thicken; add turkey, 1/2 cup celery and geeen pepper. Turn into loaf pan; chill until firm. Cook cranberries in 1 cup water until skins pop, about 7 minutes; strain through fine sieve. Add sugar; simmer for 5 minutes. Soften remaining gelatin in remaining water; dissolve in hot cranberry juice. Add lemon juice and remaining salt. Cool. Chill until mixture begins to thicken. Fold in remaining celery, apple and nuts. Pour on top of firm turkey layer; chill. Unmold onto crisp greens and serve with mayonnaise, if desired. Yield: 8-10 servings.

Mrs. Esther Sigmund
Laredo, Texas

EXOTIC LUNCHEON SALAD

3 c. mayonnaise
1 tsp. curry powder
2 tbsp. soy sauce
2 qt. coarsely cut cooked turkey or chicken
1 20-oz. can water chestnuts, sliced
2 lb. seedless grapes
2 c. sliced celery
2 to 3 c. slivered almonds
1 lge. can pineapple chunks
2 cans mandarin oranges

Mix mayonnaise with curry powder and soy sauce. Add to remaining ingredients; mix. Chill for several hours. Spoon into nests of lettuce. Sprinkle with additional toasted almonds. Yield: 12 servings.

Mrs. Paul B. MacMichael
Lubbock, Texas

EXOTIC TURKEY SALAD

4 c. coarsely cut cooked turkey
2 5-oz. cans water chestnuts
1 lb. seedless green grapes or 2 sm. cans green grapes
1 c. sliced celery
1 to 1 ½ c. toasted slivered almonds
1 ½ c. mayonnaise
1 tbsp. lemon juice
2 tsp. curry powder
1 tbsp. soy sauce
1 sm. can litchi nuts
2 c. fresh or canned pineapple chunks

Combine turkey, chestnuts, grapes, celery and almonds. Blend mayonnaise with lemon juice, curry powder and soy sauce; toss with turkey mixture. Serve litchi nuts and pineapple chunks separately to be added, as desired. Yield: 6 servings.

Mrs. Royce K. Skow
Bethesda, Maryland

TURKEY, GRAPE AND PECAN SALAD

1 ½ c. diced cooked turkey
1 c. thinly sliced celery
½ c. green seedless grapes
½ c. mayonnaise
Salt and pepper to taste
¼ c. chopped pecans

(Continued on next page)

Combine turkey, celery, grapes and mayonnaise; season to taste with salt and pepper. Add pecans and toss lightly. Serve on greens or avocado halves brushed with lemon juice, if desired. Yield: 6 servings.

Mrs. Robert S. Phillips
Amarillo, Texas

TURKEY-CURRY SALAD

6 c. diced cooked turkey
3 c. thinly sliced celery
3 c. green seedless grapes, halved
4 tbsp. lemon juice
2 tsp. salt
½ tsp. freshly ground black pepper
3 tsp. curry powder
1 c. mayonnaise
2 c. crumbled fried bacon
2 c. chopped peanuts
2 c. chopped hard-cooked eggs
2 c. finely chopped green onions
2 c. raisins
2 c. shredded coconut
2 c. chutney

Combine turkey, celery, grapes, lemon juice, salt, pepper, curry powder and mayonnaise; toss lightly. Serve on lettuce leaves. Pass remaining ingredients in separate bowls. Yield: 12 servings.

Mrs. C. H. West
Monroe, Louisiana

TURKEY SALAD

1 14-lb. turkey
Salt to taste
Celery, cut into large pieces
Onions, quartered
Parsley
1 pt. heavy cream, whipped
1 qt. salad dressing
¼ c. vinegar
¼ c. sugar
2 qt. diced celery
2 qt. seedless green grapes
18 hard-cooked eggs, diced
2 c. toasted slivered almonds

Clean turkey well; season with salt inside and out. Stuff with large pieces of celery, quartered onions and a little parsley. Place in a covered roaster; bake at 325 degrees until meat begins to leave bones. Remove from oven; cool. Cut into desired size pieces. Combine whipped cream, salad dressing, vinegar and sugar. Mix with turkey and remaining ingredients. Chill several hours before serving. Yield: 50 servings.

Mrs. K. T. Stanton
Wilmington, Delaware

TURKEY-GRAPE SALAD

2 c. diced cooked turkey
1 c. sliced celery
¼ c. French dressing
2 c. seedless grapes
Salt and pepper to taste
Lettuce or salad greens
⅓ c. mayonnaise
⅓ c. sour cream
¼ c. toasted slivered almonds

Marinate turkey and celery in French dressing for 1 hour; add grapes. Season to taste with salt and pepper. Arrange on lettuce. Mix mayonnaise with sour cream; add to salad. Garnish with sour cream; add to salad. Garnish with slivered almonds. Yield: 4 servings.

Mrs. Ernest H. Rickard
Newport, South Carolina

TURKEY-FRUIT SALAD

4 c. chopped cooked turkey
1 c. pineapple chunks
1 c. ground nuts
1 c. seedless grapes
1 c. chopped apples
1 ½ c. mayonnaise

Combine all ingredients; refrigerate. Serve on a lettuce leaf. Yield: 6 servings.

Mrs. K. B. Bellworth
Monroe, Louisiana

TURKEY GARLAND SALAD

4 c. cooked diced turkey
1 c. chopped apples
1 c. chopped walnuts
1 c. seedless grapes
1 c. drained pineapple chunks
1 c. mayonnaise
Dash of salt
Watercress
Mandarin oranges

Combine turkey, apples, walnuts, grapes, pineapple, mayonnaise and salt. Mix well. Serve on watercress; garnish with mandarin oranges. Yield: 6 servings.

Mrs. D. H. Handey
Sarasota, Florida

TURKEY SALAD

2 ½ c. diced cold turkey
½ c. diced celery
½ c. Tokay grape halves
½ c. diced apple
½ c. salad dressing
¼ tsp. salt

(Continued on next page)

Toss all ingredients very lightly with a fork. Arrange on crisp salad greens, if desired. Yield: 4-5 servings.

Mrs. Jack W. Dent
Huntington, West Virginia

Lightly toss all ingredients except potato chips and cheese. Pile in a buttered casserole. Cover with potato chips and cheese. Heat in 350 to 450-degree oven until mixture barely bubbles. Yield: 6 servings.

Mrs. J. G. Wooden
Pikeville, Tennessee

HEARTY SUPPER SALAD

1 ½ c. coarsely diced roast turkey or chicken
1 c. sliced celery
2 hard-cooked eggs, coarsely cut
3 or 4 sweet pickles, cut in strips
3 tbsp. pickle vinegar
¾ c. mayonnaise
Salt and pepper to taste

Toss all ingredients together. Add a little grated onion, if desired, and more mayonnaise if needed. Serve edged wtih lettuce. Yield: 4 servings.

Mrs. Jesse Melton
Erie, Tennessee

BAKED TURKEY SALAD

2 c. cooked diced turkey
2 c. diced celery
½ tsp. salt
1 tbsp. minced onion
½ c. chopped nuts
1 c. mayonnaise
2 tbsp. lemon juice
½ c. sliced stuffed olives
½ c. grated cheddar cheese
1 c. finely crushed potato chips

Combine all ingredients except cheese and potato chips. Spoon into buttered 1 1/2-quart casserole. Combine cheese and potato chips; sprinkle over mixture. Bake at 375 degrees for 20 minutes. Serve hot. Yield: 10 servings.

Mrs. H. B. Newton
Hollandale, Mississippi

HOT TURKEY SALAD

2 c. cubed cooked turkey
1 to 2 c. sliced celery
½ c. toasted sliced almonds
2 tbsp. chopped onion
2 tbsp. lemon juice
½ tsp. salt
¾ to 1 c. salad dressing or mayonnaise
1 c. crushed potato chips
½ c. grated American, Swiss or sharp cheese

HOT TURKEY SALAD

1 c. mayonnaise
2 tbsp. lemon juice
½ tsp. salt
½ c. cream of mushroom soup
Dash of onion salt or 2 tbsp. grated onion
2 c. diced cooked turkey
2 c. chopped celery
½ c. slivered almonds
1 c. grated cheese
1 c. crushed potato chips or Chinese noodles

Blend all ingredients except cheese and chips or noodles. Pile into 8 x 12-inch baking dish. Sprinkle cheese and chips on top. Bake at 350 degrees until bubbly. Yield: 8-10 servings.

Mrs. C. C. Lewis
Dover, Delaware

TURKEY-HAM SALAD

2 c. cooked diced turkey
1 ½ c. cooked diced ham
½ c. sour cream
3 tbsp. mayonnaise
Salt and pepper to taste
1 tbsp. capers

Combine all ingredients. Serve chilled on salad greens. Yield: 6 servings.

Mrs. R. P. Wolfe
Winston-Salem, North Carolina

TURKEY SALAD

2 c. cooked finely chopped turkey
¼ c. salad dressing
2 hard-boiled eggs, finely chopped
½ c. chopped sweet pickles
½ c. chopped onion

Combine all ingredients; serve on lettuce leaves.

Mrs. A. R. Cooke
Lawndale, North Carolina

TURKEY-MACARONI SALAD

1 8-oz. pkg. elbow macaroni
1 ½ c. diced cooked turkey
1 c. diced celery
1 sm. onion, minced
½ c. chopped green pepper
¼ c. pickle relish
Mayonnaise
Salt and pepper to taste

Cook macaroni in boiling salted water until tender; drain. Rinse in cold water; cool. Add turkey, celery, onion, pepper, relish and enough mayonnaise to moisten. Season with salt and pepper. Serve with salad greens, if desired. Yield: 6 servings.

Mrs. Reddick Lyons
Jacksonville, Florida

TURKEY SALAD

1 tbsp. unflavored gelatin
¼ c. cold water
½ c. boiling water
1 c. finely cut turkey
½ c. chopped celery
3 tbsp. mayonnaise
¼ c. chopped sweet pickle
¼ tsp. salt
Dash of pepper

Soak gelatin in cold water 5 minutes; add boiling water, stirring until dissolved. Cool. Combine turkey, celery, mayonnaise, pickle, salt and pepper. Pour gelatin over turkey mixture; mix well. Serve on lettuce. Yield: 4 servings.

Mrs. Carlie Brown
Burnsville, Mississippi

TURKEY SALAD DELUXE

1 10-oz. pkg. frozen green peas
1 10-oz. pkg. frozen asparagus
1 c. diced cooked turkey
¾ c. mayonnaise
½ tsp. salt
⅛ tsp. pepper
6 lge. tomatoes

Cook peas and asparagus separately as directed on packages; drain. Mix vegetables; chill. Add turkey, mayonnaise and seasonings; blend. Remove stem ends from tomatoes. Divide each tomato into four parts, cutting through to within 1 inch of bottom; spread petals apart. Fill tomatoes with salad mixture. Serve on crisp lettuce with additional mayonnaise, if desired. Yield: 6 servings.

Mrs. Marvin L. Henning
Hendersonville, North Carolina

TURKEY SALAD

4 c. ground turkey
½ c. chopped English walnuts
½ c. chopped dates
½ c. diced celery
1 apple, unpeeled and diced
1 tbsp. lemon juice
¼ c. cream cheese
¾ c. mayonnaise
1 c. stuffed olives

Combine all ingredients; serve on crisp lettuce. Top each salad with an olive.

Mrs. John T. Askins
Hartsville, South Carolina

TURKEY-TOMATO SALAD

½ pt. sour cream
¼ c. mayonnaise or salad dressing
2 tbsp. lemon juice
1 tsp. sugar
½ tsp. curry powder
½ tsp. paprika
½ tsp. dry mustard
½ tsp. salt
2 c. diced cooked turkey or chicken
2 c. sliced celery
2 hard-cooked eggs, chopped
½ c. sliced almonds, toasted
6 to 8 lge. tomatoes, chilled

Combine sour cream, mayonnaise and seasonings; mix well. Combine turkey or chicken, celery, eggs and almonds; add dressing. Mix lightly to coat ingredients well. Chill for several hours before serving. Cut tomatoes into sixths, three-fourths of the way through. Fill with salad mixture. Yield: 6-8 servings.

Mrs. L. W. Arnold
Columbus, Georgia

WILD RICE AND TURKEY SALAD

½ lb. wild rice
4 c. cooked chopped turkey or chicken
1 c. mayonnaise
½ c. French dressing
Salt to taste
1 5-oz. can sliced almonds
1 c. diced celery
2 cans mandarin oranges
1 No. 2 can pineapple chunks

Cook rice according to package directions. Cool. Add turkey, mayonnaise, French dressing, salt, almonds and celery. Chill. Just before serving, add oranges and pineapple. Serve on lettuce.

Mrs. Betty Nettles
Walterboro, South Carolina

SEAFOOD SALADS

Recipe for Rock Lobster Seashell Salad on Page 334

BAR HARBOR SALAD

4 firm tomatoes
1 7 ½-oz. can fish flakes
2 tbsp. capers
½ c. minced celery
2 tsp. prepared horseradish
½ c. chili sauce
Watercress

Quarter tomatoes without cutting through bottoms; scoop out center pulp. Combine fish flakes, capers, celery, horseradish and chili sauce; chill. Fill tomatoes with fish mixture; serve on watercress. Garnish with pickled onions.

Mrs. Geneva Bryant
Jacksonville, Arkansas

ESCABECHE PERUANO

2 lb. fillet of sole
24 raw shrimp, split in half
1 c. flour
Salt to taste
6 tbsp. butter
¾ c. lime juice
¾ c. orange juice
Pepper to taste
1 head lettuce
20 orange sections
16 grapefruit sections
1 tsp. chopped parsley
1 Spanish onion, chopped fine
6 scallions, chopped fine
1 green pepper, sliced thin
1 c. olive oil

Dip sole and shrimp in flour with salt to taste. Saute very fast in butter so that everything is only half cooked. Arrange all in deep pan; add lime juice and orange juice with salt and pepper. Marinate for 12 hours. Cover bottom of serving plate with lettuce leaves and place fillet of sole on top of lettuce with 6 pieces of split shrimp on each fillet leaving room between each fillet to place orange and grapefruit sections. Sprinkle chopped parsley, onion and scallions over entire dish. Place green pepper slices around edge of platter. Add olive oil to the liquid marinade and pour over the fish. Yield: 8 servings.

Photograph for this recipe on frontispiece.

FISH SALAD

2 c. cubed, flaked or canned fish
3 c. fresh or canned English peas
2 tsp. lemon juice
1 tsp. minced onion
1 ½ tsp. salt
¼ tsp. paprika
1 tsp. Worcestershire sauce
Salad dressing
Crisp lettuce

Place cubed or flaked fish in large bowl which may be rubbed with freshly cut onion. Chill. Add cold vegetables and seasonings to fish. Add salad dressing and toss together lightly with spoon and fork. Serve on crisp lettuce.

Mrs. Mary Andrews
Dothan, Alabama

FLAKED FISH

1 c. chopped cooked fish flakes
1 c. shredded crisp cabbage
½ c. chopped celery
2 tbsp. chopped sweet pickle
½ tsp. salt
⅛ tsp. pepper
2 hard-cooked eggs
2 tbsp. chopped onion
Mayonnaise
Lettuce

Mix all ingredients except lettuce. Serve over chopped lettuce in large salad bowl lined with lettuce leaves. Garnish with tomato wedges and ripe olives, if desired. Yield: 4-5 servings.

Flora T. Loftus
Miami, Florida

HALIBUT SALAD

1 lb. halibut steaks
2 hard-cooked eggs
Celery
Sweet relish
Salt and pepper
Salad dressing
½ lemon

Using cold tap water, bring fish to a boil. Drain. Repeat, using small onion in water. Boil 20 minutes. Drain. Squeeze lemon juice over fish. Remove bones and flake. Add remaining ingredients after fish has cooled.

Mrs. Lawrence Cooper
Florissant, Missouri

HERRING SALAD

2 fillets of herring, cubed
1 ½ c. cubed boiled carrots
2 pickled cucumbers, cubed
2 c. boiled, cubed beet root
1 c. boiled, cubed potatoes
2 apples, cubed
2 hard-cooked eggs

(Continued on next page)

Mix all ingredients except 1 egg; toss lightly. Mash the reserved egg yolk and white separately with a fork; arrange in strips across the top of the salad. Prepare a sharp sauce with fresh or sour whipped cream; season with mustard, vinegar and sugar. Color the sauce red or pink with boiled beet root juice.

Mrs. N. M. Sanders
Raleigh, North Carolina

SILLISALAATI--HERRING SALAD

1 med. salt herring
1 c. diced cooked beets
1 c. diced cooked carrots
1 c. diced cooked potatoes
1 sm. onion, diced

Freshen the herring in cold water. Remove skin and large bones; dice. Toss all ingredients lightly; chill for several hours. No dressing is used, but freshly ground pepper and vinegar may be added to taste. Yield: 4 servings.

Mrs. L. S. Peterson
Little Rock, Arkansas

JELLIED FISH SALAD

3 tbsp. plain gelatin
1 ½ c. cold water
1 can cream of mushroom soup
½ c. (scant) salad dressing
1 ½ c. flaked fish, tuna or salmon
½ c. diced celery
½ c. diced cucumber
2 tbsp. olives, chopped (opt.)
2 tbsp. green pepper, chopped
Lemon juice

Dissolve gelatin in 1/2 cup water. Add remaining water to soup and bring to boiling point. Add gelatin and stir until dissolved. Cool; add remaining ingredients. Pour mixture in loaf pan; slice when set and serve on lettuce.

Karen Green
Stuttgart, Arkansas

MOCK LOBSTER SALAD

1 lge. sliced halibut
1 onion, sliced
1 c. water
1 tsp. salt
1 can tomato soup
Chopped celery
Mayonnaise
Garlic salt
Pepper

Place halibut, onion, water and salt in saucepan; cook for 15 to 20 minutes or until fish is white. Drain, reserving stock; cool. Flake fish; add soup and enough reserved stock to cover fish. Refrigerate overnight. Drain fish through a sieve, allowing fish to drain for 1 hour. Mash fish; add celery, mayonnaise, garlic salt and pepper to taste. Yield: 4-5 servings.

Mrs. S. W. Stokes
Beaumont, Texas

COTTAGE CHEESE SALMON SALAD

1 c. cottage cheese
1 c. red salmon, flaked
½ c. celery, chopped
½ c. sweet pickles, chopped
Salt
Pepper
½ c. mayonnaise

Combine ingredients in order given; chill to improve flavor. Serve with tart salad dressing on lettuce. As a variation, tuna may be substituted for salmon. Yield: 6 servings.

Mrs. O. C. Cobble
Midway, Tennessee

DELUXE SALMON MOLD

1 can tomato soup
½ lb. cheese
2 tbsp. gelatin
½ c. water
3 tbsp. lemon juice
1 c. chopped celery
1 green pepper, chopped
1 sm. onion, chopped
1 tbsp. catsup
1 c. mayonnaise
1 can red salmon

Heat soup; add cheese. Stir until melted. Soften gelatin in cold water; add to soup mixture. Stir until dissolved. Add remaining ingredients. Pour into mold; chill overnight. Yield: 10-12 servings.

Mrs. Kent Rogers
Moore, Oklahoma

FISH SALAD

1 3-oz. pkg. lemon gelatin
½ c. boiling water
½ tsp. salt
2 tsp. vinegar
1 1-lb. can salmon or 2 7-oz. cans tuna
¾ c. chopped celery
½ tsp. grated onion
3 hard-cooked eggs
½ c. mayonnaise
1 sm. can pimento or 1 tbsp. chopped red pepper

Mix gelatin, water, salt and vinegar; cool until slightly thickened. Add remaining ingredients; pour into fish mold or other 1 1/2-quart mold. Chill, preferable overnight. Two cups chopped cooked chicken may be substituted for fish. Yield: 10-12 servings.

Mrs. Herman A. Wietbrock
Memphis, Tennessee

LUNCHEON SALMON SALAD

1 1-lb. can pink salmon, drained
2 hard-cooked eggs, finely chopped
2 tbsp. chopped onion
½ tsp. celery seed
½ c. mayonnaise
Salt and pepper to taste
Sprinkle of parsley flakes
½ c. sour cream
2 tbsp. dry onion soup mix

Combine all ingredients except sour cream and dry onion soup mix; arrange on lettuce leaf. Top with sour cream; sprinkle with onion soup mix. To serve hot, place salmon mixture on 8 bread slices; place under broiler until heated. Top with sour cream and onion soup mixture. Yield: 4 servings.

Mrs. C. M. Gatsby
Dover, Delaware

SALMON-MACARONI SALAD

1 c. macaroni
1 c. shredded salmon
2 tbsp. lemon juice
2 tbsp. finely chopped onion
½ c. chopped pickles
Mayonnaise
Salt and pepper to taste
Paprika

Break macaroni into 2-inch lengths. Cook in boiling salted water until tender; drain. Cover with cold water; drain. Combine macaroni, salmon, lemon juice, onion and pickles. Moisten with mayonnaise; season to taste. Mix lightly with two forks; chill. Serve on bed of crisp shredded cabbage or lettuce. Yield: 6 servings.

Lucille A. Relyea
Annapolis, Maryland

SALMON-MACARONI SALAD

1 8-oz. can salmon, broken into pieces
⅔ c. mayonnaise
1 tsp. grated onion
2 tsp. mustard
Salt to taste
1 ½ c. peas, cooked and drained
⅔ c. elbow macaroni
2 hard-cooked eggs, diced

Drain salmon, reserving liquid. Remove bones from salmon. Beat mayonnaise with onion, mustard, salt and salmon liquid. Combine salmon, peas, macaroni and eggs. Pour dressing over and mix lightly; chill. Serve on salad greens. Yield: 4 servings.

Mrs. Verla Ostberg
Seguin Texas

SALMON SALAD

2 c. salmon
3 hard-cooked eggs, chopped
1 ½ c. cooked macaroni
¼ c. diced pickles
½ c. diced celery
1 sm. onion, diced
¼ c. salad dressing
½ tsp. salt
¼ tsp. pepper

Combine all ingredients in mixing bowl; mix lightly. Pile onto crisp salad greens and garnish with paprika. Yield: 6 servings.

Louise O. Gurley
Monroe, North Carolina

SALMON SALAD

1 can pink salmon
1 ½ c. cooked macaroni
½ c. chopped pimentos
½ c. chopped sweet pickles
½ c. mayonnaise
Salt and pepper to taste

(Continued on next page)

Flake salmon; cook macaroni according to package directions. Drain. Combine all ingredients; chill. Yield: 6 servings.

Mrs. C. T. Walker
Pavo, Georgia

SEAFOOD-MACARONI SALAD

½ lb. elbow or shell macaroni
½ c. mayonnaise
¾ c. milk
½ c. French dressing
½ tsp. salt
½ tsp. pepper
1 c. flaked cooked salmon
1 c. thinly sliced celery
2 onions, thinly sliced
3 hard-cooked eggs, sliced
2 c. shredded cabbage

Cook macaroni as directed on package; drain and chill. Combine mayonnaise, milk, French dressing, salt and pepper; add macaroni and toss. Add salmon, celery, onions, eggs and cabbage. Toss and refrigerate. Yield: 8 servings.

Mrs. Don Hosler
Corinth, Mississippi

SALMON CAESAR SALAD

1 clove of garlic or ¼ tsp. garlic powder
⅔ c. oil
2 qt. torn romaine lettuce
½ tsp. salt
Freshly ground pepper
1 onion, thinly sliced
2 eggs
¼ c. lemon juice
½ c. grated Parmesan cheese
1 ½ c. dry bread croutons
1 1-lb. can salmon, flaked

Combine garlic and oil; let stand at room temperature for 3 hours. Place washed and drained salad greens in a large bowl; dry off excess water with paper towels. Add salt, pepper and onion. Add oil; toss well. Cook eggs for 1 minute. Add eggs and lemon juice to salad; toss well. Sprinkle with cheese. Add croutons and salmon. Toss just until mixed. Serve immediately. Yield: 4 servings.

Mrs. Lawrence Graham
Portsmouth, Virginia

SALMON-COTTAGE CHEESE SALAD

1 pkg. lemon gelatin
1 ½ c. hot water
2 tbsp. lemon juice
1 8-oz. can salmon
½ onion, grated
½ cucumber or ½ c. pickle relish
3 stalks celery
1 doz. stuffed olives
1 c. cottage cheese
½ c. mayonnaise

Dissolve gelatin in hot water. Stir in lemon juice. Chill until gelatin has consistency of unbeaten egg whites. Drain salmon and remove bones and skin. Break in small pieces. Chop onion, cucumber and celery fine; cut olives in thin slices. When gelatin is ready to set, stir in salmon, onion, cucumber, celery, olives and cottage cheese. Add mayonnaise and mix well. Spoon into ring mold; chill until firm. Unmold onto crisp greens and garnish with cucumber slices, radish roses, stuffed eggs or tomato wedges.

Mrs. R. B. Elliott
Livingston, Alabama

SALMON-COTTAGE CHEESE SALAD

1 1-lb. can salmon, drained, boned and flaked
¾ c. chopped sweet pickle
½ c. chopped celery
1 tsp. salt
1 ¼ c. cottage cheese
½ c. Cooked Salad Dressing

Lightly mix all ingredients. Chill. Serve on salad greens. Garnish with radish roses, carrot sticks, sliced hard-boiled eggs or cucumber slices. Yield: 6 servings.

COOKED SALAD DRESSING:

2 tbsp. sugar
1 tsp. salt
1 tsp. mustard
1 ½ tbsp. flour
1 egg, slightly beaten
¾ c. milk
¼ c. vinegar
1 tbsp. butter

Combine sugar, salt, mustard, flour, egg and milk in top of double boiler; blend thoroughly. Stir in vinegar gradually. Cook over hot water, stirring constantly until thick, about 10 minutes. Remove from heat; add butter. Blend. Cool; refrigerate. Yield: 1 1/4 cups.

Bonnie Butts
San Antonio, Texas

SALMON MOLD

1 can salmon
2 pkg. gelatin
4 c. hot water
2 hard-boiled eggs
1 c. celery, chopped
½ c. chopped olives
½ c. sweet pickles
1 onion, chopped fine
½ c. salad dressing
¼ c. catsup
2 drops hot sauce

Flake salmon. Dissolve gelatin in hot water; add salmon and next 5 ingredients. Pour into ring mold. Let set until firm. Unmold on crisp salad greens. Fill center of mold with dressing made with combination of remaining ingredients.

Mrs. Myers Clark
Corbin, Kentucky

SALMON MOUSSE

2 pkg. unflavored gelatin
½ c. cold water
2 c. red salmon
Dash of paprika
Dash of pepper
2 tbsp. vinegar
2 tbsp. catsup
1 c. mayonnaise
2 hard-cooked eggs, chopped
20 sliced stuffed olives
2 tbsp. sweet pickle relish
1 c. heavy cream, whipped

Soften gelatin in cold water; place pan over hot water, stirring until gelatin is dissolved. Remove skin and bones from salmon; flake into small pieces. Combine salmon, seasonings, vinegar, catsup and mayonnaise. Blend in eggs, olives, relish and dissolved gelatin. Chill until partially set; fold in whipped cream. Pour into a 1-quart fish mold which has been oiled. Chill overnight. Unmold onto lettuce greens; garnish with tomato slices and green pepper. Yield: 8 servings.

Mrs. M. J. Blount
Athens, Georgia

SALMON AND RICE LOAF

½ envelope unflavored gelatin
¼ c. cold water
¾ c. milk, heated
1 tsp. salt
½ tsp. pepper
1 can salmon
1 c. cooked rice
1 tbsp. melted butter

Soak gelatin in cold water for 10 minutes; dissolve by adding hot milk. Add remaining ingredients. Pour into a wet mold; chill until set. Serve cold on lettuce as a salad or with a hot tomato sauce in place of meat at dinner.

Mrs. Minnie Allen
Bay St. Louis, Mississippi

SALMON SALAD

2 c. salmon, flaked
½ c. diced celery
2 tbsp. diced sweet pickle
2 c. corn flakes
¾ c. mayonnaise
2 tbsp. lemon juice

Combine salmon, celery, pickle and corn flakes. Blend mayonnaise and lemon juice; mix with salmon mixture. Serve immediately. Yield: 6 servings.

Mrs. Paul Kruse
Orlando, Florida

SALMON SALAD

¼ c. cold water
1 envelope unflavored gelatin
¾ c. hot water
¾ c. mayonnaise
1 c. red salmon
½ c. celery, chopped fine
½ c. green peppers, chopped fine
2 tbsp. olives, sliced
½ tsp. salt
¼ tbsp. mild vinegar

Put cold water in bowl. Sprinkle in gelatin; stir in hot water. Let stand until congealing begins. Add mayonnaise. Add remaining ingredients. Put in mold; set in refrigerator. Serve on lettuce. Top with additional mayonnaise and whole olives.

Mrs. S. M. Harris
Charlottesville, Virginia

SALMON SALAD LOAF

1 pkg. lemon gelatin
3 tbsp. vinegar
½ c. mayonnaise or salad dressing
¼ tsp. salt
1 1-lb. can salmon, drained and coarsely flaked
1 c. chopped celery
¼ c. chopped parsley
¼ c. chopped onion

(Continued on next page)

Dissolve gelatin in 1 cup hot water. Add 1/2 cup cold water, vinegar, mayonnaise and salt. Beat well. Chill until partially set; beat until fluffy. Fold in remaining ingredients. Pour into 8 1/2 x 4 1/2 x 2 1/2-inch loaf pan. Chill until set. Unmold onto crisp greens. Yield: 6 servings.

Mrs. Annette Lons
Savannah, Georgia

SALMON SUPREME

LIME GELATIN LAYER:

- 2 pkg. lime gelatin
- ¾ c. boiling water
- 3 c. ice cubes and water
- 1 tbsp. lemon juice
- ½ tsp. salt
- ½ c. chopped sweet pickles or relish

Dissolve gelatin in hot water. Add ice cubes and water, lemon juice and salt; chill until thickened. Add sweet pickles. Pour into mold which has been oiled and rinsed in cold water. Chill until firm.

SALMON LAYER:

- 1 tbsp. unflavored gelatin
- 2 tbsp. cold water
- 1 c. mayonnaise
- ½ c. chopped sweet pickles or relish
- 1 ¾ c. red salmon
- 1 tsp. salt
- 1 tsp. grated onion
- ½ c. sliced celery
- ¼ c. finely chopped green pepper
- 1 ½ tbsp. vinegar

Soak gelatin in cold water; dissolve over hot water in double boiler. Mix with mayonnaise. Add all remaining ingredients. Pour carefully onto gelatin layer. Each layer should be at least 1-inch thick. Chill several hours until firm. Invert to unmold. Garnish with avocado slices and deviled eggs. Shrimp may be substituted for salmon.

Gladys R. Olson
Ozark, Alabama

SOUTHERN SALMON SALAD

- 1 sliced banana
- ¼ c. diced pineapple
- ¾ c. flaked salmon
- ¼ c. finely chopped celery
- 1 tbsp. finely chopped pickles
- ¼ tsp. salt
- 1 tbsp. mayonnaise
- 1 tsp. prepared mustard

Mix banana slices and pineapple lightly; add salmon, celery, pickles and salt. Mix together mayonnaise and mustard; add to salmon mixture. Toss together lightly. Serve on crisp lettuce or other salad greens. Garnish with radish roses, sliced banana and parsley. Yield: 2 servings.

Mrs. Mary P. Murray
De Funiak Springs, Florida

COLD SALMON WITH CUCUMBER DRESSING

- 2 med. cucumbers
- ½ c. heavy cream
- ¼ c. mayonnaise
- 1 tsp. salt
- 2 tbsp. vinegar
- Dash of Tabasco sauce
- 1 can salmon

Grate cucumbers; drain for 15 minutes. Whip cream; fold in mayonnaise, salt, vinegar, Tabasco sauce and cucumbers. Chill salmon overnight; drain and remove skin and bones. Arrange on lettuce beds and garnish with lemon, if desired. Serve with cucumber dressing. Yield: 6 servings.

Mrs. G. B. Sidney
Miami, Florida

GOOD SALAD

- 1 c. peas, drained
- 1 head cabbage, cut fine
- ½ c. salmon
- 1 med. cucumber, cut fine
- 1 stalk celery, cut fine

Combine all ingredients and mix with salad dressing 1 hour before serving. Chill in refrigerator.

Mrs. Juanita Watson
Paris, Tennessee

SALMON-CUCUMBER SALAD

- 1 1-lb. can salmon
- 1 med. cucumber, pared and diced
- 4 stalks celery, chopped
- ¼ c. mayonnaise
- 2 tbsp. lemon juice
- 1 to 2 tbsp. capers
- 1 tbsp. grated onion
- 1 tsp. monosodium glutamate
- Dash of pepper

(Continued on next page)

Mix all ingredients well; chill thoroughly. To serve, pile lightly on serving platter. Garnish with melon balls and watercress.

CREAMY CELERY SEED DRESSING:

½ c. sugar
1 tsp. dry mustard
1 tsp. salt
¼ tsp. monosodium glutamate
4 ½ tbsp. cider vinegar
1 tsp. grated onion
1 c. salad oil
1 tbsp. celery seed

Mix sugar, dry mustard, salt and monosodium glutamate; stir in 2 tablespoons cider vinegar and onion. Gradually add salad oil, beating constantly. Beat until thick and light. Beat in remaining vinegar and celery seed. Serve over salad. Yield: 4-6 servings.

Eugenia Aull
Richmond, Virginia

SALMON-POTATO SALAD

4 c. sliced cooked potato
1 small onion, minced
Salt and pepper to taste
¼ c. French dressing
1 c. sliced celery
2 tbsp. chopped parsley
¾ c. mayonnaise
1 1-lb. can salmon, drained and chunked
½ tsp. paprika

Put potato and onion in bowl. Sprinkle with salt and pepper. Mix lightly with French dressing and chill 1 hour or longer. Toss lightly with next four ingredients; season. Sprinkle with paprika. Yield: 6 servings.

Mrs. J. L. Stringfield
Cottageville, South Carolina

SALMON SALAD

1 can salmon, drained
3 c. cooked Irish potatoes
2 boiled eggs
Sweet pickles, cut in small pieces
1 small onion (opt.)
1 sm. jar mayonnaise

Mix together first 6 ingredients; add mayonnaise. Stir.

Ruby Harkness
Garden City, Alabama

SALMON SALAD

2 tbsp. gelatin
¼ c. cold water
2 c. boiling water
2 c. shredded red salmon
1 ¼ c. chopped celery
1 c. finely shredded cabbage
⅔ c. chopped sweet pickle
1 ½ tsp. salt
1 tbsp. lemon juice
1 tbsp. vinegar
Mayonnaise

Soften gelatin in cold water. Add hot water; stir until dissolved. Cool until partially set. Add salmon, vegetables, pickle, salt, lemon juice and vinegar. Mix lightly with 2 forks. Pour into mold. Chill until firm. Serve on crisp lettuce with mayonnaise. Garnish with paprika.

Mrs. Charles Lewis
Marlow, Oklahoma

SALMON SALAD MOLD

2 3-oz. pkg. seasoned tomato gelatin
2 c. boiling water
1 c. cold water
3 tbsp. lemon juice
1 1-lb. pink salmon, drained and flaked
½ c. sour cream
¼ c. mayonnaise
2 tbsp. minced onion
1 ½ tsp. dill weed

Dissolve gelatin in boiling water. Add cold water and lemon juice. Chill until very thick. Mix salmon with sour cream, mayonnaise, onion and dill. Blend into thickened gelatin. Pour into 1 1/2-quart ring mold or fish shaped mold. Chill until firm, at least 3 hours. Serve with crisp lettuce. Yield: 6-8 servings.

Mrs. Lillian Herman
Bay City, Texas

SALMON SALAD PLATTER

1 lge. can red salmon
¼ c. minced onion
½ c. diced celery
¼ c. French dressing
Salad greens
3 hard-cooked eggs
3 tomatoes
1 sm. cucumber
Paprika

Remove bones and skin from fish. Combine fish, onion and celery with dressing. Chill for an hour. When ready to serve, arrange on bed of greens. Garnish with eggs, tomatoes, cucumber and paprika.

Alice Cox
Vanceburg, Kentucky

SALMON-VEGETABLE SALAD

1 7 ¾-oz. can salmon, drained and flaked
1 c. English peas
½ c. grated carrot
⅓ c. chopped celery
¼ c. chopped sweet pickle
6 ripe olives, chopped
1 tsp. lemon juice
1 tsp. French dressing
¼ c. mayonnaise

Toss salmon and vegetables together lightly with a combination of lemon juice and French dressing. Chill for at least 1 hour. Add mayonnaise. Serve on crisp greens. Yield: 3-4 servings.

Mrs. L. D. Grimes
Maud, Texas

SARDINE SALAD

4 med. sardines
2 hard-cooked eggs, quartered
Lettuce leaves
½ c. mayonnaise

Drain sardines; cut each into 4 pieces. Place sardines and eggs on lettuce; top with mayonnaise. Yield: 4 servings.

Mrs. Hollis Corbin
Birmingham, Alabama

FAVORITE TUNA SALAD

¾ c. mayonnaise
¼ c. cider vinegar
1 tbsp. grated onion
½ tsp. salt
½ tsp. pepper
2 cans drained tuna
½ c. sliced celery
¼ c. chopped green pepper
¼ c. diced sweet gherkins
Crisp salad greens
1 tomato, sliced
2 hard-cooked eggs, cut into wedges
Chopped parsley

In medium bowl, combine mayonnaise, vinegar, onion, salt and pepper; mix well. Add tuna, celery, green pepper and gherkins; toss until well blended. Refrigerate, covered, about 2 hours to blend flavors. At serving time, line serving platter with salad greens; mound salad in center. Garnish with tomato slices, egg wedges and parsley. Yield: 6 servings.

Kathy Mashburn
Powhatan, Arkansas

CHICKEN SOUP SALAD

1 pkg. lemon gelatin
½ c. hot water
1 10 ½-oz. can cream of chicken soup
1 6 ½-oz. can tuna
½ c. diced celery
½ c. chopped walnuts
½ c. salad dressing
2 tbsp. chopped pimento

Dissolve gelatin in hot water; cool. Add remaining ingredients; mix well. Refrigerate until set. Yield: 6 servings.

JoAnn R. Merrill
Suffolk, Virginia

FISHERMAN'S SALAD AND DRESSING

1 head lettuce, broken
1 head romaine, broken
1 cucumber, sliced
1 sm. onion, sliced
3 stalks celery, sliced
2 7-oz. cans tuna
½ c. sour cream
¼ c. mayonnaise
2 tbsp. chili sauce
1 tsp. Worcestershire sauce
2 tbsp. horseradish, drained
1 tbsp. lemon juice
1 tsp. curry powder (opt.)
2 tbsp. chopped ripe olives
1 tbsp. chopped parsley

Toss vegetables lightly. Cover and chill until ready to serve; add tuna. Mix remaining ingredients; serve with salad. Yield: 10 servings.

Mona McGee
Slick, Oklahoma

FISH SALAD

1 c. lettuce or cabbage, shredded
1 c. finely cut radishes
1 c. finely cut celery
1 c. finely cut cooked fish
4 eggs, beaten
¾ c. sugar
1 tbsp. butter
Mustard
Salt
Cayenne
½ c. vinegar

(Continued on next page)

Combine first 4 ingredients. Cook remaining ingredients until thickened. Add dressing to salad, tossing thoroughly.

Eva T. Wightman
Romney, West Virginia

DEEP SEA SALAD RING

- 2 7-oz. cans tuna
- 2 hard-cooked eggs, chopped
- ½ c. chopped stuffed olives
- ½ c. finely chopped celery
- ½ tbsp. minced onion
- 1 tbsp. unflavored gelatin
- ¼ c. cold water
- 2 c. mayonnaise
- ¼ tsp. liquid hot pepper seasoning
- Crisp lettuce
- Tomatoes
- Avocados

Drain tuna and combine with eggs, olives, celery and onion. Sprinkle gelatin over cold water; let soften 5 minutes. Place softened gelatin in pan of boiling water; stir until dissolved. Stir gelatin into mayonnaise. Add tuna mixture and hot pepper seasoning. Pour into 1 1/2-quart ring mold. Refrigerate until firm. Unmold on platter, garnish with lettuce. Cut tomatoes into wedges and slice avocados; place in center of ring and around platter. Yield: 6 servings.

Diane Jones
Grannis, Arkansas

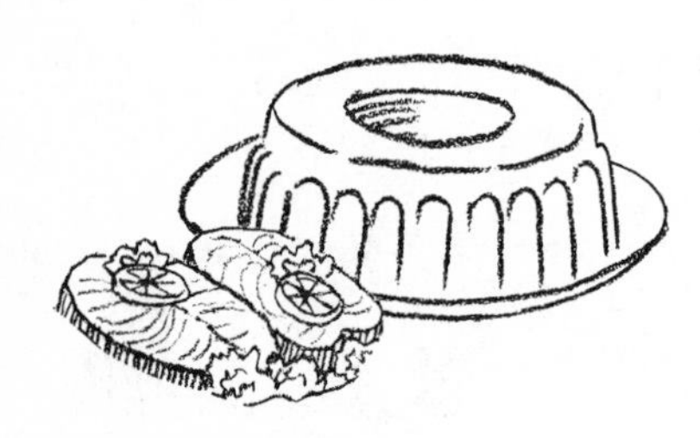

RED, WHITE AND BLUE SALAD

- 1 can tuna
- 2 hard-boiled eggs
- ½ green sweet pepper, cut up fine
- 1 lge. Delicious apple, washed and cut fine
- 1 c. grapes or raisins
- 1 tsp. salt
- 1 tsp. pepper
- ½ c. mayonnaise

Mix all ingredients thoroughly; serve.

Madine Maddux Johnson
Brownwood, Texas

TOSSED GUACAMOLE SALAD

- ½ med. head lettuce
- 2 tomatoes, cut in wedges
- ½ c. sliced, pitted ripe olives
- ¼ c. chopped green onions
- 1 6 ½ to 9 ¼-oz. can tuna, drained
- 1 c. corn chips
- 1 recipe Avocado Dressing
- ½ c. shredded cheddar cheese

Break lettuce into bowl. Add tomatoes, olives and onions. Just before serving, add tuna and corn chips; toss lightly with Avocado Dressing and garnish with shredded cheese and additional olives.

AVOCADO DRESSING:

- ½ c. mashed ripe avocado
- ½ c. sour cream
- 1 clove garlic, crushed, or garlic salt
- ½ tsp. chili powder
- 1 tbsp. lemon juice
- ⅓ c. salad oil
- ½ tsp. sugar
- ¼ tsp. salt
- ¼ tsp. Tabasco sauce

Combine all ingredients. Beat with electric beater or blender. Yield: 4-6 servings.

Mrs. Harold Dalbom
Clovis, New Mexico

TROPICAL TUNA SALAD

- 1 tbsp. mayonnaise
- 1 tsp. salt
- 1 tbsp. prepared mustard
- 1 ½ c. flaked tuna
- ½ c. diced celery
- ½ c. diced pineapple
- 1 c. sliced bananas
- 2 tbsp. chopped sweet pickles
- 1 head crisp lettuce, shredded or lettuce cups

Mix mayonnaise salt and mustard; add remaining ingredients. Blend lightly. Serve on beds of shredded lettuce or in lettuce cups. Yield: 4-6 servings.

Mrs. R. T. Norland
Charlotte, North Carolina

TUNA SALAD

- 1 c. canned tuna
- Celery hearts, minced
- 1 lge. sweet white onion, minced
- 1 lge. dill pickle, minced
- ¾ c. apple, minced
- ¼ c. mayonnaise

(Continued on next page)

Mash tuna; add other ingredients. Salt to taste and mix well. Serve on lettuce with crackers and potato chips or on white or whole wheat bread. Garnish with dill pickle slices. Yield: 3 servings.

Lucy Quillin
Memphis, Tennessee

TUNA-FRUIT SALAD

1 6 ½ or 7-oz. can white tuna
½ c. drained pineapple chunks
½ c. seedless grapes
½ c. diced celery
¼ c. chopped pecans
3 tbsp. thinly sliced stuffed olives
⅓ c. salad dressing or mayonnaise

Break tuna into chunks; combine with remaining ingredients. Mix lightly. Serve on lettuce and garnish with lemon wedges and whole pecans if desired. Yield: 4-5 servings.

Mrs. N. P. Morris
Nashville, Tennessee

TUNA SALAD

1 can tuna
1 med. apple
1 c. celery, cut in small pieces or shredded cabbage
½ c. chopped nuts
1 tsp. pimento
French dressing
Mayonnaise

Mix first 6 ingredients together and marinate with French dressing. Chill. Arrange on bed of shredded lettuce or cabbage; serve with mayonnaise and garnish with sliced stuffed olives. Salmon may be substituted for tuna.

Mrs. Mary Alice Walters
Bonnieville, Kentucky

TUNA SALAD WAIKIKI

2 7-oz. cans solid pack tuna
1 c. diagonally sliced celery
2 tbsp. diced pimento
2 tbsp. chopped crystalized ginger
¾ c. slivered toasted almonds
¼ c. sour cream
¼ c. mayonnaise
1 tbsp. white wine vinegar
1 tsp. seasoning salt or monosodium glutamate
6 to 8 slices pineapple

Drain tuna; separate into large pieces. Combine tuna with celery, pimento, ginger and almonds. Mix sour cream, mayonnaise, vinegar and seasoning salt; combine thoroughly with tuna mixture. Chill. Heap tuna mixture on pineapple slices. Garnish with ripe olives, radishes or maraschino cherries, if desired.

Mrs. H. B. Wilkerson
Dover, Delaware

JELLIED TUNA SALAD

1 tbsp. unflavored gelatin
¼ c. cold water
½ tsp. salt
½ tsp. celery seed
¼ c. vinegar
¼ c. water
2 eggs, beaten
2 c. flaked canned tuna or other canned or cooked fish

Sprinkle gelatin in cold water and let soak a few minutes. Add seasonings, vinegar and water to eggs. Cook over boiling water until thickened, stirring constantly. Add gelatin and stir until dissolved. Add fish and mix thoroughly. Pour into individual molds or large ring mold; chill. Yield: 4 servings.

Charlie Wayne Lucas
Terrell, Texas

LEMON GELATIN SEAFOOD SALAD

2 pkg. lemon gelatin
2 ½ c. hot water
1 tbsp. grated onion
1 tsp. salt
1 tbsp. lemon juice or vinegar
½ c. chopped green pepper or pickles
3 hard-cooked eggs, cubed
1 c. grated cheese
1 c. chopped nuts
½ lb. tuna, crab meat, shrimp or chicken, diced
1 sm. bottle stuffed olives, sliced
2 c. chopped celery
½ c. salad dressing
1 c. heavy cream, whipped

Dissolve gelatin in hot water. Add onion, salt and lemon juice; let set until syrupy. Add remaining ingredients. Pour into a mold, rectangular pan or individual molds. Chill until firm. Serve on lettuce leaf. Yield: 16 servings.

Bernice Stevenson
Columbus, Georgia

MACARONI SALAD

2 c. uncooked shell macaroni
1 c. Tokay grapes, halved and seeded
1 c. diced celery
1 sm. onion, finely chopped
1 6 ½-oz. can chunk tuna
½ c. mayonnaise
3 tbsp. sugar

Cook macaroni in salted water until tender; rinse and cool. Add grapes, celery, onion and tuna to macaroni. Mix mayonnaise and sugar; pour over macaroni. Mix well. Drained fruit cocktail may be substituted for grapes. Yield: 10-12 servings.

Mrs. James Varvel
Arkadelphia, Arkansas

MACARONI-TUNA SALAD

3 c. cooked macaroni
4 gherkins, diced
4 hard-cooked eggs, diced
1 sm. can tuna fish
1 sm. onion, diced
Salt and pepper to taste
1 c. salad dressing
¼ c. mustard
2 tbsp. catsup
Paprika

Combine macaroni, gherkins, eggs, tuna fish and onion. Add salt and pepper to taste. Combine salad dressing, mustard and catsup until thoroughly mixed. Pour over salad; mix well. Put salad into clean bowl and top with paprika. Sliced hard-cooked egg may also be arranged on top. Yield: 6 servings.

Mrs. Estelle Czoski
Yazoo City, Mississippi

TOASTED TUNA-CURRY-MACARONI SALAD

1 8-oz. pkg. elbow macaroni
3 qt. boiling water
2 6 ½-oz. cans tuna, flaked
1 c. cooked peas
½ c. sliced ripe olives
½ c. toasted almonds
½ c. chopped celery
½ c. coconut, toasted
1 c. mayonnaise
1 ½ tsp. curry powder
Salt and pepper to taste

Cook macaroni in boiling water with 1 tablespoonful salt until tender. Drain; rinse with cold water. Drain and chill. Combine tuna, macaroni and remaining ingredients. Mix lightly, but thoroughly. Chill well. Yield: 6-8 servings.

Mrs. Francis Plapp
Sanford, Florida

TUNA-MACARONI-PEA SALAD

1 7-oz. can tuna
3 to 4 c. cooked shell macaroni
1 No. 2 can peas, drained
5 hard-cooked eggs
½ c. celery
1 med. onion, chopped
Salt to taste
Mayonnaise

Combine all ingredients; add enough mayonnaise to bind. May be served hot or cold. Yield: 6 servings.

Mrs. Donald Brown
Monroeville, Alabama

TUNA-MACARONI SALAD

1 sm. pkg. elbow macaroni, cooked
½ c. mayonnaise or salad dressing
½ c. sour cream
½ tsp. celery seed
½ tsp. onion salt
1 7-oz. can tuna, drained
1 17-oz. can peas, drained
¾ c. diced mild cheddar cheese
2 tbsp. minced green pepper
1 tbsp. diced pimento

Cook macaroni according to directions on package. Drain and chill. Stir in mayonnaise or salad dressing blended with sour cream and seasonings. Gently stir in remaining ingredients. Chill thoroughly. Yield: 6-8 servings.

Mrs. Hulon Adams
Newborn, Georgia

TUNA SALAD

1 can tuna, minced
1 c. finely chopped celery
3 hard-cooked eggs, chopped
1 box elbow macaroni, cooked
Salt and pepper to taste
Dash of garlic salt
Mayonnaise

(Continued on next page)

Combine all ingredients except mayonnaise. Add enough mayonnaise to moisten. Yield: 6 servings.

Mrs. Ollie Hutton
San Antonio, Texas

MOCK CHICKEN SALAD

1 6-oz. pkg. lemon gelatin
3 c. boiling water
⅔ c. lemon juice
1 ¼ tsp. salt
4 7-oz. cans tuna, drained and flaked
3 ½ c. diced celery
½ c. sweet pickle relish, well drained
2 tbsp. minced pimento
4 hard-cooked eggs, diced
1 c. salad dressing

Dissolve gelatin in boiling water; add lemon juice and salt. Chill until partially thickened. Fold in remaining ingredients. Chill until firm. Serve on crisp lettuce. Yield: 16-20 servings.

Mrs. Elladean Ray
Gay, West Virginia

MOLDED EGG AND TUNA SALAD

1 envelope sour cream sauce mix
½ c. milk
2 tsp. prepared mustard
½ tsp. onion salt
1 tbsp. unflavored gelatin
¼ c. cold water
2 tbsp. mayonnaise
3 hard-cooked eggs
1 7-oz. can tuna, flaked
½ c. finely diced celery
2 tbsp. chopped sweet pickle
Pimento
Crisp lettuce

Empty sour cream sauce mix into bowl. Add milk slowly, stirring with fork until smooth. Blend in mustard and onion salt. Let stand 10 minutes. Soften gelatin in water; let stand 5 minutes. Dissolve over hot water or low heat. To sour cream, add mayonnaise, dissolved gelatin and 2 diced eggs. Add flaked tuna, celery and sweet pickle to sour cream mixture; prepare custard cups by circling bottom with strips of pimento. Add 1 tablespoon additional chopped pimento to tuna-egg mixture. Spoon mixture into cups; chill. Unmold on lettuce leaf and garnish with mayonnaise. Cut reserved egg in sections and place on top of each mold.

Mrs. Rudell Harville
Alamo, Georgia

MOLDED TUNA LOAF

3 7-oz. can grated tuna
4 hard-cooked eggs, chopped
¼ c. stuffed olives, chopped
2 tbsp. minced onion
1 c. diced celery
2 tbsp. gelatin
½ c. cold water
2 c. mayonnaise
Parsley
Celery curls

Combine first 5 ingredients. Sprinkle gelatin on cold water, using small bowl. Set bowl over hot water; stir gelatin until dissolved. Stir into mayonnaise. Add to tuna mixture and blend well. Turn into 9 x 5 x 3-inch loaf pan. Chill. Unmold and garnish with parsley and celery curls. Yield: 10 servings.

Mrs. Betty Temple
Marietta, Georgia

MOLDED TUNA SALAD

1 tbsp. gelatin
2 tbsp. cold water
2 c. tuna
½ c. chopped celery
¼ c. pickle relish
½ tsp. salt
⅛ tsp. paprika
½ c. mayonnaise dressing

Soak gelatin in cold water 5 minutes and dissolve over boiling water; flake tuna. Add tuna, celery, relish, salt, paprika and mayonnaise. Add dissolved gelatin; mix well and put into individual molds which have been dipped in cold water. Place in refrigerator until ready to serve. Unmold in nests of lettuce and garnish with celery curls and rings of green pepper.

Mrs. Wilbur Jenkins
Sadieville, Kentucky

MOLDED TUNA SALAD

2 tbsp. unflavored gelatin
½ c. cold water
1 can cream of chicken soup
¼ c. lemon juice
1 tbsp. prepared mustard
1 tsp. salt
1 c. mayonnaise
½ c. grated cucumber
¼ c. chopped bell pepper
1 c. coarsely chopped celery
2 6 ½-oz. cans tuna, drained and flaked

(Continued on next page)

Soften gelatin in cold water. Heat soup until boiling. Remove from heat and add softened gelatin, stirring to dissolve. Blend in lemon juice, mustard and salt. Chill until partially set. Add mayonnaise; fold in remaining ingredients. Pour into oiled 8 1/2 x 4 1/2 x 2 1/2-inch loaf pan or into individual molds and chill until firm. Unmold and serve on bed of salad greens. Yield: 8 servings.

Hazel Bussey
Alice, Texas

MOLDED TUNA SALAD

1 pkg. lime gelatin
2 c. hot water
1 can tuna, flaked
1 tsp. lemon juice
½ tsp. salt
¼ tsp. paprika
1 c. chopped celery
2 hard-cooked eggs, chopped
1 green pepper, diced
1 sm. onion, diced
1 cucumber, chopped
1 sprig parsley

Dissolve gelatin in hot water. Chill until slightly thickened. Combine tuna, lemon juice, salt and paprika. Add tuna mixture, celery, eggs, green pepper, onion and cucumber to gelatin. Pour into a mold; chill until firm. Garnish with parsley. Yield: 8 servings.

Mrs. William H. Golson
Williamsburg, Virginia

MOLDED TUNA SALAD

1 sm. pkg. lemon gelatin
½ c. boiling water
1 can tuna, drained
1 can chicken gumbo soup
2 tbsp. chopped green pepper
1 tbsp. chopped onion
2 tbsp. chopped celery
½ c. whipped cream
½ c. mayonnaise

Dissolve gelatin in boiling water. Fold in remaining ingredients. Pour into greased molds; chill until set. Serve in lettuce cups. Yield: 8 servings.

Patricia Beesley
Columbus, Georgia

RICE AND TUNA SALAD RING

3 hard-boiled eggs
2 ½ c. cooked rice, cooled
1 6-oz. can tuna, grated
½ c. chopped green peppers
¼ c. diced pimento
⅓ c. diced celery
2 tbsp. chopped parsley
2 tsp. minced onion
1 8-oz. pkg. cream cheese, room temperature
½ c. mayonnaise
3 tbsp. catsup
1 tsp. lemon juice
Salt and pepper to taste

Shell eggs while hot; mash. Cool. Mix rice, tuna, green pepper, pimento, celery, parsley and onion. Mash cream cheese and stir in mayonnaise, catsup, lemon juice and eggs. Combine with rice mixture. Season to taste with salt and pepper. Put in ring mold; chill for at least 4 hours. Loosen around edge with spatula and turn out on lettuce leaves. Yield: 8 servings.

Clara Habetz
Rayne, Louisiana

SEAFOOD-GELATIN SALAD MOLD

2 tbsp. unflavored gelatin
½ c. cold water
¾ c. mayonnaise
Salt and pepper
1 tbsp. lemon juice
1 c. flaked tuna, salmon or shrimp
1 c. finely chopped celery
½ c. chopped olives
3 tbsp. chopped pimento
½ c. heavy cream, whipped

Soak gelatin in cold water; dissolve over hot water. Cool. Add mayonnaise, salt, pepper and lemon juice. Stir well and chill until thickened. Add tuna, celery, olives and pimento. Fold in whipped cream. Grease mold with salad dressing and fill with mixture. Refrigerate until ready to serve. Double recipe for large fish mold. Decorate fish with sliced ripe olives and strips of pimento to resemble eyes, fins and tail.

Alice D. Griffin
Lamesa, Texas

ST. PATRICK'S SALAD

1 pkg. lime gelatin
1 ¾ c. boiling water
Salt to taste
3 tbsp. vinegar
1 c. chopped celery
½ c. chopped cucumber
¼ c. chopped olives
1 c. flaked tuna or chicken
¾ c. mayonnaise

(Continued on next page)

Dissolve gelatin in boiling water; add salt, vinegar, celery, cucumber and olives. Pour half of mixture into mold; chill until firm. Add tuna and mayonnaise to remaining mixture. Pour on first layer; chill. Unmold on lettuce. Serve with mayonnaise sprinkled with paprika. Yield: 8 servings.

Mrs. W. R. King
Fayette, Alabama

TUNA-ASPIC MOLD

1 envelope unflavored gelatin
2 ½ c. cold water
1 tsp. prepared mustard
1 7-oz. can tuna
1 c. chopped celery
2 tbsp. lemon juice
¼ tsp. salt
¼ tsp. paprika
½ c. salad dressing

Soften gelatin in 1/4 cup cold water. Add remaining water and all ingredients. Chill until set.

TOMATO ASPIC:

1 pkg. lemon gelatin
2 c. tomato juice, heated
Cloves
Onion
Salt to taste
Celery salt

Dissolve gelatin in tomato juice; add remaining ingredients. Cool; pour over tuna salad. Chill until firm.

Mrs. Helen E. Buss
Charleston, South Carolina

TUNA SALAD

4 6 ½-oz. cans tuna, chunk-style
1 c. chopped celery
3 hard-cooked eggs, chopped
½ c. pecans, broken
Mayonnaise to blend
Salt and pepper to taste
8 sweet pickles, sliced

Combine ingredients; chill. Garnish with pickle strips. Yield: 10 servings.

Mrs. Grace Gibson
Bruceton Mills, West Virginia

TUNA CRUNCH LOAF

2 envelopes unflavored gelatin
½ c. cold water
1 can cream of celery soup
¼ c. lemon juice
1 tbsp. prepared mustard
1 tsp. salt
Dash of pepper
1 c. mayonnaise or salad dressing
2 6 ½-oz. cans tuna, flaked
1 c. chopped celery
½ c. grated cucumber
¼ c. chopped green pepper

Soften gelatin in cold water. Heat soup just to boiling; add gelatin and stir to dissolve. Stir in lemon juice, mustard, salt and pepper. Chill until partially set. Add mayonnaise. Fold in tuna, celery, cucumber and green pepper. Pour into 8 1/2 x 4 1/2 x 2 1/2-inch loaf pan. Chill until firm; unmold. Yield: 8 servings.

Mrs. Pat Wilhelmi
Atlanta, Georgia

TUNA MOUSSE

1 3-oz. pkg. lemon or lemon-lime gelatin
½ tsp. salt
1 ¾ c. boiling water
Dash of cayenne
2 tbsp. vinegar
⅓ c. heavy cream, whipped
⅓ c. mayonnaise
1 7 ¾-oz. can tuna, flaked and drained
1 c. finely chopped celery
1 tbsp. chopped pimento

Dissolve gelatin and salt in boiling water. Add cayenne and vinegar; chill until very thick. Fold whipped cream and mayonnaise into gelatin, blending well. Fold in remaining ingredients. Pour into 1-quart mold or individual molds. Chill until firm. Unmold. Yield: 4 servings.

Martha Cook
Mobile, Alabama

TUNA SALAD

4 c. shredded salad greens
2 7-oz. cans tuna
4 med. tomatoes
3 hard-cooked eggs
Salt and pepper to taste
¼ c. lemon juice
½ c. mayonnaise

Arrange greens in large salad bowl. Cover with tuna; flank with quartered tomatoes and hard-cooked egg slices. Sprinkle with seasonings; drizzle lemon juice over salad. Serve with mayonnaise.

Mrs. R. T. Darnell
Morristown, Tennessee

TUNA SALAD

1 pkg. lemon or lime gelatin
¼ tsp. salt
1 c. boiling water
¾ c. cold water
1 tbsp. lemon juice
½ c. mayonnaise
1 tsp. grated onion
½ c. chopped cucumber
1 can tuna, drained and flaked
¼ c. sliced olives
2 tbsp. chopped pimento
Salad greens

Dissolve gelatin and salt in boiling water. Blend in cold water, lemon juice, mayonnaise and onion. Chill until very thick. Fold in remaining ingredients. Pour into 1-quart mold or bowl. Chill until firm. Serve on salad greens with additional mayonnaise. Yield: 4 servings.

Elsiemae Cunningham
Austin, Texas

TUNA SALAD

2 tbsp. gelatin
4 tsp. cold water
1 c. boiling water
1 tsp. sugar
½ tsp. salt
1 tbsp. vinegar
¼ tsp. paprika
1 c. chopped fine celery
2 hard-boiled eggs, diced
3 tbsp. chopped sweet pickles
½ c. salad dressing
1 can tuna

Soak gelatin in cold water; dissolve in hot water. Add sugar, salt and vinegar; cool. Before mixture thickens, add other ingredients, mixing in salad dressing last. Pour into wet loaf pan and let stand in refrigerator overnight. Cut into squares to serve.

Mrs. J. R. Adamson, Sr.
Hall Co., Texas

TUNA SALAD MOLD

1 3-oz. pkg. mixed vegetable gelatin
1 ½ c. boiling water
½ c. mayonnaise
2 tbsp. onion juice
2 tbsp. vinegar or lemon juice
1 ½ tsp. Worcestershire sauce
½ tsp. salt
⅛ tsp. pepper
1 7-oz. can tuna
¼ c. chopped black olives
½ c. diced celery
2 tbsp. diced pimento
2 tbsp. chopped green pepper

Dissolve gelatin in boiling water; add mayonnaise, onion juice, vinegar, Worcestershire sauce, salt and pepper. Mix well. Chill until mixture begins to congeal. Stir in tuna, olives, celery, pimento and green pepper. Pour salad mixture into mold. Chill for 2 to 3 hours or until firm. Yield: 6 servings.

Mrs. John C. Robinson
Perry, Florida

TUNA STAR SALAD

1 envelope unflavored gelatin
½ c. cold water
1 can condensed tomato soup
1 8-oz. pkg. cream cheese, cut in chunks
1 c. salad dressing or mayonnaise
½ c. diced green pepper
½ c. diced celery
½ c. chopped onion
¼ c. drained pickle relish
1 can tuna, drained

Soften gelatin in cold water. Heat soup. Add cream cheese; heat, beating with rotary beater until smooth. Add gelatin and stir until dissolved. Remove from heat; stir in salad dressing. Chill until partially set. Add remaining ingredients. Pour into a 5 1/2-cup star or other mold. Chill until set. Unmold on lettuce. Trim with stars cut from pimento and chilled. Yield: 8 servings.

Mrs. Callie Henderson
New Brockton, Alabama

FLAKED TUNA SALAD

2 med. potatoes, boiled
1 egg, hard-boiled
1 sm. cucumber pickle
1 tsp. celery seed
1/8 tsp. cayenne pepper
1 c. flaked tuna
Mayonnaise

Cut potatoes, egg and pickle into small cubes or pieces; add celery seed, pepper and tuna. Add enough mayonnaise to moisten. Serve on lettuce leaves. Garnish with beets rubbed through a sieve or with small squares of green pepper or pimento.

Florence Bowling
Fogertown, Kentucky

GAY CONTINENTAL SALAD

6 cucumbers, cut in half lengthwise
1 lge. can tuna
1 onion, chopped fine
1 c. diced cooked potatoes
3 hard-cooked eggs, chopped fine
1/2 green pepper, chopped fine
1/2 c. celery, chopped fine
1/4 c. olive oil
3 tbsp. apple cider vinegar
1 tsp. capers
1/2 tsp. salt
1/4 tsp. black pepper

Hollow out cucumber halves; place in ice water until ready to serve. Mix tuna with onion, potatoes, eggs, green pepper and celery. Mix remaining ingredients for salad dressing. Cover tuna mixture with dressing; fill hollowed cucumber halves. Serve on crisp lettuce leaves; garnish with pimento-stuffed olives and sprigs of parsley.

Mrs. Forest Cruse
Austin, Texas

JELLED TUNA SALAD

1 pkg. lemon gelatin
1 c. hot water
1/4 tsp. salt
4 tsp. vinegar
1/2 c. cold water
Dash of black pepper
1/2 c. mayonnaise
1 c. shredded carrots
1 c. shredded cabbage
1/4 c. cucumber or pickle
1 green pepper, chopped
1 tbsp. onion
1 can tuna or salmon

Combine gelatin, hot water and salt; stir to dissolve. Add remaining ingredients and mix well. Refrigerate till firm. Slice; serve on lettuce.

Mrs. S. A. Bone
Des Arc, Arkansas

KIDNEY BEAN-TUNA SALAD

1 1-lb. can red kidney beans, drained
1 7-oz. can chunk tuna, drained
6 anchovy fillets, quartered
1 c. sliced celery
2 tbsp. instant minced onion
1/4 tsp. instant minced garlic
1/4 tsp. pepper
1 1/2 tsp. salt
1 1/2 tsp. basil leaves
1 tsp. vinegar
1/4 c. mayonnaise
Tomato wedges
Lettuce

Combine all ingredients except tomato and lettuce; mix lightly. Chill for at least 1 hour; serve on lettuce. Garnish with tomato wedges. Yield: 6 servings.

Mrs. P. E. Bryan
Muskogee, Oklahoma

MOLDED TUNA WITH CUCUMBER DRESSING

2 envelopes unflavored gelatin
1/2 c. cold water
1 10 1/2-oz. can cream of mushroom soup
1 7-oz. can light chunk tuna, drained
1 pt. cottage cheese
1 c. finely diced celery
1 sm. jar pimento, diced
1 sm. onion, grated
1 c. mayonnaise
Salt to taste

Soften gelatin in cold water. Heat soup; add gelatin. Stir until gelatin is dissolved. Cool; fold in remaining ingredients. Spoon into lightly oiled fish mold; refrigerate for 24 hours. Unmold onto platter; garnish with crisp greens.

CUCUMBER DRESSING:

1/2 c. whipped cream
1/4 c. mayonnaise
1 tbsp. lemon juice
1/4 tsp. salt
1/4 tsp. paprika
1 c. finely diced drained cucumbers

(Continued on next page)

Blend cream, mayonnaise, lemon juice, salt and paprika; fold in cucumbers. Serve over tuna salad. Yield: 10-12 servings.

Mrs. John Pace
Bristol, Virginia

STUFFED TOMATO SALAD

4 sm. tomatoes
1 7-oz. can tuna
1 sm. onion, chopped
3 sweet pickles, chopped
Dash of salt
2 or 3 tbsp. mayonnaise

Prepare tomatoes by removing top slice and center core from each. Scoop out pulp. Mix pulp, tuna, onion, pickles, salt and mayonnaise well. Fill tomato cups and serve on lettuce leaves. Yield: 4 servings.

Mrs. Erlene Head
Cleveland, Alabama

STUFFED TOMATO WITH TUNA

1 can tuna, flaked
2 hard-cooked eggs, chopped
6 to 8 crackers, crumbled
1 tsp. onion, chopped
1 tbsp. parsley, chopped
3 tbsp. celery, chopped
2 tbsp. mayonnaise
6 med. tomatoes

Combine all ingredients except tomatoes. Cut top off tomatoes; scoop out center pulp. Fill each tomato with tuna mixture; serve in lettuce cups. Yield: 6 servings.

Mrs. Marian E. Causey
Centreville, Mississippi

SUMMER SALAD BOWL

½ lb. fresh string beans
3 hard-cooked eggs
2 green peppers, cut into thin strips
1 med. onion, sliced
2 lge. tomatoes, cut into wedges
8 ripe olives, seeded
1 2-oz. can anchovies, drained and rinsed
1 can tuna
3 tbsp. olive oil
1 tbsp. wine vinegar
Salt and pepper to taste

Cook green beans, uncovered, for 20 minutes in rapidly boiling salted water; drain and cool. Cut 1 egg into slices; peel and quarter remaining eggs. Combine beans, eggs, peppers, onion, tomatoes, olives, anchovies and tuna. Combine olive oil and vinegar; pour over salad. Toss lightly; season to taste. Yield: 4 servings.

Mrs. James J. Gibbons
Lexington, Kentucky

TUNA-BEAN BOWL

1 med. can white tuna
1 No. 303 can pork and beans
½ c. chopped sweet pickles
1 head lettuce, chopped
1 c. mayonnaise

Break tuna into lima bean-sized chunks; combine all ingredients in a large bowl. Mix gently. Yield: 6 servings.

Mrs. C. K. Lindsey
Phoenix, Arizona

TUNA CRUNCH SALAD

1 No. ½ can tuna
4 ½ tbsp. chopped sweet or dill pickles
1 ½ tbsp. minced onion
½ c. mayonnaise
1 ½ tbsp. lemon juice
1 ½ c. shredded cabbage
1 sm. bag potato chips, coarsely crushed
Lettuce
Tomato wedges

Combine tuna, pickles, onion, mayonnaise and lemon juice; chill in covered dish. When ready to serve, add cabbage and toss together. Add part of crushed potato chips; toss. Heap in shallow lettuce-lined bowl; sprinkle remaining potato chips on top and garnish with tomato wedges. Yield: 6 servings.

Shirley Woodward
Aiken, South Carolina

TUNA MEAL-IN-ONE

1 9 ¼-oz. can light tuna, flaked
1 No. 303 can green peas, drained
3 cooked potatoes, diced
2 sweet pickles, chopped
½ med. onion, chopped
½ c. chopped celery
Salt to taste
Juice of ½ lemon
Salad dressing or mayonnaise
½ head lettuce

(Continued on next page)

Combine all ingredients except lettuce and toss lightly. Chill thoroughly. Serve on lettuce leaf.

Beatrice Robinson
Lake City, Florida

TUNA-NUT SALAD

1 pkg. frozen cut green beans
2 c. shredded cabbage
3 tbsp. chopped chives
1 lge. dill pickle, chopped
½ c. chopped walnuts
1 tsp. minced parsley
½ c. mayonnaise
1 tbsp. cream
1 tsp. lemon juice
½ tsp. salt
1 sm. can solid-pack tuna

Cook green beans until tender but crisp; drain. Chill. Combine beans with cabbage, chives, dill pickle, walnuts and parsley. Toss. Mix mayonnaise with cream, lemon juice and salt. Mix lightly into salad. Drain tuna; break into large pieces and add to salad. Serve on lettuce. Garnish with additional parsley. Yield: 4 large servings.

Mrs. Thomas Fleming
Norfolk, Virginia

TUNA SALAD

1 med. head lettuce
1 sm. onion
1 8-oz. can peas
1 can tuna
2 tbsp. salad dressing
1 tsp. sugar
Dash of salt
Dash of pepper

Chop lettuce and onion into large mixing bowl; add peas and tuna. Toss. Mix salad dressing and sugar; add salt and pepper. Pour over salad. Toss and chill. Yield: 6 servings.

Kaye English
Columbus, Georgia

TUNA SALAD

1 9-oz. can tuna
4 hard-cooked eggs, chopped
2 lge. carrots, grated
¾ c. diced celery
2 tsp. celery seed
2 tbsp. frozen chives
2 tbsp. (heaping) mayonnaise
Salt and pepper to taste

Drain tuna; add remaining ingredients. If mixture is too dry, blend in additional mayonnaise. Crab meat or lobster may be substituted for tuna. Yield: 4 servings.

Mrs. Pauline Caldwell
Ohatchee, Alabama

TUNA SALAD IN PEPPER CUPS

6 med. green peppers
¾ c. instant rice
1 6 ½ or 7-oz. can tuna
½ c. chopped celery
2 tbsp. finely chopped onion
2 tbsp. finely chopped pimento
¾ c. mayonnaise
½ tsp. salt
Dash of pepper
⅓ c. finely crushed potato chips

Cut peppers into halves lengthwise; remove stems and seed. Cook peppers in small amount of boiling salted water for 5 minutes. Drain; lightly sprinkle insides with salt. Prepare rice according to package directions; combine with tuna, celery, onion and pimento. Blend mayonnaise, salt and pepper. Add to rice mixture; toss lightly. Spoon salad mixture into green pepper halves; sprinkle with potato chips. Place peppers in 10 x 6 x 1 1/2-inch baking dish. Barely cover bottom of pan with water. Bake at 350 degrees for 35 minutes. Yield: 6 servings.

Mrs. Creel A. Pickel
Dallas, Texas

TUNA SALAD IN TOMATO CUPS

1 7-oz. can light meat tuna
½ c. diced celery
½ c. chopped cucumber
1 tbsp. minced onion
1 tsp. lemon juice
1 tbsp. sweet pickle relish
Salt and pepper to taste
¼ c. mayonnaise
4 tomatoes

Mix tuna with celery, cucumber, onion, lemon juice, relish, salt and pepper. Toss together; add mayonnaise. Mix lightly until blended. Cut tops off tomatoes; scoop out center. Fill with tuna salad and serve on lettuce. Yield: 4 servings.

Mrs. Howard Riley
Shelby, North Carolina

TUNA-VEGETABLE SALAD

½ c. mayonnaise or salad dressing
2 tbsp. lemon juice
2 6½ to 7-oz. cans tuna
2 tsp. grated onion
½ tsp. salt
½ tsp. dried leaf thyme
½ c. chopped cucumber
¾ c. grated carrots
Salad greens

Combine mayonnaise and lemon juice in a bowl; blend well. Add next 5 ingredients and 1/2 cup carrots. Mix well; set aside. Spread salad greens on large serving dish; pile tuna-vegetable mixture onto greens. Top with remaining grated carrots.

Lucille Gross
Richmond, Kentucky

TUNA WALDORF SALAD

2 6½ or 7-oz. cans tuna, drained and flaked
1 c. diced apples
½ c. chopped celery
¼ c. chopped nuts
½ c. mayonnaise or salad dressing
Lettuce

Combine all ingredients except lettuce. Serve on lettuce. Yield: 6 servings.

Ellen Marie Penuel
Kinston, North Carolina

CLAM SALAD

1 cucumber, peeled and sliced
3 ribs celery, sliced
2 carrots, sliced
1 root lotus, sliced (opt.)
2 doz. med. uncooked clams, chopped into lge. pieces
1 c. vinegar
⅔ c. sugar
2 tbsp. lemon juice
½ tsp. monosodium glutamate

Combine cucumber, celery, carrots, lotus and clams. Combine remaining ingredients for dressing; toss with clam mixture. Chill; serve in lettuce cups if desired. Yield: 6 servings.

Mrs. Henry W. Mays
Oklahoma City, Oklahoma

BEACHCOMBER SALAD

1 10-oz. can tomato soup, undiluted
1 6-oz. can minced clams with liquor
1 8-oz. pkg. cream cheese
2 envelopes unflavored gelatin
½ c. cold water
¾ c. mayonnaise
1 c. chopped celery
2 hard-cooked eggs, chopped
6 stuffed green olives, chopped
½ tsp. minced onion
1 tsp. lemon juice
⅛ tsp. pepper
Salt to taste
Dash of paprika
Worcestershire sauce to taste
4 stuffed green olives, sliced

Empty tomato soup in saucepan. Add clam liquor and enough water to equal 1 soup can. Bring to boil. Add cream cheese; simmer gently, stirring until cheese is softened and partially dissolved. Remove from heat and beat with egg beater until mixture is thoroughly blended. Soften gelatin in cold water. Dissolve in the hot soup mixture. Cool and chill to syrupy consistency. Stir in remaining ingredients except sliced olives. Decorate bottom of 1 1/2-quart mold with olives. Pour in salad mold and chill until firm. Serve unmolded on salad greens.

Anna Hall
Springfield, Virginia

CRAB LOUIS

DRESSING FOR CRAB LOUIS:

¼ c. finely chopped onion
¼ c. finely chopped green pepper
2 tbsp. chopped green olives
1 c. mayonnaise
¼ c. chili sauce
1 tbsp. lemon juice
1 tsp. Worcestershire sauce
1 tsp. prepared horseradish
¼ tsp. salt

Blend all ingredients; chill thoroughly.

CRAB LOUIS:

Crab meat, chilled
Lettuce, shredded
Olives
Hard-cooked eggs, cut in wedges
Tomato wedges
Lemon wedges

Arrange crab on beds of lettuce on individual salad plates. Spoon a generous amount of dressing over each serving. Garnish with ripe olives, wedges of hard-cooked eggs, tomato and lemon. For an interesting variation, stir 1/4 cup sparkling white grape juice into dressing.

Mrs. Warren E. Williams
San Perlita, Texas

CRAB LOUIS

3 6 ½-oz. cans cooked crab meat, flaked
6 c. shredded lettuce
2 hard-cooked eggs, diced
2 tbsp. chopped onion or chives
1 ⅓ c. mayonnaise
⅓ c. heavy cream
½ c. chili sauce
2 tbsp. horseradish
4 tsp. lemon juice
1 tsp. salt
¼ tsp. pepper
¾ tsp. Worcestershire sauce
Tomato wedges

Combine crab meat, lettuce, eggs and onion in a large salad bowl. Combine mayonnaise with cream, chili sauce, horseradish, lemon juice, salt, pepper and Worcestershire sauce; mix well. Pour mayonnaise mixture over crab meat mixture; toss lightly. Garnish with tomato wedges. Serve on individual salad plates. Yield: 6 servings.

Mrs. May Round
Laurel, Mississippi

CRAB AND OLIVE SALAD

1 13-oz. can crab meat
⅔ c. chopped ripe olives
1 ⅔ c. diced celery
¼ c. mayonnaise or salad dressing
Salt and pepper
Romaine

Flake crab meat, removing bits of membrane; Combine with olives, celery and mayonnaise. Season with salt and pepper. Serve on romaine.

Mrs. Geneva Bryant
Jacksonville, Arkansas

CRAB MEAT ASPIC SALAD

2 pkg. lemon gelatin
3 c. water
½ c. mayonnaise
1 tbsp. onion juice
4 tbsp. vinegar
½ tsp. salt
2 tbsp. chopped pimento
1 ½ c. chopped celery
1 lge. can crab meat

Dissolve gelatin in water; let stand until partially set. Add remaining ingredients. Pour into 9-inch ring mold; chill for 1 hour. Yield: 8 servings.

Mrs. Ellen Bensley
Fort Wolters, Texas

CRAB MEAT SALAD

1 3-oz. pkg. lemon gelatin
1 ½ c. boiling water
3 tbsp. white vinegar
½ tsp. salt
½ tsp. onion juice
2 c. crab meat
¾ c. finely cut celery
1 tbsp. pimento

Dissolve gelatin in boiling water. Add vinegar, salt and onion juice; cool until thickened. Add crab meat, celery and pimento. Pour into 6 individual salad molds; chill until firm. Unmold onto lettuce. Yield: 6 servings.

Mrs. Eckert Irving
Baltimore, Maryland

CRAB MEAT SALAD

1 3-oz. pkg. lemon or lemon-lime gelatin
¼ tsp. salt
1 c. boiling water
½ c. cold water
Dash of pepper
1 tbsp. lemon juice
½ c. cottage cheese
1 ¼ c. canned crab meat
½ c. diced celery
¼ c. mayonnaise

Dissolve gelatin and salt in boiling water; add cold water, pepper and lemon juice. Chill until very thick. Fold in cottage cheese, crab meat, celery and mayonnaise. Pour into 1-quart mold. Chill until firm. Unmold onto salad greens. Yield: 4 servings.

Mrs. Cecil Grainger
Conway, South Carolina

CRAB SALAD

1 c. ripe olives
1 ½ c. thinly sliced celery
1 c. flaked crab meat
⅓ c. mayonnaise
1 ½ tbsp. catsup
1 tsp. lemon juice
Lettuce

(Continued on next page)

Cut olives into wedges; combine with celery and crab meat. Toss lightly with mayonnaise blended with catsup and lemon juice. Serve in lettuce cups. Yield: 4 servings.

Mrs. Ernest Senkel
Cameron, Texas

CRAB SALAD

1 can cream of mushroom soup
2 pkg. cream cheese
1 c. mayonnaise
1 pkg. gelatin
¼ c. cold water
Grated onion
Dash of Worcestershire sauce
1 can crab meat

Heat soup, cream cheese and mayonnaise in double boiler. Soften gelatin in cold water; add to mixture. Add onion, Worcestershire sauce and crab meat. Pour into individual molds. Serve on a slice of cranberry sauce. Yield: 6 servings.

Mrs. John Everett
Panama City, Florida

CRAB SALAD MOLD

1 pkg. unflavored gelatin
½ c. cold water
½ c. boiling water
1 c. mayonnaise
1 c. chili sauce
1 c. crab
4 hard-cooked eggs
2 tbsp. Worcestershire sauce
¼ c. chopped olives
1 can pimento

Soak gelatin in cold water; add boiling water. Add remaining ingredients; pour into mold. Chill. Yield: 6 servings.

Mrs. Kathryn Smette
Durham, North Carolina

CRAB-WILD RICE SALAD

1 c. King crab meat
1 c. cooked wild rice
½ c. mayonnaise
¼ tsp. dry mustard
2 tbsp. vinegar
Salad greens
2 avocados, sliced or halved

Remove any cartilage from crab, leaving in fairly large pieces. Toss crab with rice. Blend mayonnaise, mustard and vinegar; mix with crab and rice. Chill. Serve on lettuce; garnish with avocado slices. Yield: 4 servings.

Mrs. David B. Savage
Georgetown, Kentucky

CRAB AND TOMATO SOUP SALAD

1 can tomato soup
1 8-oz. pkg. cream cheese
2 tbsp. unflavored gelatin
½ c. water
1 c. mayonnaise
1 c. chopped celery
1 c. chopped green peppers
1 c. chopped onions
1 c. crab meat
½ c. chopped olives (opt.)
½ c. chopped pickles

Heat soup and cream cheese, beating until cream cheese is melted. Add gelatin dissolved in water. Cool; add remaining ingredients. Turn into individual molds. Chill until set. Yield: 8 servings.

Mrs. Jean McCormick
Little Rock, Arkansas

CRAB TOWER SALAD

1 6 ½-oz. can crab meat, flaked
2 tbsp. tarragon vinegar
½ tsp. salt
¼ tsp. pepper
3 tbsp. chopped pimento
2 tbsp. chopped chives or onion
2 tbsp. chopped gherkins
½ c. mayonnaise or salad dressing
1 tbsp. capers
Shredded lettuce
2 lge. tomatoes, sliced
1 hard-cooked egg, sieved

Moisten crab meat with vinegar; let stand for 15 minutes. Drain vinegar from crab meat; add salt, pepper, pimento, chives, gherkins, mayonnaise and capers to crab meat. Blend well. Arrange lettuce on four salad plates; center a tomato slice on each. Top each with 1/2 cup salad. Top with sieved egg; garnish with additional pimento. Yield: 4 servings.

Mrs. Joyce Grinde
Gainesville, Florida

CALIFORNIA CRAB SALAD

1 clove garlic, minced
1 tsp. salt
2 tbsp. capers
2 tbsp. chopped canned green chilies
2 tbsp. chopped pimento
2 tbsp. wine vinegar with tarragon
½ c. olive or salad oil
Freshly ground pepper to taste
Dash of Tabasco sauce
8-oz. canned or frozen cooked crab
1 lge. avocado, quartered and sliced
1 med. red onion, sliced
2 tomatoes, sliced into thin wedges
1 ½ to 2 qt. salad greens

Combine garlic, salt, capers, chilies, pimento, vinegar, oil, pepper and Tabasco sauce in jar; shake until well blended. Place remaining ingredients in large salad bowl; toss with dressing. Yield: 3-4 servings.

Mrs. Thomas A. Bell
Gallup, New Mexico

CRAB IMPERIAL

1 c. mayonnaise
¼ c. finely chopped onion
¼ c. finely chopped green pepper
½ tsp. dry mustard
3 tbsp. lemon juice
½ tsp. salt
Dash of pepper
2 c. cooked fresh, frozen or canned crab meat, drained
2 hard-cooked eggs, chopped
4 med. avocados
1 c. soft bread crumbs
2 tbsp. melted butter

Combine mayonnaise, onion, green pepper, mustard, 2 tablespoons lemon juice, salt and pepper. Mix in crab and eggs. Cut avocados into halves; remove seed. Cut a thin slice off bottom of each, so avocado will set level. Brush cut surfaces with 1 tablespoon of lemon juice. Mound crab meat mixture on avocado halves. Combine bread crumbs and melted butter; sprinkle over crab meat. Bake at 350 degrees for 10 to 15 minutes or until crumbs are lightly browned. Serve at once. Yield: 8 servings.

Mrs. William E. Perry
Statesville, North Carolina

CRABBY AVOCADO RING

4 boxes lemon gelatin
4 c. hot water
2 ¼ c. cold water
1 tsp. salt
¼ c. lemon juice
¼ tsp. Tabasco sauce
5 ripe avocados
¾ c. mayonnaise
1 c. sour cream

Dissolve gelatin in boiling water; add cold water, salt, lemon juice and Tabasco sauce. Chill thoroughly. Sieve 4 avocados; add to gelatin with mayonnaise and sour cream. Beat with rotary beater until blended. Pour into a 3-quart ring mold; chill overnight. Unmold onto salad greens. Garnish with strips of remaining avocado.

CRAB MEAT DRESSING:

1 ½ c. mayonnaise
⅔ c. milk
1 tbsp. lemon juice
½ tsp. paprika
6-oz. crab meat
Parsley

Combine mayonnaise, milk, lemon juice, paprika and crab meat. Serve with salad; sprinkle with parsley.

Mrs. Howard Finn
Cherry Point, North Carolina

CRAB-PEAR SALAD WITH HOT VINAIGRETTE DRESSING

1 7 ½-oz. can Alaska King crab, drained and sliced
1 c. chopped celery
2 hard-cooked eggs, chopped
¼ tsp. powdered mustard
1 tsp. salt
⅛ tsp. pepper
¼ tsp. garlic powder
1 tbsp. chopped chives
½ c. salad oil
2 tbsp. vinegar
2 tbsp. fresh lemon juice
1 1-lb. 13-oz. can Bartlett pear halves, drained

Toss crab with celery and eggs. Blend mustard, salt, pepper, garlic powder, chopped chives, salad oil, vinegar and lemon juice; heat to boiling. Add pear halves; simmer for 5 minutes. Remove pears to platter. Pour hot sauce over crab mixture, tossing lightly. Heap crab in center of pear platter. Garnish with crisp celery greens. Yield: 4 servings.

Mrs. William R. Swift
Bowling Green, Kentucky

CRAB SALAD

1 pkg. lemon gelatin
1 ½ c. boiling water
3 sm. pkg. cream cheese
1 can crab meat or shrimp
1 can crushed pineapple
1 c. mayonnaise
1 c. chopped celery
Onion juice or powder

(Continued on next page)

Dissolve gelatin in boiling water; beat in cream cheese. Stir in remaining ingredients. Chill until firm. Yield: 4-6 servings.

Mrs. Richard E. Mallon
Huffman, Texas

CRAB-STUFFED AVOCADO

½ c. mayonnaise
½ c. minced celery
¼ c. minced pimento
Lemon juice
⅛ tsp. Worcestershire sauce
Dash of Tabasco sauce
2 ripe avocados
Lettuce
1 ½ c. crab meat
¼ tsp. salt

Combine mayonnaise, celery, pimento, 2 teaspoonfuls lemon juice, Worcestershire sauce and Tabasco sauce. Cut avocados lengthwise; remove seed and peel. Dip in lemon juice. Arrange a bed of lettuce on four separate dishes. Place avocado on lettuce. Fill with crab meat. Sprinkle lightly with salt. Spoon sauce over top and serve. Yield: 4 servings.

Jessie A. Silva
El Paso, Texas

CRAB-STUFFED AVOCADO

2 cans King crab
1 hard-cooked egg, minced
¾ dill pickle, finely chopped
1 sm. onion, minced
6 sm. celery stalks, chopped
30 to 40 capers
3 tbsp. mayonnaise
3 cloves of garlic, pressed
1 tbsp. tarragon vinegar
3 ripe avocados

Combine all ingredients except avocados; add salt and pepper to taste. Split avocados; remove seed. Stuff with crab filling. Serve on lettuce leaves. Yield: 6 servings.

Mrs. John Hanlin
Albuquerque, New Mexico

GRAPEFRUIT-CRAB COCKTAIL

1 c. frozen crab meat, thawed
1 tbsp. lemon juice
1 1-lb. can grapefruit sections, chilled and drained
1 c. mayonnaise or salad dressing
2 tbsp. catsup
1 tbsp. lemon juice
Few drops of Tabasco sauce

Flake crab meat; sprinkle with lemon juice. Alternate grapefruit sections and crab meat in cocktail glasses. Combine remaining ingredients; pour over grapefruit and crab meat. Yield: 6-8 servings.

Mrs. James Osborn
El Paso, Texas

MOLDED CRAB-AVOCADO SALAD

3 envelopes gelatin
1 ½ c. water
2 6 ½-oz. cans crab meat
1 c. mashed avocado
1 c. sour cream
1 c. mayonnaise
3 tbsp. chopped onion
½ c. diced cucumber
¼ c. lemon juice
¼ c. chopped celery
1 ½ tsp. salt

Sprinkle gelatin in water; let stand for 5 minutes. Heat until gelatin is dissolved. Chill until mixture begins to stiffen; add remaining ingredients. Congeal in molds. Serve on lettuce. Yield: 8 servings.

Mrs. Walter N. Hess
Orlando, Florida

MOLDED CRAB MEAT SALAD

1 envelope unflavored gelatin
⅓ c. water
1 tbsp. vinegar
½ c. mayonnaise
½ c. finely diced celery or cucumber
½ c. grapefruit or orange pulp
½ c. finely diced canned pineapple
2 tsp. salt
Pepper
Paprika
1 6 ⅓-oz. can crab meat, flaked
Crisp salad greens
Tomato wedges

Soften gelatin in water; dissolve over hot water. Stir in vinegar and mayonnaise slowly, beating well after each addition. Stir in celery, grapefruit and pineapple; season with salt, pepper and paprika to taste. Stir in flaked crab meat. Pack mixture into an oiled mold. Chill until set. Serve on lettuce; garnish with tomato wedges. Yield: 6-8 servings.

Mrs. Theodore Bielen, Jr.
Lafayette, Louisiana

STUFFED AVOCADOS

2 10-oz. cans consomme, chilled
1 6-oz. pkg. King crab meat, thawed, drained and flaked
1 tbsp. lemon juice
2 avocados, halved and peeled
1 head Bibb lettuce
Watercress

Combine chilled consomme with crab meat and lemon juice. Brush avocado halves with additional lemon juice; fill with consomme mixture. Place on lettuce leaves; garnish with watercress. Yield: 4 servings.

Mrs. James Lynch
Gadsden, Alabama

HIS 'N' HERS SALAD

1 c. cooked or canned King crab or lobster meat
1 tsp. lemon juice
1 tsp. grated onion
¼ tsp. celery seeds
2 crisp lettuce cups
1 c. sliced radishes
2 deviled eggs

Combine crab meat, lemon juice, onion and celery seeds; arrange in lettuce cups. Garnish with radishes and deviled eggs. Yield: 2 servings.

Kathi Wilkins
Vandervoort, Arkansas

HOLIDAY SALAD

1 pkg. lemon gelatin
¾ c. boiling water
1 lge. pkg. cream cheese
1 can tomato soup
¾ c. salad dressing
1 can crab meat, tuna or shrimp
1 c. mixed diced celery and green pepper
1 med. jar stuffed olives, sliced

Dissolve gelatin in water in large bowl. Mash cream cheese; add to gelatin mixture while still hot. Add soup; cool. Add remaining ingredients. Pour into buttered or oiled molds and chill. Yield: 12 servings.

Ruth McBride
Oklahoma City, Oklahoma

BAKED CRAB SALAD

1 c. flaked crab meat
1 c. soft bread crumbs
1 c. cream or top milk
1 ½ c. mayonnaise
6 hard-cooked eggs, diced
1 tbsp. parsley
1 tsp. minced onion
⅛ tsp. black pepper
Few grains of red pepper
½ c. buttered crumbs

Combine all ingredients except buttered crumbs. Place in greased 2-quart casserole; sprinkle with crumbs. Bake at 350 degrees for 20 minutes or until crumbs are golden brown. Yield: 8 servings.

Mrs. Bobby Wilkerson
Los Lunas, New Mexico

BAKED CRAB SALAD

1 ½ lb. crab meat
2 c. finely chopped celery
1 c. chopped green onions
1 c. finely cut green peppers
2 c. mayonnaise
1 tsp. Worcestershire sauce
Salt and pepper to taste
1 12-oz. pkg. noodles, cooked
1 lge. pkg. potato chips, crushed

Mix crab meat, vegetables, mayonnaise and seasonings. Layer noodles, crab mixture and potato chips in large buttered casserole. Bake at 250 degrees for 1 hour and 30 minutes. Increase temperature to 325 degrees and bake for 15 minutes longer. Yield: 16 servings.

Mrs. Wesley B. Moore
Gatlinburg, Tennessee

HOT CRAB SALAD

2 sm. cans crab or 2 sm. pkg. frozen crab
2 hard-cooked eggs, finely chopped
½ c. chopped almonds
2 tbsp. butter
2 tbsp. flour
2 c. milk
Cracker crumbs

Cut crab into small pieces; add eggs and almonds. Blend butter and flour; gradually add milk. Cook until thickened, stirring constantly. Pour over crab mixture; place in casserole. Sprinkle with cracker crumbs. Bake at 400 degrees for 20 minutes. Serve on lettuce leaves with mayonnaise. Yield: 6 servings.

Mrs. W. J. Scarpino
Atlanta, Georgia

BAKED SEAFOOD SALAD

2 c. diced cooked crab, shrimp or tuna
¾ c. chopped green peppers
2 tbsp. finely chopped onion
1 c. diced celery
½ tsp. salt
⅛ tsp. pepper
¾ c. salad dressing
1 tbsp. lemon juice
¼ c. finely crushed potato chips
¼ c. grated sharp cheese

Combine all ingredients except potato chips and cheese. Place in 6 individual serving shells or a baking dish. Sprinkle with grated cheese and crushed potato chips. Bake at 350 degrees for 30 minutes. A combination of seafoods may be used.

Mrs. Freda L. Juchau
Atlanta, Georgia

HOT CRAB SALAD BOATS

1 lb. lump crab meat
1 c. diced celery
1 c. canned or cooked peas
¼ lb. process Swiss cheese, cubed
¼ c. chopped parsley
¾ c. mayonnaise
6 long hero-type rolls
¼ c. butter or margarine, melted
Lemon wedges
Ripe olives

Combine crab meat, celery, peas, cheese and parsley in bowl; fold in mayonnaise. Cut a slice from top of each roll; cut out middle with sharp knife to make a boat-shaped shell. Brush inside of roll shells with melted butter. Fill with crab meat mixture; wrap each separately in foil. Bake at 400 degrees for 15 minutes. Thread a lemon wedge and 2 ripe olives on wooden toothpick and serve with each boat. Yield: 6 servings.

Mrs. Joseph B. Medagliani
Halifax, Virginia

OCEAN BAY SALAD

1 ½ c. flaked crab meat
1 c. chopped cooked shrimp
¾ c. salad dressing
½ c. chopped green pepper
2 tbsp. finely chopped onion
2 tbsp. finely chopped pimento
1 tsp. Worcestershire sauce
½ tsp. salt
½ c. chow mein noodles
Lime twists

Combine crab meat, shrimp, salad dressing, green pepper, onion, pimento, Worcestershire sauce and salt; mix well. Place in 1-quart casserole or 4 individual baking dishes; sprinkle with chow mein noodles. Bake at 350 degrees for 25 minutes. Garnish with lime twists. Yield: 4 servings.

Pearl Scott
Gainesville, Florida

SEAFOOD SALAD

½ c. chopped green pepper
¼ c. minced onion
1 c. chopped celery
1 c. cooked flaked crab meat
1 c. cooked shrimp
1 c. mayonnaise
½ tsp. salt
1 tsp. Worcestershire sauce
2 c. cornflakes
¼ c. butter
Paprika

Combine green pepper, onion, celery, crab meat, shrimp, mayonnaise, salt and Worcestershire sauce; mix well. Place mixture in individual shells or shallow baking dish. Cover with crushed cornflakes; dot with butter. Sprinkle paprika over top. Bake at 350 degrees for about 30 minutes. Serve with slices of lemon. Yield: 7-8 servings.

Mrs. Mary P. Murray
De Funiak Springs, Florida

KING CRAB IN ASPIC

2 c. V-8 juice
2 c. chili sauce
Juice of 1 lemon
2 tbsp. horseradish
6 drops Tabasco sauce
2 envelopes unflavored gelatin, softened
4 tbsp. water
½ c. chopped onion
½ c. chopped celery
1 6-oz. pkg. frozen crab meat

Heat V-8 juice, chili sauce, lemon juice, horseradish and Tabasco sauce in pan. Dissolve gelatin in water; add to hot mixture. Let set until slightly congealed; add onion, celery and crab meat. Pour into greased mold; chill until firm. Unmold onto bed of endice. Yield: 8 servings.

Mrs. A. P. Herrewig
Raleigh, North Carolina

MOLDED CRAB SALAD

2 envelopes unflavored gelatin
½ c. hot chicken broth
2 eggs, separated
1 6½-oz. can crab meat
½ c. mayonnaise
1 stalk celery, coarsely cut
1 med. onion, sliced ¼ in. thick
1 tbsp. parsley
1 tbsp. marjoram
1 c. cream or milk

Blend gelatin and broth; add egg yolks, crab, mayonnaise, celery, onion, parsley and marjoram. Blend in blender for 15 seconds; add cream. Continue blending; fold into stiffly beaten egg whites. Refrigerate for 1 hour.

FISH DRESSING:

¼ c. salad oil
½ c. spinach
½ c. parsley
1 clove of garlic
2 tbsp. chives
1 ¼ c. mayonnaise

Blend all ingredients except mayonnaise in blender until finely chopped. Add mayonnaise. Serve with crab salad. Yield: 6 servings.

Ethel Harker
Eureka, Texas

SEAFOOD SALAD

1 5-oz. can lobster, drained and boned
1 5-oz. can shrimp, drained and cleaned
1 6½-oz. can crab meat, drained, boned and flaked
1 c. diced celery
1 tbsp. minced onion
1 tbsp. lemon juice
1 tsp. salt
¼ tsp. pepper
Mayonnaise or salad dressing

Cut lobster into bite-sized pieces. Combine seafood, celery, onion, lemon juice, salt, pepper and 3/4 cup mayonnaise in medium bowl. Toss until mixed; cover and chill thoroughly. Line salad bowl with lettuce; fill with salad mixture. Garnish with additional mayonnaise. Sprinkle with paprika. Yield: 4-6 servings.

Mrs. Margie Gugino
North Little Rock, Arkansas

TOMATO-CRAB MEAT ASPIC

1 c. tomato juice
1 slice onion
1 bay leaf
1 stalk celery, quartered
1 tbsp. unflavored gelatin
2 tbsp. cold water
¾ c. beef bouillon or consomme
1 tbsp. lemon juice
Salt and pepper to taste
1 6½-oz. can crab meat, flaked
4 stuffed olives, sliced

Heat tomato juice with onion, bay leaf and celery; strain. Soften gelatin in cold water; stir into tomato mixture until gelatin dissolves. Add bouillon, lemon juice and seasonings; cool until partially set. Add crab meat and olives. Chill in individual molds until firm. Unmold onto lettuce. Yield: 6 servings.

Mrs. Henry E. Le Febvre
Wilmington, North Carolina

CRAB LEG SALAD

Shredded lettuce
1 slice tomato
Cooked asparagus tips
Cut green beans
Cauliflowerets
Green peas
1 artichoke heart
5 or 6 crab legs, chilled
Red and green pepper strips
Sliced hard-cooked eggs

Arrange a bed of lettuce on salad plate; top with tomato. Combine asparagus, green beans, cauliflowerets and green peas; stuff artichoke with mixture. Arrange crab legs on vegetables. Place artichoke on tomato; garnish with pepper and eggs. Yield: 1 serving.

Mrs. Frank J. Valois, Jr.
Las Vegas, New Mexico

CAPERS-CRAB MEAT SALAD

6 med. tomatoes
1/3 c. French dressing
2 c. flaked crab meat
1/2 c. diced celery
6 tbsp. mayonnaise
1/4 c. capers
Paprika
Watercress

Scald, peel and chill tomatoes; scoop out centers to form cups. Marinate inside of tomatoes with French dressing for 30 minutes. Mix crab meat, celery and French dressing gently so crab meat will not be broken. Stuff tomatoes; garnish with mayonnaise, capers and paprika. Place on a bed of watercress on salad plates. Yield: 6 servings.

Patricia A. Glass
Dill City, Oklahoma

CRAB LOUIS

1 lb. crab meat
1 head lettuce, shredded
1/2 tsp. salt
4 tomatoes, sliced
1 cucumber, sliced
3 hard-cooked eggs, sliced
1 c. mayonnaise
3 tbsp. catsup
2 tbsp. chopped sweet pickle
1 tbsp. lemon juice

Remove any shell or cartilage from crab meat. Place lettuce in a large shallow bowl; sprinkle with salt. Arrange crab meat over lettuce. Place alternate slices of tomatoes, cucumbers and eggs around edge of bowl. Combine remaining ingredients; chill. Spread over crab mixture. Yield: 6 servings.

Mrs. Nancy Frizzell
Cleburne, Texas

CRAB SALAD

2 eggs, beaten
1/2 c. sugar
1/2 tsp. salt
1 tsp. dry mustard
Juice of 1 lemon
1 tbsp. butter
1 lb. cooked crab meat
1/2 c. diced celery
1/3 c. chopped walnuts
1 c. peas

Place eggs, sugar, salt, mustard, lemon juice and butter in top of double boiler. Cook and stir until thickened. Chill. Mix dressing with crab meat, celery, nuts and peas. Yield: 4 servings.

Jo Ann Wentker
Santa Fe, New Mexico

CUCUMBER BOATS WITH CRAB MEAT

3 cucumbers
2 c. crab meat, flaked, fresh cooked or canned
2 tbsp. lemon juice
2 tsp. grated onion
1 c. remoulade sauce

Carefully cut cucumbers lengthwise; remove seeds and scoop out center gently. Mix remaining ingredients together with dressing, saving some for garnish. Arrange filled cucumber boats on beds of lettuce. Garnish with chopped parsley. Yield: 4 servings.

Mrs. Hazel Tilghman
Kinston, North Carolina

KING CRAB SALAD

1 pkg. lemon gelatin
2 pkg. cream cheese
1 can tomato soup
1 can crab meat
1/2 c. celery, diced
1 tbsp. green pepper, diced
1 tbsp. minced onion
1 c. canned peas
1 c. mayonnaise
1 tbsp. vinegar
1/2 tsp. salt

Dissolve gelatin in 3/4 cup boiling water. Melt cheese in double boiler with tomato soup; cool. Mix crab, diced celery, diced green pepper, onion, peas, mayonnaise, vinegar and salt. Add all ingredients together. Pour in greased mold. Yield: 6-8 servings.

Ruth I. Lamb
Gadsden, Alabama

SURPRISE SALAD

2 c. flaked cooked crab meat
1 sm. onion, chopped
1 c. diced celery
1/2 c. diced raw carrots
1 tbsp. diced green pepper
1 1/2 c. Special Mayonnaise
Lettuce
Stuffed olives

Mix crab meat, onion, celery, carrots and green pepper with just enough Special Mayonnaise to moisten. Shape into round balls and serve on crisp lettuce leaves. Garnish with sliced stuffed olives and additional Special Mayonnaise.

(Continued on next page)

SPECIAL MAYONNAISE:

1 c. mayonnaise
2 tbsp. chopped, green olives
4 tbsp. pimento, chopped fine
1 hard-cooked egg, sieved
3 tbsp. mashed Roquefort cheese
½ tsp. black pepper
1 sm. clove garlic, pressed
2 tsp. wine vinegar

Mix all ingredients together.

Mrs. Lillian Herman
Bay City, Texas

LOBSTER ASPIC PARISIENNE

3 envelopes unflavored gelatin
1 ⅓ c. cold water
2 cans bouillon, heated
2 tbsp. lemon juice
2 tsp. Worcestershire sauce
1 ½ lb. lobster, cooked
1 ½ c. cooked peas
1 c. diced cooked carrots
1 ½ c. diced cooked potatoes
2 tsp. salt
⅔ c. mayonnaise

Soften gelatin in water; dissolve in bouillon. Add lemon juice and Worcestershire sauce. Chill until thick. Pour 1 cup gelatin mixture into 4-cup mold. Arrange pieces of lobster, red-side down, in gelatin mixture. Chill until almost set. Dice remaining lobster; add peas, carrots, potatoes, salt and mayonnaise. Add to remaining gelatin mixture. Carefully pour over firm gelatin. Chill until firm. Unmold onto lettuce; garnish with wedges of tomato, hard-cooked eggs, ripe olives and lemon wedges if desired. Yield: 8-10 servings.

Mrs. James B. Miller
Santa Fe, New Mexico

BAKED LOBSTER SALAD BUNS

3 c. cooked lobster
2 c. sliced celery
½ c. sliced stuffed olives
1 tsp. minced onion
1 c. mayonnaise
½ c. French dressing
Salt to taste
Lemon juice
6 oval hard rolls
½ c. chopped walnuts

Combine all ingredients except rolls and walnuts; refrigerate. Using sharp knife, cut out centers of rolls leaving shells. Spoon lobster mixture into shells. Wrap in foil; place on cookie sheet. Bake at 350 degrees for 30 minutes. Unwrap; sprinkle with walnuts. Yield: 6 servings.

Mrs. F. William Francke
Baton Rouge, Louisiana

LOBSTER IN CUCUMBER

½ sm. onion
Juice of 1 lime
2 ¼ c. mayonnaise
¾ c. chili sauce
Salt and black pepper to taste
Cayenne pepper
10 7 to 8-in. cucumbers
1 ½ lb. lobster, cooked and diced
¾ c. minced celery
3 tbsp. minced parsley
3 tbsp. minced dill

Mince onion in bowl until almost pureed; turn into a cloth dampened with cold water. Press out all the juice into a larger bowl. Add lime juice, mayonnaise and chili sauce; mix well. Season to taste with salt, pepper and cayenne pepper. Peel cucumbers; cut into halves. Hollow out cucumbers to make 20 shallow boats. Mix lobster, minced celery and 2 cups dressing. Fill cucumber boats with lobster mixture. Sprinkle each boat with mixed parsley and dill. Chill. Serve on lettuce with remaining dressing. Yield: 10 servings.

Mrs. Anne Cunningham
Ft. Walton, Florida

LOBSTER-MELON SALAD WITH PUFFS

½ c. mayonnaise
¼ c. sour cream
2 tbsp. chopped green onion
2 tbsp. finely chopped parsley
1 tbsp. tarragon vinegar
1 tbsp. lemon juice
1 sm. clove of garlic, crushed
¼ tsp. salt
Pepper
2 5 ½-oz. cans lobster, drained
2 c. cantaloupe or honeydew melon balls
¾ c. self-rising cornmeal
¾ c. self-rising flour
1 c. water
½ c. butter
4 eggs

(Continued on next page)

Blend mayonnaise, sour cream, onion, parsley, vinegar, lemon juice, garlic, salt and pepper. Stir in lobster; refrigerate. Just before serving, fold in melon balls. Mix cornmeal and flour. In saucepan, bring water and butter to a boil, stirring until butter melts. Add dry ingredients all at once. Reduce heat; cook and stir until mixture is smooth and forms a ball. Remove from heat; cool slightly. Add eggs, one at a time, beating well after each addition. Drop batter by rounded tablespoonfuls onto baking sheet to make 10 shells. Bake at 350 degrees for 30 to 35 minutes or until firm to touch. Cool on wire rack. Cut tops off shells; remove soft interiors. Divide lobster salad among shells. Refrigerate until ready to serve.

Mrs. Chester C. Rice
Fort McPherson, Georgia

LOBSTER MOLD

1 tbsp. unflavored gelatin
¼ c. cold water
1 10-oz. can tomato soup
1 lge. pkg. cream cheese
⅓ c. chopped celery
1 tsp. onion salt
1 tsp. Worcestershire sauce
2 cans lobster
1 c. mayonnaise

Soak gelatin in cold water. Heat soup; stir in gelatin until completely dissolved. Beat in cream cheese; cool. Fold in remaining ingredients. Place in an oiled fish mold. Chill until set. Turn out onto lettuce leaves; use olives for eyes of fish, if desired. Yield: 6 servings.

Mrs. James Richardson
Phoenix, Arizona

LOBSTER-ORANGE SALAD PUFFS

2 c. cubed cooked lobster
2 c. diced orange sections
¼ c. minced green onions
2 tbsp. minced parsley
1 c. sour cream
¼ c. mayonnaise
1 ½ tsp. salt
1 tsp. hot pepper sauce

Combine lobster, orange sections, onions and parsley. Combine sour cream, mayonnaise, salt and pepper sauce, blending well. Add to lobster mixture; blend well. Chill until ready to fill shells.

PUFF SHELLS:

1 c. water
½ c. butter or margarine
1 c. sifted flour
Dash of salt
4 eggs

Bring water and butter to a boil in a heavy saucepan, stirring until butter melts. Add flour and salt all at once. Reduce heat. Cook and stir until mixture is smooth and forms a soft ball, 1 to 2 minutes. Remove from heat and cool mixture slightly. Add an egg at a time, beating well after each addition. Drop batter by rounded tablespoonfuls in 8 mounds onto lightly greased baking sheet. Bake at 400 degrees for 40 to 45 minutes or until firm to the touch. Cool; cut off tops of shells and scoop out insides. Fill with chilled lobster mixture. Refrigerate until ready to serve. Yield: 8 servings.

Mrs. Lloyd Sorenson
Columbus, Mississippi

LOBSTER MOUSSE

3 3-oz. pkg. cream cheese
1 can tomato soup
2 tbsp. gelatin
1 c. cold water
½ to ¾ c. chopped celery
2 tbsp. chopped green onion
¼ to ½ c. chopped green pepper
1 ½ c. cooked or canned lobster
1 c. mayonnaise
Salt and pepper to taste
Tabasco sauce to taste
Worcestershire sauce

Blend cheese and soup; heat until smooth. Soak gelatin in cold water; add to hot mixture. Chill until mixture begins to congeal. Add celery, onion, green pepper and lobster. Add mayonnaise and seasonings to taste. Pour into 2-quart fish mold; chill until firm.

Mrs. Everett W. Holstrom
Fort Polk, Louisiana

LOBSTER-POTATO SALAD

½ tsp. powdered mustard
2 tbsp. instant minced onion
2 tbsp. water
2 c. cooked chopped lobster
1 c. cold diced cooked potatoes
2 tbsp. fresh lemon juice
1 ½ tsp. salt
¼ tsp. garlic powder
⅛ tsp. pepper
⅓ c. mayonnaise
1 head lettuce
Paprika

Soak mustard and onion in water for 10 minutes; add lobster, potatoes, lemon juice, salt, garlic, pepper and mayonnaise. Mix lightly; serve on lettuce. Garnish with paprika. Yield: 6 servings.

Mrs. L. R. Scott
Jacksonville, Florida

LOBSTER SALAD

1 ½ c. lobster or shrimp
1 c. coarsely chopped celery
½ c. sliced stuffed olives
4 hard-cooked eggs, diced
Mayonnaise
Salt to taste

Mix lobster, celery, olives and eggs; chill until ready to serve. Add mayonnaise and salt. Serve on crisp lettuce leaf with lemon slice. Yield: 4 servings.

Mrs. Eugene Lee
Baltimore, Maryland

LOBSTER SALAD

1 ½ c. diced lobster
Vinegar
½ c. diced celery
Mayonnaise
Lettuce

Sprinkle lobster with a very little vinegar. Mix lobster and celery; stir in enough mayonnaise to moisten and flavor. Arrange salad on center of crisp white lettuce bed bordered with green lettuce leaves. Pour on additional mayonnaise. Yield: 6 servings.

Theresa Suedekum
Lakeland, Florida

LOBSTER SALAD

1 sm. can lobster
1 tomato, cut into small pieces
1 hard-cooked egg, chopped
Chopped lettuce
Salad dressing

Mix lobster with tomato, egg, lettuce and enough salad dressing to moisten. Serve on buttered toast.

Mrs. Theodore Pembroke
Marion, Alabama

LOBSTER SALAD

¼ c. butter
¼ c. lemon juice
¼ c. brown sugar
Lobster
1 lge. fresh, cubed or 1 qt. canned chunk pineapple
1 ⅓ c. diced celery
1 ½ c. cottage cheese
½ tsp. salt
1 ⅓ c. green grapes, seeded

Melt butter; add lemon juice and brown sugar. Boil. Remove from heat; add lobster cut in pieces. Combine remaining ingredients; toss in lobster mixture. Serve on lettuce.

Utha Richardson
Braman, Oklahoma

LOBSTER SALAD IN PINEAPPLE SHELLS

1 ripe pineapple
2 c. sour cream
2 tbsp. lemon juice
1 tsp. salt
1 tbsp. curry powder
½ c. chopped green mango chutney
4 c. chopped cooked lobster
1 c. sliced pimento-stuffed olives
½ c. toasted almonds

Halve pineapple and crown lengthwise, leaving crown on pineapple. Carefully cut out fruit in wedges, leaving 1/2-inch shell. Remove core; cut fruit into 1 1/2-inch wedges. Blend sour cream, lemon juice, salt, curry powder and chutney; toss lightly with lobster, sliced olives and pineapple wedges. Heap into pineapple shells; sprinkle with almonds. Yield: 6 servings.

Mrs. Allen Goodson
Fort Hood, Texas

LOBSTER SALAD WITH TOMATO ASPIC RING

1 c. chopped cooked lobster
¼ c. French dressing
1 c. chopped celery
2 hard-cooked eggs, chopped
Mayonnaise

Marinate lobster in French dressing for 1 hour. Drain. Add chopped celery and eggs. Moisten with mayonnaise.

ASPIC RING:

2 tbsp. unflavored gelatin
3 ½ c. cold tomato juice or V-8 juice
½ c. hot tomato juice or V-8 juice
1 c. chopped celery
2 tbsp. lemon juice

Soak gelatin in cold juice. Dissolve in hot juice. Chill until slightly thickened. Add celery and lemon juice. Pour into oiled 4 1/2 to 5-cup ring mold. Chill until firm. Unmold onto lettuce leaves and fill center with lobster salad. Yield: 4 servings.

Mrs. W. R. Massey
Tulsa, Oklahoma

LOBSTER SALAD TROPICALE

1 c. diced cooked lobster meat
1 grapefruit, separated into segments
1 avocado, sliced
½ c. slivered toasted almonds
½ c. mayonnaise
1 tsp. horseradish
Dash of cayenne pepper
Salt to taste
Mixed salad greens

Mix lobster, grapefruit, avocado and almonds lightly. Mix mayonnaise, horseradish and pepper; fold into lobster mixture. Add salt; serve on greens. Yield: 4 servings.

Mrs. J. E. Swaim, Jr.
England, Arkansas

ROCK LOBSTER SEASHELL SALAD

6 3-oz. South African rock lobster tails
1 8-oz. pkg. macaroni shells
½ c. green pepper, finely diced
1 tsp. onion juice
½ c. stuffed olives, sliced
½ c. mayonnaise
¼ c. catsup
½ tsp. Augostura aromatic bitters
Salt and pepper to taste

Drop lobster tails in boiling salted water. When water reboils, simmer 3 to 5 minutes. Drain immediately and drench in cold water. With kitchen shears, cut along each edge of thin membrane and remove. Pull meat from shell in 1 piece. Dice rock lobster meat. Cook macaroni shells according to package directions. Drain in colander and rinse with cold water. Chill. Mix together macaroni, rock lobster pieces, green pepper, celery, onion juice and olives. Combine mayonnaise, catsup and bitters; add to salad. Toss all together lightly but thoroughly. Chill well. At serving time decorate bowl with empty rock lobster shell. Yield: 6 servings.

Photograph for this recipe on page 303.

PINEAPPLE SOUTH SEAS SALAD

1 c. rice
2 ½ c. chicken broth
1 14-oz. can pineapple tidbits
1 c. cooked peas
¼ c. chopped green onion
½ c. thinly sliced celery
1 c. cooked lobster
¼ c. chopped macadamia nuts or peanuts
Soy dressing

Heat rice in skillet, stirring until golden. Add chicken broth. Heat to boiling. Cover tightly; reduce heat to low and cook 20 minutes. Fluff rice with fork. Cool. Cover and chill. When ready to serve, add remaining ingredients including soy dressing. Toss gently but thoroughly. Serve in crisp lettuce cups. Yield: 6 servings.

June Lunsford
Mena, Arkansas

TOSSED FRESH VEGETABLE AND SEAFOOD SALAD

Salad greens
1 ½ c. sliced celery
1 c. shredded carrots
1 ½ c. cooked potato balls or diced potatoes
⅓ c. chopped green onions, bulbs and tops
2 c. fresh or canned lobster, shrimp, crab meat or tuna
1 ½ tbsp. fresh lemon juice
4 tbsp. salad or olive oil
1 ½ tsp. salt
¼ tsp. ground black pepper
Tomato slices or wedges
Fresh parsley
Mayonnaise (opt.)

Line a bowl with washed dry salad greens. Top with the vegetables and seafood. Combine lemon juice, oil, salt and black pepper. Pour over salad. Toss lightly. Garnish with tomato slices and fresh parsley. If desired, serve with mayonnaise. Yield: 6 servings.

Photograph for this recipe on cover.

OYSTER SALAD

1 pt. oysters, washed and drained
2 c. chopped celery
French dressing
Lettuce
8 slices lemon
8 sprigs parsley

Place oysters in saucepan with a little water; simmer until edges begin to curl. Cool; drain and cut into quarters. Add celery; moisten with French dressing. Place on lettuce; garnish with lemon slices and parsley. Yield: 8 servings.

Phebie L. Ward
Pine Bluff, Arkansas

OYSTER SALAD

1 can oysters
2 tbsp. vinegar
½ tsp. salt
2 tbsp. butter
Dash of black pepper
½ c. cracker crumbs
3 hard-boiled eggs, chopped
3 sm. sweet cucumber pickles, chopped
3 tbsp. salad dressing
Paprika

Drain oysters; mix juice with vinegar, salt, butter and pepper. Cook juice mixture 2 minutes. Mash oysters. Add cracker crumbs, eggs, pickles and salad dressing. Mix all ingredients together; sprinkle with paprika.

Mrs. Oscar Grisham
Elmwood, Tennessee

SCALLOP SALAD

2 lb. sea scallops, cooked
1 c. sliced celery
1 c. diced cucumbers
¼ c. sliced stuffed olives
½ c. French dressing
1 c. mayonnaise
Salt to taste
Lemon juice to taste
Watercress

Cut scallops into chunks; combine with celery, cucumbers and olives. Add French dressing; chill for several hours. Add mayonnaise, salt and lemon juice. Serve on watercress in scallop shells. Yield: 6 servings.

Sharon Hernandez
New Braunfels, Texas

CELERY ROOT-SHRIMP SALAD

2 lge. celery roots
Bleu cheese dressing
1 green onion, chopped
1 tsp. Tabasco sauce
1 lb. cleaned shrimp
2 tbsp. mayonnaise
Parsley

Boil celery root in the skin until soft; peel and mash. Mix with bleu cheese dressing. Add onion, Tabasco sauce and a few broken shrimp. Fill sherbet glasses half full with mixture. Put remaining shrimp on top. Garnish with mayonnaise and parsley. Yield: 8 servings.

Elsie Schmidt
New Orleans, Louisiana

FLORIDIAN SHRIMP SALAD

3 c. small cooked deveined shrimp, or cut larger ones
6 hard-cooked eggs, sliced
1 sm. bunch celery, cut fine
6 sm. sweet pickles, chopped
1 sm. bottle stuffed olives, chopped fine
1 tsp. mustard
1 c. chopped pecans
Mayonnaise
Lettuce
Paprika

Mix first 8 ingredients well; season to taste with salt and pepper. Chill. Serve on lettuce leaves and sprinkle paprika over each serving.

Mrs. Russell O. Behrens
Apalachicola, Florida

AVOCADO-SHRIMP SALAD

1 med. can deveined shrimp
1 sm. box macaroni, cooked
1 avocado, cut in sm. pieces
1 stalk celery, chopped
1 onion, chopped
½ green pepper, diced
4 hard-cooked eggs, sliced
1 c. salad dressing
2 tsp. evaporated milk
½ tsp. white vinegar
½ tsp. sugar
Paprika

Mix shrimp, macaroni, avocado, celery, onion, green pepper and eggs in large glass bowl. Using wooden spoon, mix salad dressing, milk, vinegar and sugar; beat thoroughly. Add to salad. Cover and refrigerate for 4 hours. Sprinkle with paprika. Yield: 8 servings.

Mrs. M. K. Conrad
Talladega, Alabama

FIFFLER'S GREEN STUFFED AVOCADOS

Avocados
Small shrimp or crab meat
1/3 c. chili sauce
2/3 c. mayonnaise
Dash of lemon juice
Capers (opt.)

Cut avocados into halves lengthwise; do not peel. Remove seed. Combine remaining ingredients; fill avocado halves.

Mrs. B. A. Phillips
Paducah, Kentucky

AVOCADO WITH SHRIMP

2 med. avocados, pared and cut lengthwise
Shredded lettuce
Lettuce leaves
20 shrimp
1/2 c. chopped celery
2 hard-cooked eggs, chopped
2 tbsp. mayonnaise
2 hard-cooked eggs, sliced
Ripe or stuffed olives

Lay avocados on bed of shredded lettuce in a lettuce leaf. Combine shrimp with celery and chopped eggs; stir in mayonnaise. Place mixture on avocado halves. Garnish with egg slices and olives.

Mrs. K. C. Hawkins
Arkadelphia, Arkansas

CURRIED SHRIMP SALAD

4 lb. cooked shrimp
2 tbsp. lemon juice
1/2 tbsp. grated onion
1 1/2 tbsp. salt
1 1/2 tbsp. curry powder
6 tbsp. sour cream
1 c. mayonnaise
1 c. melon balls
1/2 c. chopped celery
1/2 c. pineapple chunks
French dressing

Combine shrimp, lemon juice, onion and salt; chill overnight. Mix curry powder, sour cream and mayonnaise; let stand for several hours. Marinate melon balls, celery and pineapple chunks in French dressing for several hours. One hour before serving, combine all ingredients; chill until serving time. Yield: 8 servings.

Mrs. S. A. Chandler
Meridian, Mississippi

CURRIED SHRIMP AND MELON SALAD

1 1/2 tbsp. mild curry powder
6 tbsp. sour cream
4 c. cooked cleaned shrimp
1 c. mayonnaise
1 1/2 tbsp. grated onion
2 tbsp. lemon juice
1 1/2 c. chopped celery
1 1/2 tsp. salt
1 lge. honeydew melon
1 c. chopped nuts
1 c. grated coconut
1 c. chutney

Blend curry powder into sour cream; mix with shrimp, mayonnaise, onion, lemon juice, celery and salt; chill for several hours. Scoop balls out of melon. Remove remaining melon from shell; fill shell with salad. Garnish with melon balls. Serve with chopped nuts, grated coconut and chutney as condiments. Yield: 8 servings.

Mrs. James L. Jarnagin
Cascade, Maryland

LIME-SHRIMP SALAD

1 1-lb. 13-oz. can pear halves
1 3-oz. pkg. lime-flavored gelatin
1 c. boiling water
1 12-oz. pkg. frozen cooked shrimp, thawed
2 c. cottage cheese
1 tbsp. lemon juice
1/2 tsp. grated lemon rind
1/2 tsp. salt
1 envelope unflavored gelatin
2 tsp. lime juice
1/2 tsp. grated lime rind
1/2 tsp. salt
1 c. sour cream

Drain pears, reserving syrup. In mixing bowl, dissolve lime gelatin in boiling water; stir in 3/4 cup pear syrup. Pour into salad mold and chill until mixture begins to set. Cut 4 pear halves in half. Arrange pear quarters in gelatin mixture in sunburst fashion. Chill until set. Set aside 8 shrimp. Dice remaining shrimp and pear halves. In a mixing bowl, blend together cottage cheese, lemon juice, lemon rind, salt, diced pears and diced shrimp. In saucepan, sprinkle unflavored gelatin over 1/2 cup pear syrup. Stir over low heat until dissolved. Stir into cottage cheese mixture. Arrange reserved shrimp around edge of mold. Carefully pour cottage cheese mixture over the lime layer and chill until firm. Unmold onto greens on a chilled plate. In mixing bowl, gently fold lime juice, grated lime rind and salt into sour cream. Chill. Sprinkle with additional grated lime rind before serving with salad. Yield: 8 servings.

Martha Hooper
Gray Court, South Carolina

HAWAIIAN SHRIMP SALADS

1 ½ c. cooked cleaned shrimp
1 c. sliced celery
1 c. fresh, frozen or canned pineapple chunks
½ c. broken pecans
½ tsp. minced onion
½ c. mayonnaise
¼ c. French dressing
Salt
Lemon juice to taste
¼ c. sliced stuffed olives (opt.)
Lettuce
2 papayas or 2 avocados (opt.)

Combine all ingredients except lettuce and papayas. Refrigerate until well chilled. Serve in lettuce cups or place in halves of chilled seeded and pared papayas arranged on lettuce. Yield: 4 servings.

Mrs. J. B. Murray
Huntington, West Virginia

MANDARIN-SHRIMP SALAD

⅓ c. heavy cream, whipped
½ c. mayonnaise
2 lb. shrimp, boiled and cleaned
1 5 ¼-oz. can water chestnuts, drained and thinly sliced
1 11-oz. can mandarin oranges, drained
2 dashes of Tabasco sauce
Salt
White pepper
Lettuce leaves
1 bunch watercress
1 2-oz. jar pimento strips, drained

Fold whipped cream into mayonnaise. Combine shrimp, mayonnaise mixture, water chestnuts, orange segments and Tabasco sauce; add salt and white pepper to taste. Marinate for 30 minutes in refrigerator. Line cold serving plates with lettuce leaves; spoon salad onto lettuce. Place 2 large sprigs of watercress on each salad at opposite sides of serving plates. Place pimento strips on top of salad just before serving. Yield: 4 servings.

Mrs. R. C. Graham
Columbia, South Carolina

SHRIMP AND AVOCADO SALAD

1 lb. cooked shrimp
½ c. finely chopped celery
1 tbsp. minced onion
⅓ c. mayonnaise
3 tsp. lemon juice
1 tbsp. chili sauce
2 lge. ripe avocados
Salad greens

Chill shrimp; add celery, onion, mayonnaise, 1 teaspoon lemon juice and chili sauce. Toss well. Cover; refrigerate for 1 hour. Cut avocados into halves lengthwise; remove pits. Sprinkle with remaining lemon juice. Top each half with one-fourth of shrimp mixture, mounding high. Serve on salad greens. Yield: 4 servings.

Mrs. W. O. Edwards
Tucson, Arizona

MOLDED SHRIMP AND AVOCADO SALAD

1 ½ envelopes unflavored gelatin
½ c. cold water
1 c. boiling water
1 ½ tsp. salt
¼ c. lemon juice
¼ tsp. Tabasco sauce
¼ tsp. Worcestershire sauce
½ c. mayonnaise
2 c. mashed avocados
1 c. shrimp
½ c. chopped celery
2 hard-cooked eggs, chopped
¼ c. chopped parsley
1 tsp. grated onion

Sprinkle gelatin on cold water to soften; add boiling water and salt. Stir until dissolved. Add lemon juice, Tabasco sauce and Worcestershire sauce; cool. Mix mayonnaise and mashed avocados; combine with shrimp, celery, eggs, parsley and onion. Stir into cooled gelatin mixture. Turn into 2-quart mold; chill until set. Yield: 6-8 servings.

Mrs. Caleb Baker
Meridian, Mississippi

SHRIMP HAWAIIAN

1 14-oz. can pineapple chunks
6 c. broken salad greens
2 5-oz. cans deveined shrimp, drained
1 5-oz. can water chestnuts, drained and coarsely chopped
½ c. mayonnaise or salad dressing
¼ c. crumbled Roquefort cheese

Drain pineapple, reserving 2 tablespoons syrup. Place salad greens in a large bowl; pile shrimp, pineapple chunks and water chestnuts in rows on top. Blend reserved pineapple syrup into mayonnaise and cheese. Drizzle over salad mixture; toss lightly to mix. Yield: 6 servings.

Mrs. J. R. Pennington
Myrtle Beach, South Carolina

SHRIMP AND MANDARIN ORANGE SALAD

2 7-oz. pkg. frozen shrimp
1 8-oz. can mandarin orange sections, drained
1 tbsp. minced onion
1 tbsp. minced celery
Dash of garlic powder
Mayonnaise to moisten

Cook shrimp according to directions on package; place in bowl. Add remaining ingredients; mix well. Chill in the refrigerator; serve on leaf lettuce, if desired. Yield: 3 servings.

Mrs. F. C. Whitehouse
Dover, Delaware

SHRIMP PARADISE SALAD

1 pineapple, halved lengthwise
1 avocado, halved lengthwise
1 tbsp. orange juice
2 oranges, peeled and diced
¾ lb. cooked peeled shrimp, chilled

Remove core and meat from pineapple, reserving shell. Remove seed from avocado; peel and slice. Sprinkle with orange juice to prevent discoloration. Combine pineapple, oranges and avocado. Fill reserved pineapple shell with fruit mixture. Top with shrimp. Yield: 6 servings.

Carolyn Bassett
Jacksonville, Florida

SHRIMP AND PINEAPPLE SALAD

1 ½ c. cooked shrimp
1 ½ c. diced pineapple
2 sprigs chives, chopped
½ tsp. salt
⅛ tsp. paprika
Crisp lettuce
French dressing

Combine shrimp, pineapple, chives, salt and paprika; mix well. Chill; serve on bed of lettuce with French dressing. Yield: 6-8 servings.

Mrs. Robert Willhoite
Panama City, Florida

SHRIMP SALAD

1 5 ¾-oz. can or fresh shrimp
1 c. finely diced celery
1 tsp. minced onion
1 lge. orange, sectioned
Mayonnaise

Devein shrimp; chill. Add celery, onion and orange sections. Add mayonnaise to moisten. Serve on lettuce. Yield: 4 servings.

Mrs. S. M. Harris
Charlottesville, Virginia

SHRIMP-PINEAPPLE SALAD

1 ½ c. canned shrimp
French dressing
1 ½ c. diced pineapple
1 ½ c. shredded cabbage
½ tsp. salt
⅛ tsp. paprika
Mayonnaise

Devein shrimp; marinate in French dressing. Chill. Combine pineapple, shrimp and cabbage. Add salt, paprika and enough mayonnaise to moisten. Mix lightly with 2 forks. Serve on crisp lettuce; garnish with sliced, stuffed olives. Yield: 6 servings.

Mrs. Goldie Hall
Olive Hill, Kentucky

SHRIMP SALAD

2 7-oz. cans shrimp
5 stalks celery, diced
1 No. 303 can pineapple chunks, drained
1 c. pecans
Mayonnaise

Chill all ingredients; mix lightly. Serve in lettuce cup. Yield: 4-6 servings.

Mrs. Gary Wiltse
Jackson, Mississippi

SUPREME SHRIMP SALAD

1 can frozen shrimp soup
1 8-oz. pkg. cream cheese
1 lb. shrimp, cooked, deveined and cooled
Garlic salt to taste
2 avocados
2 tbsp. lemon juice

Thaw frozen, undiluted soup to jelly-like consistency and whip with softened cream cheese by hand. Season shrimp with garlic salt and combine with cream cheese mixture. Serve on avocado half, sprinkled with lemon juice. Yield: 4 servings.

Mrs. Lillian Herman
Bay City, Texas

BAKED SHRIMP SALAD

1 tbsp. finely chopped onion
¼ c. finely chopped green pepper
1 c. finely chopped celery
Butter
1 lb. cooked cleaned shrimp
1 tbsp. finely chopped pimento
1 tbsp. lemon juice
¼ tsp. Worcestershire sauce
1 c. mayonnaise
Salt and pepper to taste
Bread crumbs

Saute onion, green pepper and celery in a small amount of butter until golden brown. Mix all ingredients except crumbs. Place in a greased 8 x 2-inch or 9 x 1 1/2-inch pan. Sprinkle with bread crumbs. Bake at 350 degrees for 25 minutes or until slightly brown. Yield: 4-6 servings.

Mrs. T. S. Clark
Wilmington, Delaware

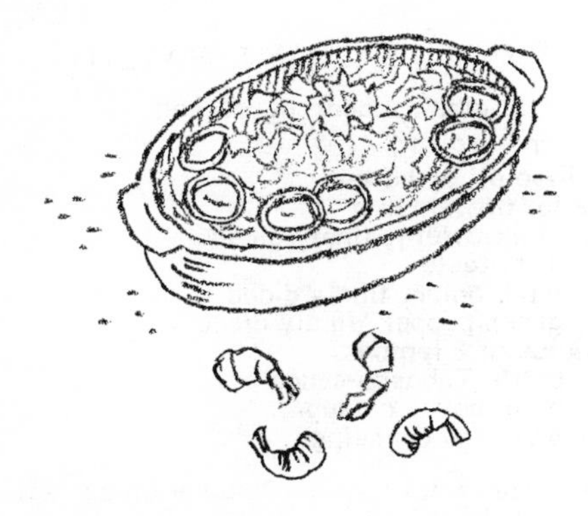

HOT SHRIMP SALAD BOATS

1 can frozen cream of shrimp soup
1 can cream of mushroom soup
1 tsp. Worcestershire sauce
1 tbsp. lemon juice
2 c. diced celery
⅓ c. diced green pepper
⅓ c. diced pimento
⅓ c. sliced ripe olives
⅓ c. toasted slivered almonds
3 c. diced cooked shrimp
Salt and pepper to taste
10 oblong hard rolls
Melted butter
Lettuce

Combine soups in heavy saucepan. Add Worcestershire sauce and lemon juice. Simmer until thoroughly blended, stirring frequently. Stir in remaining ingredients except rolls. Season mixture to taste. Keep warm over hot water until serving time. Hollow out hard roll and brush centers with butter. Place under broiler until lightly toasted. Line with lettuce leaves and fill with hot shrimp salad. Sprinkle with cardamom seed, if desired. Yield: 10 servings.

Mrs. J. M. Dunn
Pine Bluff, Arkansas

SHRIMP SALAD BOAT

1 loaf Italian bread, unsliced
4 hard-cooked eggs, diced
1 c. chopped shrimp
1 c. diced celery
2 tbsp. chopped dill pickle
2 tbsp. chopped stuffed olives
1 tbsp. minced scallions
½ tsp. garlic salt
¼ tsp. dry mustard
½ c. mayonnaise
2 tbsp. melted butter

Cut off top of loaf of bread. Hollow out leaving a 1 inch thick shell. Measure 1 cup bread crumbs from center of loaf and combine with remaining ingredients except butter. Spoon lightly into loaf; replace top. Brush entire loaf with melted butter and wrap in aluminum foil. Bake at 450 degrees for 30 minutes. Cut into 6 thick slices and serve at once. Chicken, ham or tuna may replace shrimp. Yield: 6 servings.

Mrs. R. C. Lewis
Augusta, Georgia

MACARONI SALAD WITH SHRIMP

Cooked macaroni
¾ c. mayonnaise
1 tbsp. lemon juice
1 tbsp. salad oil
1 tbsp. vinegar
Salt and pepper to taste
2 c. diced celery
Celery leaves
1 med. onion, finely diced
1 tbsp. parsley flakes
4 hard-cooked eggs, mashed
1 med. can shrimp, drained, washed and diced
Paprika

Rinse macaroni with cold water; drain. Add mayonnaise, lemon juice, salad oil, vinegar, salt and pepper; mix. Combine celery, a small amount of celery leaves, onion, parsley, eggs and shrimp. Blend thoroughly. Add a few tablespoonfuls cold water if salad seems too dry. Garnish with paprika; chill until ready to serve. Serve on lettuce if desired. Yield: 6-8 servings.

Mrs. Virgil Harkins
Miami, Florida

SAVORY SHRIMP SALAD

3 c. cooked macaroni
¼ lb. sharp cheddar cheese, cut into 1-in. cubes
4 hard-cooked eggs, quartered
¾ c. chopped celery
½ c. chopped sweet pickle
2 tbsp. chopped pimento
1 6½-oz. can shrimp, chopped
2 tsp. lemon juice
1 tbsp. chopped onion
Salt and pepper to taste
Mayonnaise

(Continued on next page)

Gently mix all ingredients, using enough mayonnaise to moisten. Serve on bed of lettuce. Garnish with olives and radishes. Yield: 8 servings.

Mrs. Clyde Parks
Louisville, Kentucky

SEAFOOD SALAD

1 ½ c. macaroni
1 ½ c. celery hearts
½ c. green pepper
2 sm. pieces pimento
2 tbsp. minced parsley
2 cans white meat tuna
1 lb. cooked shrimp
2 hard-cooked eggs
Salt
Pepper
Garlic salt
1 ½ tbsp. vinegar
Mayonnaise

Cook macaroni until tender in salted water. Pour cold water over macaroni and drain. Add chopped celery hearts, chopped pepper, pimento and parsley. Run hot water over tuna to remove oil. Rinse in cold water; drain. Mix tuna and shrimp; add chopped egg white. Press egg yolk through sieve. Season to taste; add vinegar and mayonnaise to moisten. Serve on lettuce. Garnish with additional eggs, olives, green pepper, pimento strips and lemon slices.

Mrs. Thomas T. Jones
Milford, Delaware

SHELL MACARONI AND SHRIMP SALAD

1 7-oz. pkg. shell macaroni
½ c. mayonnaise
2 tsp. prepared mustard
2 tbsp. minced onion
2 c. sliced celery
1 c. shrimp, chicken or ham
⅓ c. sweet pickle relish
½ c. chopped green pepper
½ c. green stuffed olives, whole
Lettuce cups

Cook shell macaroni as directed on package. Cool. Blend mayonnaise and mustard until smooth. Combine with remaining ingredients and macaroni. Toss until coated with dressing. Serve in lettuce cups, garnished with hard-cooked eggs, pimento and paprika. Yield: 6 servings.

Mrs. Charles H. Anderson
Manor, Texas

SHRIMP DINNER SALAD

4 c. shell macaroni, cooked
½ c. French dressing
2 c. raw cauliflowerets
1 c. thinly sliced scallions
1 tsp. salt
¼ tsp. pepper
2 lb. cooked shrimp
1 c. sliced ripe olives
1 c. mayonnaise
½ c. chili sauce

Toss macaroni with French dressing; chill for 1 hour. Add cauliflower, scallions, salt, pepper, shrimp and olives. Blend mayonnaise and chili sauce; pour over salad. Toss to mix. Yield: 10 servings.

Mary Nell Fleming
Atlanta, Georgia

SHRIMP-MACARONI SALAD

1 ½ lb. elbow macaroni, cooked and drained
Olive oil or butter
2 lb. tiny shrimp
⅓ stalk celery, finely diced
Salt to taste
1 med. onion, finely diced
1 green pepper, finely diced
Juice of 2 lemons
⅛ bottle Tabasco sauce
1 med. bottle catsup
1 pt. salad dressing

Mix macaroni with olive oil. Combine all ingredients; mix well.

Mrs. H. L. Voelkert
High Point, North Carolina

SHRIMP-MACARONI SALAD

1 pkg. ring macaroni
1 c. cooked and broken shrimp
1 tomato, finely cut
½ c. diced celery
⅓ c. cucumber, chopped
¼ c. finely sliced green onion
1 sm. green pepper, finely cut
¼ c. sliced radishes
½ c. mayonnaise
½ tsp. salt
⅛ tsp. pepper

Cook macaroni; rinse with cold water and drain. Add shrimp and vegetables. Fold in mayonnaise. Season with salt and pepper; chill. Serve on lettuce. Yield: 4-6 servings.

Mrs. Peter Johnson
Nashville, Tennessee

SHRIMP SALAD

3 c. cooked macaroni
½ c. shredded carrots
½ c. chopped celery
¼ c. finely chopped onion
2 cans salad shrimp
2 tbsp. sweet pickle relish
½ to 1 c. mayonnaise
Salt and pepper to taste

Combine all ingredients in large bowl. Cover and refrigerate until ready to serve. Yield: 6 servings.

Mrs. Norman Pfleger
Chattanooga, Tennessee

SHRIMP SALAD

2 c. cooked macaroni or 1 ½ boxes juniorette macaroni, cooked
1 c. chopped celery
1 sm. or med. onion, chopped
¼ c. finely sliced green onion
¼ c. chopped pimento
¼ c. French dressing
3 c. cooked or 2 4-oz. cans shrimp
2 to 5 hard-cooked eggs, sliced
½ tsp. salt
Pepper to taste (opt.)
¼ tsp. paprika (opt.)
1 c. salad dressing or mayonnaise

Chill macaroni; add remaining ingredients. Mix well. Yield: 4-6 servings.

Mrs. Fred Stoffel
Virginia Beach, Virginia

SHRIMP SALAD

1 lb. elbow macaroni, cooked
1 lge. can English peas, drained
1 14-oz. jar salad olives, drained
1 jar sweet pickles, chopped
¼ c. chopped onion
1 c. chopped celery
1 8-oz. jar pickled onions, drained
2 cans shrimp
2 bottles French dressing
Mayonnaise

Combine all ingredients except French dressing and mayonnaise. Mix well. Marinate in French dressing overnight. Add enough mayonnaise to moisten. Serve cold. Yield: 20 servings.

Elizabeth D. Ivey
Dover, Tennessee

SHRIMP SALAD

1 sm. pkg. macaroni
1 can peas
1 lb. boiled shrimp
Mayonnaise

Cook macaroni as directed on package; drain well. Add peas, shrimp and enough mayonnaise to moisten. Chill. Yield: 6-8 servings.

Mrs. F. M. Howard
Louisville, Kentucky

MOLDED CHEESE AND TOMATO SALAD

1 tbsp. gelatin
¼ c. cold water
1 can tomato soup
1 c. smooth cottage cheese
½ c. mayonnaise
½ c. heavy cream, whipped
Dash of salt
⅓ c. chopped green pepper
⅓ c. chopped celery
⅓ c. chopped onion
1 sm. cucumber, peeled and diced
1 c. shrimp or crab meat (opt.)

Soak gelatin in cold water. Heat soup; stir. Add gelatin, stirring until dissolved. Beat in cottage cheese. Cool. Fold in remaining ingredients. Place salad in wet ring mold. Chill until set. Serve with mayonnaise, if desired. Yield: 8 servings.

Mrs. L. S. Kirkland
Atlanta, Georgia

ORIENTAL SALAD

1 c. shredded lettuce
2 c. cleaned cooked shrimp
4 slices boiled ham, cut into thin strips
1 c. celery strips
½ c. green pepper strips
½ c. toasted, blanched slivered almonds or macadamia nuts
1 can crisp chow mein noodles

Combine lettuce, shrimp, ham and vegetables; chill. Just before serving, add nuts, noodles and desired dressing. Yield: 4 servings.

Mrs. O. C. Norman
Clearwater, Florida

QUICK SHRIMP SALAD

1 sm. head lettuce, shredded
2 sm. tomatoes, chopped
1 green pepper, chopped (opt.)
2 sticks celery, chopped
1 sm. onion
1 sm. can shrimp

Combine all ingredients; toss lightly. Serve with favorite salad dressing. Yield: 8 servings.

Mrs. Robert Kern
Baton Rouge, Louisiana

COLD RICE AND SEAFOOD SALAD

1 c. shrimp, crab meat or lobster
1 c. drained canned peas
¼ c. diced pimento
¼ c. chopped ripe olives
1 ½ c. cooked rice
2 tsp. grated onion
1 tsp. salt
Dash of pepper
2 tsp. lemon or lime juice
⅔ c. mayonnaise
1 lge. head lettuce
Green pepper strips

Combine all ingredients except lettuce and green pepper strips. Chill. Wash lettuce; cut out core to make a cavity large enough for stuffing. Pack cold salad into lettuce cavity. Chill; cut into wedges. Garnish with green pepper strips. Yield: 4 servings.

Jane Johnston
Decatur, Georgia

NEW ORLEANS SHRIMP SALAD

½ c. uncooked rice
1 4 ½-oz. can shrimp, drained
½ green pepper, finely chopped
1 sm. onion, finely chopped
1 c. caulifloweret s
6 stuffed olives, sliced
Juice of 1 lemon
Salt and pepper to taste
Dash of Tabasco sauce
¼ to ½ c. mayonnaise

Cook rice in boiling salted water; drain and cool. Combine shrimp, rice, green pepper, onion, cauliflowerets, olives and lemon juice; add seasonings and mayonnaise. Stir very carefully. Chill for at least 4 hours. Yield: 4 servings.

Mrs. Frank L. Jones
Alexandria, Louisiana

SET SHRIMP SALAD

1 pkg. lemon or vegetable gelatin
1 ½ c. boiling water
½ c. heavy cream, whipped
½ c. salad dressing or mayonnaise
1 sm. pkg. cream cheese
3 hard-cooked eggs, chopped
2 c. chopped celery
1 can shrimp
2 c. chopped nuts
1 tsp. grated onion

Dissolve gelatin in hot water; chill until mixture begins to thicken. Add whipped cream. Add salad dressing and softened cream cheese. Add remaining ingredients. Chill in individual molds or large mold. Yield: 10 servings.

Carol Shenton
Arlington, Virginia

SHRIMP ASPIC

2 envelopes unflavored gelatin
½ c. cold water
2 ½ c. tomato juice
1 tsp. prepared horseradish
¼ tsp. red pepper
1 tsp. salt
2 tbsp. lemon juice
1 tsp. Worcestershire sauce
1 ½ c. cooked shrimp
¼ c. diced celery
¼ c. finely chopped green pepper

Soften gelatin in cold water. Heat 1 cup tomato juice and pour over gelatin until dissolved. Add remaining tomato juice and seasonings. Chill until mixture begins to thicken; add remaining ingredients. Pour into oiled mold and chill until set.

Mrs. Roy Waitz
Alexandria, Louisiana

SHRIMP CUCUMBERS

3 lge. cucumbers
1 lge. pkg. cream cheese
Milk
1 can shrimp or crab meat, cut into small pieces

Remove seed and interior from cucumbers; score peel with fork. Soften cream cheese with milk; add shrimp. Stuff cucumbers with mixture; cool in refrigerator. Before serving, cut into circles. Yield: 8 servings.

Linda Nelson Kirklin
Richmond, Virginia

SHRIMP IN LIME RING

2 tbsp. unflavored gelatin
3 c. water
1 6-oz. can frozen limeade, thawed
½ c. sweet pickle liquid
¼ c. vinegar
⅓ c. plus ¼ c. chopped sweet mixed pickles
Salt and pepper
2 tsp. prepared horseradish
1 c. sour cream
2 5-oz. cans shrimp, drained

Soften gelatin in 1/2 cup water; add remaining water. Cook over low heat until gelatin dissolves. Add limeade concentrate, 1/4 cup pickle liquid and vinegar; mix well. Chill until slightly thickened. Fold in 1/3 cup pickles, 1 teaspoon salt, 1/8 teaspoon pepper and horseradish; mix well. Turn into 8-inch ring mold. Chill for 2 to 3 hours or until set. Combine sour cream, remaining pickle liquid, chopped pickles and salt and pepper to taste; mix well. Chill. Unmold gelatin ring; fill center with shrimp. Serve with sour cream dressing.

Mrs. Joan Browning
Savannah, Georgia

SHRIMP SALAD

2 tbsp. gelatin
¾ c. cold water
1 can tomato soup
1 3-oz. pkg. cream cheese
1 c. mayonnaise
1 tbsp. lemon juice
½ c. celery
½ c. pimentos
½ c. stuffed olives
2 tbsp. chopped green onion
Dash of garlic salt
Salt
1 pkg. shrimp, chopped

Soften gelatin in cold water; dissolve in soup which has been heated to boiling point. Beat in cream cheese with rotary beater until smooth. Chill to consistency of unbeaten egg whites; fold in remaining ingredients. Serve on salad greens.

Karen Green
Stuttgart, Arkansas

SHRIMP LUNCHEON SALAD

1 c. shelled pecans
½ lb. fresh shrimp
1 3-oz. can sliced, boiled mushrooms
¼ c. French dressing
1 c. diced celery
½ tsp. salt
⅛ tsp. curry powder
¼ c. mayonnaise

Cover pecans with water; bring to boil. Drain and slice with very sharp knife. Clean shrimp and cook; place nuts, drained mushrooms and shrimp in a bowl. Add dressing and mix thoroughly. Toss lightly with fork. Cover and refrigerate at least 2 hours. When ready to serve, add celery, salt, curry powder and mayonnaise. Garnish with watercress or parsley.

Mrs. Forest Cruse
Austin, Texas

SHRIMP REMOULADE

2 lb. jumbo shrimp
3 slices lemon
1 bay leaf
6 peppercorns
Pinch of thyme
4 hard-cooked eggs, minced
1 c. mayonnaise
1 tbsp. anchovy paste
2 tbsp. chopped parsley
2 tbsp. chopped green pepper
2 tbsp. finely chopped onion
2 tbsp. finely chopped celery
1 tsp. dry mustard
¼ tsp. mashed garlic
1 tsp. Worcestershire sauce
Salt and pepper to taste

Place shrimp in salted water; add lemon, bay leaf, peppercorns and thyme. Cook until shrimp are done. Remove shrimp; cool and clean. Place shrimp on lettuce bed, if desired. Combine remaining ingredients; chill. Serve over shrimp. Yield: 4 servings.

Mrs. Ben Harrell
Fort Belvoir, Virginia

SHRIMP SALAD

1 can tomato soup
1 lge. pkg. cream cheese
2 envelopes plain gelatin
1 c. cold water
¾ c. chopped celery
1 green pepper, chopped
2 tbsp. onion juice
1 c. mayonnaise
1 tsp. Worcestershire sauce
½ tsp. salt
2 c. cooked chopped shrimp

Heat soup and cream cheese until well dissolved, stirring constantly. Soak gelatin in cold water and add to soup mixture. Immediately remove from heat and let cool. Add remaining ingredients and place in mold.

Mrs. Louis McMenamy
Shallowater, Texas

SHRIMP SALAD

1 pkg. lemon gelatin
1 c. boiling water
½ c. cream
½ c. mayonnaise
1 sm. onion, grated
1 c. shrimp, cut up
1 jar pimento cheese
½ tsp. salt
3 hard-boiled eggs, chopped
1 c. celery, chopped
1 tbsp. green pepper, chopped

Mix gelatin and boiling water. When slightly cooled, add all remaining ingredients. Place in mold which has been oiled with mayonnaise. Chill till firm; serve on bed of lettuce. Garnish with wedges of tomato and olives.

Mrs. Charlie Rider
Del Rio, Texas

SHRIMP SALAD

1 c. cooked deveined shrimp
French dressing
¼ c. diced cucumber
¼ c. diced celery
½ c. mayonnaise
Iceberg lettuce wedges
Cherry tomatoes
Capers

Moisten shrimp with French dressing; chill. At serving time, mix with cucumber, celery and mayonnaise. Spoon onto chilled lettuce wedges; garnish with tomatoes and capers.

Mrs. J. W. Prince
Iuka, Mississippi

SHRIMP SALAD

2 lb. boiled cleaned and chopped shrimp
1 c. diced celery
½ c. olives, chopped
½ c. pickles, chopped
¼ c. pimento, chopped
¼ c. chopped green pepper
3 hard-cooked eggs, diced
½ c. almonds, split
Salt and pepper to taste
1 c. mayonnaise
8 lettuce cups

Combine shrimp, celery, olives, pickles, pimento, green pepper, eggs and almonds. Season with salt and pepper; mix well. Add mayonnaise and toss lightly to coat all ingredients. Chill before serving. Serve on lettuce. Yield: 8 servings.

Mrs. Walker E. Downs
Oxford, Mississippi

SHRIMP SALAD

1 ½ c. coarsely chopped cooked shrimp
1 hard-cooked egg, chopped
¼ c. finely chopped onion
½ tsp. salt
⅛ tsp. pepper
¾ c. mayonnaise
1 tbsp. vinegar
Sprigs of watercress

In a medium bowl, combine chopped shrimp, egg, onion, salt and pepper. Stir in mayonnaise and vinegar. Cover and refrigerate until serving time. Serve with tomato aspic ring. Garnish with watercress. Yield: 6 servings.

Jo Ann Carter
Folkston, Georgia

SHRIMP SALAD

1 ½ lb. shrimp
1 c. mayonnaise
2 tbsp. horseradish
1 c. finely chopped celery
½ tsp. pepper
½ c. corn oil
2 tbsp. mustard
1 c. finely chopped onion
1 tsp. salt
½ tsp. sugar

Boil shrimp in salted water 3 to 5 minutes. Peel, clean and set aside. Blend all other ingredients together thoroughly. Chop shrimp into several pieces if large and add to mayonnaise mixture. Chill well before serving on lettuce leaf. Yield: 6 servings.

Mrs. Darrell Methvin
League City, Texas

SHRIMP SALAD

1 lb. cooked shrimp
2 c. sliced celery
¼ tsp. salt
2 tsp. sugar
½ tsp. dry mustard
⅛ tsp. paprika
2 tsp. horseradish
⅓ c. oil
2 tbsp. vinegar
Lettuce

Prepare shrimp and celery. Mix dry ingredients together; add horseradish, oil and vinegar. Blend well. Pour over shrimp; let stand 2 hours in refrigerator. Add celery; serve on lettuce.

Virginia Redden
McCool, Mississippi

SHRIMP SALAD

½ med. head cabbage
2 c. boiled shrimp
1 c. mayonnaise
½ c. chopped sweet pickles
1 tbsp. vinegar
½ tsp. salt
¼ tsp. sugar
1 tbsp. grated onion
1 tsp. black pepper
½ c. diced celery
2 ripe tomatoes

Shred cabbage; chop shrimp. Blend with next 8 ingredients. Chop tomatoes and toss lightly. Chill 30 minutes and serve. Yield: 6 servings. PERSONAL COMMENT: This is a blue ribbon recipe.

Mrs. Jessie B. Barkley
Whiteville, North Carolina

SHRIMP SALAD

Lettuce
1 c. cooked cut-up shrimp
¼ c. cut-up celery
¼ c. cut-up green onions
1 hard-cooked egg, chopped
1 tbsp. Worcestershire sauce
1 tbsp. mayonnaise
Dash of mustard
¼ to ½ c. bread or cracker crumbs (opt.)
Salt and pepper to taste

Arrange lettuce on small individual plates. Combine remaining ingredients. Place on lettuce. Yield: 2-3 servings.

Jo Giamanco
Vidalia, Louisiana

SHRIMP SALAD

7 cooked shrimp
Green pepper strips
Celery, sliced
Tomatoes, diced
Thousand Island dressing
Lettuce cup

Combine shrimp with vegetables. Moisten with dressing; chill. Serve on lettuce cup.

Nita Carol Sammons
Forest Hills, Kentucky

SHRIMP SALAD BOWL

1 lb. cooked shrimp, peeled
1 head lettuce
¼ head curly lettuce
12 stuffed olives, sliced
2 hard-cooked eggs, sliced

Chill shrimp. At serving time, combine well-chilled greens, shrimp and olives in a salad bowl. Toss lightly with Piquant Mustard Dressing. Garnish with eggs.

PIQUANT MUSTARD DRESSING:

1 c. cold evaporated milk
1 tbsp. lemon juice
1 tbsp. chopped chives
3 tbsp. prepared mustard
½ tsp. salt
¼ tsp. cayenne pepper

Blend evaporated milk and lemon juice in mixing bowl. Stir in remaining ingredients. Chill. Yield: 4-6 servings.

Mrs. Nina T. Smith
Picayune, Mississippi

SHRIMP SALAD WITH LEMON

1 ½ lb. cooked fresh or 3 6-oz. cans shrimp
3 tbsp. chopped fresh parsley
1 ½ c. chopped celery
1 ½ tsp. salt
¼ tsp. ground black pepper
1 ½ tbsp. olive or salad oil
1 ½ tbsp. fresh lemon juice
3 tbsp. mayonnaise
1 head lettuce
Olives
3 hard-cooked eggs, sliced

Peel, devein and dice shrimp. Add parsley and celery. Combine salt, black pepper, olive oil, lemon juice and mayonnaise. Mix well; pour over shrimp. Toss lightly to coat. Serve on lettuce topped with olives and encircled with sliced boiled eggs.

Mrs. George Hunt
Corpus Christi, Texas

SHRIMP SALAD MOLD

2 pkg. lemon gelatin
1 ½ c. boiling water
½ c. light cream
1 8-oz. pkg. cream cheese
1 c. sliced ripe olives
1 c. diced celery
1 c. heavy cream, whipped

Dissolve gelatin in boiling water. Chill until slightly thickened. Add light cream to cream cheese; mix. Add to gelatin mixture with olives and celery. Fold in whipped cream. Place in 9-inch square pan; chill for 1 hour. Cut into squares; place on lettuce leaf.

TOPPING:

1 ½ c. chopped shrimp, drained
1 c. mayonnaise
2 tbsp. lemon juice
3 tbsp. chopped pimento
2 tbsp. onion

Combine all ingredients; pour over shrimp salad. Yield: 9 servings.

Colleen Tachovsky
Dallas, Texas

SHRIMP WILLIAM

½ c. olive oil
½ c. wine vinegar
½ c. grated onion
1 tbsp. curry powder
Garlic to taste
½ c. chili sauce
2 tbsp. salt
2 tbsp. mustard
5 lb. shrimp, cooked and chilled

Warm olive oil; add vinegar, onion, curry powder, garlic, chili sauce, salt and mustard. Toss with shrimp; marinate overnight. Sprinkle with paprika and serve on a bed of lettuce, if desired. Yield: 8 servings.

Mrs. T. E. Williams
Shreveport, Louisiana

SOUTHERN DRAWL SHRIMP SALAD

1 6-oz. pkg. curried rice mix
½ c. mayonnaise
½ c. sour cream
½ c. diced celery
¼ c. diced green pepper
1 tbsp. finely chopped green onion tops
¼ tsp. seasoned pepper
⅛ tsp. seasoned salt
2 4-oz. cans small shrimp, drained
1 egg, hard boiled
Pickled beet juice (opt.)

Cook rice mix according to package directions. Cool. Blend mayonnaise, sour cream, celery, green pepper, onion, pepper and salt. Add cooled rice and shrimp. Mix lightly. Chill. Serve on lettuce leaves. Garnish with egg slices, soaked in pickled beet juice. Pimento strips and pickle slices may also be used for garnish. Yield: 6 servings.

T. O. Davis
Waynesboro, Mississippi

SPECIAL SALAD

1 lge. head iceberg lettuce
8 cooked jumbo shrimp
2 cooked chicken breasts
1 clove garlic, cut
2 c. watercress leaves
1 hard-cooked egg, sliced
4 anchovies
1 c. tomato juice
½ c. creamed cottage cheese
3 tbsp. wine vinegar
1 tsp. salt
⅛ tsp. Worcestershire sauce

Cut up lettuce. Cut shrimp and chicken in small pieces; combine in garlic-rubbed bowl or individual salad bowls. Add watercress, egg and anchovies. Toss with dressing made from combination of remaining ingredients.

Vera Meeks
Frederick, Oklahoma

TOMATO-SHRIMP ASPIC

Juice of 1 lemon
1 can shrimp
1 pkg. strawberry gelatin
2 c. tomato juice
2 tsp. horseradish
½ tsp. salt
¾ c. chopped celery
1 sm. bottle Spanish olives

Pour lemon juice over shrimp. Dissolve gelatin in 1 cup boiling tomato juice; add 1 cup cold tomato juice. Add remaining ingredients. Pour into large mold or individual molds. Chill until firm. Serve on lettuce leaf; top with mayonnaise or favorite dressing. Yield: 6-8 servings.

Dorothy Nelson
Jacksonville, Florida

TOMATO-SHRIMP SALAD

1 round Holland rusk
Cream cheese
Tomato slice
Shredded lettuce
Boiled, peeled, deveined shrimp
¾ c. salad oil
½ c. chili sauce
½ c. sugar (about)
¼ c. vinegar
1 tsp. salt
¼ c. water
1 tsp. paprika
Juice of 1 onion

Spread Holland rusk round with cream cheese; top with slice of tomato. Place lettuce and boiled shrimp over all. Combine remaining ingredients; shake well. Serve dressing over salad.

Mrs. Kenny F. Pate
Cleveland, Mississippi

BEAN AND SHRIMP SALAD

1 1-lb. can wax beans, drained
1 15-oz. can garbanzo beans, drained
1 1-lb. can green beans, drained
1 1-lb. can red kidney beans, drained
1 med. onion, sliced and separated into rings
1 lb. shrimp, cooked, cleaned and deveined
1 pkg. Parmesan salad dressing mix

Combine all ingredients except dressing mix. Prepare dressing mix according to package directions. Toss with salad. Marinate for 8 to 12 hours. Yield: 12 servings.

Mrs. M. C. Davis
Knoxville, Tennessee

COLESLAW AND SHRIMP SALAD

1 can shrimp, drained and rinsed
¼ tsp. sugar
⅛ tsp. salt
⅛ tsp. pepper
1 sm. onion, finely chopped
½ head lge. cabbage, finely cut
¼ green pepper, finely diced
1 stalk celery, finely cut

Combine all ingredients, mixing well.

TANGY DRESSING:

2 eggs
¼ c. sugar
1 tsp. salt
2 tsp. flour
1 tsp. dry mustard
¼ tsp. pepper
½ c. vinegar
2 tsp. butter
1 c. whipped cream

Combine all ingredients except butter and cream; cook until thickened. Add butter; chill. Add whipped cream. Pour over salad. Yield: 4 servings.

Mrs. A. D. Griffin
Sherman, Texas

FAR EAST SHRIMP SALAD

1 c. mayonnaise
1 tsp. curry powder
1 tbsp. soy sauce
1 can bean sprouts
2 c. cooked shrimp
3 hard-cooked eggs, chopped
⅓ c. blanched slivered almonds
Lettuce
Tomato wedges

Combine mayonnaise, curry powder and soy sauce; toss lightly with bean sprouts, shrimp, eggs and almonds. Serve on lettuce with tomato wedges. Yield: 6 servings.

Mrs. G. R. Patton
Austin, Texas

GREEN GODDESS SALAD

½ head romaine
1 stalk chicory
1 head lettuce
1 c. plus 2 tbsp. cooked shrimp
3 med. tomatoes, peeled and quartered
½ c. julienne beets
1 clove garlic
¼ tsp. garlic puree
¼ to ½ tsp. salt
1 tsp. Worcestershire sauce
2 tbsp. anchovy paste
1 c. mayonnaise
2 to 3 tbsp. chopped chives or green onions

(Continued on next page)

Tear romaine, chicory and lettuce into bite-sized pieces. Arrange on salad plates with 1 cup shrimp, tomatoes and beets on top. Combine remaining ingredients; mix well. Serve dressing with salad.

Mrs. R. B. Nevil
McKinney, Texas

HELP YOURSELF SALAD

½ med. tomato, sliced
½ c. shrimp
½ c. cooked green beans
1 hard-cooked egg, sliced
Salad greens
6 slices cucumber
1 radish, sliced
2 tbsp. French Dressing

Toss first 4 ingredients; serve on salad greens garnished with cucumber and radish slices. Drizzle French Dressing over all.

FRENCH DRESSING:

1 tsp. salt
½ tsp. sugar
½ tsp. paprika
¼ tsp. pepper
¼ c. vinegar
¾ c. salad oil

Combine ingredients in covered jar and shake well. Yield: 1 cup dressing.

Mrs. J. E. Wilson
Chidester, Arkansas

SHRIMP SALAD

5 artichokes
Salt
1 tbsp. lemon juice
2 5-oz. cans shrimp
1 c. mayonnaise
1 tsp. chopped cloves
1 tsp. chopped pimento
Lettuce
5 lge. tomato slices
2 hard-boiled eggs
3 tbsp. chili sauce

Snap off artichoke leaves; trim heart. Cook artichoke hearts in boiling water with salt and lemon juice about 35 minutes or until tender. Drain; rinse with cold water. Chill. Drain and rinse shrimp; chill. Combine mayonnaise, cloves and pimento. Arrange lettuce on salad dishes; top with tomato slice. Fill artichoke heart with shrimp and place on tomato. Top shrimp with chopped boiled egg; drizzle with chili sauce.

Margaret Ann Mattingly
Lebanon, Kentucky

SHRIMP SALAD

1 pkg. lemon gelatin
1 c. boiling water
1 can tomato soup
3 3-oz. pkg. cream cheese
1 c. mayonnaise
1 c. diced celery
1 green pepper, chopped
1 can shrimp, cut up
1 No. 2 can peas, drained
1 onion, minced

Dissolve gelatin in boiling water; cool slightly. Heat soup until it simmers. Beat cream cheese into soup; cool and add mayonnaise. Add to gelatin mixture. Stir in remaining ingredients. Chill until firm.

Mrs. Leo Shultz
Memphis, Tennessee

SHRIMP SALAD WITH PEAS

Mayonnaise
Cream
2 c. fresh cooked shrimp
1 c. diced celery
4 hard-cooked eggs, diced
1 c. cooked peas
Salt and pepper to taste
Lettuce

Thin mayonnaise with cream. Combine shrimp, celery, eggs and peas. Season; moisten with mayonnaise. Serve on lettuce. Yield: 8 servings.

Mrs. P. S. Finley
Charleston, South Carolina

SHRIMP-VEGETABLE SALAD MOLD

1 pkg. lemon gelatin
1 c. hot water
1 glass pimento cheese spread
1 tbsp. lemon juice
2 cans shrimp, finely chopped
¼ c. diced green pepper
1 c. diced celery
½ c. diced cucumber
1 c. cooked peas
2 hard-cooked eggs, sliced
½ c. baby lima beans (opt.)
½ c. chopped pecans (opt.)
½ c. heavy cream, whipped
½ c. salad dressing

Dissolve gelatin in water; chill until partially firm. Add remaining ingredients; pour into individual molds. Chill until completely firm. Serve on lettuce leaf. Garnish with mayonnaise and a wedge of hard-cooked egg. Tuna may be substituted for shrimp.

Suzanne H. Stagg
Fort Campbell, Kentucky

CHEESE, EGG, CEREAL AND PASTA SALADS

Recipe for Macaroni Fruit Buffet Salad on Page 361

BAKED EGG SALAD

8 hard-boiled eggs, chopped
1 ½ c. diced celery
¼ c. broken pecans
2 tbsp. chopped parsley
⅔ c. mayonnaise
¼ tsp. pepper
½ tsp. salt
1 c. grated cheese
1 c. crushed potato chips

Combine all ingredients except cheese and potato chips; toss lightly. Turn into greased casserole dish. Sprinkle cheese over top. Sprinkle potato chips over cheese. Bake at 375 degrees for 25 minutes. Yield: 4 servings.

Mrs. Alpine A. Redmond
Swansea, South Carolina

CHEESE DEVILED EGGS

6 hard-cooked eggs, chilled
1 tsp. mustard
1 tbsp. chopped parsley
¼ tsp. salt
⅛ tsp. pepper
½ c. finely crushed cheese crackers
½ c. mayonnaise
Paprika

Halve eggs lengthwise; remove yolks. Press yolks through a fine sieve; add mustard, parsley, salt, pepper and half the crumbs and mayonnaise. Refill centers of whites with yolk mixture; press 2 halves together. Dip one end of each egg into remaining mayonnaise and into crumbs. Sprinkle with paprika. Yield: 6 servings.

Barbara Widmyer
Richmond, Virginia

COSTAIN'S EGG RING SALAD

1 envelope unflavored gelatin
¼ c. cold water
½ c. boiling water
6 hard-cooked eggs, chopped
1 c. mayonnaise
1 tbsp. catsup
Juice of ½ lemon
½ c. chopped watercress or parsley
Salt to taste
¼ onion, chopped
½ clove garlic, chopped
½ tsp. Worcestershire sauce

Soak gelatin in cold water; dissolve in boiling water. Combine all ingredients. Pour into mold; chill until firm. Yield: 8 servings.

Mrs. William T. Page
Baltimore, Maryland

BOILED EGG SALAD

3 hard-boiled eggs, cold and diced
2 tbsp. mayonnaise
2 tbsp. vinegar
1 c. chopped radishes
Salt and pepper to taste

Combine eggs, mayonnaise, vinegar, radishes, salt and pepper. Serve on fresh lettuce and radishes.

Kathy Bebout
Salem, Kentucky

DEVILED EGG SALAD

1 envelope unflavored gelatin
½ c. boiling water
1 ½ tsp. salt
2 tbsp. lemon juice
1 tsp. Worcestershire sauce
⅛ tsp. cayenne
¾ c. mayonnaise
½ c. coarsely chopped celery
½ c. coarsely diced green pepper
2 pimentos
4 hard-cooked eggs

Place gelatin and boiling water in blender. Cover; blend at high speed for 40 seconds. Add remaining ingredients except eggs. Cover; blend well. Add 1 egg at a time; blend well after each addition. Pour into 3-cup mold; chill until firm. Yield: 4 servings.

Mrs. Harold M. Johnson
Wichita Falls, Texas

DEVILED EGGS IN TOMATO ASPIC

6 hard-cooked eggs
¼ c. mayonnaise
2 tsp. prepared mustard
2 tbsp. minced onion
¼ tsp. salt
Dash of pepper
2 tbsp. chopped stuffed olives
1 3-oz. pkg. seasoned tomato gelatin

Cut eggs into halves lengthwise; remove and mash yolks. Blend yolks with mayonnaise, mustard, onion, salt, pepper and olives. Stuff yolk mixture into egg whites; place halves together. Chill. Prepare gelatin according to package directions. Pour 1/2 cup gelatin into 1-quart ring mold. Chill until almost set. Arrange eggs in mixture; pour remaining gelatin over eggs. Chill until firm. Unmold; garnish. Yield: 4-6 servings.

Mrs. Wilbur Williams
Baton Rouge, Louisiana

EGG AND CHEESE SALAD

6 hard-cooked eggs, mashed
¼ c. chopped chives
¾ c. sm. curd cottage cheese
½ c. salad dressing
3 tbsp. vinegar
1 tbsp. white sugar
Salt and pepper to taste

Combine eggs, chives and cottage cheese. Blend salad dressing, vinegar, sugar, salt and pepper. Combine mixtures. Serve on lettuce as salad or use as sandwich spread. Yield: 8 servings.

Dorothy Tenniswood
Las Vegas, New Mexico

EGG AND CHEESE SALAD LOAF

1 clove garlic, cut
8 hard-cooked eggs
½ lb. cheese
8 crackers
1 sm. can pimento
6 sweet pickles
Salt
Mayonnaise or salad dressing

Rub the interior area of a bowl with garlic. Mix next 5 ingredients in the bowl; add seasonings and enough mayonnaise to bind ingredients together. Press into paper-lined pan; chill. Serve as squares or slices on lettuce.

Mrs. Thelma Ranson
Hamlet, North Carolina

EGG AND PEANUT SALAD

6 hard-boiled eggs
2 tsp. vinegar
1 tsp. mustard
6 tbsp. mayonnaise
½ c. chopped peanuts

Cut eggs in half; remove yolks. Combine yolks with vinegar, mustard and mayonnaise; blend in peanuts. Fill egg whites with mixture. Serve on lettuce leaves surrounded with celery curls; garnish with peanut halves. Pickle slices may be added if desired.

Lorraine T. Carter
Raleigh, North Carolina

EGG SALAD

5 hard-cooked cold eggs, chopped
¼ c. mayonnaise
½ tsp. prepared mustard
¼ c. chopped onion
⅛ tsp. pepper
¼ tsp. salt

Combine all ingredients; mix well.

Clarice Froedge
Marrowbone, Kentucky

EGG SALAD

4 hard-cooked eggs, chopped
¾ c. diced celery
2 tbsp. chopped sweet pickle
½ tsp. grated onion
Salt and pepper to taste
2 tbsp. salad dressing

Mix eggs with next three ingredients. Season with salt and pepper; add salad dressing to moisten.

Mrs. Donald Warder
Wallingford, Kentucky

EGG SALAD

6 hard-cooked eggs
French dressing

Cut eggs in half crosswise, keeping whites in pairs. Remove yolks; mash. Add enough French dressing to moisten. Refill whites with mixture; arrange on bed of lettuce. Serve with mayonnaise dressing.

Dena G. Owen
Decatur, Georgia

EGG SALAD

12 to 15 hard-cooked eggs, chopped
1 c. diced celery
1 tsp. Worcestershire sauce
Dash of Tabasco sauce
2 tbsp. grated onion
2 tbsp. chopped parsley
¼ c. pickle relish
2 tbsp. lemon juice
¼ c. chopped green pepper
1 envelope unflavored gelatin
½ c. cold water
2 c. mayonnaise
¾ tsp. salt
Pepper

(Continued on next page)

Combine eggs, celery, sauces, onion, parsley, relish, lemon juice and green pepper. Soften gelatin in coldwater; dissolve over boiling water. Beat in mayonnaise; combine egg mixture and mayonnaise mixture. Add salt and pepper. Place in mold; chill until firm. Yield: 12 servings.

Mrs. H. H. Hankins
Rogers, Arkansas

EGG SALAD

6 hard-boiled eggs
½ tsp. dry mustard
½ tsp. celery salt
1 pkg. lemon gelatin
2 tsp. vinegar
½ tsp. paprika
1 tsp. salt
1 c. boiling water
⅔ c. salad dressing

Dissolve gelatin in boiling water; mix remaining ingredients well. Pour mixture over sliced eggs. Chill until firm.

Donna Campbell
Green Forest, Arkansas

EGG SALAD AND LETTUCE IN BUNS

⅓ c. mayonnaise or cooked salad dressing
2 tbsp. finely chopped sweet gherkins
2 tbsp. chopped onion
2 tbsp. chopped parsley
1 ½ tbsp. sweet gherkin juice
½ tsp. salt
½ tsp. mustard
⅛ tsp. pepper
6 hard-cooked eggs, chopped
4 lge. buns, split and buttered

In medium bowl, combine mayonnaise, gherkins, onion, parsley, gherkin juice, salt, mustard and pepper; mix well. Add eggs; mix until well blended. Fill buns with salad, using lettuce if desired. Yield: 4 servings.

Kathy Mashburn
Powhatan, Arkansas

FLUTED EGG SALAD

6 hard-cooked eggs
1 tsp. mustard
3 tbsp. relish spread
⅓ tsp. salt
Paprika
Mayonnaise

Flute eggs by cutting with end of knife in saw-tooth fashion around egg, cutting through to yolk. Remove and mash egg yolks. Combine with remaining ingredients. Refill whites with egg yolk mixture. Place in nest of lettuce, using 3 halves per serving. Sprinkle with paprika; garnish with mayonnaise. Yield: 6 servings.

Mrs. Minnie Lou Honeycutt
Monroe, North Carolina

EGG SALAD MOLD

1 ½ envelopes unflavored gelatin
⅓ c. cold water
Juice of 2 lemons
2 c. mayonnaise
2 tsp. salt
1 tsp. sugar
Dash of cayenne pepper
2 tbsp. Worcestershire sauce
1 dozen hard-cooked eggs, grated or riced
4 tbsp. chopped parsley

Dissolve gelatin in water; add lemon juice. Combine with mayonnaise, salt, sugar, cayenne pepper and Worcestershire sauce. Mix in eggs and parsley. Pour into greased 5 or 6-cup mold. Refrigerate until firm. Yield: 8-10 servings.

Mrs. Robert Walsh
Portsmouth, Virginia

MOLDED EGG SALAD IN TOMATO CUPS

8 hard-cooked eggs, coarsely chopped
1 c. finely diced celery
¼ c. salad dressing
1 tsp. Worcestershire sauce
1 tbsp. lemon juice
1 tsp. scraped onion
Salt and pepper to taste
Paprika
6 thick tomato slices
Salad greens
Celery curls

Combine eggs, celery, dressing and all seasonings except paprika. Press into molds and chill. Unmold on tomato slices placed in a bed of salad greens. Sprinkle with paprika; garnish with celery curls and additional seasoning. Yield: 6 servings.

Zelda Leigh Powell
Mandeville, Louisiana

EGG SALAD IN TOMATO CUPS

6 ripe tomatoes
1 3-oz. pkg. cream cheese
¼ green sweet pepper, chopped
1 sm. cucumber, chopped
1 tbsp. chopped green onion
½ c. chopped celery
1 tbsp. chopped red sweet pepper
3 hard-cooked eggs, chopped
¼ c. salad dressing
Salt to taste

Peel tomatoes; cut slice from top and scoop out insides. Chill. Mix remaining ingredients except cream cheese. Add cream cheese, blending well. Fill chilled tomatoes; serve on lettuce leaf.

Mrs. E. F. Mulvehill
Morris, Alabama

JELLIED EGG SALAD

2 3-oz. pkg. lemon gelatin
1 ¼ c. boiling water
2 c. cold water
3 tbsp. lemon juice
1 c. mayonnaise
4 tbsp. pickle relish, drained
1 tsp. salt
¼ c. chopped onion
2 tbsp. pimento
6 hard-cooked eggs

Dissolve gelatin in boiling water; add cold water and chill until syrupy. Stir in lemon juice, mayonnaise, pickle relish, salt, chopped onion and pimento. Fold in sliced eggs, reserving 1 egg yolk. Spoon into 2-quart mold; chill until firm. Garnish with sieved egg yolk. Yield: 8 servings.

Mrs. Birtie Wilkerson
Moulton, Alabama

PEARL'S MOCK LOBSTER SALAD

15 crackers, crumbled
1 c. tomato juice
1 c. chopped celery
1 onion, chopped
1 pepper, finely cut
3 boiled eggs, chopped
½ c. salad dressing or more
Chopped pickles

Cover crackers with tomato juice; let set a few minutes. Add remaining ingredients. Mix well.

Mrs. Olen Fryar
Big Spring, Texas

STUFFED EGGS CURRY

12 hard-cooked eggs
1 c. mayonnaise
1 tsp. chicken seasoned stock base
¼ tsp. instant onion powder
¼ tsp. white pepper
1 tsp. curry powder
½ tsp. salt
1 c. finely minced cooked chicken (opt.)
Anchovies
Olive slices
Capers

Cut eggs into halves, crosswise; slice small cap off ends. Remove yolks; mash or force through sieve. Add mayonnaise, stock base, onion powder, pepper, curry powder, salt and chicken; mix thoroughly. Refill egg whites, piling yolk mixture high. Cap with smaller portion of white; top each with rolled anchovies, sliced ripe or stuffed olives and capers. Yield: 24 servings.

Mrs. A. C. Crowe
Ft. Walton, Florida

TOMATOES STUFFED WITH EGG SALAD

6 hard-cooked eggs, chopped
½ c. finely chopped celery
⅓ c. sliced stuffed green olives
¼ c. minced green onions
½ tsp. salt
Dash of pepper
¼ c. mayonnaise
6 med. tomatoes

Combine eggs, celery, olives and onions; season with salt and pepper. Add mayonnaise; mix well. Scoop out centers of tomatoes; fill with egg salad. Top with additional olive slices. Chill. Yield: 6 servings.

Mrs. Joseph F. Smith
Santa Fe, New Mexico

ANITA'S NO-FUSS SALAD

1 pkg. lime gelatin
1 ½ c. boiling water
1 pt. cottage cheese
¼ c. finely chopped onion
2 tbsp. finely chopped green pepper
½ c. mayonnaise
½ c. chopped pecans
10 to 12 stuffed olives, sliced

Dissolve gelatin in boiling water; add remaining ingredients. Pour into a 9 x 13-inch shallow dish. Chill until firm; serve on bed of lettuce. Yield: 12 servings.

Mrs. David A. Rich
Charlotte, North Carolina

BEST-EVER SALAD

2 tbsp. gelatin
½ c. water
1 c. grated cheese
2 pimentos, chopped
½ c. chopped nuts
½ c. chopped ripe olives
¼ tsp. prepared mustard
Dash of cayenne
1 tsp. Worcestershire sauce
1 c. whipping cream

Soak gelatin in water 5 minutes. Dissolve over hot water. Blend together cheese, pimentos, nuts, olives and seasonings. Add dissolved gelatin to whipped cream; fold in cheese mixture. Pour into mold and chill. Yield: 8 servings.

Mrs. Charles A. Houghton
Aztec, New Mexico

CAMEMBERT MOUSSE

¼ c. cold water
1 envelope unflavored gelatin
2 1 ⅓-oz. wedges Camembert cheese
3 1 ¼-oz. wedges Roquefort cheese
1 tsp. Worcestershire sauce
1 egg, separated
½ c. heavy cream, whipped

Pour cold water into measuring cup; add gelatin. Set cup in pan of hot water until gelatin dissolves. Blend cheeses together until smooth. Beat in Worcestershire sauce, egg yolk and gelatin. Beat egg white until stiff; fold egg white and cream into cheese mixture. Pour into 4 individual molds or one 2 or 3-cup mold. Refrigerate overnight. Unmold onto lettuce leaves or watercress. Yield: 4 servings.

Mrs. Harry S. Dennis, Jr.
West Palm Beach, Florida

CHEESE AND BLACK WALNUT SALAD

1 pkg. cream cheese or
 1 carton cottage cheese
Cream
Salt and pepper to taste
1 ⅓ c. finely chopped black walnuts

Mash cream cheese; moisten with a little cream. Season to taste. Mix with walnuts; shape into small balls. Arrange on lettuce bed; serve with mayonnaise dressing.

Dena G. Owen
Decatur, Georgia

CHEESE ASPIC

1 pkg. lime gelatin
1 pkg. lemon gelatin
3 c. hot water
3 tsp. vinegar
1 ½ tsp. salt
1 c. mayonnaise
2 tsp. minced onion
1 c. milk
1 c. grated American cheese

Dissolve gelatins in hot water; add vinegar and salt. Chill until partially set; add mayonnaise, onion, milk and cheese. Beat until smooth. Pour into wet molds; chill until firm. Serve with mayonnaise on bed of lettuce. Yield: 10-12 servings.

Mrs. M. A. Rogers
Cambridge, Maryland

CHEESECAKE SALAD

2 ¼ tsp. unflavored gelatin
6 tbsp. sugar
½ c. lemon gelatin
1 c. boiling water
¾ c. pineapple juice
3 tbsp. fresh lemon juice
½ tsp. grated lemon rind
1 tbsp. grated orange rind
1 c. smooth cottage cheese
½ c. cream cheese
¾ c. crushed pineapple
3 c. green and red gelatin cubes
1 c. heavy cream, whipped

Mix unflavored gelatin with sugar and lemon gelatin; add boiling water. Stir until dissolved. Add juices and fruit peels; mix until well blended. Chill until syrupy. Cream cottage cheese and cream cheese until smooth; fold into thickened mixture. Add pineapple and gelatin cubes. Fold in whipped cream. Pour into a 2-quart mold; chill overnight. Unmold. Yield: 8-10 servings.

Mrs. Lewis M. Epperson
Savannah, Georgia

CHEESE MOLD SALAD

2 c. cottage cheese
1 3-oz. pkg. cream cheese,
 softened
1 tbsp. unflavored gelatin
¼ c. cold water
½ tbsp. grated onion
½ c. mayonnaise
½ tbsp. lemon juice
Cayenne pepper
Salt
2 tbsp. chopped green pepper
 (opt.)
Few drops of green coloring

(Continued on next page)

Remove lumps from cottage cheese with electric beater; beat in cream cheese. Dissolve gelatin in cold water; melt over hot water. Add remaining ingredients, tinting pale green with food coloring.

PUERTO RICAN DRESSING:

- ¼ c. powdered sugar
- 1 tbsp. steak sauce
- ¼ c. tarragon wine vinegar
- ½ tsp. grated onion
- Paprika
- 1 tbsp. lemon juice
- 1 tsp. Worcestershire sauce
- ⅓ c. catsup
- 1 tsp. salt
- ½ c. salad oil

Place all ingredients except oil in jar; blend thoroughly. Add oil; shake well. Yield: 4 servings.

Mrs. Howard Persons
Macon, Georgia

CHEESE AND NUT SALAD

- 1 c. American cheese or cream cheese, softened
- ½ c. sweet cream
- 1 tbsp. melted butter
- Salt and pepper to taste
- ½ c. chopped pecans
- ⅓ c. chopped pimento
- ⅓ c. chopped olives

Mash softened cheese with cream and melted butter; season with salt and pepper. Add nuts, pimento and olives; press into mold. Let stand for 2 hours in refrigerator. Cut in slices; serve on lettuce with mayonnaise dressing.

Edith De-Berry
De Witt, Arkansas

CHEESE-NUT SALAD

- 1 3-oz. pkg. lemon gelatin
- 1 c. hot water
- ½ c. cold water
- 1 c. cream-style cottage cheese
- 2 tbsp. mayonnaise
- ¼ c. chopped green pepper
- ¼ c. chopped walnuts
- 2 tbsp. diced pimento

Dissolve gelatin in hot water. Add cold water; chill until partially set. Add remaining ingredients. Refrigerate until firm.

Mrs. T. W. Taylor
Abbeville, South Carolina

CHEESE-OLIVE SALAD

- 8 oz. cream cheese
- 1 tsp. salt
- ½ c. sugar
- ½ c. cold water
- 1 envelope unflavored gelatin
- ½ c. cream or milk
- ½ c. chopped nuts
- 2 tbsp. grated onion
- 1 red or green pepper, chopped
- 1 sm. bottle olives
- 2 lb. cottage cheese

Cream the cream cheese, salt and sugar. To cold water, add gelatin. Heat. Add to cream mixture. Add cream, nuts, onion, pepper, olives and cottage cheese. Pour into mold which has been greased with oil. When set, invert on serving dish. Garnish with lettuce, radishes and olives.

Mrs. Sara Dale Casey
Shelbyville, Kentucky

CHEESE SALAD

- 2 ½ to 4 c. crushed pineapple
- 1 pkg. lemon gelatin
- 1 sm. can pimento
- 2 3-oz. pkg. cream cheese
- ½ c. celery, chopped
- ⅔ c. walnuts or pecans, chopped
- 1 c. whipped cream
- ⅛ tsp. salt

Heat juice drained from pineapple. Add gelatin and dissolve. Cream pimento and cheese; add to juice-gelatin mixture. Combine all ingredients and pour in molds. Chill several hours. Yield: 10-12 servings.

Mrs. Johnie Dismuke
Lytle, Texas

CHEESE WHIP SALAD

- 2 glasses pimento cheese
- 1 sm. can crushed pineapple, drained
- 1 8-oz. pkg. miniature marshmallows
- ½ c. salad dressing
- 1 c. heavy cream, whipped

(Continued on next page)

Mix cheese and pineapple thoroughly; add marshmallows and salad dressing. Fold in whipped cream. Let stand overnight. Serve on lettuce. Yield: 8-10 servings.

Mrs. A. B. Joyner, Jr.
Southport, North Carolina

CINNAMON-CHEESE SALAD

½ c. cinnamon candies
½ c. boiling water
1 box strawberry gelatin
1 c. cold water
1 4-oz. pkg. cream cheese
½ c. apples, diced
½ c. celery, diced
½ c. nuts, chopped

Melt cinnamon candy in boiling water. Add to gelatin; stir to dissolve. Add cold water and cream cheese. Beat until smooth. Chill until thickened; add apples, celery and nuts. Chill until firm. Yield: 6 servings.

Twyla M. Regula
Lakeland, Florida

COEUR A LA CREME

1 lb. cottage cheese
1 lb. cream cheese
2 c. heavy cream
Salt
Mint
Strawberries or raspberries

Beat cottage cheese and cream cheese until smooth; gradually add cream. Season with salt. Line a heart-shaped basket with cheesecloth; fill with cheese. Place basket on a plate; refrigerate overnight. Unmold onto glass platter; remove cheesecloth. Garnish with mint and strawberries or raspberries. Yield: 6 servings.

Mrs. James B. Saum
Saint Joseph, Louisiana

COTTAGE CHEESE DELIGHT

1 c. cottage cheese
½ c. coconut
½ c. crushed pineapple
2 tbsp. sour cream or half and half cream

Mix all ingredients well; serve on lettuce leaf.

Mrs. H. Derrick
Huntsville, Alabama

COTTAGE CHEESE LOAF

1 tbsp. gelatin
¼ c. cold water
2 c. cottage cheese
2 hard-cooked eggs
1 tbsp. onion
½ c. diced cucumber
½ c. chopped celery
½ c. nuts
¼ c. pimento
¼ c. parsley
¼ c. mayonnaise
1 ½ tsp. salt

Soften gelatin in cold water and dissolve over hot water. Mix all ingredients and add dissolved gelatin. Pour into mold greased with salad oil and chill. Serve on platter garnished with lettuce.

Mrs. Wilbur Jenkins
Sadieville, Kentucky

COTTAGE CHEESE SALAD

2 c. cottage cheese
1 c. chopped dates
1 c. chopped tart red apples
Mayonnaise dressing
Whipped cream

Combine cheese, dates and apples; moisten with mayonnaise. Mix lightly with 2 forks. Serve on crisp lettuce. Top each serving with 1 teaspoonful whipped cream. Yield: 6 servings.

Mrs. Goldie Hall
Olive Hill, Kentucky

COTTAGE CHEESE SALAD

1 pkg. lime gelatin
1 ½ c. hot water
½ c. mayonnaise
1 tbsp. vinegar
1 ½ c. celery, diced
¼ tsp. salt
¼ c. walnuts
1 c. cottage cheese
½ c. pineapple juice
¼ c. pimento, chopped

(Continued on next page)

Let gelatin dissolve in hot water and set. Whip and add remaining ingredients. Chill until firm.

Mrs. Juanita Watson
Paris, Tennessee

COTTAGE CHEESE SALAD BOWL

3 med. carrots
1 med. head lettuce, shredded
1 c. chopped celery
1 ½ c. cottage cheese
Salt and pepper to taste
French dressing

Cut carrots in tiny strips 1-inch long. Toss lettuce, carrots and celery lightly in large bowl. Just before serving, add cottage cheese. Season with salt and pepper. Add French dressing as desired. Yield: 8-10 servings.

FRENCH DRESSING:

¼ c. vinegar
¾ c. salad oil
¼ tsp. paprika
½ tsp. salt
1 tsp. sugar

Combine ingredients thoroughly. Shake before servings.

Shirlynn Roberts
Dike, Texas

CREAM CHEESE SALAD

1 pkg. lime gelatin
1 pkg. lemon gelatin
1 c. hot water
2 c. cold water
2 sm. pkg. cream cheese, softened
1 sm. jar stuffed olives, sliced
1 c. chopped walnuts
1 pt. heavy cream, whipped

Dissolve gelatins in hot water; add cold water. Cool until slightly thickened; add cream cheese, olives and nuts. Fold in whipped cream; mold and chill until firm. Serve on lettuce leaf with salad dressing. Yield: 8 servings.

Mrs. Edward Godbold
Raleigh, North Carolina

CREAM CHEESE SALAD

1 pkg. lime gelatin
½ c. crushed pineapple, drained
1 pkg. cream cheese, crumbled
½ c. pecans, broken

Prepare gelatin according to directions on package, substituting pineapple juice for part of the cold water. Mix cream cheese, pineapple and pecans; add to gelatin. Chill until firm. Garnish with maraschino cherries and parsley. Yield: 4-6 servings.

Mrs. Jo Nell Baker
Kemp, Texas

DRUSILLA'S LIGHT GREEN SALAD

1 3-oz. pkg. lime gelatin
1 8-oz. pkg. cream cheese, softened
1 tsp. finely chopped onion
½ c. sliced stuffed olives
1 tsp. vinegar
Salt and pepper to taste

Prepare gelatin as directed on package; gradually blend into cream cheese. Chill until slightly thickened; add remaining ingredients. Pour into 6 individual molds. Chill until firm. Unmold into lettuce cups. Yield: 6 servings.

Mrs. W. B. Leclaire
Houston, Texas

GAINESVILLE CREAM CHEESE SALAD

2 c. crushed pineapple
1 pkg. lemon gelatin
1 tbsp. cold water
1 tbsp. unflavored gelatin
Juice of 1 lemon
¼ tsp. salt
2 pkg. cream cheese, broken in pieces
¼ c. pimento, chopped
½ c. nuts, chopped
1 stalk celery, chopped
6 marshmallows
½ pt. whipped cream

Drain pineapple. Combine juice and enough water to make 2 cups liquid. Heat to boiling point; pour over lemon gelatin. Mix cold water and unflavored gelatin; combine with lemon gelatin mixture. Add lemon juice and salt; chill until partially set. Mix pineapple, cream cheese, pimento, nuts, celery and marshmallows. Add to gelatin mixture. Fold in whipped cream. Pour into mold. Chill. Yield: 8 servings.

Mrs. Marie M. Mingledorff
Douglas, Georgia

JELLIED SALAD

2 cans cream tomato soup
1 box lemon gelatin
1 pt. cottage cheese
1 c. chopped celery
1 c. chopped bell pepper
1 c. chopped onion
1 c. mayonnaise

Heat soup to bubble stage. Do not boil; add gelatin and stir well. Pour into a large bowl and add remaining ingredients. Chill until firm. Serve on lettuce leaves. Yield: 20 servings.

Mrs. S. A. Bone
Des Arc, Arkansas

MARY MINNICK'S SALAD

1 pkg. lime gelatin
1 c. hot water
1 c. ginger ale
1 16-oz. carton creamed cottage cheese
1 sm. can crushed pineapple, drained
½ c. celery, finely diced
½ c. nuts. chopped

Dissolve gelatin in hot water. Let cool. Add ginger ale, cottage cheese, pineapple, celery and nuts. Chill until firm. Yield: 9 servings.

Nancy Kimbrell
Tallahassee, Florida

MOLDED CHEESE SALAD WITH FRESH FRUIT

3 envelopes unflavored gelatin
1 ¼ c. cold water
1 ⅔ c. boiling water
2 c. grated cheddar cheese
¾ c. mayonnaise
1 tsp. powdered mustard
1 tsp. salt
Speck of cayenne
3 tbsp. chopped pimento
3 tbsp. chopped stuffed olives
1 tbsp. fresh lemon juice

Soften gelatin in cold water. Add boiling water and stir to dissolve gelatin. Chill until mixture begins to thicken. Beat gelatin with an electric or rotary beater. Combine cheese, mayonnaise, mustard, salt and cayenne. Mix well. Fold into the beaten gelatin along with pimento and olives. Turn into an oiled 1-quart mold. Chill until firm and ready to serve. Turn out onto a serving plate. Arrange assorted fresh fruit around the mold; sprinkle fruit with lemon juice. Yield: 6-8 servings.

Photograph for this recipe on cover.

PIMENTO CHEESE PARTY SALAD

1 pt. whipping cream, whipped
3 3-oz. jars pimento cheese
2 sm. cans crushed pineapple, drained
1 can grapes, drained
1 c. miniature marshmallows

Combine whipped cream and cheese; mix thoroughly. Fold in remaining ingredients; chill. Yield: 8-12 servings.

Mrs. Noah McFodden
Paris, Texas

PIMENTO CHEESE SALAD

1 4-oz. can pimento, finely chopped
1 lb. American cheese, grated
⅓ c. salad dressing

Add pimentos, liquid also, to cheese. Add salad dressing; blend together. Serve on lettuce or cabbage.

Mrs. J. C. Clouse
Manchester, Tennessee

PIMENTO AND CHEESE SALAD

½ lb. cheese, grated
1 can pimento, finely chopped
3 apples, finely chopped
3 hard-boiled eggs, finely chopped
3 pickles, finely chopped
1 egg
1 tsp. salt
1 tsp. sugar
½ c. cream or milk
½ tsp. black pepper
2 tbsp. flour

Set aside small amount cheese. Combine remaining cheese, pimento, apples, hard-boiled eggs and pickles. Combine remaining ingredients; heat in double boiler to custard consistency. Cool. Combine dressing with salad mixture; sprinkle with grated cheese.

Mrs. L. D. Grimes
Maud, Texas

PIMENTO CHEESE SALAD

2 lb. Velveeta cheese
1 4-oz. can pimentos, including liquid
1 pt. mayonnaise
1 tbsp. vinegar
2 to 3 tbsp. sugar

(Continued on next page)

Grind cheese and pimento fine with food grinder. Add other ingredients; mix with fork until smooth. Serve on lettuce.

Mrs. Robert Chapman
Uniontown, Kentucky

ROYAL FROSTED FRUIT MOLD

1 c. milk
2 envelopes unflavored gelatin
2 12-oz. cartons cream-style cottage cheese
½ c. crumbled bleu cheese
1 6-oz. can frozen limeade concentrate, thawed
½ c. broken pecans, toasted and salted
6 drops green food coloring
1 c. whipped cream

Pour milk into large saucepan. Sprinkle gelatin over milk to soften. Place over low heat and stir until gelatin is dissolved. Remove. Beat cottage cheese and bleu cheese together until well blended. Stir in gelatin mixture and add limeade concentrate, pecans and food coloring. Fold in whipped cream. Turn in 6-cup ring mold and chill until firm, about 4 to 6 hours. Unmold on serving plate and garnish with frosted grapes and mint leaves. Yield: 10 servings.

Mrs. F. L. Love
Miami, Florida

STUFFED LETTUCE SALAD

1 sm. firm head lettuce
1 4-oz. pkg. Roquefort or bleu cheese
1 3-oz. pkg. cream cheese
1 3-oz. pkg. pimento cream cheese
1 tbsp. chopped chives
1 tbsp. milk

Wash lettuce; drain well. Hollow out center from stem end, leaving 1 to 1 1/2 inches of shell. Blend softened cheeses with other ingredients; pack into center of lettuce. Wrap tightly in foil, waxed paper or plastic bag; chill well. Cut into wedges; serve with French dressing. Yield: 4-6 servings.

Mrs. Charles W. Evans
Tuscaloosa, Alabama

SUMMER CHEESE DELIGHT

1 envelope unflavored gelatin
¼ c. cold water
2 3-oz. pkg. cream cheese
¾ c. sugar
1 c. evaporated milk
½ c. boiling water
1 6-oz. can frozen lemon-strawberry punch concentrate
Blueberries
Sliced sugared peaches

Sprinkle gelatin over cold water. Soften cream cheese to room temperature in medium mixing bowl; add sugar and blend well. Beat in evaporated milk; whip until smooth. Add boiling water to softened gelatin; stir until dissolved. Add to cheese mixture, stirring to blend. Stir in frozen fruit punch, mixing well until dissolved. Pour into oiled 4-cup ring mold. Chill until set, 3 to 4 hours. Serve with fresh fruits.

Mrs. Flint Johnston
New Hebron, Mississippi

SUMMER SALAD

1 c. cottage cheese
1 med. tomato, diced
2 eggs, scrambled
1 med. cucumber, diced
Salt and pepper to taste

Mix all ingredients just before serving time. Yield: 4 servings.

Mrs. Otis Allen
Stroud, Oklahoma

TANGY COTTAGE CHEESE SALAD

1 3-oz. pkg. lemon gelatin
1 3-oz. pkg. lime gelatin
1 c. boiling water
1 No. 2 can crushed pineapple
1 1-lb. carton cottage cheese
1 c. salad dressing
1 c. milk
2 tbsp. horseradish

Dissolve lemon and lime gelatins in boiling water. Drain pineapple, reserving 1 cup juice. Add pineapple juice to dissolved gelatin; stir in pineapple. Chill until almost congealed. Combine cottage cheese, salad dressing, milk and horseradish. Fold into gelatin-pineapple mixture. Turn into 6 1/2 x 10 x 2-inch loaf pan. Chill until firm. Yield: 8 servings.

Mrs. Malcolm L. Blessing
Oxford, Mississippi

GOOD VEGETABLE SALAD

1 5-oz. pkg. egg noodles
1 c. diced pickled beets
½ c. chopped celery
1 c. cooked cold cauliflower
¼ c. chopped green onion
2 c. shredded lettuce
¾ c. French dressing

Cook noodles until tender. Mix with remaining ingredients. Add enough French dressing to coat each piece.

Mrs. T. W. Foshee
Albuquerque, New Mexico

CHEESE-MACARONI SALAD

2 c. cooked, seasoned macaroni
1 c. diced celery
1 c. cooked peas
¼ c. shredded carrots
1 green pepper or pimento, shredded
Salt and pepper to taste
Mayonnaise
Cheese balls or stuffed olives

Chill macaroni; combine with celery, peas, carrots and green pepper. Season to taste. Moisten with mayonnaise; mix lightly with two forks. Serve on crisp salad greens; garnish with cheese balls or diced stuffed olives. Yield: 6 servings.

Mrs. G. E. Black
Winchester, Kentucky

EASY MACARONI SALAD

1 c. uncooked shell macaroni
½ c. finely chopped onion
½ clove of garlic, minced
1 tbsp. salad oil
1 tbsp. vinegar
1 tbsp. salt
½ c. chopped celery
¼ c. chopped dill pickles
6 radishes, thinly sliced
¼ c. mayonnaise

Cook macaroni according to package directions; drain well. Combine ingredients; chill. May be garnished with radishes. Yield: 6-8 servings.

Mrs. William E. Fox
Valdosta, Georgia

LUNCHEON SALAD

1 c. finely chopped celery
½ c. cooked peas
½ c. finely chopped carrots
1 sm. onion, finely chopped
2 tomatoes, pared and cut in wedges
2 hard-cooked eggs, chopped
½ c. grated snappy cheese
1 ½ c. cooked macaroni, cut in pieces
Salad dressing
Lettuce

Mix all ingredients. Use enough salad dressing to moisten. Serve on lettuce.

Mrs. J. K. Galbraith
Arkadelphia, Arkansas

MACARONI-CARROT SALAD

1 box shell or elbow macaroni
1 lge. green pepper, chopped
4 sm. carrots, sliced
1 sm. can pimento, chopped
3 stalks celery, finely cut
4 sm. green onions, cut round or 1 med. dry onion, chopped
½ tsp. salt

Cook macaroni 15 minutes; drain and cool. Add other ingredients. Serve with mayonnaise.

Mrs. T. W. Taylor
Abbeville, South Carolina

MACARONI-EGG SALAD

1 lb. macaroni
1 lge. cucumber
1 green pepper
6 hard-cooked eggs
2 ripe tomatoes
3 or 4 sweet pickles
2 tbsp. salad dressing
Salt and pepper to taste

Cook macaroni until tender; drain and cool. Chop cucumber, green pepper, eggs, tomatoes and pickles. Add to macaroni; mix well. Add salad dressing and seasonings. Yield: 8 servings.

Vivian Blankenship
Ocean, West Virginia

MACARONI-CUCUMBER SALAD

1 c. uncooked shell macaroni
½ c. salad dressing
2 hard-cooked eggs, chopped
1 green pepper, chopped
1 cucumber, chopped
1 med. onion, chopped

(Continued on next page)

Cook macaroni according to package directions; drain. Add remaining ingredients. Chill. Garnish with additional hard-cooked egg and green pepper. Yield: 6 servings.

Lois Witt
Heber Springs, Arkansas

MACARONI-FRUIT BUFFET SALAD

Salt
4 to 6 qt. boiling water
4 c. elbow macaroni
2 c. sour cream
2 c. creamed cottage cheese
¼ c. chopped pecans
½ tsp. cinnamon
2 c. orange sections
2 1-lb. 12-oz. cans apricot halves, drained
3 tbsp. pineapple syrup
Crisp salad greens
2 1-lb. 14-oz. cans apricot halves, drained

Add 2 tablespoons salt to rapidly boiling water. Gradually add macaroni so water continues to boil. Cook, uncovered, stirring occasionally, until tender. Drain in colander. Rinse with cold water; drain again. Mix together macaroni, sour cream, cottage cheese, nuts, 1 teaspoon salt and cinnamon. Add orange sections, pineapple and pineapple syrup. Toss lightly and chill. Mound on salad greens; surround with apricots. Sprinkle with paprika. Garnish with cinnamon, if desired. Serve with additional sour cream, if desired. Yield: 12 servings.

Photograph for this recipe on page 349.

MACARONI-OLIVE SALAD

4 c. cooked elbow macaroni
1 c. mayonnaise
Salt to taste
Dash of cayenne pepper
¼ c. sliced stuffed olives
2 tbsp. grated onions
2 c. diced, firm ripe tomatoes
1 c. finely chopped celery (opt.)
1 c. grated med. or sharp cheese

Place cooked and drained macaroni in refrigerator until cold. Combine macaroni with mayonnaise, salt and cayenne pepper. Gently stir in other ingredients; keep refrigerated until serving time.

Mrs.T. W. Nicholson
Eastman, Georgia

MACARONI AND PEA SALAD

12 oz. shell macaroni
1 tbsp. seasoned salt
2 lge. onions, chopped
1 tsp. salt
8 hard-cooked eggs, sliced
2 c. celery, chopped
½ c. pimento, sliced
1 c. green pepper, sliced
2 No. 2 ½ cans English peas, drained
1 ½ c. mayonnaise

Boil macaroni in salted water until tender. Drain; blanch with cold water and drain again. Add seasoned salt, onions, salt, eggs, celery, pimento and green pepper. Toss lightly. Add English peas; toss lightly. Gently mix in mayonnaise. Chill several hours before serving. Yield: 12 servings.

Mrs. Oleta M. Smith
O'Donnell, Texas

MACARONI-PICKLE SALAD

1 16-oz. pkg. elbow macaroni, cooked
2 c. cooked salad dressing
8 hard-cooked eggs, diced
1 ½ c. med. cut celery
½ c. finely chopped onion
1 tsp. salt
¼ tsp. paprika
½ c. diced canned pimento
1 c. sweet chopped pickle
Crisp lettuce

Mix macaroni with salad dressing. Add other ingredients except lettuce. Cover; chill for 2 or more hours. Serve on crisp lettuce. Yield: 8-12 servings.

Mrs. Lindon Baker
Santa Fe, Tennessee

MACARONI-RELISH SALAD

1 ⅔ c. shell macaroni
1 10 ½-oz. can cream of celery soup
¼ c. milk
1 ½ tbsp. vinegar
½ c. pickle relish

Cook macaroni according to package directions; drain. Dilute soup with milk; heat. Add vinegar and relish. Pour over hot macaroni; mix well. Yield: 5-6 servings.

Chlois McInnish
Talladega, Alabama

MACARONI SALAD

1 sm. pkg. shell or elbow macaroni
¼ lb. grated cheese
1 c. milk
½ stick margarine
¼ c. minced onion
¼ c. sweet pickles, chopped
2 hard-boiled eggs, chopped
1 bell pepper, chopped
½ c. mayonnaise

Cook macaroni according to package directions; drain and set aside. Combine cheese, milk and margarine; melt over low heat. Add onion, pickles, eggs, pepper and mayonnaise to macaroni; mix thoroughly. Pour cheese mixture over macaroni; mix thoroughly. Serve on lettuce leaves. Yield: 6 servings.

Judy Szanfill
Beech Bluff, Tennessee

MACARONI SALAD

3 c. shell macaroni, cooked, drained and cooled
1 sm. onion, finely chopped
1 green pepper, finely chopped
1 med. cucumber, finely chopped and soaked in salt water overnight
3 lge. tomatoes, finely chopped
2 lge. stalks celery, finely chopped or ¾ tsp. celery seeds
Salad dressing

Drain cucumber. Cook macaroni in salted water until well done, but do not overcook. Drain; cool. Add onion, pepper, cucumber, tomatoes and celery. Add enough salad dressing to be sure all ingredients are well mixed. The salad is of a soft texture.

Nita Carol Sammons
Forest Hills, Kentucky

MACARONI SALAD

1 pkg. shell macaroni
4 to 5 stalks celery, finely chopped
1 green pepper, chopped
2 pimentos, chopped
4 hard-boiled eggs, chopped
1 cucumber pickle, diced
2 tbsp. vinegar
Salt, pepper and sugar to taste

Cook macaroni according to package directions. Combine macaroni with remaining ingredients. Serve.

Carrye B. Conyers
Milltown, Kentucky

MACARONI SALAD

2 c. cooked macaroni, seasoned with salt
½ c. diced cheese
⅓ c. diced bell pepper
1 lge. tomato, diced
2 tbsp. mayonnaise or salad dressing
Black pepper or paprika

Toss all ingredients together; sprinkle with black pepper or paprika. If desired, chopped ham may be added. Serve in salad dish or on individual lettuce leaves. Yield: 6 servings.

Mrs. Annie Ruth Myers
Fayette, Alabama

MACARONI SALAD

3 c. cooked elbow macaroni
2 hard-cooked eggs
6 slices bacon, fried crisp and crumbled
½ c. chopped celery
¼ c. chopped parsley
¼ c. chopped green pepper
½ c. sliced radishes
2 tbsp. chopped onions
Salt to taste

Cook macaroni until soft; rinse with hot water. Place in bowl; add remaining ingredients. Add salad dressing; toss with a fork. Garnish with pepper rings and more radish slices.

DRESSING:

½ c. sugar
1 tsp. salt
1 tbsp. flour
⅛ tsp. black pepper
½ c. vinegar
½ c. water
2 eggs, beaten
1 tsp. prepared mustard

Mix dry ingredients in top of double boiler; add vinegar, water, eggs and mustard. Cool ingredients until thick; cool slightly. Yield: 6 servings.

Alberta Cromer
Townville, South Carolina

MACARONI SALAD DELUXE

2 c. raw macaroni cooked
6 hard-cooked eggs
1 c. diced celery
1 green pepper, diced
1 sm. onion, diced
2 carrots, shredded
Sliced olives
1 c. cooked drained peas

Drain macaroni; rinse under cold water. Peel eggs; reserve 2 whole yolks. Chop remaining eggs; combine with macaroni and all remaining ingredients.

DRESSING:

1 c. mayonnaise
¼ c. milk
1 tbsp. vinegar
1 tsp. salt
¼ tsp. pepper
Paprika
Parsley sprigs

Combine all ingredients except paprika and parsley. Mix well with salad. Force reserved egg yolks through sieve; sprinkle over top. Sprinkle with paprika; garnish with parsley sprigs. Yield: 12 servings.

Mrs. Betty Lou Kirkpatrick
Dahlgren, Virginia

PICCADILLY SALAD

1 8-oz. jar Cheez Whiz
¼ c. milk
1 7-oz. pkg. elbow macaroni, cooked
½ c. chopped onion
½ c. sliced sweet pickles
2 tbsp. chopped pimento
¼ c. chopped celery
4 hard-cooked eggs, chopped

Heat Cheez Whiz with milk over low heat; stir until sauce is smooth. Add remaining ingredients; mix well. Garnish with egg slices and pimento. Yield: 6 servings.

Pearl Scott
Gainesville, Florida

SALAD SUPREME

1 c. macaroni
1 c. chopped celery
6 tbsp. chopped sweet pickle
3 tbsp. chopped pimento
6 tbsp. chopped green pepper
1 c. diced sharp cheese
½ c. cooked green peas
½ c. salad dressing

Cook macaroni according to package directions. Drain and chill for 2 hours. Add celery, pickle and pimento. Toss lightly. Add remaining ingredients; toss. Chill. Yield: 6 servings.

Mary Nan Fitch
Electra, Texas

MAINLY MACARONI SALAD

8 oz. salad macaroni
¼ c. green pepper, chopped
1 4½-oz. can olives, chopped
1 med. onion, finely chopped
¼ c. celery, chopped
3 hard-cooked eggs, sliced
Mayonnaise
Vinegar
Salt
Pepper
Paprika

Cook macaroni according to package directions; rinse. Combine next 5 ingredients, reserving some egg slices for garnish. Add mayonnaise, vinegar, salt and pepper to taste. Garnish with egg slices and paprika. Let stand several hours before serving. Yield: 8 servings.

Helena Tidrow Raine
Perry, Florida

SUMMER MACARONI SALAD

7 or 8-oz. uncooked elbow, shell or ring macaroni
1 c. cubed cheddar cheese
1 c. sliced gherkins
½ c. minced onion
½ c. mayonnaise
1 10 or 12-oz. pkg. frozen peas, cooked and drained
Salt and pepper to taste

Cook macaroni; drain and rinse with coldwater. Add remaining ingredients; season with salt and pepper. Chill. Serve in lettuce cups. Yield: 4-6 servings.

Wilma Mansel
West Columbia, Texas

SWEET MACARONI SALAD

2 c. cooked macaroni
2 c. miniature marshmallows
½ c. maraschino cherries, quartered
⅓ c. mayonnaise
Light cream
1 or 2 bananas, sliced

(Continued on next page)

Combine macaroni, marshmallows and cherries. Thin mayonnaise with cream; combine with macaroni mixture. Chill thoroughly. Add bananas. Mix lightly. Yield: 6-8 servings.

Mrs. Judd Morris
Jacksonville, Florida

SWEET AND SOUR MACARONI SALAD

4 to 5 tbsp. mayonnaise or salad dressing
4 tbsp. vinegar
2 to 3 tbsp. sugar
1 to 2 tbsp. water
½ c. chopped green pepper
½ c. chopped onion
½ c. shredded carrots
¾ lb. macaroni, cooked and drained

Combine mayonnaise, vinegar, sugar and water in bowl. Add green pepper, onion, carrots and macaroni; mix thoroughly. Chill for 2 to 3 hours. Yield: 10-12 servings.

Mrs. John R. Fitzgerald
New Smyrna Beach, Florida

ZIPPY MACARONI SALAD

1 8-oz. pkg. elbow macaroni
1 c. chopped celery
½ green pepper, chopped
½ red pepper, chopped
½ c. chopped onions
½ c. French dressing
½ c. sour cream
½ c. mayonnaise
1 tsp. prepared mustard
½ tsp. salt
Dash of pepper
½ c. chopped parsley

Cook macaroni according to package directions; drain. Combine with celery, green pepper, red pepper and onions. Cover with French dressing; toss lightly to mix. Cover; chill several hours or overnight. At serving time, combine sour cream, mayonnaise, mustard, salt and pepper; stir to blend. Fold in chopped parsley. Combine with macaroni mixture; serve.

Mrs. Muriel Lycan
Terra Alta, West Virginia

WALNUT-MACARONI SALAD

1 ½ c. uncooked elbow macaroni
2 c. chopped celery
½ c. diced sweet pickles
¼ c. chopped onion
Salt and pepper to taste
¾ c. chopped walnuts
½ c. mayonnaise
1 tsp. prepared mustard
2 tbsp. lemon juice
1 hard-boiled egg

Cook macaroni; drain and run cold water through it. Add celery, pickles, onion and salt and pepper. Add chopped walnuts. Mix mayonnaise, mustard and lemon juice. Add to salad; mix lightly. Chill. Serve in lettuce-lined bowl; garnish with egg and walnut halves. Yield: 5-6 servings.

Mrs. Robert Chapman
Uniontown, Kentucky

WESTERN MACARONI SALAD

1 c. ripe olives
¾ c. raw shell macaroni, cooked
½ tsp. parsley
¼ c. chopped sweet red onion
4 hard-cooked eggs, coarsely chopped
1 c. salad dressing
1 tbsp. prepared mustard
2 tsp. vinegar
½ tsp. salt
¼ tsp. chili powder
½ lb. bacon, cooked and crumbled

Cut olives into wedges; combine with macaroni, parsley, onion and eggs. Mix salad dressing with mustard, vinegar, salt and chili powder. Pour over macaroni mixture; add bacon. Toss lightly; chill. Yield: 6 servings.

Mrs. Gerald P. Brannon
Sante Fe, New Mexico

CURRIED RICE SALAD

1 ½ c. cooked rice
¼ c. minced onion
1 tbsp. vinegar
2 tbsp. salad oil
1 tsp. curry powder
2 tsp. salt
1 c. chopped celery
1 c. cooked green peas
½ c. salad dressing or mayonnaise

Combine rice, onion, vinegar, salad oil, curry powder and salt; chill for several hours. Add remaining ingredients just before serving. Yield: 4-6 servings.

Mrs. John R. Snow
Fort Monroe, Virginia

EGG-RICE SALAD

¼ c. minced green onions
¼ c. diced cucumbers, or stuffed olives
6 hard-cooked eggs, chopped
1 c. diced celery
Pickles, chopped
2 c. cooked rice, cooled
¾ c. mayonnaise
Salt and pepper to taste

Combine onions, cucumbers, eggs, celery, pickles, rice and mayonnaise. Season to taste. Serve on crisp lettuce.

Julia A. Olson
Columbia, Kentucky

GOLDEN RICE SALAD

¾ c. plus 2 tbsp. raw rice
½ c. plus 2 tbsp. chicken stock
2 tbsp. salad oil
1 tbsp. vinegar
¼ tsp. salt
⅛ tsp. pepper
½ c. ripe olives, cut in large pieces
1 hard-cooked egg, diced
¾ c. celery, chopped
2 tbsp. dill pickle, chopped
¼ c. pimento, chopped
¼ c. green onions, chopped
¼ c. mayonnaise
1 tbsp. prepared mustard

Cook rice in chicken stock. Blend salad oil, vinegar, salt and pepper. Pour over hot rice; mix well. Cool. Add remaining ingredients; toss lightly. Chill thoroughly. Yield: 8 servings.

Edna C. Hathorn
Crowley, Louisiana

GOLDEN RICE SALAD

¼ c. salad oil
2 tbsp. vinegar
2 tbsp. prepared mustard
1 ½ tsp. salt
⅛ tsp. pepper
4 ½ c. hot cooked rice
1 c. ripe olives, cut in lge. pieces
2 hard-cooked eggs, diced
1 ½ c. diced celery
¼ c. chopped sweet pickles
1 sm. onion, chopped
½ c. mayonnaise

Blend salad oil, vinegar, mustard, salt and pepper; pour over hot rice. Toss; set aside to cool. Add remaining ingredients; toss. Chill thoroughly. Serve on lettuce leaf; garnish with extra sliced eggs. Yield: 8 servings.

Mrs. H. B. Taylor
Georgiana, Alabama

MILLION DOLLAR RICE SALAD

1 lge. pkg. marshmallows, diced
1 lge. can crushed pineapple, drained
1 8-oz. pkg. cream cheese
2 tbsp. sugar
1 tbsp. mayonnaise
2 c. cooked rice
Maraschino cherries
1 c. whipping cream
Nuts (opt.)

Cut marshmallows into small pieces; add pineapple. Cream together cheese, sugar and mayonnaise until smooth. Add rice, cherries and marshmallow mixture. Fold in whipped cream and nuts. Chill.

Miss Karen L. Durst
Grantsville, Maryland

OLIVES 'N' CHEESE

4 pkg. lime gelatin
7 c. boiling water
1 sm. carton cottage cheese
1 med. can crushed pineapple, drained
2 stalks celery, finely chopped
1 sm. bottle stuffed olives, sliced
1 sm. pkg. cream cheese

Dissolve gelatin in boiling water; cool. Add cottage cheese, pineapple, celery and olives. Roll cream cheese into small balls; add to mixture. Pour into large mold or 11 x 14-inch pan. Top with mayonnaise thinned with pineapple juice, when ready to serve, if desired. Yield: 12 servings.

Mrs. N. M. Mason
Phoenix, Arizona

RICE AND OLIVE HONOLULU

2 c. cooked rice
¼ c. chopped stuffed green olives
¼ c. mayonnaise

(Continued on next page)

Combine cold rice, olives, and enough mayonnaise to hold ingredients together. Pack individual molds with the rice. Chill for several hours. Turn over just before serving. Garnish with watercress.

Leland Buckner
Dallas, North Carolina

PARTY PINEAPPLE-PECAN SALAD

2 c. cooked hot rice
¼ c. creamy French dressing
1 1-lb. 4-oz. can pineapple tidbits, drained
⅓ c. coarsely chopped toasted pecans
Salad greens
Red or green maraschino cherries (opt.)

Mix rice, French dressing and pineapple together; cool. Cover well; refrigerate. Just before serving, stir in pecans. Serve on salad greens; garnish with maraschino cherries.

Robert H. Pryor
Kensett, Arkansas

RICE MOLD

1 pt. water
1 tsp. butter
½ tsp. salt
½ c. rice
½ c. sugar
1 box orange-pineapple gelatin dissolved in ¾ amount water required on gelatin pkg.
1 sm. can crushed pineapple

Bring water to boil; add butter, salt and rice. Let simmer 20 minutes or till tender. Stir in sugar; remove from heat. Stir rice into gelatin while rice is still hot. When gelatin mixture is cool, add pineapple. Place in refrigerator to congeal.

Mrs. W. L. Kester
Pryor, Oklahoma

RAISIN-RICE SALAD

1 envelope unflavored gelatin
2 tbsp. sugar
¼ tsp. salt
1 c. water
½ c. mayonnaise
2 tbsp. lemon juice
1 c. cooked rice
1 apple, peeled and chopped
½ c. chopped raisins

Blend gelatin, sugar, salt and water; heat in saucepan, stirring until dissolved. Remove from heat; stir in mayonnaise and lemon juice. Blend with rotary beater; chill quickly in freezer tray for 15 minutes until slightly jelled. Beat until fluffy; fold in remaining ingredients. Chill until firm. Serve with salad greens; garnish with mayonnaise.

M. K. Brown
Miami, Florida

RICE-PINEAPPLE SALAD

1 c. rice, cooked with salt
1 No. 2 can pineapple, drained
1 lge. bottle maraschino cherries, sliced
1 box Dream Whip, whipped

Combine rice, pineapple, maraschino cherries and Dream Whip. If salad is too dry, add a little pineapple or cherry juice.

Mrs. Annie M. Ramsey
Gretna, Virginia

RICE SALAD

3 c. cooked rice
6 hard-cooked eggs, coarsely chopped
½ c. chopped onion
¼ c. pimento, chopped
¼ c. chopped green pepper
¼ c. chopped celery
¼ c. chopped dill pickle
1 tsp. salt
Dash of pepper
¼ c. French dressing
⅓ c. mayonnaise or salad dressing
2 tbsp. prepared mustard

Combine first 9 ingredients. Blend French dressing, mayonnaise and mustard; add to rice mixture and toss to coat ingredients. Chill well. For individual servings, lightly pack rice mixture into a custard cup; immediately turn out on crisp lettuce. Yield: 6 servings.

Mrs.Bryan A. Erickson
Clifton, Texas

RICE SALAD

½ c. salad dressing
1 tbsp. mustard
1 tbsp. pickle juice
2 c. cooked rice
4 hard-cooked eggs
4 sweet pickles
1 tbsp. onion, diced
¼ c. green pepper, diced
¼ c. celery, diced
1 tsp. salt
½ tsp. black pepper
½ c. chopped pecans (opt.)

Mix salad dressing, mustard and pickle juice. Mix with remaining ingredients. Chill. Yield: 8 servings.

Mrs. Dorothy Weikal Bickerstaff
Mariana, Arkansas

RICE SALAD

4 c. cooked cold rice
⅓ c. minced celery
2 tbsp. minced onions
1 tbsp. minced green pepper
1 tbsp. pimentos
2 tbsp. French dressing
4 tbsp. sweet relish
¼ tsp. black pepper
Salt to taste
Salad dressing

Combine all ingredients with enough salad dressing to hold together. Yield: 8 servings.

Mrs. Melvin Giesenschlag
Somerville, Texas

STUFFED TOMATO SALAD

6 lge. tomatoes
1 ½ c. cooked brown rice
2 tbsp. chopped celery
1 tsp. onion juice or garlic clove, finely, chopped
1 ½ c. cooked brown rice
1 tbsp. basil

Gently scoop out center of tomatoes. Mix rice and other ingredients together; stuff into tomatoes. Serve on lettuce, watercress or shredded cabbage. Serve with cottage cheese yogurt dressing or plain cottage cheese dressing. Yield: 6 servings.

Mrs. Hazel Tilghman
Kinston, North Carolina

RICE SALAD

1 lge. pkg. colored marshmallows, diced
1 lge. can crushed pineapple, drained
1 8-oz. pkg. cream cheese
2 tbsp. sugar
1 tbsp. mayonnaise
2 c. cooled, salted rice
12 or more maraschino cherries
1 c. chopped pecans
1 c. cream, whipped (opt.)

Combine marshmallows, pineapple, cheese, sugar and mayonnaise. Add rice, cherries and nuts. Fold in whipped cream. Chill overnight.

Mrs. Herman Maynard
Winder, Georgia

RICE SALAD

2 c. cooled, chilled rice
⅓ c. chopped sweet peppers
⅓ c. chopped sweet pickles
3 tbsp. salad dressing
¾ c. grated American cheese
Crisp lettuce leaves
4 tomatoes, peeled

Combine rice, peppers, pickles and salad dressing; mix well. Add 2/3 cup grated cheese; mix lightly. Place lettuce leaves on plates. Cut tomatoes in wedges, not cutting all the way through tomato, to resemble flower petals. Place tomatoes on lettuce leaves; fill with rice mixture. Sprinkle salads with remaining cheese.

Mrs. Frank Baker
Weiner, Arkansas

SWEET RICE SALAD

1 c. rice
1 c. sugar
Milk
2 pkg. strawberry gelatin
1 pt. whipping cream
1 lge. can crushed pineapple

Cook rice with 1/2 cup sugar. Cover rice with milk; set aside to cool. Prepare gelatin; chill until firm. Whip cream, adding remaining sugar. Mix gelatin, rice, whipped cream and undrained pineapple. Refrigerate.

Mrs. John Faber
Greenfield, Iowa

RICE SALAD VINAIGRETTE

2 c. cooked rice
¼ c. chopped onion
¼ c. diced celery
¼ c. seeded diced cucumber
¼ c. diced green pepper
Vinaigrette sauce
Fresh garlic pods, chopped
Parsley, chopped

Combine rice, vegetables and vinaigrette sauce; mix well. Arrange on salad dish; Sprinkle with chopped garlic pods and parsley. Yield: 6 servings.

VINAIGRETTE SAUCE:

3 tbsp. olive oil
1 tbsp. wine vinegar
1 tsp. salt
½ tsp. pepper

Blend olive oil and wine vinegar with salt and pepper to suit your salad.

Mrs. Helen G. Morris
Prescott, Arkansas

SPAGHETTI SALAD

1 12-oz. pkg. spaghetti
1 sm. jar olives
2 hard-boiled eggs
1 sm. jar pimento
1 sm. jar mayonnaise
1 sm. onion, minced

Cook spaghetti according to package directions; drain well. Combine all ingredients; serve warm.

Mrs. Sam W. Borland
Cedar Grove, North Carolina

TROPICAL RICE SALAD

1 c. uncooked rice
2 c. orange juice
¼ tsp. salt
1 tsp. grated lemon rind
1 tbsp. lemon juice
1 c. coarsely chopped dates
½ c. toasted slivered almonds
6 thin cantaloupe slices, peeled
6 thin honeydew melon slices, peeled

Combine rice, orange juice and salt in 3-quart saucepan. Bring to boil; stir gently with a fork. Cover tightly; reduce heat to simmer. Cook about 20 minutes, or until rice is tender. Chill. Mix in lemon rind and juice, dates and nuts. Serve in ring of alternating slices of cantalope and honeydew melon topped with Minted Sour Cream Dressing.

DRESSING:

1 c. sour cream
1 tbsp. finely chopped mint
2 tbsp. sugar
1 tsp. lemon juice
Pinch of salt

Combine all ingredients; chill.

Ella Stanley
Coeburn, Virginia

SPAGHETTI SALAD

1 9-oz. pkg. spaghetti
3 hard-cooked eggs, chopped
2 stalks celery, chopped
2 sweet pickles, chopped
2 scallions or green onions, chopped
3 tbsp. Parmesan cheese
Parsley sprigs
1 c. mayonnaise
1 tsp. salt
Dash of pepper
1 tbsp. vinegar
1 tsp. Worcestershire sauce

Break spaghetti into short lengths; cook in boiling salted water until tender. Drain; cool. Add eggs, celery, pickles, onions, cheese and parsley. Combine mayonnaise, salt, pepper, vinegar and Worcestershire sauce. Add to spaghetti mixture; mix thoroughly. Yield: 6-8 servings.

Mrs. Dean Fuller
Frederick, Maryland

SPAGHETTI-VEGETABLE SALAD

1 pt. canned green beans
3 hard-cooked eggs, diced
1 c. cooked spaghetti
½ c. diced canned pickled beets
½ c. diced American cheese
6 sweet pickles, diced
1 sm. onion, minced
⅔ c. salad dressing

Boil canned beans in liquid for 10 minutes; drain and cool. Combine beans with remaining ingredients; serve with salad dressing on lettuce leaf.

K. B. McElroy
Hugo, Oklahoma

SPECIAL OCCASION SALADS

Recipe for Wedding Luncheon Salad Plate on Page 378

BRIDE'S SALAD

1 pkg. lime gelatin
1 c. crushed pineapple
1 c. shredded cheddar cheese
1 c. chopped pecans
¾ c. mayonnaise

Prepare gelatin according to package directions. When partially congealed, add pineapple, cheese, nuts and mayonnaise. Mix well. Pour into molds. Refrigerate until firm.

Annette Braswell
Monroe, Georgia

BRIDE'S SALAD

1 pkg. miniature marshmallows
1 lge. can crushed pineapple, drained
12 maraschino cherries, chopped
1 3-oz. pkg. cream cheese
2 tbsp. sugar
2 tbsp. mayonnaise
½ pt. whipped cream, whipped
½ c. chopped pecans (opt.)

Combine marshmallows and pineapple. Mix cherries, cream cheese, sugar and mayonnaise together. Add to pineapple mixture. Fold whipped cream into pineapple mixture. Add pecans if desired. Chill. Yield: 8 servings.

Mrs. Maury Watkins
New Edinburg, Arkansas

CANDLESTICK SALAD

8 pineapple rings, drained
8 lettuce leaves
4 bananas, cut in halves crosswise
8 strawberries, maraschino cherries or candied cherries
Shredded coconut
½ c. whipped cream or fruit salad dressing

Arrange a slice of pineapple on lettuce for the candle base or holder. Dip bananas in pineapple juice to prevent discoloration. Place half of banana in pineapple ring to make candle. Add strawberry for flame. Put coconut in strawberry for wick. Dribble whipped cream down banana to make it look as if candle is melting. For a colorful Christmas salad, red or green candied apple rings may be used instead of pineapple, and lemon juice used on banana.

Mrs. L. A. Boyd
Vernon, Texas

CHERRY CHRISTMAS SALAD

Juice drained from cherries
⅓ c. orange juice
Juice of 1 lemon
1 c. sugar
1 pkg. lemon gelatin
1 1-lb. can sour cherries, drained
1 c. chopped celery
1 c. chopped pecans

Combine cherry, orange and lemon juices; heat to boiling. Dissolve sugar and gelatin in hot liquid. Chill. Fold in cherries, celery and pecans. Refrigerate until firm. Yield: 8 servings.

Mrs. Joanne Odell
Knoxville, Tennessee

CHRISTMAS APRICOT SALAD

1 pkg. lime gelatin
1 c. boiling apricot juice
Juice of 1 orange
Juice of 1 lemon
1 pkg. cream cheese
¼ c. finely chopped maraschino cherries
¼ c. finely chopped pecans
¼ c. finely chopped dates
2 tbsp. mayonnaise
16 canned apricot halves

Dissolve gelatin in boiling apricot juice; cool. Combine orange and lemon juice, cordial and enough water to make 1 cup liquid. Add to gelatin mixture. Mix cheese, cherries, nuts and dates with mayonnaise; form into balls. Stuff half of the apricots with cheese-mayonnaise mixture; cover with remaining apricot halves. Place 2 stuffed apricots in each individual mold. Pour gelatin over apricots. Chill until firm. Serve on lettuce cups topped with mayonnaise. Garnish with cherries cut to resemble poinsettias.

Mrs. Mabel Kitchrigs Owen
Monticello, Arkansas

CHRISTMAS BELL SALAD

1 No. 2 ½ can crushed pineapple, drained
1 pkg. lemon gelatin
2 3-oz. pkg. cream cheese
1 4-oz. can pimento, chopped
½ c. chopped celery
½ c. chopped mixed pecans and walnuts
⅛ tsp. salt
1 c. whipped cream

(Continued on next page)

Heat juice drained from pineapple; add gelatin and stir until dissolved. Chill until mixture starts to congeal. Soften cheese with pineapple. Add pimento, celery, nuts and salt. Combine gelatin and cheese mixture. Fold in cream. Turn into oiled molds; chill until firm.

Mrs. Sara Hollman
Monetta, South Carolina

CHRISTMAS CRANBERRY SALAD

1 3-oz. pkg. red gelatin
1 c. hot water
½ c. cold water
1 orange, peeled and diced
½ c. crushed pineapple
½ c. cut celery
½ c. white grapes
¼ c. chopped nuts
1 can jellied or whole cranberry sauce

Dissolve gelatin in hot water. Add the cold water. Partly chill. Remove all membrane from the orange; fold in gelatin. Add remaining ingredients. Pour into individual molds. Yield: 6 servings.

Mrs. Marie Goodrich
North Ft. Myers, Florida

CHRISTMAS LAYER SALAD

LIME LAYER:

1 pkg. lime gelatin
1 c. hot water
1 c. pineapple tidbits, drained
⅓ c. pineapple juice

Dissolve gelatin in hot water. Add pineapple and juice. Chill until firm.

CHEESE LAYER:

1 ½ tsp. unflavored gelatin
2 tbsp. cold water
1 8-oz. pkg. cream cheese
¼ c. milk

Sprinkle gelatin over cold water to soften. Add cream cheese softened with milk. Spread over firm lime layer.

CRANBERRY LAYER:

2 pkg. strawberry gelatin
2 c. hot water
1 can whole cranberries

Dissolve gelatin in hot water. Add cranberries. Cool. Pour over cheese layer. Chill until firm. Yield: 9-10 servings.

Joyce Niedenthal
Fort Lauderdale, Florida

CHRISTMAS RING SALAD

1 c. pineapple juice
1 lge. pkg. cream cheese
1 pkg. lime gelatin
1 or 2 pkg. unflavored gelatin
4 slices pineapple, finely cut
1 small bottle cherries
1 head lettuce
1 lge. bottle stuffed olives

Bring pineapple juice and cream cheese to a boil. Stir to dissolve cheese. Make lime gelatin according to package directions. Dissolve unflavored gelatin in cold water; add to lime gelatin mixture. Blend gelatin mixture into cheese mixture until smooth. Stir in pineapple and whole cherries. Mold in a 9-inch ring mold. Chill until firm. Unmold on a bed of lettuce; fill the center with olives. Yield: 10 servings.

Mrs. Ben Stanton
Red Springs, North Carolina

CHRISTMAS SALAD

1 pkg. cherry gelatin
1 No. 2 can fruit cocktail, drained
1 8-oz. pkg. cream cheese
Mayonnaise
Milk
Juice of 1 garlic button
1 c. chopped pecans
1 pkg. lime gelatin
1 No. 2 can pear sections, drained
1 No. 2 can crushed pineapple, drained

Prepare cherry gelatin according to directions on package substituting the juice from fruit cocktail for part of the liquid. Add fruit cocktail. Pour into mold; let congeal. Moisten cream cheese with mayonnaise and milk to desired spreading consistency. Add garlic juice and pecans. Spread cheese mixture over cherry gelatin. Prepare lime gelatin according to package directions substituting the juice from the pears and pineapple for part of the liquid. Add pears and pineapple. Pour lime mixture over cheese-cherry layer. Chill until firm. Yield: 12 servings.

Mrs. Rowena McCarty
Beaumont, Mississippi

CHRISTMAS SALAD

1 pkg. lime gelatin
1 lge. pkg. cream cheese
1 sm. can crushed pineapple
3 tbsp. mayonnaise
1 pkg. cherry gelatin

Prepare lime gelatin according to package directions; let set until firm. Mix cream cheese, pineapple and mayonnaise; spread over lime gelatin. Chill. Prepare cherry gelatin according to package directions; spread over the cheese-lime layer. Chill. Yield: 8-10 servings.

Mrs. Myrtle D. Webb
Jacksonville, Florida

CHRISTMAS SALAD

1 pkg. lime gelatin
1 pkg. lemon gelatin
½ pt. whipped cream, sweetened
1 3-oz. pkg. cream cheese, softened
½ c. chopped nuts
½ can crushed pineapple, drained
1 pkg. strawberry gelatin

Dissolve lime gelatin according to package directions. Chill until thoroughly set. Dissolve lemon gelatin according to package directions. Add whipped cream, cream cheese, nuts and pineapple. Pour lemon mixture over lime gelatin. Chill until firm. Dissolve strawberry gelatin according to package directions. Pour over lemon-lime layers. Chill until firm. Yield: 12 servings.

Bonnie Warner
Wells, Texas

CHRISTMAS SALAD

1 c. hot water
1 pkg. lime gelatin
½ lb. marshmallows
1 c. pineapple juice and water
1 9-oz. pkg. cream cheese
3 tbsp. salad dressing
1 No. 2 can crushed pineapple, drained
½ pt. whipping cream, whipped
1 pkg. cherry gelatin

Pour hot water into lime gelatin; add marshmallows. Stir until marshmallows are dissolved. Add pineapple juice and water. Let set. Soften cream cheese with salad dressing; add pineapple. Fold in whipped cream; pour over the firm lime gelatin mixture. Mix cherry gelatin according to directions on package. Pour over cheese-lime layer. Chill until firm. Yield: 24 servings.

Mrs. Eva Jo Woody
Frankston, Texas

CHRISTMAS SALAD

1 can sliced pineapple, diced
3 oranges, sectioned and broken
1 jar maraschino cherries, halved
2 c. miniature marshmallows

Chill fruits; drain. Mix lightly with marshmallows.

COOKED DRESSING:

1 egg
3 tbsp. vinegar
3 tbsp. sugar
1 c. whipped cream

Beat egg slightly; add vinegar and sugar. Stir constantly over low heat until mixture thickens. Cool. Pour over fruits, coating all pieces well. Fold in whipped cream. Refrigerate until ready to serve. Yield: 8-10 servings.

Lois G. Salter
Zwolle, Louisiana

CHRISTMAS TREES

1 pkg. lime gelatin
1 c. boiling water
1 c. pineapple juice and water
1 c. whipped cream
½ c. cottage cheese, drained
1 c. crushed pineapple, well drained
½ c. broken pecans
Mayonnaise
Whipped cream for garnish
½ c. chopped maraschino cherries

Dissolve gelatin in boiling water; add juice-water mixture. Chill until partially set. Fold in whipped cream. Fold in cottage cheese which has been put through a fine sieve, pineapple, nuts and cherries; blend well. Pour into pointed waxed paper cups to chill. Unmold on a bed of lettuce; garnish with mayonnaise and fluff whipped cream. Let a small amount run down the sides of each tree. Top with a cherry wedge. Yield: 10 servings.

Mrs. Vera Troyer
Columbia, South Carolina

CHRISTMAS TREE SALAD

2 c. pineapple syrup plus water
1 pkg. lime gelatin
16 marshmallows, cut up
1 sm. can crushed pineapple, drained
1 c. whipped cream
8 lge. maraschino cherries

Heat pineapple syrup to boiling; dissolve gelatin in hot liquid. Add cut up marshmallows and dissolve. Add crushed pineapple. Chill until very thick. Fold in whipped cream. Place cherry in bottom of a paper cone-shaped mold. Pour mixture in mold; chill until set. Serve by peeling off mold; garnish with colored whipped cream or mayonnaise. Yield: 8 servings.

Alice Allison Kealhofer
Bentonia, Mississippi

CHRISTMAS TREE SALAD

1 c. hot water
1 pkg. lime gelatin
1 c. juice drained from pineapple
1 8-oz. pkg. cream cheese, whipped
1 can crushed pineapple, drained
½ c. chopped pecans
1 sm. bottle red cherries, quartered
6 lge. marshmallows, quartered
½ pt. whipped cream

Combine hot water and gelatin; stir. Add juice; chill until mixture is syrupy. Add whipped cheese-pineapple mixture, nuts, cherries and marshmallows to gelatin. Chill; fold in whipped cream. Pour into pointed paper cup molds; place cups in juice glasses to chill. Save a little whipped cream to decorate trees, using a cake decorator. Whipped cream may be tinted with cake coloring if desired. Yield: 6 servings.

Mrs. R. G. Hunt
Gazoo City, Mississippi

CRANBERRY CANDLES

1 1-lb. can whole cranberry sauce
1 3-oz. pkg. cherry or orange gelatin
1 c. boiling water
¼ tsp. salt
1 tbsp. lemon juice
½ c. mayonnaise
1 apple or orange, peeled and diced
¼ c. chopped walnuts

Heat cranberry sauce; strain. Set berries aside. Dissolve gelatin in hot juice and water. Add salt and lemon juice. Chill until thickened enough to mound slightly when dropped from a spoon. Beat in mayonnaise with rotary beater until light and fluffy. Fold in cranberries, fruit and nuts. Divide mixture evenly into eight 6-oz. fruit juice cans. Chill 4 hours or longer. Unmold. Garnish with mayonnaise to taste. To flame: Cut thin birthday candles in half; insert tops in cranberry candles. Light. Yield: 8 servings.

Margaret Allen Shanks
Orrville, Alabama

HALLOWEEN SALAD

½ c. chopped green peppers
½ c. chopped celery
½ c. chopped tart apples
½ c. chopped walnuts
½ c. cabbage heart
½ c. cold, chopped, boiled potatoes
½ c. chopped beets
½ c. chopped carrots
½ tsp. salt
Mayonnaise
Lettuce
8 eggs
Cloves
Tomato or red pepper
1 lge. red apple
1 parsley sprig

Combine first 9 ingredients with desired amount of mayonnaise; mix well. Form mound; place in center on lettuce lined serving platter. Boil eggs 10 minutes; remove shells. Make faces on eggs by using cloves for eyes and small pieces tomato for mouths. Stand eggs around mound, pressing them to stand. Remove inside of apple with sharp spoon; cut out eyes and mouth like a jack-o-lantern. Stand apple on top of mound with a tiny candle inside; light before serving. A cupped lettuce leaf makes a hat for the apple; pin up one side of front and trim with a sprig of parsley.

Mrs. Hubert Hiers
West Palm Beach, Florida

HAPPY HOLIDAY SALAD

1 3-oz. pkg. cream cheese
1 tbsp. milk, cream or mayonnaise
½ c. chopped pecans
1 pkg. strawberry gelatin
1 c. hot water
1 10-oz. pkg. frozen strawberries

(Continued on next page)

Thoroughly mix cream cheese, milk and pecans; shape into balls about the size of small walnuts. Dissolve gelatin in hot water; chill until it begins to congeal. Add strawberries. Alternate layers of gelatin and balls into a large mold. Chill until firm. Unmold onto a plate; garnish with whole strawberries and dressing. Yield: 8 servings.

Pauline K. Brown
Lone Wolf, Oklahoma

HOLIDAY CRANBERRY SALAD

- 1 lb. fresh cranberries, ground
- 3 to 4 med. apples, ground
- 1 c. chopped nuts
- 1 10-oz. pkg. miniature marshmallows
- 1 ½ c. sugar
- 1 pt. whipped cream or 2 pkg. dessert topping mix

Combine cranberries, apples and nuts. Add marshmallows and sugar; mix well. Gently fold in whipped cream. Chill.

Betty Brown
Dallas, Texas

HOLIDAY SALAD

FIRST LAYER:

- 1 pkg. lime gelatin
- 1 ¼ c. hot water
- 1 c. crushed pineapple

Dissolve gelatin in hot water. Add pineapple. Chill until firm.

SECOND LAYER:

- 1 pkg. unflavored gelatin
- ¼ c. water
- ¾ c. pineapple juice
- 1 6-oz. pkg. cream cheese
- ½ c. mayonnaise
- ½ c. pecans

Mix gelatin, water and pineapple juice; bring to a boil. Remove from heat; add cream cheese. Cool. Add mayonnaise and pecans. Pour on top of firm lime layer. Chill until firm.

THIRD LAYER:

- 1 pkg. cherry gelatin
- 1 ½ c. hot water
- 1 c. crushed pineapple
- ⅔ c. cranberry sauce
- ¼ c. sugar
- ½ c. chopped celery
- ¼ c. chopped pecans

Dissolve cherry gelatin in hot water. Add remaining ingredients. Chill until partially set. Spoon over cheese layer. Chill until firm. Yield: 8 servings.

Mrs. Lucille Jordan
Cary, North Carolina

HOLIDAY SALAD

- 1 pt. maraschino cherries, cut up
- 1 c. pecans, chopped
- 1 lge. can crushed pineapple, drained
- 1 box lemon gelatin
- 1 c. boiling water
- 1 c. whipped cream

Combine cherries, nuts and pineapple; chill for 30 minutes. Dissolve gelatin in boiling water. Chill until partially set. Combine cherry mixture with gelatin. Fold in whipped cream. Mold and congeal. Yield: 8 servings.

Mrs. Carnell Barnes
Maud, Oklahoma

HOLIDAY SALAD

- 2 pkg. cherry gelatin
- 1 No. 2 can applesauce, heated
- 1 No. 2 can crushed pineapple
- 1 ½ c. ginger ale

Dissolve gelatin in hot applesauce. Add remaining ingredients. Chill. Yield: 15 servings.

Mrs. Lalah H. Newman
Pulaski, Virginia

HOLIDAY SALAD

- 1 egg yolk, well beaten
- 1 pkg. small marshmallows
- 2 tsp. vinegar
- 1 pkg. cherry gelatin
- 1 c. water
- ½ c. chopped nuts
- 1 med. can fruit cocktail, drained
- 1 sm. can crushed pineapple, drained
- ½ pt. whipped cream

(Continued on next page)

Pour egg yolk over marshmallows; add vinegar. Boil gelatin in 1 cup water for 1 minute. Pour gelatin over marshmallow mixture; allow to congeal slightly. Add nuts, fruit and cream to other ingredients. Mix well. Chill until firm.

Margie Alford
Spearman, Texas

HOLIDAY SALAD

- 12-oz. orange gelatin
- 1 qt. boiling water
- 1 qt. cold water
- 1 No. 2 ½ can crushed pineapple
- 8-oz. dates, chopped
- 8-oz. lemon rind, grated
- ½ stalk celery, finely chopped
- 4-oz. pecans, chopped
- 4-oz. miniature marshmallows, chopped
- 4-oz. candied cherries, chopped
- 4-oz. orange rind, grated

Dissolve gelatin in one quart boiling water; add cold water. Add remaining ingredients. Chill. Cut into squares. Serve with Whipped Cream Dressing.

WHIPPED CREAM DRESSING:

- ½ c. whipped cream
- ½ c. mayonnaise
- Lemon juice to taste

Thoroughly blend ingredients.

Mrs. Anna B. Whitescarver
Flemington, West Virginia

MERRY CHRISTMAS SALAD

- 1 pkg. lime gelatin
- 1 c. boiling water
- 1 No. 2 can crushed pineapple
- 1 c. cottage cheese or 1 pkg. cream cheese
- ½ c. finely sliced celery
- 1 tbsp. chopped pimento
- ½ c. chopped nuts

Dissolve gelatin in boiling water; cool. Stir in remaining ingredients. Chill until firm. Yield: 8 servings.

Mrs. Prince A. Hodgson
Elberton, Georgia

HOLIDAY SQUARES

- 1 pkg. cherry gelatin
- 1 3-oz. pkg. cream cheese, crumbled
- 1 c. boiling water
- 1 No. 2 can whole cranberry sauce
- 1 apple, finely chopped
- ¼ c. chopped nuts
- 3 stalks celery, finely chopped
- ½ c. miniature marshmallows
- ½ pkg. Dream Whip
- ¼ c. cold milk
- 1 tbsp. sugar

Combine gelatin and cheese. Add boiling water; whip until completely dissolved. Place in square dish; chill to syrupy stage. Fold in fruit, nuts, celery and marshmallows. Whip Dream Whip and milk; add sugar. Fold into salad. Chill overnight. Cut into squares. Serve on shredded lettuce. Yield: 12 servings.

Mrs. LaVerne Stokes
Palestine, Texas

KRIS KRINGLE SALAD

- 1 ¼ c. water
- ½ c. sugar
- ¼ c. red cinnamon candies
- 2 apples, pared and cut in wedges
- 1 avocado, cut in wedges

Makes syrup of water, sugar and cinnamon candies. Add apples; cook till just tender. Chill. Alternate apples and avocado on lettuce. Serve with French dressing. Yield: 4 servings.

Mrs. Pecola L. Scott
Dallas, Texas

QUICK CHRISTMAS CRANBERRY CANDLES

- 1 3-oz. pkg. raspberry gelatin
- 1 No. 101 can whole cranberry sauce
- Lettuce leaves
- Salad dressing or whipped cream

(Continued on next page)

Prepare gelatin according to package directions. Chill until mixture is consistency of egg whites. Add cranberry sauce; blend well. Pour into small frozen juice cans or small paper cups. Let set several hours or overnight. Unmold on lettuce leaves and garnish with salad dressing. Yield: 4 servings.

Mrs. Martha F. Jenkins
Hildebran, North Carolina

PEACHY HOLIDAY DELIGHT

1 pkg. lime gelatin
1 c. hot water
1 tbsp. lemon juice
1 bottle 7-Up
¼ c. chopped celery
¼ c. chopped nuts
½ c. miniature marshmallows
1 c. drained, diced sweetened peaches

Dissolve gelatin in hot water. Add lemon juice and 7-Up. Chill until slightly thickened. Fold in celery, nuts, marshmallows and peaches. Mold and chill. Yield: 6-8 servings.

Eula Mae Lincecum
Amarillo, Texas

RAGGEDY ANN SALAD

½ deviled egg, cut lengthwise
Whole cloves
Pimento
Carrot, grated
1 bite-size cheese wafer
Tomato, sliced
Stuffed olives, sliced
Chicken, ham or tuna salad
Lettuce leaf
Pickle or asparagus strips
Almonds or cashew nuts

Make Raggedy Ann's head with a halved deviled egg. Use cloves for eyes and nose; a small piece of pimento for mouth. Grated carrot for hair; a cheese wafer hat. The body is a big tomato slice with 3 buttons of olive slices. Add a skirt of chicken salad on lettuce leaf, strips of pickles for arms and legs. Almonds for hands and feet complete Raggedy Ann. Yield: 1 serving.

Mrs. James A. Cox
Chatham, Virginia

RECEPTION SALAD

Juice from drained pineapple
1 c. hot water
1 pkg. lemon gelatin
1 sm. can pimento
2 3-oz. pkg. cream cheese
½ to 1 c. finely chopped celery
⅔ c. chopped nuts
1 med. can crushed pineapple, drained
⅛ tsp. salt
½ pt. whipped cream

Heat pineapple juice and water to boiling. Dissolve gelatin in juice. Cool. Mash pimentos and cream cheese together. Mix celery, nuts, pineapple and salt with thickened gelatin. Add cream. Allow to chill before serving. Yield: 6-8 servings.

Sammie Saulsbury
Odessa, Texas

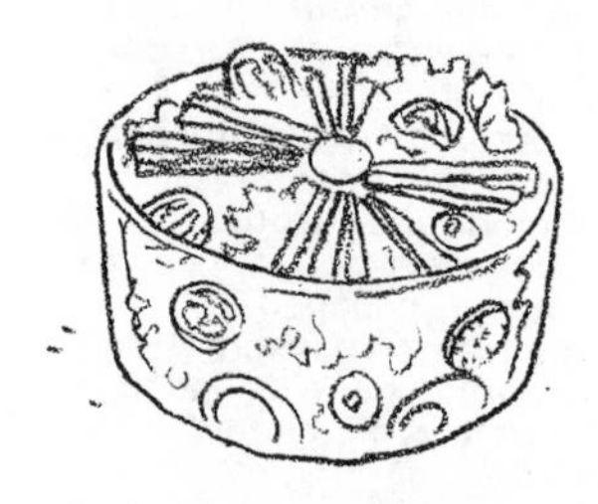

ST. NICK SALAD RING

2 pkgs. strawberry gelatin
3 ½ c. boiling water
2 tbsp. lemon juice
1 tbsp. vinegar
1 tbsp. grated onion
1 tsp. salt
2 3-oz. pkg. cream cheese
⅓ c. chopped parsley
2 grapefruit, sectioned
1 c. diced celery
1 avocado, diced
1 medium unpared apple, diced

Dissolve gelatin in boiling water; stir in lemon juice, vinegar, onion and salt. Chill until syrupy. Shape cream cheese into small balls about the size of marbles; roll in parsley. Lightly oil 1 1/2-quart ring mold. Alternate cheese balls and grapefruit sections around bottom of mold, rounded side of fruit down. Spoon syrupy gelatin around design to depth of about 1/4 inch. Chill until firm. Fold celery, avocado and apple into remaining syrupy gelatin. Pour into mold. Chill several hours.

SNOW CREAM DRESSING:

1 c. sour cream
2 tbsp. mayonnaise
2 tsp. sugar
2 tsp. lemon juice
½ tsp. salt

Combine all ingredients; chill to blend flavors. Serve with St. Nick salad ring. Yield: 8-10 servings.

Mrs. M. R. Turner
Tulsa, Oklahoma

ST. PATRICK'S SALAD

1 pkg. lime gelatin
1 c. hot water
½ tsp. salt
½ c. pineapple juice
1 c. pineapple, drained
1 pkg. cream cheese
½ c. evaporated milk
2 tbsp. lemon juice

Dissolve gelatin in hot water; add salt and pineapple juice. Chill until mixture begins to thicken. Put 1 to 2 tablespoons of gelatin mixture in each individual mold. Chill until firm. Mix pineapple, cream cheese, milk and lemon juice together; fold into remaining gelatin. Fill each mold with cheese-gelatin mixture. Chill until firm. Yield: 10-12 servings.

Mrs. Maudine C. Jackson
Camden, South Carolina

THANKSGIVING CRANBERRY SALAD

2 pkg. cherry gelatin
2 c. hot water
1 c. cold water
Juice from drained pineapple
2 tbsp. lemon juice
½ tsp. salt
¾ c. sugar
2 c. cranberries, ground
1 orange, finely ground
1 c. orange section halves
1 9-oz. can pineapple tidbits, drained
¾ c. sliced celery
⅓ c. chopped California walnuts

Dissolve gelatin in hot water. Add cold water, pineapple juice, lemon juice and salt. Chill until partially set. Add sugar to ground fruits. Add fruits, celery and nuts to gelatin. Pour into 2 1/2-quart mold. Chill until firm. Yield: 12 servings.

Mrs. Faye D. Decker
Virginia Beach, Virginia

THANKSGIVING CRANBERRY SALAD

2 boxes cherry gelatin
2 c. sugar
1 lb. cranberries, ground
1 orange, peeled and ground
1 orange, unpeeled and ground
2 apples, diced
½ c. celery
Pecans or walnuts
1 sm. can crushed pineapple

Prepare gelatin as directed on package. Add sugar; stir until dissolved. Combine cranberries, oranges, apples, celery, nuts and pineapple. Add cranberry mixture to gelatin. Chill until firm. Garnish with frosted grapes and cheese pumpkins. To frost grapes, dip grapes in egg whites. Then roll in granulated sugar. To make cheese pumpkins, mold grated American cheese with the hands to form a small ball which is slightly flattened to look like a pumpkin. With the dull side of knife, make ridges on the sides to resemble the ridges of a pumpkin. Use a whole clove for the stem. Yield: 12 servings.

Evelyn B. Willey
Gatesville, North Carolina

VALENTINE SALAD

Juice from drained pineapple
1 pkg. cherry gelatin
1 pkg. raspberry gelatin
2 No. 2 cans crushed pineapple, drained
1 pt. small curd cottage cheese
½ pt. whipped cream
1 c. pecans or walnuts

Bring pineapple juice to a boil; pour over gelatins. Cool. Add pineapple and cottage cheese. Fold in whipped cream and nuts. Chill until firm. Salad will keep for several days in refrigerator. Yield: 12 servings.

Mrs. Fay Cansler
Pollok, Texas

WASHINGTON'S BIRTHDAY CHERRY SALAD

1 c. diced canned peaches, drained
1 8 ¾-oz. can pineapple tidbits, drained
½ c. chopped maraschino cherries
1 3-oz. pkg. strawberry-flavored gelatin
½ tsp. salt
1 c. boiling water
¼ c. drained peach syrup
¼ c. drained pineapple syrup
1 tbsp. maraschino cherry syrup
1 tbsp. lemon juice
1 3-oz. pkg. cream cheese, softened
2 tbsp. mayonnaise
1 c. miniature marshmallows
½ c. heavy cream, whipped

(Continued on next page)

Chill a buttered 9-inch pie pan. Mix peaches, pineapple and cherries; chill. Combine gelatin and salt; add boiling water, stirring until completely dissolved. Combine peach syrup, pineapple syrup, cherry syrup and lemon juice; blend into gelatin. Stir frequently over ice water until consistency of thick unbeaten egg whites. Combine cream cheese and mayonnaise; beat until fluffy. Slowly add by tablespoons cheese mixture to gelatin; beat constantly until well blended. Stir in fruit and marshmallows. Gently fold in whipped cream. Turn into pie pan, spreading evenly to edges. Cover with a moisture, vapor-proof material; freeze until firm, about 4 hours. Cut into wedges; serve on chilled salad plate lined with crisp greens. Serve with Mallow-Grenadine Dressing.

MALLOW-GRENADINE DRESSING

- 2-oz. or 8 marshmallows
- 2 tbsp. grenadine syrup
- ⅔ c. sour cream

Heat marshmallows and syrup in top of double boiler over simmering water until melted, stirring frequently. Remove from heat; blend in sour cream. Chill thoroughly. Yield: 8-10 servings.

Mary Lee Cheatwood
Fruithurst, Alabama

WEDDING LUNCHEON SALAD PLATE

- 1 pkg. lemon gelatin
- 1 c. boiling water
- 1 ½ tsp. grated lemon rind
- 2 tbsp. lemon juice
- Dash of salt
- 2 c. canned applesauce
- ½ c. diced celery
- ¾ c. chopped orange wedges
- ¼ c. chopped maraschino cherries
- 2 1-lb. pkg. cottage cheese
- Toasted almonds
- Watercress
- Strawberries
- Fruit Salad Dressing

Dissolve gelatin in boiling water; add lemon rind, lemon juice and salt. Mix well. Add applesauce, celery, oranges and cherries. Mix well. Pour into individual molds; chill until set. Mound cottage cheese in a large bowl; sprinkle cheese with toasted almonds. Surround bowl with watercress on round platter. Unmold applesauce molds; arrange around cheese. Between each mold arrange strawberries. Serve with Fruit Salad Dressing. Yield: 8 servings.

FRUIT SALAD DRESSING:

- Mayonnaise
- Whipped cream

Combine equal parts mayonnaise and whipped cream. Mix well. Serve over salad.

Photograph for this recipe on page 369.

VALENTINE SALAD

- ¼ c. red-hot cinnamon candies
- 1 c. boiling water
- 1 pkg. lemon gelatin
- 1 c. unsweetened applesauce
- 1 3-oz. pkg. cream cheese
- 2 tbsp. cream
- 2 tbsp. mayonnaise

Dissolve cinnamon candies in boiling water. Pour over lemon gelatin. Dissolve; allow to cool. Add applesauce. Put half of mixture in heart-shaped mold. Chill until set. Combine cheese, cream and mayonnaise. Spread on set gelatin mixture. Pour remaining gelatin on top of cheese. Chill until firm. Yield: 6 servings

Mrs. Helen M. Godwin
Greensboro, North Carolina

VALENTINE SALAD

- 1 ½ tbsp. gelatin
- ¼ c. cold water
- 2 c. crushed pineapple
- ½ c. sugar
- 2 tbsp. lemon juice
- 2 tbsp. cherry juice
- 12 lge. maraschino cherries, finely cut
- 1 6-oz. pkg. cream cheese, softened
- ½ pt. whipped cream

Soak gelatin in cold water. Heat crushed pineapple with sugar. Add gelatin; stir until melted. Add lemon and cherry juice. Cool. Add cherries to the cheese; fold into pineapple mixture. Chill until slightly thickened. Fold in cream. Mold and chill. Yield: 6 servings.

Carolyn Holley
Heflin, Louisiana

INDEX

FRUIT, 61-90, 94-130, 216-236, 370-378

MEAT, 238-268

MIXED FRUIT AND VEGETABLE, 194-214, 216, 373

POULTRY, 270-302, 376

SALAD DRESSINGS, 47-54

SEAFOOD, 217, 304-348

SPECIAL OCCASION, 370-378

VEGETABLE, 132-168, 170-192, 217